D1464872

24487

BTEC Nationals
for
IT Practitioners

Geoffrey Knott BA, AIB, Cert Ed
Nick Waites BSc, MSc, Cert Ed

Brancepeth Computer Publications
2002

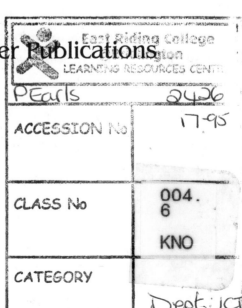

East Riding College
LEARNING RESOURCES CENTRE

PEarls	2426
ACCESSION No	17.95
CLASS No	004.6 KNO
CATEGORY	

Dept: ICT02.

©Geoffrey Knott and Nick Waites 2002

ISBN 0-9538848-2-1

Cover Design by Nick Waites
Graphical illustrations by Nick Waites and Geoffrey Knott
Production and Editing by Geoffrey Knott

Published in Great Britain by

Brancepeth Computer Publications Limited
Brancepeth Castle
Durham
DH7 8DF

Tel: 0191 378 3363
Fax: 0191 378 2972
E-mail: enquiries@bcpublications.co.uk
Web site: www.bcpublications.co.uk

All rights reserved. No part of this publication may be reproduced, stored in a retrieval system
or transmitted in any form or by any means, electronic, mechanical, photocopying, recording or
otherwise, without the prior consent of Brancepeth Computer Publications Limited.

British Cataloguing-in-Publications Data

A catalogue record for this book is available from the British Library

Printed in Great Britain by Athenaeum Press, Gateshead

Foreword by Douglas Kay

Qualification Leader for ICT, Edexcel Foundation

Before joining Edexcel I taught and managed IT and Computing courses in FE for 10 years, and in that capacity I became very familiar with the work of Geoffrey Knott and Nick Waites. I used their book, Computer Studies for BTEC, as my course text during that time, and now, in my capacity as Edexcel's developer of IT and Computing qualifications, I am delighted to be able to write this foreword to their latest publication. The authors' first textbook, "Computer Studies for BTEC" was published in 1987 and was followed by three further editions, the 4th in 1998. During that period it became the favoured text for the course of that title. In 2000, Edexcel was pleased to endorse its successor, BTEC Nationals in Computing and we are very happy to do the same for this new title.

During their 15 year writing partnership, Geoffrey Knott and Nick Waites have concentrated on producing Computing and ICT texts for courses which formed the basis of their combined 45 years of teaching experience. It is difficult for one author to adequately cover all the subject matter involved in Computing and ICT courses and it is a major strength of their writing partnership that each author brings to it complementary skills, knowledge and experience.

If you are a student studying for one of the BTEC National qualifications for IT Practitioners you will find that this book comprehensively covers Edexcel's requirements for a course text. If, on the other hand, you are a lecturer teaching on one of the BTEC Nationals for IT Practitioners courses, you can with confidence recommend this book to your students.

Edexcel does not lightly give their endorsement to textbooks for their courses, but we had no hesitation in doing so for this excellent publication. I am sure that you will be as delighted with it as I am.

To Carolyn and Anne with love

The Authors

Geoffrey Knott and Nick Waites have long experience in Computing and IT education and have been producing highly successful course text books for over a decade. They are authors of Computer Studies, BTEC Nationals in Computing, AS/A2 Information and Communication Technology, Advanced VCE Information and Communication Technology, GNVQ Advanced Information Technology, GNVQ Intermediate Information Technology, Information Processing, Computing, Small Business Computer Systems, Information Technology Skills - A Student Guide, GCSE Information Systems and co-authors of Business GNVQ Advanced and Core Skills for GNVQ.

Acknowledgements

We are grateful to our friend and colleague Jim Morton for his careful technical editing.

Contents

Unit 6: Systems analysis and design

Unit 1: Language and communications

Assessment Evidence Grid

Grade E	Grade C	Grade A
Give a presentation and consider your choice of vocabulary, sentence construction and style of delivery in meeting the needs of your audience.	Give a presentation and adjust appropriately your choice of vocabulary, sentence construction and style of delivery to the needs of your audience.	Give a presentation and match your choice of vocabulary, sentence construction and style of delivery to the needs of your audience and to present arguments persuasively.
When presenting written and/or graphical information, describe the relative advantages and disadvantages of using one type of software package in preference to another.	Compare and contrast the benefits and drawbacks of using one type of package as opposed to another to produce a given type of document.	Produce a detailed evaluation of the relative benefits and drawbacks of two different types of package for the production of a given type of document.
Use appropriate standard conventions and styles of writing to present work and write coherently.	Use appropriate standard conventions and styles of writing to present work. Write coherently and structure documents appropriately.	Show originality and creativity in structuring and presenting work, write coherently and use standard conventions and styles of writing.
Select and appropriately use a range of written research materials from a range of resources.	Spell, punctuate and use the rules of grammar with accuracy, using a range of specialist terms coherently and with precision.	Spell, punctuate and use the rules of grammar with accuracy, using a range of grammatical constructions and using a range of specialist terms coherently and with precision.
Present research findings in different presentation formats.	Select and appropriately use a range of written research materials from a range of resources.	Select and appropriately use a range of written research materials from a range of resources.
Draw upon different sources and present the combined information.	Present findings clearly in different presentation formats.	Use sophisticated presentation skills to present findings in a variety of different presentation formats.
	Identify, analyse and select appropriate resources.	Identify, evaluate and select appropriate resources.
	Synthesise information from different sources and present findings in a structured manner.	Synthesise information from a variety of sources and present it within a coherent structure.

Chapter 1
Written and graphical communication

When you are preparing a document, you need to keep in mind:

- ❑ its purpose. What is the document meant to communicate?
- ❑ the reader. Who is meant to read and understand its contents?

To ensure that the documents you produce are readable, you will need to:

- ❑ pay careful attention to spelling;
- ❑ ensure that your sentences convey the meanings you intend;
- ❑ use a language style which is appropriate to the subject and the reader;
- ❑ use document layouts which present the information clearly and effectively.

To produce an effective document, you must have a clear understanding of the information you are trying to communicate and be familiar with the requirements of your readers. For example, this text book would be unlikely to be useful to you if we, the authors, had little knowledge of our subject, or the contents of the BTEC Nationals course.

Spelling, grammar and meaning

Careful attention to spelling and good use of grammar are also important for clear communication. For example, you can probably work out the intended meaning of "The hows is neer the toun horl", but you can't be absolutely sure.

The aim of grammar is to ensure that the words of a sentence are arranged to convey a single meaning. Apart from giving a very bad impression to the reader, poor use of grammar can obscure meaning or convey a completely different, and unintended, message. Consider the following note provided by a parent to explain his child's absence from school. "Albert has to stay at home today because he has diarrhoea through some bad fish."

We know what he means, but the sentence construction gives a completely different and peculiar message. A clearer explanation might have been: "As a result of eating some bad fish, Albert has diarrhoea and is unable to attend school." For a business, such careless use of language in communications with customers not only damages its image of professionalism, but may also result in serious financial loss or contractual misunderstanding. Consider the following statements made by the Sales Manager of Global Supplies Limited to a customer.

"The goods we sold to you were supplied by Acme Systems. We believe that the goods are a disgrace to the company and that you should be able to sue for damages." The Sales Manager intends to say that the goods are a disgrace to Acme Systems and that the customer should be able to sue that company for damages. However, the statements could suggest an admission that the poor quality goods disgrace Global Supplies and that they are prepared to be sued.

Writing style

This book is written in a style which makes the content easier to read, that is, one with relatively short sentences and a friendly tone. We also avoid the unnecessary use of 'difficult' vocabulary and provide numerous examples to illustrate ideas. On the other hand, the book has a serious purpose and an over-friendly, perhaps 'jokey' style, would simply be patronising and some-times less common vocabulary can be used to express ideas more briefly. For example, the words "intercede" or "mediate"can be used instead of the phrase "to plead in favour of". As a general rule don't use 'big' words simply to impress, especially if you are not sure what they mean. The Thesaurus tool (see later) in a word processor will suggest alternative vocabulary and you should use it with extreme care.

Some documents are not trying to communicate ideas or concepts and require simple state-ments of fact, without explanation. For example, the Table of Contents in this book simply lists chapter titles and main headings, together with the relevant page numbers. Similarly, you would expect notice of an important staff meeting to briefly identify basic information, such as the subject of the meeting, for example, 'New car parking arrangements', its location, date and time. However, a notice advertising a newly released film would include slogans such as, "A real weepy", or "You'll never sleep again.", to encourage people to go and see it.

Personal writing style

A memorandum example

Although writing is a skill and rules of grammar and spelling are vitally important, it is also a highly creative process and if practised sufficiently can be as clear a part of your personality as the way you speak. Those who need to use sign language can bring their own personalities to they way in which they use their hands and facial expressions to express simple or complex in-formation, feelings and emotions. Admittedly, some documents such as invoices do not call for personal style, but most do. Even a brief memorandum asking people to attend a meeting can aggravate, annoy, or cause resentment if it is badly phrased.

Consider the following contrasting examples and judge what your response might be to each.

<u>**Memorandum**</u>

To: All Accounts staff

From: Mrs. V. Uptight, Accounts Department Manager

Subject: Upgrade of accounting software   **Date:** 14 June 2000

There will be a meeting at 5.30 p.m. tomorrow and all Accounts staff must attend. There is a lot to discuss and the meeting will take around two hours. Come and see me if you feel that you have an excuse for not attending.

<u>**Memorandum**</u>

To: All Accounts staff

From: Iris Pectu, Accounts Department Manager

Subject: Meeting 5.30 p.m. 15 June - Upgrade of accounting software   **Date:** 14 June 2000

I realise that this meeting is being called at very short notice, but the delay in the delivery of the software means that we have even less time than planned to complete the change to the new system. To ensure that the changeover to the new accounting software runs smoothly and does not disrupt services to our customers (and the vitally important task of receiving their invoice payments!), we need to discuss a number of different operating procedures. I cannot over-emphasise the importance of this meeting, so if you think that you may be unable to attend, please talk to me today and we will try to get the information to you some other way.

Unfortunately, the meeting is likely to take around 2 hours so I have arranged for sandwiches and coffee to keep us going.

Neither memo is likely to be welcome, but the first is abrupt, inconsiderate and does not even explain why the meeting is so important. It suggests little 'team spirit' and the dictatorial style of the memo probably reflects the Head of Department's management style. The memo would almost certainly cause resentment and if its tone is typical will not ensure that the operational changes to the accounting system go smoothly. The second memo appeals to the loyalty of staff and makes a real effort to explain the reasons for the meeting and the short notice given. The last two sentences demonstrate a care for the staff as individuals and a willingness to treat them as colleagues. Although the memos say a great deal about contrasting management styles, which is not relevant here, personal writing style is difficult to force and will, as with other forms of communication, reflect your own personality. Mrs. V Uptight would probably have great difficulty in writing the second memo.

Of course, you need to apply your personal style appropriately, to a number of different documents types and target readers. The following section provides examples of formal and informal styles for a range of document types.

Choosing a style and form of presentation

Although presentational techniques such as page layout and font styles are dealt with later in this chapter the following examples illustrate the use of style and presentation to meet different communication needs, such as attracting attention, writing to impress and gathering information through questionnaires.

Attracting attention in advertisements

Example 1: Hair care products

Study the two example advertisements in Figures 1.1 and 1.2. They are for similar types of product but each is aimed at a very different audience. To be effective, advertisements must capture your attention, but the methods used will depend largely on the age, lifestyle and personal values of their intended readers.

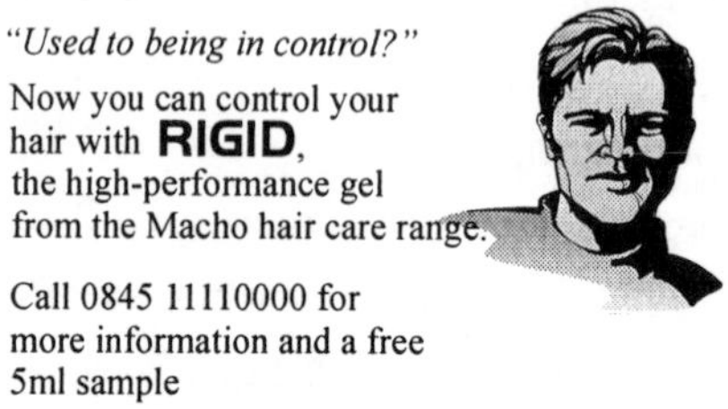

"Used to being in control?"

Now you can control your hair with **RIGID**, the high-performance gel from the Macho hair care range.

Call 0845 11110000 for more information and a free 5ml sample

Figure 1.1

The advertisement for RIGID hair gel in Figure 1.1 is short and to the point, and uses a 'no-nonsense' writing style designed to emphasise the gel's ability to keep your hair in one place. The opening question "Used to being in control?" is not a complete sentence, but is perfectly acceptable in the context of a 'punchy' advertisement. This question form of headline is often used in advertisements because it is an effective way of grabbing your attention. Simple phrases are often used in newspaper headlines, such as "Man bites dog" - put in this way it could be open to misinterpretation. (Does the man bite the dog repeatedly?) The sentence "Yesterday, a man bit a dog." would be clearer but would lack the same impact. Further impact in the RIGID advertisement is achieved both with the graphic of the 'lantern-jawed' man, to highlight the 'strength' element and the bold and stark (*sans-serif*) font used for the word '**RIGID**'. A sans-serif font lacks the short strokes at the ends of individual letters; the Arial font is of this type. The body text in this book is Times New Roman, which is a *serif* font.

The advertisement in Figure 1.2 for shampoo also uses a graphical image and capitalises the font to highlight the name of the product. However, the font is serif, in italics and is not in bold type, which is suited to the gentle tone of the message. Considerable detail is given about the product, and its highlighted (by underscoring) benefits for the environment are obviously aimed at a particular category of reader.

The advertisement uses well constructed and flowing sentences which assume the information is important to the reader in deciding whether or not to buy the shampoo. The reader's attention is probably drawn by the image and the word 'Natura' in the company's name. The Italian word 'Indulgente' hints at a slightly luxurious element in the product, despite its ecological soundness.

Natura Hair www.naturahair.co.uk

We understand that you care about your health and the environment, so we developed a shampoo that protects the environment and looks after your hair, NATURALLY.

INDULGENTE

only uses <u>natural products</u> which are <u>not harmful to the environment</u>. Indulgente is <u>kind to your hair</u> and washes without destroying the natural oils that give your hair vitality.

Call our hair consultancy team on **0345 888999** for more information on how you can look after your hair and care for our planet. 2% of our profits go to the Global Nature Foundation www.globalnature.org.

Figure 1.2

Neither of these advertisements require technical or other detail, but some products, such as computers and financial services cannot be sold by simple slogans. Before making a purchase, potential buyers will want to know, for example, the capabilities, features and quality of the product being advertised. The next examples illustrate this point.

Example 2: Advertisements for computers and financial services

The first advertisement in Figure 1.3 gives the precise technical information which is needed to make an informed choice.

Writing style is of minimal importance as the information comprises a simple list of technical features. To attract attention to what would otherwise be a fairly boring image of a computer system, it uses a jet aircraft which helps to reinforce the im-

Botisha

Phantom 700

Only £625
(£734.38 inc VAT)

Ref: AZ3995

- Intel Pentium III 700MHz
- 128 MB SDRAM
- HDD 13 GB
- 17inch monitor, 0.28 dot pitch
- O/S Win 98
- MS Intellimouse
- 56 KBPS Modem
- ATI Rage 128 graphics

Figure 1.3

pression of speed and perhaps, rather less credibly, the real-life quality of the graphics. The price is enclosed in an exploding star to indicate that the system is a real bargain. No time is spent on explanation, partly because it would require considerable space to do so for every technical feature and the seller is assuming that most readers of this particular advert will be familiar with the terminology.

Financial services legislation requires that certain information, such as the interest rate (using a standard method of calculation called the APR), must be included in advertisements for loan facilities. Advertisements for investments are also heavily controlled concerning the claims which can be made on the projected value of an investment, say, after 10 years.

Figure 1.4 shows some typical features of an investment advertisement. The style is more restrained, friendly but not over-familiar and emphasises security with a castle logo and a family picture. The amount of £9,365 in large, bold type is clearly designed to attract attention. The asterisk next to the amount is very important as it points to the fact that it relates to a past investment, which is no guarantee of what would be received in 5 years if the same amount were again invested. Apart from the statement, invariably in very small print, at the bottom of the advertisement, financial services legislation requires numerous other statements which qualify what is claimed in the main text.

Safe as Houses

How secure is your future?

If you are aged between 23 and 65 and have £2500 or more to invest for 5 years you could gain rich rewards with a Safe As Houses Investment Bond.

If you had invested £5,000 in 1995, it would now be worth

£9,365*

Contact us on 0800 11 00 22 for further information.

* Past performance is not a guarantee of future returns, as these depend on bonuses yet to be earned.

Figure 1.4

Summarising information

Summarising refers to the process of preparing a shorter or condensed version of a body of information. To summarise information effectively, you must:

- ❑ thoroughly understand the information;
- ❑ select the main themes and major facts. You must not add to the content or alter any factual content;
- ❑ write the summary clearly and concisely (which is the whole point of a summary). The summary should 'flow' and read as a whole, not as a collection of disconnected sentences. A wide vocabulary will obviously help.

Minutes

Summarising is an important skill in many aspects of work. For example, the discussions at a formal meeting are recorded in the *minutes*, which then have to be agreed at the next meeting as a true record of what took place. Some minutes are referred to as Action Minutes and detail tasks to be completed and the names of the persons responsible for carrying them out, so it is important that minutes are accurately recorded and corrected if found to be in error. Consider the problems that may be caused if Mr. X was incorrectly quoted as admitting that he had failed to contact an important customer and lost valuable business as a result. The problem would be worse if he was not at the next meeting to put matters right. Minute taking is not an easy skill, especially if the meeting is not well managed and several people try to speak at the same time. The minutes secretary must be able to distinguish the important from the unimportant and learn to ignore flippant, indiscrete or irrelevant comments which are clearly not meant to be recorded. An example minutes document is given on the next page (it relates to the Parish Council Agenda in the next section).

At each meeting, the second item on the Agenda refers to the minutes of the previous meeting. Examples of other occasions when information needs to be summarised are given below.

- ❑ A member of staff attends a one-day conference on new VAT regulations and then has to pass on what he or she learned to the Financial Director.
- ❑ After numerous complaints to sales staff about the non-delivery of an order, a customer rings the Sales Manager, who then asks the Sales supervisor for a summary of the events since the first complaint was made.

AMBRIDGE PARISH COUNCIL MINUTES

OF THE MEETING of the PARISH COUNCIL held on MONDAY 19 JUNE 2000 at 7.30 p.m.

PRESENT	Councillors Smith, Brown, Ginelli, Jones (in the Chair), Patel and Kenelly.
	An apology for absence was received from Cllr Redman.
MINUTES	The Minutes of the meeting held on 19 May were agreed.
FINANCE	Agreed payment of fees to Cullen and Brown, solicitors of £1,654.50 for work done on Compulsory Purchase Order and £356 to Borchester County Council for installation of new lamp in Main Street.
PLANNING APPLICATIONS	Agreed no objection to extension at 13 Hayseed Cottages and that Cllr Patel look into the matter of the outhouse which has been constructed at the rear of Buttercup Way. It appears that planning permission has not been sought.
CORRESPONDENCE	Noted County Council report on government housing needs and the County Structure Plan. To be viewed by all members before next meeting.
AOB	None
NEXT MEETING	18 July 2000

Giving notice and details of meetings

Agendas

The quality and effectiveness of a meeting tends to be improved if the chairperson takes proper control and prevents members from speaking over one another. The meeting is also likely to be more productive if all members have proper notice of what is to be discussed and this is done through the agenda.

If there are reports to be considered, these should be submitted for distribution to members before the meeting, rather than 'tabled'(presented at the meeting itself); this enables members to read them in advance and so, hopefully, be more able to make informed comment at the meeting. An example agenda follows.

AMBRIDGE PARISH COUNCIL

A MEETING of the **PARISH COUNCIL** will be held in the Village Hall, Ambridge on **MONDAY 26 JUNE 2000** at **7.30 p.m**

AGENDA

1. Apologies for absence.
2. Minutes of the meeting held on 19 May 2000 (copy attached).
3. Matters arising.
4. Finance.
5. Planning applications.
6. Correspondence.
7. Traffic and safety reports.
8. Any other business.
9. Date of next meeting.

Albert Benbow, Clerk to the Parish Council,   18 June 2000

Item 2, 'Minutes of the last meeting ...', is the point at which members must agree that the minutes are an accurate record or what was discussed and agreed at the last meeting. If there are any corrections, these are made and the Chairperson signs them as a correct record. Item 3, 'Matters Arising' relates to the discussion of items in the meetings of the last meeting which may need further discussion.

Public meeting notices

The above agenda includes the notice details of the meeting, but for public meetings it is impractical to issue agendas and there is often only one topic. The format of such notices is largely up to the producer, but it must include all information that people need in order to attend, that is the location, date and time. For people travelling some distance, directions will also be valuable. Obviously, the subject of the event or meeting is crucial.

Writing to impress

When applying for a job or a place at university, for example, your letter of application and *curriculum vitae* (CV) are usually the only means by which the employers or admissions tutors can initially judge your suitability for selection. If you fail to impress at this stage, you may well not be asked to proceed to the next stage of application, which is normally an interview. If this happened, you might say to yourself, "If only they had had the chance to meet me and talk to me, they would have seen that I was perfect for the job/course." Letters of application and cv's, even interviews, are very imperfect tools for selecting people, but for most organisations they are often the only practical way of doing so. As with most things, practice will improve your letter writing skills.

Preparing a cv is a little more straightforward, as the contents and layout are fairly standard, but you will need to think very carefully about the content. It is likely that you will have to modify your cv, not only as your experience, achievements and qualifications increase, but also to suit the requirements of different applications. If you are applying for a post as a sports club trainer, you would emphasise your athletic achievements, whereas an application for a position as a computer technician would tend to place these achievements in the 'Outside interests/activities' section of the cv.

A curriculum vitae (CV)

A CV is a brief account of a person's career and personal development. It normally accompanies letters of job application, but the content may need to be incorporated in a special application form, if one is provided for the purpose. A CV is also useful in support of a general letter of enquiry about job availability in a particular organisation. A typical CV is likely to include the following:

1. personal details;   2. education;   3. qualifications;

4. work experience;   5. interests, hobbies;   6. supplementary information.

Curriculum Vitae

Name: Shahin Hussain

Age: 19   Date of Birth:18.4.81
Marital Status: Single
Nationality: British
Home Address: 12 Neville View, Ambridge, BC1 4LS
Telephone Number: 0141 654321
E-mail: shahin@talk21.com

Education

1992 - 1997	Wood Lane Comprehensive School, Felpersham. Captain of school cricket team 1996-1997
1997 - 1999	Borchester College of Further Education, Felpersham. Secretary of Students Union Management Committee and member of Borchester College Soccer Team.

Qualifications

1997	GCSE Information Technology Grade A * GCSE English Grade B GCSE Mathematics Grade B GCSE History Grade C GCSE Art Grade C GCSE Geography Grade D (All with Welsh Joint Education Committee)
1998	Royal College of Music Piano Grade 7
1999	GNVQ Advanced Information Technology (Pass with Merit): Information Technology Systems; Systems Analysis; Using Information Technology; Software; Organisations and Information Technology; Database Development; Communications and Networking; Information Technology Projects and Teamwork; Programming; Multimedia Systems.

Work Experience

1998	Work experience placement for 4 weeks as part of college course, with Kitchen Systems Ltd, Ambridge Road, Borchester, involved in IT support work in IT Services Department.
1998- to date	Assistant Network Engineer with Kitchen Systems Ltd, Ambridge Road, Borchester. (Present salary £9,800 p.a.)

Interests

I have a keen interest in all outdoor sports, particularly cricket. I am captain of the Ambridge Cricket Club's first team which plays in the Borchester League. I also play the piano for my own pleasure.

General Information

Career opportunities with my present employer are limited and I am seeking to develop my career in network engineering. I am taking a 1 week course next month (as part of my holiday entitlement) on a Novell Network Engineering course on 4 July 2000. I have to give 2 weeks notice to terminate my present job.

Referees

Mr Roger Pearson, Human Resources Manager, National Farmers Union, Felpersham Road, Borchester, Tel: 0141 364789

Mrs Anne McDonald, Course Leader, Advanced VCE in ICT, Borchester College of Further Education, Felpersham, Tel: 0141 349821

Letters of application

Such letters are essentially formal, although as explained earlier, provided that your personal writing style makes a positive contribution to the tone of the letter, then let it come through. However, although e-mail communication is leading to greater informality in communication, it has to be assumed that the recipient of a job application expects to see a formal letter. The first example, given below, is properly constructed, presented and written in an appropriate style.

12 Neville View
Ambridge
Borchester
BC1 4LS

28 June 2000

(i) Mrs. M. Marconi
Human Resources Manager
Ambridge Bathrooms Ltd
32-34 Downham Road
Felpersham
Borchester, BC2 3LD

(ii) Your ref: MM/NE1

(iii) Dear Mrs Marconi,

(iv) I wish to apply for the post of Assistant Network Administrator which was recently advertised in the Borchester Chronicle.

(v) I have enclosed my curriculum vitae in support of my application.

(vi) My present post is Network Support Technician at Kitchen Systems Ltd in Felpersham, where I have worked since completing my GNVQ Advanced Information Technology course at Borchester College in June 1999. I believe that my experience and the further qualification I hope to gain next month as a Novell Accredited Network Administrator would enable me to take on the duties you require with confidence and skill. Your advertisement indicates that you use the Novell network operating system, which is also that used by Kitchen Systems Ltd.

(vii) I have to give two weeks notice to terminate my present job and can arrange to be available for interview at any time convenient to you.
Yours sincerely,

Shahin Hussain

(The numbering is simply to cross reference with the comments which follow the letter.) Shahin's letter contains the following points:

(i) The name, status and address of the recipient.

(ii) The company reference, to enable the recipient to identify the matter to which the letter relates.

(iii) The salutation. If the name of the recipient is not known, you would have to use 'Dear Sir/Madam and use the close 'Yours faithfully'. It is now usual to use the slightly less formal, 'Yours sincerely' when addressing people by name. There may be circumstances, however, when you judge it safer to use 'Yours faithfully'.

(iv) A formal application statement to identify the post and where he heard about it.

(v)   Reference to any enclosures, in this case his CV.

(vi) A brief account of his educational qualifications and work experience, even though this information is provided in more detail in the CV. Although the CV is important, the letter will be read first and should make sufficient impact to encourage further consideration of your application. The statement of confidence, provided it is justified, will help to do this.

(vii) A closing paragraph which indicates a willingness to attend for interview and thereby a keen desire to be considered for the post..

Contrast the previous letter with following application for a Web Designer position.

> 12 Neville View
> Ambridge
> Borchester

Dear Madam,

I saw the advert of the job about Web Design in the Borchester Chronicle and I think that I would be good at it. I done a course on computers and the Internet at college and really liked it. I am 19 now and got 5 GCSE at school. I nearly passed the course at college. I would have passed but the tutor had it in for me. I don't really like working with peeple, so I thought the a computer job would be ideal. If you want to contact me you can get me on my mobile (0788 478590), but my top-up card might run out soon. Better still by e-mail at rodgerthedodger@supermail.com. If you want you can look at my personal website on www.rogerspalace.super.net, but I am still working on it and some of the links don't work.

Yours sincerley,

Roger Hutchinson

As you will notice, there are a number of major flaws in the letter:

- ☐ The name and address and reference of the recipient are missing and the letter is undated.

- ☐ The job is not clearly identified. The company may be advertising for several staff to work in the area of Internet and Web support.

- ☐ Roger refers to his GCSE's, but does not provide grades. The information about the course is obviously not helpful and the statements concerning his relationships with people and the course tutor suggest that he would not be able to work as part of a team.

- ☐ The contact information is not likely to inspire confidence and the use of silly names for his e-mail and web site address are clearly inappropriate as illustrations of his work.

- ☐ There are spelling mistakes and grammatical errors and the style is more appropriate for an e-mail to his friends.

Gathering information through questionnaires

A questionnaire is used to conduct a survey on an area of interest or research. It is a means of gathering information, and it consists of a number of questions that are to be answered by a single person. Sometimes the questions are of a personal nature, to do with people's opinions on various things such as the quality of television programmes, or the effectiveness of the government; at other times a questionnaire is used to gather factual information on such things as what banks people use, how often they visit their bank and for what main purposes, or what household products they generally purchase. Sometimes questionnaires will be posted to individuals (the *respondents*) who will complete and return them within a certain time span; on other occasions a questionnaire will be used by an interviewer to ask individuals questions directly.

Questionnaire design

There are a number of distinct stages in designing a questionnaire:

1. Identify the population.

    The *population* is the type of person to which the survey applies. It could be small, such as the members of a football team, or it could be all the students in a certain college. If the population is large, then it will generally be necessary to reduce the number of people involved. The usual method of doing this is to take a sample, that is, a proportion of the population selected according to some scheme. There are many methods of sampling, some designed to allow statistical analysis to be performed, others for convenience. In fact, one of the simplest methods, if the results of the survey are intended to give only a rough idea about something, is called convenience sampling, in which, as the name suggests, the interviewer uses the questionnaire on any suitable person who happens to be available. It is definitely not a reliable method, but it has the advantage of being quick and easy to use.

2. Design the layout of the questionnaire. Things to think about here are:

    (i)   For interviewer administered questionnaires, using a front sheet to record the interviewer, the date and time, the length of the interview, and any other relevant information.

    (ii) A statement of the purpose of the survey.

    (iii) The number of questions. Too many will be both time consuming and tedious for the respondent as well as an interviewer.

    (iv) The order of the questions. Generally start with broad, easy to answer, impersonal questions before going on to less interesting questions and then sensitive, personal and open-ended questions.

3. Design the format for the answers. The following pages show some examples of different questions and answers.

Example 1

1. **Please indicate your opinion of the importance of being able to use the college's computers for word processing assignments:**

CIRCLE ONE	
No opinion	1
Not desirable	2
Fairly desirable	3
Very desirable	4

This limits responses to defined categories and, by assigning a different number to each response, makes it easier to analyse the final survey results. It is best to limit the number of categories in this type of question to between three to seven, because people often find it difficult to discriminate between the categories when there are too many.

Example 2

The following method may be used to filter out people to whom a question does not apply, to reduce the number of questions to be answered.

2.   **Have you ever made use of the college's computers?**

RING	
Yes	1
No	2

If Yes: What types of software have you used?

Wordprocessor	3
Spreadsheet	4
Desktop publishing	5
Graphics	6
Other (specify)....................	7

Example 3

An alternative is to indicate which question to answer next, depending on the answer to the current question:

3.   **Have you ever made use of the college's computers?**

RING ONE		
Yes	1	GO TO Q10
No	2	GO TO Q15

Example 4

Sometimes open-ended questions are appropriate:

4.   **What do you most like about your course?**

....

....

This type of question increases the amount of work required in the analysis phase of the survey because the answers must somehow be categorised and allocated a suitable code after the questionnaires have been administered. It is generally advisable to limit the number of this type of question and rely mainly on forced response questions like the other examples given earlier.

Example 5

Another possibility for responses is to provide a numeric scale to indicate how well or how badly something is rated:

5.   **How relevant was the course you took to your current employment?**

	Highly relevant				Irrelevant
CIRCLE ONE	1	2	3	4	5

The phrasing of the questions is very important. Here are a few things to avoid:

Double questions: Do you own a computer and do you use it just for playing games?

Vague questions: What do you think of the computer services section?

      What sort of computers do you think the college should have?

Leading questions: Why did you enjoy your course so much?

Coding the questions

If a computer is to be used for analysing the completed questionnaires, it is important that each response to each question is given a unique code. This must be done at the design stage and incorporated into the questionnaire in order to reduce the amount of work required in the analysis stage of the survey. The code could simply be the question number followed by the response for a question. For instance, in Example 5, if the *Highly relevant box* (1) had been ringed, the code would simply be 51 representing question 5, response 1. Of course coding may not be necessary at all if the analysis of the questionnaires is to be done manually.

Questionnaire presentation

Apart from expressing questions clearly and unambiguously, the questionnaire needs to be clearly presented to encourage simple and accurate completion. Consider the medical questionnaire shown in Figure 1.5 and then compare it with the improved version in Figure 1.6. The layout in Figure 1.5 is cluttered and is likely to lead to mistakes in its completion, Notice particularly that the list at the bottom of the form leaves little room to circle individual items.

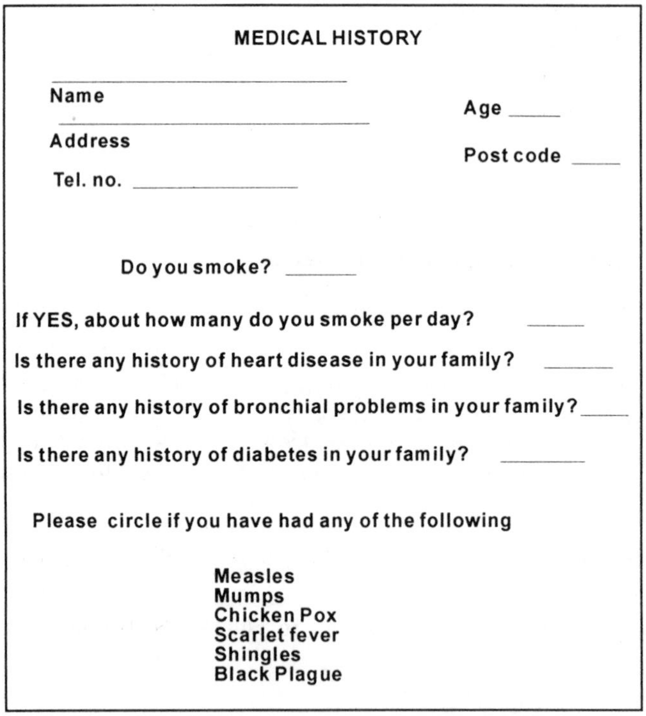

```
                    MEDICAL HISTORY

        _____
        Name                              Age _____
        _____
        Address                           Post code _____

        Tel. no. _____


            Do you smoke?  _____

    If YES, about how many do you smoke per day?       _____

    Is there any history of heart disease in your family?    _____

    Is there any history of bronchial problems in your family?_____

    Is there any history of diabetes in your family?    _____


        Please circle if you have had any of the following

                    Measles
                    Mumps
                    Chicken Pox
                    Scarlet fever
                    Shingles
                    Black Plague
```

Figure 1.5. *A poorly designed and presented questionnaire*

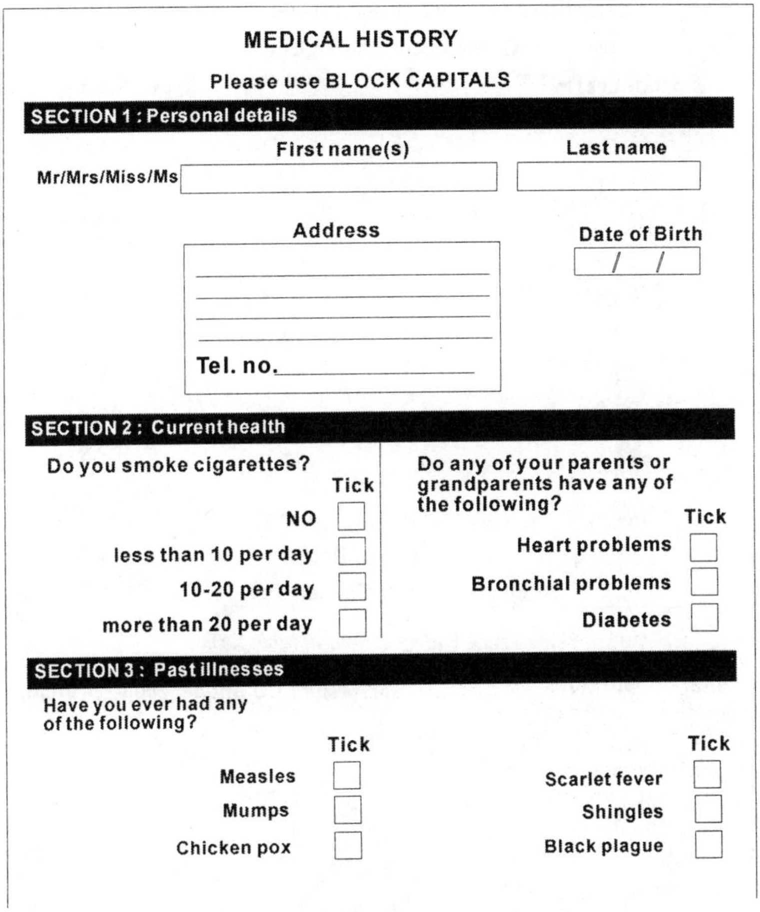

MEDICAL HISTORY

Please use BLOCK CAPITALS

SECTION 1 : Personal details

Mr/Mrs/Miss/Ms First name(s) Last name

Address

Tel. no.

Date of Birth / /

SECTION 2 : Current health

Do you smoke cigarettes? Tick

NO

less than 10 per day

10-20 per day

more than 20 per day

Do any of your parents or grandparents have any of the following? Tick

Heart problems

Bronchial problems

Diabetes

SECTION 3 : Past illnesses

Have you ever had any of the following? Tick

Measles

Mumps

Chicken pox

Tick

Scarlet fever

Shingles

Black plague

Figure 1.6. *A well-designed and presented questionnaire*

The form in Figure 1.6 is uncluttered, pleasing in appearance and the use of tick boxes should encourage accurate completion. Note also that some of the questions in Figure 1.5 are rather vague and have been re-phrased.

Presenting facts

Tabular and graphical presentation

Facts and figures are often presented in table form which reflects the structure of the information and makes it easier to interpret. The example on the next page (Table 1.1) shows how Borsetshire County Council use a table presentation to set out details of their planned budget and inform council tax payers of how their money is to be spent.

Borsetshire County Council Budget 2000-2001				
Gross Expenditure	Government Grant for Specific Services	Charges for Services	Net Expenditure	Net Expenditure
£m	£m	£m	£m	£m
Education 210.1	10.2	16.2	**183.7**	145.2
Fire 12.3	1.2	0.5	**10.6**	8.1
Highways 22.3	5.6	5.2	**11.5**	9.5
Police 36.5	18.1	8.6	**9.8**	7.2
Social Services 42.1	8.1	4.4	**29.6**	22.3
Other Services 15.1	3.1	2.2	**9.8**	6.7
Contingencies 20.8	3.2	2.8	**14.8**	12.4
Total Expenditure 359.2	49.5	39.9	**269.8**	211.4
Less:	Government Block Grant		**134.5**	112.3
	Use of Balances		**1.3**	3.8
	To be raised from Council Tax		**134.0**	95.3

Table 1.1. *A budget set out in table form*

The table presentation provides tax payers with detailed information, which is important for some people, but others may prefer to see be presented with, for example a pie chart (Figure 1.7) to show the distribution of spending or a bar chart (Figure 1.8) to compare the amounts of planned spending on the various services, with the spending figures for the previous year.

Borsetshire CC Budget 2000-2001 (£m)

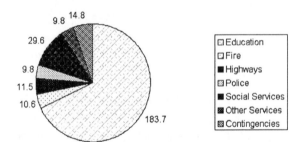

Figure 1.7. *Pie chart showing distribution of budget*

Reports

Although reports may be delivered verbally, they are usually written. A report is a document which examines a particular topic or group of topics to: communicate information; report findings; make suggestions or put forward ideas. Usually, a report will conclude by making recommendations for action. Reports can be classified according to whether they are routine, such as an Annual Company Report to Shareholders, or special, such as a Royal Commission to investigate the problem of child poverty. Reports do not have to be concerned with such major subjects and can be quite short, for example, in the case of a sports club treasurer's report on the club's financial position and the ways in which it can be improved. Reports can also be classified as formal or informal, although both must be structured.

Formal and informal reports

Formal reports are more heavily structured and generally longer than informal reports. The greater the level of detail in a report, the greater the need for structure. Representing a work of research, argument and recommendation, report writing is a significant test of anyone's communication skills. Because every report identifies its author and may be circulated to colleagues and superiors, it can be highly influential in making or breaking a person's reputation in an organisation. A highly structured report may contain the following sections:

(i)   Title page.

(ii) Contents page.

(iii) Summary of recommendations.

(iv) Introduction and Terms of Reference (the objectives of the report).

(v)   The information on which the report is based.

(vi) Conclusions.

(vii) Recommendations.

(viii) Appendices.

(ix) Reference section (references to information sources on which the report relies).

Routine and special reports

Reports which are produced routinely, for example, to give annual sales figures or report balance of trade figures are generally standardised and ideal for production by computer systems Routine reports are normally built into a business's information systems, to be output on demand or automatically at regular intervals or specified times.

Special reports, by definition, are not about standard issues and the structure tends to be less standardised. All reports, however, must be based on Terms of Reference or objectives. A special report be sequenced as follows:

(i)   Terms of Reference.

(ii) A logically presented statement of facts or arguments concerning the subject of the investigation.

(iii) Findings. These identify possible solutions to the problem, giving the benefits and drawbacks or each solution.

(iv) Reasoned recommendations.

Draft report

A 'draft report' is the report before it has been put in its final presentation form. At this stage, the author is concerned with getting the content right, rather than obtaining a highly polished report. Its conclusions may also not be completely finalised and may be altered following further consultation and feedback from those who have commissioned the report. The term 'draft' can be used to refer to any document which is not yet in its final form.

Communicating by e-mail

E-mail etiquette (netiquette)

The word 'etiquette' refers to rules of correct behaviour in society or amongst members of a profession. These rules are not about being 'stuffy' but about observing courtesies which communicate respect and consideration for others. Of course, as society changes so do the rules of etiquette and today many people are happy to be addressed without titles or formality. This is not a problem in face-to-face communication because gestures, body language, facial expression and eye contact can all be used to communicate respect, consideration and friendliness without the constraints of more formal forms of address. Even on the telephone, tone of voice can be used to express feelings and emotions which are difficult to put directly into words. When writing to a stranger, you may have no way of knowing how they wish to be addressed or how they will respond to your usual style of writing, which may convey friendliness or cold formality. Either may be appropriate or inappropriate depending on the recipient of your document. Preparing a document for delivery by 'snail mail', that is, conventional post, takes preparation and effort and provides plenty of time for redrafting or even a decision not to send it at all. If the document is contentious in any way, such as a letter of resignation, or a complaint then the adage "sleep on it" is good advice; a difficult situation often appears very different the next day. E-mail is electronic and once a message is transmitted it may be in the recipient's mailbox seconds later. The first 'netiquette' rule of e-mail is "Think before you send." Some other important rules are:

- ❑ Check your e-mail regularly to ensure that you respond quickly to messages. Of course this applies to normal letter communications as well.

- ❑ If you can't reply immediately, send a quick acknowledgement.

- ❑ If you don't use encryption, be careful about what you say. A building society has been sued for libellous comments e-mailed by one of its employees. Laws on copyright, personal privacy, libel, pornography and incitement of racial hatred also apply to electronic communication.

- ❑ Use your words carefully, especially if you are angry or irritated. As explained earlier, e-mail does not provide the opportunities for body language or voice intonation to 'fine-tune' what you say. If you write something in jest, for example, "You are bone idle, you haven't replied to my e-mail", it is wise to use a 'smiley' (see later) to indicate that you are only joking.

- ❑ Keep your messages fairly brief. If you need to communicate a large amount of information send it as an attachment.

E-mail writing style

E-mail communications are encouraging informality, but you should always try to use wording and style which communicate respect. Because the medium is so quick, many e-mail users become very careless about spelling and grammar, which is probably acceptable between friends but is still unwise in business communication. Abbreviations are common, for example, BTW for "By the way", FAQ for "Frequently asked question", FWIW meaning "For what it's worth" and IMO for "In my opinion".

Smileys

These are ASCII or plain text characters formed into facial expressions to convey a variety of emotions. Suppose that you sent the following message:

"She has gone on holiday."

You might mean

"SHE has gone on holiday" (said with bitterness")

"She HAS gone on holiday" (confirming something that had been in doubt)

" She has gone on HOLIDAY" (said incredulously)

Even with capital letters, each of these could indicate different emotions from those suggested. Here are some examples of smileys which may help to more accurately express the emphasis in what you want to say. To get the effect you need to turn your head to view them sideways. (They look best in the `Courier New` font.)

```
:-)     Happy face - don't take what I said too seriously.
;-)     The smile with a wink implies sarcasm or irony.
:-(     The frown means that you don't like what was said to you.
8^0     The open mouth and wide eyes suggests that you are shocked.
```

Proofing documents

Some of the most commonly used proofing signs are shown in Figure 1.9.

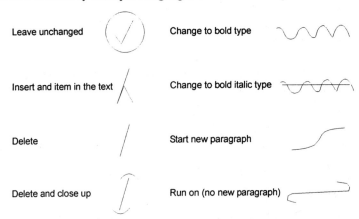

Figure 1.9. *Standard proofing symbols*

To produce readable and presentable documents you need to develop the skill of *proofing* or searching for errors. Generally, except for very short documents, it is very difficult to carry out all proofing on screen and you will probably need to print a draft copy to read. With hard copy, you can use a ruler to guide your eye as you scan each line. If someone else is to carry out the corrections, it is helpful to use standard correction signs which are recognised and used by those involved in writing and publishing. Proofing requires concentration and systematic searching for several types of error which commonly occur. They are detailed below, together with examples.

Spelling

You may have little trouble with spelling, but most people have a 'blind spot' with certain words and some common errors are listed alongside. Apart from checking for misspellings, you should try to be consistent where a word has more than one acceptable spelling. Frequently, for example, you will find that the letter '*s*' can sometimes be used in place of '*z*'. The Oxford Eng-

Correct spelling	Common misspelling
sep*a*rate	separate
stationery	stationary (referring to paper)
station*a*ry	stationery (if you mean stopped)
sincer*e*ly	sincerly
lia*i*son	liason
person*n*el	personel

lish Dictionary will give you the word 'organization', but you will frequently see it spelt as 'organi*s*ation'. Similar examples include, 'specialize' or 'speciali*s*e', 'emphasize' or 'emphasi*s*e'. These are only examples and not demonstration of a rule. For example, 'adverti*s*e' is correct, 'advertize' is wrong and 'advi*z*e' is *not* an alternative to 'advise'.

Typographical or keying errors

Categories of typographical errors include words or individual characters out of order (*transposed*), missing or surplus words or characters and inappropriate or inconsistent use of lower case and capital letters. Look carefully at the two sentences which follow and you should be able to identify at least one example of each category of typographical error.

> "Apart from being late, he was also poorly dressed."

> "apart form being late, HE was was aslo dressd poorly ."

Punctuation errors

You need to look for incorrect and missing punctuation. Some rules, such as the use of a full stop at the end of a sentence, are absolute. Rules on the use of, for example, commas are less clear. Generally, they are used to improve the readability of a document and are often a matter of personal judgement. For example, the sentence

> "Apart from being late he was also poorly dressed."

would not be incorrect but would be more readable if a comma was used as follows.

> "Apart from being late, he was also poorly dressed."

Spacing errors

This relates to the incorrect omission of space or the inclusion of surplus space between words, sentences, lines or paragraphs. Generally, you should leave a single space between words and between a full stop and the beginning of the next sentence. You should also leave a blank line between paragraphs. (Alternatively, you can format the paragraph style to include additional space after each carriage return). Your word processor may provide the option to display characters which are normally *hidden*. These include spaces, tabs and carriage returns, and can make proofing for spacing errors easier. Figure 1.10 shows some hidden characters, with a space represented by a • and a carriage return by a ¶.

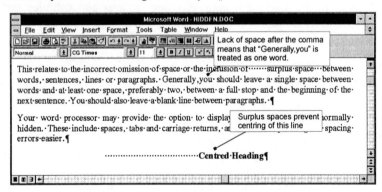

Figure 1.10. *Spacing errors*

Two possible consequences of erroneous spacing can be identified in the Figure.

- ❑ 'Centred Heading' is off centre because the preceding spaces are taken as characters and included as part of the heading.

- ❑ The lack of a space after a comma means that the word before and after it, and the comma itself, are taken as one word; this would mean, for example, that the word processor's spell checker would highlight 'Generally,you', in Figure 1.10, as a misspelling. To correct it you would have to insert the required space.

Spellchecker

All word processors and many other packages include a *spell checking* facility. You may find that, for example, it throws up words like 'organization' as being incorrectly spelled and indicates that only 'organisation' is correct. This does not mean that you cannot use the 'z' form. It simply means that the spellchecker's rules have not allowed for it. Spell checkers will identify as misspelled any word that does not appear in its *dictionary* (stored on disk). Thus, you may find that proper names, such as 'Wilkinson', or abbreviations like 'VCE', as well as many specialist technical terms, are highlighted as being incorrect. Most spell checkers allow you to add words to the dictionary, so that they are not identified as misspellings. If you misspell a word and it happens to be the correct spelling for another word, then the computer will not detect it. For example, 'stationery' and 'stationary' are both correctly spelled but have entirely different meanings. Such errors can only be found by careful proofing.

Thesaurus

Apart from a built-in spell checker, your word processor may also have a *Thesaurus*, which allows you to check the meanings of words and suggests alternatives. This facility should be used with great care, to avoid the use of unusual words which may obscure what you are trying to say. Further, it should only be used to jog your memory for an alternative word. If you use a word with which you are not familiar, you may discover that the word has a similar, but not identical, meaning to the original. For example, the meaning of the following sentence is quite clear.

"She was studious and passed all her examinations."

If you checked the Thesaurus for the word 'studious', it may throw up the suggestions such as, assiduous, diligent, industrious, determined, hard-working, busy, contemplative, intent and tireless. The adjectives do not necessarily relate to the activity of studying. To keep the meaning similar, you could change both adjectives to adverbs and keep the verb 'to study'. Possible alternatives of this form are shown below.

"She studied industriously and passed all her examinations."

"She studied diligently and passed all her examinations."

"She studied assiduously and passed all her examinations."

Even with these forms, the meaning is changed slightly. In the original, it is inferred that she was studious by nature, whereas the others suggest that she was studious for a limited period. The original is probably the easiest to read and best expresses the intended meaning. However, provided you clearly understand the meanings of the words suggested by the Thesaurus and that they are not simply 'wordy' alternatives, then the facility can make your language more varied and lively.

Grammar checker

The grammar checking process is usually an additional option within the spellchecker facility and can be useful for picking up some of the more obvious errors, which could also be picked up by careful proofing. These errors include, for example:

❑ using two full stops at the end of sentence;

❑ using a lower case letter at the start of a sentence;

❑ repeating the same word in succession.

Generally, however, the grammar checker should be used with extreme care as it will often make suggestions which may conform to the rules of grammar but if adopted would make complete nonsense of what you are trying to say. The grammar tool is only useful for identifying possible errors and you need to be confident in your use of grammar in order to determine whether an error actually exists. After the grammar checker has completed scanning a document it can be set to display readability statistics, as shown in Figure 1.11.

The 20% 'Passive sentences' figure relates to the use of sentences such as:

> An example is shown in the next Figure.

To use the 'active voice', which many word processors encourage, you would have to say:

> The next Figure shows an example.

Either is acceptable and which you use is a matter of personal preference but using the active voice can improve readability. Sometimes, the active voice is completely inappropriate, and you need to know when to ignore the grammar checker's warning against the passive voice. For example, the sentence

> You calculate the area of a rectangle by multiplying the width by the length.

is in the active voice but if I don't wish to address the reader directly, I would write

> The area of a rectangle is calculated by multiplying the length by the width.

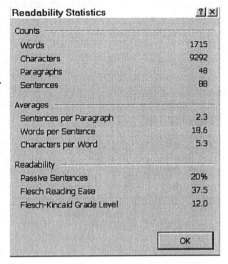

Figure 1.11. *Readability statistics*

Each of the US readability measures (Flesch Reading Ease and Flesch-Kincaid) is based on the average number of syllables per word and words per sentence. Readability also has to do with choice of words and the ways in which sentences are constructed, but the measures do provide a crude guide to readability. Again you need to use your own judgement in assessing readability and only shorten sentences or use words with fewer syllables if it will not destroy the flow and style of your writing. As explained earlier in this chapter, you need to tailor your style to suit the reader. For example, you would not expect to achieve the same readability score for a document aimed at university professors as you would for one aimed at young children.

✍ Exercises

1. Using illustrative examples, suggest two reasons why correct spelling is important.
2. What is meant by proofing and why is it an important process?
3. a. Briefly describe the operation of a spell checker.
   b. With the aid of suitable examples, explain the limitations of a spell checker for proofing purposes.
4. Identify **three** types of document when a personal writing style may be important and **three** types of document when it would not be relevant.
5. Distinguish between a *serif* and *sans-serif* font, giving an example of each.
6. What rules concerning content should you bear in mind when summarising a document.
7. What is the purpose of meeting minutes.
8. What standard items would you expect to see on an agenda?
9. List the sections would you expect to see in a curriculum vitae to support a job application.

10. Suggest items of information you would expect to see in a job advertisement.

11. List the main components of a formal letter.

12. a. Give three examples of information gathering which would be suited to the use of questionnaires.

    b. Give an example of a question which can be answered using an opinion scale.

    c. Give an example of a leading question.

13. Distinguish between a bar chart and a pie chart and give an example of numerical information for which each would be appropriate.

14. List the main headings you would expect to find in a formal report.

15. What is a *draft* document?

16. Give two examples of e-mail etiquette.

17. What is a smiley?

18. a. When would you use a Thesaurus?

    b. When may a Thesaurus be of little use?

19. With the use of examples, distinguish between the 'passive voice' and the 'active voice'.

20. Suggest why a word processor's grammar checker cannot be wholly relied upon for correct grammar.

Chapter 2
Oral communication

Presentations

A presentation is only one of a number of ways which can be used to provide information for an audience, and as with other methods it has its own strengths and weaknesses. Printed material, such as textbooks, handouts, leaflets and pamphlets, and electronic systems, such as websites and CD-ROM resources, provide cost-effective ways of delivering information to mass audiences. However, the effectiveness of a textbook is usually improved if the reader has the opportunity to ask questions and receive clarification from a teacher. A major benefit of a presentation is that it involves 'live' contact between presenter and audience. Of course, some presentations may allow for little interaction between presenter and audience and if its subject comprises the presentation of purely factual information, there may be little need for any. In such an event, it is reasonable to suggest that a printed report would have served just as well and avoided the need for audience and presenter to meet at all.

Commercial organisations are likely to make presentations for a variety of reasons and to a variety of audiences. For example, when a manufacturer launches a new product, this may warrant several different presentations, each one tailored to a particular audience. For example, one presentation can inform sales staff of the product's main selling points, another can advise maintenance staff of the product's maintenance requirements and another can promote the product to potential distributors. Although all the presentations are dealing with the same subject, the details, delivery method and style are likely to be different for each. To be effective, a presentation's content needs to be relevant and of interest to its audience and the presenter must develop a number of presentation skills,. such as speaking clearly and responding effectively to audience feedback. Making a presentation is rather like giving a performance on stage and presenters, like stage actors, often make use of 'props' to support delivery of the message. Commonly used props for presentations include slides for display using an overhead projector (OHP) and computer displays developed with presentation software such as Microsoft PowerPoint. Flip charts and marker pens are useful tools for recording audience questions and feedback.

Structure and sequence

A presentation should have a clear structure with an *introduction*, followed by the *main body* of material, with a *conclusion* or summary of points at the end. The introduction informs your audience of the general subject, perhaps using a main title and sub-title; it should also identify the presenter. If you simply launch into the detail of the subject, for example, with a slide announcing that customer complaints reached record levels in 1999, the audience may well be confused and fail to establish the point of the presentation until several more slides have been viewed. In any case, it is usual to give an oral introduction to the purpose and subject of your presentation, hopefully establishing a rapport with your audience at the same time.

Visual aids

Overhead projector slides and computer slide shows are there to reinforce the content of your presentation, to establish key points and provide a framework for your commentary. It is likely that your spoken commentary will expand on bullet points and include questioning and requests for audience feedback. An example of a structured presentation follows. The presentation includes sample introduction, body and closing slides, presenter script and key points for improving the quality of your own presentations.

Example presentation

This short presentation deals with the topic of e-commerce and is targeted at a group of SME (small to medium enterprise) proprietors and managers. The title slide identifies the topic, a theme and the presenter.

Title slide and introduction

Once the audience is seated, the presenter can introduce himself/herself and the purpose of the presentation. The presenter should be facing the audience and in a position which does not obscure the slides. With the title slide displayed, the presenter may begin by saying:

> ### E-commerce for small businesses
> *"Size need not be important."*
>
> Peter Lansing
> Electronic Futures Limited

"Hello and welcome. My name is Peter Lansing. I am e-commerce consultant for Electronic Futures Limited and run my own on-line business selling helicopter spares. Our company specialises in providing a competitive consultancy service for SMEs such as yourselves. The presentation I am about to make will show you how the Internet and e-commerce can give your business access to global markets, reduce your costs and increase your competitiveness. E-commerce allows you to compete with larger businesses. Remember, size need not be important".

☞ **Set the scene, give your audience a focus and a reason for staying awake**. This means stating the subject of the presentation and its relevance for the audience. It is helpful to establish a theme for the entire presentation. In this example, the catch phrase "Size need not be important" is meant to achieve this aim. It emphasises that e-commerce allows small enterprises the same commercial opportunities as large businesses.

☞ **Establish your credentials and give your audience confidence in what they are about to hear.** Peter Lansing points out his company's association with SMEs and the real benefits that e-commerce can bring. He also gives his own credentials (he is experienced in business) and thereby his qualifications for advising people on the subject of e-commerce. Even if you are not an expert on the subject of your presentation, you need to ensure that you have researched it well and present a confident image to your audience. If you appear hesitant, your audience will have little confidence in what you have to say. This is particularly important when your presentation is part of an interview process.

Body slide 1

The first slide (see next page) in the main body of the presentation begins with a question and then lists key points relating to it. The presenter script may be as follows.

"Stated simply, e-commerce is <u>conducting business transactions over electronic networks</u>. E-commerce is fundamentally changing the way we do business. E-commerce can improve the efficiency of all stages of the business process, from design and manufacture to retailing and distribution.

The major catalyst for the expansion of international electronic retailing is the Internet. Its users, the number of which is rapidly increasing, can communicate with the Web sites of countless organisations all over the world, and it is through these World Wide Web sites that companies can provide 'virtual stores', with product catalogues, 'virtual shopping baskets' and secure credit card payment systems."

Keep slide titles and key points concise. Slide images are vitally important because your audience will remember what they see much more readily than what they hear, no matter how interesting the topic or your voice.

Use slide titles and key points as a guide for your talk. Don't simply read what is on the slide; your listeners will soon start to fidget and mutter that you might as well have printed it out for them to read. The above example script appears to be quite lengthy, but would last less than a minute. So, you need to 'flesh out' the slide bullet points, but don't swamp your listeners with too much detail.

What is e-commerce?

◎ Business transactions that are conducted over electronic networks.

◎ E-commerce is fundamentally changing the way we do business.

◎ Internet stores provide virtual shopping baskets and secure credit card payment systems.

Closing slide

At this point, the presenter should review the key points which are of primary interest to the audience. However effective your presentation, they will not remember all of what you have said and the final slide should be used to provide impact points which they will remember. If they need to check on details later, this can be handled at the end in a question and answer session.

Business benefits

◎ A shop window to the world

◎ Direct contact with customers

◎ Access to new markets

◎ Lower costs

The end of your presentation should be designed for impact, so avoid detail and emphasise the key points. If you are using a computer to support your presentation, then slides can easily include graphics to increase impact, as the alternative closing slide example in Figure 2.1 shows.

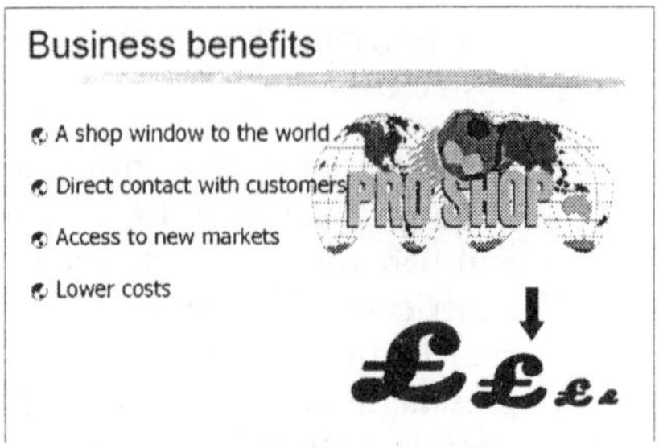

Business benefits

꙼ A shop window to the world

꙼ Direct contact with customers

꙼ Access to new markets

꙼ Lower costs

Figure 2.1. Closing slide with graphics

Using slide presentation software

A computer slide presentation, for example with PowerPoint, needs to be carefully designed to take into account its content and the target audience. It is helpful to consider the following questions and guidelines.

1. Is the user going to browse through and control the flow of the presentation or will the show be controlled by a presenter with spoken commentary? The answer to this question will affect the content of slides - if there is spoken commentary, supplementary information can be provided without cluttering up the slide with too much information.

2. Is the information provided in the presentation regarded as important or of real interest to the audience? Careful use of animation and, where possible, sound can provide impact and prevent the audience from slipping into a deep sleep. On the other hand, fancy

effects can distract the audience from the content of a message.

3. Images should be carefully chosen to suit the subject and the target audience. Cartoon images can add a little humour, but may distract from a serious message. On the other hand effective use of cartoon images can 'lighten' the presentation of what is otherwise a serious subject.

4. Text font styles and sizes should be consistent and appropriate to the presentation. A wild array of several font styles will simply make the text more difficult to read.

5. Don't pack too much information onto one slide and keep the font size large enough for the audience to read, taking into account the distance that they will be from the screen.

6. Good use of colour is more difficult for some, but provided colours are not too garish and text fonts contrast sufficiently with the background to make text legible, then the effect should never be too objectionable.

7. Timing of slide changes and animations within slides is also important if the user is not controlling its progress. You will need to check time delays to give the audience time to absorb the message on each slide. Excessive delays between slide changes are likely to be irritating.

Personal style

Even if you are making a formal presentation, your own personality is bound to come through and it is generally a bad idea to fake it, at least too much. Some presenters have personalities which are highly suited to the task, with a keen sense of wit and an ability to appear enthusiastic, even on the dullest of subjects. They can also quickly establish a relaxed and friendly rapport with an audience. Of course, extroverts may need to exert some restraint in more formal situations, such as interviews. Most people are not blessed with these gifts and have to work a great deal harder to deliver effective presentations. You can be confident and appear so without being an extrovert, but no matter what your personality, careful preparation and a thorough grasp of the subject are vital to a competent performance. Preparation, together with carefully designed slide support, will help you to gain confidence, but speaking to an audience is a skill which can only be improved with practice.

Using your voice effectively

Without microphone support, you will need to make your voice project to everyone in the audience, not just the people in the front row. The first thing to make people 'switch off' is an inability to hear what the presenter is saying and most people are reluctant to say, "Can you speak up? I can't hear you."

Enunciation and articulation

Although you should avoid shouting, you will need to raise the volume and clearly enunciate. This means speaking clearly, emphasising the consonants, particularly the letters B P T D K and G and separating words. An example of fading or dropping of consonants is the pronunciation of Sco-land instead of Scotland or 'wha' instead of 'what'. In normal conversation most of us slur our speech to some extent, sometimes merging words into one another and fading out consonants. It is worth practising speaking your script beforehand and checking with friends whether they can clearly hear what you are saying, even at the far end of the room. Of course, it is possible to overdo the volume and enunciation, such that the audience may become more fascinated by the unnatural form of speaking than they are by the content of the presentation. Just place a little more emphasis on consonants and if you do have a tendency to gabble, it should help to slow you down.

Inflexion

Inflexion, or varying the pitch of your voice, is important for emphasis and to maintain interest. Listening to monotone speech **is** monotonous and will quickly lead to boredom and loss of interest. Some people put inflexion into their speech quite naturally but others who normally speak in a monotone can find it difficult to use inflexion naturally. Forcing your voice to go up and down may sound rather strange, but some gentle raising of pitch to emphasise particular words can be effective. For example, in the following sentence, speaking the underlined word at a very slightly higher pitch would create greater impact than maintenance of a monotone throughout.

The company doubled its profits in one year.

Rehearsing the presentation

Rehearsal is vital for your confidence and the success of your presentation. You should try to give the whole presentation in advance, preferably in the location planned for the real presentation and using some friends or colleagues as audience. Hopefully, they will give you constructive advice if it needs improvement. By rehearsing, you will ensure that you are confident in using the equipment, such as an overhead projector, that your slides are clear and legible even from the back row of the audience, that the sequence and organisation of your material is as it should be, and that you have a thorough knowledge of your subject. This latter point is particularly important if you expect to answer questions from the audience. Rehearsal will also give you the opportunity to test the suitability of your appearance and body language.

Appearance and body language

You should be dressed in a way which suits the audience, which may be formal or informal, but you should dress with care and appropriately. You need to feel comfortable, confident and project a professional image to your audience. Your body language is very important and the following list of guidelines may be helpful.

1. Stand straight and don't hunch your shoulders.

2. Keep your feet slightly apart. This will steady you and help to calm your nerves.

3. Look at your audience, not over them. Making brief eye contact with individuals shows that you are interested in their response and allows you to judge their response.

4. Change your position occasionally, but give your audience a reasonably consistent range on which to focus. Walking backwards and forwards will distract your audience from the subject of your presentation.

5. Avoid jangling keys or other nervous movements, but do use suitable gestures for emphasis. Expansive gestures such as briefly holding your hands wide apart in front of you when asking, "Are there any questions on that point?", for example, can make the audience feel involved. However, making stabbing gestures with your finger can appear aggressive.

6. If you need to glance behind you to check the computer screen or the overhead display, stop talking and wait till you are facing the audience before you start speaking again. Talking with your back to the audience can appear rude and will probably mean that some people do not hear what you say.

Managing the presentation

If you are using an OHP:

1. Before the presentation, make sure that the bulb is working and that you know how to

switch it on. Make sure that the cable is out of harm's way and that you, or any member of the audience, will not trip over it.

2. Ensure that all members of the audience will be able to see the display.

3. Get used to putting the slides the correct way up and positioning them.

4. Check that the slides focus properly on the display board and that the content is large enough to be legible.

5. It is useful to use a pencil or wand to indicate a particular point on the display. Practise pointing at the slide film on the OHP, rather than at the projected image and ensure that the wand is long enough to prevent your hand from obscuring part of the image.

6. Make sure that your slides are in the correct order and that you have somewhere to discard each one as the presentation proceeds.

7. During the presentation, switch the OHP off when you are not using it for lengthy periods. The cooling fan can be quite noisy.

If you are using a computer-generated presentation, the ideal solution is to use an overhead display which will project the computer image onto a display board. When using an OHP you would stand, but for computer-generated displays, you need to be seated. If such equipment is not available, it is helpful if you have one screen to view and control the presentation and the audience has another. If there is only one screen audience numbers should be limited to five or six and you will have to sit to one side to avoid obscuring the screen.

Keeping the audience interested

Variety helps to keep an audience interested. Without it, boredom will quickly set in. So, vary the pace of the presentation. If you come to a part which requires greater emphasis or is more difficult to explain, slow the pace a little. Another section may simple list a number of fairly simple points which require little explanation and the pace can be quickened.

> **Business benefits**
>
> ◎ A shop window to the world
> ◎ Direct contact with customers
> ◎ Access to new markets
> ◎ Lower costs

If you know that your audience has some knowledge or experience of the subject, ask them for comments to further illustrate a particular bullet point. For example, the second bullet point in the adjacent slide could allow the presenter to ask:

"Do you know what proportion of your customers have access to e-mail? How many of you use e-mail at present?"

The first question might obtain no response, but the second will probably result in the raising of hands. Questioning in this way is a bit of a 'fishing expedition' and you hope that someone will 'bite' and provoke a short discussion. Of, course, if time for the presentation is limited, or the audience is large (discussion requires some feeling of closeness and intimacy), you may have to avoid such breaks in continuity. Be enthusiastic. If you look bored, the feeling will quickly transfer to your audience. Make sure that your materials are well organised and that if there is some distraction, such as someone walking into the room, you can deal with the interruption and continue confidently from where you left off. Interruptions or distractions can destroy a presentation, but if you respond with good humour, they can act as 'ice breakers' and make both you and the audience feel more relaxed.

Closing questions and handouts

Oral presentations, even with visual aids, can lead to 'information overload' and you may need to provide handouts. If you plan to give handouts at the end of the presentation, tell your audience at the outset or they may spend the entire time trying to take notes and failing to listen to your commentary. It can be helpful to give your audience paper copies of the slides, to help them keep track of the presentation, but it is generally a bad idea to provide detailed notes during the presentation. Some people will spend time reading those instead of listening to you; more detailed handouts can be issued afterwards. The presentation needs to add something to the information which appears in the handout. Hopefully, this something will include your personality, extra examples, additional explanation, humorous comments, emphasis of key points and the opportunity for audience members to ask questions. Otherwise, the presentation could have been substituted by a handout.

It is usual to allow the audience to ask questions afterwards, so it is important that you understand everything you have said in your presentation. You may be able to answer some questions immediately, or it may be necessary for you to re-display a slide and quickly review one aspect of the presentation. If someone asks you a question which is outside the range of your topic, be honest and don't pretend that you know the answer. If you think that you can find the answer later, say something like, "I'm sorry, I don't know the answer to that question but I will try and find out and get back to you." A question may be completely outside the range of your presentation and it is perfectly acceptable to say, politely, that you can't answer it. It is important that you control the questioning and ensure that any individual does not prolong the session, particularly with questions which are not of general interest. You can always offer to answer such questions as others are leaving.

Interview skills

Whether you are applying for a place at college or university, or for a job, good interview skills are vital for your chances of success. It is important that you prepare for a job interview by:

- ☐ finding out all you can about the employer. You will want to know the size of the organisation, its product or service range, its branch network (if any) and where you might be located. If the organisation has a Web site, this can be an effective way of obtaining information, but you may also be able to obtain company brochures or consult the local Chamber of Commerce. The more research you have done the more the employer will be impressed.

- ☐ finding out details about the advertised post. There should be a job description, salary structure and so on in the advertisement. You may be unsure whether or not you really want the job so it is important to have questions to ask the employer in more detail, such as career structure, training etc.

- ☐ clearly identifying your own ambitions and career interests. It is as well to practise expressing these clearly. This may be quite a lengthy process but you need to try and anticipate what you responses would be to typical questions such as "What qualities do you think you can bring to this job?"

- ☐ identifying your own strengths and weaknesses in relation to the advertised post. If you have a significant weakness, for example, a lack of familiarity with a particular piece of software, try to identify a strength which will reduce the significance of the weakness. For example, you may have a high level of skill with other software and are able to pick up new skills very rapidly.

Good preparation should enable you to answer questions confidently and in a conversational manner. Interview formats vary and may include the requirement for a presentation. They also vary in formality and structure. A typical 30 minute interview would include 2 to 3 minutes 'warm up' with general pleasantries, 15 minutes questions from the interviewer(s), 5 to 10 minutes for your questions and 2 minutes for concluding comments. During the interview, it is desirable to:

1.   show knowledge and interest in the employer's business;

2.   show friendliness, confidence, enthusiasm, calm and quiet assertiveness;

3.   have and be able to express clear career goals and particular interests;

4.   maintain appropriate levels of eye contact;

5.   use a tone of voice which projects the qualities in 2;

6.   be relaxed and take an interest in what is being said;

7.   be well groomed and have a neat, professional appearance;

8.   have a clear grasp of your own skills and experience and their relationship to work in general and to the advertised post. Even if you don't have work experience, it is helpful if you can point to activities in which you have taken responsibility. For example, you may have had some organisational responsibility in a sports club.

Answering questions

It is impossible to anticipate all the question which you may be asked, but you can prepare for some typical ones. It is not a good idea to memorise prepared answers because they will probably sound that way and it is better that you maintain a conversational tone and at least give the impression that you are responding naturally. Try to be honest, but use your discretion. For example, when asked, "How did you choose your college course?", the truth may be that you chose it to be with your friends but later found that the course was what you wanted to do. Rather than saying, "It's what I have wanted to do since I was 10", it would be better to say that you were unsure when you first joined the course but after a few weeks you realised that you had made the right choice. It's probably best to leave out any reference to your initial desire to be with your friends, but you could elaborate by saying that you found that you had many friends on the course and that this added to your enjoyment.

Don't ramble and try not to repeat yourself. Use examples to illustrate your answers - this adds interest - but be succinct and stick to the question. Always keep the requirements of the advertised post in mind. Hopefully, your interviewer will be friendly and the atmosphere relaxed, but don't take this as a signal to lay back in your chair and make careless conversation.

Common interview pitfalls

Here are some avoidable mistakes which may lead to rejection of a candidate: poor knowledge and preparation; lack of enthusiasm; little or no eye contact; arrogance, 'showing off' and insincerity; vague answers.

Discussions

"The earth is not flat." Although this was a subject of scientific discussion several hundred years ago, we now know that the earth is round and is, therefore not something to be argued about. For a subject to be discussed, it must be possible for people to have different opinions about it. Effective discussion requires the expression of opinions which are supported by arguments. A debate is a particularly formal type of discussion where a *motion* is put before the 'house' (the group participating in the debate) and following the presentation of arguments for and against the motion, the 'house' votes to accept or reject it. For example, a motion may state, "This house believes that the national speed limit should be reduced to 50 mph." A proposer and seconder present arguments to support the motion and another proposer and seconder argue to reject it. The discussion may then be thrown open to the 'floor' (the other people taking part in the debate) before a vote is taken to accept or reject the motion. This is the basis for deciding on new laws in the House of Commons and the quality of the debate is determined by the effectiveness of the speakers and the quality of the arguments and facts they present to support their opinions. An important part of debate is listening to the opinions and arguments of others. Of course, discussions can also take place in a much less formal way and the following paragraphs provide suggestions for making them effective.

The point of discussion is to come to a conclusion on some issue or to decide on a particular course of action, weighing the arguments for and against each option. Generally, the participants in a discussion are aware of rules that they will adopt, such as a majority vote or, consensus (general agreement). Majority voting is commonly used by committees, boards of directors and other groups charged with the responsibility of managing organisations. Majority voting may also be used by completely informal groups such as friends trying to decide which club they are going to or the destination for a holiday. In formal situations, it is less important to "keep everybody happy" and decisions will often be made with which not everyone agrees. The group of friends discussing where to go on holiday will obviously be very concerned about one another's feelings and will attempt to come to an agreement with which all are content. The success of any agreement is more likely if all the participants feel that they have had an opportunity to put their points of view and that the others listened and took them into account before coming to a conclusion. If this does not happen, some members may be left feeling resentful and become 'awkward' or even try to make trouble when other decisions are to be made. In the case of discussions between friends or work colleagues, such feelings can lead to the breakup of the group or loss of 'team spirit' and for committees or boards of directors, less effective management of the organisation.

Speaking and listening

Effective discussion, indeed communication in general, requires skill on the part of the speaker and the listener. Ideally, a speaker should:

- ❏ have a wide vocabulary and choose words which the listener will understand;

- ❏ pronounce words correctly;

- ❏ speak fluently and without too much hesitation;

- ❏ speak at a speed which suits the listener, not so slowly as to cause irritation and not so quickly as to cause the listener to lose much of what is being said;

- ❏ use inflexion or intonation in the voice to give variety of expression. Speaking without any variation in tone can be boring for the listener, but it also makes it difficult for the listener to interpret the true meaning of what the speaker is saying. For example, the sentence "I think that people should drive their cars less." spoken in a monotone would suggest, possibly incorrectly, that the speaker is unconvinced about it. With intonation, perhaps with the final word "less" being spoken at a higher pitch and slightly louder, would indicate a strong opinion on the subject.

- ❏ keep some eye contact with the listener, to judge their response to what is being said and to give the listener opportunity to intervene. However, maintaining permanent eye contact can be intrusive or threatening and can cause the other party embarrassment.

A listener should:

- ❏ concentrate on what the speaker is saying;

- ❏ respond with comments as necessary and interject if it is helpful to the flow of the discussion. By maintaining some eye contact, the speaker is able to see when the listener wishes to interject and can respond accordingly. In a lively discussion, there can be a tendency for a speaker to 'hog' the conversation or for a listener (who is not really listening) to continually interrupt and 'get their oar in'. Such tendencies should be avoided if proper discussion is to take place.

❑ respond non-verbally to what is being said, for example, nodding to signify understanding or approval, or smiling to provide encouragement.

Managing discussions

Discussion requires that all participants are given the opportunity to present their views, argue their case and comment on the views of others. For a discussion between two individuals, this requirement can be met quite easily, but where several people are involved, there is often a need for a chairperson. The job of the chairperson is to manage the discussion and determine that only one person speaks at a time. The chairperson should also try to channel discussion towards a conclusion and may well summarise views periodically to find points of agreement and identify points which need further discussion. Suppose, for example, a sports club committee holds a meeting to decide on whether to increase membership subscriptions and by how much. At a particular point, the chairperson may say, "We seem to be moving towards a view that we should increase the subscription. I'll ask each one of you for your final comments and then we will put it to the vote." At this point, less confident people are given a clear opportunity to express the opposing view. Sometimes stronger personalities will dominate general discussion, and a good chairperson will ensure that before a vote is taken, each person is invited to speak.

Generating ideas

Discussion is a productive way of generating and refining ideas. When an idea comes to us, we can think about it, turn it over in our minds and consider the potential benefits and pitfalls. Before we use the idea, we will often want to discuss it with others. Apart from gaining the benefit of other views on the idea, the process often leads us to re-examine the idea and perhaps reject it or see new possibilities which improve it. It is likely that every great inventor, having conceived an initial idea, has spent some time developing it through discussion with at least one other person.

Brainstorming

Brainstorming can be effective in generating new ideas or suggestions. Ideas are accepted without discussion and typically, written directly onto a flip chart or board so that everyone can see. The pool of ideas can then be examined, unworkable ideas rejected and those with potential discussed further.

Team building

A team has common objectives, for example, the development of a new software package, or the building of a new swimming pool for a local community. Each member needs to know and understand the team's objectives, his or her own role and the roles of others in achieving them. Discussion at regular meetings is an essential part of a team's progress towards the achievement of its objectives. Progress needs to be monitored and individual members need opportunities to report on their own work and identify and resolve difficulties. Building a team involves the development of:

❑ ways of working to improve efficiency and productivity;

❑ co-operative and supportive relationships;

❑ mutual respect for each others' strengths;

❑ recognition of one's own weaknesses and the need to use the strengths of others;

❏ the team's adaptability to changes in circumstances, such as a cut in its operating budget.

Achieving consensus through negotiation

Making decisions by consensus is desirable, but not always achievable, at least in the sense of absolute and unreserved agreement. Consensus can only be obtained when each member of a group has clearly expressed his or her views and disagreements, listened to and understood those of the others, and presented any alternatives they wish to be discussed. When, through discussion and negotiation a decision, which everyone understands, is reached then we can say a consensus decision has been made.

Negotiation can take many different forms, from the confrontational to the co-operative. Negotiation generally means compromise, that is, a willingness between parties to modify their own requirements to come to a common agreement. The most successful negotiations are those which leave all parties content and without feelings of resentment. If one party feels that he or she has been forced into an unwilling acceptance of an 'agreement', it is more likely that the agreement will be broken. Successful labour relations between employers and employees are based on good negotiating skills. Some general pointers towards good negotiation are given below:

❏ Each party should be clear about the objectives and wishes of the others.

❏ Identify areas of particular difficulty and resistance to any compromise. Attempt to find areas of agreement first and then work on the areas of resistance.

❏ Keep personalities out of the discussion. In other words, try not to allow personal likes and dislikes of others to obstruct negotiations.

❏ Avoid using threats and giving in to anger and frustration. If your counterpart gives in to such emotion, remain calm and patient and try to return attention to the areas of agreement and mutual benefit.

❏ Pay attention to you own body language and that of the other negotiators.

❏ Before making a proposal try to anticipate the possible responses. As in chess, it is important to think a few moves ahead.

❏ Emphasise the positive qualities in your own proposals and the benefits for your counterpart, but also admit the benefits for yourself.

Body language

Being able to read the body language of others and use body language yourself are very important communication skills. Of course, body language is something we use without thinking much of the time, but self-awareness is important if you don't want the wrong signals to be given out. Although too deliberate use of body language will probably be recognised as such, it is helpful to be aware of some simple codes which you can use and recognise. By way of illustration, participants in business negotiations would probably use and recognise the following example body language codes (the meanings of postures and gestures vary with different cultures and those described below relate to the Western culture).

Posture	Meaning
Seated, leaning forward, feet flat on floor, hands open on knees	Acceptance
Seated, leaning forward, pointing or fists clenched	Aggressive rejection

Seated, legs slightly apart, feet under chair and leaning forward	Eager acceptance
Slumped in chair, gazing into space, doodling	Boredom
Standing with arms behind back, legs slightly apart and smiling	Attentive
Stroking chin, looking up and to the right	Evaluating and thinking of response

Exercises

1. Suppose that you are required to make a presentation to a group of 15 school students who are considering following the BTEC Nationals course next year.

   (a) List the items of equipment and support materials which you may require, briefly identifying the purpose of each item.

   (b) Suggest a title for the presentation, a short and memorable 'catch phrase' for the title slide.

   (c) Write a suitable opening script, which includes your personal introduction, a statement of the purpose of the presentation and your credentials.

   (d) Rehearse the script with a member of your group and modify it until you are both satisfied that it uses an appropriate style for the audience.

   (e) Word process (use the Outline feature if the package has one) an outline structure for the presentation. Make sure that the structure and sequence are quite clear.

   (f) Suggest 3 methods you may use to try and maintain the interest of your audience.

   (g) Identify any problems you can envisage with the physical arrangements for the presentation. Assume that you are to make the presentation in your usual class room or laboratory.

   (h) Distinguish between articulation and inflexion and explain why each would be important for the success of your presentation.

2. Suppose that you have applied for a job with a local Internet Services company and have been asked to attend for interview.

   (a) Suggest two ways in which you can prepare for the interview, briefly suggesting why each is important.

   (b) Identify 4 aspects of your behaviour (be reasonable) during the interview which are likely to:

      (i) improve your chances of success;

      (ii) damage your chances of success.

3. Suppose that you are a member of a team which is responsible for the production of a your employer's company web site. A team meeting has been called to identify ways in which the web site could be used to improve marketing and customer support services. The meeting will include a 'brainstorming' session to help in this task.

   (a) What is meant by 'brainstorming' and what is it meant to achieve?

   (b) Consider your own personality and in particular, your confidence to take part in discussions generally. Suggest two ways in which your confidence in making a contribution may be:

      (i) increased;

      (ii) reduced.

Chapter 3
Study skills

The effectiveness of your study can be improved by careful attention to:

- ❏ planning and time management;
- ❏ efficient searching of information sources, both conventional and electronic;
- ❏ discriminatory use of information sources;
- ❏ the layout and presentation of your work, both in note form and as formatted documents.

There are also different methods of reading which can make the tasks of information gathering and learning easier. Note taking is an important skill for recording key pieces of information which you identify in a research text. Summarising is essential if you are to extract more detail and obtain a true interpretation of the text. It therefore requires more careful examination of a text than simple note taking.

Planning and time management

Planning requires that you identify the tasks you are required to complete, draw up a schedule which shows when each has to be completed and then analyse each one to determine its work requirements. Apart from scheduled tasks, you will obviously have to take account of the time taken up by lectures, workshops, meal and coffee breaks, travel, sleep, social activities and so on. If we suppose that all the tasks are to be completed by the same date, it will be necessary to analyse each one to determine its inputs. These will include, for example, research from texts in the library (you need to be available when its open), research from the Web (unless you have your own computer, check when you can have access), consultation with your tutor to check on progress (this will tie you to a particular time), investigation of the facilities provided by a software package, expanding on notes or summaries and word processing final documents. Here are some simple do's and don'ts.

Not everyday follows the same pattern, so you will need to get used to a different plan for each day. If you know that you have a complete afternoon free on a Thursday, make sure that you are prepared to work on a task which requires a longer, uninterrupted effort.

Some people can think more clearly in the mornings than the afternoons, so try to fit tasks which require careful thought and concentration into the times which suit you.

Make good use of your time and don't let the work pile up.

Try to understand concepts the first time that they are presented to you. Further review of the concepts will then further establish your understanding. Don't daydream in lectures and rely on reading the handout or textbook to learn later.

Research

Although there are many sources of information (the Internet is examined later), the text book is still the most important. When you are researching a topic, you will probably consult the library indexes, perhaps by entering key words into a computerised search system, or by consulting the manual subject indexes.

Although browsing the shelves is useful once the general location has been found, you should always aim to narrow your search as quickly as possible. It is best to research a topic from a variety of sources, although you will probably concentrate on one as your primary source, consulting others to obtain additional information, to verify the accuracy of stated facts and evaluate the worth of stated opinions. This is important even in subjects such as computing which are regarded as mainly factual. If the results of your researches are to be worthwhile, then you will need to evaluate the information you find and be discriminating in selecting or rejecting it. You should reject information which:

- ❏ is not relevant;
- ❏ is beyond the scope of your task;
- ❏ includes detail which you do not understand;
- ❏ repeats what is already there;
- ❏ is simply 'padding'.

Effective and efficient reading

There are different reading techniques to suit different purposes and text sources. For example, 'skimming' is useful for quickly finding a key word or phrase in a document, but useless for learning about a new and difficult topic. When undertaking research, you will need to examine a range of sources, first making a quick check to see if each is likely to be useful and then examining those selected in more detail. Suppose that you have picked up a book because its title seemed to fit with the topic your are researching. There are a number of stages (in a typical top-down approach) you can go through to determine whether it may actually be useful.

1. Check how the book is organised, its general content, author (who may be familiar to you from other texts you have read) and publication date (an old text may be suitable for basic concepts but hopeless for current technologies).

2. The Preface may give you an overall idea of the aims of the book and the target readers.

3. The Table of Contents and Index are obvious ways of checking for your required topic.

4. If you find a suitable page reference, go to it and judge whether the level of detail is what you want and whether you find it readable.

Some tasks require careful, word-by-word reading, but there are techniques which can be used to increase the rate at which you can absorb the information you need.

Speed reading

There are two main approaches to speed reading. With *expanded* reading, you use your peripheral vision to take in 2, 4 or even 6 words in at a glance. You may well do this to a limited extent already when the text is familiar or you don't need to take in every word - often referred to as "getting the gist of it". Speed reading trainers state the practical limit using this technique is around 700 words a minute. To read dynamically, you need to be trained to use your peripheral vision both horizontally and vertically, effectively viewing sections of a page at a time and absorbing up 20 or more words at a glance. Reading speeds of between 1500 and 10,000 words per minute are achievable. Although most people are not going to take the trouble to obtain formal training, it can be useful to practice using your horizontal peripheral vision and gain an appreciable increase in reading speed. Of course, the purpose of reading is to take in information, so there is no point in using skimming or expanded reading if you are not achieving that purpose. It is worth trying to improve your reading speed, but you need to choose a method which suits the material you are studying. Reading requires concentration, so remember to pace yourself, taking a break or carrying on with a different task when necessary.

Unit 1 Assignments

1.1. Documents and writing style

Following the merger of Silicon Software with Omega Business Systems, the first board meeting of the new company, Silicon Business Software Limited, resulted in a number of important changes being implemented. One of the changes is to establish a Human Resources department. Previously, neither company had operated corporate personnel systems, but had left personnel matters to indvidual departments. You have been transferred to this new department, where your job involves you working as a senior assistant to the Human Resources Manager, Ann Robinson. After your initial meeting with Mrs Robinson, at which a variety of issues were discussed, you received the following internal memorandum.

Memorandum

To: Senior Personnel Assistant

From: Human Resources Manager

Re: Establishment of corporate materials

Date: 14 June 2000

I have given thought to our conversation on the need for standardised letters and forms to meet the functions of the new department. I am satisfied that we cannot standardise job advertisements, but want you to provide me with drafts of the following:

Forms:

a job application form that all job applicants would have to complete (I would want it to contain sufficient information to enable me to use it as an employee record form).

a staff appraisal form to record job performance.

Letters to fulfil the following tasks:

invite applicants for job interviews;

inform an applicant that he/she is not being called for interview;

inform an interviewee that he/she is not being offered the job;

offer the job to the successful interviewee;

issue a formal warning to an employee who is guilty of misconduct, stating that dismissal will result from a repetition of the conduct complained of;

issue a dismissal;

inform an employee that he/she is being made redundant;

I am aware that this is a substantial task but would ask you to complete it as a matter of urgency.

Tasks

1. Draft the forms and letters requested in the memorandum, using a content, tone and style appropriate to each of them.
2. Write a memorandum to the Human Resources Manager indicating that you expect the work to take considerable time to complete.
3. Obtain examples of some of the above documents, letters and forms used by public and private sector organisations in your area. Compare these in order to produce a dossier

containing an example of each document, letter or form which combines the examples of best practice in each.

1.2. Meeting documents

Draw up and word process an agenda for a meeting to discuss an issue relating to your course. For example, you will probably appoint one or more of your fellow students as representatives to attend Course Team meetings and will need to inform them of matters which you wish to pass on to Tutors. You should appoint a chairperson and minutes secretary (this job can be taken by a different person for each meeting). The minutes should be word processed by the minutes secretary after each meeting and be distributed to the rest of the group before the next meeting. As minute taking is a difficult skill, you will need to record the main points only and the name of the person who made each contribution. At the next meeting, the minutes of the previous meeting will be checked for accuracy before being signed by the chairperson.

1.3. Questionnaires

This assignment concerns the design and use of a questionnaire to carry out a survey on some area of interest.

1. Design a questionnaire to survey opinion on an area of interest to you. Think carefully about the aims of the survey, the size of the survey and how the results are to be analysed, because these factors will greatly influence the design of the questions and how they are to be coded.
2. Apply the questionnaire to a suitable population or sample of a large population.
3. Calculate the percentages of response to each question and present the calculations in tabular form for easy reference.
4. Calculate any other useful statistics, such as means, medians or modes.
5. Produce appropriate statistical charts to illustrate the results of the survey.
6. Write a report describing the results of your survey and explain the reasoning behind your conclusions.

1.4. Presentation

As a member of the ICT support team employed by a recruitment agency, HFC Ltd, you have been asked to give a presentation to recruitment and administrative staff on ONE of the following topics.

1. Viruses, their types, their effects and the measures which can be taken to protect the company's systems against attack.
2. Hacking, the motives of hackers and the measures which HFC Ltd can take to protect their systems.
3. The Internet and the opportunities and dangers it presents for the future of the company.

Unit 2: Computer systems

Assessment Evidence Grid

Grade E	Grade C	Grade A
State the basic concepts and principles involved in the representation of data (including 2's complement and fixed and floating point forms for numeric data, ASCII, bit masks, and bit maps) within a computer system.	Explain the concepts and principles involved in the representation of data within a computer system, the role played by each format and the possible errors caused by inappropriate use of each format.	Describe in detail the function of the fetch-decode-execute cycle and its relationship to the workings of a microprocessor, making detailed reference to the role played by hardware and software in this relationship.
Specify and select components, and build, conforming to safety standards, a PC to meet a technical specification.	Describe, with the aid of diagrams, the hardware (including logic gates, registers, buses, CU, ALU and memory) and its function within a model microprocessor.	Evaluate the work you have done in building and configuring a computer system to a given specification including how well the finished system met the specification, what went well and what went less well in your work and what improvements could be made to the resulting system.
Install and configure an operating system and software to meet a client specification.	Describe the functions of an operating system within a modern computer system.	Write coherently and comprehensively, include accurate drawings which enhance your text and show a good command of technical language.
Convert numbers between binary, denary and hexadecimal notation.	Write programs in a low level programming language which include data transfer, arithmetic, jump and branch instructions.	
Use 2's complement notation to add and subtract fixed point binary numbers, use floating point representation to perform addition, subtraction, multiplication and division of denary numbers, use floating point representation to add and subtract binary numbers.		
Write very basic programs (such as fetching and adding together two numbers, and storing the result) in a low level language.		

Chapter 4

Basic concepts

A computer system is a collection of devices (the *hardware*) controlled by a computer program (the *software*). But what actually happens inside a computer to cause all these components to work together? How does a program control the hardware? How is data stored in the memory of a computer? This chapter provides the answers to these and other questions regarding the fundamental operation of a computer. However, a computer system is in a way like a jigsaw puzzle: the pieces of the puzzle are theoretical concepts embracing mathematics and physics, and they must be understood and fitted together in a certain way before the whole picture can be seen. So, to begin with, we will identify and describe a number of important ideas to provide a basis for understanding how they fit together to make a computer.

Binary numbers

If there is a single concept that can be said to be the basis of the operation of a modern digital computer, then it must be the *binary numbering system*. Incredible as it might seem, the operation of a computer is based entirely on the numbers 0 and 1. A computer "remembers" only the numbers 0 and 1; a computer does arithmetic using only the numbers 0 and 1; indeed, the notorious logical abilities of a computer rely solely on the numbers 0 and 1. This is the reason for the emphasis on binary numbers and binary arithmetic in Chapter .

So in terms of the operation of a computer what is the significance of all this? The point is that there are many simple ways that only two digits can be represented. For example, opposites such as big and small, positive and negative, up and down, or on and off can all be used. What all of these examples have in common is that they have two different states that can be used to represent the binary digits 0 and 1. In an electronic device such as a computer, the two states most commonly used are

- [ ] the presence of an electrical voltage (above a certain value, such as five volts); this is used to represent binary 1, and

- [ ] the absence (or near absence) of an electrical voltage, which represents binary 0.

If we can find some means of storing and reading these voltage states using some kind of electronic device, then we have the potential for making computer memory. Of course this device exists: it is constructed from *gates* which in turn use transistors. When a number of gates are linked together in a certain way they form a device called a *flip-flop,* which is able to "remember" a binary digit. One type of flip-flop has a single input by which electrical signals are used to *set* the device to store a logic 1, or *reset* it to store a logic 0. Once a flip-flop has been set or reset, it

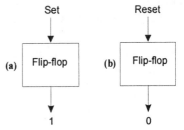

Figure 4.1. *Binary digits stored using a flip-flop*

stays that way until further signals change it; in other words, it "remembers" a binary digit - it stores a single *bit*. Figure 4.1 shows two flip-flops, one set to store a binary 1 and the other reset to store a binary 0.

Figure 4.1(a) shows a logic 1 signal applied to the *set* input in order to set the flip-flop to store a binary 1. In (b) a logic 0 signal is applied to the *reset* input to make the device store 0.

The memory size of a computer is frequently specified in terms of a number of *kilobytes* (K) or *megabytes*(M). A *byte* is a group of eight flip-flops regarded collectively as a unit of memory. So, rather than storing a single *bit* (that is, a single 1 or a single 0) in memory, a byte is usually the smallest amount of data that is stored. A kilobyte is approximately one thousand bytes (1024 bytes, actually) and a megabyte is approximately a thousand kilobytes (1024 x 1024 bytes). In order to store a byte of data in memory, the data needs to be presented to the eight flip-flops as a group of eight simultaneous signals; Figure 4.2 illustrates this.

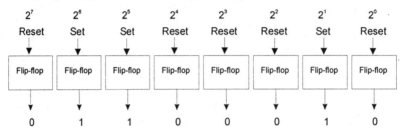

Figure 4.2. *Eight flip-flops used to store a byte of data*

Figure 4.2 shows a set of eight flip-flops organised to represent an eight bit binary number. The leftmost unit represents 2^7, or 128, and the rightmost unit represents 2^0, or 1. The whole eight-bit number therefore represents

$$0 \times 2^7 + 1 \times 2^6 + 1 \times 2^5 + 0 \times 2^4 + 0 \times 2^3 + 0 \times 2^2 + 1 \times 2^1 + 0 \times 2^0$$
$$= 0 + 64 + 32 + 0 + 0 + 0 + 2 + 0 = 98$$

The largest number that we can store in this way, using a single byte of memory is

$$1 \times 2^7 + 1 \times 2^6 + 1 \times 2^5 + 1 \times 2^4 + 1 \times 2^3 + 1 \times 2^2 + 1 \times 2^1 + 1 \times 2^0$$
$$= 128 + 64 + 32 + 16 + 8 + 4 + 2 + 1 = 255$$

However, we can store larger numbers by using several bytes and treat them as a single number. Moreover, by using numeric codes to represent alphabetic characters and other symbols such as punctuation marks, we are able to store text as well as numeric data. Table 4.1 shows part of a commonly used method for storing textual data; it is called the ASCII character set (American Standard Code for Information Interchange). Each letter in the table has its own unique code.

character	ASCII	character	ASCII	character	ASCII	character	ASCII
a	01100001	h	01101000	o	01101111	v	01110110
b	01100010	i	01101001	p	01110000	w	01110111
c	01100011	j	01101010	q	01110001	x	01111000
d	01100100	k	01101011	r	01110010	y	01111001
e	01100101	l	01101100	s	01110011	z	01111010
f	01100110	m	01101101	t	01110100		
g	01100111	n	01101110	u	01110101		

Table 4.1. *Extract from ASCII character set*

Thus, if the binary code 01100010 shown in Figure 4.2 was being used to store a character rather than a number, it would represent the letter b.

So now we are able to store numeric data or text, depending on how we choose to regard the memory contents. Yet another possibility is to view the contents of memory as instructions forming a computer program. For example, a certain combination of bits might mean add two numbers; another combination might mean move a number from one part of memory to another, or transfer the contents of a memory location to an output device such as a printer, or read the keyboard and store the ASCII code of the key that has just been pressed. In this way it is possible to store instructions to perform a large number of simple tasks, and we can specify more complex tasks by grouping these simple operations into sequences forming computer programs.

We now need to consider how a set of instructions stored in the memory can be interpreted and performed one after another by the computer automatically. In other words, how can a computer program be executed? We have seen that logic gates can be combined in order to store binary data, and other combinations of gates can be used to perform switching operations to direct data to different parts of a computer system, depending on the a combination of bits in a memory location being used to store a program. Yet other combinations of gates can be used to perform arithmetic operations, and in fact gates are so important that we will spend some time looking at the characteristics of a number of different types in order to show how they may be applied inside a computer to perform some essential tasks such as executing a stored program. Figure 4.3 summarises what we have discussed so far regarding computer memory devices.

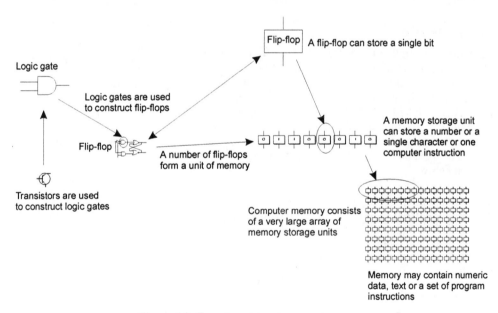

Figure 4.3. *From transistors to computer memory*

Gates: the building blocks of computers

Gates are simple electronic devices that respond in a certain way to inputs in the form of electrical signals. These electrical signals represent either a binary 1(called logic 1) when the signal voltage is high or a binary 0 (called logic 0) when the signal voltage is low. For example, one type of gate called an *OR gate* works like this: it has two or more inputs and a single output such that if at least one of the inputs is at logic 1 then the output is logic 1, otherwise the output is logic 0. Figure 4.4 shows all the possible combinations of two inputs to an *OR* gate with their corresponding outputs.

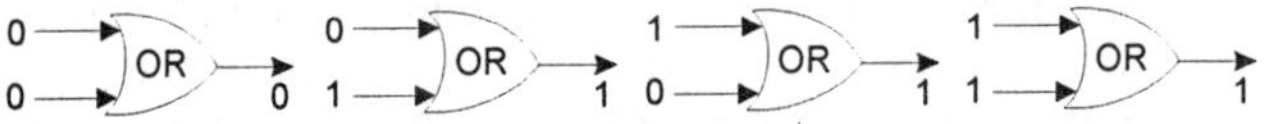

Figure 4.4. *Operation of an OR gate*

Thus, when at least one of the pair of inputs is at logic 1, then the output is at logic 1: only when both inputs are zero is the output zero. A gate with different input/output characteristics is the *AND* gate, shown in Figure 4.5.

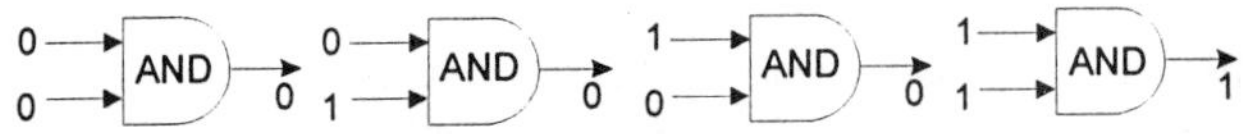

Figure 4.5. *Operation of an AND gate*

The AND gate only produces an output of 1 when both inputs are 1. So, if at least one input is 0, the output is 0. A third important type of gate is the *NOT* gate, sometimes called an *inverter*. Figure 4.6 shows that the gate simply inverts the input, so that if the input is 1, the output is 0, and if the input is 0, the output is 1.

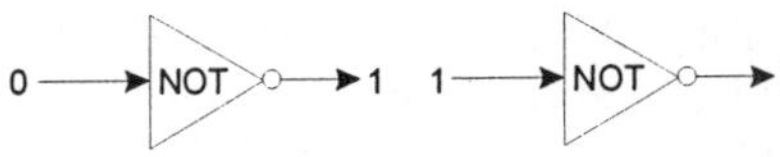

Figure 4.6. *Operation of the NOT gate*

Truth tables

The diagrams illustrating the operation of the AND, OR and NOT gates described in the previous section can be neatly summarised using *truth tables*. Truth tables show the output or outputs from a logic circuit for every possible input. For example, the truth table on the right defines the operation of an OR gate with two inputs X and Y. You can see that the table matches the inputs and outputs shown in Figure 4.4 exactly. The truth tables for an AND gate and a NOT gate are shown below.

X	Y	OUTPUT (X + Y)
0	0	0
0	1	1
1	0	1
1	1	1

Truth table for an OR gate

X	Y	OUTPUT (X.Y)
0	0	0
0	1	0
1	0	0
1	1	1

Truth table for an AND gate

X	OUTPUT ($\overline{X}$)
0	1
1	0

Truth table for a NOT gate

Truth tables are used later in this chapter and also in Chapter 6, Computer Logic, to define more complex gates and logic circuits.

Using gates to interpret stored instructions

We saw earlier that computer instructions can be stored in memory just like any other type of data. How a set of program instructions can be automatically performed in sequence will be explained a little later, but for the moment let us assume that an instruction has been retrieved from memory and is ready to be interpreted and executed.

Suppose also that the three most significant bits (that is, the three leftmost bits) of the instruction specify what action is to be performed.(Normally there will be more bits than three to specify an action, but the principle about to be explained would still apply). Because the pattern of these three bits uniquely identifies the action to be performed, we could use a combination of gates such as that shown in Figure 4.7 to generate a signal to trigger the computer circuitry which performs the action. The outputs from the three flip-flops containing the code for the required operation are fed into a three-input *AND* gate with the middle input inverted using a *NOT* gate to make it logic 1. Thus, only if the code in these three bits is 101 will the inputs to the *AND* gate be all 1's, producing an output of logic 1 from the *AND* gate; only then will the appropriate circuitry be triggered to perform the operation. A logic circuit used in this way is called a *decoder*. The outputs from the three operation

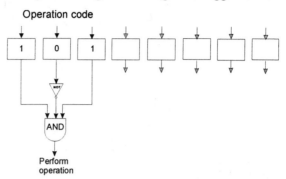

Figure 4.7. *Simple decoder for a three-bit instruction code*

code flip-flops will be simultaneously fed into other decoders, each one dealing with a different operation code. Because each operation code will have its own unique decoding circuitry, only one decoder will produce a logic 1 output to trigger the required operation. Eight decoders would be required for our simple three-bit instruction code, one each for the codes 000, 001, 010, 011, 100, 101, 110 and 111.

We have yet to consider how the instructions stored in memory can be executed one after another automatically. This involves the *fetch-execute cycle* discussed in the next section.

Fetch-execute cycle

The sequence of events described below is usually termed the *fetch-execute cycle*, in which each instruction in turn is *fetch*ed from memory and then *execute*d until a *Halt* instruction is encountered. Figure 4.8 summarises the way that a program is automatically executed.

Every computer contains circuitry to perform a number of distinct tasks. On of these tasks, the overall co-ordination and control of the computer, is performed by the *Control Unit*. One of its functions is to transfer the contents of memory locations into a special storage location called the *Current Instruction Register* (CIR) which is like a very small, special-purpose section of memory, but it is located in the Control Unit itself. Another register, called the Program Counter (PC) tells the Control Unit which memory location to copy into the CIR. (Memory locations are numbered and the PC holds a number which represents the next instruction to be fetched.) Once an instruction has been transferred into the CIR, the Control Unit triggers the decoding circuitry as described in the previous section. The PC is incremented to point to the next instruction to be loaded into the CIR, the appropriate operation is then performed, again under the direction of the Control Unit, and the next instruction is transferred into the CIR. This sequence of operations continues until one of the program instructions loaded into the CIR is a *Halt* instruction, which tells the Control Unit that the program is complete. In other words, once the Control Unit has started to execute the program, the program itself must contain an instruction to terminate the process.

Notice that the circuitry which is responsible for executing any arithmetic or logic operations required by the current instruction is called the Arithmetic and Logic Unit (ALU) and in the next section we will describe a little of what happens inside the ALU by showing how the addition of two 8-bit numbers might be performed using logic gates.

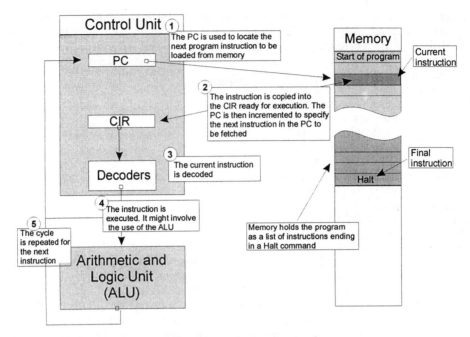

Figure 4.8. *The fetch-execute cycle*

Using logic gates for binary addition

Computer arithmetic is described in some detail in Chapter 8, *Internal Numbers and Computer Arithmetic,* and in Chapter 6, *Computer Logic*, we introduced the idea of logic gates and their use in binary addition. In this section we look at binary addition, emphasising the role of logic components in performing calculations. Table 4.2 summarises the result of adding two binary digits X and Y.

X	Y	Carry	Sum
0	0	0	0
0	1	0	1
1	0	0	1
1	1	1	0

Table 4.2. *Operation of a Half Adder*

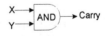

Figure 4.9. *Half Adder*

When we add two single binary digits, we obtain one of the values 00, 01 or 10 as shown in the table. The left digit can be regarded as a carry, though most the time it will be zero. If we regard the 1's and the 0's as binary signals, then an electronic unit which adds two binary digits requires two inputs *X* and *Y*, and two outputs, *Carry* and *Sum* as in Figure 4.9. This device is usually called a *Half Adder*, but how can gates be used to construct it? To begin with, the table above shows that a single *AND* gate with two inputs X and Y would produce the column labelled *Carry*. Figure 4.5 shows that this is true, so we can easily implement part of the *Half Adder* by just using one *AND* gate, as shown in Figure 4.10.

Figure 4.10. *Carry term of a Half Adder*

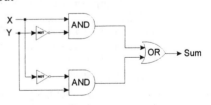

Figure 4.11. *Sum term of a Half Adder*

The *Sum* term of a *Half Adder* can be produced by the logic circuit shown in Figure 4.11.

To help to understand how it works, look at Figure 4.12. It shows how the circuit uses all four possible combinations of the inputs X and Y.

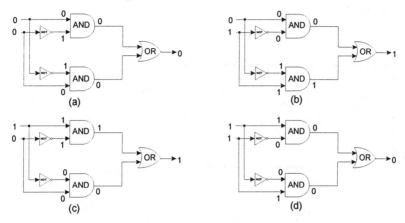

Figure 4.12. *Operation of the circuit for the Sum output of a Half Adder*

Figure 4.12a shows how the X and Y inputs, both at logic 0, are affected as they go through the circuit. As required, the *Carry* and *Sum* outputs are both logic 0.

In Figure 4.12b, X is at logic 0 and Y is logic 1; the carry output is still logic 0, but the sum output becomes 1 as required. As you would expect, when X is 1 and Y is 0 as in Figure 4.12c, the same *Sum* and *Carry* outputs occur. Finally, in Figure 4.12d, when both inputs are at logic 1, the *Carry* output is 1 and the *Sum* output is 0.

When we put the two logic circuits for the *Sum* and *Carry* outputs together in Figure 4.13, we obtain the complete circuit for a *Half Adder*.

However, this circuit is capable of only adding two bits; in binary addition, we need to cope with adding three bits: the bits in the two numbers plus a possible carry from the addition of the two bits to the right. In other words, we really need a *Full Adder*.

Fortunately, once we have designed a Half Adder, it is simply a matter of combining two of them in the manner shown in Figure 4.14 in order to have a Full Adder.

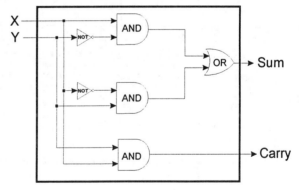

Figure 4.13. *Complete logic circuit for a Half Adder*

As shown in Figure 4.14a, the two digits to be added are used as the inputs to the first *Half Adder. The Sum* output of *Half Adder 1* and the *Carry* output from the previous addition are used as the inputs to the second *Half Adder*. The *Sum* output from the second *Half Adder* is the final *Sum* output from the *Full Adder*, and the final *Carry* output is produced by *OR*ing the *Carry* outputs from both *Half Adders*. Figure 4.14b shows the *Full Adder* as a unit with three inputs and two outputs as required.

Now, all that remains is to show how several *Full Adders* can be combined to enable two binary numbers, each consisting of a number of digits, to be added and the result stored. We will assume for simplicity that the two numbers to be added are a maximum of eight bits long and that they are already stored in two eight-bit registers. The resulting number will be transferred to another eight-bit register.

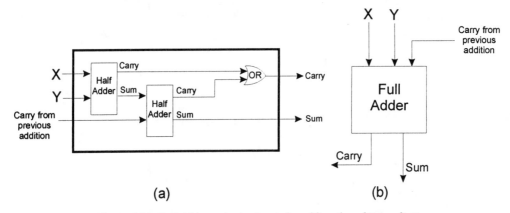

Figure 4.14. *Full Adder: a logic circuit for adding three binary digits*

The logic circuit is shown in Figure 4.15. Each pair of digits, together with the carry from the previous addition are added by one full adder, the sum digit being transferred to register 3 in the diagram. The carry bit from this addition is transferred to the next full adder to the left. This is called *parallel addition* because all of the bit pairs are added at the same time, that is, in parallel.

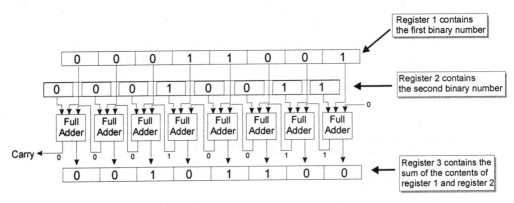

Figure 4.15. *Logic circuit for the addition of two eight-bit numbers*

✎ Exercises

1. Why is the binary numbering system important to the construction and operation of a computer?
2. What is the purpose of a flip-flop?
3. Name and explain the operation of 3 types of gate.
4. What is the function a half-adder and a full adder?
5. Describe the fetch-execute cycle, naming and explaining the purpose of important registers.
6. How can gates be used to decode computer instructions?

Chapter 5
Number Systems

Although the denary number system has proved to be the simplest for people to use, it is more convenient for computers to use the binary number system. The electronic components used in computers can be in either one of two physical states, permitting the representation of 0 and 1, the two symbols of the binary number system. This chapter explains the basis of this and other number systems relevant to the subject of computing.

The base of a number system

The denary system has ten symbols, 0, 1, 2, 3, 4, 5, 6, 7, 8 and 9 and the *base* or *radix* of a number system is identified by the number of different symbols it uses. Thus, the denary number system has base of 10. To identify a number as denary it can be written as, for example, 123_{10}.

Place value

Each symbol can be given a weight or place (or positional) value, according to its position within any given number. In the denary system, each place value is a power of ten. Remember that the base of the denary number system is ten. Thus, for denary integers each place value is ten raised to a power. Starting from the least significant digit on the right, there are units (10^0), tens (10^1), hundreds (10^2), thousands (10^3) and so on. The idea of place value can be illustrated with examples of integer (whole) numbers. Table 5.1 shows that 1263_{10} can be expressed as one thousand, plus two hundreds, plus six tens and three units, or $1 \times 1000 + 2 \times 100 + 6 \times 10 + 3 \times 1 = 1263_{10}$.

power 10^3	10^2	10^1	10^0
thousands	hundreds	tens	units
1	2	6	3

Table 5.1. *Place values example 1263_{10}*

power 10^3	10^2	10^1	10^0
thousands	hundreds	tens	units
0	4	8	7

Table 5.2. *Place values example 487_{10}*

Similarly, Table 5.2 shows that 487_{10} is the same as zero thousands, plus four hundreds, plus eight tens and seven units, or $0 \times 1000 + 4 \times 100 + 8 \times 10 + 7 \times 1 = 487_{10}$. Note that any number ($n$) raised to the power of zero (n^0) is equal to 1. This can be seen from Tables 5.1 and 5.2 and from the place value tables shown later, for each of the binary, octal and hexadecimal number systems. The *fractional* component of a number is also determined by position, except that the power is negative, as shown in Table 5.3.

	10^{-1}	10^{-2}	10^{-3}
decimal point	tenths	hundredths	thousandths
.	6	2	5

Table 5.3. *Fractional place values example 0.625_{10}*

Table 5.3 shows that 0.625_{10}, can be seen as: $6 \times \dfrac{1}{10} + 2 \times \dfrac{1}{100} + 5 \times \dfrac{1}{1000} = \dfrac{5}{8}$

Binary system

The binary system uses only two symbols, 0 and 1. Each digit in a binary number is known as a binary digit or *bit*. An example binary number is 11001_2, which is equivalent to 25_{10}. The binary system has a base of 2, so each place value is a power of two. The next two tables each show a range of integer place values and an example binary number. Table 5.4 demonstrates that the binary number 11101_2 is equivalent to denary $1\times16 + 1\times8 + 1\times4 + 0\times2 + 1\times1$ or 29_{10}. Table 5.5 shows that the binary number 01100111_2 is equivalent to $0\times128 + 1\times64 + 1\times32 + 0\times16 + 0\times8 + 1\times4 + 1\times2 + 1\times1 = 103_{10}$.

2^4	2^3	2^2	2^1	2^0
16	8	4	2	1
1	1	1	0	1

Table 5.4. *11101_2 or 29_{10}*

2^7	2^6	2^5	2^4	2^3	2^2	2^1	2^0
128	64	32	16	8	4	2	1
0	1	1	0	0	1	1	1

Table 5.5. *01100111_2 or 103_{10}*

Binary *fractions* can also be represented and an example is shown in Table 5.6.

binary point	2^{-1}	2^{-2}	2^{-3}	2^{-4}
	half	quarter	eighth	sixteenth
.	0	1	1	1

Table 5.6. *Fraction 0.0111_2*

We can see from this that 0.0111_2 is equivalent to $0\times\dfrac{1}{2}+1\times\dfrac{1}{4}+1\times\dfrac{1}{8}+1\times\dfrac{1}{16}=\dfrac{7}{16}$

Table 5.7 shows the binary equivalents of 0 to 9 in the denary system.

base$_{10}$	base$_2$	base$_{10}$	base$_2$	base$_{10}$	base$_2$	base$_{10}$	base$_2$	base$_{10}$	base$_2$
0	0000	1	0001	2	0010	3	0011	4	0100
5	0101	6	0110	7	0111	8	1000	9	1001

Table 5.7. *Denary symbols and binary equivalents*

Using the place values for the binary system shown in Tables 5.4 and 1.5, it can be seen how each of the denary numbers in Table 5.7 equates with its binary representation.

Rules of binary arithmetic

Addition rules are given, together with example sums, in Table 5.8. The rules for binary addition are needed when studying computer arithmetic in Chapter 8.

addition rules	carry	example sum	example sum
$0 + 0 = 0$		0 1 1 0 1 0	1 0 1 1 0 0
$0 + 1 = 1$		+ 1 1 0 1 0 0	+ 0 0 0 0 1 0
$1 + 0 = 1$		1 0 0 1 1 1 0	1 0 1 1 1 0
$1 + 1 = 0$	1		

Table 5.8. *Binary addition rules and examples*

Octal and hexadecimal numbers

These number systems are often used as a shorthand method for representing binary numbers. As can be seen from the binary numbers in the earlier tables, they are very confusing to the eye and it is sometimes difficult, even with small groupings, to distinguish one pattern from another. Where it is necessary for the computer's binary codes to be written or read by programmers, for example, it is invariably more convenient to use alternative coding methods. Octal and hexadecimal (*hex*) notations are used in preference to denary because they are more readily converted to or from binary. It must be emphasised that computers can only handle binary forms of coding. Therefore octal and hexadecimal codes must be converted to binary before they can be handled by the computer.

Octal coding

The octal number system has a base of 8, using 0, 1, 2, 3, 4, 5, 6 and 7 as its symbols. Each place value is a power of eight; some of the place values are shown in Table 5.9.

8^4	8^3	8^2	8^1	8^0	8^{-1}	8^{-2}	8^{-3}
4096	512	64	8	1	$^1/_8$	$^1/_{64}$	$^1/_{512}$

Table 5.9. *Some octal place values*

Octal coding uses three bits at a time, allowing 8 or 2^3 (see Table 5.10) different patterns of bits.

Binary	0 0 0	0 0 1	0 1 0	0 1 1	1 0 0	1 0 1	1 1 0	1 1 1
Octal	0	1	2	3	4	5	6	7

Table 5.10. *Octal symbols and binary equivalents*

To represent any given value, a binary number can be split into groups of 3 bits, starting from the right-hand side, as the two 16-bit examples in Table 5.11 show. Because the 16 bits will not divide exactly into groups of 3, the left-most or *most significant bit* (MSB) can only take the values 0_8 or 1_8.

0111001101100110_2	0	1 1 1	0 0 1	1 0 1	1 0 0	1 1 0
Octal code	0	7	1	5	4	6
1101010100101011_2	1	1 0 1	0 1 0	1 0 0	1 0 1	0 1 1
Octal code	1	5	2	4	5	3

Table 5.11. *Octal coding examples*

Hexadecimal coding

The hexadecimal number system has a base of 16, and uses the following symbols: 0, 1, 2, 3, 4, 5, 6, 7, 8, 9, A, B, C, D, E and F. The six letters, A to F, are used instead of the

16^3	16^2	16^1	16^0	16^{-1}	16^{-2}	16^{-3}
4096	256	16	1	$^1/_{16}$	$^1/_{256}$	$^1/_{4096}$

Table 5.12. *Hexadecimal place values*

denary numbers 10, 11, 12, 13, 14 and 15, respectively. This brings the number of hexadecimal symbols to sixteen. Some place values, each being a power of 16, are shown in Table 5.12.

A group of 4 bits provides 16 unique binary patterns, the number required to represent all 16 symbols of the hexadecimal number system. The symbols and their binary equivalents are given in Table 5.13.

Binary	0 0 0 0	0 0 0 1	0 0 1 0	0 0 1 1	0 1 0 0	0 1 0 1	0 1 1 0	0 1 1 1
Hexadecimal	0	1	2	3	4	5	6	7
Binary	1 0 0 0	1 0 0 1	1 0 1 0	1 0 1 1	1 1 0 0	1 1 0 1	1 1 1 0	1 1 1 1
Hexadecimal	8	9	A	B	C	D	E	F

Table 5.13. *Hexadecimal symbols and binary equivalents*

Therefore, a binary number can be coded by grouping the bits into groups of four and using the appropriate hexadecimal symbol for each group, as the examples in Table 5.14 show.

1100001111110110_2	1 1 0 0	0 0 1 1	1 1 1 1	0 1 1 0
Hexadecimal code	C	3	F	6
0101011010111101_2	0 1 0 1	0 1 1 0	1 0 1 1	1 1 0 1
Hexadecimal code	5	6	B	D

Table 5.14. *Hexadecimal coding examples*

In practice, hexadecimal is used in preference to octal code because computers organise their internal memory in 8-bit groupings (*bytes*) or multiples of bytes. These groupings conveniently divide into 4-bit *nibbles* which can be coded in the shorthand of hexadecimal. A knowledge of hexadecimal is essential for the interpretation of computer manufacturers' manuals, which use the coding system extensively to specify memory and backing storage features. Programmers using low level languages, such as assembly code, also need to be familiar with this number system.

Number base conversion methods

Conversion of binary numbers into their hexadecimal and octal equivalents is described in the preceding section. The following section provides methods and examples of conversion from:

❏ denary to binary;   ❏ denary to octal;   ❏ denary to hexadecimal.

Denary to binary

Method 1 - using conversion tables

Table 5.15 contains a range of place values for integer conversion; Table 5.16 can be used for fractions.

2^{14}	2^{13}	2^{12}	2^{11}	2^{10}	2^9	2^8	2^7	2^6	2^5	2^4	2^3	2^2	2^1	2^0
16384	8192	4096	2048	1024	512	256	128	64	32	16	8	4	2	1

Table 5.15. *Denary to binary conversion table - integers*

2^{-1}	2^{-2}	2^{-3}	2^{-4}	2^{-5}	2^{-6}	2^{-7}	2^{-8}	2^{-9}
½	$1/4$	$1/8$	$1/16$	$1/32$	$1/64$	$1/128$	$1/256$	$1/512$

Table 5.16. *Denary to binary conversion table - fractions*

To convert a denary number to binary requires the identification of those place values which, when added together, will equal the denary number. By reference to the appropriate table, a binary 1 is placed in each position, where the value is required and a binary 0 is recorded in each of those remaining. Starting with the largest value in the table, which is less than, or equal to the denary number, successive values to the right are selected and accumulated until the sum is obtained; a binary 1 is placed in each such position. Table 5.17 provides an integer example.

2^{14}	2^{13}	2^{12}	2^{11}	2^{10}	2^9	2^8	2^7	2^6	2^5	2^4	2^3	2^2	2^1	2^0
16384	8192	4096	2048	1024	512	256	128	64	32	16	8	4	2	1
		1	0	1	0	0	1	1	0	0	1	1	1	0

Table 5.17. *Integer 5326_{10} converted to 1010011001110_2*

Obviously, any value which will result in the required sum being exceeded is skipped, a binary 0 being placed in the relevant position. The place values containing a binary 1 can be summed and the result checked as follows.

$1\times4096 + 0\times2048 + 1\times1024 + 0\times512 + 0\times256 + 1\times128 + 1\times64 + 0\times32 + 0\times16 + 1\times8 + 1\times4 + 1\times2 + 0\times1 = 5326_{10}$

Similarly, Table 5.18, shows a denary fraction converted to binary.

	2^{-1}	2^{-2}	2^{-3}	2^{-4}	2^{-5}
binary point	½	$^1/_4$	$^1/_8$	$^1/_{16}$	$^1/_{32}$
•	0	1	1	1	0

Table 5.18. *Fraction $^7/_{16}$ converted to •01110$_2$*

Again, the binary 1 place values can be totalled and the result confirmed, as follows.

$$0\times\frac{1}{2}+1\times\frac{1}{4}+1\times\frac{1}{8}+1\times\frac{1}{16}+0\times\frac{1}{32}=\frac{7}{16}$$

Method 2 - successive division by the base

Integers

This technique requires that the denary number is successively *divided by 2*, the base of the binary system, until the result of a division is zero. If a division leaves a *remainder* of denary 1, a binary 1 is placed in the next available position in the binary number being formed; if there is a denary 0 remainder, a binary 0 is entered. Table 5.19 illustrates the process. Note that the binary number should be read, beginning with the most significant bit (MSB), from the bottom of the table, to the least significant bit (LSB).

The binary number is written as follows: $1273_{10} = 10011111001_2$, the last binary 1, at the bottom of Table 5.19, being the most significant bit (MSB).

denary	divided by	equals	remainder	binary	
1273	2	636	1	1	LSB
636	2	318	0	0	
318	2	159	0	0	
159	2	79	1	1	
79	2	39	1	1	
39	2	19	1	1	
19	2	9	1	1	
9	2	4	1	1	
4	2	2	0	0	
2	2	1	0	0	
1	2	0	1	1	MSB

Table 5.19. *Integer 1273_{10} to 10011111001_2*

Real number conversion

Tables 5.20 and 5.21 show how a *real* (having a fractional component) denary number is converted; the integer and fractional parts must be dealt with separately and differently. The *integer* part of 34.375_{10} is converted as shown in Table 5.20, by successive division (as in the previous example in Table 5.19). The *fractional* part is converted by a process of successive *multiplication*, as shown in Table 5.21; this table shows that, if a multiplication results

denary	divided by	equals	remainder	binary	
34	2	17	0	0	LSB
17	2	8	1	1	
8	2	4	0	0	
4	2	2	0	0	
2	2	1	0	0	
1	2	0	1	1	MSB

Table 5.20. *Conversion of 34_{10} (integer part of 34.375_{10})*

in a 1 appearing before the decimal point, the 1 is placed in the next available place to the right of the binary point; otherwise, 0 is placed there. Note that the binary fraction is read from the top of the table, identified by MSB. The process is complete when a product of denary 1 is obtained (much of the time, an exact figure will not be achieved and the process is continued until the desired accuracy is reached).

denary	multiplied by	equals	binary	
0.375	2	0.75	0	MSB
0.75	2	1.5	1	
0.5	2	1.0	1	LSB

Table 5.21. *Conversion of 0.375 (fractional part of 34.375₁₀)*

Looking at Tables 5.20 and 5.21 together, the result can be seen to be as follows: $34.375_{10} = 100010.011_2$.

Conversion with limited precision

Sometimes, a decimal fraction cannot be converted to its precise binary equivalent (as achieved in Tables 5.20 and 5.21). This topic is dealt with, in more detail, in the section on *floating point arithmetic*, in Chapter 8.

Table 5.22 shows the conversion of denary 0.425 to its binary equivalent, but with some loss of precision. The level of precision is determined by the number of place values allocated for the storage of the binary fraction; more places would allow a greater degree of precision.

Table 5.22 shows that, in this example, absolute precision cannot be achieved (the Product column will continue with the pattern shown and denary 1 will never be reached) and that, using the precision limit in the Table, 0.425_{10} is approximately equal to 0.011011001_2.

denary	multiplied by	equals	binary	
0.425	2	0.85	0	MSB
0.85	2	1.7	1	
0.7	2	1.4	1	
0.4	2	0.8	0	
0.8	2	1.6	1	
0.6	2	1.2	1	
0.2	2	0.4	0	
0.4	2	0.8	0	
0.8	2	1.6	1	LSB

Table 5.22. *Denary to binary conversion with loss of precision*

Referring to the place values in Table 5.16, it can be seen that the binary fraction is, in fact, equal to the following expression.

$$0 \times \frac{1}{2} + 1 \times \frac{1}{4} + 1 \times \frac{1}{8} + 0 \times \frac{1}{16} + 1 \times \frac{1}{32} + 1 \times \frac{1}{64} + 0 \times \frac{1}{128} + 0 \times \frac{1}{256} + 1 \times \frac{1}{512} = \frac{217}{512} = 0 \cdot 423828125$$

The difference is $0.425_{10} - 0.423828125_{10}$ or 0.001171875_{10}. A greater degree of precision (although not absolute) could be obtained by continuing the process shown in Table 5.22 and using more significant digits.

Denary to octal

Method 2 (successive division by the base), described in the denary to binary section, is also used here, in each case using the relevant base of 8. Table 5.23 shows an example of denary to octal conversion. LSD and MSD stand for least significant *digit* and most significant *digit*.

denary	divided by	equals	remainder	octal	
1273	8	159	1	1	LSD
159	8	19	7	7	
19	8	2	3	3	
2	8	0	2	2	MSD

Table 5.23. *Integer 1273₁₀ converted to octal 2371₈*

8^3	8^2	8^1	8^0
512	64	8	1
2	3	7	1

Table 5.24. *Integer 2371$_8$ and place values*

That $1273_{10} = 2371_8$, is proved, with the following expression (and by reference to the place values shown in Table 5.24).

$$2371_8 = 2 \times 512 + 3 \times 64 + 7 \times 8 + 1 \times 1 = 1273_{10}.$$

Denary to hexadecimal

Method 2 (successive division by the base), described in the denary to binary and denary to octal sections, is also used here, in this case using the relevant base of 16. Table 5.25 shows an example of denary to hexadecimal conversion. Remember that the symbol 'F' is equivalent to denary 15.

denary	divided by	equals	remainder	hex	
1273	16	79	9	9	LSD
79	16	4	15	F	
4	16	0	4	4	MSD

Table 5.25. *Integer 1273$_{10}$ to 4F9$_{16}$*

That $4F9_{16} = 1273_{10}$ can be proved by the following expression (the relevant place values appear in Table 1.26).

$$4F9_{16} = 4 \times 256 + 15(F) \times 16 + 9 \times 1 = 1273_{10}.$$

16^2	16^1	16^0
256	16	1
4	F	9

Table 5.26. *Integer 4F9$_{16}$ and place values*

✍ Exercises

1. Calculate the *denary* equivalents of the following binary numbers:

a. 11001110	d. 00000100	g. 00100000	j. 11111111
b. 10101011	e. 00001000	h. 01000000	k. 11110000
c. 01001100	f. 00010000	i. 10000000	l. 00001111

2. Using the conversion tables provided in the text, write down the *octal* and *hexadecimal* equivalents of the binary values in 1.

3. Using *successive division by the base*, convert 2165_{10} to binary.

4. Convert the real number values 26.325_{10} and 0.4685_{10} to binary. Comment on the results.

5. Use hexadecimal notation to represent the denary numbers 325_{10} and 2967_{10}.

6. Why is hexadecimal notation used in preference to other number bases, to represent binary codes?

Chapter 6

Computer logic

In Chapter 4, *Basic Concepts,* we introduced the idea of logic gates and showed how combinations of AND, OR and NOT gates are used in the construction of logic circuits for binary addition. In this chapter we look at the design of more complex logic circuits and introduce three more gates that are of practical importance in the construction of computer circuitry.

We then show in detail how logic circuits can be designed to perform binary addition. The chapter concludes with an introduction to flip-flops and some of their uses. Note that it is necessary to have some knowledge of Boolean algebra in order to fully appreciate the Boolean expressions included in this chapter, and how such expressions can be simplified. However, because a treatment of Boolean algebra is beyond the scope of this text, only an indication of how Boolean expressions are simplified has been included for completeness .

The design of logic circuits

The complete process of designing a logic circuit may be summarised as follows:

(i)   Identify Boolean variables equivalent to the inputs to the circuit required.

(ii)   Identify the outputs from the circuit.

(iii) Draw a truth table to define the output required for each possible combination of the input variables.

(iv)   Derive an expression from the truth table for the output in terms of the input variables.

(v)   Simplify this expression using Boolean algebra

(vi)   Draw the circuit using the appropriate gate symbols.

The following problem illustrates the process.

Four binary signals A, B, C, D represent a single Binary Coded Decimal (BCD) digit. A logic circuit is required to output logic 1 on the occurrence of an invalid combination of the signals, that is, when they represent a number in the range 10 to 15.

(i) The inputs to the circuit are clearly defined and it is assumed that A is the most significant digit and D the least significant digit.

(ii) The single output is to be 1 when the binary number represented by ABCD is in the range 10 to 15, that is, 1010 to 1111 in binary.

(iii) The truth table in Table 6.1 has 16 entries, representing the numbers 0 to 15.

A	B	C	D		OUTPUT	
0	0	0	0	(0)	0	
0	0	0	1	(1)	0	
0	0	1	0	(2)	0	
0	0	1	1	(3)	0	
0	1	0	0	(4)	0	
0	1	0	1	(5)	0	
0	1	1	0	(6)	0	
0	1	1	1	(7)	0	
1	0	0	0	(8)	0	
1	0	0	1	(9)	0	
1	0	1	0	(10)	1	$A.\overline{B}.C.\overline{D}$
1	0	1	1	(11)	1	$A.\overline{B}.C.D$
1	1	0	0	(12)	1	$A.B.\overline{C}.\overline{D}$
1	1	0	1	(13)	1	$A.B.\overline{C}.D$
1	1	1	0	(14)	1	$A.B.C.\overline{D}$
1	1	1	1	(15)	1	$A.B.C.D$

Table 6.1

(iv) The expression for the output is given by

$$\text{OUTPUT} = A.\overline{B}.C.\overline{D} + A.\overline{B}.C.D + A.B.\overline{C}.\overline{D} + A.B.\overline{C}.D + A.B.C.\overline{D} + A.B.C.D$$

(v) This expression translates to the logic diagram in Figure 6.1.

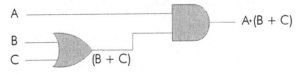

Figure 6.1

More logic gates

The gates that have yet to be defined are the NOR(Not OR), NAND(Not AND) and XOR (eXclusive OR) gates.

The truth table for the NOR gate (Table 6.2) shows that its outputs are the inverse of those for the OR gate.

Algebraically, the NOR gate is written $(\overline{X+Y})$. Thus the gate appears to be formed from one OR gate and one NOT gate inverting the output from the OR gate.

In practice, however, the OR gate outputs are generated from a single simple circuit and not by the combination of an OR gate followed by a NOT gate.

The symbol for the NOR gate is shown in Figure 6.2(a).

The truth table for the NAND gate (Table 6.3) shows that its outputs are the inverse of those for the AND gate.

X	Y	X NOR Y
0	0	1
0	1	0
1	0	0
1	1	0

Table 6.2. *NOR gate truth table*

In Boolean Algebra, the gate is written $(\overline{X.Y})$. The comments above regarding the construction of the NOR gate similarly apply here: the NAND gate is not constructed from an AND gate followed by a NOT gate, but consists of a single circuit no more complex than the other gates.

The symbol for the NAND gate is shown in Figure 6.2(b).

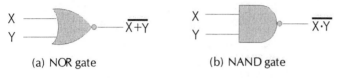

X	Y	X NAND Y
0	0	1
0	1	1
1	0	1
1	1	0

(a) NOR gate   (b) NAND gate

Figure 6.2. *Symbols used for NOR and NAND gates*

Table 6.3. *Truth table for NAND gate*

The importance of the NAND gate and NOR gate

The importance of these gates may be attributed to two factors:

(i)   each may be manufactured cheaply and easily;

(ii)   each can be used in the production of any circuit using AND/OR/NOT logical components. In other words, NOR gates and NAND gates can be used in the place of AND, OR or NOT gates.

These two properties mean that a logic circuit using, for instance, NOR gates only, can be produced more easily and cheaply than the same circuit using combinations of three different types of components (AND, OR and NOT gates). A unit using a number of the same component is much easier to manufacture than one using several different components. The logic diagrams in Figure 6.3, (a), (b) and (c), show how NOR gates may be used to represent the functions of NOT, AND and OR gates.

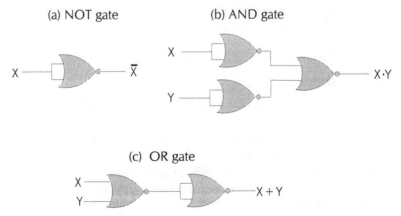

Figure 6.3. *NOR gates to represent functions of NOT, AND and OR gates*

The logic diagrams in Figure 6.4, (a), (b) and (c), show how NAND gates may be used to represent the functions of NOT, AND and OR gates.

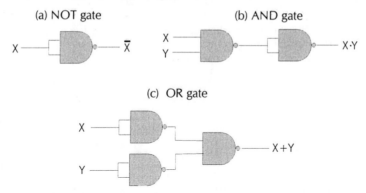

Figure 6.4. *NAND gates used to represent functions of NOT, AND and OR gates*

It may appear from the diagrams shown above that circuits using NAND or NOR gates will generally require more gates than when using AND/OR NOT components. This may be true on occasions, but at other times fewer gates may be required. The number of gates required often may be reduced by transforming the Boolean expression into a more suitable form. For example, the following expression, when implemented directly using NOR gates, uses more gates than the expression requires using AND/OR/NOT logic:

$$X.\overline{Y} + \overline{X}.Y \text{ (2 AND gates, 2 NOT gates, 1 OR gate = 5 gates)}$$

However, it can be shown that the following identity is true:

$$X.\overline{Y} + \overline{X}.Y = \overline{\left(\overline{\overline{X} + \overline{Y}}\right) + \left(\overline{X + Y}\right)}$$

which may not look very helpful but, in fact, shows that the original expression can be transformed into one much more suited to implementation by NOR gates. As Figure 6.5 shows, the circuit based on this transformed expression has only five NOR gates.

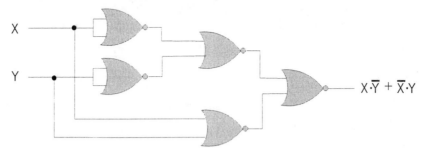

Figure 6.5.

The Exclusive OR gate

This is usually abbreviated to XOR or EOR. The truth table for the XOR gate is shown in Table 6.4. The exclusive OR gate is so named because, of its output values, the case where both inputs are logic 1 is excluded; in the OR gate these inputs produce an output of 1. In effect, the XOR gate has an output of logic 1 when the inputs are different; when the inputs are the same, the output is logic 0.

X	Y	X XOR Y
0	0	0
0	1	1
1	0	1
1	1	0

Table 6.4. *Truth table for XOR gate*

Algebraically, the XOR gate is $X.\overline{Y} + \overline{X}.Y$ and the symbol that is frequently used is shown in Figure 6.6.

X
Y
$X.\overline{Y} + \overline{X}.Y$

Figure 6.6. *Symbol for XOR gate*

As an example of its use, suppose that it is required to generate an even parity bit for a four bit word ABCD. The truth table for this problem is shown in Table 6.5.

The expression for even parity is thus

Parity bit =

$\overline{A}.\overline{B}.\overline{C}.D + \overline{A}.\overline{B}.C.\overline{D} + \overline{A}.B.\overline{C}.\overline{D} + \overline{A}.B.C.D +$
$A.\overline{B}.\overline{C}.\overline{D} + A.\overline{B}.C.D + A.B.\overline{C}.D + A.B.C.\overline{D}$

If the terms are grouped together as follows, a pattern begins to emerge.

Parity bit =

$\overline{A}.\overline{B}.(\overline{C}.D + C.\overline{D}) + \overline{A}.B.(C.D + \overline{C}.\overline{D}) + A.\overline{B}.(\overline{C}.\overline{D} + C.D) + A.B.(\overline{C}.D + C.\overline{D})$

Rearranging the terms,

parity bit $= \overline{A}.\overline{B}.(\overline{C}.D + C.\overline{D}) + A.B.(\overline{C}.D + C.\overline{D}) + \overline{A}.B.(C.D + \overline{C}.\overline{D}) + A.\overline{B}.(C.D + \overline{C}.\overline{D})$

A	B	C	D	parity bit	
0	0	0	0	0	
0	0	0	1	1	$\overline{A}.\overline{B}.\overline{C}.D$
0	0	1	0	1	$\overline{A}.\overline{B}.C.\overline{D}$
0	0	1	1	0	
0	1	0	0	1	$\overline{A}.B.\overline{C}.\overline{D}$
0	1	0	1	0	
0	1	1	0	0	
0	1	1	1	1	$\overline{A}.B.C.D$
1	0	0	0	1	$A.\overline{B}.\overline{C}.\overline{D}$
1	0	0	1	0	
1	0	1	0	0	
1	0	1	1	1	$A.\overline{B}.C.D$
1	1	0	0	0	
1	1	0	1	1	$A.B.\overline{C}.D$
1	1	1	0	1	$A.B.C.\overline{D}$
1	1	1	1	0	

Table 6.5

The first two and the last two terms can be grouped together to give:

$\qquad$ parity bit $= (\overline{A}.\overline{B} + A.B).(\overline{C}.D + C.\overline{D}) + (\overline{A}.B + A.\overline{B}).(\overline{C}.\overline{D} + C.D)$

Notice that two of the terms in brackets are immediately recognisable as XOR functions. In addition it can be shown that

$$\overline{\overline{X}.Y + X.\overline{Y}} = \overline{X}.\overline{Y} + X.Y$$

Using this identity, the expression for parity becomes:

$\qquad$ parity bit $= \overline{\left(\overline{A}.B + A.\overline{B}\right).\left(\overline{C}.D + C.\overline{D}\right)} + \left(\overline{A}.B + A.\overline{B}\right).\overline{\left(\overline{C}.D + C.\overline{D}\right)}$

Now each bracketed term looks like an XOR gate and, treating each bracketed term as a unit, the complete expression has the form

$\qquad$ $\overline{X}.Y + X.\overline{Y}$, where X = $(\overline{A}.B + A.\overline{B})$ and Y = $(\overline{C}.D + C.\overline{D})$

Thus the whole expression, and every term within it, represent XOR gates.

The equivalent circuit is shown in Figure 6.7.

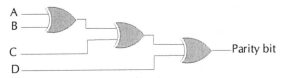

Figure 6.7.

Designing logic circuits for binary addition

The logic circuits which perform the function of addition in the Arithmetic and Logic Unit of the Central Processing Unit are called *adders*. A unit which adds two binary digits is called a *half adder* and one which adds together three binary digits is called a *full adder*. In this section each of these units will be examined in detail, and it will be shown how such units are combined to add binary numbers.

Half adders

In Chapter 4, *Basic Concepts*, the construction of a half adder was explained in order to illustrate how electronic circuits can be used to perform arithmetic operations. Remember that the function of a half adder is to add two binary digits and produce as output a Sum term and Carry term. The operation of the half adder is defined by the truth table in Table 6.6(a).

X	Y	Sum		Carry	
0	0	0		0	
0	1	1	$\overline{X}.Y$	0	
1	0	1	$X.\overline{Y}$	0	
1	1	0		1	$X.Y$

Table 6.6(a).

Thus, the expressions for the Sum and Carry terms are given by:

$$\text{Sum} = \overline{X}.Y + X.\overline{Y}$$

$$\text{Carry} = X.Y$$

The symbol in Figure 6.8 will henceforth be used for a half adder.

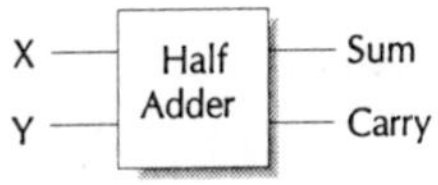

X ── Half Adder ── Sum
Y ──   ── Carry

Figure 6.8. *Symbol used for a Half Adder*

Full adders

Table 6.6(b) shows the truth table for the addition of three binary digits.

X	Y	Z	Sum		Carry	
0	0	0	0		0	
0	0	1	1	$\overline{X}.\overline{Y}.Z$	0	
0	1	0	1	$\overline{X}.Y.\overline{Z}$	0	
0	1	1	0		1	$\overline{X}.Y.Z$
1	0	0	1	$X.\overline{Y}.\overline{Z}$	0	
1	0	1	0		1	$X.\overline{Y}.Z$
1	1	0	0		1	$X.Y.\overline{Z}$
1	1	1	1	$X.Y.Z$	1	$X.Y.Z$

Table 6.6(b). *Truth table for addition of three binary digits*

Considering the Sum term first, the expression derived from the truth table is

$$\text{Sum} = \overline{X}.\overline{Y}.Z + \overline{X}.Y.\overline{Z} + X.\overline{Y}.\overline{Z} + X.Y.Z$$

Grouping together the first and third terms, and the middle two terms gives

$$\text{Sum} = \overline{Z}.(\overline{X}.Y + X.\overline{Y}) + Z.(\overline{X}.\overline{Y} + X.Y)$$

Using the identity

$$\overline{\overline{X}.Y + X.\overline{Y}} = \overline{X}.\overline{Y} + X.Y \quad \text{(this can easily be proved using a truth table)}$$

the Sum term can be written

$$\text{Sum} = \overline{Z}.\left(\overline{X}.Y + X.\overline{Y}\right) + Z.\overline{\left(\overline{X}.Y + X.\overline{Y}\right)}$$

which is of the form

$$\overline{Z}.S + Z.\overline{S} \quad \text{where } S = \overline{X}.Y + X.\overline{Y}$$

In other words, S is the sum term from a half adder with inputs X and Y, and Sum is one of the outputs from a half adder with inputs Z and S. The Sum term can now be produced using two half adders, as shown in Figure 6.9.

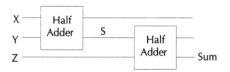

Figure 6.9. *Using two half adders to produce Sum term*

Returning to the Carry term, the expression derived from the truth table is

$$\text{Carry} = \overline{X}.Y.Z + X.\overline{Y}.Z + X.Y.\overline{Z} + X.Y.Z$$

Again gathering terms,

$$\text{Carry} = Z.(\overline{X}.Y + X.\overline{Y}) + X.Y.(\overline{Z} + Z)$$

$$= Z.(\overline{X}.Y + X.\overline{Y}) + X.Y \text{ since } \overline{Z} + Z = 1 \text{ and } X.Y.1 = X.Y$$

Substituting S for $\overline{X}.Y + X.\overline{Y}$ as before, the expression becomes

$$\text{Carry} = Z.S + X.Y$$

Both of these terms look like the carry term from a half adder: Z.S is the carry term from a half adder with inputs Z and S (the carry term from the second half adder in the diagram above); X.Y is the carry output from the first half adder in the diagram. The two carry outputs merely need to be ORed together, to give the final circuit in Figure 6.10.

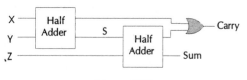

Figure 6.10.

Adding binary numbers

So far, the circuits for addition have only been capable of adding two or three binary digits; more complex schemes are necessary in order to add two binary numbers each comprising several digits. Two approaches will be considered. The first adds numbers bit by bit, one pair of bits after another and is termed *serial addition*; the other accepts as inputs all pairs of bits in the two numbers simultaneously and is called *parallel addition*.

Serial addition

Suppose that the numbers to be added have a four-bit wordlength, and the two numbers A and B have digits a3, a2, a1, a0, and b3, b2, b1, b0 respectively. The circuit for a four-bit serial adder is shown in Figure 6.11.

In this particular design, a single full adder is presented with pairs of bits from the two numbers in the sequence a0 b0 , a1 b1 , a2 b2 , a3 b3 . As each pair of bits is added, the sum term is transmitted to a shift register to hold the result, and the carry term is delayed so that it is added in to the next addition operation. Though this method is cheap in terms of hardware requirements, it is not often (if at all) used in modern digi-tal computers because of its slow operation. The degree to which hardware prices have dropped in recent years has resulted in the almost universal adoption of parallel addition.

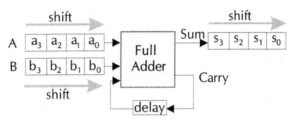

Figure 6.11. *Four-bit serial adder*

Parallel addition

In parallel addition, a separate adder is used for the addition of each digit pair. Thus for the addition of two four-digit numbers, one half adder and three full adders would be used. In this type of circuit, all the digits are input simultaneously, with the carry term from each stage being connected directly to the input of the next stage. This is shown in Figure 6.12.

Though faster than serial addition, one fault of the type of parallel adder

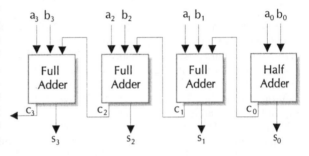

Figure 6.12. *Circuit for parallel addition*

shown above is the successive carry out to carry in connections which cause relatively long de-lays; more elaborate schemes are capable of overcoming this problem (at the expense of added circuitry).

The efficiency of the addition circuits is of particular importance in microprocessors where the functions of multiplication and division, as well as subtraction, often use these circuits. Most computers have special purpose circuitry for multiplication and division.

Flip-flops

One of the fundamental functions performed by digital computers is the storage of data in memory. The electronic component which is usually used for this purpose is called a *flip-flop*. Other names for the same device are *bistable*, *latch* and *toggle*, but flip-flop is the most com-monly used name.

A flip-flop is capable of storing, in electrical form, a single binary digit. Thus, a collection of eight flip-flops can store a byte of data. As well as being used for memory, flip-flops form the basis of other useful CPU components, such as *shift registers* and *binary counters*.

Flip-flops are frequently constructed with gates, but using *sequential logic* rather than the *combinational logic* described in the previous part of this chapter. As we have seen, a combinational logic circuit produces an output which is entirely dependent on the current inputs; with sequential logic, because of the use of feedback, the output from a sequential logic circuit depends on its current state in addition to the current inputs. In other words, the output from a sequential logic circuit is partly determined by the previous inputs it received.

In this section we describe the operational characteristics of the simplest type of flip-flop, the *SR flip-flop*, before going on to show how it may be constructed using NAND gates. We then discuss the synchronous version of the SR flip-flop, the *clocked SR flip-flop* before showing how shift registers, binary counters and memory units may be fabricated using them.

Though there are a number of different types of flip-flops in common use, including JK, Master-Slave and D-type flip-flops, essentially they are all based on the SR flip-flop, and it is beyond the scope of this book to discuss the precise differences between them and why one type is preferred over another for certain types of application.

Operation of the SR flip-flop

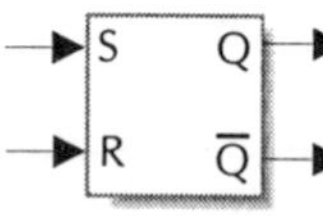

The term flip-flop derives from its characteristic of being in one of two stable states at any instant, and hence the alternative name, *bistable*. These two states we conveniently designate 0 and 1. In state 1, the device is said to be *set*, and in state 0, *reset*, hence SR flip-flop. If the flip-flop is in state 1, it will remain in that state until an input causes it to change to state 0, in which state it will also remain until changed. Thus it remembers its current state until some signal causes it to change state. Figure 6.13 shows the symbol generally used for an unclocked SR flip-flop. The two outputs are labelled Q and $\overline{Q}$ because each is the complement of the other. The current state of the device is by convention that of the Q output. The input lines, S and R, are used to control the state of the flip-flop. If a signal is applied to the S line, the flip-flop is set (ie Q=1); a signal on the R line resets it (ie Q=0). The absence of any signal leaves the state of the flip-flop unchanged. Applying a signal to both lines simultaneously is not allowed. Table 6.7 illustrates these rules with a sequence of input signals and the resulting state of the flip-flop.

Figure 6.13.
Unclocked SR flip-flop

S	R	Q	Effect of input
1	0	1	set
0	0	1	remains in same state
0	0	1	remains in same state
0	1	0	reset
0	0	0	remains in same state
1	0	1	set
1	0	1	already set so no effect
0	1	0	reset
0	1	0	already set so no effect

Table 6.7. *Effect of input signals on SR flip-flop*

Construction of the SR flip-flop

A simple form of an SR flip-flop may be implemented using two NAND gates connected as shown in Figure 6.14. The operation of this flip-flop is defined by Table 6.8.

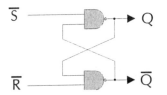

Figure 6.14. *Construction of SR flip-flop*

S	R	Q'
0	0	Q
0	1	0
1	0	0
1	1	not defined

Table 6.8. *Operation of SR flip-flop*

The current state of the circuit is denoted by Q and the resulting state, due to the two inputs, is Q'. We can verify the operation of the circuit by tracing each pair of inputs and comparing them with the outputs shown:

(i) $\overline{S}$=1, $\overline{R}$=1 and Q=1. This corresponds to the null input, self-sustaining state. The inputs to the lower NAND gate are both 1, producing an output, Q', of 0. This means that the inputs to the upper NAND gate are 1 and 0, producing an output of 1; no change in the outputs. If the current state is Q=0, the lower gate has inputs 0 and 1, producing an output of 1, and the upper gate now has both inputs at logic-1, producing an output of 0; again no change.

(ii) $\overline{S}$=0 and $\overline{R}$=1. This is the *set* condition. Because $\overline{S}$=0, the upper gate must output logic-1; the inputs to the lower gate both being 1, the output is 0.

(iii) $\overline{S}$=1 and $\overline{R}$=0. This is the *reset* condition. Because $\overline{R}$=0, the lower gate must output logic-1 this time, and the two logic-1 inputs to the top gate produce an output of 0.

(iv) $\overline{S}$=0 and $\overline{R}$=0. In this instance the output from the flip-flop cannot be determined; the resulting state will be unpredictable and will depend on such factors as temperature and component tolerances.

The clocked SR flip-flop

Figure 6.15 shows the symbol for a clocked SR flip-flop. It has an additional input designated *clock* or *enable*. The circuit for a clocked SR flip-flop is shown in Figure 6.16.

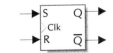

Figure 6.15. *Clocked SR flip-flop*

The extra input allows the operation of the flip-flop to be controlled by a timing signal which is used to synchronize the operation of the separate components of a circuit. Circuits controlled by a clock are called *synchronous* circuits; where a clock is not used the circuit is *asynchronous*.

Because of the added complexity of asynchronous circuits, most circuits are of the synchronous variety.

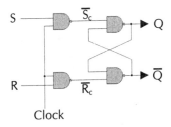

Figure 6.16. *Construction of Clocked SR flip-flop*

The effect of the additional gates in the circuit is to hold the S and R inputs at the null state ($\overline{S}$=$\overline{Q}$=1) until a clock pulse is applied to the first two gates, at which time set and reset signals are applied to the flip-flop. In effect, the clock pulse *enables* the flip-flop to assume a new state.

Shift registers

A four stage shift register is shown in the Figure 6.17.

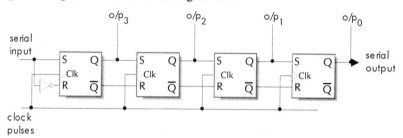

Figure 6.17. *A four-stage shift register*

A sequence of signals representing a binary number is applied to the input. Each input is set up while the clock is at logic-0. When the clock pulse becomes logic-1, each flip-flop is enabled and assumes the value of the signal being applied to the S input. Therefore, the complete contents of the flip-flops are shifted along by one bit at every clock pulse. The current state of each flip-flop is available on the lines labelled O/P0 to O/P3. Table 6.9 illustrates the process with the binary sequence 1101, assuming that the initial contents of the shift register is 0000.

clock pulse	input	O/P0	O/P1	O/P2	O/P3
		0	0	0	0
1	1	1	0	0	0
2	0	0	1	0	0
3	1	1	0	1	0
4	1	1	1	0	1

Table 6.9. *Operation of a four-stage shift register*

Binary counters

A binary counter consists of a collection of flip-flops each of which is associated with a bit position in the binary representation of a number. If there are n flip-flops in a binary counter, the number of possible states is 2^n and the counting sequence is from 0 to 2^n-1. If the maximum value is exceeded, the counting sequence starts at 0 again. A simple form of a binary counter is based on an SR flip-flop connected to act as a *toggle circuit* shown in Figure 6.18.

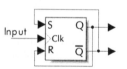

Figure 6.18. *Toggle*

Each pulse applied to the clock input inverts the output, Q, of the circuit; in effect, this is dividing the input frequency by two by performing alternate *set* and *reset* operations. Table 6.10 shows how the output changes after each logic-1 input, assuming that the current output is logic-0. Notice that logic-0 inputs have no effect on the output. A four-bit counter uses four toggle circuits connected in series. (See Figure 6.19)

The output from the first toggle circuit alternates between 0 and 1 as shown in the previous table. Each time a logic-1 is output from the first toggle component, the second one is enabled and its output inverts; each time the output from the second component is logic-1, the third one is enabled and its output inverts, and so on. Therefore, the first component inverts after each logic-1 input, the second one inverts after two logic-1 inputs, the third after four and the fourth after eight. Table 6.11 shows how the outputs of each of

	input	output (Q)
		0
1	1	1
2	0	1
3	1	0
4	0	0
5	1	1
6	0	1
	etc	

Table 6.10. *Operation of a toggle*

the toggle circuits, A, B, C and D change for a sequence of logic-1 inputs.

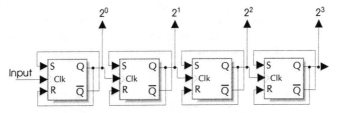

Figure 6.19. *Four-bit binary counter*

Thus, A represents the least significant bit of the 4-bit number and D the most significant bit. The counter thus counts up from 0 to 15 cyclically.

Memory circuits

One of the fundamental characteristics of the digital computer is its ability to store data and programs in random-access memory. We have seen already that sequential circuits are capable of storing binary signals and that collections of such components may be used to store bytes or larger words of data. Large arrays of such circuits constitute the internal memory of a computer. Figure 6.20 shows one possible arrangement for a random-access memory unit. The *Address Lines*, typically 16 or 32 for a microcomputer, specify which particular memory word is to be accessed; a *Chip Enable* line (not shown) enables the chip if it is logic-1, or disables the chip if it is logic-0; when enabled, the chip may be written to, by making *Write=1* and read from, using Write=0.

Each horizontal row of memory elements represents a word of memory which may be selected by an Address Decoder. So for an 8-bit word there will be a row of eight memory elements. When an address is input to the address decoder, it selects the corresponding

input	A	B	C	D
	0	0	0	0
1	1	0	0	0
2	0	1	0	0
3	1	1	0	0
4	0	0	1	0
5	1	0	1	0
6	0	1	1	0
7	1	1	1	0
8	0	0	0	1
9	1	0	0	1
10	0	1	0	1
11	1	1	0	1
12	0	0	1	1
13	1	0	1	1
14	0	1	1	1
15	1	1	1	1
16	0	0	0	0
17	1	0	0	0
etc.				

Table 6.11. *Outputs for toggle circuits*

word. For a 16-bit address, the decoder will select one line from 2^{16} possibilities. If a read operation is required, the word, corresponding to the states of the eight memory elements, will appear on the *Out* lines; a write operation will cause the eight memory elements to take on the binary values on the *In* lines. The construction of the memory elements, each storing a single bit, is shown in Figure 6.21.

Each element comprises a flip-flop and a number of other gates to control the transfer of data between the flip-flop and the common internal data lines. Notice that the AND gates are used to control the passage of signals; only when all inputs to an AND gate are 1 will the output become 1. Each *word-select* line is used to enable all elements in a row for reading or writing, and each column has two internal data lines, one for reading - data-in - and one for writing - data-out. The data-out line takes the value of the element in the currently enabled word.

Thus, when *Word select=1* the Q output from the memory element is ORed with the data-out line. A word is written into a memory location by presenting the appropriate address to the decoder (which enables the word memory elements), the bit pattern of the word to the data-in lines and then setting *Write=1*. Two AND gates in each memory element allow its state to be changed to the value on the data-in line providing *Write* and *Word select* are both at logic-1.

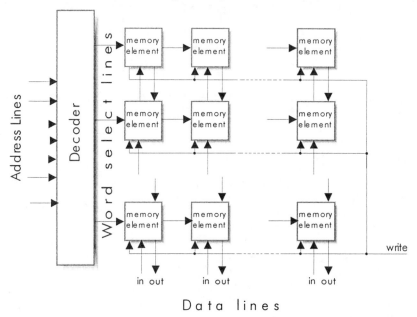

Figure 6.20. *Random access memory*

Integrated circuits

The logic elements described earlier in this chapter are fabricated using semi-conductors - transistors in particular. The speed of operation of transistors, which act as electronic switches in logic circuits, is dependent on their size; power consumption, heat generated and cost are also dependent on their size. Since size is such a critical factor, a great deal of research has been done to reduce the size of a transistor as far as possible. The result of this research has been the steady evolution of the Integrated Circuit (IC). Though invented in 1959, integrated circuits were first used in computers in the late 1960s. The PDP-11 was one of the first commercial machines to use such devices. At that

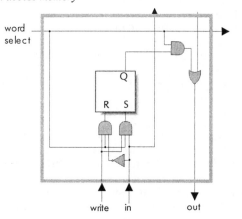

Figure 6.21. *Construction of a single-bit memory element*

time an integrated circuit contained less than one hundred transistors; today, microprocessors are constructed from chips containing millions of transistors. Electronic devices are constructed using combinations of components such as resistors, capacitors and transistors. The most common material of microelectronic circuits is silicon, the same type that is found in ordinary sand. The silicon is first refined and made into thin discs which form the base material, the *substrate*, for a number of ICs. The manufacturing process produces several identical ICs, each perhaps only a quarter of an inch square, on one wafer of silicon. The circuit to be set into the silicon is first designed with the aid of a computer to minimize the number of components before being used to prepare a series of masks.

After being photographically reduced to the actual chip size, the masks are used in a photographic process which sequentially isolates each chip from its immediate neighbours, defines the position of the components, modifies the structure of the substrate to give it the required semiconducting characteristics and interconnects the components using etched metallic films. Further stages are required to test the circuits, separate them and package them into the familiar 'bug' shape. Table 6.11 is a rough guide to the five generations of ICs, in terms of chip complexity.

generation	no. of components
Small Scale Integration (SSI)	2 - 64
Medium Scale Integration (MSI)	64 - 2000
Large Scale Integration (LSI)	2000 - 64,000
Very Large Scale Integration (VLSI)	64,000 - 2,000,000
Ultra Large Scale Integration (ULSI)	2,000,000 - 100,000,000

Table 6.11. *Generations of integrated circuits (ICs)*

Since its invention in 1959, the IC has undergone rapid growth, its complexity following a progression known as Moores Law which states that the maximum number of components on a microprocessor chip doubles about every one and a half years. Of course there is a limit to how small an electronic component can be made, and therefore the maximum speed at which a microprocessor can be made to operate, so that eventually it will be impossible to make circuits smaller. However, just as the development of the transistor resulted from advances in theoretical physics, there is evidence that further advances will produce technological innovations that will again revolutionise the construction of computers.

 **Exercises**

1. For each of the following expressions, draw a truth table:
   (i) $X.Y.\overline{Z} + X.Y.Z + X.\overline{Y}.Z$
   (ii) $A.B.C + A.\overline{B}.C + A.B.\overline{C} + \overline{A}.\overline{B}.C + \overline{A}.B.C$
   (iii) $A.B.C.D + A.B.\overline{C}.D + A.B.C.\overline{D} + \overline{A}.B.\overline{C}.D + \overline{A}.B.C.\overline{D} + A.\overline{B}.\overline{C}.\overline{D}$
   (iv) $\overline{W}.X + X.\overline{Y} + X.\overline{Y}.Z + \overline{W}.\overline{Y}.\overline{Z} + W.X.\overline{Y}.\overline{Z}$

2. Given two binary signals, X and Y, produce a truth table to define the difference of the two digits for every combination. There will be two outputs representing the difference and a 'borrow'.

   Produce a truth table which defines the 4-bit product when two numbers are multiplied together (the largest number produced will be $3 \times 3 = 9$, which requires 4 bits).

3. Draw a truth table for a circuit that will generate an odd parity bit for a 4-bit word ABCD (see section on the XOR gate).

4. Describe the operation of the SR flip-flop.

5. What determines whether a circuit is synchronous or asynchronous?

6. Name 3 types of computer circuits that use flip flops. Briefly describe their operation.

Chapter 7

Data Representation

Data, in the context of this chapter, is a general term which covers any data or information which is capable of being handled by the computer's internal circuitry, or of being stored on backing storage media such as magnetic tape or disk. To be processed by computer, data must be in a form which the computer can handle; it must be *machine-sensible*.

Forms of coding

To be machine-sensible data has to be in *binary*, using the digits 0 and 1. Both main memory and external storage media, such as magnetic disk and tape, use electrical/magnetic patterns representing the binary digits 0 and 1 to record and handle data and instructions.

Why binary? - bi-stable devices

Computer storage uses two-state or bi-stable devices to indicate the presence of a binary 0 or 1. The circuits inside a computer represent these two states by being either conducting or non-conducting, that is, current is either flowing or is not flowing through the circuit. A simple example of a bi-stable device is an electric light bulb. At any one time it must be in one of two states, on or off. Magnetic storage media use magnetic fields and the two possible polarities (north and south) are used as bi-stable devices to represent 0 and 1. Denary is not practicable because a computer's circuitry would have to use and accommodate ten clearly defined physical electronic states. Extremely reliable components would be needed to avoid the machine confusing one physical state with another. With bi-stable devices, slight changes in performance do not prevent differentiation between the two physical states which represent 0 and 1.

Character and numeric codes

Much of the data processed by computer and stored on backing storage are represented by *character* codes. The codes used inside the computer are referred to as *internal* codes, whereas those used by various peripherals are termed *external* codes. Data transferred between peripheral devices and the processor may use a variety of binary character codes, but when processing data the processor will tend to use a particular internal code, which will vary with machines of different manufacture. Sometimes, an external character code may continue to be used for storage of data in main memory; alphabetic data remains in character code form during computer processing. On the other hand, numeric data, presented by a peripheral in character code form, is converted to one of a number of numeric codes for processing purposes. Code conversion may be executed within a peripheral, within the *interface* device between a peripheral and the processor, or within the processor itself. Characters may be:

❏ alphabetic (upper and lower case); numeric (0 to 9); special characters (apostrophe, comma, etc.); control characters and codes.

Control characters are used in data transmission, perhaps to indicate the start or end of a *block* of data; *control codes* can be used to affect the display of data on a VDU screen and include those which cause, for example, carriage return, delete, highlight or blinking. Control characters and control codes do not form part of the data which are to be usefully processed, but are needed for control. The range of characters which can be represented by a computer system is known as its *character set*.

The ASCII (American Standard Code for Information Interchange) code uses seven binary digits (*bits*) to represent a full range of characters. Data passing between a peripheral and the computer is usually in character code, typically ASCII. Extracts from the ASCII character set are given in the Chapter on Basic Concepts, but a smaller sample is shown in Table 7.1

character	ASCII	character	ASCII	character	ASCII	character	ASCII
0	0110000	9	0111001	I	1001001	R	1010010
1	0110001	A	1000001	J	1001010	S	1010011

Table 7.1. *Extract from ASCII character set*

Parity checking of codes

The ASCII is a 7-bit code. An additional bit, known as the *parity bit* (in the left-most or most significant bit position), is used to detect *single bit* errors which may occur during data transfer. Such errors may result from a peripheral fault or from corruption of data on storage media.

The parity scheme used for detecting single bit errors is simple. There are two types of parity, odd and even, though it is of little significance which is used. If odd parity is used, the parity bit is set to binary 1 or 0, such that there is an odd number

data with no parity	parity bit	data with odd parity	parity bit	data with even parity
1 0 0 1 0 1 0	0	1 0 0 1 0 1 0	1	1 0 0 1 0 1 0
0 1 0 1 1 0 1	1	0 1 0 1 1 0 1	0	0 1 0 1 1 0 1

Table 7.2. *Examples of data with odd and even parity*

of binary 1s in the group. Conversely, even parity requires that there is an even number of binary 1s in the group. Examples of these two forms of parity are provided in Table 7.2.

The parity bit for each group is in bold. If even parity is being used and main memory receives the grouping 10010100 then the presence of an odd number of binary 1s indicates an error in transmission. Provided that the number of bits corrupted is odd, all transmission errors will be detected. However, an even number of bits in error will not affect the parity condition and thus will not be revealed. Additional controls can be implemented to detect multiple bit errors; these controls make use of parity checks on blocks of characters; known *as block check characters* (BCC), they are used extensively in data transmission control.

Data storage in main memory

Character codes, such as the ASCII code , are primarily of use during data transfer between a peripheral and the main memory. They are also generally used to represent non-numeric data inside the computer. Numeric data is usually converted to one of a number of *numeric codes*, including binary coded decimal (BCD) and floating point formats.

Internal parity checks

Most mini and mainframe computers use parity bits to detect and sometimes correct, data transfer errors within the computer, so the actual length of codes is extended to allow for this. Parity checking, built into the circuitry of the memory chips is a feature of many microcomputer systems. Memory chips can develop faults, so it is important that a user is made aware of parity errors (which may indicate major memory faults), before significant data loss occurs.

Binary coded decimal (BCD)

As the name suggests, BCD uses a binary code to represent each of the decimal symbols. It is a 4-bit code, using the natural binary weightings of 8, 4, 2 and 1 and is only used for the representation of numeric values. Each of the ten symbols used in the decimal system is coded with its 4-bit binary equivalent, as shown in Table 7.3.

denary	0	1	2	3	4	5	6	7	8	9
BCD	0000	0001	0010	0011	0100	0101	0110	0111	1000	1001

Table 7.3. *BCD equivalents of denary symbols*

In this way, any decimal number can be represented by coding each digit separately. An example is given in Table 7.4.

denary	6	2	4
BCD	0110	0010	0100

Table 7.4. *BCD representation of* 624_{10}

BCD arithmetic

Floating point arithmetic can introduce small inaccuracies which can be a problem in financial data processing applications. For example, an amount of 120.50 stored in floating point form may return a value of 120.499999; although the application of *rounding algorithms* can adjust the figure to the required number of significant figures, the rounding is being carried out on the binary representation, when it is the decimal form which should be rounded.

For BCD numbers, each decimal character is separately coded and their addition cannot be accomplished with the normal ADD instruction; more complex electronics are needed to carry out arithmetic on data in BCD form than are necessary for pure binary numbers. BCD numbers also take more memory space than pure binary numbers. For example, with a 16-bit word the maximum BCD number is 9999_{10}, while using binary it is 65535_{10}. Numbers with a fractional element *(real* numbers) use an implied decimal point which can be located between any of the 4-bit groupings.

Boolean values

Apart from characters and numeric values, binary code can also represent the *Boolean* values of *true* or *false, the former by 1 and the latter by 0. Boolean variables can be used to indicate, for example, the condition of a flag register* used to signal the occurrence of an overflow condition after an arithmetic operation, or an *interrupt* from a peripheral indicating its need for servicing by the processor.

Bit-mapped graphics

Bit-mapping is the pixel-level control of displayed output. A monochrome VDU screen with a resolution of 720 pixels by 350 rows needs 252,000 bits of memory, each bit capable of being set to 1 for white or 0 for black. Colour screens need to use more bits for each pixel, to allow the setting of a variety of colours; one *byte* (eight bits) per pixel permits 256 (2^8) separate colours to be used. By definition, bit-mapped device control is inflexible and very device-dependent, but its use is essential for graphical work, word processing and text output which uses a variety of sophisticated fonts. Since large amounts of memory are needed, particularly for high resolution colour display, graphics adapter cards provide additional VRAM (*video RAM*) for screen memory.

The structure of main memory

Main memory is divided into a number of cells or *locations*, each of which has a unique name or *address* and is capable of holding a unit or grouping of bits which may represent data or an instruction. Memory locations are normally addressed using whole numbers from zero upwards. The *size* of memory location used varies from one make of computer to another and is related to the coding methods employed and the number of bits it is designed to handle as a unit.

Memory words and bytes

A *memory word* is a given number of bits in memory, addressable as a unit. The addresses of memory locations run consecutively, starting with address 0 and running up to the largest address. Each location contains a word which can be retrieved by specification of its address. Similarly, an instruction to write to a location results in the storage of a word into the quoted address. For example, the word 01100110 may be stored in location address 15 and the word 11000110 in location address 16. A memory word may represent data or an instruction.. The memory's *word length* equates with the number of bits which can be stored in a location. Thus, memory which handles words of 16 bits is known as 16-bit memory, whilst that which makes use of 32-bit words is known as 32-bit memory. In practice, a machine may use words of different lengths for different operations. Word length is one of the most important design characteristics of computers, in that it can be fundamental to the efficiency and speed of the computer. Generally, the larger and more powerful the computer, the greater the word length. Until recently, 32-bit and 64-bit words were largely used by mainframe and minicomputer systems exclusively. When first introduced, microcomputers were 4-bit or 8-bit machines, but advances in technology have made 32-bit and 64-bit microcomputers commonplace.

Even if a machine normally handles words of 16 or 32 or 64 bits, reference sometimes needs to be made to a smaller unit, the *byte*, which is 8 bits. Programming in a low level language requires separate identification of bytes. Table 7.5 illustrates the formation of a 16-bit word, with byte subdivisions. The leftmost bit in a word is referred to as the most significant bit (MSB) and the rightmost as the least significant bit (LSB). The most significant *byte* in a 16-bit word is identified as the *high order byte*, the least significant byte as the *low order byte*.

high order byte								low order byte							
MSB															LSB
15	14	13	12	11	10	9	8	7	6	5	4	3	2	1	0

Table 7.5. *High and low order bytes*

A 32-bit word would be divided into byte-1 (the lowest order byte), byte-2, byte-3 and byte-4 (the highest order byte). A number of different memory structures have been used, based on different word lengths, which have sufficient flexibility to accommodate the requirements of both numeric and non-numeric data.

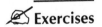 **Exercises**

1. Why do computers use binary in preference to, for example, the denary system?
2. (i) Differentiate between *internal* and *external* codes.
   (ii) What is the name of a device which converts an external code to its internal equivalent and vice versa?
   (iii) What is the purpose of *parity checking*?
3. Give two examples of the use of *control codes*, one relating to display screens and the other to data transmission.
4. In the context of computer storage and processing, what does *word length* mean and why is it important?

Chapter 8

Internal Numbers and Computer Arithmetic

A number stored without indication as to whether it is positive or negative, but simply as having a given magnitude (25_{10}, 129_{10}, for example,) is known as an *unsigned number*. To be of practical use, a computer must be able to store, manipulate and differentiate between positive and negative numbers (*signed numbers*). There are a number of different ways this can be done. The most common are: sign and magnitude; complementation.

Sign and magnitude

With this method, the MSB position is occupied by an explicit *sign bit*; binary 0 and binary 1 are used to indicate, respectively, a positive and a negative number. The remainder of the binary word holds the *absolute* (independent of the sign) *magnitude* of the number. The examples in Table 3.1 illustrate this method, using a 16-bit word.

	MSB															LSB
$+0_{10}$	0	0	0	0	0	0	0	0	0	0	0	0	0	0	0	0
$+33_{10}$	0	0	0	0	0	0	0	0	0	0	1	0	0	0	0	1
-33_{10}	1	0	0	0	0	0	0	0	0	0	1	0	0	0	0	1
$+85_{10}$	0	0	0	0	0	0	0	0	0	1	0	1	0	1	0	1
-85_{10}	1	0	0	0	0	0	0	0	0	1	0	1	0	1	0	1
bit	15	14	13	12	11	10	9	8	7	6	5	4	3	2	1	0
	sign	<					m a g n i t u d e									>

Table 8.1. *Sign and magnitude format*

Note from the top row in Table 8.1, that the number zero uses a positive sign (0).

Two's complement numbers

To follow the computer arithmetic examples in this chapter, you need to know the rules for binary addition, which can be found in Chapter 5. Table 8.2 shows two 8-bit examples of two's complement negative and positive numbers.

	MSB	place values						LSB
	-128_{10}	64_{10}	32_{10}	16_{10}	8_{10}	4_{10}	2_{10}	1_{10}
$+33_{10}$	0	0	1	0	0	0	0	1
-33_{10}	1	1	0	1	1	1	1	1
$+85_{10}$	0	1	0	1	0	1	0	1
-85_{10}	1	0	1	0	1	0	1	1
bit	7	6	5	4	3	2	1	0

Table 8.2. *Examples of two's complement, positive and negative numbers*

A computer can carry out *addition*, using *two's complement* notation. *Subtraction* can also be effected, through addition (by first negating the number to be subtracted). A two's complement number has an *implicit sign bit*. In other words, it has a place value which contributes to the magnitude of the number, as well as indicating its sign (positive or negative). The positive number examples (+33 and +85) in Table 8.2 contain a binary 0 in the sign bit position, so the place value of -128 does not contribute to the magnitude of the numbers.

The negative number examples (-33 and -85) contain a binary 1 in the sign bit position, so its place value of -128 forms part of each number's value. The negative value is calculated by adding the negative place value of the sign bit to the positive values of the remaining bits, which contain a binary 1. These points can be illustrated with the following analysis of the numbers.

$$+33_{10} = 00100001_2 = 0 + 0 + 32 + 0 + 0 + 0 + 0 + 1$$

$$-33_{10} = 11011111_2 = -128 + 64 + 0 + 16 + 8 + 4 + 2 + 1$$

$$+85_{10} = 01010101_2 = 0 + 64 + 0 + 16 + 0 + 4 + 0 + 1$$

$$-85_{10} = 10101011_2 = -128 + 0 + 32 + 0 + 8 + 0 + 2 + 1$$

Subtraction, using two's complement numbers uses the following method. The second number (the *subtrahend*) is negated and is added to the first (the *minuend*). This is equivalent to expressing in denary, for example,

$$(+55) - (+25) \text{ as } (+55) + (-25).$$

Conversion of binary to two's complement

The two's complement of a binary number is obtained through the following stages:

Stage 1

The number is converted to its *one's complement* representation by inverting the values of all the bits in the number. In other words all ones are flipped to zeroes and all zeroes are flipped to ones. The examples in Table 8.3 illustrate the one's complements of some binary numbers.

	Example (i) +13$_{10}$	Example (ii) +36$_{10}$	Example (iii) +76$_{10}$
binary number	00001101	00100100	01001100
one's complement	11110010	11011011	10110011

Table 8.3. *One's complement of binary numbers*

Stage 2

The one's complement of the binary numbers in Table 8.3 can then be converted to *two's complement* by adding 1, as shown in Table 8.4.

	Example (i) +13$_{10}$	Example (ii) +36$_{10}$	Example (iii) +76$_{10}$
one's complement	11110010	11011011	10110011
+	1	1	1
two's complement	11110011	11011100	10110100

Table 8.4. *Converting from one's to two's complement*

The two's complement numbers in each example now represent the following denary values.

two's complement of 13_{10} is $-128 + 64 + 32 + 16 + 0 + 0 + 2 + 1 = -13_{10}$

two's complement of 36_{10} is $-128 + 64 + 0 + 16 + 8 + 4 + 0 + 0 = -36_{10}$

two's complement of 76_{10} is $-128 + 0 + 32 + 16 + 0 + 4 + 0 + 0 = -76_{10}$

Integer arithmetic using two's complement

Binary subtraction

Subtraction can be carried out by negating the second number (the *subtrahend*), in this case by conversion to two's complement form and adding it to the first number (the *minuend*). The ease with which binary numbers can be switched from positive to negative and vice-versa, by complementation, makes subtraction by addition suitable for computers.

Consider the examples in Tables 8.5 and 8.6, assuming a 6-bit word length.

minuend	0 1 1 1 0 1		$+29_{10}$
subtrahend	0 0 0 1 1 1		$+7_{10}$
one's complement of subtrahend	1 1 1 0 0 0		
	1	+	
two's complement of subtrahend	1 1 1 0 0 1	=	-7_{10}
minuend	0 1 1 1 0 1	+	$+29_{10}$
result	1 0 1 0 1 1 0	=	
ignore carry (c)	0 1 0 1 1 0		$+22_{10}$

Table 8.5. *Two's complement arithmetic* $29_{10} - (+)7_{10} = 22_{10}$

The result in Table 8.5 (the carry is ignored) can be proved as follows.

$$010110_2 = 0_{10} + 16_{10} + 0_{10} + 4_{10} + 2_{10} + 0_{10} = 22_{10}.$$

Now consider the example in Table 8.6, where the minuend is smaller than the subtrahend, resulting in a negative answer.

minuend	0 0 0 1 1 1		$+7_{10}$
subtrahend	0 0 1 0 0 1	−	$+9_{10}$
one's complement of subtrahend	1 1 0 1 1 0		
	1	+	
two's complement of subtrahend	1 1 0 1 1 1	=	-9_{10}
minuend	0 0 0 1 1 1	+	$+7_{10}$
result	1 1 1 1 1 0	=	-2_{10}

Table 8.6. *Two's complement arithmetic example* $+7_{10} - (+9_{10}) = -2_{10}$

The result in Table 8.6 can be proved as follows.

$$111110_2 = -32_{10} + 16_{10} + 8_{10} + 4_{10} + 2_{10} + 0_{10} = -2_{10}$$

Number range and arithmetic overflow

The *number range* for any given word is determined by the number of bits in the word and the fact that the MSB is needed to indicate the sign (unless, of course, the number is unsigned). This applies whatever method is used to indicate the sign of numbers. The number range which can be stored in any given word length can be readily calculated. In an 8-bit word using *two's complement* (Table 8.7), the maximum number which can be represented is either $+127$ ($2^{n-1} - 1$) or -128 (-2^{n-1}), where n = word length.

$01111111_2 =$	$0_{10} + 64_{10} + 32_{10} + 16_{10} + 8_{10} + 4_{10} + 2_{10} + 1_{10} = +127_{10}$
$10000000_2 =$	-128_{10}
	sign bit (bit-8) implicit (-128)

Table 8.7. *Two's complement number range in an 8-bit word*

With *sign and magnitude*, the range is $\pm 127_{10}$ $(\pm 2^{n-1} - 1)$, as shown in Table 8.8.

$01111111_2 =$	$+(64_{10} + 32_{10} + 16_{10} + 8_{10} + 4_{10} + 2_{10} + 1_{10}) = +127_{10}$
$11111111_2 =$	$-(64_{10} + 32_{10} + 16_{10} + 8_{10} + 4_{10} + 2_{10} + 1_{10}) = -127_{10}$
	sign bit (bit-8) explicit $(0 = +, 1 = -)$

Table 8.8. *Sign and magnitude number range in an 8-bit word*

Detection of overflow

If the result of an operation involving two numbers exceeds the maximum permitted by the word, then overflow occurs. For example, with the use of 16-bit words and two's complement arithmetic, overflow occurs if the result is outside of the range -32768_{10} (-2^{16-1}) to $+32767_{10}$ $(2^{16-1}-1)$. Similarly, a 24-bit word would permit a range of -8388608_{10} (-2^{24-1}) to 8388607_{10} $(2^{24-1}-1)$.

Overflow needs to be detected by the computer so that an incorrect result is not overlooked. The hardware in the arithmetic logic unit (ALU) detects an overflow condition by comparing the states of the *carry in* to, and the *carry out* from, the sign bit. If they are not equal, overflow has occurred and the answer is incorrect.

Consider the two's complement examples in the next two tables, assuming an 8-bit word length. The sum in Table 8.9 shows a correct result, but the example in Table 8.10 appears to result in a negative sum (-96); this incorrect result is a consequence of overflow, indicated by the conflicting *carry in* and *carry out* states. Overflow will also occur when two *negative* numbers are added to produce a sum beyond the range of the word.

	64_{10}	0 1 0 0 0 0 0 0
+	4_{10}	0 0 0 0 0 1 0 0
=	68_{10}	0 1 0 0 0 1 0 0
carry		0 0

	96_{10}	0 1 1 0 0 0 0 0	
+	64_{10}	0 1 0 0 0 0 0 0	
=	-96_{10}	1 0 1 0 0 0 0 0	incorrect answer
carry		0 1	carries differ - overflow

Table 8.9. *Sum with no arithmetic overflow*

Table 8.10. *Incorrect sum resulting from overflow*

An *overflow flag* (a single bit) in the *condition codes*, *status* or *flag register* is set as soon as an overflow occurs. Thus, following the execution of an arithmetic process, a low level programmer can include a single test on the overflow flag to determine whether or not incorrect results are due to arithmetic overflow. Other machines may use the flag to implement an *interrupt*, which interrupts the CPU operation, to suspend processing and display an error message. The problem of limited number range and the need for accuracy can be overcome by the use of two or more words of memory to store a single number.

Real numbers

The first part of this section has concentrated on the storage and handling of *integers*. Although a programmer could choose to restrict numbers to integer format, all general-purpose computers must be able to deal with *real numbers*. Real numbers include all the integers and fractions of a number system, that is, all numbers above and below zero and including zero. Many computer applications require the use of numbers with a fractional element, that is, real numbers. Clearly, this can provide for a greater level of accuracy than is permitted by integer numbers, but at the cost of increased storage requirements. There are two basic methods of representing real numbers in computer storage:

❑ fixed-point and floating-point representation.

Fixed-point representation

Fixed-point numbers use what can be seen as a conventional format. The binary point is *assumed* to be immediately to the right of the integer part, which is where we would locate the decimal point if we were expressing real denary values. A programmer can require the binary point to be in any position within a memory word, according to the number of bits he or she wishes to assign to the integer and fractional parts. If more bits in a memory word are assigned to the fractional part, greater precision is possible; on the other hand fewer bits are then available for the integer part and this reduces the magnitude range. Conversely, increasing the proportion of a word given to the integer part increases the magnitude range, but reduces the possible level of precision. Table 8.11 illustrates fixed point format.

integer part	·	fractional part

Table 8.11. *Fixed point format*

Of course, a programmer may equally assume a given memory word to be entirely integer, with no fractional part. The binary point is said to have an *assumed* position which gives meaning to a number. Using 8-bit words, the programmer may instruct that the binary points for two numbers, labelled (i) and (ii), are located as shown in Table 8.12.

	integer part	·	fractional part
(i) 2.75$_{10}$	0 0 0 0 1 0	·	1 1$_2$
(ii) 28.25$_{10}$	0 1 1 1 0 0	·	0 1$_2$

Table 8.12. *Fixed point numbers*

If the programmer then relocates the binary points, as shown in Table 8.13, the same binary groupings take on different values. The point for number (i) is shifted one place to the left, which *halves* its value; the point in number (ii) is shifted one place to the right, which *doubles* its value. Therefore, a pro-

	integer part	·	fractional part
(i) 1.375$_{10}$	0 0 0 0 1	·	0 1 1$_2$
(ii) 56.5$_{10}$	0 1 1 1 0 0 0	·	1$_2$

Table 8.13. *Fixed point numbers after moving point*

grammer using fixed point numbers must keep track of the point position in order to know their value. This problem is of particular concern to the programmer using low level languages.

If a programmer is using fixed point numbers, this simply means that the decisions on the degree of precision are made by the programmer. If no floating point facility is available, the programmer must use integer arithmetic (see earlier) and set the precision after each calculation. The practicalities of this are of concern to the low level programmer, but briefly, involve the *scaling* of numbers to remove any fractional part, carrying out integer arithmetic and then re-scaling the result to the required number of fractional places. Today, all computers provide a floating point number facility, but there was a time when a programmer had to represent all real numbers in fixed point form. As explained later, floating point numbers require a longer word length than 8 bits, which was the norm, for example, for the first generation of microcomputers.

Number range and precision of fixed point numbers

Continuing with the topic of fixed point numbers, consider a 16-bit word with the binary point assumed to be between the bit-4 and bit-5 positions; sign and magnitude format is being used, so the sign bit (shown in bold) occupies the most significant bit position, which leaves 10 bits for the integral part and 5 bits for the fractional part of the number. The number range which can be represented is limited to that given in Table 8.14.

Positive 0_{10} to $+1023.96875_{10}$	Negative 0_{10} to -1024_{10}
$00000000000 \cdot 00000_2$	$00000000000 \cdot 00000_2$
$01111111111 \cdot 11111_2$	$10000000000 \cdot 00000_2$
sign	**sign**

Table 8.14. *Example sign and magnitude range*

Precision is limited by the number of bits allocated to the fractional part of the number and no matter what word length is used, some loss of precision is, occasionally inevitable.

Arithmetic overflow

Consider the multiplication of two denary values in Table 8.15, where only 1 place is available for the integer part and 3 places for the fractional part. The max-

$1 \cdot 363_{10} \times 8 \cdot 112_{10} = 11 \cdot 057_{10}$	**The 10s digit is lost**

Table 8.15. *Multiplication resulting in overflow*

imum positive value the location can hold is $9 \cdot 999_{10}$. Although such a location is large enough to hold each of the two numbers to be multiplied, the product of $11 \cdot 057$ (after rounding to 3 decimal places) results in an arithmetic overflow error. Given a particular word length for *fixed point* numbers, the allocation of more bits to the fractional part improves precision but at the cost of reduced number range. Conversely, the result of the above multiplication could be accommodated if 2 places are given to the integer part, but this would leave one less bit for the fractional element and consequently, reduced precision.

Arithmetic underflow

$0 \cdot 125_{10} \times 0 \cdot 005_{10} = 0 \cdot 000625_{10}$	**underflow error**

Table 8.16. *Arithmetic underflow*

This condition occurs when a number (a fraction or a negative number) is too small to fit into a given length word. The denary example in Table 8.16 illustrates underflow which results from the smallness of a fraction. Provision is made for a maximum of 3 decimal places. Multiplication of the two decimal fractions gives a product which underflows, giving an erroneous result of zero. Another example illustrates how a negative number can underflow and result in more serious error; given the provision of only two integer places, $-99_{10} \times 2_{10}$ gives a product of -198_{10}, which does not fit.

The main drawback of fixed point form is the small range of numbers which can be represented. *Floating-point* number representation helps overcome this problem at the cost of slightly slower computation and some reduction in precision; this latter point is discussed later.

Floating-point representation

A *mantissa* and *exponent* (or *index*) can be used to represent a number. Denary numbers, written in *standard index* form, reveal a format similar to that used for the storage of binary floating point numbers. Examples of binary floating point and denary standard index numbers are given in Table 8.17. Note that the formats are not exactly the same.

binary	binary floating point			denary	denary standard index	
	mantissa *m*	exponent r^e			mantissa	exponent
$101 \cdot 0101_2$	$0 \cdot 1010101_2$	$\times 2^3$		$6,800,000_{10}$	$6 \cdot 8_{10}$	$\times 10^6$
$0 \cdot 0011001_2$	$0 \cdot 11001_2$	$\times 2^{-2}$		$0 \cdot 0000564_{10}$	$5 \cdot 64_{10}$	$\times 10^{-5}$

Table 8.17. *Binary floating point and denary standard index examples*

In floating-point notation, the point is not fixed by the programmer. Instead it remains in a position at the left of the mantissa. Floating-point notation is based on the expression: $m \times r^e$, where *m* is positive or negative and *e* is positive or negative, *m* is the mantissa, *r* is the radix or base and *e* is the exponent (power). In binary, the radix is 2 (see Chapter 5).

Fixed-point numbers can be converted to floating-point numbers by a process of *normalisation*. As the first example ($101 \cdot 0101_2$) in Table 8.17 shows, if the number is *greater than* 1_2 then the point floats to the left (actually achieved by shifting the mantissa to the right), to a position immediately before the most significant bit. This part becomes the mantissa (m).The point in Table 8.17 has moved 3 places to the left, the mantissa is now $0 \cdot 1010101_2$ and the exponent (*e*) is therefore, 3. The second example ($0 \cdot 0011001_2$) in Table 8.17 shows that, if the number is a *fraction* and a binary 1 does not immediately follow the point, then the point floats to the right (actually achieved by shifting the mantissa to the left) of any leading zeros, until the first non-zero bit is reached; the mantissa becomes $0 \cdot 11001_2$. The point has moved 2 places to the right, so the exponent (*e*) is -2. Two more examples are given in the next two tables.

In Table 8.18, the point moves four places to the left, so the exponent is 4.

In Table 8.19, the fraction is normalised by moving the point three places to the right, so the exponent is -3. The floating point format (there are alternatives) used in this text follows a number of rules.

fixed point	binary floating point	
	mantissa *m*	exponent r^e
$1110 \cdot 001_2$	$0 \cdot 1110001_2$	$\times 2^4$

Table 8.18. *Fixed point > binary 1 converted to floating point*

❑ With normalised *positive* numbers the binary point must not be followed immediately by a binary 0. Only positive, floating point number examples have been provided so far.

fixed point	binary floating point	
	mantissa *m*	exponent r^e
$0 \cdot 000111_2$	$0 \cdot 1110000_2$	$\times 2^{-3}$

Table 8.19. *Fixed point < binary 1 converted to floating point*

❑ Conversely, normalised *negative* numbers require that the binary point is not followed immediately by a binary 1. The next section, on storage of floating point numbers, describes the format for negative numbers in more detail.

❑ Any normalised binary mantissa must be a fraction falling within the range $+0.5$ to less than $+1$ for positive values and -1 to less than -0.5 for negative values. The range of possible normalised 4-bit mantissas is shown in Table 8.20.

positive mantissas	denary equivalent	negative mantissas	denary equivalent
$0 \cdot 100_2$	$+\frac{1}{2}$	$1 \cdot 000_2$	-1
$0 \cdot 101_2$	$+\frac{5}{8}$	$1 \cdot 001_2$	$-\frac{7}{8}$
$0 \cdot 110_2$	$+\frac{3}{4}$	$1 \cdot 010_2$	$-\frac{3}{4}$
$0 \cdot 111_2$	$+\frac{7}{8}$	$1 \cdot 011_2$	$-\frac{5}{8}$

Table 8.20. *Range of possible normalised, 4-bit mantissas, with zero exponent*

Storage of floating-point numbers

As already indicated, floating-point numbers are stored in two parts:

- ❑ The *mantissa*, the length of which is determined by the precision to which numbers are represented. Clearly, if fewer bits are allocated to the mantissa (which is always a left-justified fraction) then less precision is possible.

- ❑ The *exponent*, which is usually allocated one-third to one-half of the number of bits used for the mantissa.

Table 8.21 assumes the use of a 16-bit word for the storage of each floating-point number, in two's complement form, 12 bits being used for the mantissa and 4 bits for the exponent.

	sign	mantissa (fraction)										exponent (integer)			
bit	15	14	13	12	11	10	9	8	7	6	5	4	3	2	1	0

Table 8.21. *Example floating point format using a 16-bit word*

The binary point in the mantissa fraction is immediately to the right of the sign bit, which is 0 for a positive and 1 for a negative floating-point number. Table 8.22 illustrates these points.

positive floating point form		negative floating point form	
12 bits	4 bits	12 bits	4 bits
$0 \cdot 1 * * * * * * * * * *$	$* * * *$	$1 \cdot 0 * * * * * * * * * *$	$* * * * *$
mantissa	exponent	mantissa	exponent

Table 8.22. *Positive and negative representation in floating point form*

In two's complement form, the most significant digit to the right of the binary point is 1 for a positive and 0 for a negative floating-point number. It should be noticed that the sign bit and the most significant non-sign bit differ in both cases. As explained earlier, any representation where they are the same indicates that the mantissa needs to be normalised. This may be necessary after any floating-point arithmetic operation.

Floating-point conversion

To obtain the denary equivalent of a number held in floating point form requires the mantissa to be multiplied by 2, raised to the *power* of e, which has the value stored in the exponent part of the number. For example, the floating point number in Table 8.23, which uses 8 bits for the mantissa and 4 bits for the exponent, converts to denary as follows.

8-bit mantissa	4-bit exponent
$0 \cdot 1 1 0 1 0 0 1$ $\times$	$0 1 0 1$ (2^5)

Table 8.23. *Floating point number*

$0 \cdot 1101001_2 \times 2^5 = 11010 \cdot 01_2$ (moving the binary point 5 places to the right)

$= (16 + 8 + 2 + \frac{1}{4}) = 26 \frac{1}{4}$

Therefore, the floating point number $0 \cdot 1101001_2 \times 2^5$ is equivalent to fixed point $11010 \cdot 01_2$. If 4 bits are allocated to the exponent, e can have a value between +7 and −8 (assuming two's complement form). Alternatively, in a 16-bit machine, two words with a total of 32 bits may be used to store each floating-point number, the mantissa occupying 24 bits, and the exponent, 8 bits. In such a representation, the exponent e could have a value between +127 and −128 (assuming two's complement). The earlier section entitled Number Range and Arithmetic Overflow gives an explanation of these calculations.

Alternative floating-point forms

Different machines may use different methods for coding floating-point numbers. The mantissa may be coded in two's complement, as described previously, or it may be stored as sign and magnitude. The advantage for machine arithmetic of storing numbers in two's complement form has already been identified, but machines with the circuitry to handle floating-point numbers may also have the facility to carry out subtraction without two's complement representation. The above illustrations of floating-point numbers assume that the exponent is also stored in two's complement form. In practice, the exponent is often stored in sign and magnitude.

Floating-point arithmetic

The floating point addition and subtraction examples used in this section assume the use of a 6-bit mantissa and a 4-bit exponent. Both mantissa and exponent are expressed in two's complement form.

Addition

To add two floating-point numbers, they must both have the same value exponent. If they differ, the necessary *scaling* is achieved by *shifting*, to the right (equivalent to the binary point floating to the left), the mantissa of the number with the smaller exponent and *incrementing* the exponent at every shift until the exponents are equal.

The addition procedure consists of equalising the exponents by scaling, adding the mantissas and then, if necessary, normalising the result. Tables 8.25 to 8.26 illustrate the floating-point addition procedure with the example sum in Table 8.24.

	mantissa		exponent	
6.75_{10}	$0 \cdot 1 1 0 1 1_2$	$\times$	$0 0 1 1_2$	2^3
$+12.50_{10}$	$0 \cdot 1 1 0 0 1_2$	$\times$	$0 1 0 0_2$	2^4

Table 8.24. *Binary floating point sum $6.75_{10} + 12.5_{10} = 19.25_{10}$*

❑ *Scaling.* In Table 8.25, the mantissa with the smaller exponent is shifted one place to the right and the exponent is incremented. As a result, a binary 1 is lost from the least significant bit position.

mantissa		exponent			mantissa		exponent
$0 \cdot 1 1 0 1 1_2$	$\times$	$0 0 1 1_2$	scales to		$0 \cdot 0 1 1 0 1_2$	$\times$	$0 1 0 0_2$
6.75_{10}		2^3			**LSB (1) lost**		2^4

Table 8.25. *Equalise the exponents by scaling*

❑ *Add the mantissas.* Table 8.26 shows that this is clearly incorrect, because the sign bit is now 1, indicating a negative value, when the result should be positive. The method by which the computer detects this type of error is explained earlier in the section on Arithmetic Overflow.

mantissa		exponent	
$0 \cdot 0 1 1 0 1_2$	$\times$	$0 1 0 0_2$	2^4
$+\ \ 0 \cdot 1 1 0 0 1_2$	$\times$	$0 1 0 0_2$	2^4
$=\ \ 1 \cdot 0 0 1 1 0_2$	$\times$	$0 1 0 0_2$	2^4

Table 8.26. *Mantissas added*

❑ Normalise the result (1.00110_2) shown in Table 8.26, which is beyond the permitted range (see Table 8.20) for a positive number. Table 8.27 shows the result of shifting the mantissa one place to the right and incrementing the exponent.

mantissa		exponent	
$0 \cdot 1 0 0 1 1_2$	$\times$	$0 1 0 1_2$	2^5

Table 8.27. *Result normalised*

The floating-point result in Table 8.27 can be expressed as follows.

$0 \cdot 1 0 0 1 1_2 \times 2^5 = 1 0 0 1 1_2$ (moving the binary point 5 places to the right)

$= 16+2+1 = 19_{10}$

Some loss of accuracy has resulted (19_{10} instead of $19 \cdot 25_{10}$). The loss of accuracy results from the right-shift operation required to equalise the exponents (Table 8.25); a significant bit is lost when the binary value for $6 \cdot 75_{10}$, ($0 \cdot 1 1 0 1 1_2 \times 2^3$) becomes $6 \cdot 5_{10}$ ($0 \cdot 0 1 1 0 1_2 \times 2^4$). The decimal value of this discarded bit is its fractional value of 1/32, multiplied by the exponent (before scaling) of 2^3(8), giving a result of $0 \cdot 25_{10}$. Although a further right-shift is needed to normalise the result (Table 8.27), the discarded bit is a 0 and does not produce any additional inaccuracy.

Subtraction

The procedures for subtraction are the same as for addition except that the mantissas are subtracted. This can be achieved by negating the subtrahend and then adding it to the minuend. In denary, this is the same as saying $12 \cdot 5_{10} + (-6 \cdot 75_{10}) = 5 \cdot 75_{10}$. Consider this example, shown in Table 8.28. The procedures for carrying out this subtraction, using floating point arithmetic are illustrated in Tables 8.29 to 8.32.

	mantissa		exponent	
$12 \cdot 50_{10}$	$0 \cdot 1 1 0 0 1_2$	$\times$	$0 1 0 0_2$	2^4
$-6 \cdot 75_{10}$	$0 \cdot 1 1 0 1 1_2$	$\times$	$0 0 1 1_2$	2^3

Table 8.28. *$12.5_{10} - 6.75_{10} = 5.75_{10}$*

❑ Scale the mantissa (Table 8.29) with the smaller exponent and increment the exponent, repeatedly if necessary, until the exponents of the two numbers are equalised. In this case, one right-shift is needed.

mantissa		exponent			mantissa		exponent
$0 \cdot 1 1 0 1 1_2$	$\times$	$0 0 1 1_2$	scales to	$0 \cdot 0 1 1 0 1_2$	$\times$	$0 1 0 0_2$
6.75_{10}		2^3		LSB (1) lost		2^4

Table 8.29. *Scale mantissas*

❑ Negate the subtrahend by finding the two's complement of its mantissa (Table 8.30).

	mantissa
6.75_{10}	$0 \cdot 0 1 1 0 1_2$
One's complement	$1 \cdot 1 0 0 1 0_2$
+	1_2
Two's complement	$1 \cdot 1 0 0 1 1_2$

Table 8.30. *Convert subtrahend to two's complement*

❏ Add the mantissas, as shown in Table 8.31; the carry of binary 1 is ignored.

	mantissa		exponent	
	$0 \cdot 1 1 0 0 1_2$	$\times$	$0 1 0 0_2$	2^4
+	$1 \cdot 1 0 0 1 1_2$	$\times$	$0 1 0 0_2$	2^4
=	$1 0 \cdot 0 1 1 0 0_2$	$\times$	$0 1 0 0_2$	2^4
	carry ignored			

Table 8.31. *Add the mantissas*

❏ If necessary, normalise the result. In this case, the answer is not in normal form because the sign bit and the most significant bit to the right of the binary point, are the same. The result is normalised by carrying out a left-shift of one on the mantissa and decrementing the exponent accordingly; the result is shown in Table 8.32.

The result in denary = $0 \cdot 11000_2 \times 2^3 = 110 \cdot 00_2$ (moving the binary point 3 places to the right) = 2+4 = 6_{10}. Note that a zero (in bold) is inserted into the least significant bit position of the mantissa. This floating point example has resulted in some significant loss of accuracy (and answer of 6_{10} instead of $5 \cdot 75_{10}$). In reality, inaccuracies of this order would clearly be intolerable and techniques are used to ensure that floating point arithmetic operations produce the degree of precision needed for the most demanding applications. Some aspects of these techniques are introduced in the next section.

mantissa		exponent	
$0 \cdot 1 1 0 0 0_2$	$\times$	$0 0 1 1_2$	2^3
zero inserted in LSB position			

Table 8.32. *Normalise the result*

Fixed point versus floating point representation

Precision. As stated earlier, given a particular word length, fixed point representation allows greater precision than is possible with floating point form. Consider, for example, a word length of six bits, used to store wholly fractional numbers. In fixed point form, all the bit positions can be used by significant digits, but in floating point form, if two bits are reserved for the exponent, this leaves only four bits for the mantissa and thus a maximum of four figure precision.

Range. As is demonstrated in the previous section, a major advantage of floating point form is the facility for storing an increased number range.

Maintenance of floating point arithmetic precision

Floating-point arithmetic precision can be improved by: increasing the number of bits allocated to the mantissa; rounding; double precision numbers and arithmetic.

Mantissa length

Increasing the number of bits allocated to the *mantissa* will improve precision but inaccuracies can never be completely eliminated. In practice, memory words are much longer than those used for illustration here and where memory words are of insufficient length to ensure acceptable accuracy, two adjacent locations may be used. Machines which make use of this method are providing what is referred to as *double-precision floating-point* facilities.

Rounding

The subtraction example in Tables 8.28 to 8.32 demonstrates a loss of accuracy through *truncation*; a significant bit 1 is lost when the mantissa is shifted one place to the right, in order to equalise the exponents of the minuend and the subtrahend. If a computer process requires a series of calculations, each using the results of previous ones, repeated truncation may accrue considerable inaccuracy and this will be reflected in the final result. As can be seen from the example of floating-point addition in Tables 8.24 to 8.27, the process of normalising the result also requires the shifting or justification of the mantissa.

Consider the example in Table 8.33, which only shows the mantissas to illustrate the normalisation process. In Table 8.33, normalisation has resulted in the loss of a binary 1 from the least significant bit position (a 0 is inserted into the sign bit position) and consequent loss of accuracy. Rounding dictates that, if during an arithmetic shift the last bit to be discarded (the *most significant* of those which are lost) is a 1, then 1 is added to the *least significant* retained bit.

	mantissa	
	0.1001_2	
+	0.1100_2	
=	1.0101_2	sign bit now 1
	0.10101_2	right shift of 1

Table 8.33. *Normalisation of mantissa*

	7 bits	1010111_2
101011101_2	6 bits	101011_2
rounded to	5 bits	10110_2
	4 bits	1011_2

Table 8.34. *Rounding*

Consider an 8-bit mantissa, rounded as in Table 8.34. The accumulated errors caused by repeated truncation of values during a lengthy arithmetic process can partially, though not entirely, be avoided by rounding. In practice, rounding can sometimes result in greater inaccuracies than would result without rounding. Many rounding algorithms exist to try to overcome this problem and the type of inaccuracy which occasionally occurs will depend on the rounding algorithm.

Double precision numbers and arithmetic

As the term (also known as *double length numbers*) suggests, where a single memory word is of insufficient length to accommodate a number, two contiguous words are used. Double precision numbers may be used to increase precision or when the product of a multiplication operation will not fit into a single location. The example addition in Table 8.35 provides a basic idea of double precision arithmetic; in the example, each number occupies two contiguous 4-bit *nibbles*. The procedure is also described with the pseudocode algorithm in Listing 8.1.

Listing 8.1. Double precision arithmetic

```
{double precision}
add least significant halves of numbers {1}
if carry = 1 then
  add 1 to most significant half {2}
```

```
set carry bit to 0 {3}
endif
add most significant halves of numbers {4}
```

most significant half		least significant half		
0	1 0 1	0	0 1 0	$1 0 1 0 1 0_2 = 42_{10}$
0	0 0 1	0	1 1 1	$0 0 1 1 1 1_2 = 15_{10}$
0		1	0 0 1	{1}
0	0 0 1			{2}
0	0 1 0			{2}
0		0	0 0 1	{3}
0	1 0 1			{4}
0	1 1 1	0	0 0 1	{4} $1 1 1 0 0 1_2 = 57_{10}$
sign		carry		

Table 8.35. *Double precision arithmetic*

Floating-point multiplication and division

To multiply two floating-point numbers, the mantissas are multiplied and their exponents are added. For simplicity, the multiplication process is illustrated using denary, but the principles are the same for binary floating point numbers. Tables 8.36 to 8.38 illustrate the process.

mantissa		exponent		mantissa		exponent
$0 \cdot 3$	×	10^3	multiplied by	$0 \cdot 2$	×	10^4

Table 8.36. *Floating point multiplication $300_{10} \times 2000_{10}$*

❏ Multiply mantissas and add exponents.

mantissa		exponent
$0 \cdot 06$	×	10^7

Table 8.37. *Result of multiplying mantissas and adding exponents*

❏ Normalise the result; the exponent is decremented each time the mantissa is shifted one position to the left.

mantissa		exponent
$0 \cdot 6$	×	10^6

Table 8.38. *Normalise result*

Tables 8.39 to 8.41 show a second example.

mantissa		exponent		mantissa		exponent
$0 \cdot 237$	×	10^2	multiplied by	$0 \cdot 415$	×	10^3

Table 8.39. *Floating point multiplication $23 \cdot 7_{10} \times 415_{10}$*

❏ Multiply mantissas and add exponents.

mantissa		exponent
$0 \cdot 098355$	×	10^5

Table 8.40. *Result of multiplying mantissas and adding exponents*

❏ Normalise the result; the exponent is decremented each time the mantissa is shifted one position to the left.

mantissa		exponent
$0 \cdot 98355$	×	10^4

Table 8.41. *Normalise result*

Floating-point division is carried out by dividing the mantissas and subtracting their exponents.

Hardware and software control of computer arithmetic

The execution of computer arithmetic operations often involves a mixture of hardware and software control. However, all modern computers are equipped with additional circuitry to handle floating-point numbers directly.

✍ Exercises

1. (i) If a computer uses a 16-bit word to represent integers, show how the numbers 30_{10} and 362_{10} would be represented in *binary coded decimal* (BCD).

   (ii) Show how the same computer would represent the values –30, –72 and –473 in (a) *sign and magnitude* and (b) *two's complement*.

2. Using two's complement representation and an 8-bit word, calculate the following:

   (i)   42 + 74;

   (ii)   74 – 42;

   (iii) 35 – 46.

3. Use the addition 75 + 96 to illustrate *arithmetic overflow* and explain how the computer's circuitry might detect the condition. Assume use of an 8-bit word.

4. What would be the denary, integer *number range*, for a 12-bit word, using two's complement representation?

5. Why is the number range for sign and magnitude different from that for two's complement?

6. If real numbers are to be represented in fixed point format, how does the low-level programmer determine the degree of precision?

7. How does floating point notation allow greater number range, for a given word length, than fixed point notation?

8. Given a particular word length, why does fixed point notation allow greater precision than floating point notation? Use an example to illustrate.

9. A particular computer uses a 16-bit word to store floating point numbers, allocating 10 bits to the mantissa and 6 bits to the exponent; both parts are stored in two's complement notation. Numbers are normalised when the bit immediately to the right of the binary point has a value of 1. The format is illustrated on the next page.

sign	binary point														
mantissa								**exponent**							

(i)   Calculate the denary values of:

      a.   0110100101000011

      b.   1010010100100101

      c.   0001010101 0011101

(ii) Write down the bit patterns to represent the following numbers, in normalised form:

      a.   +5.4

      b. -0.625

(iii) Add the numbers in part (ii), showing each stage, as described in the text.

(iv) Subtract 4.25 from 10.75, showing each stage as described in the text.

10. In the context of floating point arithmetic, what is meant by *arithmetic underflow*? Give an example of this condition.

11. How can the precision of floating point numbers be improved?

12. Convert the following floating point numbers to fixed point notation:

    (i) 0.1101011×0110

    (ii) 0.1001111×1100

    (iii) 1.010011×1010

    (iv) 1.011101×0011

Chapter 9

Computer systems architecture

The term "Computer Systems Architecture" refers to the composition of computer systems and the mechanisms by which components communicate electronically with each other. A computer system is a collection of a large number of separate components. Many of these are electro-mechanical or electronic, that is physical, components collectively termed the *hardware*. The remaining components are the electronically stored *software* items that either control the hardware (computer programs) or are used by other pieces of software (data). A separate chapter is devoted to the subject of software. Computer systems such as desktop computers (PCs) are general-purpose machines, capable of performing a wide range of data processing tasks. Computer programs make this versatility possible by controlling the hardware in different ways. For instance, many modern computer games control the components of the computer system that allow animated graphics to be displayed on the visual display unit. On the other hand, a company payroll program controls those hardware components required for processing and printing numeric and text-based data. A knowledge of the characteristics of the many different forms of hardware and software components is essential to the task of understanding and specifying computer system configurations for specific purposes. In this chapter we provide a broad introduction to the many different forms of hardware that can be found in typical PC systems; subsequent chapters deal with some of these subjects in more detail. Throughout this and subsequent chapters in this Unit, particular emphasis is placed on hardware and software used in typical personal computer systems.

Computer system components

The term *hardware* is used to describe all the physical devices that form a computer system. Figure 9.1 shows a few familiar examples. Although computer hardware catalogues list many examples of hardware devices, each one is likely to be concerned with a particular functional area from the following categories:

❑ input, output and backing storage devices, collectively known as *peripherals*;

❑ internal memory;

❑ motherboard and processor.

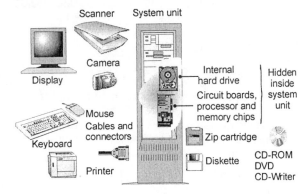

Figure 9.1. *Examples of computer hardware*

Input, output and backing storage

Figure 9.2 illustrates the functions of input, output and storage devices for communication with the central processing unit (CPU).

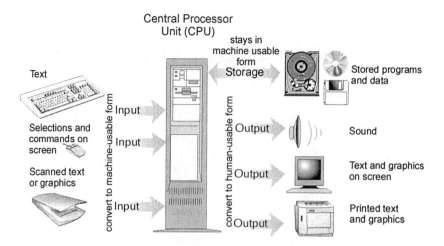

Figure 9.2. *How the CPU communicates with the outside world*

The job of each group of devices is as follows

❏ *Input* devices take data (text, graphics, sound and so on) from the outside world and convert it into the internal codes used inside the computer. Each device is designed to meet particular user requirements, so a microphone allows data entry through sound waves and a keyboard responds to keystrokes. Apart from working in a different way, they are designed to accept different kinds of data, so a microphone can accept speech input or be used to capture music. All input devices convert the data from the user's form into computer-sensible form.

❏ *Output* devices convert computer-sensible data into the forms users require. For example, a speaker converts data to sound and a screen produces a visual display. Of course, the data must be appropriate for the devices, so a music recording cannot be output to a display screen, although with appropriate software, the sound waves could be graphically displayed.

❏ *Backing storage* devices provide permanent storage for computer programs (software) and data files. A magnetic disk, for example, allows large amounts of data to be stored in magnetic form, so data is not lost when the computer is switched off. Programs are held on backing storage and are only loaded into the computer's memory when the user needs them. Data files, such as word processed documents or a company's payroll records are also held on backing storage and are called into memory as required by the program(s) in use.

Input, output and backing storage devices are known as *peripherals* because they are outside, or peripheral to, the central processing unit (CPU). Even though disk and CD-ROM drives are usually held inside the system unit casing, they are still classed as peripherals.

Input/output ports

Obviously, all of these types of devices must be connected to and be able to communicate electronically with the Central Processing Unit. Input/output ports are the connection points for peripheral devices, such as the mouse, printer or modem (for communication with other remote computers via a communications network such as the public telephone system).

Serial port

Microcomputers usually have at least two serial ports, one for connecting a mouse and the other for a modem. Serial ports transfer data in a single stream (one binary digit after another) as Figure 9.3 illustrates.

Figure 9.3. *Serial mouse*

Parallel port

The parallel port, known as a Centronics interface, is used to connect a printer. The port can also be used to communicate with some externally attached disk drives. The data is transferred as parallel groups of bits (each one representing a character), as shown in Figure 9.4. Another parallel port is normally specially reserved for connecting the display screen.

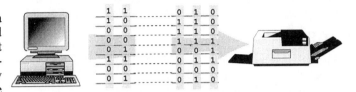

Figure 9.4. *Computer sending data from a parallel port to a printer*

PC I/O connectors

Figure 9.5 shows the rear of a typical system unit casing with its various ports and connectors. One side of a connection is *male*, with pins and the other *female*, with holes to match the pin pattern.

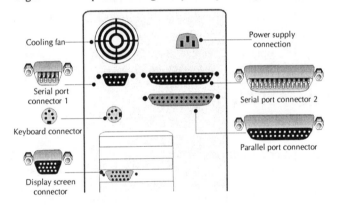

Figure 9.5. *Rear of system unit showing ports and types of connectors*

Controllers and interfaces

Controllers

These are electronic devices that control the transfer of data between a computer and peripherals. For example, disk drives, display screens, keyboards, and printers all require controllers.

In personal computers, the controllers are often single chips. Motherboards incorporate all the necessary controllers for standard components, such as the display screen, keyboard, and floppy disk drives. Hard disk drives and CDROM drives that use the *PCI* bus have controllers built in; they communicate with the CPU via an *IDE* interface integrated within the motherboard. Some devices, including certain types of hard drives and optical storage devices, use *SCSI* interfaces that may need to be provided on expansion cards. Controllers are designed to communicate with the computer's expansion bus (See **Buses**). Consequently extra controllers for additional devices must be compatible with a particular computer's expansion bus architecture.

IDE interfaces

The Intelligent/Integrated Drive Electronics (IDE) interface is specifically for mass storage devices, in which the controller is integrated into the mass storage device. Basic PCs usually provide IDE interfaces for up to four devices.

SCSI interfaces

Pronounced "scuzzy", SCSI (Small Computer System Interface) is a fast parallel interface standard used by PCs, Apple Macintosh computers, and many UNIX systems for attaching peripheral devices to computers. Many Apple Macintosh computers come with a SCSI port for attaching devices such as disk drives and printers. SCSI interfaces provide faster data transmission rates than standard serial and parallel ports and many devices can be linked to a single SCSI port. SCSI devices can be attached to a PC by inserting a SCSI board in one of the expansion slots. Many high-end new PCs come with SCSI built in.

AGP interfaces

The abbreviation for Accelerated Graphics Port, *AGP* is a new interface specification developed by Intel Corporation. Based on PCI, AGP is designed especially for 3-D graphics. AGP has a number of important system requirements:

❏ The motherboard chipset must support AGP.

❏ The motherboard must be equipped with an AGP bus slot or must have an integrated AGP graphics system.

❏ The operating system must be Windows 95 (version 2.1), Windows 98, 2000 or Windows NT 4.0. Currently, many professional Macintoshes support AGP.

Internal Memory

RAM

A computer can only run a program when it is in memory or *RAM* (*Random Access Memory*). Data needed by the program is also held in RAM. An important characteristic of RAM is that it is *volatile*. This means that the contents of the main memory can be destroyed, either by being overwritten as new data is entered for processing and new programs used, or when the machine is switched off. It is not practical to store data files and programs permanently in main memory because of its volatility.

DRAM

Pronounced "dee-ram", DRAM stands for Dynamic Random Access Memory, the type of memory used in most personal computers. DRAM chips are available in several forms. Each is appropriate to particular types of applications. The most common forms of DRAM are:

❏ DIP (Dual In-line Package). The DIP-Style DRAM package was popular when it was common for memory to be installed directly on the computer's system board. DIPs are through-hole components, which means they install in holes extending into the surface of the printed circuit board. DIPs can be soldered in place or seated in sockets.

❏ SOJ (Small Outline J-lead), and TSOP (Thin, Small Outline Package). These are components which mount directly onto the surface of the printed circuit board. TSOP and SOJ gained in popularity with the advent of the SIMM. Of the two, the SOJ package is by far the most popular..

EDO DRAM

This abbreviation stands for Extended Data Output Dynamic Random Access Memory. Unlike conventional DRAM which can only access one block of data at a time, EDO RAM can start fetching the next block of memory at the same time that it sends the previous block to the CPU. This makes EDO RAM faster than conventional DRAM.

FPM RAM

An abbreviation for Fast Page Mode RAM, FPM RAM is a fast form of DRAM It is sometimes called Page Mode Memory and is generally slower than EDO DRAM. FPM RAM is being superceded by newer types of memory, such as SDRAM.

SDRAM

SDRAM stands for *Synchronous* DRAM, a new type of DRAM that can run at much higher clock speeds. SDRAM is capable of running at 133 MHz, about twice as fast as EDO DRAM. SDRAM is replacing EDO DRAM in many newer computers.

RDRAM

Short for Rambus DRAM, a type of memory developed by Rambus, Inc. Whereas the fastest current memory technologies used by PCs (SDRAM) can deliver data at a maximum speed of about 133 MHz, RDRAM transfers data at up to 600 MHz.

Types of Memory Modules

Modern motherboards have banks of special slots for memory modules. Currently there are two main forms of these modules:

- ❑ SIMMs (Single Inline Memory Modules) and, more recently,
- ❑ DIMMs (Dual Inline Memory Modules).

Each module is a board onto which are soldered a number of memory chips. DIMMs are very high density memory modules that have two banks of chips soldered to the circuit board. Because they require less space than SIMMs, they are likely to supercede SIMMs in the near future. Figure 9.6 shows an example of a SIMM containing nine memory chips. One of the chips is usually used for parity checking.

Figure 9.6. *Example of a SIMM*

The table below summarises the major characteristics of SIMMs and DIMMs. As you can see, SDRAM DIMMS are much faster than EDO DRAM SIMMs (*ns* stands for nanosecond, one thousandth of a millionth of a second). Currently, megabyte for megabyte, DIMMs are also much cheaper than SIMMs.

Type	Capacity range (MB)	Approx. access speed (ns)	Type	Pins
SIMM	8 - 64	60	EDO RAM	72
DIMM	8 - 256	8	SDRAM	168

Most new motherboards accept only 168-pin DIMMs, but some also accept 72-pin SIMMs. Motherboard documentation will specify the type of RAM that it supports: typically FP DRAM or EDO DRAM for SIMMs, or EDO DRAM or SDRAM for DIMMs.

Cache memory

Cache Memory is a special high-speed memory designed to accelerate processing of memory instructions by the CPU. The CPU can access instructions and data located in cache memory much faster than instructions and data in main memory. For example, on a typical 100-megahertz system board, it takes the CPU as much as 180 nanoseconds to obtain information from main memory, compared to just 45 nanoseconds from cache memory. Therefore, the more instructions and data the CPU can access directly from cache memory, the faster the computer can run. Cache can be internal or external. Internal cache is built into the computer's CPU, and external cache is located outside the CPU.

ROM and flash memory

ROM is a type of memory designed to hold data more permanently than RAM. With most types of ROM, the data is built into the memory when it is manufactured and cannot be changed. For this reason it is *non-volatile*, so the contents are not lost when power is removed. ROM is used to hold the *BIOS* (Basic Input/Output System) and the *bootstrap loader*. Flash memory also retains its contents when power is removed, but unlike ROM, its contents can be changed by software. Most modern microcomputers use flash memory to allow the BIOS to be changed automatically when new hardware devices are added.

Central processing unit (CPU)

Also known as the *processor*, the CPU is the heart of the computer and has two part main parts:

Control unit

The control unit:

- ❏ fetches program instructions from memory and decodes and executes them, calling on the ALU (see below) when calculations or comparisons need to be carried out on data;
- ❏ controls the flow of data both within the CPU and to and from peripheral devices such as printers, disk drives and keyboards;
- ❏ ensures that devices operate according to program instructions, by sending electrical control signals to them as required.

Arithmetic/logic unit (ALU)

The ALU contains circuitry to carry out important tasks such as addition, subtraction, multiplication and division of numbers fetched from RAM or held in registers in the processor. It can also, for example, compare two numbers and discover whether or not they are equal and perform logical operations, such as AND, OR and NOT. The data-flow routes between various hardware components and the CPU are illustrated in Figure 9.7.

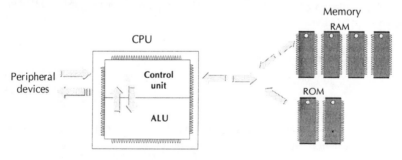

Figure 9.7. *The data flows between hardware devices*

Co-processors

In order to speed certain types of computations, a computer system might incorporate one or more co-processors. For example, a graphics accelerator card (see **Expansion Cards**) will usually include its own processor to deal with graphics computations independently of the main motherboard processor. Modern processors include a maths co-processor to deal with floating-point computations, though earlier PCs sometimes had a separate chip on the mother-board for this purpose.

Motherboard

The motherboard is the main circuit board inside a microcomputer's system casing. A number of major hardware components are plugged into it, including the CPU, the BIOS memory and RAM. It also has a number of *expansion slots*, into which plug-in circuit boards can be inserted. These are slots into which *expansion boards* or *cards* can be plugged, to add extra features to a system. Note the following points regarding motherboards:

- ❑ The motherboard has printed circuits (not shown) which provide the electrical connections between all the components plugged into it. One or more *buses* are built into the motherboard to provide fast connections between components. Buses are discussed in more detail in the next section.

- ❑ All replaceable components must be compatible with the motherboard. This often prevents certain upgrading of the machine. For example, one type of memory called EDO RAM uses 72 pins to contact with the motherboard, but SDRAM, which allows data to be accessed more quickly than EDO RAM, uses 128 pins and therefore a different sized socket. (Memory is discussed in more detail in **Types of RAM).** In the same way, when a new processor becomes available, upgrading a machine from an older type will often mean replacing the motherboard.

- ❑ The processor chip plugs into a ZIF (Zero Insertion Force) socket; this allows the processor to be inserted or removed without damage.

- ❑ RAM chips are fixed to a small circuit board called a SIMM (Single In-line Memory Module). For example, a 64MB SIMM has 8 × 8MB memory chips attached to it. In the motherboard map, there are two memory *banks*, each with two slots, so 4 SIMMs could be attached. If 64MB SIMMs were used, this would allow the computer to have 256MB of RAM.

- ❑ Modern motherboards often incorporate interfaces and functions that required separate expansion boards in the past. For example, a motherboard may include two IDE interfaces for hard drives and CD ROM drives in addition to a floppy disk interface. Many motherboards now also include sound chips that also used to require a separate card in the past.

Expansion Cards

Figure 9.8 shows a typical expansion card. Some of these circuit boards may be used for controlling peripheral devices, but there are many other boards available for a wide range of applications. Because each pin on an expansion slot is connected to the same pin on all the other expansion slots by a printed circuit, a board can be plugged in to any compatible slot. Expansion slots are connected to the system bus (it makes electrical contact), so when an expansion card is plugged in, it becomes part of the system. Here are some common examples of expansion cards:

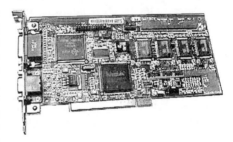

Figure 9.8. *A plug-in expansion card*

- ❑ modem cards for connection to the Internet and for receiving and transmitting faxes;
- ❑ graphics cards (video adapters, graphics accelerators) for accelerating graphics-based

applications such as games and for capturing video sequences from external sources such as VCRs and video cameras;

❑ TV cards to allow the computer to show TV programs on the monitor;

❑ network cards to allow several computers to be linked in a network;

❑ sound cards for capturing and playing high quality sound sequences;

❑ SCSI (Small Computer System Interface) card, a fast parallel interface standard for connecting peripheral devices. (see **Controllers and Interfaces**).

Two of these, video adapters and sound cards, are described in more detail below.

Video Adapters

A video adapter is a board that plugs into an expansion slot of a personal computer's motherboard to give it display capabilities when connected to a monitor. These display capabilities depend on both the electronics provided in the video adapter and the display monitor. For example, a monochrome monitor cannot display colours whatever the quality of the video adapter. Adapters usually provide two basic categories of video modes:

❑ text mode - a monitor can display only ASCII characters;

❑ graphics mode - a monitor can display any bit-mapped image.

So that large quantities of the computer's RAM is not used for storing display data, modern video adapters contain their own memory. The amount of memory determines maximum resolution and the number of colours that can be displayed. At lower resolutions a monitor can display more colours. Some accelerators use conventional DRAM, but others have video RAM (VRAM), which enables both the video circuitry and the processor to access the memory simultaneously. A typical graphics card might contain 4MB to 8MB of VRAM. In addition, most adapters have their own graphics coprocessor for performing graphics calculations. Such adapters are often called graphics accelerators. Because of the growth of multimedia software and games requiring high-resolution graphics, most computer manufacturers now include a graphics accelerator with their systems.

Sound cards

These are expansion boards that enable computers to capture, play and edit high quality sound. As mentioned earlier, a motherboard might incorporate sound capabilities, but if not a sound card will be necessary, particularly if the computer includes a CD-ROM. Sound cards include sockets for speakers to play sound files and a microphone for recording sound on disk. Bundled software allows sound files to be loaded, edited, stored and played. The majority of sound cards support the MIDI standard for representing music electronically, and most sound cards are compatible with the Sound Blaster card which has become the standard for PC sound.

Buses

Though all computers have the same basic functional components, the architectural details in some are far more complex than in others. A particular area of variation relates to the arrangement of the bus systems which permit communication between the various parts of the computer system. A number of features concerning buses can be identified:

❑ a bus is a group of parallel wires, one for each bit of a word, along which data can flow (as electrical signals);

❑ the *system* bus comprises a number of such communication channels, connecting a computer's processor and its associated components of memory and input/output(I/O) devices;

- ☐ a single bus may carry data for different functions at separate times or it may be dedicated to one function. A computer will usually have several buses, used for specific purposes, for example, the I/O bus or main memory-to-processor bus;

- ☐ some buses are *bi-directional*, that is data can flow in both directions;

- ☐ the *width* of a bus determines the length of word which can be handled at one time. So, a processor which used a 16-bit bus, but required a 32-bit word to address memory, would combine two 16-bit words in two separate fetch operations.

Communication is required within a processor, to allow movement of data between its various registers, between the processor and memory and for I/O transfers. In a *single* bus system, both I/O and memory transfers share the same communication channel, whereas in a *two-bus* system, I/O and memory transfers are carried out independently; similarly, in small systems with few I/O devices, they usually share the same bus, but a larger system requires several I/O buses to ensure efficient operation.

Each of the separately identified functions of memory, register-to-register and I/O transfers (assuming that the I/O bus is shared by a number of devices), must have the use of:

- ☐ a *data bus*, for the transfer of data subject to processing or manipulation in the machine;

- ☐ an *address bus* which carries the address of, for example, a memory word to be read, or the output device to which a character is to be transmitted;

- ☐ a *control bus*, which as the name suggest, carries signals concerning the timing of various operations, such as memory write, memory read and I/O operations.

All signals on a bus follow strict timing sequences, so some operations take longer than others.

Bus architecture - a brief history

This concerns the internal structure of a computer, that is the way in which the various components are connected and communicate with one another. As technological advances improve the performance of certain components, so the architecture has to change to take advantage of these improvements.

Micro channel architecture (MCA)

MCA aimed to overcome the limitations of the old, Industry Standard Architecture (ISA), IBM AT (Advanced Technology) machines as well as a myriad of clones produced by IBM's competitors. IBM used MCA in their 32-bit PS/2 (Personal System 2) range.

System bus width and system performance

One of the many differences with the MCA approach concerns the width of the *system bus*. This bus is a communication link between the processor and system components and is an essential, but passive, part of system architecture. The active components, such as the processor, disk controller and other peripherals are the primary determinants of system performance. As long as the data transfer speed along the bus matches the requirements of these devices and does not create a bottleneck, the bus does not affect system performance. The MCA bus is 32 bits, compared with the AT's 16 bits, and the wider data path allows components within the system to be accessed twice as quickly. The MCA bus also uses bus-mastering controllers to handle data transfers more quickly. The wider bus is also compatible with the 32-bit external bus used on more recent processors. The bus can be controlled by separate *bus master* processors, relieving the main processor of this task.

MCA is also radically different from AT architecture in many other respects. For example, the expansion slots in the PS/2 range which allow the user to insert extra features, perhaps for networking or for extra memory, are physically different from those in the AT and PC machines and their expansion cards will not fit in the PS/2 machines. The problem for existing AT and PC users was that they could not buy new PS/2 machines and still make use of their existing expansion cards. This incompatibility also meant that few manufacturers produced MCA versions of their expansion cards. IBM and Apricot were the biggest proponents of the MCA standard, but it never became the standard architecture.

Extended industry standard architecture (EISA)

A consortium of IBM's competitors including Compaq, Zenith, NEC and Olivetti amongst others, established a new architecture (EISA - Extended Industry Standard Architecture) which aims to give the benefits of MCA and to retain compatibility with existing AT expansion cards. EISA also uses a 32-bit bus, thus providing the same data transfer benefits as MCA, particularly for hard disk controllers (a very important contributor to overall system performance). Both EISA and MCA machines were more expensive than the ISA-based microcomputers, and tended to be used where extra power was needed, as *file servers* in networked systems. Most small business users found that ISA machines were adequate for their needs, particularly as the use of *local bus* technology was further increasing their power.

Local bus

A local bus is a high speed data path connecting the processor with a peripheral. Local bus design is used, primarily, to speed communications with hard disk controllers and display adapters. The need for local bus derives from the imbalance between the clock

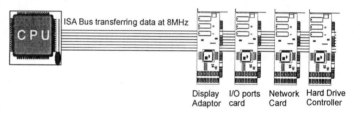

Figure 9.9. *ISA bus*

speed of a 32-bit processor (typically, in excess of 100MHz) and the ISA 16-bit system bus (operating at 8 MHz). The ISA system is illustrated in Figure 9.9. This imbalance can result in the processor idling while waiting for data to be transferred from disk, or the display adapter waiting for screen data. The widespread use of Windows, a *graphical user interface* and software

packages which make intensive use of the hard disk (such as databases) and screen graphics (computer-aided design), has highlighted the deficiencies of such imbalanced computer systems.

A local bus provides a wider data path, currently 32 bits and an increased clock speed, typically 33MHz or more. The first local bus systems appeared in 1992, with manufacturers following a standard referred to as *VL-bus*, developed by VESA (Video

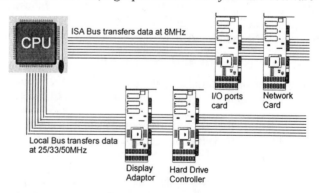

Figure 9.10. *Local bus*

Electronics Standards Association). Figure 9.10 illustrates the principle of a local bus system.

In 1993, Intel backed the development of a new industry standard called **PCI**. The PCI standard encourages the development of computer systems which allow local bus connection to any high-speed peripheral. Apart from speeding communication with screen graphics controllers, PCI local bus can be used with, for example, hard disk, network and motion video controllers (up to 10 devices in total).

***USB**,* short for Universal Serial Bus, is a new external bus standard that supports data transfer rates of 12 Mbps (12 million bits per second). A single USB port can be used to connect up to 127 peripheral devices, such as mice, modems, and keyboards. USB also supports *Plug-and-Play* installation and *hot plugging* (adding and removing devices while the computer is running and have the operating system automatically recognise the change - also called *hot swapping*). USB is expected to completely replace serial and parallel ports.

Exercises

1. What is meant by the term 'hardware'?
2. Name 3 types of device that are generally connected to a computer system. Give two examples of each type.
3. What two types of memory are commonly found in a computer? For each type, give an example of what it stores.
4. A CPU has two main components. Name and briefly explain the function of each part.
5. Explain the purpose of a port.
6. What is the name of the main circuit board inside a computer?
7. What is the function of a Controller?
8. Name three types of interfaces for peripherals and say for what types of peripherals each interface has been designed.
9. What do the following abbreviations mean?
   DRAM
   EDO RAM
   FPM RAM
   SDRAM
   RDRAM
   VRAM
10. Name two types of commonly used memory modules. Typically, what types of RAM are used in each case?
11. Explain the function of Cache memory.
12. What is *Flash Memory*?
13. Give two typical uses of Co-processors.
14. What are the main upgradable components of a motherboard?
15. Name 4 types of expansion cards.
16. Define a Bus. Name and describe the uses of three common PC buses.

Chapter 10

Input and output devices

Input and output devices allow users to communicate with the computer, in different ways, according to their requirements. For a given type of device, such as a printer, there are many different product specifications, each designed to meet a particular need. For example, when judging a printer specification, you need to consider its speed of output and the quality of the print it can produce. The first part of the chapter deals with input devices and the second with output devices. For each type of device there is

❏ a general description of the device and details of the main products of that type. For example, when examining printers, you need to be aware of differences between laser and inkjet products;

❏ where necessary, an explanation of technical terms found in product specifications and guidance on matching device specifications to users' needs.

Input devices

Input devices enable information to be entered into a computer for processing or storage on magnetic media. The computer can only process or store information if it is in an electronic, binary coded form, so input devices are needed to convert, for example, letters of the alphabet, digits in our number system, the sounds of the human voice or musical instruments, into the computer's code.

The most commonly used input device is the keyboard, which converts key presses into the computer's code. So, for example, pressing the 'A' key produces electrical signals which the computer uses to represent that letter. The computer uses a different code for each character on the keyboard. The ASCII (American Standard Code for Information Interchange) binary code is recognised by all computers. Similarly, a *scanner* allows typed or hand-written documents to be read into a computer and a microphone enables the entry of sounds, perhaps to give voice commands to the computer. Each input device needs its own software to make it work on a particular computer system.

Computer keyboards

A number of alternatives are available to suit different ways of working, different work conditions and special applications.

Standard keyboard

A typical standard computer keyboard is shown in Figure 10.1. The arrangement of keys on the main part of the keyboard is the same as for any typewriter. This QWERTY layout comes from mechanical typewriters and has little to do with the requirements of a computer

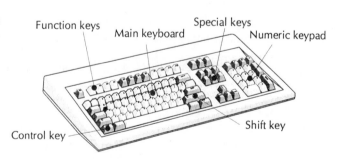

Figure 10.1 *A typical standard keyboard*

keyboard. It has continued as the favoured design because many people are used to it and changing the layout of the keys would mean retraining for millions of keyboard users. The computer keyboard does have other keys, specifically designed for the computer. Function keys, for example, are programmable and are used by software packages to access particular options, such as Help menus. Some common examples of keyboard use are:

☐ entering text and numbers into the computer, perhaps using a word processor;

☐ entering keywords into a *search engine,* a type of program used to find information on the World Wide Web;

☐ controlling animated graphics characters in computer games;

☐ entering commands to an operating system such as MS-DOS.

Microsoft Natural keyboard

An alternative keyboard design has been developed by Microsoft. Its shape and main features are illustrated in Figure 10.2. The Natural keyboard splits the keys into two main areas and angles the keys slightly, allowing the user to keep a straighter, more comfortable wrist posture. The keyboard also slopes and provides palm support, which puts less strain on the wrists and allows the shoulders to relax. Repetitive strain injury (RSI) is a common complaint of keyboard users and a comfortable wrist posture helps to

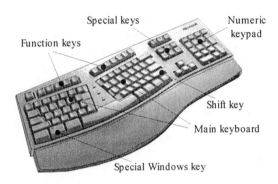

Figure 10.2. *Microsoft Natural keyboard*

avoid it. The design was based on *ergonomic* research, which is the "study of efficiency of workers and working arrangements" (Oxford English Dictionary).

Membrane keyboard

This is a keyboard covered by a transparent, plastic cover, to protect the keys from dirt. Membrane keyboards are used in factories or other locations where the dirt from users' fingers or the surroundings may damage them. The membrane makes its difficult to type accurately and quickly, so these keyboards are not used in a normal office environment.

Concept keypads

In specialist applications, the standard keyboard is not always the most convenient method of input. In a factory, for example, a limited number of functions may be necessary for the operation of a computerised lathe. These functions can be set out on a touch-sensitive pad and clearly marked. This is possible because all inputs are anticipated and the range is small. The operator is saved the trouble of typing in the individual characters which form instructions.

Concept keypads are used in shops, restaurants and bars. For example, each key position on the pad can be assigned to a particular drink. Pressing a key automatically enters the charge for the specified drink. Concept keypads are also useful in education, particularly for the mentally and physically handicapped. Different overlays, which can set different areas of the keypad to different functions, allow its use for different educational programs. For example, if the responses required by a user are limited to 'yes' and 'no', the overlay is simply divided into two parts, one for each response. The cells have to be programmed to match the overlay in use. Figure 10.3 illustrates this idea.

The grid shown on the keypad is divided into a grid of 16 × 8 (128) programmable cells and the example overlay shows that the grid is to be programmed into 4 areas. Each area occupies 32 cells (128 ÷ 4) and pressure on any of the cells in one area indicates that the user has selected a particular picture. This may result, for example, in the matching word being displayed on screen. Alternatively, the input may be the user's response to the word shown on screen.

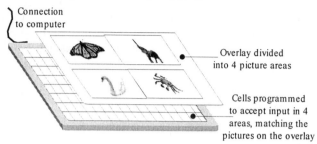

Figure 10.3. Educational concept keypad with sample overlay

Choosing a keyboard

The desirable qualities of a keyboard are reliability, quietness and light operating pressure and in these terms keyboards vary considerably. If the keyboard is for a normal office use then a standard or Microsoft keyboard is appropriate. Computerised tills in restaurants, pubs and hotels often use concept keypads tailored for all the items they sell. This ensures accurate pricing, as well as quicker service. Gas and electricity meter readers also use concept keypads to collect the readings. Security systems often include a concept keypad, for entry of pass codes. Dirty environments in factories or on building sites, for example, need equipment with extra protection, so membrane keyboards are used.

Pointing devices

Apart from the keyboard, which is an essential part of every computer system, pointing devices are the next most popular option for input. The devices in this group use different mechanisms and technologies, but they all allow the user to draw, erase, select and format text and graphics on screen. Figures 10.4 and 10.5 illustrate two such actions. Pointing devices are an essential component for the effective use of modern software. Two of the most popular types are described next.

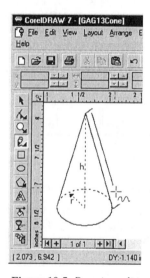

Figure 10.5. Drawing a line

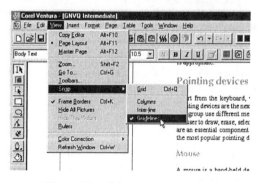

Figure 10.4. Selecting a menu option

Mouse

A mouse is a hand-held device which the user can move on a flat surface to direct a pointer on the computer screen. It has two or more buttons, which allow the user to draw, erase, select and format text and graphics on screen. Most computer systems are equipped with a mouse facility and many packages, including those for art, design, word processing and desktop publishing can only be operated effectively with a mouse or similar device. Graphical user interfaces such as that provided by the Windows 95/98 operating system, also depend heavily on its use.

Tracker ball

A tracker (or roller) ball is another variation of a mouse and is used for the same purposes. As shown here, a tracker ball is a bit like an up-side-down mouse, with the ball visible on the top of the base. To use a tracker ball you simply move the ball in the required direction using your fingers. Buttons are supplied just like on a mouse. Like joysticks, tracker balls have the advantage over mice that a flat surface is not required for its operation, and for this reason they are often used with portable computers.

Tracker ball

Other pointing devices

Although the mouse and tracker ball are very popular, they are not the most suitable for every application. Three other pointing devices are described below.

☐ *Touch screen.* A touch sensitive display allows selection of screen options with a finger. It is commonly used in banks and tourist agencies to allow customers to obtain information on certain topics.

☐ *Digitising tablet.* A stylus (pen-like device) is used to 'draw' on the tablet; the movements of the stylus are reflected on screen. Used by architects and designers, it allows more precise drawing than a mouse.

☐ *Light pen.* This pointing device is moved over the screen and uses a light sensitive tip to allow the computer to track its movements. It can only be used with cathode ray tube (CRT) displays and cannot be used with laptop or notebook computers.

Choosing a pointing device

For most users, the mouse is standard equipment, but for architects, graphic artists and other designers, the mouse does not provide the precision control possible with a graphics tablet. The light pen is a possible alternative to the graphics tablet; it is cheaper but is not capable of the same accuracy. The roller or tracker ball is suitable for a portable computer because it does not need a flat surface. Touch-sensitive screens are suited to public display information systems, because no keyboard or other input device is needed. The user simply uses a finger to touch the required option on screen.

Sensors and ADCs

Sensors are used to detect continuously varying values, such as temperature, pressure, light intensity, humidity, wind speed and so on. These sensors detect analogue signals which are not compatible with digital computers. So, apart from several other components, an *analogue-to-digital converter* (ADC) is needed to convert analogue signals into the digital values a computer can understand.

Suppose that the temperature of a washing machine is computer controlled, using a built-in microprocessor programmed for that purpose. The microprocessor can only

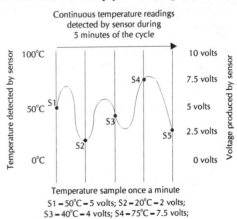

Continuous temperature readings detected by sensor during 5 minutes of the cycle

Temperature sample once a minute
S1 – 50°C – 5 volts; S2 – 20°C – 2 volts;
S3 – 40°C – 4 volts; S4 – 75°C – 7.5 volts;
S5 – 25°C – 2.5 volts

Figure 10.6. *Washing machine temperature variation, with a sample reading every minute*

handle discrete, that is separate, values, so the ADC in this machine takes a sample from the sensor every minute. Figure 10.6 illustrates the analogue wave form which represents the temperature variations detected by the sensor, over a 5 minute period. The figure also shows the temperature readings at each sample point (S1 to S5). For example, at the 3rd minute sample S3 = 40^0C.

Figure 10.7 shows a temperature sensor immersed in the water. The electrical signal (after being strengthened by an amplifier) produced by the sensor is converted by the ADC into an equivalent digital value for the microprocessor. Therefore, for each temperature sample, the microprocessor receives an equivalent digital value. It can then use these values to control the washing machine's heater.

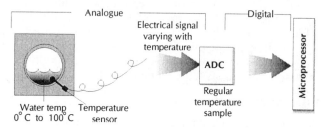

Figure 10.7. *Sensor detects variations in temperature and ADC digitises sample values*

Microphone

Figure 10.8 illustrates the use of a microphone connected to a computer. Just as the temperature sensor produces a voltage which varies with the temperature, so a microphone acts as a sensor, converting sound waves to equivalent electrical voltage levels. The voltages are sampled and converted by the sound card inside the system casing into the binary codes which the computer can store and process. Most personal computers are equipped with a microphone to allow, with appropriate software, sound recording or the input of commands and text.

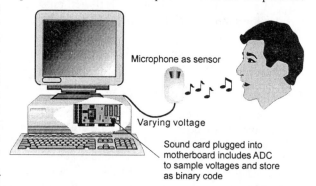

Figure 10.8. *Microphone as sensor for sound input*

Digitiser

The term *digitiser* is used to describe more complex ADCs used for capturing video sequences (the digitiser is a *video capture card*) and scanning documents. Scanners are briefly described in the next section.

Other input devices

There are a number of devices designed to capture information, in the form of pictures or text, already printed on paper. These devices include the following.

❏ *Scanners.* These devices allow whole documents to be scanned optically and converted into digital images. Text can be captured in this way and then converted for use in a word processor. The conversion is carried out by *optical character recognition (OCR)* software.

❏ *Optical mark reader (OMR).* An OMR is designed to read simple pencil marks placed in pre-set positions on a document. A common application for OMR is a multi-choice examination paper, where the answer to each question has to be indicated by a pencil mark in one of several boxes located after the question number. The OMR can then scan the paper for the pencil marks and work out a grade. National Lottery tickets are completed and checked in a similar fashion.

☐ *Bar code readers.* Bar codes are commonly used to store a variety of data such as prices and stock codes relating to products in shops and supermarkets. A sticker with the relevant bar code is attached to each product, or alternatively, the packaging may be pre-coded. By using the data from the code, the cash register can identify the item, look up its latest price and print the information on the customer's receipt.

Output devices

Just as input devices allow human beings to communicate with computers, so output devices convert computer code into the information we can use. In this section we describe the devices that form part of typical personal computer systems, namely, *visual display units* (*VDUs*), *printers* and *loudspeakers*.

Visual display unit

The most commonly used device for communicating with a computer is the *visual display unit* (VDU). The term VDU *terminal* is normally used to describe the screen and keyboard as a combined facility for input and output. On its own, the screen is called a *monitor* or *display*.

Technical features of VDUs

Screen size

A screen's size is quoted as a measurement across the diagonal, as shown. In practice, part of the screen is covered by the casing and the part of the screen you can see is usually at least an inch less. Some screen specifications quote this smaller measurement as the 'viewable area'. For desktop personal computers, 14" or 15" is standard, but 17", 19" and 21" are also available. The larger screens are needed for applications such as computer-aided design (CAD). This is because the level of detail on some designs cannot be properly seen on a standard screen.

Notebook computer screens, which use a different technology to desktop models, are obviously smaller and typically around 12" (12 inches) across the diagonal.

Screen resolution

A screen's *resolution* is one measurement indicating the clarity or sharpness of displayed text or graphics. Images are formed on the screen with pixels (picture elements). A pixel is one dot in a graphic image. A display screen is divided into thousands or millions of such pixels, organised in rows and columns. By varying the colours and luminosity (brightness) of individual pixels, text and graphic images are displayed. A high resolution screen packs pixels more densely to produce sharper images. A lower resolution will produce a more 'grainy' image, rather like a photograph which has been enlarged to many times its original size. To illustrate the idea of resolution, examine Figure 10.9, showing two pictures of a puma.

They are both the same size, but the top picture uses fewer pixels than the other. For this reason, the top picture is much less clear than the other. In fact, the resolution is so poor that the jagged edges of pixels can be seen.

The resolution of each image is indicated by the number of pixels in each row and column. So, the top picture has a resolution of 72×48 and the bottom picture has a resolution of 192×128. Expressed as an area, the low resolution picture is formed from 3,456 pixels (72×48) and the higher resolution picture from 24,576 pixels (192×128). As you would expect the higher resolution picture is sharper, more clearly defined.

Any given screen has a *maximum resolution*. This is the number of pixels it is capable of displaying. This maximum may be reduced, depending on several other things, such as the number of colours to be used and the amount of memory on the graphics card. The software which controls the graphics card can then be used to set the screen's resolution to the user's requirements (up to the screen's maximum). A higher resolution allows the user to 'zoom in' and obtain a greater level of detail.

Screen size and resolution

A resolution of more than 1024 × 768 is only practical for screen sizes of 17" or larger. This is because higher resolutions on a small screen make the images too small to see.

Refresh rate

The contents of a display must be continually refreshed, that is re-displayed. Flicker occurs when the eye can detect a gap between each screen refresh cycle. If the refresh rate is quick enough, the eye will not detect any flicker. A screen may, for example, be refreshed 75 times every second (75 Hz), which is the minimum for modern displays.

Non-interlaced and interlaced display

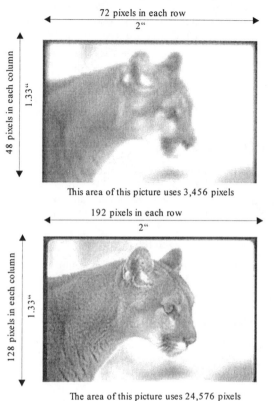

72 pixels in each row
2"

48 pixels in each column
1.33"

This area of this picture uses 3,456 pixels

192 pixels in each row
2"

128 pixels in each column
1.33"

The area of this picture uses 24,576 pixels

Figure 10.9. *Two pictures of the same size, but formed from different numbers of pixels*

When a screen's contents are refreshed, as described in the last paragraph, this involves a scanning process inside the monitor. Put simply, the image is built up line by line, although the process is too quick to be noticed. There are two main types of scanning used by monitors. Most monitors are of the *non-interlaced* type, which means that all the lines that form the complete screen image are produced in a single refresh scan. An *interlaced* screen refreshes the screen in two separate passes.

The lines in Pass 1 leave alternate blank lines. Pass 2 fills in these blank lines. An interlaced screen can produce the same resolution as a non-interlaced one, but does it more cheaply by only replacing half the lines each time the screen is refreshed. A disadvantage of an interlaced screen is that it takes longer to completely refresh the display (two refresh cycles). Although this is not a problem for many applications, animation, video and redraws of complex diagrams are likely to produce noticeable flicker.

Monochrome and colour

A monochrome monitor uses one colour for the text or graphic images and one for the background, for example, white, green or amber on black. Colour monitors use red, green and blue, which can be mixed together in different quantities to produce different colours. For example, when red, green and blue are mixed in exactly the same quantities, we see white light; red and green in equal quantities produces yellow; two parts red and one part green gives orange. In fact, by varying the quantities and the mixtures, any colour can be produced.

Resolution and colour range

The more colours a screen can display, the more memory is required, so graphics cards (or adapters) have their own memory. In practice, the maximum number of colours, which can be up to 16·7 million, is set by the graphics adapter. Higher resolutions also use more memory, so although a graphics card may allow 16·7 million colours at a resolution of 1024 × 768, it may only permit 256 colours when the resolution is increased to 1600 × 1200. Typically, such a graphics card would have several megabytes of its own special RAM.

Text mode

For some applications, graphics display is not needed and when operated in text mode, the computer system needs to use less power and memory. This is an advantage when numerous VDUs are controlled by a central computer. In text mode, characters are formed using a matrix of *pixels* and the clarity of individual characters is determined by the number of pixels used. The same principle is used in character printers, such as the ink-jet (see Printers). Selected dots within the matrix are illuminated to display particular characters. There are various main text modes, including one that displays 40 characters and another that displays 80 characters in each of 25 rows.

LCD Monitors

These monitors are very thin (about 1.5 inches thick) and oc-cupy about a third of the space that CRT monitors require. They use much less energy than CRT monitors and because they are based on Thin Film Transistor (TFT) technology, they give off only one-third as much heat as many traditional moni-tors. Even more importantly, they produce virtually no electromagnetic emissions. In addition the flicker-free view-ing of the TFT technology make them much easier on the eyes. Many LCD monitors swivel so that they can be used in either portrait or landscape orientation. Figure 10.10 shows two col-our LCD monitors produced by IBM.

Figure 10.10. *LCD monitors*

LCD monitors are capable of high resolutions such as 1280 x 1024 and can display millions of colours. Their extremely compact dimensions and energy-efficient features make them ideal for space- or energy-conscious environments. At the moment, however, they are considerably more expensive than equivalent conventional CRT monitors, though prices are coming down as they become more popular.

Choosing a monitor

Although specific recommendations cannot be given here, it is possible to provide advice for broad application areas.

Text-based applications

These are likely to be standard applications, such as ordering, sales and stock control systems. There is no graphics requirement. You are likely to see text-based displays at supermarket checkouts or a in a car parts department.

General office applications

These include use of word processors, spreadsheets and database. They all run under operating systems such as Windows 95, through a mouse-driven, graphical interface. For general office applications, a 15" monitor is probably the norm. Although larger screens are generally better, they take up more desk space and, of course, are more expensive. A resolution of 800 × 600 is probably the best resolution to give the necessary clarity and image size. Although the graphics card may support higher resolutions, their use may well make icons, buttons and other images so small that viewing the screen may result in eye strain. The refresh rate is important, but provided it is 75Hz or more, the screen should be flicker-free.

To obtain the cheapest alternative, an interlaced screen could be chosen, because the applications do not require complex graphics and most users will not notice screen flicker. To avoid flicker on an interlaced screen, a higher refresh rate is usual. However, a non-interlaced screen should still provide a steadier image and this is important for users' eyesight.

Graphics-intensive applications

These include computer-aided design (CAD), photo-editing, graphic design, desktop publishing, video-editing and animation. Larger monitors, from 17" to 21" are essential for these applications. Higher resolutions of 1024×768, 1280×1024 and 1600×1200 need greater screen areas to ensure that images are large enough to allow detailed work on them. At the two highest resolutions, a refresh rate of 85Hz is desirable, to avoid screen flicker (the higher the resolution, the more pixels that have to be refreshed).

Printers

Computer printers vary according to: the technology they use for the printing process; the quality of their printed output; the speed of printing; whether they can print in black and shades of grey, or in colour, or both. We now examine, in some detail, ink-jet and laser printers. At the end of this section, a brief summary is provided of the other types of printer.

Ink jet printers

Liquid inkjet

Ink jet printers spray high-speed streams of ink droplets from individual nozzles in the print head onto the paper to form individual characters or smooth graphical images. Individual text characters are formed by the print head as a matrix of dots. By a series of passes and adjustments to the head's position, graphics can also be produced. Although the output quality is high, print speeds for graphical work are very slow.

Liquid inkjets produce their best quality output on special paper, which is considerably more expensive than standard copier paper. The fastest liquid inkjets can print 20 or more pages per minute (ppm) although colour printing at the best resolutions of 1200 dots per inch (dpi) is a little slower. At such a resolution, near photographic quality can be achieved.

Solid inkjet

A *solid inkjet* uses sticks of ink (rather like crayons) and these are turned to liquid by being heated. In contrast to the more common liquid inkjet, the solid inkjet is quick at 16 to 20 ppm and provides resolutions up to 1200 dpi. In comparison with laser and liquid inkjet printers, the technology provides more uniform, round-shaped, dots to give smoother colour blends and dot colour and shape are unaffected by paper type.

Buffer memory

To enable the printer to print bi-directionally, that is from left to right and then right to left, alternately, it must have enough of its own *buffer memory* to store at least a complete line.

How colour printing works

Most inkjet printers print in monochrome, shades of grey and in colour. In colour printers, the ink is often supplied from two cartridges, one holding black ink and the other containing three colours (cyan, magenta and yellow). As explained in the section on colour displays, a few colours can be mixed to produce all the others. As explained in the section on VDUs, colour displays use the RGB (red, green, blue) model. Colour printing uses a different colour mode to produce the full colour range; it is called CMYK (cyan, magenta, yellow and black -K).

Figure 10.11 shows a dialogue box from CorelDRAW for the CMYK model. The displayed colour is navy blue, which is produced from different proportions of cyan, magenta and black.

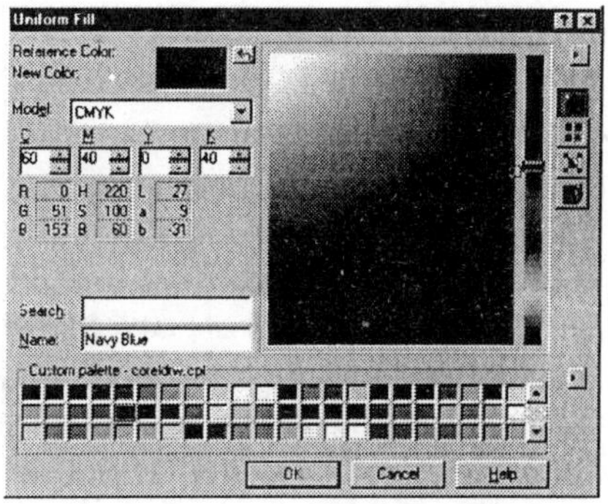

Laser printers

Laser printers are called *page printers*, because they effectively print a complete page at one time. To do this, the printer must have received the contents of an entire page from the controlling computer, before it starts printing. This is illustrated in Figure 10.12. Laser printers may be monochrome only or both monochrome and colour and print 20 or more ppm, with similar quality output to the liquid inkjet printer.

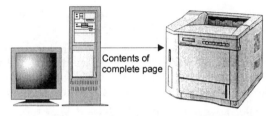

Figure 10.11. *CMYK model*

Network laser printer

Some models of *network* laser, designed to serve the printing needs of many users, can print 50 or more ppm at 600 or 1200 dpi. The lower of these two resolutions in perfectly good for standard printing, including invoices and general correspondence. However, such printers are relatively expensive and aimed at high volume use, say a maximum of 900,000 pages per month. Figure 10.13 shows an example of a large network printer.

Figure 10.12. *Typical laser printer receiving complete page into its memory before printing*

Contents of complete page

Colour laser printer

Resolutions are similar to the monochrome models, up to 1200 dpi. An advantage of colour lasers over liquid inkjets is that they can produce the best quality on standard paper. The quality of liquid inkjet printing depends on the quality of paper used. As you would expect, these advantages are gained at a price, colour laser printers costing significantly more than monochrome models. However, the speed of the laser printer allows it to be shared on a network, so the cost per user for colour printing may be little more than that of buying a personal inkjet for each user. Running costs are also much lower than for inkjet printers.

Figure 10.13. *High volume, network laser printer*

Printer memory

As a page printer, the laser printer must be able to hold the data for an entire page at one time. If the page has a large proportion of graphics, then the memory requirements for one page can be very large. Most laser printers are equipped with a basic memory of 2MB, but this is often insufficient for complex graphical documents; extra memory can be added if necessary. Some printers also make use of the computer's own RAM and thereby remove the need for buying extra, expensive, printer memory.

Printing speeds - quoted and real

Print speeds quoted as pages per minute (ppm) in manufacturer specifications cannot be used as a rule for all kinds of printing. The following points should be noted. Print speed will vary considerably, depending on the mix of graphics and text on a page. A small logo at the top of a page may not slow the printout much, but a full-page poster is likely to reduce the printing rate drastically.

Printing a text page with a little colour highlighting will mean that the entire page is printed as a colour document and will take much longer than if it were plain text.

Other types of printers

Line impact. As the name suggests, this type of printer uses hammers to print the characters onto the continuous stationery, a complete line at a time. They are used as system printers, for internal, high volume reports and can achieve speeds of between 500 and 1400 lines per minute (lpm).

Large format (plotters). Used for design work, a large format printer can handle poster images up to 150 feet long and 54 inches wide. Monochrome and colour models are available. Figure 10.14 shows a typical example.

Figure 10.14. *Large format printer*

Choosing a printer

Although specific recommendations cannot be given here, there follow some typical user examples and suggested choices.

Personal computer printing. The user needs to print a few letters and perhaps produce the occasional colour poster. The choice is fairly straightforward here. Until recently, the choice would have included the impact dot matrix (not dealt with in this text), but the liquid inkjet provides excellent quality output, with the option of colour.

Publishing and graphics for a single user system. The user needs to print large, monochrome publications, including some complex graphics. A laser printer is the necessary choice for this user, because an inkjet printer would be much too slow and the running costs too high; print cartridges have a much higher cost per page than the toner used in a laser printer.

Network monochrome printing. Again, the only choice is a laser printer. Which model is chosen would depend on the number of users and the type of printing required. For text documents, a printer would support more users than would be the case for graphical work.

Near-photographic quality printing. Both liquid inkjet and laser printers will produce the necessary quality at up to 1200 dpi. If colour printing is needed by a number of users, then the higher cost of the colour laser could be shared by placing it on a network. The alternative is to provide as many liquid inkjet printers as there are users who need access at the same time.

General-purpose colour printing. Either the solid inkjet or the colour laser printer would provide the necessary speed and the 300 dpi quality for general business graphics.

✍ Exercises

1. Explain the need for input devices.
2. Name as many input devices as you can.
3. Why is an ADC necessary when using a sensor to capture temperature values?
4. Explain the need for output devices.
5. Name as many output devices as you can.
6. What is meant by the screen resolution of a monitor?
7. What is the difference between an interlaced and a non-interlaced monitor?
8. What advantages do LCD monitors have over traditional CRT monitors?
9. Name two types of printers commonly used. Give a typical print resolution and output speed (in pages per minute) for each one. What other factors need to be considered when choosing a printer?

Chapter 11

Storage systems

As explained in Chapter 9, backing storage is needed to hold programs and data files, from where they can be recalled as necessary by the computer. They are all *non-volatile* - their contents are not lost when power is removed. The purpose of main memory or RAM, which is volatile, is to hold programs and data currently in use - it is not a permanent storage area. A wide range of different backing storage systems is available, to suit every kind of computer system and user requirement. They vary according to:

- ❏ the technology they use and the way they operate;
- ❏ the speed with which they can record and retrieve data;
- ❏ capacity, that is, the amount of data they can hold;
- ❏ whether they are: *read-only* - contents cannot be changed or *read-write* - contents can be changed.

The storage systems described in this chapter (there are numerous others) are those using:

- ❏ magnetic disk, including hard and removable media, such as floppy, Zip and Jaz.
- ❏ magnetic tape.
- ❏ optical media, including: CD-ROM (read only memory); CD-R (recordable - once only); CD-E (erasable - read and write); DVD (digital versatile disk).

A common feature of all disk storage systems is the way in which they are addressed by the computer system. Magnetic disk addressing principles are described in the following section.

Magnetic disk

All disk storage systems provide *direct access* to data. This is in contrast to tape systems where data has to be accessed *serially*, that is, in the order in which it is organised. When data is to be written to or read from disk, a specific *location* can be identified, by its *address*. Tape devices do not have locations which can be addressed, so data can only be accessed serially.

Magnetic disk addressing

In a similar fashion to the first line of a typical postal address of house number and street, magnetic disks use *sector* and *track*. This structure is illustrated in Figure 11.1. The figure illustrates a simplified magnetic disk structure, with 8 sectors numbered 0 to 7 and a number of tracks, numbered from 0, starting with the outermost track. In reality, on a hard disk, there would be hundreds of

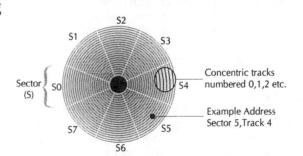

Figure 11.1. *Addressing structure on disk surface*

tracks. The Figure also shows an example address, Sector 5, Track 4. To read from or write to a disk location directly, the software must specify the address.

Hard disks and other high capacity systems use a number of disks within the one device and this makes the address structure slightly more complicated (not dealt with in this text).

Hard disk

A typical microcomputer has an internal hard disk with a capacity measured in gigabytes (GB). An illustration of its internal components is provided in Figure 11.2. The illustration shows the top surface of a pack of hard disks on a central spindle. The disks are rotated at high speed, between 4,500 and 10,000 revolutions per minute (rpm). The read/write heads, through the use of a motor, can be moved in or out across the surface of the disk. This is how particular tracks are reached.

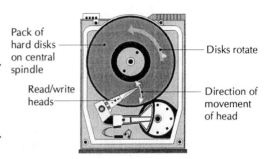

Pack of hard disks on central spindle — Read/write heads — Disks rotate — Direction of movement of head

Figure 11.2. *Components of a microcomputer's hard disk drive*

Access speed

The speed with which data can be read from, or written to, a hard disk is measured as the *average seek time*, in thousandths of a second, or milliseconds (ms). This means that to access a location, the read/write heads have to move to the required track. The time taken to reach the track is known as the *seek time*. A typical average seek time is between 7 ms and 10 ms. The seek time is usually better in systems which use higher spin speeds. This means that the correct sector comes into position more quickly. Figure 11.3 illustrates seek time and spin speed delay. Another major influence on the speed of a disk drive is its *controller*. This is the interface between the disk drive and the computer system. The topic is not discussed further here, but well-known interface standards are SCSI (Small Computer Systems Interface), Ultra Wide SCSI, and UDMA (Ultra Direct Memory Access).

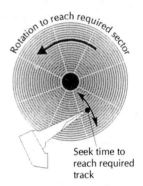

Rotation to reach required sector — Seek time to reach required track

Figure 11.3. *Effects of seek time and spin speed*

Capacity

Modern software, with its provision of an ever-increasing range of features and the use of multimedia images, such as photographs and video clips, demands larger capacity disk drives. Typical capacities used to be measured in megabytes (MB), but are now measured in gigabytes (GB) - thousands of megabytes.

To understand how capacities can be increased in this way, you need to be familiar with some basic ideas about how the data is stored on magnetic disk. The binary codes used to represent data in a computer are stored as magnetic dots along the length of disk tracks. Figure 11.4 illustrates the tracks and magnetic dots

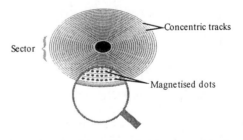

Concentric tracks — Sector — Magnetised dots

Figure 11.4. *Disk surface showing magnetic dots representing binary data*

which represent the data. Different methods are used to make the magnetic dot represent binary 1 or binary 0. One method uses polarity, positive for a 1 and negative for a 0. Increased capacity is achieved by packing the magnetic dots more closely together, that is, more densely. Until recently, it was thought that optical media, such as CD-ROM would far outstrip capacities of hard disk drives. This has not been the case, because technical advances mean that the magnetic dots can be packed more densely than was previously thought possible.

Usage

The hard disk, with its huge capacity and fast access times, remains the best product for the *primary drive* in a computer system, holding the operating system and main applications programs.

Removable magnetic disk

Floppy disk

The floppy disk has, until recently, been the main product for securing small files. The 1·44 MB capacity of the 3·5" floppy disk is insufficient for many users. A graphics image, for example, is often too large to fit on a floppy. It also provides very slow access times, with a spin speed of only 360 rpm.

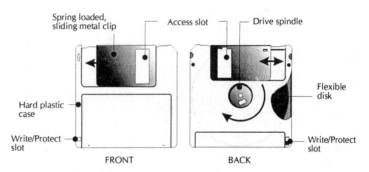

Figure 11.5. *3·5" floppy disk*

Floppy disks are extremely cheap and a 3·5" drive is still standard equipment in a microcomputer system. For many home and small business users, it is adequate for making backup copies of data files held on the primary hard drive and passing copies of data files to other users. The increasing use of e-mail, which allows the *attachment* of such files, is likely to reduce the need for this practice. For many other users, who need to produce and store multimedia data and backup large parts of their primary hard drive, the 1·44 MB floppy disk is inadequate.

Data compression programs

It is possible to compress files so that they will fit onto a floppy disk, through the use of data compression programs, such as WinZip. Bitmap files, in particular will compress to about 2% or 3% of their original size. Compression may allow, for example, text and graphics files with a total capacity of 50MB (which would take at least 35 disks) to be stored on around 10 disks. Backing up to even 10 disks is still a laborious task and likely to discourage the vital task of frequent and regular backup.

Iomega Zip

A Zip disk cartridge holds 100MBor 250MB of data on its single platter, the equivalent of approximately 70 × 1·44MB floppy disks. The Zip drive can be attached *externally*, to the parallel printer port. The printer and Zip drive connectors can be 'piggy backed' to allow both to connect to the port. It can also be attached *internally*, as another drive, to the hard disk controller.

Attached externally, the Zip drive is still relatively slow, but when attached internally to the main hard drive controller, it has a seek time of around 30 ms. This compares with a typical hard drive seek time of between 7 and 12 ms.

Its 100 or 250MB capacity makes it ideal for users who need to store large files, such as those producing design and multimedia presentations. The quickness of the internal drive encourages regular backup and although not matching the hard disk drive, allows it to be used as an extension to the on-line storage system. Files could be efficiently retrieved from the Zip without first copying them to the hard drive.

Iomega Jaz

A single Jaz cartridge contains two platters and will store 1GB of data (2GB with data compression). It can be attached internally or externally, but only to a SCSI drive controller.

The Jaz drive has an average seek time of between 10 and 12 ms, making it as quick as most fixed hard disks.

Its huge capacity and hard drive performance make the Jaz drive a true extension to on-line storage. Files can be retrieved from a Jaz cartridge as quickly as from the main hard drive. It is also suitable for backing up the contents of the primary hard drive.

Magnetic tape

In contrast to disk, tape does not have locations which can be separately *addressed*. For this reason tape storage systems provide only *serial access* to data, that is, the order in which it is stored. This is illustrated in Figure 11.6.

The figure shows that to reach a particular item of data on tape requires the device to read all the data that comes before it. Although magnetic tape systems can be used for

Figure 11.6. *Serial access to data*

some data processing applications, such as payroll, which do not need direct access, the systems described here are for backing up network servers, mini and mainframe computers. Although the arrangement of data on tape is different from that on disk, the magnetic storage principles are the same.

Tape backup systems

To prevent permanent loss of data, it is vital that a computer system's main hard drive is regularly backed up. The more frequently the contents of files change, the more frequent should be the backups. For a single microcomputer hard drive, a single tape is often sufficient. A single tape device is often referred to as a *tape streamer*. When several tapes are required for a complete backup, such as for a large network server a *tape library* is essential. This device includes an *autochanger*, which rather like a juke box, automatically loads the next tape. The alternative is to insert new tapes manually, which for a process that may take hours, is not desirable.

Capacity

The most popular tape backup systems use Digital Audio Tape (DAT) cartridges. For example, a 120 metre tape can store up to 4GB, and 8GB using data compression. A tape library system, capable of holding 8 such tapes, would be able to backup 64GB of data.

Data transfer rate

Typically, tape backup systems can transfer data to the tape at between 35 and 60MB per minute. If compression is being used the rate will vary during backup, because some kinds of data take longer to compress than others. At an average of 50MB per minute, a 4GB drive would take 80 minutes (4000MB ÷ 50MB).

Optical media

Instead of using magnetism to record data, optical media are read or re-corded using laser light. To *record*, a high intensity laser beam burns tiny holes into the surface of the disk, each hole representing a binary 1 or a binary 0. To *read*, a lower intensity laser is used to detect the holes and the binary digits they represent. The binary digits are recorded along tracks in a similar fashion to magnetic disk, but instead of using concentric tracks, optical disks use a spiralling track, similar to the old gramophone records. This is illustrated in Figure 11.7.

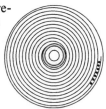

Figure 11.7. *Optical disk with spiralling track*

Compact disk (CD)

CDs are optical media and a single disk can hold approximately 650MB of data. Although data transfer rates are continually being improved, CD drives are slower than hard magnetic disks. There are three types of CD.

CD-ROM (compact disk-read only memory). As the name indicates, the data is recorded dur-ing manufacture and can only be read by a CD-ROM drive. The main uses of the CD-ROM are for:

- ❑ multimedia applications, such as games and encyclopaedia.
- ❑ software installation. The large memory requirement of many software packages means that delivery on floppy disk is impractical, whereas one CD-ROM disk is often sufficient to deliver an entire package

CD-R (recordable - once only). This is a CD which can be written to once, with a suitable CD-Writer. Provided the contents do not need to be updated, this can be a useful medium for ar-chiving documentary and other material. The falling cost of CD-Writers and the small cost of each disk, makes it possible for businesses and other organisations to produce their own multi-media training programmes.

CD-R/W (read and write). Because data can be erased and updated, this type of CD is an alter-native to magnetic disk, although its data transfer rates are still relatively slow.

DVD (Digital versatile disk)

Using the same basic principles as the CD, DVD packs the data more densely and can store 4.7GB, compared with the CD's 650MB. With this capacity and its quicker data transfer rate, a single DVD disk can hold 133 minutes of video, with Dolby surround sound. It is probable that DVD drives will be an increasingly important removable storage device, particularly with the increasing use of video in multimedia products.

✍ Exercises

1. What main factors determine the type of backing storage device to use for a particular IT application?
2. List as many types of backing-storage devices as you can.
3. How is data organised on a magnetic disk?
4. How is data organised on magnetic tape?
5. Give a major use of magnetic tape.
6. What is a tape streamer?
7. What is the main difference between CD ROM and magnetic disks for data storage?

Chapter 12

Setting up a computer system

This chapter deals with the following aspects of setting up a computer system:

- ❏ Connecting the hardware.
- ❏ Powering up the system.
- ❏ Installing device drivers, such as printer drivers.
- ❏ Tailoring a GUI 'desktop'.
- ❏ Installing and configuring applications software.

Connecting the hardware

Although some additional devices, such as a scanner and camera may be included in a system, the guidelines which follow deal with a typical minimum configuration. The connections to be made are:

- ❏ system unit;
- ❏ monitor;
- ❏ keyboard;
- ❏ mouse;
- ❏ printer;
- ❏ power supplies for the printer, monitor and system unit.

Figure 12.1 illustrates the connection of these devices. Obviously, safety requires that the entire task must be carried out without connection to the power supply.

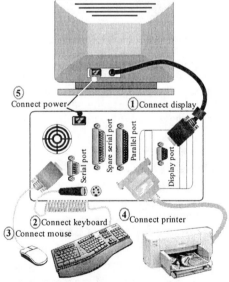

Monitor connection

The system unit communicates with the monitor through a *data cable*. The data cable is permanently attached to the monitor as shown. The other end usually has a 15 pin, male, D-type plug to connect it to the 15 pin, female, D-type socket on the system unit. This is labelled 'Display port' in the figure. The 'D' shape of the plug and socket mean that the connection can only be made in one way. The screws on the side of the plug are used to secure the connection.

Keyboard connection

Keyboard to system unit; this is sometimes a coil stretch cable as shown in Figure 12.1. The cable is fixed to the keyboard. The other end has a 5 pin, male, round connector which connects to the

Figure 12.1. *Connecting computer hardware*

5 pin, female socket on the system unit. The plug simply pushes into the socket.

Mouse connection

A serial mouse connects to the serial port, commonly known by its MS-DOS name of COM1. The mouse has a fixed cable. The other end has a 9 pin, female, D-type plug which connects to the 9 pin male socket on the system unit. Screws are used to secure the connection. If the mouse is to be connected to the other serial port (labelled 'Spare serial port' in the figure), which has 25 pins, an adapter must be used. This port is known as COM2 and can be used to attach other serial devices, such as an external *modem*.

Parallel printer connection

Although some printers allow either serial or parallel connection, the parallel port is the usual connection point. Data can be transferred to a printer more quickly in parallel than it can serially. The parallel port is often known as a Centronics interface. The printer cable is not fixed to the printer and is usually bought separately. The printer end of the cable is a 25 way, (not pins) male plug which attaches to the 25 way, female socket on the printer. The system unit end of the cable has a 25 pin male plug which attaches to the 25 pin female socket on the system unit. Spring clips secure the cable to the printer. Screws are used to secure the cable to the system unit.

Power connections

The system unit, monitor and printer each have a separate power supply and these should be the final connections.

Powering up the system

Having checked that all components are properly connected, the power supply and switches on the printer, monitor and system unit should be switched on.

Power on self-test

The system goes through a self-checking procedure and if properly set up will load the operating system. If errors or faults are detected, a suitable error message may be displayed. Although you would need to check the computer manufacturer's user manual, the following table shows some example errors, possible causes and solutions.

Error	Possible cause	Possible solution
Keyboard error	Not properly connected	Push home connection
Non-system disk or disk error	Floppy disk left in drive on power up	Remove floppy disk
C: drive failure	Corruption of software on hard disk	Run ScanDisk
C: drive failure	Damaged hard disk	Call manufacturer
HDD controller failure	Hard disk ribbon cable or power supply not properly connected	Open system unit and check cables properly connected
FDD controller failure	Floppy drive ribbon cable or power supply not properly connected	Open system unit and check cables properly connected

Installing device drivers

Device drivers are programs which control the way a device works. All attached devices, including for example, the graphics card (to control the display), sound card, disk drive controller and printer need device drivers. For example, without the appropriate driver, the computer system will be unable to take advantage of all the printer's features. So, a particular make of printer, with facilities to print text and graphics at a resolution of 600 dpi, will only provide all those facilities with the correct driver. The incorrect driver may prevent printing of graphics or even print gobbledygook.

A printer driver can be installed with the installation program provided by the printer manufacturer, or with the appropriate operating system utility.

Printer install program

A new printer will include its associated software on disk, and the driver is installed through the use of this software.The following notes illustrate a typical printer install process.

1. The operating system is instructed to 'Run Setup.exe'. In this case the setup program is on the first floppy disk supplied with the printer (Figure 12.2).

2. The setup program prompts for the parallel port to be used by the printer. In this case, the system only has one such port, LPT1, so this is the only option (Figure 12.3).

3. The user is asked to confirm the hard disk directory into which the programs will be installed. Generally, the default is chosen, unless there is a particular reason for changing it.(Figure 12.4)

4. The setup continues with the copying of files from the floppy to the named directory on hard disk (Figure 12.5).

5. If the setup programs occupy more than one floppy disk, the user is prompted when the next one is needed.

6. When the setup is complete, various configuration files may be altered and the process is completed.

7. For the changes to take effect, the operating system has to be restarted. Figure 12.6 shows the prompt to restart. This is because the changes to the configuration files are detected when the operating system is first loaded.

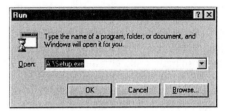

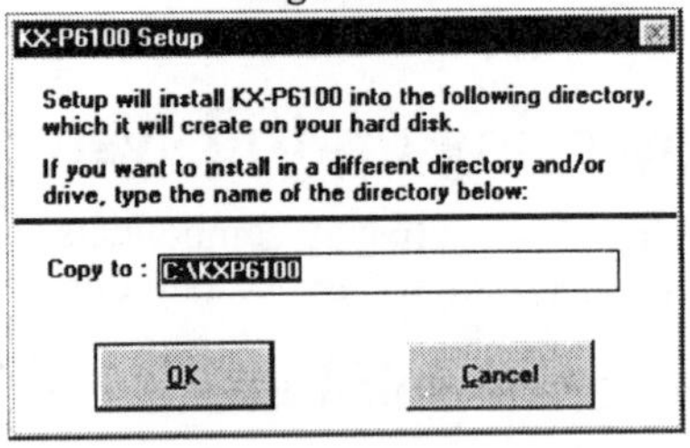

Figure 12.2

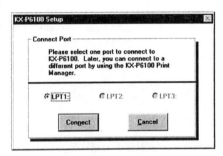

Figure 12.3

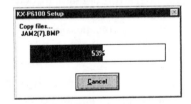

Figure 12.4

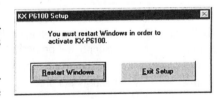

Figure 12.5

Figure 12.6

Printer install utility

In the case of the Windows operating systems, a new printer can be installed with printer Install Wizard. Figure 12.7 shows the Printers window with two installed printers and the 'Add Printer' utility. Running the 'Add Printer' utility, calls up the Wizard. This provides the options of selecting a driver already available on the hard drive, or one held on another disk (such as that provided by the manufacturer).

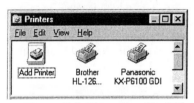

Figure 12.7. *Printer install utility*

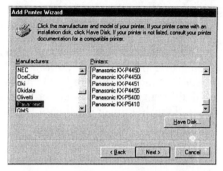

Figure 12.8 shows a list of drivers already available on the hard drive.

Figure 12.8. *List of available printer drivers*

Downloading drivers from the Internet

Figure 12.9 shows the download page on the Brother.com Web Site. Manufacturers often modify their device drivers to improve the features or performance of the devices they control. It is often worth downloading the latest device driver from the manufacturer's Web site, to take advantage of such improvements. Obtaining the latest graphics driver can improve the performance of a computer system, for example, by speeding up screen redraws. To download a particular driver, the user simply clicks on the appropriate driver name.

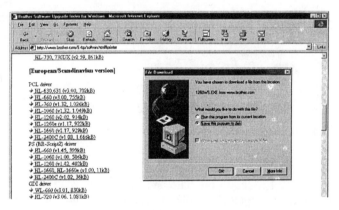

Figure 12.9. *Downloading drivers from the a Web site*

The figure shows that the user has requested the download of the Brother 1260 printer driver. The dialogue box indicates that the downloaded file can be copied straight to memory or to the hard disk. The downloaded file will normally include a program to automate the installation process.

Setting GUI preferences

A major benefit of a GUI is that its appearance can be altered to suit an individual user or a group of users. If the settings are made for a group, then a generally accepted appearance has to be agreed. If one user in the group decides to change settings, without proper agreement, this can be annoying or even confusing for the other members of the group. There are too many different settings to deal with them all here, so we will concentrate on some of the most important. The examples used here refer to the Windows GUI.

Display properties

The Windows Display Properties window is shown in Figure 12.10. Each tab deals with a different aspect of the display. The displayed tab gives access to *Screen Saver* and energy saving controls. Setting a screen saver prevents a static image from remaining on screen and burning a permanent shadow into it. Energy saving features can only be used if the screen is compatible. This switches the monitor power down or off after a certain period. The *Settings* tab allows the user to control the appearance of the screen display, including screen resolution, number of colours and the font size. The figure also shows an MGA settings tab, which is specific to the installed graphics card, an MGA Matrox Millennium. It provides more varied controls than the standard Settings tab. Figure 12.11 shows the *Appearance* settings can be selected from a number of different standard models, or the user can alter individual parts of the screen, such as the colour of the desktop or spacing of icons.

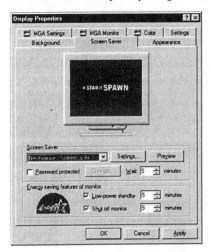

Figure 12.10. *Display properties window*

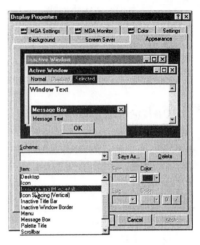

Figure 12.11. *Appearance tab*

Date and time

Figure 12.12 shows the date and time window in Control Panel. Figure 12.13 shows the MS-DOS prompt and the alteration of the date and time through typed commands.

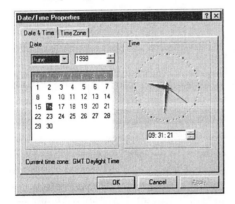

Figure 12.12. *Setting the date and time*

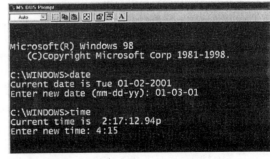

Figure 12.13. *Using DOS prompt to set date and time*

Software installation

Much of this process is automated through an *install program*. Figure 12.14 is an example.

Install settings

Some installations are quite straightforward and the only major decision to be made concerns the drive and folder in which the programs are to be stored. The default is usually C:, but another drive or partition can be chosen if there is limited space on the C: drive. Although the drive and directory can be changed from that suggested by the install program, it is usually sensible to accept the default. The C:\ drive is normally the preferred location for applications programs, but another hard drive, or partition of the hard drive can be used. If an alternative is chosen, the operating system will still require some files on its own drive, usually the C: drive.

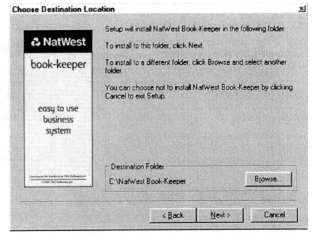

Figure 12.14. *A software install program*

Other entries include:

☐ acceptance of licence arrangements. This restricts the number of machines on which the software can be installed at the same time.

☐ user name and company; these details are required for technical support from the software supplier.

☐ key code. This is supplied to the licensee and is designed to discourage pirate copies. The key code must be entered before the installation can continue.

Type of installation

The *typical* installation is useful if you wish to be certain that the facilities required by most users are provided. However, if you are knowledgeable about the facilities, a custom installation is usually better. Custom installation ensures that all the facilities you require are installed (your needs may not be typical) and that facilities you do not need are not installed. This can save considerable disk space.

Testing the installation

Completion on installation involves:

☐ copying of program files to the named directory;

☐ alteration of configuration files which 'tell' the operating system that the program is installed and where it is located.

Sometimes, the system needs to be restarted for the settings to be detected by the operating system. Once the above tasks are completed, the program can be run and tested with sample tasks or data. Whether the installation meets all of the user's requirements cannot be thoroughly checked until the full range of tasks has been attempted. Obviously, if the range of tasks is wide, this may take a considerable time. If a required option has not been installed, the install program may:

❑ require the full installation to be repeated;

❑ allow the additional option to be installed without full installation.

Removing programs

Most commercial programs provide an *uninstall* program. The uninstall program should be used wherever possible. It is generally a bad idea to simply delete the program files. The configuration files will still contain details and the operating system will still 'think' that the program is installed. At best, only space will be wasted. At worst, the operating system may display error messages on startup, which although not damaging are a great nuisance.

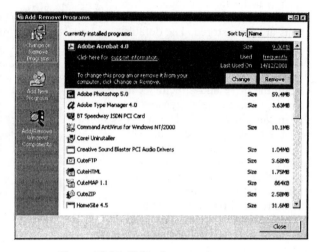

Figure 12.15. *Utility for removing programs*

Figure 12.15 shows the Windows operating system utility for starting the removal of programs from the system, with a list of the installed software.

System security

Loss of important data can be disastrous for an organisation. For example, if a business loses its sales accounting records, it may prevent collection of sales debts (amounts owed by customers for goods bought on credit). The loss of income may then prevent it from paying its suppliers, resulting in bankruptcy or liquidation. The causes of data loss are varied, but the computer *virus* is one important threat. An important part of the protection system is the virus protection program.

Data loss can also result when unauthorised persons gain access to a computer system. Protection systems include physical methods, such as the use of security staff and locked doors, and software methods, including passwords.

✎ Exercises

1. When setting up a typical PC what connections need to be made?

2. What are device drivers?

3. What is the main purpose of a screen saver program?

4. How are most modern commercial programs removed from computer systems?

5. What do you understand by the term computer virus?

6. What methods can be used to protect PCs from viruses?

7. Why are passwords often used in computer systems?

Chapter 13

PC assembly and upgrade

Modern PCs are designed to be assembled and upgraded quickly and easily. System cases, whether standard desktop or tower, have brackets, screw holes and connector slots that allow all essential, basic components to be fitted easily and without the need for special tools or extensive experience and training. In this chapter we describe the steps required to fit and connect basic PC components. Diagrams and photographs will help to identify standard PC components and show how they are fitted and connected. We describe fitting and connecting the:

- ❑ motherboard;
- ❑ expansion boards;
- ❑ memory modules;
- ❑ hard drive, floppy drive and CD ROM drive.
- ❑ processor chip;

It is assumed that the system case already has a suitable power supply and fan fitted since PC cases are usually sold this way.

Before you start

Precautions

There are three very important precautions that you must take before starting to work on assembling or modifying a computer:

1. **Make sure that you have made backups of any essential files held on your system**. Things can go wrong when upgrading a computer so assume the worst and make backups of important files if you have not already done so.

2. **Make sure that the power cable to the computer is physically disconnected.** Do not just switch off the power supply at the power socket - physically pull out the power supply lead from the power socket at the rear of the computer case. Always put the cover back on the case before re-connecting the power supply.

    These precautions are essential to remove the risk of getting an electric shock when working on components installed inside the case.

3. **Draw a diagram of the back panel leads and connectors before you disconnect anything**. It is easy to forget which lead goes where. A good idea is to attach numbered labels to leads and use a marker pen to write corresponding numbers near to the appropriate back panel sockets.

4. **Make sure that you have neutralised any electrostatic charge that might have built up in your body.** Without knowing it you can easily build up thousands of volts of static electricity on your body and if you have done so, and you touch an electronic component such as a memory module, you could easily damage it. You can easily discharge yourself by touching a metal object that is plugged into a wall socket. For example, you could touch a metal part of a lamp or a power tool. The object does not need to be turned on for this purpose.

Tools

The only tools that you are likely to need are a Phillips screwdriver, a flat blade (ordinary) screwdriver and a pair of long-nosed pliers.

The Motherboard components and connectors

Figure 13.1 shows the structure of a typical motherboard for a Pentium processor.

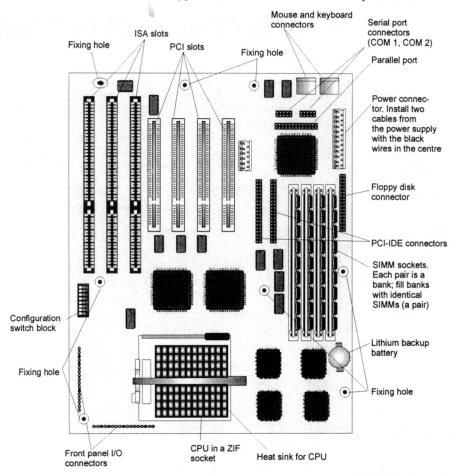

Figure 13.1. *Example layout of a motherboard for a Pentium processor*

Features of importance to the placement and connection of components are described below. This information is important when assembling a PC as described in a later section (see **Assembling a PC**)

Expansion board slots

The motherboard illustration shows three ISA and four PCI slots for expansion boards.

The photograph in Figure 13.2 shows two empty PCI expansion board slots on a motherboard.

Figure 13.2. *PCI slots*

CPU in ZIF socket

The photograph shown in Figure 13.3 shows a Pentium processor package in a ZIF socket with its own cooling fan on top. Depending on the particular processor, there may not be a cooling fan mounted on the unit.

SIMM sockets

Figure 13.4 shows a bank of four SIMMs. SIMMs (or DIMMs for more recent motherboards) are plugged into the four sockets. This motherboard requires SIMMs to be installed in identical pairs. These pairs can be FPM or EDO SIMMs and either parity checking or non-parity checking. (parity-checking SIMMs

Figure 13.3. *CPU in ZIF socket with fan*

have eight chips on a single module, eight of them being memory chips and the ninth a parity checking chip; non-parity checking SIMMs have eight memory chips). For example the SIMM banks could contain two 16MB EDO SIMMs and two 8MB FPM SIMMs. Motherboard documentation will usually specify SIMM requirements.

Figure 13.4. *SIMM banks*

Primary and secondary IDE connectors

These are connectors for connecting hard drives, CDROM drives and backup drives such as ZIP drives. These connectors are shown in Figure 13.5.

Ribbon cables are used to connect devices to the motherboard connectors. See the section on installing drives for more information about connecting and configuring hard drives and other types of drive.

The secondary connector can be used for a CDROM or ZIP drive or both if they are daisy chained together.

Figure 13.5. *IDE connectors*

Floppy disk connector

In addition to the Primary and Secondary IDE connectors, Figure 13.5 also shows the smaller connector for the floppy disk drive.

Power supply connectors

There are two main forms of power supply plugs. The photograph in Figure 13.6 shows the old type of connector type that uses twin power supply plugs.

These plugs can be fitted incorrectly - when plugged in correctly, the four black wires are in the centre.

The other type of plug, which is for an ATX power supply, is a single unit that can only be fitted one way.

Figure 13.6. *Power supply connectors*

Port connectors

There are three port connectors shown in Figure 13.7. There are two serial port connectors, COM 1 and COM 2, and a single parallel port connector. These connectors are linked to sockets on the back of the PC chassis by means of ribbon cables as shown in Figure 13.7. Some motherboards have the port sockets mounted on them so that no ribbon cables are required.

Figure 13.7. *Port connectors*

Front panel connectors

These are connected to the various switches and indicators on the front of the PC case by means of small connectors. For instance there are connectors for the hard disk drive activity light, for the reset switch and for the internal speaker. There is also a connector for the internal fan. The uses of the pins are labelled on the motherboard or described in the documentation. Figure 13.8 shows a photograph of some of the front panel connectors on a typical motherboard.

Configuration switch block

This is a bank of tiny switches that change various motherboard and processor parameters. For instance some of the switches are used to specify processor speed for motherboards that can take processor upgrades. The function of each switch is dependent on the type of motherboard and will be described in documentation. You may need to use a small screw driver or a ballpoint pen cap to flip the switches if they need altering.

Figure 13.8. *Front panel connectors*

Installing and removing SIMMS

SIMM connectors pivot forward to allow memory modules to be installed and removed more easily. When installing SIMMs, angle the connector at about 45° and push the module in, as shown in Figure 13.9, until it snaps into position and is held by the two metal clamps at the two ends of the connector.

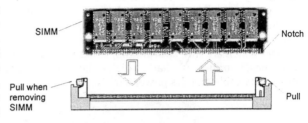

Figure 13.9. *A SIMM and connector*

To remove a memory module, first gently release the metal clamps at the ends of the socket. Then tilt the module forward and lift it out. The metal clamps **must** be released first to avoid damage to the module.

Installing and removing a processor

Inserting the processor

ZIF sockets have an integral handle to facilitate seating and removing the processor chip. Before installing the processor, unlatch and raise the handle.

Align the processor over the socket making sure that all the pins match the pin holes in the socket. Then push the processor into place being very careful not to bend any of the pins. Then lower and lock the handle. A heat sink and fan for the processor may also need to be locked in place over the processor once it is inserted in the socket.

Removing the processor

If there is a fan over the processor, release the sprung wire retaining brackets and lift the fan away. Then if necessary remove the heat sink from the top of the processor. The ZIF socket handle must then be unlatched and lifted to release the processor.

Installing and removing drives

PCs can accommodate a number of different types of drives, including hard disk drives, floppy disk drives, CDROM drives and ZIP drives. All of these drives are installed and removed in much the same way. The main difference is that since hard drives do not use removable media such as floppy disks or CD ROMs they do not have a face plate in the front panel of the computer; all of the other types of drives need to be accessed from the front of the computer so that disks or cartridges can be inserted or removed.

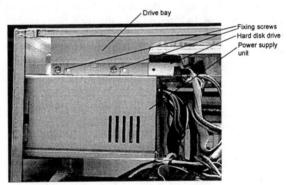

Figure 13.10. *Hard Disk Drive mounted above PSU*

Installing a hard disk drive

Hard disk drives are usually located behind the front panel of the computer or in a bay above the power supply unit as illustrated in Figure 13.10. Before fixing the drive in place, make sure that the jumper settings are correct.

Usually the main hard drive (the one that is used to boot the system on startup) is connected to the Primary IDE connector on the motherboard and a second hard drive can be daisy-chained to it using the same ribbon cable. Hard drive ribbon cables usually have two connectors at one end for this purpose. If two hard drives are being connected in this way, the main drive must be configured as the Master drive and the other as the Slave drive. These settings are made using *jumpers* which are tiny two-pin plugs that join pairs of connections on the hard drive jumper pins. The illustration of a hard drive in Figure 13.11 shows the connections for the jumpers, the ribbon data cable and the power supply.

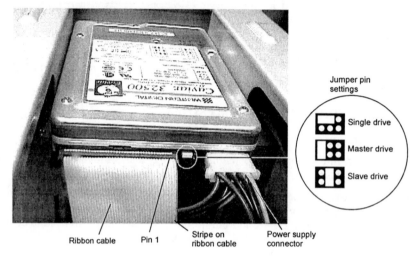

Figure 13.11. *Hard drive connections and jumper settings*

The jumper settings in the illustration will probably be different for other makes of hard drive. The settings are usually written on the casing of the hard drive or included in documentation for the device.

When plugging in the ribbon cables, make sure that they are the right way round; some connectors are constructed so that it is impossible to get them the wrong way round, but this is not always the case. In Figure 13.11 the right hand side of the ribbon cable connector, closest to the jumper pins, is Pin 1 and it corresponds to a stripe on the ribbon cable. The motherboard IDE connectors have the pins labelled from 1 to 40. (See Figure 13.5). Getting the connector orientation wrong won't damage the hard drive, but of course it won't work. (When you try to start the system, the hard drive light usually stays on permanently if the connector is the wrong way round).

Before installing the hard drive check the location of Pin 1 on the 40 pin socket so that the stripe on the ribbon cable can be aligned with it later.

Four small screws (two on each side) secure the drive unit to the drive bay as illustrated in Figure 13.10. The ribbon data cable and power supply connectors need to be plugged in once the drive is fixed in place.

Installing a CDROM drive

Before installing the CDROM drive, set any jumpers or switches. Details of jumper and switch settings should be included in the documentation for the device. Remember that if more than one CDROM drive or an IDE hard drive are to be installed on the same cable, they must be configured as master and slave.

The CDROM drive occupies one of the front panel bays. If necessary, remove a blank panel to allow the drive to be slid in from the front as shown in Figure 13.12. Once positioned flush with the front of the case, use the fixing screws to fix the unit in place and attach the 40 pin data ribbon cable and the power cable. As with hard drives, ensure that the ribbon cable stripe is positioned at pin 1 of the CDROM drive connector.

The secondary IDE connector on the motherboard is usually used for drives other than hard drives or floppy disk drives. In addition, so that the CDROM drive can output sound, an audio cable must be connected to

Figure 13.12. *CDROM drive being installed*

the sound card, if there is one, or to the motherboard if it includes sound circuitry. Figure 13.13 shows an audio cable connected to a sound card from the CDROM drive.

Installing a floppy disk drive

The procedure for installing a floppy disk drive is essentially the same as that for a CDROM drive, the main difference being that the ribbon cable has a split in it at the end that connects to the floppy drive A: and the other end goes into the floppy disk connector on the motherboard

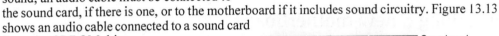

Figure 13.13. *Audio cable from CDROM drive*

(see Figure 13.5) or to a floppy disk controller expansion board . The ribbon cable will usually have a connector in the middle for a possible second floppy disk drive B:. Check that any jumper settings are correct (usually the factory settings are appropriate) as detailed in the drive's documentation. Also note the position of pin 1 which is probably labelled on the case or circuit board of the floppy disk drive; the coloured wire of the ribbon cable goes to this pin.

For old-style cases it may be necessary to use an expansion frame for a 3.5 inch drive if the drive bay is too wide. Some older cases also require plastic or metal slide rails on each side of the bracket assembly. Four screws are used to secure the drive in position.

Attach the end of the ribbon cable with the twist to the floppy disk connector and plug in the power cable.

Installing Expansion boards

Expansion boards plug into the ISA or PCI slots on the motherboard. Figure 13.14 shows an expansion board prior to being installed. Expansion boards are positioned such that the metal bracket at the end of the board (where there are usually connectors for peripheral devices) can be held in position by a single screw (Figure 13.15). If the position for the bracket on the rear of the chassis is covered by a plate, prise it off with a small flat-blade screwdriver (or unscrew it if possible). Then align the board over the appropriate expansion socket and gently push the connector strip of the board into the socket. Make sure that the connector strip is fully inserted into the expansion socket before securing the board with a screw.

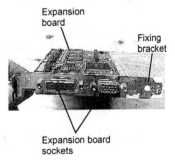

Figure 13.14. *Expansion board prior to installation*

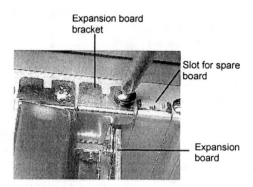

Figure 13.15. *Securing an expansion board*

Installing a new motherboard

Precautions

If you intend to upgrade a PC by installing a new motherboard in the old system case, before buying the motherboard it is a good idea to check the following details:

❑ CPU compatibility - if you are not changing the processor, make sure that it is compatible with the new motherboard. This includes the type of socket required as well as the type of processor.

❑ Power supply requirements - new motherboards (for Pentium IIs and above) generally require an ATX power supply which provides different voltages and motherboard connector from the older type power supply units. In addition ATX motherboards may not fit an older type system casing. If the new motherboard does require the ATX power supply, it is probably advisable to buy a new ATX system case with the power supply unit already installed.

❑ CMOS settings - modern hard disk drives auto-configure on startup. In other words they are able to provide the CPU with the drive type and the number of cylinders and tracks they have automatically; this information is essential to accessing data on the drive. For many older drives this information needs to be provided manually to the CMOS setup program (see Chapter 12). Just to be sure that there is no risk of losing essential setup information, make a copy of the current CMOS settings on paper before replacing the motherboard.

Read through **both** of the following two sections before removing and/or installing a motherboard; this is so that you know in advance what needs to be done in both cases. The section on the Motherboard Components and Connectors, referenced in the following sections, contains essential information for installing a motherboard. If you assume that anything that can go wrong, will go wrong, and take all possible precautions, you are more likely to be able to install a new motherboard without any major hitches.

Removing a motherboard

If there is already a motherboard installed in the system casing, first attach labels to all cables and draw a diagram of the connectors to which they were attached. This will be of great help when trying to connect the new motherboard. Then disconnect all cables attached to the motherboard.

Next, remove all expansion boards, first making a note of which expansion slots they occupied and labelling any connectors that need to be removed. The motherboard is usually secured to the PC chassis by a combination of several plastic standoffs (see Figure 13.16) that fix into slots and two or more screws that go through the motherboard and screw into hexagonal metal standoffs attached to the chassis. Figure 13.17 is a sectional view of a PC chassis showing a plastic and metal standoff.

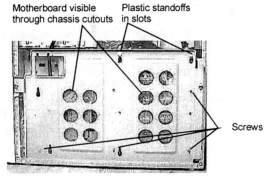

Motherboard visible through chassis cutouts

Plastic standoffs in slots

Screws

Figure 13.16. *Installing and removing a motherboard*

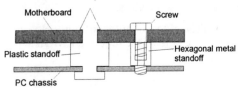

Motherboard

Screw

Plastic standoff

Hexagonal metal standoff

PC chassis

Figure 13.17. *Motherboard standoffs*

Remove the screws and slide the motherboard sideways to free the plastic standoffs. The motherboard can then be lifted out.

Installing a motherboard

This is more or less the reverse of the process of removing a motherboard described in the previous section. First set any switches or jumpers that are needed to configure the system; these settings should be explained in the documentation that came with the new motherboard.

Fit memory modules if not already installed. (See **Installing and removing SIMMs**).

If there are no standoffs already on the motherboard, push three or four of them into the motherboard fixing holes that align with appropriate chassis slots. Again if necessary, screw in and tighten two or three hexagonal metal standoffs into chassis screw holes. The metal and plastic standoffs should be evenly distributed over the motherboard, the intention being to keep the printed circuits on the underside of the motherboard from touching the metal casing, and also to prevent the motherboard from flexing too much when components such as expansion boards and memory modules are being fitted later.

Now align the motherboard with the plastic standoff holes and metal standoffs. Lower the motherboard so that the wide bases of the plastic standoffs go through the wide parts of the chassis slots and then slide the motherboard sideways so that the plastic standoffs are firmly engaged in the slots. Now fix the motherboard in position with metal screws that screw into the hexagonal metal standoffs attached to the chassis.

Connect the front panel LED wires and the internal speaker wires. The motherboard should have some markings to indicate where each of the small connectors is located.

Next connect the power supply cable or cables (see **Power supply connectors** earlier) making sure that where two connectors are required the black wires of both are together in the middle.

If IDE controllers are on the motherboard, connect ribbon cables from the appropriate drives to these. (See **Primary and secondary IDE connectors**). Also attach the cable from the floppy disk drive to the motherboard connector if appropriate.

If there are pins on the motherboard for serial and parallel ports, attach the ribbon cables to these. (See **Port connectors**).

Now re-install all expansion boards and connect any cables that were disconnected when the old motherboard was removed.

Before replacing the cover, check that all cables are connected and that all connectors are seated properly. Finally, replace the cover and reconnect cables to peripheral devices.

When you switch the machine on, you may get error messages regarding unrecognised disk drives. This has two most probable causes:

1. IDE and floppy drive connectors have not been replaced properly. You will need to open the case and check that connectors are seated properly and that drives are configured correctly. Also check that the ribbon cables are connected to the drives the right way round, with the striped wire to pin 1 of the drive connectors.

2. The CMOS memory requires drive information if drives do not autoconfigure. Before removing the old motherboard you should have made a note of the required CMOS settings for just this eventuality.

✍ Exercises

1. Explain safety precautions that should be taken before adding or removing components from the inside of a PC?
2. What connectors are usually provided on a motherboard?
3. What two main types of expansion board slots are usually provided on motherboards?
4. What is a ZIF socket?
5. What restriction often applies to installing SIMMs of different memory sizes on a motherboard?
6. What is usually connected to the Primary IDE connector?
7. When the motherboard's power supply socket requires two connectors, how should they be plugged in?
8. What is the purpose of the *Configuration Switch Block* on a motherboard?
9. What is the significance of Master and Slave disk drives? How is a hard disk drive set to be a single drive, a Master drive or a Slave drive.
10. What is the guideline for fitting a hard drive ribbon cable?
11. What precautions should be taken before installing a new motherboard?

Chapter 14
Assembly language programming

In this chapter we describe a simplified instruction set and assembly language for a hypothetical 16-bit microprocessor, the BEP/16. The BEP/16 instruction set has been shortened to allow us to present some typical microprocessor instructions, and to illustrate simple programming tasks. The ATL1 (Assembler Teaching Language 1) assembler produces machine code for the BEP/16. Full details of the BEP/16 instruction set, the ATL1 assembler and a program that will assemble and execute ATL1 programs can be found at www.bcpublications.co.uk. The chapter concludes with a number of small assembly language programs to illustrate how some simple programming tasks may be implemented. We start by describing the general characteristics of programs and, in particular, of low-level languages.

Programming languages

At the level at which the computer operates, a program is simply a sequence of numeric codes. Each of these codes can be directly converted by the hardware into some simple operation. Built into the processor, the heart of the computer, is a set of these simple operations, combinations of which are capable of directing the computer to perform complex tasks. Computer programs, in this fundamental form, are termed *machine code*, that is code which is directly 'understandable' by the machine.

The numeric codes of the program are in binary form, or at least the electrical equivalent of binary, and are stored in the *memory* of the computer. Because this memory is volatile (in other words, it is temporary and can be changed), it is possible to exchange the program currently held in the memory for another when the computer is required to perform a different function. For this reason the term *stored program* is often used to describe this fundamental characteristic of the modern digital computer.

The numeric codes that direct the computer to perform such simple operations as those mentioned above are collectively called the *instruction set*. The instruction set of a typical computer would normally contain a number of the following types of instructions:

1. Data transfer. This allows data to be moved within the processor, between the processor and the memory of the computer system or between the processor and external devices such as printers, VDUs and keyboards.

2. Arithmetic operations. Such instructions direct the computer to perform arithmetic functions such as addition, subtraction, multiplication, division, increment, decrement, comparison and logical operations such as AND, OR, NOT and EXCLUSIVE OR.

3. Shift operations. These move data to the left or right within a *register* or memory location.

4. Transfer of control. This directs the machine to skip one or more instructions or repeat previously encountered instructions.

A program, consisting of a combination of the types of instructions outlined above, is *executed* by retrieving each instruction in turn from the memory of the computer, decoding the operation required and then performing this operation under the direction of the processor. This sequence of events is termed the *fetch-execute cycle*. On completion of each current instruction, the next instruction in the program's logical sequence of execution will be fetched from store automatically. This process ends, under normal circumstances, when a halt instruction in the program is recognised by the computer. The example in Table 14.1 illustrates the form of a machine code program. Suppose that a computer has currently in its main store memory a simple machine code program to load two numbers into internal registers from memory, add them and store the result in memory.

Each instruction in turn, starting with that resident in memory location 1000, would be fetched from memory, decoded and executed. This process would continue until the halt instruction in location 1007 was decoded. The particular binary code or combination of binary digits (0's or 1's) in the instruction (shown in hexadecimal notation in the example) causes the decoding circuitry of the CPU to transmit to other components of the hardware the sequence of control signals necessary to perform the required operation.

Memory location	Contents (Hex)	Comments
1000	220F	Load R0 from ..
1001	2000	..memory location 2000
1002	221F	Load R1 from ..
1003	2001	..memory location 2001
1004	0901	Add R1 to R0
1005	351F	Store R0 in ..
1006	2002	..memory location 2002
1007	FFFF	Halt execution

Table 14.1. *Example machine code program*

When it is considered that a typical program might contain tens of thousands of machine code instructions, it might seem that programming is a formidable task, well beyond the capabilities of all but the most determined and meticulous of computer professionals. Indeed, if machine code were the only computer language in use, it is extremely unlikely that society would today be experiencing such a widespread presence of computers in almost every aspect of industrial, commercial, domestic and social life. Fortunately for the computer industry, programming techniques have evolved along with advances in hardware. There is now a proliferation of programming languages designed to allow the programmer to concentrate most of his attention on solving the problem rather than on the tedious task of converting the solution to machine code form.

Low-level languages

In the history of programming languages, one of the first significant innovations was the development of *assembly languages*. A program written in an assembly language is much more readable and understandable than its equivalent in machine code. For example, a program, in some typical assembly language, equivalent to that given in Table 14.1 for the addition of two numbers, might take the form shown in Table 14.2.

Instruction	Comments
LDR R0, N1	;LoaD Register R0 with the contents of location N1
LDR R1, N2	;LoaD Register R1 with the contents of location N2
ADD R0, R1	;ADD Ro and R1 and store sum in R0
STR R0, N3	;STore Register R0 in location N3
HLT	;HaLT execution of program

Table 14.2. *Assembly language program for the addition of two numbers*

Notice that the operation codes LDR, ADD, STR and HLT (representing LOAD, ADD, STORE and HALT respectively) are now easily recognisable and easy to remember; such memory aids, or *mnemonics*, are chosen for these reasons. The references, N1, N2 and N3, relate to memory locations and are called *symbolic addresses*, and in many assembly languages it is possible to use more meaningful names such as HRS or RATE to indicate the type of data stored there. The internal registers, R0, R1, may be two of several available within the computer for use by the programmer.

The processor is unable to decode instructions in this coded form, so they must first be converted into the equivalent machine code. An *assembler* is a machine code program which performs this function. It accepts an assembly language program as data, converts mnemonic operation codes to their numeric equivalents, assigns symbolic addresses to memory locations and produces as output the required machine code program. The assembly language program is termed the *source program* and the final machine code program is the *object program*. Thus assemblers and assembly languages have removed the need to write machine code programs and a considerable burden has been removed from the programming task; the computer itself now does much of the work required to produce the object program.

Though assembly languages aid the programmer considerably, they are still closely related to machine code; there is a one-to-one correspondence between a machine code instruction and one in assembly language. In other words each machine code instruction must have a matching assembly language instruction. This fundamental correspondence has led to the term *low-level* being applied to this type of programming language.

Assemblers

Though a program written in an assembly language is much more readable and understandable than its equivalent in machine code, it is no longer directly executable by the computer. An *assembler* is a computer program which carries out the necessary translation.

The assembler accepts an assembly language program as data, converts *mnemonic* operation codes (op-codes) to their numeric equivalents, assigns *symbolic addresses* to memory locations and produces as output the required machine code program.

The assembly language program is termed the *source program* and the final machine code program is the *object program*.

Though it is true that by far the majority of computer programming today is in high-level languages such as Pascal, C or COBOL, programming in assembly languages is still essential for certain tasks. The reason for this, despite continual improvements in compiler design, is simply that the programmer, having total control over the structure of the machine code generated by the assembler, is able to write much faster and more efficient code than that produced by a compiler. The very nature of high-level languages, allowing us to deal with a greatly simplified, virtual machine, often precludes the programmer from being able to fine-tune code according to particular circumstances.

For example, a commonly used method of increasing the speed of a machine-code program is to utilize internal registers as much as possible in preference to memory locations, in order to minimize relatively slow memory accesses. While this type of code optimization is perfectly feasible in any assembly language, most high-level languages do not allow the programmer this degree of control (C is a notable exception, allowing identifiers to be specifically allocated to general purpose registers).

A consequence of the one-to-one correspondence between an assembly language instruction and its equivalent machine-code instruction is that assemblers are *machine dependent*, producing machine code for a specific type of processor. For instance, the machine code generated by an Intel 8086/88 assembler could not be used directly by a computer with a Motorola 68000 processor. For this reason, there is no single, archetypal assembler; rather, each assembler is related to the architecture of the processor for which it has been designed. Thus, if the processor supports two-address machine-code instructions, this will be reflected in the format of the assembly language instructions. In the following sections a number of fundamental

characteristics, common to most assemblers, are introduced. It uses a hypothetical microprocessor and associated assembly language to illustrate simple programs and includes an example
program to illustrate the assembly process.

Assembler tasks

Early assemblers did little more than convert instruction mnemonics to their equivalent numeric machine codes, but current assemblers do much more. Some of the most common
assembler tasks are described below:

☐ *Op-code translation.* Numeric operation codes replace the mnemonic op-codes used in
the source program.

☐ *Absolute address allocation.* Each instruction or data word in the source program must
be allocated an absolute machine address (its physical location). The assembler
maintains a *location counter* (sometimes referred to as a *load pointer*) which, having
been set to an initial base address, is incremented by the length of each data or
instruction word as it is assembled.

☐ *Symbolic operand conversion.* This refers to the assembly process of substituting any
symbolic addresses, that is, user identifiers used in place of memory locations, with
numeric machine addresses. A symbol table records each symbolic operand together
with its corresponding absolute address; a similar table logs labels and their machine
addresses. If relative addressing is used, labels and symbolic addresses are converted to
offsets from the location counter; this enables a program to be relocatable.

☐ *Converting constants to their internal forms.* This will involve conversion from textual
(ASCII, for example) representations of decimal, hexadecimal, octal or binary to pure
binary.

☐ *Replacing identifiers by user-defined macros.* If the assembly language supports the
use of *macro* instructions (a shorthand used by a programmer to express sequences of
regularly used instructions by a macro name), any such macro must be expanded by the
assembler and inserted into the source program prior to assembling it.

☐ *Obeying directives.* Many assemblers support the use of *pseudo-operations,* or
directives which are instructions not directly translatable into machine instructions.
These involve such things as reserving space for data, defining the values of identifiers
used in the program and defining where the program is to be located in memory.

☐ *Generating error messages.* If the assembler detects any syntax errors in the source
program, it must be able to issue a message indicating the source and nature of the
problem.

☐ *Producing source-code listings.* These may take various forms including listings of the
source-code, object-code and symbol table.

Assembly

The assembly process usually involves the assembler in executing several passes of the program's source code, each one carrying out certain of the tasks described above. The problem of
forward referencing (an instruction uses a symbolic operand which is not defined until later in
the program, so its address has not been allocated at that point and cannot be included in the instruction) means that assemblers usually carry out a minimum of two passes. Some assemblers,
such as our hypothetical ATL1, perform an additional initial pass to simplify the main two
passes described below.

Two-pass assembly

Pass 1. Any macro instructions are expanded as part of the pass or as a separate initial pass, making three in all. All instructions are examined and checked for syntactical correctness; any errors are recorded in a table. After each instruction has been dealt with, the location counter is incremented, and a symbol table is constructed to link any symbolic operands and labels with their corresponding absolute addresses.

Pass 2. By reference to the symbol tables, the assembler generates and outputs the object code.

A hypothetical microprocessor: the BEP/16

The BEP/16 is a simple, hypothetical 16-bit microprocessor loosely based on the Intel 8086/88. The BEP/16 processor contains the following 16-bit registers:

- ❏ 11 general-purpose registers, R0–R10
- ❏ a 16-bit Stack Pointer, SP
- ❏ a 16-bit Overflow Register, VR

- ❏ a 16-bit Program Counter, PC
- ❏ a 16-bit Flag Register, FR

Addressable RAM is limited to 64K bytes, though an additional 16K bytes are used for the stack. Memory is accessed in 16-bit words. The *flag register* contains the following flags:

- ❏ the carry flag (C)-bit0
- ❏ the sign flag (S)-bit2

- ❏ the zero flag (Z)-bit1
- ❏ the overflow flag (V)-bit3

Carry flag: the C flag is set (C=1) if there is a carry out from the most significant bit (m.s.b.) as a result of an arithmetic operation. The C flag is *cleared* (C=0) if there is no carry out.

Zero flag: the Z flag is set if the result of an operation is zero. It is cleared if the result is non-zero.

Sign flag: the S flag reflects the state of the most significant bit of the result of an arithmetic operation. S = 0 represents a positive value and S = 1 represents a negative value.

Overflow flag: the V flag is set when an arithmetic overflow occurs, that is when, as a result of a signed arithmetic operation, the most significant bit of the result is lost.

Examples of instructions using two registers are

```
MOV R1,R2        ;Data transfer
ADD R2,R4        ;Arithmetic operations
```

A subset of the instruction set is first summarized and then described in more detail in the next sections. In the summary, the flags that are affected (if any) are indicated by a hyphen (flag not used) or * (depends on the result of the instruction).

Summary

A shortened instruction set for the BEP/16 is summarised in Table 14.3.

mnemonic	operation	formats	words	flags
				V S Z C
ADD: Add	Adds reg2 to reg1	ADD reg1,reg2	1	* * * *
		ADD reg,immed		
CMP: Compare	Compares reg1 and reg2	CMP reg1,reg2	1	- * * *
	and sets flags	CMP reg,immed	2	
DEC: Decrement	Subtracts 1 from operand	DEC reg	1	* * * *
		DEC addr		

DIV: Divide	Divides reg1 by reg2	DIV reg1,reg2 DIV reg,immed	1	- - - *
	Unsigned integer division		2	
HLT: Halt	Halts execution of the program	HLT	1	- - - -
INC: Increment	Adds 1 to operand	INC reg	1	* * * *
		INC addr	2	
Jcondition	Conditional jump		2	- - - -
	Jump if equal	JEQ label		
	Jump if not equal	JNE label		
	Jump if plus	JPL label		
	Jump if minus	JMI label		
	Jump if greater or equal	JGE label		
	Jump if less than	JLT label		
	Jump if greater than	JGT label		
	Jump if less or equal	JLE label		
JMP: Unconditional jump		JMP label	2	- - - -
LDR: Load register	Copies memory address contents to register	LDR reg,addr	2	- * * -
MOV: Move	Copies reg2 to reg1	MOV reg1,reg2	1	- * * -
		MOV reg,immed	2	
MUL: Unsigned multiply	Multiplies reg1 by reg2 retaining sign of operand	MUL reg1,reg2 MUL reg,immed	1 2	- - - *
STR: Store register	Copies contents of register to memory	STR reg,addr	2	- * * -
SUB: Subtract	Subtracts reg2 from reg1	SUB reg1,reg2 SUB reg,immed	1 2	* * * *
SWI: Software interrupt	Invokes an operating system routine	SWI addr	2	- - - -

Table 14.3. *Instruction set*

reg refers to any one of the registers.

addr is an address which may be a number or a symbolic address.

immed is an immediate operand which may be a single character enclosed in single quotes, or a number, preceded by the @ symbol. Immediate numeric constants may also be preceded by the & symbol for hexadecimal constants or the % symbol for binary constants.

Data transfer instructions: MOV, LDR, STR

These instructions are for transferring data to and from memory, and between internal registers.

MOV: Copies a word from from a source operand to a destination operand. The source operand may be an immediate constant or a register, but the destination must be a register.

LDR: Copies the contents of a memory location to a specified register. For example,

LDR R1, &1234 or LDR R3, cost, where cost is a symbolic memory address;

STR: Copies the contents of a specified register to a memory location.

Arithmetic instructions: ADD, SUB, CMP, MUL, DIV, INC, DEC

This set of instructions allows simple arithmetic operations to be performed on the contents of registers. The multiply and divide instructions use the overflow register (V) to hold part of the result of the operations.

ADD:
Performs addition on two words, putting the sum in the first operand. For example, the instruction ADD R10, @3 would add 3 to the contents of R10.

SUB:
Subtracts the second operand from the first operand, putting the difference in the first operand. For example, SUB R5, R3 subtracts the contents of R3 from R5 and stores the difference in R5.

CMP:
Performs the same operation as SUB, but does not store the difference in the first operand. It is used to compare two values and set appropriate flags (V, C and Z) according to the result so that a conditional branch instruction may follow it.

MUL:
Multiplies two 16-bit unsigned numbers to produce a 32-bit product. The carry flag is set if the product exceeds the size of a 16-bit register; in this instance, the overflow (the most significant word) is stored in V, the overflow register, which is reserved for this purpose, though it may also be used as a general-purpose register.

DIV:
Divides the first unsigned operand by the second and stores the integer quotient in the first. The remainder after division is stored in V.

INC:
Adds 1 to the specified register or memory location.

DEC:
Subtracts 1 from the specified register or memory location.

Transfer of control instructions: JMP, Jcond

This set of instructions allows the normal sequential flow of instructions to be modified. Normally, the PC is incremented after every fetch cycle so that each instruction is performed in the order in which it is stored in memory; this set of instructions allows the contents of the PC to be changed to any value in the memory space so that program instructions may be executed in orders other than sequential. This allows, for instance, sections of code to be repeated in a loop.

JMP:
Causes an unconditional jump by adding a signed offset to the PC. That is, it performs a relative jump forwards or backwards. The assembler automatically converts label addresses to the appropriate offsets.

JEQ:
Performs the transfer of control only if Z=1, that is, if the result of an arithmetic operation was zero.

JNE:
Performs the transfer of control only if Z=0, that is, if the result of an arithmetic operation was not zero.

JPL:
Performs the transfer of control only if S=0, that is, the last operation produced a positive number with a sign bit of 0.

JMI:
Performs the transfer of control only if S=1, that is, the last operation produced a negative number with a sign bit of 1.

JGE:
This assumes that the previous operation used signed integers in two's complement representation. The branch is performed if the first operand was greater or equal to the second operand.

JLT:
This assumes that the previous operation used signed integers in two's complement representation. The branch is performed if the first operand was less than the second operand.

JGT:
This again assumes signed arithmetic with the first operand greater than the second.

JLE: Again assuming signed arithmetic with the first operand less than or equal to the second.

Input/output instructions: SWI

SWI: This instruction performs an indirect call to an operating system subroutine. It allows access to pre-written routines for standard tasks such as keyboard input and displaying text on the screen.

SWI getInt : get an integer from the keyboard and store in R0

SWI putInt: display the contents of R0 as an integer

SWI getChar: get a single character from the keyboard and store in R0

SWI putChar: display the contents of R0 as a character

These addresses form a table of addresses of the actual routines. The SWI instruction uses the operand provided in the instruction as a pointer to the appropriate routine. This allows for the operating system routines to be located in different areas in different machines while still retaining the same SWI call. Other SWI calls allow graphics operations to be performed and input/output devices to be used.

Other instructions: HLT

HLT: Terminates program execution, returning control to the operating system.

The ATL1 assembler

The ATL1 assembler includes the following facilities:

- ❑ the use of mnemonics for operation codes;
- ❑ the use of labels for branching instructions;
- ❑ the use of comments for annotating programs;
- ❑ symbolic memory addresses.

ATL1 assembly language instruction format

Assembly language instructions, or statements, are divided into a number of fields:

(i) *Operation code field*. This contains the instruction mnemonic and therefore must always be present in the instruction.

(ii) *Operand(s) field*. The composition of this field depends on the operation and the addressing mode. It may contain zero or more operands which may be registers, addresses or immediate operands.

(iii) *Label field*. This optional field allows the programmer to establish a point of reference in the program. Certain other instructions, such as branch instructions, use these labels in their operand field.

(iv) *Comment field*. This is another optional field, ignored by the assembler, to allow the programmer to annotate the program.

Assemblers provide varying degrees of flexibility in how these fields may be combined in program statements. Fields are separated from one another by means of *delimiters*, which are special characters (such as spaces, semi-colons or colons) recognised by the assembler as serving this function.

Listing 14.1 shows a short assembly language subroutine illustrating the concepts explained above. Internal registers are designated R0, R1, R2 etc. The subroutine adds the numbers 5 to

14 inclusive, that is, the 10 consecutive numbers starting with 5, by accumulating them in register R2.

Listing 14.1. Addition of ten consecutive numbers

label	Opcode	Operand(s)	comments
start:	MOV	R0, @10	; init loop counter
	MOV	R1, @5	; start value, R1=5
	MOV	R2, @0	; clear running total, R2=0
loop:	ADD	R2, R1	; accumulate total, R2=R2+R1
	INC	R1	; add 1 to R1
	DEC	R0	; decrement R0
	JGT	loop	; branch to label if R0>0
	HLT		; halt program

The ATL1 preprocessor

The ATL1 assembler uses a preprocessor to make an initial pass through the source program to perform the following functions:

- ❑ Remove unnecessary spaces
- ❑ Remove blank lines
- ❑ Convert text to upper case
- ❑ Process #DEF lines

These operations simplify the source program in preparation for the next two passes which produce the required machine code. The final bullet point in the list above requires some explanation.

#DEFines

The preprocessor looks for any lines starting with #DEF. It then expects to find an identifier followed by a value or another identifier. It then searches the source program and replaces any incidences of the identifier with the value following it. For example, the definition below causes all occurrences of width to be replaced by 10 in the source program.

```
#DEF width 10
```

The examples following illustrate some uses of #DEF.

Example 1

Use meaningful names for registers:

```
#DEF counter R1
```

This definition allows you to use the identifier counter instead of the register name R1. The assembler would replace every incidence of counter with R1. Thus, an instruction such as INC counter in the source program would become INC R1 after preprocessing.

Example 2

Define the values of constants used in the program:

```
#DEF asterisk '*'
```

The assembler would replace every incidence of asterisk with '*'. Thus, an instruction such as MOV R4, asterisk in the source program would become MOV R4, '*' after preprocessing.

The ATL1 assembly process

The ATL1 assembler performs three passes of the source code:

❏ *Pass 1*: Preprocessing. Comments are removed and #DEFs are processed.

❏ *Pass 2*: A symbol table is constructed, assembler directives are obeyed and instructions are converted into machine code where possible.

❏ *Pass 3*: Any forward referenced addresses are inserted with the aid of the symbol table.

The following examples illustrate a number of simple programming tasks.

Programming examples

Data transfer

Programming example 1

```
;Program to illustrate simple data transfer instructions using MOV
;LDR and STR. A register is set to zero and then stored in two
;memory locations
        #DEF n1 &1000     ; Allocate n1 to location hex 1000
        #DEF n2 &1002     ; Allocate n2 to location hex 1002
        ;
        MOV R0, @0        ; Move zero to R0
        STR R0, n1        ; Store in location n1
        STR R0, n2        ; Store in location n2
        HLT               ; Terminate program.
```

Simple arithmetic

Programming example 2

```
;Program to illustrate simple 16-bit integer arithmetic and simple
;data transfer instructions. The two numbers, a and b, are input
;from the keyboard and the program calculates a2 - b2, using
;(a+b)(a-b).
        ;
        SWI getInt        ; Operating system call to get a 16-bit
                          ; integer from the keyboard. Value is
                          ; returned in R0
        MOV R1, R0        ; Store the first value in register R1
        SWI getInt        ; Get the second value
        MOV R2, R0        ; Store in register R2
        MOV R3, R1        ; R3 = a
        ADD R3, R2        ; R3 = a+b
        MOV R4, R1        ; R4 = a
        SUB R4, R2        ; R4 = a-b
        MUL R3, R4        ; R3 = (a+b)(a-b)
        MOV R0, R3        ; Copy answer to R0
        SWI putInt        ; Operating system call to display the
                          ; 16-bit integer in R0.
        HLT               ; Terminate program.
```

Transfer of control

Programming example 3

```
;Program to illustrate conditional jump instructions. Two numbers
;are input and the smaller of the two is displayed.
        ;
        SWI getInt          ; Operating system call to get a 16-bit
                            ; integer from the keyboard. Value is
                            ; returned in R0
        MOV R1, R0          ; Store the first value in R1
        SWI getInt          ; Get the second value
        MOV R2, R0          ; Store in R2
        CMP R2, R1          ; compare numbers
        JLT L1              ; Jump to L1 if R2 < R1
        SWI putInt          ; Display second number (already in R0)
        JMP L2              ; Jump to end
L1:     MOV R0, R1          ; Move the first number into R0
                            ; ready for displaying
        SWI putInt          ; Display the first number
L2:     HLT                 ; Terminate program.
```

Loop

Programming example 4

```
;Program to illustrate a loop. Positive numbers are input and
;added to R1 until a negative number is input. Then the sum of the
;numbers is displayed
        ;
        MOV R1,@0           ; Set R1 to 0
L1:     SWI getInt          ; Operating system call to get a 16-bit
                            ; integer from the keyboard into R0
        MOV R2,R0           ; Move number to R2
        JMI L2              ; Jump to L2 if number is negative
        ADD R1, R2          ; Add number to R1
        JMP L1              ; Get next number
L2:     MOV R0, R2          ; Move total into R0 ready for displaying
        SWI putInt          ; Display the total
        HLT                 ; Terminate program.
```

✐ Exercises

1. Write a program to input two integers and output their sum, difference and product.
2. Read two integer values, a and b, and perform the following calculations.
   $2a + 3b$
   $a^2 - b^2$
   $5a^2 + 3a - 1$
3. Write a program to arrange two characters into alphabetical order.
4. Write a program to read in a set of 10 positive and negative integers then add the positive and negative numbers separately and display the two totals.

Chapter 15

Software

The word *software* is used to describe all computer programs. *Systems software* is used to make the hardware operate as a general-purpose computer system. *Applications software* makes the computer operate in partic-ular ways, for example, as a payroll, word processing, graphic design, route plan-ning or games system.

Figure 15.1 shows the sys-tems and applications software groups and some of the sub-groups belong-ing to each.

Relevant examples of com-mercial software products are shown in the figure, be-neath each sub-group. Some of the examples should be familiar and should help you to under-stand the purpose of each software group and sub-group.

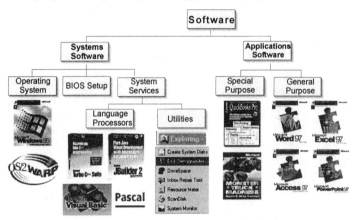

Figure 15.1. *Main categories of software, with examples*

Summary of software types

Referring to Figure 15.1, the following types of software can be identified.

- ☐ *Operating system.* This set of programs has overall control of the computer system, both hardware and applications software and acts as the *interface* between the user and the machine. Frequently the interface is graphical and known as a *graphical user interface* (GUI). Sometimes, the user may communicate through a *command-driven* interface, typing commands at a simple screen prompt.

- ☐ *Utilities.* These are programs to help the user carry out general maintenance tasks on the system. For example, Windows 9x provides *Windows Explorer* to manage the disk filing system, *Disk Defragmenter* to recover wasted space on disks, *DriveSpace* to create additional disk space and *ScanDisk* to find and repair disk recording problems.

- ☐ *BIOS* (Basic Input/Output System). The BIOS specifies the details of the installed hardware and 'fine tunes' it for best performance and user preference. Note that the BIOS software is not a category that most users deal with. The BIOS deals with the direct control of the hardware components and is normally the concern of computer manufacturers. Experienced users of computer systems may access the BIOS when installing new hardware to upgrade their system.

- ☐ *Development tools.* These are used by programmers to create and maintain systems and applications software. They include *programming language* development tools.

❑ *Special-purpose* applications software. These are programs designed for a single purpose, such as stock control, invoicing, accounts or a game.

❑ *General-purpose* applications software. These are packages which can be used for many different applications. For example, a database package could be used to hold details about holidays, food, people or dogs. The packages are 'content free' and need tailoring to each particular purpose. They are often called *generic* software.

The rest of this chapter examines all these topics in more detail. The first major section deals with systems software and the second with applications software.

Systems software

Operating system

An operating system manages and communicates with the resources of a computer system, as illustrated in Figure 15.2. You should recognise these resources as the hardware components that form a computer system (see Chapter 9).

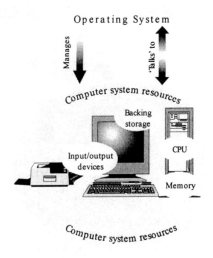

❑ *central processing unit (CPU)*. The operating system controls the CPU in its different tasks, which include, for example:

 ○ fetching program instructions and data from RAM;

 ○ starting a data transfer from an input device;

 ○ handling separate user requests for data, perhaps from the same file, in a *multi-user* system;

Figure 15.2. *Purpose of the operating system*

 ○ sharing the CPU's time between several tasks in RAM at the same time, a process known as *multi-tasking*.

❑ *Memory* or *RAM*. Programs (sometimes several) have to be accommodated in RAM, together with the data they are processing. The operating system:

 ○ loads programs (or part programs) into memory as requested;

 ○ unloads programs (or part programs) no longer required;

 ○ moves programs around in memory to make best use of the space.

❑ *Input/output devices*. The operating system requests the use of devices as required and checks for conflict, for example, when two user programs try to print at the same time.

❑ *Backing storage*. Programs and data files are held on backing storage and loaded into RAM as needed. The operating system:

 ○ manages the storage space;

 ○ supervises transfers between RAM and backing storage.

Types of operating system

Computer systems vary in size, power and the number and variety of peripherals which can be attached. The biggest computer systems are called supercomputers. Coming down the scale, there are mainframe, mini and microcomputer systems. Because the resources for each are so different and the applications for which they are used also vary widely, there is a need for different kinds of operating system. So, for example, there are:

❑ simple operating systems like MS-DOS, designed for running one program at a time for a single user.

❑ multi-tasking operating systems, which allow a user to have several programs loaded at one time. Figure 15.3 illustrates a user operating several tasks through the Windows operating system.

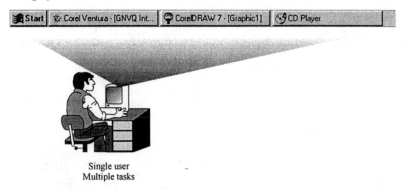

Figure 15.3. *A user multi-tasking with the Windows operating system*

❑ network operating systems, such as Windows NT, 2000 and Novell Netware which are designed to control networked computer systems. Figure 15.4 shows several computers linked to a network using the Novell Netware operating system.

❑ A network operating system has the following features:

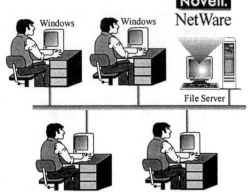

Figure 15.4. *Network controlled by a network operating system*

　　○ Facilities to control users' access to *shared resources*, including programs and data held on the network. They use login procedures to identify the user and request a password.

　　○ A user's access to the network is limited by their *network rights* and these are controlled and checked by the operating system. For example, a clerk in the personnel department may be able to view staff salary figures, but is not given access to the program which allows them to be changed.

Note from the figure that the individual workstations run their own 'local' operating system. The network operating system is designed to be able to communicate with workstations running under different *platforms*. So, for example, PCs and Macintosh workstations may be attached to the same network. There are many other operating systems, to suit every kind of use, including, for example, air traffic control, manufacturing processes and large-scale business systems such as those used by banks.

Operating system interfaces

An operating system is the interface for communication between the computer and its users and operators. The method or 'language' used for this communication can be:

❏ command driven. Commands are typed at a system prompt, such as that for the old MS-DOS operating system (often referred to as the C:\> prompt). This is a *command line interface* (CLI).

❏ graphical. A *graphical user interface* (GUI) provides a more user-friendly method of communication and avoids the need to learn complicated command sequences.

Command line interface (CLI)

Figure 15.5 shows the CLI for the MS-DOS operating system. With this type of interface, the user must enter commands. These commands may instruct the operating system to carry out some action, or provide the user with some information. At the bottom of the figure, there is a lengthy command sequence to copy a file from one directory to another. It is followed by the message "1 file(s) copied", which confirms that the command has been executed successfully.

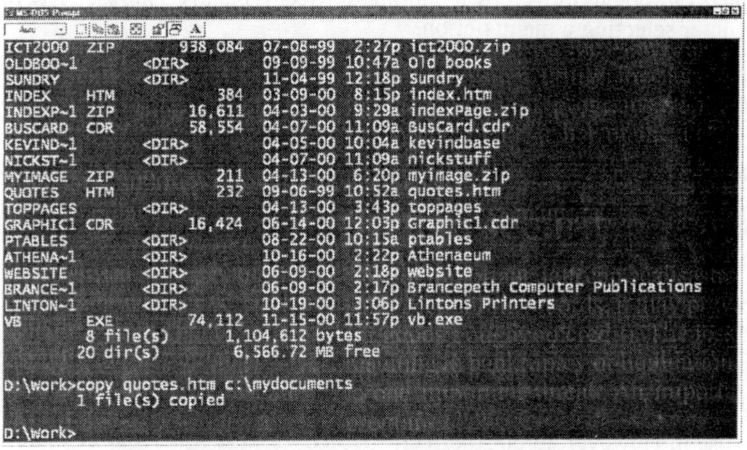

```
MS-DOS Prompt
Auto          A
ICT2000  ZIP      938,084  07-08-99  2:27p ict2000.zip
OLDBOO~1          <DIR>     09-09-99 10:47a Old books
SUNDRY            <DIR>     11-04-99 12:18p Sundry
INDEX    HTM          384  03-09-00  8:15p index.htm
INDEXP~1 ZIP       16,611  04-03-00  9:29a indexPage.zip
BUSCARD  CDR       58,554  04-07-00 11:09a BusCard.cdr
KEVIND~1          <DIR>     04-05-00 10:04a kevindbase
NICKST~1          <DIR>     04-07-00 11:09a nickstuff
MYIMAGE  ZIP          211  04-13-00  6:20p myimage.zip
QUOTES   HTM          232  09-06-99 10:52a quotes.htm
TOPPAGES         <DIR>     04-13-00  3:43p toppages
GRAPHIC1 CDR       16,424  06-14-00 12:03p Graphic1.cdr
PTABLES          <DIR>     08-22-00 10:15a ptables
ATHENA~1         <DIR>     10-16-00  2:22p Athenaeum
WEBSITE          <DIR>     06-09-00  2:18p website
BRANCE~1         <DIR>     06-09-00  2:17p Brancepeth Computer Publications
LINTON~1         <DIR>     10-19-00  3:06p Lintons Printers
VB       EXE       74,112  11-15-00 11:57p vb.exe
         8 file(s)      1,104,612 bytes
        20 dir(s)       6,566.72 MB free

D:\work>copy quotes.htm c:\mydocuments
         1 file(s) copied

D:\work>
```

Figure 15.5. *Command line interface in MS-DOS*

The main advantage of the CLI is that the short commands, though not particularly user-friendly, are ideal for rapid, expert use.

The main disadvantages of the CLI are:

❏ it is unsuitable for novice users;

❏ the commands must be learned and remembered;

❏ it can only be used with the keyboard.

Graphical user interface (GUI)

Figure 15.6 shows the graphical user interface (GUI) for the Windows operating system and illustrates the following features:

Figure 15.6. *Graphical user interface (GUI) for Windows operating system*

☐ a *pointer* on screen, moved by a pointing device, typically a *mouse*. The figure shows the pointer selecting a menu option.

☐ *icons* (small pictures) representing, amongst other things, programs, which can be run by pointing and clicking the mouse. The recycle bin icon is in the bottom right corner of the figure.

☐ *windows*. Applications run in their own self-contained areas called *windows*. There are three in the figure, one for Explorer, the Internet browser, another for CorelDRAW, a graphic design program and a third for Corel Ventura, a desktop publishing program. These are all examples of *applications software*.

☐ *pull-down menus* which provide access to standard functions. The figure shows such a menu in the Corel Ventura window.

Benefits of a GUI

Most users are not really interested in the technical details of a computer's operation and simply want to use it. However, to do so effectively, a user must learn routine maintenance tasks, such as creating folders, copying files and formatting disks as well as the use of the particular applications they need. A GUI is designed to make these tasks easier as follows.

☐ Methods of doing things are more *intuitive*. This means that a user can often anticipate what certain actions with the mouse will do. For example, selecting a file with a mouse pointer and dragging it to an *icon* (small picture) of a dustbin has the effect of deleting the selected file.

☐ Applications running under a GUI have common features, so, for example, it is easier to transfer skills learned using a word processor to those needed for a spreadsheet. Figure 15.7 shows that two entirely different packages use several of the same menus and command buttons. As the figure also shows, common package requirements, such as creating new, opening existing and saving files, whether they relate to a spreadsheet from Microsoft or a publishing package from Corel, use the same buttons. Obviously, individual packages have extra buttons and menus which relate to their particular facilities.

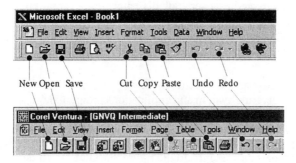

New Open Save   Cut Copy Paste   Undo Redo

Figure 15.7. *Common menus and buttons in two packages running under Windows*

Utilities

These are programs, usually included with the operating system, which do routine maintenance tasks on the computer system. The Windows Explorer, Disk Defragmenter, DriveSpace and ScanDisk utilities, provided by the Windows operating system are described in this section.

Windows Explorer

Figure 15.8 shows the Windows Explorer view of a particular computer system. This Windows 9x utility allows the user to see the disk file systems attached to the computer and carry out various maintenance tasks on the files stored there. To understand the purposes of this utility, you need to know some basic principles about a Windows disk file system.

Each physical disk drive in the system is identified by a letter. Usually, the main hard drive is C: and the floppy drive is A:. Other drives, such as the CD-ROM take other letters, D:, E: and so on. Note that a single physical drive may be partitioned into two or more drives, each with a different letter. Also, additional, compressed drives (see DriveSpace) can be created from a physical drive, each additional compressed drive being given a different letter. Note that the example system has six drive letters:

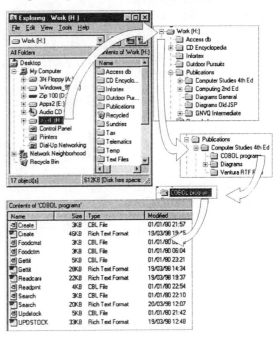

Figure 15.8. *Windows Explorer*

- ☐ A: (floppy drive);
- ☐ C: (first *partition* of the main hard drive);
- ☐ D: (a 100MB Zip drive);
- ☐ E: (second partition of the main hard drive);
- ☐ F: (CD-ROM drive);
- ☐ H: (a compressed drive - see DriveSpace, later).

Each drive letter can be treated as a separate disk and storage area. For example, the C: drive contains the operating system and usually the main applications programs. In the example system, the E: partition drive contains other applications programs and the H: drive all the main data files. The A: and D: drives use removable disks and are used for taking security backups of important files.

Each drive letter holds a hierarchical (different levels) directory or folder structure. Some folders are created for the operating system and applications programs. A user can create additional folders to organise the data files. Figure 15.8 shows Windows Explorer being used to view the various levels on the H: drive, to access files held in the COBOL directory. Clicking on a + next to a folder reveals any sub-folders, whilst clicking on a − hides its sub-folders and clicking on a folder or sub-folder reveals its contents. In the figure, the COBOL folder is opened to show the files it holds.

Files or folders can be selected and deleted, or copied or moved to other folders or drive letters. Usually, these operations use the mouse to drag the selection to the required destination.

Disk Defragmenter

This utility is extremely important for the efficient operation of the main hard drive(s) in a computer system. To understand its purpose, you need to be familiar with a number of facts relating to disk storage. Disk space is allocated in *clusters*, which are units of disk storage. For example, the cluster size may be 16 kilobytes (KB). When a file is stored on disk it takes up as many clusters as it needs. For example, if a document is of size 525 KB, it will need 525 ÷ 16 = 33 clusters (to the nearest whole cluster).

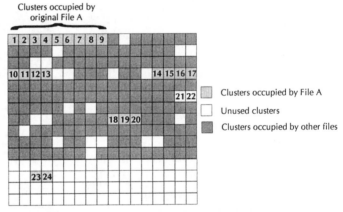

Figure 15.9. *Area of disk clusters, showing File A fragmented*

When a file is first stored on disk it is given, if possible, a *contiguous*(no gaps between) chain of clusters. Each time it is altered and made larger, it may not fit in its original place, so the extra has to be placed somewhere else. This *fragmentation* of files leads to slower disk performance, because the read/write heads may have to go to several different parts of the disk to retrieve a single file. Such a fragmented file is illustrated in Figure 15.9. Note the following points in the figure.

The figure represents a small area of disk space, with each square as a single cluster. The white squares are empty clusters. The 24 light grey squares are the clusters occupied by a particular File A. The clusters numbered 1 to 9 shows where the original version of File A is stored. Numbers 10 to 24 are clusters filled as File A has been altered and

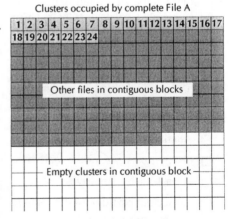

Figure 15.10. *Disk space after defragmentation*

made larger. The dark grey clusters are filled by other files.

Ideally, File A would be in a contiguous (without gaps) set of clusters, but each time it has been updated and made larger, the extra clusters have been taken from separate areas of the disk. The white clusters, although empty now, may not have been at the times File A was updated.

The defragmentation utility rearranges the disk space so that each file is held in a contiguous set of clusters. The empty space is also organised into a contiguous block of clusters. Figure 15.10 shows how the disk space may appear after defragmentation is complete.

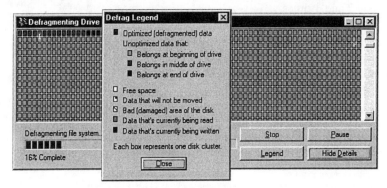

Figure 15.11. *Disk Defragmenter in progress*

Figure 15.11 shows the Windows utility, Disk Defragmenter in progress, together with a legend explaining the different states of clusters on the disk. As the legend shows, the utility also identifies any damaged areas of the disk.

DriveSpace

This utility is used to increase the amount of disk space, by compressing some of the existing physical space.

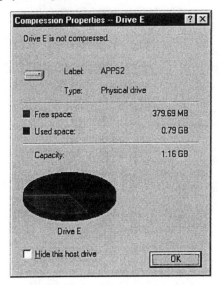

Figure 15.12. *Details of a standard, uncompressed drive*

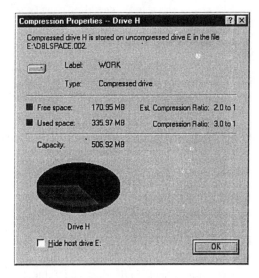

Figure 15.13. *A compressed drive H:, created from space on physical drive E:*

So, for example, using a compression ratio of 2:1, a disk can be made to hold twice as much data. An example will help to explain what happens. Figure 15.12 shows the properties of Drive E:, a physical hard drive. The figure shows that it is a 'physical', uncompressed drive with a capacity of 1.16GB and around 379MB of unused space. Figure 15.13, shows the properties for a compressed drive H: with a capacity of 506 MB, of which around 170MB is unused. The compression ratio indicates that data stored on drive H: is compressed between 2 and 3 times.

Figure 15.13 shows that physical drive E: is the *host*. This means that H: is not a new drive, simply a compressed storage area on drive E:. As a result the physical space on the host drive E: is reduced because it is storing the compressed drive H:.

Figure 15.14 of Windows Explorer shows that a compressed drive appears to the user as just another drive. Figure 15.15 shows how extra space has been created. The amount of space gained with drive H: is, in the example, 2 to 3 times that lost to the compressed drive on drive E:.

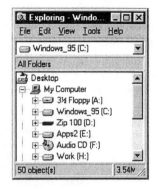

Figure 15.14. *Explorer with drives, including compressed drive H:*

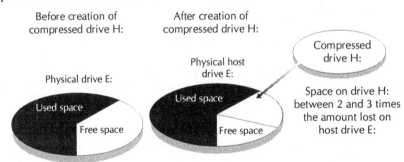

Figure 15.15. *Part of free space on physical drive E:, used to create compressed drive H:*

ScanDisk

This utility detects and repairs disk recording errors. Some locations on disk may not record data properly and if they are not found and repaired, data may be stored in those locations and be corrupted or lost. ScanDisk also finds 'lost' files. When a program 'crashes', or more seriously, when the operating system crashes, corrupted files, or bits of files, may be left on disk. These lost files take up valuable disk space and often contain meaningless information or 'garbage'. The ScanDisk dialogue box is shown in Figure 15.16. The figure shows the following options.

The *standard* check finds files and folders for errors, including 'lost' files. It is a good idea to run this check whenever the operating system crashes.

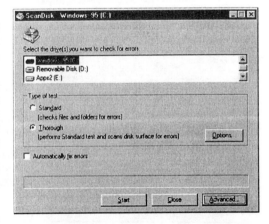

Figure 15.16. *ScanDisk with options for file and folder check and surface scan*

The *thorough* check carries out the standard check, plus a surface scan for possible disk recording errors. This check should be carried out regularly to find and fix disk recording problems before vital data is lost.

BIOS

A computer system's BIOS (Basic Input/Output System) holds details of what hardware is installed and settings for individual components. The settings are held in CMOS RAM. This is a special type of RAM, which can retain its contents with only a tiny amount of battery power - the battery is attached to the motherboard and recharged whenever the machine is switched on. The BIOS settings are used to control the *system start-up* and carry out diagnostic checks on the hardware.

System start-up

When a computer system is 'powered on' the BIOS starts the Power-On Self-Test (POST) routine. The POST routine is in two stages:

1. The *motherboard* (also known as the *system board*) and its components (processor, RAM etc.) are checked for their normal operation. The RAM test is visible on screen while it is being carried out.

2. The hardware actually installed is checked to see that it matches with the system's BIOS (Basic Input/Output System) settings.

If an error is identified, the system reports it, either with a 'beep' or an error message on screen. The Power-On Self-Test (POST) sequence checks the hardware to see that the major components, including RAM, are present and working properly.

BIOS Setup utility

The BIOS Setup utility is held in ROM so that it is not lost when the machine is switched off. The program is used to enter details of the computer system's hardware, that is, the BIOS settings. When a computer is powered on and before the operating system starts to load, the operator has the opportunity to access the BIOS Setup utility, normally by pressing the <delete> key. Because settings entered through this program are then stored in CMOS RAM, the program menu includes options for the Standard CMOS setup and the BIOS Features (or Advanced CMOS) setup.

Standard CMOS setup

Standard CMOS Setup is used to record details of the basic hardware in the computer system. The settings are recorded when the motherboard is installed, normally by the manufacturer. This is usually the first BIOS Setup menu option. An example of a Standard CMOS Setup screen is shown in Figure 15.17.

The exact settings will vary according to the computer hardware, but note the following details labelled in the figure.

❑ The Primary Master is the main hard disk drive inside the system unit and in this example, it has a capacity of 2·5 GB. The Primary Slave, in this example, is a 100MB Zip drive, which uses removable disk cartridges. There is only one floppy disk drive, designed for 1·44 MB floppy disks.

❑ The 'Halt on' setting specifies that any hardware error will cause the powering up sequence to stop, until the error is corrected. The only other options are to ignore keyboard and/or floppy disk errors. Failure of RAM or the hard disk drive, for example, would always halt the system.

❑ The RAM total is 128 MB.

❑ The screen type is EGA or VGA. These are screen resolution standards. VGA is a minimum 800 × 600 resolution.

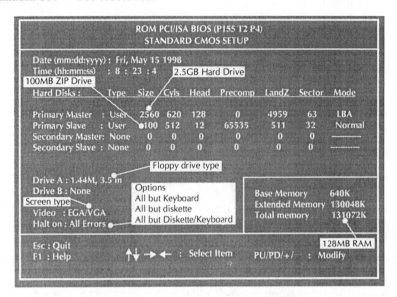

Figure 15.17. *Example Standard CMOS Setup*

The Standard CMOS Settings option would only need to be used if:

(a) the CMOS contents are corrupted or lost, perhaps through battery failure (as can happen if a machine is switched off for a long period). It is important that the settings are written down, so that if the contents are lost or corrupted, they can be re-entered. Without the correct settings, the machine may not work properly or at all;

or

(b) the system configuration is altered, perhaps through replacement of the hard disk or installation of a new motherboard.

BIOS Features setup

This option is used to 'fine tune' the hardware configuration, to improve performance and to set certain user preferences. Figure 15.18 shows an example BIOS Features screen.

The Figure is labelled with the following four features:

1. Boot sequence. Following a successful Power-On Self-Test (POST) routine, the BIOS loads the operating system, normally from the hard drive. The boot sequence dictates the order in which the BIOS checks the various disk drives to find the operating system. Setting the A: (floppy) drive as the first to be checked, allows for an emergency 'boot' if the operating system will not load from the hard drive. Windows provides an option to create such a startup or setup disk.

   To carry out the emergency boot, the setup disk is placed in the floppy drive before the machine is powered up. As soon as the BIOS finds the setup disk it boots the system from there, rather than trying to load the operating system from the hard drive. For this reason, an error message is displayed if a 'non-system' disk (one not containing special start-up files) is left in the floppy drive during start-up.

2. Floppy disk access control.

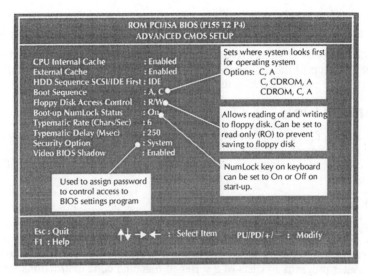

Figure 15.18. *Example BIOS Features setup*

The default setting is R/W (read/write), but to prevent users copying files from the hard drive onto floppy disk, it may be set to RO (read only). This may be done for security reasons.

3. Boot-up NumLock status. Setting the NumLock key to 'On' ensures that it is automatically on when the system is powered up. The keys on the numeric keypad then operate as such. If set to 'Off' the numeric keys have an alternate use as navigational keys (cursor left, right, page up and so on). Whatever the boot setting, the user can switch the NumLock key on or off as necessary.

4. Security option. As the earlier warning point out, altering BIOS settings has to be carried out with great care and only by someone who knows what they are doing and has the authority to do it. This option allows a password to be set. If a user tries to access the BIOS Setup program during startup, he or she will be asked for the password.

Plug and Play BIOS

Plug and Play operating systems use a BIOS which is automatically updated when a new device is added. On a Windows machine, the BIOS details then appear in the System Properties window, as shown in Figure 15.19. The Device Manager tab lists all the categories of device attached to the computer system. In the figure, three of the items are expanded, to show details of the actual attached device:

❑ The CD-ROM is identified as a TEAC CD-58E;

❑ The display adapter, or graphics card, is a Matrox Millennium;

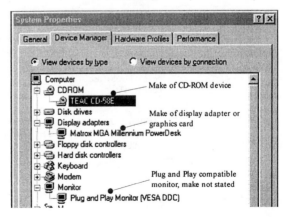

Figure 15.19. *Example BIOS details in a Windows System Properties window*

❏ The monitor is identified as Plug and Play (VESA DDC). 'VESA' indicates that it meets the Video Electronics Standards Association requirements for monitors.

Once a new device, such as a disk drive, or extra RAM, has been connected, the BIOS detects it during the next startup. If the device is not Plug and Play compatible, the installation settings have to be made through the BIOS setup utility.

Development tools

This is a group term for software which is used to develop applications and systems software. Examples of development tools are *programming languages* and *database packages*. To understand the purpose of development tools generally, you need to be familiar with the idea of a *computer program*.

Computer programs

The words *software* and *program* are often used to describe the same thing, but what exactly is meant by these two terms? To be usable by a computer, a program has to be in *machine code*. Machine code is *binary code*, a series of 1's and 0's, represented electrically inside the computer. A computer program consists of a series of machine code instructions which make the computer perform the required tasks. The program is stored in memory. It is fetched, decoded and executed, one instruction at a time, by the CPU (processor) until a Halt instruction is reached. The CPU has its own *instruction set*, which it uses to understand the instructions in a computer program. The set includes instructions for:

❏ *Arithmetic operations*, such as add, subtract, divide and multiply and logical operations, such as AND, OR, NOT.

❏ *Data transfer*, to enable data to be moved between the various devices in the computer system, including input, storage and output devices.

❏ *Transfer of control*, which allows the computer to skip one or more instructions or repeat previous instructions.

The storage of a computer program in memory and its execution by the CPU are illustrated in Figure 15.20.

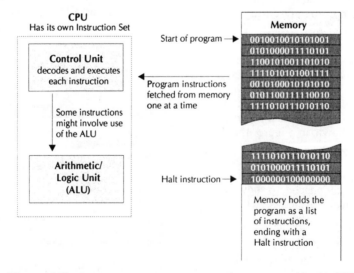

Figure 15.20. *A computer program in memory being executed by the CPU*

Writing computer programs

Although the computer needs programs to be in the binary codes it understands (according to its instruction set), it is not practical for programmers to write the same codes. Instead, programmers use *programming languages* and other development tools to write programs in a form that they understand; this is known as *source code*. The computer is then given the job of translating the source code into the machine's own code, known as the *object code*. The next section deals with the various software development tools used by programmers.

Programming languages

C++, Visual C, Visual BASIC, Pascal, Java, Delphi and COBOL are all examples of programming languages. All programming languages can be used to produce software, although some languages are suited to particular applications. For example, COBOL is mainly for business data processing applications, while Java is particularly suited to Internet applications. Pascal is used for commercial applications, but is particularly popular in education for teaching programming skills. Like English and other languages, a programming language has a *vocabulary*. These are keywords which form the language. Each keyword has a particular meaning. In Pascal, for example, the keywords `begin` and `end` are used to mark the beginning and end of a program, or separate groups of instructions within it. The words `if` and `then` are used in the writing of *conditional* statements. For example, the statement

```
if age < 16 then writeln('Junior Member');
```

will display the message in quotes if a the memory location labelled *age* contains a number less than 16. There are also rules of grammar. These are rules on the formation of program instructions. The example statement above would fail the rules for Pascal grammar if it were written as

```
if age < 16 writeln('Junior Member');
```

The word `then` must be used as part of an `if` statement. A programming language's rules for spelling and grammar are known as its *syntax*.

Program development

Programming language software includes a number of components to assist the programmer, including:

☐ an *editor* to allow entry of the source code. Figure 15.21 illustrates this process;

☐ *debugging* utilities to help find and correct errors in syntax;

☐ a *translator* to convert the source code into the object machine code. There are two main types of translator:

    ○ *compiler*. This is the most common and produces a separate machine code program which the computer can use without further use of the translator.

    ○ *interpreter*. This type does not produce an independent machine code program. The program must be translated each time it is run. Many versions of BASIC use an interpreter.

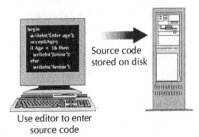

Use editor to enter source code

Figure 15.21. *Editor used for entry and storage of program source code*

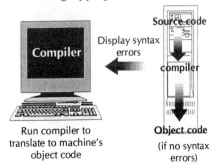

Run compiler to translate to machine's object code

Figure 15.22. *Translating the source code to the machine's object code*

A translator only checks the syntax of a program, not its *logic*. Before it can be used a program must be thoroughly tested to check that it performs exactly as required. Figure 15.22 illustrates the translation process with a compiler.

Applications software

This category of software includes all the purposes for which organisations and individuals use computers.

Specific applications packages

The needs of accounts and other special applications may be met by *specific* applications package, such as Sage Accounts and Quickbooks. Specific means that each one can only be used for a certain purpose and has no other use. Other applications in this category include, for example, payroll and stock control.

Some applications software is *tailor-made*, that is, developed specifically for a particular organisation. Off-the-shelf packages, such as QuickBooks are cheaper but they cannot always meet the exact needs of an organisation.

General-purpose software packages

Word 97 and Excel 97 are examples of *general-purpose* applications packages. General-purpose means that they can be used for a range of different purposes. Word 97 is a word processor and could be used to produce any text and graphics documents, for example, letters and reports or magazines and books with colour graphics. Excel 97 is a spreadsheet package and can be used for any number-based work, such as a sales forecast or a statistical analysis of the health of a population. It can also produce graphs or charts, to present the information in different ways. Other examples include drawing and paint packages, such as CorelDRAW and PhotoPaint and desktop publishing (DTP) packages, such as Quark Express. There are many different such packages, among the most important being: word processors; spreadsheets; databases; graphics, including desktop publishing (DTP), business graphics, graphic design and computer-aided drawing (CAD).

✍ Exercises

1. What is the function of the following types of software?
    (i)   Operating system
    (ii)   Utilities
    (iii)   BIOS
    (iv)   Development tools
    (v)   Applications
2. Name three operating systems commonly used on PCs.
3. What is an operating system interface?
4. What are the main features of a GUI?
5. Name and briefly describe the purpose of four types of utility software used by Windows 95/98.
6. What is the purpose of the CMOS settings? Typically, what information is stored by the CMOS? What BIOS settings are accessible via the CMOS?
7. Name 4 programming languages.
8. Give examples of special-purpose and general-purpose applications programs.

Unit 2 Assignments

2.1. Software installation

Task 1

Install an applications package, from floppy disk or CD-ROM, onto the hard disk of a stand-alone computer. Record the details of your experience as you go. Although your experience will vary with different packages, you should record the following.

(a) Package details, including the name and type.

(b) Operating system required.

(c) Hardware requirements for the package. The documentation should detail minimum and recommended requirements for the: amount of disk space; type of processor; type of display;

(d) How the target computer system met the requirements in (a) and (c).

(e) Initial instructions for running the 'install' or 'set-up' program.

(f) The name of the directory into which the program was installed. This is most likely to be the one suggested by the install program, but you could choose to install the package in a different directory.

(g) If options are given, which package configuration you chose. Typical alternatives are 'minimum', 'full' or 'custom' install. Record the amount of disk space taken by the chosen configuration.

(h) The action taken once installation was completed.

It is likely that the screen display driver is already installed. If so, check the resolution and colour settings. Record the settings and how you found them.

Task 2

Install the driver program for the system printer. Record the steps you followed and add them to the installation log. Re-save the log and print it.

2.2 Software applications and hardware requirements

Task 1

For this task you are to describe purposes of various kinds of application software and give examples of their uses. First, use appropriate software to create a 3-column table which lists various types of application software in the first column. In the second column, for each type, enter:

(a) a brief statement of the software's general purpose;

(b) one or more examples of typical applications.

To complete this task use a software catalogue or computer magazine to find the names of two or three commercial package examples of each type and enter the names into the third column.

Task 2

This task requires you to select hardware for different types of application software. You need to refer to two tables, the one your created in Task 1 and the one alongside, which lists a range of hardware devices.

CPU	RAM
Hard disk drive	CD-ROM drive
Mouse	DVD-drive
Laser printer	Graphics card
Monitor	Backup device
Plotter	Scanner

For each item in the table provide specification figures for commercial devices you find in hardware catalogues, computer magazines or on the Internet. For example, a hard drive has a *storage capacity*, an *average access time* and *data transfer rate*. For **each** application in Table 1, select one or more of the hardware entries from Table 2. You should only select entries which are **of particular importance** to the application. Using the information from these two tables, prepare a **User Guide** on the selection of suitable hardware for particular types of application software. The Guide should be ordered in the same sequence as the application software types in Table 1. For each type of application software, the User Guide should:

(a) describe the purpose of each type of application software;

(b) describe the hardware devices required for each type of application software, emphasising those which are of particular importance.

(c) briefly explain why the selected hardware is needed, for each application;

(d) quote some actual quality/performance figures for recent examples of the hardware devices.

2.3. Matching application requirements

In this assignment you identify system requirements from a case study. Then, you select appropriate hardware and software which meets those requirements. Before starting this assignment, read the three case studies which follow.

Case study: ComDesign

ComDesign is a graphic design company. Their work requires the use of computers to produce graphics for book covers, book illustrations, CD sleeves, brochures, posters and other similar applications. They also design and create multimedia productions and web sites. Customers provide materials for ComDesign to use in many different formats, including picture and text files on disk, CD-ROMs and paper. Consequently their computer systems must be flexible and capable of storing and handling very large multimedia files. The web design work is expanding so rapidly that they are using Internet facilities continuously for most of each working day.

Case study: Condew Properties

Condew Properties is a local estate agency. The agency sells houses on behalf of *vendors* to *buyers* who come to the agency looking for houses to buy. Records need to be kept of every house for sale, including its address, number of rooms, size of gardens, sale price and so on. When a buyer makes an offer for a house, this also needs to be recorded. Usually, there are several buyers after the same house, so all their details and the prices they have offered also need to be recorded. At any one time there may be hundreds of houses for sale and even more buyers who have put in offers for them. Condew Properties need a system which will store all this information securely and allow details of individual houses and offers to be retrieved quickly. They also need to produce posters with descriptions of the houses for sale. Pictures of the houses are not held on computer, and prints are simply stuck on the posters manually. The posters are put in the agency window to help advertise the properties. Some buyers may spend months looking for the right house and are kept informed of properties as they become available. This is done by keeping their details on a mailing list. The firm has also been considering the possibility of advertising their properties on-line to allow potential customers with Internet access to be able to view property details from their homes.

Case study: Top Flight Accountancy Services

Top flight is run by David Micawber who is a qualified accountant. The firm offers a full range of accountancy services, including the auditing of business accounts and handling of personal and business tax returns to be sent to the Inland Revenue. The law requires that businesses of a certain size must have their annual accounts checked or audited. This must be done by a professional accountant before the accounts are sent to the Inland Revenue to calculate the tax due from the business. The final accounts (a *trading and profit and loss account* and a *balance sheet*) of any particular business are similar from year to year. Although the amounts vary, the layout and the headings tend not to change. This means that David could hold the appropriate layout and headings for each client's final accounts on computer and then fill in the figures to automatically check them. Top Flight is a small firm and only has about 150 regular clients. The volume of printing is fairly low, but the quality should be good enough to give a professional image to David's clients.

Tasks

Write a report that identifies the *system requirements* for each of the three case studies - ComDesign, Condew Properties or Top Flight Accountancy Services. The report should answer the following questions.

(a) What are the main uses of the computer system?

(b) What application software would be required? There may be more than one type of software that could be used for a particular purpose, but state which one you think would be the most suitable and why.

(c) What computer hardware would be needed? Give details of keyboard; mouse; monitor type and size; processor type and speed; RAM capacity; hard drive capacity and average access time; printer type, resolution and speed; number and types of port. Justify your choice of hardware.

2.4. PC connection

Task 1

Demonstrate the connection of typical stand alone computer system components.

Task 2

Produce a report on the procedures carried out in Task 1, identifying any difficulties experienced.

2.5. PC hardware assembly and removal

In this assignment you are required to demonstrate your ability to install and remove PC hardware components located in the system case. For each of the components listed below you will need to demonstrate that you can remove it and replace it while observing appropriate safety precautions.

Each component must be safely removed and then replaced separately, and the system tested for correct operation each time. For example, when you remove and replace a particular component, you must make sure that the computer is switched off and that the power cable is disconnected and unplugged from the case before removing the case cover. You must then perform the particular task and replace the cover. Then you can reconnect external cables and switch the computer on in order to make sure that the computer functions correctly. You will need to keep a log of any problems encountered, the causes of the problems and how you dealt with them, and how you tested the computer for correct operation in each case.

Tasks

Remove and replace the following system components:

> The CPU
> A memory module (eg SIMM or DIMM)
> An expansion card
> A hard drive
> The floppy drive
> The CD-ROM drive

Unit 3: Business information systems

Assessment Evidence Grid

Grade E	Grade C	Grade A
Identify different types of organisational structure.	Provide examples of actual organisations which illustrate variations in organisational structure, from the strictly hierarchical to the 'flatter'.	Provide an analysis of the importance of information to the meeting of an organisation's business objectives. Also, by reference to example applications and siutations, explain why information needs to be communicated upwards, downwards and sideways in an organisation.
Describe and provide examples of functional areas of an organisation.	Analyse data handling and processing methods and by reference to example data handling applications, illustrate their use within organisations.	Explain how, by reference to example data handling applications, the choice of data handling and processing methods are affected by the size and structure of an organisation.
Identify and illustrate the primary information flows which take place between the main business functions in an organisation.	Describe activities which trigger example information flows between functions.	Provide examples of information flows which support operational and strategic decisions in an organisation. Also illustrate the role of ICT in supporting information flow and decision-making.
Illustrate the stages of the data processing cycle by reference to an example data handling application. Also identify an appropriate processing method.	Explain how document design can aid accuracy of data input.	For a suitable data handling application, prepare completed source documents for input, together with suitable batch control documents and explain how they help to assist accuracy and any limitations of the method. Identify and explain the stages of control from data preparation to output.
With the use of an example data handling application, illustrate the role of data control systems in maintaining the validity and accuracy of information.	Compare the physical and operational requirements of business systems and provide an overview of their importance to the business environment.	Provide an evaluation of the importance of ergonomic, security and data protection issues and state how these impact on the physical and operational aspects of business systems.
Produce the source document(s), based on prepared template(s), to capture and input data for a given data handling application.	Describe the stages of the systems life cycle and their importance to the development of organisations.	
Summarise the role of the systems life cycle and describe the stages within it.		

Chapter 16
Organisations

Need for organisations

The society in which we live is complex and sophisticated. As consumers we demand a variety of goods and services to enable us to maintain the quality of life we enjoy. In order to satisfy these demands, suppliers must produce the goods and services which the consumer wants by combining factors of production such as land, labour and capital in the most efficient manner. By this we mean producers must hire workers, rent or buy premises, perhaps invest in plant and machinery and purchase raw materials, and then organise the manufacture of the final product in such a way that they will make a profit. Society may also gain, as its scarce resources are being used in the way consumers wish rather than being wasted in producing things people do not need. Suppliers under such a system are known as commercial organisations. Many public sector organisations also provide goods and services to society and, in the same way as commercial organisations, these public sector bodies must employ staff, occupy premises and raise capital. The fundamental difference between these two types of organisation lies in the objectives they seek to fulfil. The private sector tends to be motivated by profit, while public sector organisations will often have a much less mercenary motive, such as providing for the public good and improving the state of society. If we wish to see society ordered and governed in such a way that individuals are free to express their demands and producers are able to meet such wants, it becomes necessary to form organisations to control and regulate society through a variety of administrative structures. These are the bodies which make up the organisations of the state. In the UK, these are Parliament, the Government and its Executive, the Civil Service, the Local Authorities and the Courts and justice system. These bodies are required to carry out legislative, administrative and judicial functions.

If you examine the nature and range of individual demands in an industrialised society you soon realise that most of them cannot be met other than by organisations. Individually we lack the knowledge, skills and physical resources to manufacture products that fulfil our needs, whether these are simple or sophisticated. It would be as difficult for us to make a biro or a floppy disk as it would a television or a computer. Admittedly, some goods and services can be supplied by an individual working alone. A farmer may be able to grow sufficient food to satisfy himself and his family without any help from others. But what if he requires other goods and services? It is unlikely that the farmer will also have the ability or resources to produce his own combine-harvester or tractor. If he did not have such products which are manufactured by others, his life would be much simpler, but no doubt much harder.

A similar situation exists in the supply of services. A strong and resourceful individual may try to protect himself and his property from the dangers imposed by thieves or vandals. If he cannot, however, then he may turn to the state to demand protection. Recognising that a failure to respond to such demands from its citizens would lead to an anarchic system, the government must accept the responsibility and establish a legal system incorporating law enforcement agencies to provide the protection being sought.

How, then, are these goods and services produced? It is clear that individuals working independently would be unable to meet our complex physical and social needs. Therefore society has developed a system where people join together to form organisations. These bodies are extraordinarily diverse. They manufacture products, which they distribute and sell. They also provide all the services that we need. Thus, both the BBC and the Ford Motor Company are organisations, although their products are very different.

Clearly, then, if individuals within society are to have all their various needs satisfied, there must be co-operation between workers. Each must specialise in a certain aspect of the supply process. These workers must be organised and allocated a specific role in which to perform co-ordinated tasks. These tasks are normally organised with the aim of producing a given product or service, although there are some organisations which do not specialise and which make an extremely diverse range of products. In the private sector of the economy, such businesses will usually have the objective of making a profit for their owners. Of course, this is just one example of an organisation. As we have already noted, the state is another form of organisation which is clearly more complex than a business, and it has a variety of objectives, such as increasing the wealth of citizens, improving their quality of life and protecting them if they are threatened. We are all members of organisations, some of which are formal while others are informal. Your family is an example of an informal organisation, as is the group of friends you mix with. Other more formal organisations to which you may belong or may have belonged are the school you attended as a child, your employing body, or your trade union.

The tendency to form groups is a characteristic of human nature. Human beings are highly socialised, they need to 'belong' and will generally find it uncomfortable and disturbing if they cannot find 'acceptance' within a social group. An employee who is capable and confident in his or her job, and who is in turn regarded by the employer and the rest of the work force as a professional, gains a 'role' satisfaction through identifying as a vital part of the group. So organisations have an important role to fulfil in meeting the social needs of man. However, perhaps more important in the context of this course of study is the function of organisations as the satisfiers of needs. They allow individual workers to develop their specialist skills, and this in turn allows productive capacity to increase.

Since differing organisations concentrate on the supply of different goods and services, there must be a system established whereby products can be distributed to the consumers. Thus shops, wholesalers, transport companies and so on must all be involved. The fabric of the social and economic environment is based on a process whereby individuals form organisations which are dependent upon other organisations to survive. In just the same way as the needs of the individual cannot be met by that individual alone, so the same also holds true for organisations. They are interdependent. Organisational activity involves a perpetual interaction, one organisation with another, as society steadily evolves in a direction that individually and collectively we try to guide. However, as we shall see, even though the overall aim of society is the advancement of our physical well-being, the methods for achieving this are the subject of much disagreement.

Characteristics common to all organisations

The specific reasons for the formation of organisations are many and varied, and may not, of course, always be clearly defined. Some are the result of the need for individuals to find company for a social or leisure reason, for example by forming a sporting or working-men's club. Others are formed with a more precise economic objective in mind, such as the desire to make a profit for the person who has established a business organisation. Some, such as the organisations which make up the state and government, evolve as a result of the emergence of particular needs in society which require government intervention. For example, the Government established the National Health Service in 1946 to meet the needs of society for a high standard of free health care, available to all. Nevertheless, most formal organisations have some common characteristics. These may be simply stated as follows:

(i) The establishment of an organisation is usually for a specific purpose.

For example, the Automobile Association was founded with the precise objective of promoting the interests of motorists within this country. Other organisations may be launched with one prime aim, but may later diversify in order to follow alternative causes or objectives. For instance, Guinness, the brewery company, was established to produce alcoholic drinks, but now has subsidiaries making a variety of products such as fishing tackle boxes and cassette cases. This illustrates how a business may try to evolve as the commercial environment changes and new commercial opportunities emerge.

(ii) Organisations usually have a distinct identity.

People belonging to a specific organisation can identify themselves as being part of a group either as a result of where they work or of what they do. A Manchester United footballer wears a red shirt to show he is part of the particular organisation. A member of a trade union is given a membership card to signify he belongs to that union. Manufacturing companies promote their brand names through advertising. This sense of identity, which we have already seen is an important need for most people, can produce extreme loyalty to the organisation.

(iii) Most organisations require some form of leadership.

We have seen that organisations are normally formed for a specific purpose. In order to achieve this purpose, it is necessary to co-ordinate the efforts of the members of the organisation. This requires management, or leadership. Formal organisations such as companies or a club have a specified management hierarchy which may be appointed by the owners of the organisation. For instance, the shareholders of a company appoint the directors. Alternatively, the leadership may be elected, as in the case of a club or society where the members vote to have a chairman, secretary and committee. However, once appointed this management team has the responsibility for ensuring the organisation achieves its objectives.

(iv) Organisations are accountable.

Such accountability applies both to those the management team deals with and those it employs.

Objectives of organisations

The objectives of an organisation are the targets it hopes to achieve. Clearly the objectives which are set will vary considerably between different types of organisation. As we shall see later in this section, the objectives of commercial organisations will largely be based around the goal of profit. For organisations within the public sector, profit may not be the sole aim. Factors such as benefit to the community or the creation of jobs may also feature as targets for the public sector. It should be noted, however, that the profit motive has grown substantially in importance in recent times.

A classification of organisations

Initially, it is convenient to categorise organisations as: *public service*; *commercial*; *industrial*.

Public service organisations

Many public services are provided by central and local government (the public sector) Central government takes responsibility for a wide range of services and has specific organisations, referred to as Departments, to manage each. Thus, there are separate departments, each responsible for the provision of, amongst others, health, education, defence and social welfare services. The role of local government is continually changing as successive governments pursue policies which tend to centralise power, or devolve it to locally elected council bodies. The provision of water, electricity and gas services used to be provided by 'public utilities', but they have been 'privatised' and now operate as commercial and industrial businesses. Some services, traditionally provided by the public sector, are now partly in the private sector; for example, some prisons are privately owned and private companies may carry out the work of refuse collection. Even so, overall control of such services is still the responsibility of central and local government departments. Table 16.1 lists some major central government organisations and briefly describes the responsibilities of each. Table 16.2 does the same, in respect of local government.

Government departments	Responsibilities
Education	Schools.
Transport	Road and building.
Home Office	Law and order, police and prison services policy.
Health	Hospitals.
Trade and Industry	Business and industrial policy.
Social Security	Benefits such as income support.
Treasury	Economic policy.
Defence	Armed Forces.

Table 16.1. *Central Government Departments and areas of responsibility*

It should be noted that although the government departments retain overall responsibility for the areas listed in the Table, private companies carry out some of the work. For example, some hospitals, prisons and schools are privately owned. As part of the government's 'privatisation' programme, local councils have to allow private businesses to tender for (compete for) work traditionally carried out by their own departments; this is called Compulsory Competitive Tendering (CCT).

For example, private businesses can tender for contracts to carry out street sweeping or refuse collection. In addition, some schools have 'opted out' and receive their funding directly from central governments.

Local Government departments	Responsibilities
Social Services	Home helps, children's homes, meals on wheels, day nurseries, residential homes and day centres for the mentally ill.
Education	Nursery, and secondary schools.
Housing	Council housing provides affordable accommodation for those who cannot buy their own homes.
Environmental Services	Refuse collection and disposal, street sweeping and pollution control.
Police and Fire Services	Although there is co-operation between forces, these services are still locally controlled.
Planning and Building Control	Consider applications for local building and enforce regulations on building standards.

Table 16.2. *Local Government Departments and areas of responsibility*

Industry and commerce

The term 'industry' covers a wide range of organisations which form part of a country's economy. We tend to link factories with the idea of industry, but the term also covers: *extraction* industries, such as coal-mining and fishing; *manufacturing* businesses which take raw materials and process them into finished products, such as cars and clothing, as well as those assembling ready-made components into, for example, computers and televisions; *retail* and *wholesale* businesses, concerned with buying, selling and distributing goods for personal and business consumption; *service* industries, such as hotel, catering, travel and banking. The word 'commerce' overlaps with 'industry' and includes all forms of trading organisation and those which support trade, such as banking and insurance.

Organisational structures

A structure can be defined as having component parts, which are connected in a particular way. Structures are designed to fulfil purposes. For example, a house is a structure, consisting of rooms, windows, floors, ceilings, doors and connection passages; the mix of these component parts and the way they are put together determines the design of the house. Two main types of organisational structure are considered here: *hierarchical*; *flat* (or 'flatter').

Hierarchical structure

An organisation with a hierarchical structure includes different levels of authority and responsibility. Heads of Department may be directly responsible to one of the Directors. For example, the Accounts Department Head may be subject to the authority of the Financial Director. Such authority relates to the operation of the organisation and enables tasks to be completed. There may be Section Supervisors who are responsible to their respective Heads of Department for particular functions within departments. Each section supervisor may have authority over a number of clerks. Generally, there are more 'workers' than 'bosses', so a hierarchical structure can be viewed as a pyramid, as shown in Figure 16.1. The Figure also shows an organisation chart with the same levels in the hierarchy and the various directions in which information can flow within the hierarchy, upwards, downwards, sideways and diagonally.

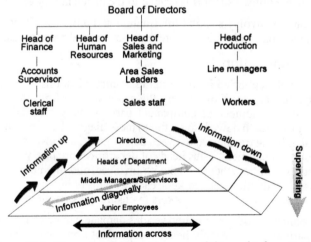

Figure 16.1. *Hierarchy of authority, responsibility and information flow*

The lower down the pyramid you descend, the larger the number of staff you are likely to find employed. The jobs at the top of the pyramid carry the most authority and the greatest responsibility for the success or failure of the organisation. Operatives and clerical staff are unlikely to have any authority in the organisation, but they have responsibility for the completion of their own jobs.

Downward communication

Figure 16.1 shows that, within the pyramid, communications go up and down. Policy decisions taken at board level by the directors are implemented by instructing the relevant departmental heads to see that the policy is carried out. The heads of department brief their middle managers and the final stage in the process is the communication between middle managers and their subordinates.

Downward communications will predominantly involve the issue of: (a) directives or general orders, such as a rule that no one below a certain level or authority shall make long distance telephone calls before 1 p.m.; (b) specific orders, such as an instruction to report a fault or clean a machine; and (c) requests. Additionally, downward communications will often involve the granting of authority to a subordinate, or confirmation of the action taken by a subordinate.

Upward communication

The communication also passes from the bottom upwards. Staff provide feedback to their seniors. This may take many forms; it may involve monitoring shortages of materials, absences of staff, production problems, grievances and suggestions for improving work methods. Anything which requires the authority or approval of someone further up the organisational hierarchy and which has been generated or identified below, will pass back up the system. Only in extreme circumstances is it likely that an issue arising at the bottom of the pyramid will pass right back to the top for consideration and decision. For the most part, an immediate senior is likely to have sufficient authority to make a decision; ultimately however, it is a question of the extent of *delegated* responsibility held by senior employees that determines whether they can deal with it personally, or must pass it back to their own superiors. As organisations grow bigger it is inevitable that communications have much further to travel. This is not ideal since it is likely to take longer to transmit information and there is greater distancing between the giver and the receiver, which can lead to a 'them and us' view of the organisation by junior staff. However, it is clear that as the organisation grows, so its communication system must be become increasingly refined. Information technology support is crucial to the efficiency of communications.

Upward communications involve seeking information and advice and obtaining authority to act, and include suggestions and criticisms presented by subordinates to superiors.

Horizontal communication

Within each of the levels identified in the pyramid, communications also take place horizontally, that is to say, between staff of broadly the same status within the bands. Since most organisations consist of a number of component parts, usually referred to as departments (which are often further broken down into sections) these diagonal communications will invariably involve messages being transferred between departments, as most of the workforce will be attached to a particular department. Thus heads of department are likely to meet regularly. Junior staff may need to work together to deal with invoices, and in an organisation engaged in production processes, production line workers, each with his or her own particular responsibility, will need to co-operate with fellow workers to ensure the smooth running of the line.

When horizontal communication is impaired serious damage can be caused to the entire enterprise, for each department is inevitably heavily dependant upon other departments if it is to function effectively. Horizontal communications are essentially concerned with information exchange, for example, the giving and receiving of data between departments, and working on joint or group projects.   .

Diagonal communication

This occurs when staff at different levels within the organisation and who work in different departments, are involved in communicating with each other. For instance a Sales and Marketing Manager may request financial information from a financial assistant in the accounts department, or a junior employee in the production department may need personal details about a newly appointed employee to the department, information which is held by the Personnel Manager. Both in the case of diagonal communications, and those across the organisation, care and tact are called for, since staff in one department are not accountable to staff in another department, so it would generally be out of order for a senior member of department A to issue an instruction to an employee in department B, or seek to discipline someone in department C.

Flatter structure

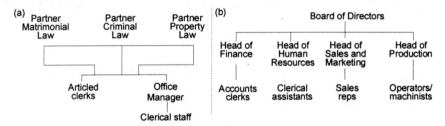

Figure 16.2. *Flatter structure*

In contrast to a hierarchy, a flatter structure generally has a single, or at the most, two levels of management, as shown in Figure 16.2. Except for the smallest organisations, very few will have an entirely flat structure. It is possible, that an organisation wishes to avoid a cumbersome hierarchy and attempts to keep the number of management levels to a minimum; they are thus aiming for a 'flatter' structure. As mentioned earlier, hierarchies with many levels of authority can make communication difficult. A flatter structure can encourage 'team spirit' through the avoidance of the 'them and us' feelings, which can be characteristic of hierarchies. Figure 16.2a represents a firm of solicitors, where each partner has the same level of authority and responsibility, specialises in a particular aspect of the law and has joint authority over the Office Manager and articled clerks ('apprentice' solicitors). The Office Manager is responsible for supervision of the clerical staff. Although there are hierarchical elements in the organisation, its structure is fairly 'flat'. Figure 16.2b represents a larger organisation which has attempted to keep the number of management levels to a minimum. One consequence of removing a level of management from a large and complex organisation may be to increase the workload of at each remaining level. On the other hand, the extra levels of management maye have resulted in some duplication of effort and unnecessary bureaucracy which stifled initiative and prevented progress and change.

✍ Exercises

1. Choose three formal organisations with which you are familiar and for each:
    (a) identify its main *purpose*;
    (b) select an aspect which gives it its distinct *identity*;
    (c) briefly describe how it is *lead* - its top management structure;
    (d) identify to whom the management are ultimately *accountable*.
2. Use the examples you gave in 1. to illustrate characterstics common to all organisations.
3. The water industry used to be in the public sector, but is now run by private companies, overseen by a regulator (OFFWAT). Briefly list features which allow   the privatised water company to be classified as both commercial and public service.
4. (a) Choose a hierarchically structured organisation with which you are familiar and using Figure 16.1 as a guide, draw a pyramid structure to show the main levels of authority.
    (b) Identify two benefits and two drawbacks of the structure for the chosen organisation.
    (c) Comment on the potential difficulties of reducing levels of management in a large organisation.

Chapter 17

Functional areas of organisations

This Chapter investigates some of the main functional areas to be found in organisations:

- ❏ financial accounting
- ❏ payroll and personnel;
- ❏ invoicing and stock control;
- ❏ design and production;
- ❏ marketing;
- ❏ ICT services.

Financial accounting

Financial accounting or 'book-keeping' is the process of recording financial transactions arising from the day-to-day operation of a business. The sale of goods to a customer and the subsequent settlement of the debt are two examples of financial transactions. More detailed information on financial accounting systems is provided in Chapter 19.

Sales accounting

Sales accounting is also known as Accounts Receivable, which is the subject of the design tutorial in Unit 6. When credit sales are made to customers, a record needs to be kept of amounts owing and paid. Payment is normally requested with an invoice, which gives details of goods supplied, quantities, prices and VAT. Credit sales are usually made on for example, a 14, 21 or 28 day basis, which means that the customer has to pay within the specified period to obtain any discounts offered. Overdue payments need to be chased, so sales accounting systems normally produce reports analysing the indebtedness of different customers. Debt control is vital to business profitability and computerised systems can produce prompt and up-to-date reports as a by-product of the main application.

Purchase accounting

Purchase accounting is also known as Accounts Payable. This function is concerned with controlling amounts owed and payments made to suppliers of services, goods or materials which are used in the main business of the company. For example, a car manufacturer will need to keep records of amounts owing to suppliers of car components and sheet steel manufacturers. Delayed payments to suppliers may help cash flow, but can harm an organisation's image, or even cut off a source of supply when a supplier refuses to deliver any more goods until payment is made.

Nominal or general ledger

The general ledger keeps control of financial summaries, including those originating from payroll, sales and purchase accounting and acts as a balance in a double entry system. Computerised systems can automatically produce reports at the end of financial periods, including a trial balance, trading and profit and loss account and balance sheet.

Other finance-related functions

Stock control

Any organisation which keeps stocks of raw materials or finished goods needs to operate a stock control system. Although stock constitutes an asset, it ties up cash resources that could be invested in other aspects of the business. Equally, a company must keep sufficient quantities of items to satisfy customer demand or manufacturing requirements. To maintain this balance a stock control system should provide up-to-date information on quantities, prices, minimum stock levels, and re-order quantities. It should also give warning of excessively high, or dangerously low levels of stock. In the latter case, orders may be produced automatically. A stock control system may also generate valuable management reports on, for example, sales patterns, slow-moving items, and overdue orders. The functions of stock control are examined in more detail in Chapter 19.

Sales order processing

This function will normally be concerned with:

☐ the validation of orders, checking, for example, that the goods ordered are supplied by the business or that the customer's credit status warrants the order's completion;

☐ the identification of individual items ordered. A customer may request several different items on the same order form and any particular item will probably appear on many different order forms, so the quantities for each are totalled to produce picking lists to enable warehouse staff to retrieve the goods for despatch;

☐ the monitoring of back orders. If an order cannot be fulfilled, it may be held in abeyance until new stocks arrive, so all outstanding back orders need to be available on request.

Invoicing

This function deals with the production of customer invoices, requesting payment for goods or services delivered. Information stored in the customer files and stock files is used to produce invoices, usually on pre-printed continuous stationery.

A detailed description and pictorial illustration of sales order processing and invoicing are provided at the beginning of the systems design tutorial Chapter 38 in Unit 6.

Payroll

Payroll systems are concerned with the production of payslips for employees and the maintenance of records required for taxation and other deductions. In a manual system, the preparation of payroll figures and the maintenance of payroll records is a labour intensive task. Although tedious and repetitive, it is a vitally important task. Most employees naturally regard pay as being the main reason for work and resent delays in payment or incorrect payments, unless of course it is in their favour! The repetitive nature of the task makes it a popular candidate for computerisation, especially with organisations which employ large numbers of people. The automatic production of reports for taxation purposes also provides a valuable benefit.

Smaller organisations with only several employees probably do not regard payroll as a high priority application for computerisation. The benefits are not as great if the payroll can be carried out by one or two employees who also carry out a number of other tasks.

Human resources or personnel

The human resources (personnel) function is responsible for the selection (usually by interview), recruitment, training and development of staff. Personnel records will store all the information needed by Salaries and Wages to make the correct payments to employees; this will include details of, for example, gross salary, tax code, statutory sick pay and holiday entitlement. Depending on the size of the organisation, information may also be held concerning: qualifications, courses attended; personal and career development plans.

Design

The design function is present where an organisation develops its own products and services; a trader who simply buys and sells goods has no need of a design team. Design is part of the research and development (R& D) function, which is vital to organisations wishing to radically develop their product range. The nature of design teams depends on the product or service being designed. The skills and talents of a car design team are clearly very different from those of a team designing a cover for a magazine.

Production

The production function should, ideally, be driven by the market for the business's products. In other words, it should be geared to produce the necessary mix and quantities of products required by customers. If goods are perishable within a short time, and large reserve stocks cannot be held, then production should be flexible and responsive to the day-to-day sales requirements. Of course, this is an ideal and production plans cannot always be changed at short notice; ships and other large items take months or years to build. The production department must know exactly what is required and when; it must also have the staff with the necessary skills and any machinery must have the appropriate facilities and production capacity. For example, a production department which is geared to produce 1000 units of a product per day, will probably find it difficult to produce 2000 units, without modification of the system of production.

Marketing

A marketing function is a vital part of many large national and international businesses; it aims to generate information, from a wide range of data sources, to support marketing decisions. Three such decision areas are:

(i) *strategic* and relating to, for example, expansion of the company's existing market share and the identification of new marketable products;

(ii) *tactical*, for example, planning the marketing mix;

(iii) *operational*, for example, day-to-day planning of sales calls and ad hoc promotions.

At the operational level, for example, data gathered from sales invoices, sales force staff and accounting information can be used to establish customer types. Thus, customers can be classified as 'low', 'medium' or 'high' volume users according to the frequency and volume of their orders. This information can help sales staff to target particular categories of customer and to plan the timing of sales calls.

At the tactical level, invoices provide information on sales variance between market segments over time or sales projections based on current patterns.

Distribution

Distribution concerns the delivery of a company's products to its customers and is obviously of great importance. An organisation can have the best products in the world and the most effective marketing campaigns, but if it cannot distribute its goods efficiently it will fail. Distribution systems include the management and control of a company's own delivery vehicles and drivers, the scheduling of deliveries to ensure rapid response to orders and efficient use of the transport fleet. If a company does not have its own vehicles, then it must arrange for suitable contracts with other companies, such as Parcel Force, UPS and Securicor. Systems must also be in place for the handling of delayed deliveries and customer complaints, order tracking (buyers can check on the progress of their order) and the return of unwanted or damaged goods.

Controlling the costs of distribution, which can be considerable, is of major importance. For example, the breakdown of distribution costs across manufacturing industry is typically as follows: administration 17%; transport 29%; handling 8%; packaging 12%; warehousing 17%; stock control 17%.

Administration

Administration systems provide support and services across the organisation. They include, for example, the handling of telephone switchboard and fax and photocopying services, document production, room booking (for meetings etc), requisitioning of equipment and consumables, and general secretarial support. ICT services are part of that administration support service.

ICT Services

Apart from small firms, most organisations need specialist staff to develop, introduce, maintain and update the various systems which make use of information technology. The term 'information communication technology' covers all computer-based information processing systems, plus those which make use of data communications, such as computer networks, fax machines, photocopiers and telephone systems. The responsibilities of ICT Services are, therefore, much broader than those traditionally held by wholly centralised computer services or data processing departments. The development of cheaper and more powerful microcomputer systems, which can be networked with one another, as well as with larger mini and mainframe systems, has resulted in computer facilities being distributed more widely. For this reason, ICT Services needs to provide a much more flexible service and support user systems at the point of use. For example, users of network workstations need support when equipment, such as a shared printer, breaks down or they may require help in the use of software on the network. This contrasts with a centralised department, which holds all the computer equipment, carries out all computer processing and restricts user access to specialised applications, run through dedicated terminals. ICT Services may be known variously as Computer Services, Management Information Services or less commonly now, the Data Processing Department.

Role of ICT Services

ICT Services fulfils a servicing function for the whole organisation. In larger organisations, there is a centralised computer facility, possibly in the shape of a mainframe or mini-computer system, with the responsibility for major applications, such as payroll and stock control. User departments may have access to the centralised facility through attached terminals or networked microcomputers. Individual members of staff may also use stand-alone microcomputer systems or portable devices, such as notebooks and personal digital assistants (PDAs). ICT Services staff need to support users in the use of these distributed facilities, as well as control the operation of any centralised system. ICT Services provides facilities to satisfy both *operational* and *managerial* information needs.

Operational requirements

Each functional area has its own operational information needs. For example, Wages and Salaries need payroll details and payslips, and Sales Order Processing require the production of customer invoices. Common examples of routine operations include:

- keeping stock records
- payroll;
- routine costing;

- sales accounting and purchase accounting;
- invoicing and production of delivery notes;
- filing of customer orders.

Managerial requirements

Routine processing work forms the bulk of the activity within ICT Services, but there is an increasing demand for management information. This includes assistance with functions which require management involvement and thinking, but which can be partially automated or assisted by computers. Examples of such functions include:

- production planning;
- setting of budgets;
- marketing decisions and sales management;
- price determination;

- short term and long term forecasting;
- decision-making on financial policies;
- factory maintenance and management;
- selection of suppliers.

Function of ICT Services

Figure 17.1 shows the typical functions within an ICT Services department.

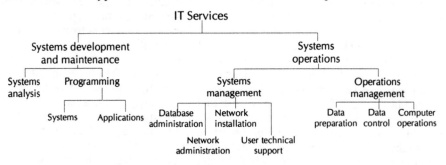

Figure 17.1. *Typical structure of ICT Services department*

Systems development

This function relates to the development of new computerised systems and the maintenance of existing ones. This function is staffed primarily by *systems analysts* and *programmers*. In small organisations, hybrid skills are often needed, so job titles such as *analyst programmer* may be used.

Systems analysis

Systems analysis is a process used in the design of new systems, as requested by corporate management. Systems analysis follows stages of *investigation*, *design* and *implementation*. Each stage should involve close consultation with potential users, in the various functional areas of the organisation, to ensure that their information and operational requirements are met.

The design stage should produce a *system specification* which, rather like an architect's plans for a building, details all necessary materials and procedures needed to fulfil the specification. The specification should detail the necessary clerical procedures, hardware requirements and the inputs, processing and outputs required of the computer software.

After implementation of a system, it will require continual monitoring and probably, occasional modification, when the operational or information requirements of users change. This maintenance task is the responsibility of the systems analysts,

Programming

Programming lacks some of the creative aspects of systems analysis and involves the use of a programming language (for example, C++, COBOL, Visual BASIC) to code the necessary computer programs. The program requirements are detailed in the *program* or *software specification*, which forms part of the system specification prepared by systems analysts.

Most programmers who work in an ICT Services department are likely to be *applications programmers*, responsible for the development or modification of applications, such as stock control or payroll. Systems programmers are concerned with the development of operating systems and utilities, which are normally developed by large computer manufacturers or software companies, such as Microsoft. An ICT Services department may also employ *systems programmers*, but they are likely to have a more limited role than applications programmers. Much software is now in commercial package form, but not all applications can be satisfied by such means and applications programmers continue to be needed for tailoring of programs specifically for their employer.

The growth of network use has created the need for *network programmers*, who have specialist knowledge of such systems. Apart from specialising in systems, applications or network programming, a programmer is likely to be skilled in the use of one or more programming languages. An organisation seeking to employ programmers will specify the language or languages they require.

System operations

This broad function is concerned with the operational, rather than the developmental aspects of the ICT systems. It is divided into *systems management* and *operations management*.

Systems management

This function deals with the general operation of all the ICT systems and is not directly concerned with particular applications.

There are a number of separate areas within this function: *network installation*; *network administration*; *intranet and extranet management*; *user technical support*; *database administration*.

Network installation and administration

Computer networks are a feature of most organisations and tasks of selecting, purchasing and installing the hardware and software, both systems and applications, may be carried out by specialist staff in this area. Staff employed in this area need to be familiar with the network operating system and its utilities. They are responsible for setting up and managing network user accounts, controlling passwords, managing printer queues, allocating and maintaining and backing up network storage and monitoring the performance of the network.

User technical support

The distribution to users, of computer resources through networks, desktop and portable computer systems has hugely expanded the need for ICT user support. Users often have access to a range of different devices, such as printers, scanners, plotters and fax modems and apart from needing initial training in their use, they also require occasional support when things go wrong. Support staff may also give guidance in the use of software and help trouble-shoot problems which users will inevitably encounter at some stage. User technical support is extremely important if users are to use ICT resources efficiently and for the benefit of the organisation.

Database administration

If applications are implemented through a database system, then specialist staff, known as database administrators, are employed to control access to the database by applications and ensure consistency in the use of data within it. Systems analysts and programmers involved in the development of database applications need to work closely with the responsible *database administrator* (DBA).

Operations management

This function, led by an operations manager, several areas of responsibility: *data control*; *data preparation*; *computer operations*; *media library* (storage of data file backups and software installation disks).

These responsibilities relate particularly to centrally controlled applications.

Data control

Data control staff are responsible for the co-ordination and control of data flowing through the operations section. For example, data received from Salaries, to update the payroll master file and produce payslips, have to be controlled to ensure their accuracy and completeness at all stages of processing.

Data preparation

Batch processing systems require the transcription and encoding of data gathered from source documents, such as order forms or invoices, on to magnetic storage. The input is then effected directly from the magnetic tape or disk on which the data has been accumulated. On-line, transaction processing systems, do not usually require this data preparation stage.

Computer operations

Computer operators are responsible for the day-to-day running of the computer hardware. In the case of mainframe computer systems, their responsibilities include the loading and unloading of magnetic tape reels or magnetic disk packs, according to the on-line requirements of applications currently in use. For example, before a payroll run, the media containing the master and transaction files have to be loaded onto the relevant devices, so that they can be accessed by the computer which is running the payroll program. The computer hardware is under the control of operating system software and an operator needs to communicate with the operating system regarding jobs to be processed and to deal with error conditions which may arise. A separate terminal is normally dedicated as an *operator console* and access to it is restricted both physically and through software-controlled passwords.

✎ Exercises

1. Machem Ltd is a large manufacturing business. It buys in raw materials from a number of suppliers and uses the raw materials to produce its range of specialist outdoor clothing and equipment, which it sells to retailers. It has a warehouse next to the factory, to store the stocks of raw materials and finished goods.

    (a) Explain the circumstances when Machem Ltd is a *debtor* and when it is a *creditor*.

    (b) Explain circumstances when Machem will receive *invoices* and when it will issue them.

    (c) List the processes involved in invoicing a retailer and settlement of the debt.

    (d) Identify features of a typical *stock control* system which Machem Ltd could use to maintain sufficient, but not excessive levels of stock.

    (e) Machem Ltd is planning to extend its range of products and needs to ensure that there will be sufficient demand for the new products to make a profit. As well as its production function, the company has its own research and development (R&D) and marketing departments. Suggest ways in which these three functions may co-operate to maximise Machem Ltd's chances of success.

2. Machem Ltd has its own *ICT Services* function, employing systems analysts, programmers, network engineers, network administrators and user technical support assistants.

    Briefly outline the likely role of each of these categories of staff at Machem Ltd.

Chapter 18

Information in organisations

Role of information

In business, making decisions or taking actions without all the relevant information can be risky. For example, if a company decides to increase the price of a product because the product is selling well and ignores information that competitors have launched similar products, it is acting without all the relevant information. Similarly, fulfilling a customer order without checking their credit record risks an increase in bad (unrecoverable) debt. Information can vary in quality and to provide the best possible basis for decision-making, organisations should attempt to control the quality of the information they use. If it is to act with any purpose, an organisation needs information about itself, its customers (or clients) and suppliers (if any) and the *environment* in which it operates. Environment includes influences which are external to an organisation, such as government legislation and bank lending rates. Without such information, an organisation cannot properly plan for the future (*strategic planning*), or control and monitor its present performance (*operational control*).

Strategic planning

Planning for the future is never risk-free, but with a range of appropriate information the risks of decision-making can be minimised. Suppose, for example, that a manufacturing company is planning its production output for the next month; it needs to specify the particular product mix and the number of units of each product to be manufactured. In making these decisions, it is likely to draw on two main sources of information:

- ❏ past sales figures;
- ❏ market research results.

Decisions of this nature are likely to be made at corporate (Board of Directors) level and fall into a category known as *strategic* decision-making.

Operational control

When a company monitors its production figures, its stocks of raw materials and finished products, its is controlling its day-to-day, manufacturing operations. Other functions in the company, such as sales, payroll and accounts require similar operational control. Operational information permits day-to-day control to be exerted and allows measurement of present performance, as opposed to future prospects. Examples of operational information include:

- ❏ balances of customer accounts;
- ❏ invoices for customer sales;
- ❏ delivery notes for goods received from suppliers.

Periodic monitoring through Annual Accounts

The production of statements, such as a Trading and Profit and Loss Account and Balance Sheet, provides information on the financial health of a company, at the time the statements are produced. These statements are a legal requirement for all but the smallest businesses, but are useful for periodic monitoring of performance. Accounting records are essential to effective decision-making and also produce information demanded by, for example, shareholders, the Inland Revenue or the VAT authorities. Not all information generated within or used by an organisation can be categorised as wholly operational or corporate. Information which is classed initially as operational can become part of corporate information. For example, the operational information that a customer has failed to pay their account in two successive months may result in a suspension of further credit. Subsequently, this information may be combined with details of similar customer accounts to produce a bad debts report, which results in a corporate decision to alter customer credit and debt collection strategy.

Information systems

The production of information needs to be a controlled process, exercised through the use of information systems. An organisation can be divided into a number of *internal* functions, such as Sales, Marketing, Production and Accounts and each function requires its own information systems or sub-systems. The information system for any one functional area should not be considered in isolation, because it forms only part of an organisation-wide information system. This is made particularly clear when database systems are used. The various information systems within an organisation interact and affect one another. An organisation also interacts with and is influenced by organisations, such as banks and the Inland Revenue, in the surrounding environment; these are *external* functions. Co-ordination of an organisation's separate information systems or sub-systems is essential if its common aims are to be achieved.

Information needs

To operate, different functions within an organisation need access to particular types of information, some examples of which are briefly described below.

Design specifications; before a product is manufactured a specification is produced detailing, for example, the types, qualities and quantities of required materials, physical features, performance requirements (such as for a car) and so on. Some products, such as computer software, need to include design features concerning, for example, the user interface.

Construction drawings. As the term indicates, these are used to guide the person or persons building or constructing the product. An architect produces construction drawings for the house builder to follow; design specification details are also included, so that the builder knows the types and quantities of materials.

Market research. This information is often gathered through surveys, either using questionnaires or monitoring consumer buying patterns. A company should carry out market research before beginning the production or sale of a new product in its range.

Advertising is essential to any organisation wishing to promote its image or product range. Advertising uses market research information to target the most appropriate areas of the population. For example, market research may indicate that a product is most likely to be bought by professional people living in the south of England; advertising can be directed, perhaps through mails shots, to that section of the population.

Sales orders detail customer order requirements, including item details, quantities and delivery dates; *purchase orders* detail the organisation's purchase requirements from suppliers.

Payments and receipts. These may relate to sales orders or purchase orders. Receipts are amounts received from debtors. Payments are made by a business to settle debts with creditors (suppliers to the business).

Transport requirements. This information will detail, for example, a goods list, the delivery address, special requirements, such as refrigeration and possibly the route to be taken.

Information flow diagrams

Figure 18.1 illustrates some information flows within a typical manufacturing and wholesaling organisation. An examination of the Figure shows that each functional area is dependent on one or more other areas for the information it needs to operate. For example, to charge the retail outlets (their customers) for the goods supplied, the Accounting function requires the necessary sales information, which is supplied by the Sales function. The information allows the Accounting function to prepare the necessary invoices to send to customers. Similarly, Purchasing must be kept informed by the Warehouse (stock control) of raw materials which need re-ordering from suppliers, to replenish stocks.

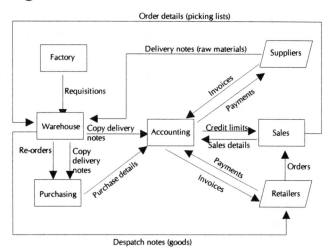

Figure 18.1. *Information flows between functions*

These examples of *operational* information allow day-to-day decisions to be made on the operation of the business. To keep the diagram fairly simple, certain vital functions, such as Production Control and Marketing, are not shown. Obviously, their inclusion would increase the number of information flows and the complexity of the diagram. The information flows shown in Figure 18.1 are all 'triggered' by *events*. For example:

   (i)   a customer order is generated when a customer orders goods;

   (ii)   credit limit details flow from Accounting to Sales, when a customer order is checked;

   (iii) an invoice is raised when goods are despatched to a customer;

   (iv) a payment to a supplier is triggered when the invoice payment falls due.

An information flow diagram may also illustrate the transmission medium or method used for each flow. For example, an interaction between two functions may be face-to-face, by e-mail, a video conferencing link, fax, electronic point-of-sale (EPOS), web site, or one of several other methods outlined at the end of this chapter.

ICT support of information flows

Teleconferencing

This service allows users to support a discussion over the telephone with a shared computer application, such as a word processor, spreadsheet or drawing package and a common whiteboard (an area of the display screen) visible to the conference users. The whiteboard is a comment or drawing area which users can use to illustrate points they wish to make. Each user has the ability to control the application, allowing co-operative development of, for example, a drawing or a spreadsheet model. Of course, such application sharing needs to be carefully managed and controlled to avoid inefficiency and time-wasting, which may result if users have different views on how the drawing or model should develop. The voice communications may be carried out over a conventional telephone network or over the Internet as part of the teleconferencing package. Microsoft's NetMeeting is built into the Explorer browser and supports all these facilities.

Video conferencing

Using computers with attached video cameras, microphones and speakers, conference participants are able to see and hear one another. The audio and video signals are carried over the Internet for real-time display as the conference takes place. The availability of cheap mini video cameras has radically increased the popularity of this service. Both tele and video conferencing have the potential to make significant savings for organisations in staffing, travel and accommodation costs. The main cost derives from local rate telephone charges.

Bibliographic databases

These databases provide information on specialised or widely ranging subjects. For example, BLAISE, which is provided by the British Library, gives information on British book publications. Euronet Diane (Direct Information Access Network in Europe) provides information extracted from publications, research documents and so on, which may be of interest to specialists, such as scientists, engineers, economists and lawyers. Each extract provides the relevant bibliographic references to allow users to access the original sources more fully.

Bulletin boards

A bulletin board (BB) is simply a means by which users can, for example, exchange ideas, pass on information and buy or sell items to one another. Frequently, no charge is made. Chat lines are often included; this means that two users can carry on a conversation, through the use of screen and keyboard.

Telex

Telex is a well established communications system which, rather like the public telephone network, allows subscribers to communicate with one another. There are over a million subscribers in this country at present. Each subscriber is given a telex code (you will often see it at the top of business letter headings next to the telephone number) and must have a teleprinter which is a combination of keyboard and printer. There is no screen, so all messages sent or received are printed onto hard copy. The transmission rate of approximately 6 characters per second is slow compared with more modern telecommunications systems, but the limitations of keyboard entry and printer speed on the teleprinter, make any faster speed unnecessary. The main benefit of telex is that a permanent record of communications is kept and the receiver does not have to be on the spot when the message arrives. Its main disadvantage is that there is no storage facility for messages. Any transmission has to be printed as soon as it is transmitted so that if the receiver is faulty, the system comes to a halt. Although it is inferior to e-mail (see next paragraph), it is still the only method (apart from telephone) of instant communication with less developed countries, where Telex machines are still widely used.

Electronic mail (e-mail) services

E-mail systems based on computer networks are paper-less (except when a user requires hard copy). A major advantage is the facility for message storage if a destination terminal is busy, or has a temporary fault. When it is free, the message can be transmitted. Certain basic features can be identified as being common to all e-mail systems:

❏ a terminal for preparing, entering and storing messages. The terminal will be intelligent, possibly a microcomputer, mainframe terminal or dedicated word processor. In any event, it should have some word processing or text editing facilities to allow messages to be changed on screen before transmission. A printer may also be available for printing out messages received over the system;

❑ an electronic communication link with other workstations in the network and with the central computer controlling the system;

❑ a directory containing the electronic addresses of all network users;

❑ a central mailbox facility (usually the controlling computer) for the storage of messages in transit or waiting to be retrieved.

Ideally, the following facilities are available to e-mail users:

❑ messages are automatically dated upon transmission;

❑ messages are automatically acknowledged as being received when the recipient first accesses it from the terminal;

❑ multiple addressing, that is the facility to address a message to an identified group, without addressing each member of the group individually;

❑ priority rating to allow messages to be allocated different priorities according to their importance.

Networks require two particular features in order to support e-mail:

❑ a message storage facility to allow messages to be forwarded when the recipient is available;

❑ compatibility with a wide range of manufacturers' equipment. Devices attached to a network have to be able to talk to the communications network using protocols or standards of communication.

Benefits of e-mail

The following major benefits are generally claimed for e-mail systems:

❑ savings in stationery and telephone costs;

❑ more rapid transmission than is possible with conventional mail;

❑ e-mail can be integrated with other computer-based systems used in an organisation;

❑ all transmissions are recorded, so costs can be carefully controlled;

❑ e-mail allows staff to telework, that is, to work from home via a terminal;

❑ the recipient does not have to be present when a message is sent. Messages can be retrieved from the central mailbox when convenient.

Electronic data interchange (EDI)

Similar to E-mail, EDI allows users to exchange business documents, such as invoices, delivery notes, orders and receipts over the telephone network. EDI can drastically reduce the volume of paperwork and business can be transacted much more quickly than is possible through the normal postal system.

Web site

The World Wide Web has made possible new ways for a business to communicate with its customers. Some sites are 'brochure' sites and are simply another way of promoting a business's corporate image, whilst some e-commerce sites are the basis of the entire business. Amazon.com is probably the most famous of such sites, selling books, CDs and other publications entirely through the Web.

Intranet and extranet

Some organisations may use their internal networks to form an intranet, effectively a private Internet. Its appearance is that of the Web and the familiar browser is its user interface. 'Out of the box' Web servers provide a convenient and relatively cheap method of developing internal network requirements and many organisations have built intranets as part of their overall Internet strategy. Employees are usually familiar with the Web and require little training to access the resources they need on the company intranet. Web tools, such as HTML (code for developing Web pages) editors, are relatively cheap and application development only becomes expensive when large and complex databases are needed, as in the case of an on-line store's product database.

To provide external access to their intranet a company may use its Web site, with suitable access controls, including the use of *firewalls* (software protection), encryption (scrambling of incoming and outgoing messages) and passwords. As an intra/extranet, outside access only requires the use of a Web browser, which is generally available. Extranets can be a valuable way of providing customer support and services. For example, the progress of a project can be monitored by the client, products can be developed by sharing information with partner organisations, customers can check on product availability, or the status of a delivery.

New generation mobile phones

Apart from voice transmission, mobile phones can be used to transmit text messages and those that support Internet Protocol (IP) or the newer WAP (Wireless Application Protocol) can be used to access Internet services, albeit very slowly. The delivery of Internet services through mobile networks is hampered by the mobile phone itself, with its slow processor, poor battery life, mono display and awkward keypad, as well as by limited bandwidth. The development of *broadband* mobile networks and more sophisticated phones will allow the Internet's multimedia content to be accessed through mobile phones. In the meantime, services are largely text-based and perfectly adequate for the viewing of such information as travel, weather, sport results, share prices and the delivery of bank, ticket and message services. New generation mobile phones are making use of larger flip-up screens with touch-sensitive input and handwriting recognition as additions to the usual keypad.

EFTPOS (electronic funds transfer at point-of-sale)

This service provides for the automatic debiting of customers' bank accounts at the checkout or point of sale. Many garages now have a device for reading the magnetic strip details on bank and credit cards. The system saves considerable time when contrasted with payments by cheque and as an alternative to cash, reduces the likelihood of theft. The retailer also has the assurance that the payment is authorised before the sale is made. Usually, a retailer will have a floor limit, or amount above which a telephone call needs to be made to the credit card company for authorisation of payment.

EFT (electronic funds transfer)

This system is used to transfer money between the branches of the same bank and between different banks. In the UK, the system is known as the Bankers Automated Clearing Service (BACS). The service is not restricted to bank use; organisations can pay their employees salaries directly into their bank or building society accounts. Business accounts can also be settled through this EFT system. Apart from the banks, other users usually link into the PSTN (Public Switched Telephone Network - the standard telephone network) through a dial-up connection (unless the volume of data justifies a leased line).

Facsimile transmission (FAX)

This service allows the transmission of facsimiles or exact copies of documents or pictures through a data communications network. Using a fax machine connected to a telephone line, the user simply dials the fax number of the recipient, waits for the correct signal and the document is fed though the fax machine and transmitted. The fax machine sends picture elements or pixels obtained by scanning the document in a series of parallel lines; a synchronised fax machine at the other end prints a facsimile from those pixels. Fax/modems allow computer communication by fax with other fax modems or with conventional fax machines.

Example of ICT support of information flow

To illustrate the role of ICT in managing information flow, we use a simple example of a small electrical company, Wingrove Electrical Ltd, based on the outskirts of London. It employs 38 people and produces electrical components for use in central heating equipment. The following examples of activities and information flows are used to show the potential benefits of using IT.

An enquiry from a potential buyer

A telephone enquiry from a potential customer is received by the company's telephonist, who attempts to connect the caller with the company sales manager, who is out of the office. She makes a note of the caller's name and the nature of the enquiry and promises to pass these details on to the sales manager when she returns to the office. Unfortunately, the paper with the message is lost and so is the potential order. Clearly, the system could have been improved by a number of methods.

If Wingrove had a local area network, the telephonist could have obtained sufficient product information to meet the initial enquiry of the potential buyer. The message could have been transmitted through the electronic mail system, for the sales manager to access when she returned. If the sales manager used a notebook computer, she could download such messages remotely, through the telecommunications or mobile phone network.

It is also possible that the customer's enquiry could have been satisfied through the company web site. Information on products, prices, anticipated delivery times, technical support details and the answers to frequently asked questions (FAQs) can be stored and kept up to date through customer support pages.

Receipt of an order

Wingrove receives a substantial order by post. The manual procedures involve copying the order, sending a copy to Accounting and a copy attached to a 'job sheet' to Production. When the order is completed and despatched, Accounting will invoice the customer and await payment. Unfortunately, when the customer eventually pays, he submits a cheque for an incorrect amount, but the clerk fails to notice that the amount on the invoice and the amount on the cheque do not agree; as a result, he processes the invoice as paid. Wingrove has thus lost some of its profit.

The company could improve its financial control by installing a computerised order processing and invoice verification system. As each order is received into the company, the appropriate details, such as customer, item, quantity, price and so on, are entered into its computer, which automatically generates an invoice, statements and increasingly harshly worded reminders, until the customer settles the debt. When the cheque arrives, its value is also entered and the program automatically checks to ensure that the amount matches both the original price quoted and the invoice value. As protection against the miskeying of the cheque amount, a further check involves the automatic reconciliation, each month, of totals for paid and unpaid invoices.

Production of a quotation

Wingrove's managing director is informed that Birmingham City Council is intending to replace the central heating systems in all its public buildings, over the next three years and is seeking tenders for the component parts of the system. Wingrove would very much like to gain the contract and decide to submit a detailed quotation document. The quotation is 28 pages long and contains an extensive amount of technical detail, as well as product specifications, prices and delivery details. Typed manually, reference would have to be made to numerous files for component specifications and prices and the inevitable modifications to the tender would involve extensive re-typing. The following improvements are possible.

Using a word processor and quotation template, the task can be completed much more quickly. Layout alterations and editing can easily be done before a final copy is printed. A high quality printer, possibly with colour facility, will contribute to a highly professional appearance and improve the image of the company. Component specification and price data can be imported from the company's database of such information, directly into the document. If speed is important, the document could be faxed or e-mailed to Birmingham City Council.

ICT applications for strategic decision-making

Management information systems (MIS)

Although computers can perform routine processing tasks very efficiently, it is generally recognised that limiting a computer's use to the processing of operational information constitutes a waste of computer power. An MIS is designed to make use of the computer's power of selection and analysis to produce useful management information. An MIS has a number of key features:

- ❑ it produces information beyond that required for routine data processing;
- ❑ timing of information production is critical;
- ❑ the information it produces is an aid to decision-making;
- ❑ it is usually based on the database concept.

The claims for MIS are sometimes excessive. It is rarely the complete answer to all a company's information needs, but when successfully implemented, it provides a valuable information advantage over competitors.

Decision support systems (DSS)

A DSS aims to provide a more flexible decision tool than that supplied by a MIS which tends to produce information in an anticipated, pre-defined form and as such, does not allow managers to make ad hoc requests for information. DSS tend to be narrower in scope than MIS, often making use of general-purpose software packages. Examples of DSS include electronic spreadsheets, such as Microsoft Excel and relational database management systems such as Access and Paradox. Additionally, *financial modelling* and statistical packages are considered to be DSS tools. A major benefit is the independence they allow for information control by individual managers and executives. When, for example, a sales manager requires a report on sales figures for the last three months, a microcomputer with database package may provide the report more quickly than a centralised data processing department.

✍ Exercises

1. Study the information flow diagram in Figure 18.1 and answer the following questions.
   (i) When a customer places an order with Sales, to which function must they refer for a credit limit?
   (ii) When a customer order is accepted why are the details passed to Accounting?
   (iii) What information does accounting need from the Warehouse function before paying an invoice sent from a supplier?
   (iv) What use does the Warehouse function make of the requisitions it receives from the Factory?
2. With the use of suitable examples, explain the role of e-mail and video conferencing in supporting communications within and between organisations.
3. Distinguish between an *Intranet* and an *Extranet* and indicate how each can be used to improve the way an organisation communicates internally and with its customers and suppliers.
4. Distinguish between EFT and EFTPOS.
5. Suggest one benefit and one drawback of using a mobile phone to access the World Wide Web.
6. List the key features of a Management Information System (MIS).
7. A Sales Manager uses a spreadsheet to identify sales patterns across each of the five areas for which she is responsible. The data will be used to identify one area which is to be targeted for a special sales drive. What is the general term for this type of information system?

Chapter 19
Data handling systems

The data processing cycle

Computer-based data handling systems employed at the *operational* level of an organisation, for example, in the areas of payroll calculation or sales order processing, frequently involve a repeated cycle of events, which can be identified as follows:

- ❏ data collection and input;

- ❏ processing of the data, including reference to and the updating of relevant files;

- ❏ reporting of output.

Data collection

Depending on the application, this stage may include one or more of the following procedures.

Source document preparation

To ensure standardisation of practice and to facilitate checking, data collected for input, for example, customer orders, are transcribed onto source documents specially designed for the purpose.

Data transmission

If the computer centre is geographically remote from the data collection point, the source documents may be physically transported there, or be keyed and transmitted through a terminal and telecommunications network to the computer.

Data encoding and verification

This involves the transcription, usually through a keyboard device, of the data onto a storage medium such as magnetic tape or disk; a process of machine verification, accompanied by a repeated keying operation assists the checking of keying accuracy. Key-to-disk and key-to-tape systems are used for encoding, commonly making use of diskette and cassette tape storage, from which media the data is then merged onto a large reel of magnetic tape or onto magnetic disk for rapid subsequent input.

Data input and validation

Data validation is a computer-controlled process that checks the data for its validity according to certain pre-defined standards. For example, an account number may have to comprise 6 digits and be within the range 500000 to 900000.

Sorting

To improve the efficiency of processing sequentially organised files, input data is sorted into a sequence determined by the primary key of each record in the relevant master file.

Processing, storage and retrieval

This stage is entirely computer controlled and involves the processing of input data according to the requirements of the program currently in use. Thus, for example, in payroll processing, data on hours worked for each employee may be input and processed against information regarding rates of pay and tax codes held on the payroll master file, to produce the necessary payslips. In addition, the payroll information regarding, for example, pay to date and tax paid to date is updated on the master file.

Reporting of output

The destination of the results of processing also depends on the application and the requirements of the users. Output may be in the form of thousands of printed payslips or invoices or it may be simply a screen display of information in response to a user enquiry.

Processing methods

Data handling systems make use of one or more processing methods, depending on the requirements of the application. The methods can be categorised according to the ways in which data is controlled, stored and passed through the system; the major categories are:

- ❑ batch processing;
- ❑ on-line processing, which includes real-time and time-share processing;
- ❑ distributed processing and centralised processing.

To allow particular methods of processing a computer must have the necessary *operating system* software; thus any particular computer system is equipped with, for example, a batch processing or real-time operating system, or even a combination of types, depending on the needs of the user organisation.

Batch processing systems

Such systems process batches of data at regular intervals. The data is usually in large volumes and of identical type. Examples of such data are customer orders, current weekly payroll details and stock issues or receipts. Although associated with large organisations using mainframe or minicomputer systems, the technique can be used by a small business using a microcomputer.

The procedure can be illustrated with the example of payroll, which is a typical application for batch processing. Each pay date, whether it is every week or every month, the payroll details, such as hours worked, overtime earned or sickness days claimed, are gathered for each employee (these details are referred to as transactions) and processed in batches against the payroll master file. The computer then produces payslips for all employees in the company. A major feature of this and similar applications is that a large percentage of the payroll records in the master file are processed during the payroll 'run'. This percentage is known as the hit rate. Generally, high hit rate processing is suitable for batch processing and if, as is usual, the master file is organised sequentially, then the transaction file will be sorted into the same sequence as the master file. In the case of magnetic tape, transactions must be sorted because the medium only allows serial (one record after another in their physical order) access.

Batch processing method closely resembles manual methods of data handling, in that transactions are collected together into batches, sent to the computer centre, sorted into the order of the master file and processed. Such systems are known as 'traditional' data processing systems. There is normally an intermediate stage in the process when the data must be encoded using a key-to-tape or key-to-disk system. A disadvantage of batch processing is the delay, often of hours or days, between collecting the transactions and receiving the results of processing and this has to be remembered when an organisation is considering whether batch processing is suitable for a particular application. Conversely, batch processing has the advantage of providing many opportunities for controlling the accuracy of data (Chapter 14) and thus is commonly used when the immediate updating of files is not crucial.

On-line processing systems

If a peripheral, such as a Visual Display Unit or keyboard, is on-line, it is under the control of the computer's processor or Central Processing Unit (CPU). On-line processing systems therefore, are those where all peripherals in use are connected to the CPU of the main computer. Transactions can be keyed in directly. The main advantage of an on-line system is the reduction in time between the collection and processing of data. There are two main methods of on-line processing: *real-time* and *time-share*.

Real-time processing

Process control in real-time

Real-time processing originally referred only to process control systems where, for example, the temperature of a gas furnace is monitored and controlled by a computer. The computer, through an appropriate sensing device, responds immediately to the boiler's variations outside pre-set temperature limits, by switching the boiler on and off to keep the temperature within those limits. Real-time processing is now used in everyday consumer goods, such as video cameras, because of the development of the 'computer on a chip', more properly called the microprocessor. The important feature common to all real-time applications is that the speed of the computer allows almost immediate response to external changes.

Information processing in real-time

To be acceptable as a real-time information processing system, the response-time (that is the time between the entry of a transaction or enquiry at a VDU terminal, the processing of the data and the computer's response) must meet the needs of the user. The delay or response time may vary from a fraction of a second to 2-3 seconds depending on the nature of the transaction and the size of the computer. Any delay beyond these times would generally be unacceptable and would indicate the need for the system to be updated. There are two types of information processing systems which can be operated in real-time. These are *transaction processing* and *information storage and retrieval*.

Transaction processing

This type of system handles clearly defined transactions one at a time, each transaction being processed completely, including the updating of files, before the next transaction is dealt with. The amount of data input for each transaction is small and is usually entered on an interactive basis through a VDU. In this way, the user can enter queries through the keyboard and receive a response, or the computer can display a prompt on the screen to which the user responds. Such 'conversations' are usually heavily structured and in a fixed format and so do not allow users to ask any question they wish.

A typical example of transaction processing is provided by an airline booking system (see Booking Systems, later).

Information storage and retrieval

This type of system differs from transaction processing in that, although the information is updated in real-time, the number of updates and the number of sources of updating is relatively small.

Consider, for example, the medical records system in a hospital. A record is maintained for each patient currently undergoing treatment in the hospital. Medical staff require the patient's medical history to be available at any time and the system must also have a facility for entering new information as the patient undergoes treatment in hospital. Sources of information are likely to include a doctor, nurses and perhaps a surgeon, and new entries probably do not number more than one or two per day.

This is an entirely different situation from an airline booking system where the number of entries for one flight record may be 200-300 and they could be made from many different booking offices throughout the world. A further example of a library system is provided later (see Library Systems).

Time-share processing

The term time sharing refers to the activity of the computer's processor in allocating time-slices to a number of users who are given access through terminals to centralised computer resources. The aim of the system is to give each user a good response time. These systems are commonly used where a number of users require computer time for different information processing tasks. The processor time-slices are allocated and controlled by a time-share operating system. The CPU is able to operate at such speed that provided the system is not overloaded by too many users, each user has the impression that he or she is the sole user of the system.

A particular computer system will be designed to support a maximum number of user terminals. If the number is exceeded or the applications being run on the system are 'heavy' on CPU time the response time will become lengthy and unacceptable. Time-share systems are possible because of the extreme speed of the CPU in comparison with peripheral devices such as keyboards, VDU screens and printers. Most information processing tasks consist largely of input and output operations which do not occupy the CPU, leaving it free to do any processing required on other users' tasks.

Distributed processing

As the term suggests, a distributed processing system is one which spreads the processing tasks of an organisation across several computer systems; frequently, these systems are connected and share resources (this may relate to common access to files or programs, or even the processing of a single complex task) through a data communications system (Chapter 7). Each computer system in the network must be able to process independently, so a central computer with a number of remote intelligent terminals cannot be classified as distributed, even though some limited validation of data may be carried out separately from the main computer. Examples of distributed systems include mini or mainframe computers interconnected by way of wide area networks, or a number of local area networks similarly linked.

Distributed systems provide a number of benefits:

❑ *Economy*. The transmission of data over telecommunications systems can be costly and local database storage and processing facilities can reduce costs. The radical reduction in computer hardware costs has favoured the expansion of distributed systems against centralised systems;

❑ *Minicomputers and microcomputers*. The availability of minicomputer and microcomputer systems with data transmission facilities has made distributed processing economically viable. An increasingly popular option, in large multi-sited organisations, is to set up local area networks of microcomputers at each site and connect them through communications networks to each other and/or to a central mainframe computer at the Head Office. This provides each site with the advantages of local processing power, local and inter-site communications through *electronic mail* and access to a central mainframe for the main filing and database systems;

❑ *Local management control*. It is not always convenient, particularly where an organisation controls diverse activities, to have all information processing centralised. Local management control means that the information systems will be developed by people with direct knowledge of their own information needs. Responsibility for the success or otherwise of their division of the organisation may be placed with local management, so it is desirable that they have control over the accuracy and reliability of the data they use.

Centralised systems

With this type of system, all processing is carried out centrally, generally by a mainframe computer. The continuing reduction in hardware costs and the increase in computer power has led the move towards distributed processing systems. This is achieved through computer networks.

Financial accounting systems

The following section describes the various financial accounting systems of a typical business and the main features of accounting software. To begin with some associated terminology is defined and some basic concepts are explained.

The ledgers

Business accounts are needed to record:

- ❑ *debtor* transactions; debtors are people or organisations who owe money to the business for goods or services provided (credit sales);

- ❑ *creditor* transactions; creditors are people or organisations to whom the business owes money, for the supply of goods (credit purchases).

These transactions are recorded in the *sales ledger* and the *purchases ledger* respectively. A third ledger, the *nominal* (or *general*) *ledger* is used to record the overall income and expenditure of the business, with each transaction classified according to its purpose.

Sales ledger

General description

The purpose of the sales ledger is to keep a record of amounts owed to a business by its trading customers or clients. It contains a record for each customer with a credit arrangement. Most businesses permit their customers to buy goods on credit. The goods are usually supplied on the understanding that, once payment has been requested, the debt will be paid for within a specified period of, for example, 14 or 30 days. Payment is requested with the use of a customer addressed *invoice*, which contains details of goods supplied, the amount owing and credit days given. Once a customer order has been accepted and processed, the total amount due for the order is recorded in the relevant customers account in the sales ledger and the balance owing is increased accordingly. When a payment is received from the customer, the amount is entered to the customer's account and the balance owing is decreased by the appropriate amount.

Software requirements and facilities

Customer master file

When setting up the Sales Ledger system, one of the first tasks is to open an account for each customer. These accounts are maintained in a sales ledger *master file*, which is updated by sales and account settlement transactions. A typical package should provide as a minimum, the following data item types for each customer record:

- ❑ *account number* - used to identify uniquely a customer record;

- ❑ *name and address* - this will normally be the customer's address to which statements of account and invoices are sent;

- ❑ *credit limit* - the maximum amount of credit to be allowed to the customer at any one time. This is checked by sales staff before an order is authorised for processing;

- ❑ *balance* - this is the balance of the customer's account at any one time.

Normally, when the file is first created, a zero balance is recorded and outstanding transactions are entered to produce a current balance. An *open item* system stores details of any unpaid invoices. Each invoice can be associated with a particular customer account through the account number.

Transaction entries

Transactions may be applied directly to customer accounts in the sales ledger (*transaction processing*) or they may be initially stored as a transaction file for a *batch* updating run. Whichever method the package uses, it should allow for the entry of the following transaction types:

- ❑ *invoice* - this is sent to the customer requesting payment concerning a particular order. The amount of the invoice is debited to the customer's account in the sales ledger, thus increasing the amount owing;

- ❑ *credit note.* If, for example, goods are returned by a customer or there is a dispute concerning the goods, a credit note is issued by the business to the customer. The amount of the credit note will be credited to the customer's account in the sales ledger, thus reducing the balance owing. Credit notes are often printed in red to distinguish them from invoices;

- ❑ *receipt* - this is any payment or remittance received from a customer in whole or partial settlement of an invoice. Such an entry will be credited to the customer's account and reduce the balance owing accordingly.

The following data may be entered with each type of transaction:

- ❑ *account number* - essential to identify the computer record. Although some packages allow for the entry of a shortened customer name (if the account number has been forgotten) the account number is still necessary to uniquely identify a record;

- ❑ *date of transaction* and *amount of transaction*;

- ❑ *transaction reference* - this is the invoice number to which the transaction relates.

Outputs

The following facilities may be expected:

- ❑ *single account enquiry* - details of an individual customer's account can be displayed on screen. Retrieval may be by account number or a search facility, using a shortened version of the customer name. If more than one record is retrieved by this method they may be scanned through on screen until the required record is found;

- ❑ *customer statement printing* - it is essential that the system can produce monthly statements for sending to customers;

- ❑ *debtors age analysis* - this provides a schedule of the total amounts owing by customers, categorised according to the time various portions of the total debt have been outstanding (unpaid). It is important for a business to make financial provision for the possibility of *bad debts*. These are debts which are unlikely to be settled and may have to be taken out of business profits. From their own experience of the trade, the proprietor of a business should be able to estimate the percentage of each debt that is likely to become bad. Generally, the longer the debt has been outstanding, the greater the likelihood that it will remain unpaid;

☐ *customers over credit limit* - this may form the basis of a black list of customers. Any new order from one of these customers has to be authorised by management. On the other hand, the appearance of certain customers on the list may suggest that some increased credit limits are needed. When a business is successful, it often needs more credit to expand further;

☐ *dormant account list* - if there has been no activity on an account for some time, it may warrant removal from the file. Alternatively, it may be useful to contact the customer to see if further business may be forthcoming.

Validation and control

The package should provide for careful validation of transactions and the protection of records from unauthorised access or amendment. Generally, for example, a customer record cannot be removed from the sales ledger while the account is still live (there is a balance outstanding). More details of validation and control are given in Chapter 20.

Purchase ledger

General description

The purchase ledger function mirrors that of the sales ledger, except that it contains an account for each *supplier*, from whom the business buys goods. When trading with a supplier, it is usually through credit arrangements, similar to those provided by the business for its own customers. Thus, the business receives an invoice requesting payment, within a certain period, for goods purchased. The amount of the invoice is credited to the supplier's account and the balance owing to the supplier is increased accordingly. When payment is made to a supplier, in full or part settlement of an invoice, the supplier's account is debited by the appropriate amount and the balance is decreased.

Most purchase ledger systems operate on an open item basis. Each supplier invoice is given a reference number and when payment is made to a supplier, the reference number can be used to allocate the payment to a particular invoice.

Software requirements and facilities

Supplier master file

The supplier master file contains the suppliers' (*creditors'*) accounts. It is updated by supplier invoices and payments to suppliers. A typical package should provide, as a minimum, the following data item types for each supplier record:

☐ *account number-* used to identify uniquely a supplier record;

☐ *name and address* - the name and address of the supplier business;

☐ *credit limit* - the maximum amount of credit allowed to the business by the supplier at any one time. A check should be kept on this to avoid rejection of orders;

☐ *settlement discount* - this is the amount of discount given by a supplier if an invoice is settled within a specified discount period;

☐ *due date* - the system may issue a reminder when payment is due. A report may be printed, on request, listing all invoice amounts due for payment within, say, 7 days;

☐ *balance* - the current balance on the account.

Transactions

Transactions may update the supplier accounts directly (transaction processing) or they may be initially stored as a transaction file for a later updating run. A purchase ledger package should allow for the following transactions:

❑ *supplier invoices* - before entry, each invoice must be checked against the appropriate order and then against the relevant delivery note, for actual receipt of goods. The balance on a supplier's account (the amount owed to the supplier) is increased by an invoice entry. Some packages allow unsatisfactory (there may be doubt about the delivery of the goods) invoices to be held in abeyance until cleared;

❑ *approved payments* - once an invoice has been cleared for payment, a voucher may be raised to ensure payment, on or before a due date, and discount for prompt payment. The entry of the payment value decreases the balance of a supplier's account and thus the amount owed by the business to the supplier. Cheques may be produced automatically on the due date, but there should be some checking procedure to ensure that payments are properly authorised;

❑ *adjustments* - to reverse entries made in error.

Outputs

The following output facilities may be expected:

❑ *single account enquiries* - details of an individual supplier's account can be displayed on screen; retrieval may be through a supplier code;

❑ *payment advice slip* - this may be produced to accompany a payment to a supplier. Each payment slip details the invoice reference, the amount due and the value of the payment remitted. Payment advice slips help the supplier, who may be using an open item sales ledger system;

❑ *automatic cheques* - the package may, with the use of pre-printed stationery, produce cheques for payment to suppliers, as and when invoices fall due. There must be a careful checking and authorisation procedure to prevent incorrect payments being made;

❑ *unpaid invoices* - a list of all outstanding invoices, together with details of supplier, amount owing and due date;

❑ *creditors' age analysis* - this is the supplier equivalent of debtors' age analysis. The report provides a schedule of total balances owing to suppliers, analysed according to the time the debt has been outstanding. The report may be used to determine which payments should be given priority over others.

Nominal ledger

General description

The nominal ledger is used to record the income and expenditure of a business, classified according to purpose. Thus, for example, it contains an account for *sales*; sales totals are entered on a daily basis. The sales ledger analyses sales by customer, whereas the *sales account* provides a cumulative total for sales, as the accounting year progresses. The *purchases account* in the nominal ledger fulfils a similar purpose for purchases by the business. Other income and expenditure accounts recorded in the nominal ledger may include, for example, *rent*, *heating* and *wages*. If some items of income and expenditure are too small to warrant separate analysis, there may also be *sundry income* and *sundry expenditure* accounts. The information held in the nominal ledger accounts is used to draw up a *profit and loss account*. This account provides information on the trading performance of the business over the year. A *balance sheet* can then be produced to give a snapshot view of the assets and liabilities of a business, on a particular date.

Software requirements and facilities

Nominal accounts master file

When an account is opened in the nominal ledger, the following should be available:

- ❑ *account code* - each account is given a code, to allow the allocation of transactions. For example, an entry for a gas bill payment may be directed to the Heating account by the code 012;

- ❑ *account name* - for example, Sales, Heating, Rent;

- ❑ *balance*.

Associated with each account are a number of transactions processed during the current accounting period.

Transactions

- ❑ *sales and purchases* - these may be entered periodically as accumulated totals or, in an integrated accounts system, values may be posted automatically, at the same time as they update customer and supplier accounts in the sales ledger and purchase ledger;

- ❑ *other income and expenditure* - entries concerning, for example, wages, rent, rates or heating.

Outputs

Typical output facilities include:

- ❑ *trial balance* - this is a list of debit and credit balances categorised by account. The balances are taken from the nominal ledger and the total of debit balances should agree with the total of credit balances;

- ❑ *transaction report* - a full list of transactions which may be used for error checking purposes, or as an audit trail, to allow the validity of transactions to be checked by an external auditor.

- ❑ *trading and profit and loss account* - a statement of the trading performance of the business over a given period;

- ❑ *balance sheet* - a statement of the assets and liabilities of a business, at a particular date.

The major benefit of the computerised nominal ledger is that these reports can be produced easily and upon request. The manual production of a trial balance, trading and profit and loss statement and balance sheet can be a laborious and time consuming task. Many small businesses, operating manual systems, have difficulty in completing their annual accounts promptly for annual tax assessment.

Apart from the basic ledgers described in the previous section, there are other applications which can benefit from computerisation. They include:

- ❑ stock control;

- ❑ sales order processing and invoicing.

Stock control

General description

Different businesses hold different kinds of stock. For example, a grocer holds some perishable and some non-perishable stocks of food and a clothing manufacturer holds stocks of materials and finished articles of clothing. Any trader's stock needs to be controlled, but the reasons for control may vary from one business to another. For example, a grocer wants to keep the full range of food items that customers expect, but does not want to be left with stocks of unsold items, especially if they are perishable. A clothing manufacturer's stocks will not perish if they are unsold, but space occupied by unwanted goods could be occupied by more popular items. On the other hand, if the manufacturer runs out of raw materials the production process can be slowed or even halted. Apart from such differences, there are some common reasons for wanting efficient stock control:

- ❏ excessive stock levels tie up valuable cash resources and increase business costs. The cash could be used to finance further business;

- ❏ inability to satisfy customer orders promptly because of insufficient stocks, can often lead to loss of custom.

It is possible to identify some typical objectives of a stock control system and these can be used to measure the usefulness of facilities commonly offered by computer packages:

- ❏ to maintain levels of stock which will be sufficient to meet customer demand promptly;

- ❏ to provide a mechanism which removes the need for excessively high safety margins of stock to cover customer demand. This is usually effected by setting minimum stock levels which the computer can use to report variations outside these levels;

- ❏ to provide automatic re-ordering of stock items which fall below minimum levels;

- ❏ to provide management with up-to-date information on stock levels and values of stock held. Stock valuation is also needed for accounting purposes.

Stock control requires that an individual record is maintained for each type of stock item held. Apart from details concerning the description and price of the stock item, each record should have a balance indicating the number of units held. A unit may be, for example, a box, 500 grammes or a tonne. The balance is adjusted whenever units of that particular stock item are sold or purchased. Manual or computerised records can only give recorded levels of stock. Physical stock checks need to be carried out to determine the actual levels. If there is a difference between the recorded stock level of an item and the actual stock of that item, it could be because of pilferage or damage. Alternatively, some transactions for the item may not have been applied to the stock file.

Software requirements and facilities

Stock master file

The stock master file contains records for each item of stock and each record may usefully contain the following data item types:

- ❏ *Stock code or reference* - each stock item type should have a unique reference, for example, A0035. The code should be designed so that it is useful to the user. For example, an initial alphabetic character may be used to differentiate between raw materials (R) and finished goods (F) and the remaining digits may have ranges which indicate particular product groupings. The stock file may also be used to record any consumable items used by a business, for example, stationery and printer ribbons. The initial character of the stock code could be used to identify such a grouping. The number and type of characters in a code, as well as its format, are usually limited by the package because the code will also be used by the software to determine a record's location within the file;

❏ *Description* - although users may become used to referring to individual products by their codes or references, a description is needed for the production of, for example, purchase orders or customer invoices;

❏ *Analysis code* - this may be used in conjunction with sales orders so that they can be analysed by product group. If, for example, a clothing manufacturer produces different types of ski jacket, it is important for production planning purposes to know the relative popularity of each type;

❏ *Unit size* - for example, box, metre, tonne, kilo;

❏ *Re-order level* - this is the stock level at which an item is to be re-ordered, for example, 30 boxes. Reaching this level may trigger an automatic re-order when the appropriate program option is run. Alternatively it may be necessary to request a summary report which highlights all items at or below their re-order level. The decision on what the re-order level should be for any particular item will depend on the *sales turnover* (the number of units sold per day or week) and the *lead time* (the time taken for delivery after a purchase order is placed with a supplier). Seasonal changes in sales figures will require that re-order levels for individual items are changed for time to time;

❏ *Re-order quantity* - this is the number of item units to be re-ordered from a supplier when new stock is required;

❏ *Bin reference* - this may be used to indicate the physical location of stock items within, for example, a warehouse;

❏ *Minimum stock level* - when an item falls to this level, a warning is given that the stock level of the item is dangerously low. As with the re-order level, the warning may be produced by a request for a special summary report which highlights such items. Even though the re-order level warning may have already been given, it is possible that no new stocks were ordered or that the supplier was unusually slow with deliveries;

❏ *Cost price* - the price paid by the business for the stock item;

❏ *Sale price* - the price charged to the customer. The package may allow the storage of more than one sale price to differentiate between, for example, retail and wholesale customers;

❏ *VAT code* - different items may attract different rates of Value Added Tax (VAT);

❏ *Supplier code* - if orders can be produced automatically, then the supplier code may be used to access a supplier file, for the address and other details needed to produce an order;

❏ *Quantity issued* - generally, several values may be entered, so that the turnover of an item can be viewed for different periods, for example, from 3 months ago to date, the preceding 3 month period and so on;

❏ *Stock allocated* - a quantity may not have been issued but may have been allocated to a customer order or factory requisition;

❏ *Quantity in stock* - the current recorded level of stock. This will change whenever an issue, receipt or adjustment transaction is entered.

Transactions

☐ *Goods received* - stock received from a supplier;

☐ *Goods returned* - for example, stock returned by a customer or unused raw materials returned from the factory;

☐ *Goods issued* - this may result from a customer order or from a factory requisition, if the business has a manufacturing process;

☐ *Stock allocated* - this will not reduce the quantity in stock figure but the amount allocated should be used to offset the quantity in stock when judging what is available;

☐ *Amendments* - for, example, there may be amendments to price, re-order level or supplier code.

The method used to update the stock master file will depend on how up-to-date the figures need to be (this will depend on how tight stock levels are) and how often the data entry operator can get at the computer. To keep the file up-to-date throughout the day, physical stock changes have to be notified immediately to stock control and the transactions have to be entered as they occur. Unfortunately, this means that a single-user system would be unavailable to any other users, such as sales staff, who needed to know quantities in stock. A networked system with central file storage, would allow continual updating and enquiry access. If the stock levels are sufficiently high to allow differences to arise between physical and book totals without risking shortages, then daily batch updating may be acceptable. In such a situation, an enquiry on a stock item may reveal, for example, a book stock of 200 units, when the physical stock is only 120 units (80 having been issued since the last update at the end of the preceding day).

Outputs

Typical outputs from a stock control package include:

☐ *Stock enquiry* - details concerning a stock item may be displayed on screen, or printed;

☐ *Stock out report* - a list of stock items which have reached a level of zero;

☐ *Re-order report* - a list of stock items which have fallen to their re-order level, together with supplier details and recommended re-order quantities;

☐ *Stock list* - a full or limited (for example, within a certain stock code range) list of stock items, giving details of quantities held and their value. The value may be calculated using the cost or sale price, depending on the costing method used by the business;

☐ *Outstanding order report* - a list of all purchase orders not yet fulfilled and the dates ordered. This may be used to chase up orders when stocks are falling dangerously low.

This is not an exhaustive list and some packages offer many other analytical reports which can help a business to maintain an efficient customer service and plan future production and purchasing more effectively.

A stock control case study

The Astex Homecare chain of DIY stores has branches all over the country and each branch maintains stocks of thousands of items used in the home. These items range from building materials such as sand and cement to bedroom furniture, fitted kitchens, bathroom suites, ceramic wall and floor tiles, lights and light fittings, garden materials such as plants, plant pots and garden furniture, nails, screws, paint, wallpaper and numerous other common household goods.

Each branch has its own small computer system dedicated to dealing with the *point of sale* (POS) terminals located at the customer tills. The POS terminals are used to record purchases and provide customer bills by scanning the bar code on each purchase using a hand-held scanner. The stock number contained in the bar code is fed by the POS terminal to the local computer which returns the description and price to be printed on the customers' receipts as well as the bill totals.

Each branch maintains its own stock file on the local computer but ordering stock is controlled by a mainframe computer at the Astex head office. Each Astex branch is laid out according to a *merchandise layout plan* (MLP) in which the store is organised into a large number of four foot sections, each having its own MLP code. Each item of stock is allocated to one MLP section and its computer record contains the MLP code together with the minimum and maximum stock level for that particular section of the store. When an item has been sold, the relevant information is transmitted automatically by the local computer to the mainframe at head office. The head office computer determines from the MLP data whether the item needs to be re-ordered from a supplier. It uses the MLP information regarding minimum and maximum stock levels in order to determine how many of a particular item to order.

Overnight, while the stores are closed, the head office computer transmits suggested ordering information back to the individual branches where order sheets are printed out on local laser printers, so that they can be checked manually by the appropriate personnel before stock is ordered. This manual monitoring of computer-generated information allows the information system to cope with unexpected situations and prevents the occurrence of gross errors. About ninety percent of all orders can be made electronically using communication links to the computers used by suppliers. Other suppliers not linked to the central Astex computer are contacted manually by telephone.

The security of the Astex information systems are ensured in two major ways. Firstly, because of the importance of the local computer system for producing customer bills, a backup processor is always available for use in the event of the primary processor failing. Secondly, access to the various users of the computer systems is provided on several different levels. Each person who uses the computer system has his or her own access code which provides access to only those areas he or she is authorised to use. These measures are essential to maintain the security and reliable operation of such large-scale systems.

Some sophisticated stock control systems enable the supply of materials just before they are needed for manufacture. Nissan car plants operate using this *just in time* principle, using satellite supply companies located around or near the main plant.

Sales order processing and invoicing

Sales order processing

Sales order processing is concerned with the handling of customers' sales orders. It has three main functions:

- ❑ validation of orders. This means checking, for example, that the goods ordered are supplied by the business or that the customer's credit status warrants the order's completion;

- ❑ to identify quantities of individual items ordered. A customer may request several different items on the same order form. An item will probably appear on many different order forms and the quantities for each need to be totalled to provide lists (picking lists) for warehouse staff to retrieve the goods;

- ❑ to monitor back orders. If an order cannot be fulfilled it may be held in abeyance until new stocks arrive. The system should be able to report all outstanding back orders on request.

The efficient processing of customer orders is of obvious importance to the success of a business and in whatever form an order is received, the details should be immediately recorded. Preferably, the details should be recorded on a pre-designed order form which ensures that all relevant details are taken. The order details should include:

- ❏ the date the order is received;
- ❏ the customer's order number;
- ❏ a description of each item required including any necessary stock references or codes;
- ❏ the quantity of each item ordered;
- ❏ the price per item excluding VAT;
- ❏ the total order value excluding VAT;
- ❏ any discount which is offered to the customer;
- ❏ the VAT amount which is to be added to the total price;
- ❏ the total order value including VAT;
- ❏ the delivery date required.

Invoicing

The invoice is the bill to the customer, requesting payment for goods or services supplied by the business. The following section describes typical package facilities which allow the integration of the sales order processing and invoicing systems.

Package requirements and facilities

To be effective, the sales order processing system needs to have access to the customer file (sales ledger) for customer details and to the stock file, so that prices can be extracted according to stock item codes entered with the order. This latter facility means that the system may also be integrated with invoicing.

Files

- ❏ *Customer file.* When a customer account number or name is keyed in with an order, the package usually accesses the customer file and displays the address details, so that the operator can confirm the delivery address or type in an alternative address if this is required. The process also ensures that all orders are processed for registered customers;
- ❏ *Stock file.* As stock item codes are entered from an order form, the system accesses the price and displays it on the screen for confirmation by the operator. Access to the stock file also ensures that only valid stock codes are used;
- ❏ *Completed order file.* This is used for the generation of invoices after an order's completion;
- ❏ *Back order file.* This is needed to ensure that orders which cannot be fulfilled immediately are kept on file and processed as soon as goods become available.

Transactions

- ❏ *Sales order* - details concerning an individual order, including customer number, items required (by item code), quantity of each item, delivery date, discount allowed and the date of the order.

Outputs

- ❏ *Invoice* - an invoice can be generated by using the details of customer number, stock codes and quantities from the order, together with information retrieved from the customer and stock files;

❑ *Back order report* - a report can be requested detailing all unsatisfied orders. This is useful for planning production schedules or generating special purchase orders;

❑ *Picking list* - a summary of the quantities required of each item ordered. These are used by warehouse staff to extract the goods needed to make up orders for delivery;

❑ *Sales data* - details of each customer's order need to be extended to include the financial ledgers (sales, purchase and nominal ledger). Such integration should not usually be attempted all at once but full integration does reduce the number of inputs necessary and automates many of the updating procedures.

Payroll

The task of calculating wages for a large company having hundreds or even thousands of employees is an enormous task. It involves taking into account some or all of the following factors:

❑ number of hours worked;
❑ amount of overtime;
❑ bonus payment;
❑ sickness leave;
❑ type of employee (for example, waged or salaried, shop floor or management);
❑ deductions (for example, national insurance contributions and union fees);
❑ holidays;
❑ tax code;
❑ tax rate;
❑ cash analysis.

The gross pay is calculated from the hours worked and hourly pay rate, for weekly paid employees, and is a standard sum for salaried employees. Added to this gross payment are any allowances from overtime or bonuses, for example. Tax is calculated and subtracted from the total earnings and other deductions such as national insurance, union fees and pension contributions are also taken from it. Thus the total calculation is quite complicated, and it will probably be different for each employee. Producing payslips manually is therefore very time consuming and prone to error, so computers are particularly well suited to the task. Most computerised payroll systems use batch processing in which long-term employee information held on a master file is used in conjunction with a transaction file containing recent information such as hours worked and overtime details. The transaction file changes from week to week or month to month but most of the information on the master file either does not change at all or changes only occasionally. If employees are paid weekly, at the end of each week details of hours worked, bonus payments, overtime payments and deductions are recorded on a payroll transaction file which contains a record for every employee.

This sequential transaction file is then sorted into employee number order so that it is in the same order as the payroll master file. The two files are then used by the computer to calculate and print the payslips, and to update the master file which must keep track of such things as tax paid to date, total national insurance contributions and holiday and sickness leave for each employee for the current tax year. A *systems flowchart*, as illustrated in Figure 19.1, is often used to describe business data processing systems such as this. The systems flowchart shows the computer operations involved in a payroll run. Payroll systems normally use batch processing when the majority of the employees need to be paid. This lends itself to the use of magnetic tape devices (the flowchart does not specify the medium) which are restricted to sequential access. The payroll data is first stored on the *transaction file* using keyboards as the input devices.

Each employee's pay information is stored in a separate record identified by employee number. Because the *master file* records are stored on tape in order of employee number, the transaction file must also be sorted into the same order. This is to avoid having to search for matching master file and transaction file records for each employee - because both files are in the same order, the next record in each file should be for the same employee. The sorted transaction file must be validated by the computer before processing the payroll data to produce payslips. This process performs various checks on the transaction file to ensure that only correct data will be processed. Any errors detected at this stage must be corrected before the payslips are generated.

Finally, the validated and sorted transaction file is processed against the payroll master file in order to produce the payslips. In addition to updating the master file, the payroll system might also produce summary reports for the management personnel of the company, and, if employees are paid by cash rather than by cheque or transfer to a bank account, a *cash analysis* might be produced. The cash analysis calculates exactly how many of each currency denomination will be required for all the pay packets, so that the correct money can be obtained from a bank. Each payslip would also have a corresponding breakdown for a single pay packet to make it easier for the cashiers to make up the pay packets.

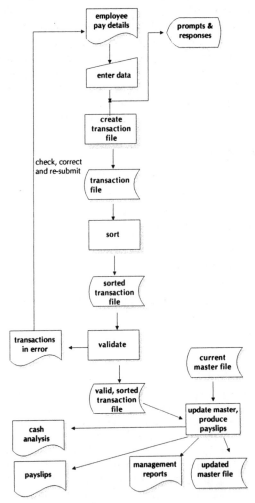

Figure 19.1. *Systems flowchart for payroll system*

A large company will probably use a mainframe computer for the task of processing the payroll information. Data entry will often be carried out using key-to-tape systems by a number of data entry clerks, and the output of the payslips will probably be by means of pre-printed stationery used on a line printer for speed. Backing storage will normally be in the form of magnetic tape or magnetic disk, but sequential *batch processing* will almost invariably be used. Of course, small companies having only a few employees might use a microcomputer system for the payroll, or even produce the payslips manually without the use of a computer at all.

Booking systems

Travel agents

If you go to a travel agent to book a seat on a major international airline, the travel agent will need to check the airline for the availability of the flight that you require. This normally involves communicating with the airline's computer to obtain up-to-date flight information. Remember that the same thing can be happening from all over the world: numerous travel agents could be accessing the same airline's computer at the same time, several of them even trying to book seats on the same flight that you want. To cope with this type of demand, the airline will use a mainframe computer allowing on-line communication with each travel agent via the public telephone network. Each travel agency will have one or more terminals connected by modem to the airline's computer. Flight reservations will be performed in *real-time*, that is, the mainframe's flight and passenger information will be updated immediately to prevent the possibility of double-booking a seat on a particular flight. This ensures that the information that the travel agent obtains will be completely accurate and reliable. This form of processing, where a master file is updated immediately, is called *transaction processing*.

The process of reserving a seat on a flight is further complicated by the fact that several airlines might have scheduled flights to your destination, each offering different flight times, facilities and costs. Rather than contacting each one separately, a process that could take a considerable amount of time, the travel agent links into a wide area network(WAN) which connects the main computers of the different airlines. This allows the agent to choose the most appropriate flight for you and book it immediately. Though each airline in the system might have a different passenger reservation information system, the network software presents the same information format to the travel agents and takes care of transferring data in the correct format to the individual computer systems of the airlines.

When you have decided on your choice of airline and flight, your details are entered at the travel agent's terminal. While this is happening, other travel agents are prevented from accessing that particular flight record. On completion of the reservation, the flight record becomes available again. Booking cancellations and changes are handled in the same way. Your ticket, which will have been produced by the airline's computer, is usually sent out to you a few days prior to the departure date. Individual airline's computers also produce passenger lists automatically for use at the departure airports. An airline's master passenger reservation and flight information file will be held on a high-capacity magnetic disk drive. For backup purposes, in case the master file is in some way lost or partly erased, or the disk drive fails, a separate disk drive will be used to hold an exact duplicate of the master file, and this duplicate file will be updated at the same time as the other master file. This duplication is necessary because the master file will be in constant use, night and day, and there will be no opportunity to stop updating it in order to make a backup on magnetic tape. For the same reasons of security, there will also be a duplicate main computer immediately ready to be used if the other one fails for some reason. Because of the importance of the fast response time required of the system, it will almost certainly be used exclusively for passenger booking purposes, and it will have been designed to operate without break, 24 hours a day, every day of the year.

Similar real-time systems are used by holiday firms, some of which are able to offer thousands of holidays all over the world. Travel agents must have access to accurate information regarding the availability of all the holidays on offer. Again it is important to ensure that exactly the same holiday is not sold to more than one customer, so the booking file held on the holiday company's main computer must be completely up-to-date.

Hotel booking

Hotels frequently use booking systems for keeping track of room reservations made by guests. These systems generally provide additional facilities relating to hotel management, typically keeping track of guests' accounts and producing hotel room usage information. When someone reserves a room in the hotel, a record is created in the guest file. The file contains three types of data:

- details of the guest, such as name, address, telephone number;

- room details, such as type (single, double etc.), number, period of occupancy;

- charges incurred by the guest during the stay at the hotel. For each charge, the item code, cost and date will be recorded.

The first two types of data are entered at the time the reservation is made; items and services bought by the guest during his or her stay, such as telephone calls, drinks, newspapers and extra meals, are recorded as and when they occur. When the guest leaves, the hotel system calculates the total bill and prints out an itemised list that the guest can check.

A hotel management system such as this can easily be implemented with a microcomputer system, though large hotel chains might also have a large central computer at their headquarters for general accounting purposes (such as producing financial reports covering the whole chain of hotels, and for payroll calculations).

Library systems

Dotherstaff College is a split site college of further and higher education. Each site has a large library which has recently been supplied with a microcomputer network for a library automation system called Alice, produced by a software company called Softlink. The software has a number of interlinked modules covering all aspects of typical library operation.

- Catalogue and Classification - managing the book database;

- Circulation - managing borrowers;

- Enquiries - information retrieval;

- Acquisition - ordering books;

- Reports and utilities- producing reports of publishers' details, author details and library usage figures;

- Periodicals- managing the ordering of magazines.

Catalogue and classification

This module is mainly used for the addition of new titles to the book database. Book details can be created, edited and deleted, as well as allowing the file to be browsed through, or searched.

Circulation

The circulation module is used for managing borrowers' details. To borrow a book from the library a borrower must produce his or her ticket on which there is a unique bar code. This bar code is scanned by a librarian and the borrower's record then appears on the screen. When the bar code of the book is scanned, the code is stored in the borrower's record. To return a book, the bar code of the book is scanned or typed in and the book is automatically removed from the borrower's record. The system also allows the display of all books currently borrowed by any person. Periodically, about every two weeks, the borrower file is searched for overdue items so that reminders can be generated automatically.

Enquiry

The enquiry module is used by staff and students to search the book database for books satisfying certain criteria. For example, a user can type in the name of an author and obtain a list of all books in the library written by that person. The title of a book, or part of the title can be entered and a list of books closely matching the title will be displayed. Alternatively, one or more keywords can be used to produce a list of books which contain the keywords in the title. The book information retrieved by an enquiry is summarised on the screen in several sections containing such things as the book titles, subjects covered and author(s). Any book selected from the list can have its full details displayed on screen or printed. This type of enquiry facility can save a great deal of time searching shelves or catalogues for specific information.

The network used for the library information system currently supports about 20 terminals, but it is also linked to the main college networks which provide access to other software such as word processors and spreadsheets.

E-commerce

Many businesses including, for example, supermarkets, travel agents, wine merchants, booksellers and car sales companies now sell their products through e-commerce web sites. With a computer, Internet connection and Web browser, consumers can visit these virtual stores and view, select and pay for goods which can often be delivered within 24 to 48 hours. Until the 1960s it was common practice for shops to make home deliveries or orders taken over the telephone and Internet shopping has the potential to reduce the volume of traffic visiting, for example, out of town shopping centres. It is extremely unlikely that demand for conventional 'bricks and mortar' will disappear because Internet shopping provides no social interaction and many consumers will wish to view and handle many types of goods before buying.

More formally, e-commerce can be defined as *"conducting business transactions over electronic networks"*. E-commerce is fundamentally changing the way business operates. Because of e-commerce, businesses of all sizes are changing their internal operations and their relationships with suppliers and customers. When properly implemented, e-commerce can improve the efficiency of all stages of the business process, from design and manufacture to retailing and distribution.

E-commerce is playing a major role in the establishment of a global economy. The major catalyst for the expansion of international electronic retailing is the Internet. Its users, the number of which is rapidly increasing, can communicate with the Web sites of countless organisations all over the world, and it is through these *World Wide Web* sites that companies can provide 'on-line stores'. The Web-based on-line stores are accessible by Web browsers, such as Microsoft Explorer and Netscape Communicator. An Internet store provides all the facilities that the customer needs, including a product catalogue, a 'virtual shopping basket' and a secure credit card payment system.

Business to business e-commerce

Business to business e-commerce is well established and one of the fastest growing areas. Many office equipment and consumables suppliers, for example, are able to take orders on-line and provide direct delivery to business customers. Because transactions such as the submission and settlement of invoices are all conducted electronically, the participating businesses enjoy significant cost savings.

Benefits of e-commerce for business

Businesses can benefit tremendously from e-commerce in many important ways, reducing costs and improving efficiency. For instance, expensive printed catalogues and service guides can be replaced by a single, up-to-date electronic product database that is accessible at all times. Many businesses use mail shots to inform customers of new products or special offers, a time consuming and expensive exercise. Instead the latest information can be held on the company web site and existing customers can obtain up-to-date information on new products or services at any time. A business can maintain closer contact with its customers and suppliers, and direct communication allows improved pre- and post-sales support.

Direct selling shortens the supply chain so delivery times and costs are reduced. Staffing costs can be a fraction of those for conventional sales outlets. For example, Web site software can handle routine sales transactions automatically, leaving sales staff to deal with more complex orders. E-commerce also provides opportunities for entirely new products and services. These include network supply and support services, web site design and hosting, and various types of on-line information services.

Business to consumer e-commerce

Business to consumer e-commerce, or electronic retailing, is expanding rapidly as businesses become informed of the new opportunities it presents for market expansion. Physical products, information and various services are all available for purchase over the Internet. For example, consumers can buy cars, books, CDs, wine, stock market information and computer software from numerous Internet shops.

Benefits of e-commerce for consumers

Consumers can gain considerable benefits from electronic commerce. The range of products that can be bought on-line is continually being extended. There are virtual stores all over the Internet offering a wide range of goods, including books, wine, newspapers, cakes, computer hardware, software and even cars. Similarly, numerous services are available on-line. These include education, entertainment and information services.

There is the convenience of 24-hour home shopping and access to a wider range of goods and services than is conventionally available within their locality. A conventional shopping chain rarely offers its full product range at every shop, whereas a virtual shop can make its full product range available globally. The consumer is given global choice. If a product or service is available from a number of suppliers, the consumer can choose without regard to geographical location.

Consumers may benefit from lower prices because electronic commerce drastically reduces transaction costs. A transaction involving human interaction may be measured in £s, but the same transaction carried out electronically can cost a few pence.

Orders may be fulfilled more quickly. Direct supply from manufacturer to customer can also be effected with mail order or telephone order catalogues, but the human and paper-based transactions are more costly and involve longer delays than is possible with e-commerce. For products that can be delivered electronically, such as software, video and newspapers, the time delay between order and delivery can be reduced to an absolute minimum, and intermediaries in the traditional supply chain are entirely redundant. By bringing products and services to the home, electronic commerce also has the potential to benefit the disabled, the elderly and those living in remote areas.

Social and employment costs of e-commerce

Clearly, some of the above benefits will not apply to all consumers and there will be social costs as well.

- ❏ If residents of rural communities choose to shop on the Internet local stores may be unable to compete and have to close. Not everyone will have, or wish to have, access to the Internet and such closures will bring serious social deprivation to some.

- ❏ Many aspects of electronic shopping are automated and fewer staff are needed to process orders. Much customer support can be provided through the Web site, which further reduces staff requirements. Of course, e-commerce will also create jobs, but the skills and working practices are very different from those in many traditional businesses.

❑ E-commerce businesses may have access to global markets, but they may also be subject to global competition. This means that the business must be able to respond much more quickly to changes in consumer demand and to the activities of its competitors. Working practices, therefore, tend to demand a much more flexible and multi-skilled approach than is usual in traditional business.

E-commerce relies entirely on the operation and effectiveness of electronic systems and there are greater demands for people with suitable technical skills. If an e-commerce business is to keep its customers, a rapid and reliable delivery system is vital and as a result, employment in distribution is likely to increase.

An organisation's network needs to be secure against unauthorised access to maintain the integrity and confidentiality of its resources and protect the privacy of any clients whose details they hold. There are general security issues which apply to all networks, closed and open, but here we are concerned with the particular problems thrown up by the Internet and the new security measures developed to cope with those problems.

Objectives of data handling systems

A number of general objectives can be identified as being of relevance to most applications, in most organisations:

❑ Improved *operational efficiency*. *Speed* and *accuracy* of operations should be radically improved. This is not automatic as the computer-based system may be badly designed and the staff may be ill-trained, but given proper design and implementation, administrative systems will normally be more efficient.

❑ Better *control of resources*. Administrative systems such as those for financial control and the control of resources such as staff and raw materials, benefit particularly from the rapid production of up-to-date information by computer.

❑ Improved *productivity*. Redundancy does not always follow computerisation, particularly if the organisation is an expanding business. Computer-based systems should permit large increases in the volumes of business which can be handled without the need for extra staff.

❑ Improved *security of information*. With proper physical security, clear operational procedures to restrict access to computer facilities to those properly authorised, and with sophisticated use of software control mechanisms such as passwords, information can be made more secure than equivalent manual systems.

❑ Opportunities to *share data*. This is most likely where database systems and networked computer systems are employed.

❑ Improved *quality of information* for *decision taking* at the operational, strategic and corporate levels in an organisation. *Operational decisions* concern day-to-day operations, such as handling of customer orders or delivery of new stocks. At the *strategic level*, decisions may relate to issues such as production planning and the selection of suppliers. *Corporate decision* examples include the setting of prices, targeting of markets and the manufacture of new products. Most systems generate a range of management information reports, drawn from the routine processing of transactions and these are primarily of use at the strategic level, but may also help with corporate decisions. Accounts software, for example, produces reports on outstanding debts, potential bad debtors, dates when payments to suppliers are due and analysis of sales patterns.

❑ Improved *external image*. An organisation can improve its external image by the improved presentation of correspondence and by an improved service to its customers or clients, but badly designed procedures can also make life more difficult for them.

❑ Improved *working conditions*. This is highly debatable in respect of an office environment, but computer-based manufacturing systems usually provide a less dirty and dangerous environment for employees, as much of the work is done by robots and other computer-controlled machinery.

Choosing a system type

Whether batch processing, one of the on-line types, or distributed processing is appropriate depends on a number of factors:

❑ the type and size of organisation. Large organisations generally have larger volumes of data to handle, than do small ones. Batch processing is efficient in the sense that it is a concentrated activity and if transactions can be accumulated and handled together, then it may be more efficient than dealing with each transaction as it arises. On the other hand, delay may prevent achievement of an important objective, such as the provision of up-to-date management information. Distributed processing through computer networks is an increasingly popular option for a medium or large organisation, because it gives local control to branches and allows data to be shared and communicated across the whole organisation.

❑ the activity (for example, financial accounts, hotel booking);

❑ the objectives of the activity (see previous section).

A batch processing system provides numerous opportunities to ensure the accuracy of data, as it passes through the system. In this way, the type satisfies one of the main objectives of many systems and if this were the only criterion for selection, all systems would use batch processing. Of course, there are other criteria which must be applied to the selection process, including: system purpose(s); size and type of organisation; other objectives, such as security, speed, or the provision of extra management information. For example, an airline's passenger reservation system cannot be effective unless files are updated at the time each reservation is made and transaction processing is found to be appropriate. An organisation's stock control system may need to reflect stock changes on the same basis as the airline reservation system, particularly if delivery has to be immediate. Discount stores, such as Argos, sell a huge range of consumer items and some are expensive; it is not desirable to hold high stock levels, because this ties up large amounts of cash, so the stock records need to be updated as goods are delivered and sold. In some organisations, stock movements (stock received and stock issued) do not have to be instantly reflected in stock records, because delivery times to customers can be longer, perhaps up to several weeks. If the goods are not of high value, then it may be convenient to hold larger stocks, which ensure the satisfaction of customer demand. For example, if the stock record for an item shows 1000 units and 50 units is the maximum customer requirement, then a physical stock level which is only 800 units, is not an immediate problem.

The size of the organisation is also a significant factor in determining the most appropriate type of data handling system. A small plumbing firm, perhaps consisting of two partners and a couple of employees is unlikely to include anyone to keep the accounts; this will probably be the job of one of the partners, who will only have time to do the work at weekends. Thus, customer invoices and payments are dealt with in a batch, perhaps every week. As a small firm, a major objective will be to collect customer debts as quickly as possible and the computerised system can help to do this, in the limited time that the partner has to deal with such matters.

✍ Exercises

1. Which *ledger* would a business use to record:
   (a) balances owing by customers for goods bought on credit?
   (b) expenditure on heating, light and wages?
   (c) balances owing to suppliers for goods bought on credit.?
2. Name the type of document which is sent to a customer:
   (a) requesting payment for goods bought on credit;
   (b) to show a refund on their account to the value of goods returned.
3. Which accounting package report would be useful for identifying potential *bad debts*?
4. Which report details the assets and liabilities of a business on a particular date?
5. Which report shows the profit made by a business over a specified period?
6. Which fields in a stock record are concerned with maintaining optimum levels of stock?
7. List three transaction types which may be entered into a stock control system.
8. (a) Assuming a fully integrated financial accounting system, identify the files which would need to be accessed to produce an invoice.
   (b) What data would be extracted from each file identified in (a), to produce the invoice?
9. List the components an organisation needs to support an e-commerce operation.

Chapter 20
System controls

Computerised information systems present particular problems for the control of data entering the system, because for much of the time this data is not in human-readable form and even when it is stored, the information remains invisible unless it is printed out or displayed on a VDU screen. If proper system controls are not used, inaccurate data may reach the master files or unauthorised changes to data may be made, resulting in decision-making which may be based on incorrect information. System controls can be divided into two main types, according to the purposes they serve: data control; data security.

Data control

A number of data control mechanisms, including for example, the validation of input data, can be employed. Controls should be exerted at all stages in the data processing cycle, which commonly recognises the following stages: (i) data *collection*; (ii) *input*; (iii) *processing*, including file processing; (iv) *output*. Controls can be implemented by clerical and software procedures. It is only through the combined application of both clerical and software controls that errors can be minimised, although their entire exclusion can never be guaranteed.

Data collection and input procedures

Before describing the controls it is necessary to outline the activities which may be involved in the collection and input of data. Depending on the application these may include one or more of the following:

- [ ] Source document preparation. To ensure standardisation of practice and to facilitate checking, data collected for input, for example, customer orders, are clerically transcribed onto source documents specially designed for the purpose.

- [ ] Data transmission. If the computer centre is geographically remote from the data collection point, the source documents may be physically transported there, or be keyed and transmitted through a terminal and telecommunications link to the computer.

- [ ] Data encoding and verification. This involves the transcription, usually through a keyboard device, of the data onto a storage medium such as magnetic tape or disk; a process of machine verification accompanied by a repeated keying operation assists the checking of keying accuracy. *Key-to-disk* and *key-to-tape* systems are used for encoding, commonly making use of diskette and cassette tape storage, from which media the data is then merged onto a large reel of magnetic tape or a disk pack for subsequent rapid input.

- [ ] Data input and validation. Data validation is a computer controlled process which checks the data for its validity according to certain pre-defined parameters, so it must be input to the computer first. The topic of validation is examined in more detail later.

- [ ] Sorting. In order to improve the efficiency of processing, input data is sorted into a sequence determined by the *primary key* of each record in the relevant master file; this is always necessary for efficient sequential file processing, but direct access files allow records to be processed by transactions in the same order that they are received.

Collection and input controls

Transcription of data from one medium to another, for example, from telephone notepad to customer order form, or from source document to magnetic disk, provides the greatest opportunity for error. A number of strategies can be adopted to help limit data collection and input errors:

❑ minimising transcription. This may involve the use of automated input methods such as bar code reading. Another solution is to use *turnaround documents*, which are originally produced by the computer and later become input documents, for example, remittance advices which, having been sent to customers, are then returned with their payments. Because these remittance advices already show customers' details, including account numbers, only the amounts remitted need to be entered for them to become complete input documents;

❑ designing data collection and input documents in ways which encourage accurate completion;

❑ using clerical checking procedures such as the re-calculation of totals or the visual comparison of document entries with the original sources of information;

❑ using codes with a restricted format, for example, customer account numbers consisting of two alphabetic characters, followed by six digits, permits easy validation;

❑ employing *batch* methods of input which allow the accumulation and checking of batch control totals, both by clerical and computerised methods;

❑ using screen verification before input data is processed and applied to computer files. Screen dialogue (the form of conversation between the computer and the user) techniques, which allow data verification and correction at the time of entry, can be used to provide this facility;

❑ checking input data with the use of *batch* or *interactive* screen validation techniques;

❑ ensuring that staff are well trained and that clerical procedure manuals are available for newly trained staff;

❑ controlling access to input documents. This is important where documents are used for sensitive applications such as payroll. For example, input documents for changing pay rates should only be available to, say, the Personnel Manager.

File processing controls

Once validated data has entered the computer system, checks have to be made to ensure that it is; (i) applied to the correct files; (ii) consistent with the filed data.

Header records

Files can have header records which detail the function, for example, Sales Ledger, *version number* and *purge date*. The purge date indicates the date after which the file is no longer required and can be overwritten. Thus, a file with a purge date after the current date should not be overwritten. Such details can be checked by the application program to ensure that the correct file is used and that a current file is not accidentally destroyed.

File validation checks

Some validation checks can only be made after data input when reference can be made to the relevant master file data. These are described in the later section on data control in batch processing systems.

Data integrity

The printing of all master file changes allows the user department and auditors to check that all such changes are *authorised* and *consistent* with transaction documents. All data used by applications for reference purposes should be printed periodically; price lists, for example, may be held as permanent data on master files or in table form within computer programs.

Output controls

It might reasonably be supposed that input and file processing controls are sufficient to ensure accurate output. Nevertheless, a number of simple controls at the output stage can help to ensure that it is complete and is distributed to the relevant users on time. They include:

- ❑ the comparison of *filed* control totals with *run* control totals. For example, when an entire sequential file is processed, the computer counts all processed records and compares the total with a stored record total held in a *trailer record* at the end of the file;

- ❑ the *conciliation* of control totals specific to the application, with totals obtained from a related application. For example, the sales transactions total posted to the Sales Ledger for one day should agree with the total sales transactions recorded in the Sales Day Book or Journal;

- ❑ the following of set procedures for the treatment of error reports;

- ❑ the proper checking and re-submission of rejected transactions.

Data control in batch processing

It is extremely important that all relevant data is processed and that accuracy is maintained throughout the data processing cycle. The controls which are used will depend on the type of processing method in operation, but batch processing provides the greatest opportunity for exerting control over the data, from the input stage through to the output stage.

Amongst the control methods outlined above, there are two which are particularly important - *verification* and *validation*. These control methods can be used to maximum advantage in a batch processing system and typical procedures are described below.

The stages involved in a batch processing *system cycle* are illustrated in Figure 20.1 with a systems flowchart for a payroll run.

The following controls can be used at certain stages within the cycle.

Clerical controls

These can be used at any stage in the cycle when the data is in a human-readable form. The types of check include:

- ❑ visual checking of source documents to detect missing, illegible or unlikely data values, an example of the latter being a total of 100 in the weekly overtime hours entry for an individual worker;

- ❑ the verification of entries by checking them against another source, for example, the price catalogue for the price of a stock item on an invoice;

- ❑ the re-working of calculations on a source document, for example, the checking of additions which make up the total quantity for an item on an order form.

Verification

Before processing, data has to be transcribed from the source documents onto a
computer input medium, usually involving a keying operation to encode the data
onto magnetic tape or magnetic disk. This
stage can be prone to error, particularly if
large volumes of data are involved and
verification, which is usually a machine-assisted process, can ensure that
data is encoded accurately. Magnetic tape
encoders (*key-to-tape* systems), for example, can operate in two modes, *record*
and *verify*. The operation involves one
person keying the data in the record
mode, after which a second person
re-keys the data with the machine in verify mode. In effect the machine reads the
data from the first keying operation and
then checks it against the second keying
as it occurs. The machine signals if characters do not agree, thus indicating a
possible transcription error. *Key-to-disk*
systems operate on a similar principle, either with stand-alone workstations or
through terminals linked to a minicomputer and usually incorporate some
facility for *validation* of data.

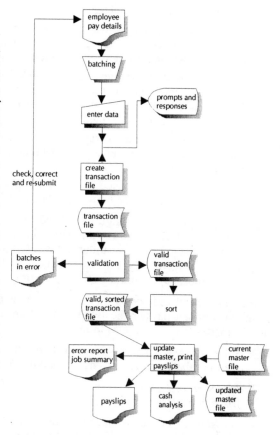

Figure 20.1. *System flowchart of batch payroll system*

Validation

This process is carried out after the data
has been encoded onto the input medium and involves a program called the *data vet* or *validation program*. Its purpose is to check that the data falls within certain parameters defined by the
systems analyst. A judgement as to whether or not data is valid is made possible by the validation program, but it cannot ensure absolute accuracy. That can only be achieved by the use of all
the clerical and computer controls built into the system at the design stage. The difference between *validity* and *accuracy* can be illustrated by the following example.

Example of validation

A company has established a Personnel file. Each record in the file may contain a field for the
Job Grade. The permitted values of job grade are A, B, C or D. An entry in an individual's record may be *valid* and accepted by the system if it is recorded as A, B,C or D, but of course this
may not be the *correct* grade for the individual worker concerned. Whether or not the grade is
correct can only be established by the clerical checks discussed earlier.

Types of validation check

Character, field and record checks

- ❑ *Size*. The number of characters in a field is checked. For example, an account number
  may require 6 characters and if there are more or less than this, then the item is rejected.

- ❑ *Mode*. It may be that particular fields must contain particular types of character, for
  example alphabetic or numeric. If the system is programmed to accept only numbers

then letters would be rejected.

☐ *Format*. This refers to the way characters within a field are organised. For example, an Item Code may consist of 2 alphabetic characters followed by 6 numeric characters, so the system would reject any entry which did not correspond to this format.

☐ *Reasonableness*. Quantities can be checked for unusually high or low values. For example, a gas consumer with one small appliance may have a meter reading appropriate to a consumer with a large central heating system and a reasonableness test could be used to reject or highlight it.

☐ *Presence*. If a field must always have a value then it can be checked for existence. For example, the field 'Sex' in a Personnel record would always have to have an M(ale) or F(emale) entry.

☐ *Range*. Values are checked for certain upper and lower limits, for example, account numbers may have to be between 00001 and 10000.

☐ *Check digit*. An extra digit calculated on an account number can be used as a self checking device. When the number is input to the computer, the validation program carries out a calculation similar to that used to generate the check digit originally and thus checks its validity. This kind of check will highlight transposition errors caused by, for instance, keying digits in the wrong order.

All the above checks can be carried out prior to the master file updating stage. Further checks on data can be made through the use of a validation program at the *update* stage, by comparison with the master file. They are as follow:

☐ *new records*. When a new record is to be added to the master file, a check can be made to ensure that a record does not already use the entered record key .

☐ *deleted records*. It may be that a transaction is entered for which there is no longer a matching master record.

☐ *consistency*. A check is made that the transaction values are consistent with the values held on the master record which is to be updated. For instance a deduction for pension contributions by an employee who is not old enough to be in a pension scheme would obviously be inconsistent.

Validation using batch controls

Batch totals

The purpose of batch totals is to allow a conciliation of manually produced totals for a batch with comparable computer-produced totals. Differences are signalled and the batch is rejected for checking and re-submission. Following the arrangement of source documents into batches of say 30 in each batch, totals are calculated on add-listing machines for each value it is re-quired to control. On an order form, for example, quantities and prices may be separately totalled to provide two control totals. Totals may also be produced for each account number or item code simply for purposes of control although they are otherwise meaningless. For this rea-son such totals are called hash or nonsense totals.

The totals are recorded on a *batch control slip* (Figure 20.2), attached to the batch, together with a value for the number of documents in the batch and a batch number. The batch number is kept in a register held by the originating department so that missing or delayed batches can be traced. It should be noted that *hash totals* may produce a figure which has a large number of digits, so extra digits over and above the original length of the data item are truncated.

Reconciliation of batch totals

The details from each batch control slip are entered with each batch of transactions at the encoding stage. The serial transaction file which results may be arranged as in Figure 20.3.

The serial transaction file is processed from beginning to end by the validation program. The sum of the transaction records relating to each batch should match the batch total. If any validation error is detected, either by differences in

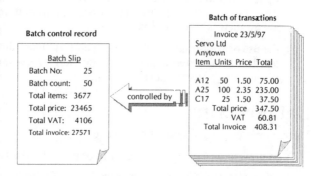

Figure 20.2. *Batch control slip*

batch totals or through the field checks described earlier, the offending batch is rejected to be checked and re-submitted. Rejected batches are reported on a computer printout.

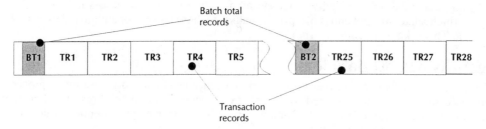

Figure 20.3. *Arrangement of serial transaction file, with batch totals*

Validation during updating

Checks can be made in the manner described earlier, on transactions for deleted or new records, or on data which is inconsistent with the relevant record on the master file. These controls can be used in conjunction with proper clerical procedures to ensure that as far as possible, the information stored on the master files is accurate.

File controls

In addition to controlling the accuracy of data entering the system it is essential to check both that the data is complete and that all relevant data is processed. This can be done through the use of file controls on the transaction file. Following the validation of the batches of transactions, correct batches are written to another file to be sorted and used for updating the relevant master file. During validation, the validation program accumulates totals for all the correct batches. These can be used during the update run to ensure that the whole transaction file is processed.

Validation in on-line systems

On-line systems, as described in the Chapter on Processing Methods, tend to be interactive and transactions are processed immediately against the master files at the data entry stage. The main controls which can be introduced to such systems include:

- ❑ the character, field and record validation checks described earlier. Error messages are displayed on the screen at the time data is entered and require immediate correction at that time;

- ❑ visual verification. At the end of each transaction entry, the operator is given the opportunity to scan the data on the screen and to re-enter any incorrect entries detected. This usually takes the form of a message at the bottom of the screen which is phrased in a way such as "Verify (yes or no)";

☐ the use of well-trained data entry operators. They should have sufficient knowledge of the data being entered and the application it serves, to respond to error messages and make corrections to data accordingly.

Data security

The controls used have several main functions:

☐ to prevent loss of files by software or procedural errors, or by physical hazards;

☐ to protect data from accidental or deliberate disclosure to unauthorised individuals or groups;

☐ to protect the data from accidental or deliberate corruption or modification. This is known as maintaining *data integrity*;

☐ to protect the rights of individuals and organisations to restrict access to information which relates to them and is of a private nature, to those entitled or authorised to receive it. This is known as *data privacy*.

Security against data loss

The loss of *master files* can be an extremely serious occurrence for any organisation so properly organised security procedures need to be employed. Among commercial organisations that have lost the major part of their information store, a large percentage subsequently go out of business. The main causes of data loss are as follow:

☐ environmental hazards such as fire, flood and other natural accidents;

☐ mechanical problems, for example the danger of disk or tape damage caused by a drive unit malfunction;

☐ software errors resulting from programming error;

☐ human error. A wrong file may be loaded, the wrong program version used, a tape or disk mislaid, or physical damage caused to tape or disk;

☐ malicious damage. It is not unknown for staff to intentionally damage storage media or to misuse programs at a terminal.

The standard solution to such problems is to take regular copies of master files and to store the copies in a separate secure location. It is also necessary to maintain a record of transactions affecting a file since the last copy was taken, so that if necessary they can be used to reconstruct the latest version of the file.

Magnetic tape file security

When a tape master file is updated by a tape transaction file the physical nature of the medium makes it necessary for a new tape file to be produced. As Figure 20.4 illustrates, the updating procedure provides a built-in security system referred to as the Grandparent, Parent and Child (*generation*) system.

In the first run, Master File 1 is updated by the transactions file to produce Master File 2 as its Child. Master File 1 is the Parent. Should the Child file be damaged and the data lost, it can be re-created from the Parent master file and the relevant transactions. At the end of the second run, Master File 1 becomes the Grandparent, Master File 2 becomes the Parent and Master File

3, the Child. Each generation provides security for subsequent files. The number of generations used will depend on the policy of the organisation. Three generations are usually regarded as providing sufficient security and the oldest files are re-used by being overwritten as each cycle of generations is completed.

Internal header labels

Internal header labels are designed to deal with two major areas of concern:

1   It is important that the correct file is used in a file processing operation to ensure correct results. Thus, the *subject* of the file and the *version* must be identifiable. For example, it is no good producing monthly payslips using information from a payroll master file three months out of date.

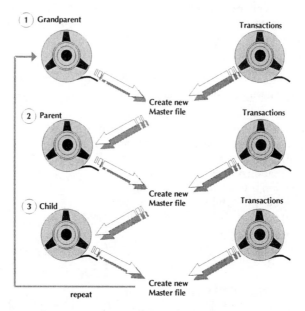

Figure 20.4. *Generation security system for tape files*

2.   A tape file must be protected against accidental erasure. This may occur because tapes are re-usable and when a file is no longer required it can be overwritten by new information.

To ensure that the correct file is used for any particular job, a tape file usually has an internal header label. The label appears at the beginning of the tape and identifies it. The identifying information in the label is usually recorded under program control or by a data encoding device.

A tape header label usually contains the following items of information:

❑   file name e.g. Payroll, Stock, Sales;

❑   date created;

❑   purge date - the date after which the tape is no longer required and may be re-used.

The label is checked by the program, before the file is processed, to ensure that the correct tape is being used.

File protection ring

A device called a file protection ring can be used to prevent accidental erasure. When tapes are stored off-line, the rings are not fitted. To write to a tape, the ring must first be fitted to the centre of the reel. A tape can be read by the computer whether or not a ring is fitted. The simple rule to remember is 'no ring, no write'.

Magnetic disk file security

Security back-ups

Disk files can be treated in the same way as tape files in that the updating procedure may produce a new master file leaving the original file intact. On the other hand, if the file is updated *in-situ* (which in so doing overwrites the existing data), then it will be necessary to take regular back-up copies as processing proceeds. The frequency with which copies are taken will depend on the volume of transactions affecting the master file. If the latest version of the master file is corrupted or lost, then it can be re-created using the previous back-up together with the transaction data received since the back-up.

Transaction logging

A systems flowchart in Figure 20.5 illustrates a transaction logging procedure.

In an on-line system, transactions may enter the system from a number of terminals in different locations, thus making it difficult to re-enter transactions for the re-creation of a damaged master file. One solution is to log all the transactions onto a serial transaction file at the same time as the master file is updated. Thus, the re-creation process can be carried out without the need for keying in the transactions again.

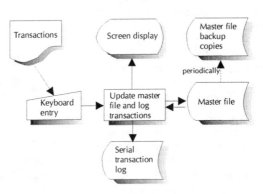

Figure 20.5. *Backup and transaction logging*

Access controls

Unauthorised access to a system may: provide vital information to competitors; result in the deliberate or accidental corruption of data; allow fraudulent changes to be made to data; result in loss of privacy for individuals or organisations. To avoid such hazards an information system should be protected *physically*, by *administrative procedures* and *software*. To detect any unauthorised access or changes to the information system:

- ❏ users should require *authorisation* (with different levels of authority depending on the purpose of access);
- ❏ the computer should *log* all successful and attempted accesses;
- ❏ users should be *identifiable* and their identity *authenticated*;
- ❏ the files should be capable of being *audited*;
- ❏ the actions of *programmers* should be carefully controlled to prevent fraud through changes to software.

Physical protection

These include the use of security staff, mechanical devices, such as locks and keys and electronic alarm/identification systems.

Computer systems with terminals at remote sites present a weak link in any system and they must be properly protected and here software plays an important protection role. Disk and tape libraries also need to be protected, otherwise it would be possible for a thief to take file media to another centre with compatible hardware and software. A variety of methods may be used to *identify* and possibly *authenticate* a system user. They include:

- ❏ Identity cards. Provided that they cannot be copied and have a photograph, they can be effective and cheap. The addition of a magnetic strip which contains encoded personal details including a *personal identification number* (PIN), which the holder has to key in, allows the user to be checked by machine. This method is used to allow access to service tills outside banks. Of course, the user of the card may not be the authorised holder, possession of the PIN being the only additional requirement; the following methods allow authentication as well as identification.

❑ Personal physical characteristics. Voice recognition or fingerprint comparison provide effective, if expensive, methods of identification and authentication.

Such methods are only effective if the supporting administrative procedures are properly followed.

Software protection

Ideally, before a user is given access to a system, the log-in procedures should check for: *authorisation*; *identification*; *authentication*.

Authorisation is usually provided by an account code, which must be keyed in response to a computer prompt; similar prompts may appear for a user-id *(identification)* and a password *(authentication)*.

Further control can be exerted with *fixed terminal identifiers*, whereby each terminal and its location is physically identifiable by the controlling computer, thus preventing access from additional unauthorised locations. Such controls can also be used to restrict particular terminals to particular forms and levels of access.

Password controls

Access to files can be controlled at different levels by a series of passwords, which have to be keyed into the terminal in response to a series of questions displayed on the screen. For example, a clerk in a Personnel Department may be given authority to display information regarding an employee's career record but only the Personnel Manager is authorised to change the information held on file.

Passwords should be carefully chosen, kept secure (memorised and not divulged) and changed frequently. Using people's names, for example, may allow entry by trial and error. Characters should not be echoed on screen as the password is entered.

Handshaking is a technique which requires more than a simple password and may be used between two computers or a computer and a user, as a means of access control. In the latter case, the user would be given a pseudo-random number by the computer and the expected response would be a transform, of that random number. The transform may be to multiply the first and last digits of the number and add the product to a value equal to the day of the month plus 1. Provided the transform is kept secret, handshaking provides more security than simple passwords.

One-time passwords. The computer will only accept a password for *one access occasion*; subsequently, it will expect the user to provide a different password for each additional access, in a pre-defined sequence. Provided the password list and their expected sequence list are kept separate, then possession of one list only will not be of any assistance. The number of attempts at logging-on should be controlled, so, for example, after three unsuccessful attempts, the user should be locked out and a record kept of the time and nature of the attempt.

Authorisation tables

These are held with the relevant files and detail the kinds of access permitted by particular users or groups of users - read only, read and write or delete. Control may also be exerted at a record or field level.

Data encryption

If data signals being transmitted along the telecommunication links are not properly protected, *hackers* can pick up the signals and display them on their own machines. To prevent such intrusion, data encryption methods are used to protect important financial, legal and other confidential information during transmission from one centre to another. Encryption scrambles the data to make it unintelligible during transmission. As the power and speed of computers has increased, so the breaking of codes has been made easier.

Code designers have produced methods of encryption which are currently unbreakable in any reasonable time period, even by the largest and most powerful computers available. An example of such an elaborate coding system is illustrated by the operation of the Electronic Funds Transfer (EFT) system. This is used by banks and other financial institutions to transfer vast sums of money so these transmissions are protected by the latest data encryption techniques. The Data Encryption Standard (DES) was approved by the American National Bureau of Standards in 1977, but as costs of powerful computers have fallen and come within the reach of criminal organisation, EFT makes use of the DES standard, plus additional encryption techniques.

Security to maintain data integrity

Data integrity refers to the accuracy and consistency of the information stored and is thus covered by the security methods outlined above. A major threat to data integrity comes from a variety of computer viruses.

Computer viruses

A computer virus is program code designed to create nuisance for users, or more seriously, to effect varying degrees of damage to files stored on magnetic media. Generally, the code

- [ ] is introduced through portable media, such as floppy disks, particularly those storing pirated or shareware programs; files downloaded from *bulletin boards* on the Internet may be infected and uncontrolled use of these services is likely to result in the receipt of viruses;

- [ ] transfers itself from the infected medium into the computer's main memory as soon as the medium is accessed;

- [ ] transfers from memory onto any integral storage device, such as a hard disk and commonly conceals itself in the boot sector (and sometimes in the partition sector where it is less likely to be traced), from where it can readily infect any other media placed on line in that computer system, whether it be stand-alone or networked. Naturally, any write-protected media cannot be infected.

Some virus codes are merely a nuisance, whilst others are developed specifically to destroy, or make inaccessible, whole filing systems. They pose a serious threat to any computer-based information system, but a number of measures can be taken to minimise the risk:

- [ ] only use proprietary software from a reliable source;
- [ ] write-protect disks being used for reading purposes only;
- [ ] use virus detection software, although this is only effective in respect of viruses using known storage and proliferation techniques;
- [ ] use diskless workstations on networks;
- [ ] control access to portable media and forbid employees to use their own media on the organisation's computer system.

Security to maintain privacy of data

The rights of individuals and organisations concerning their confidential records are similarly protected by the security controls outlined earlier. In addition, legislation by parliament (the Data Protection Act- see Chapter 22 - attempts to exert some control by requiring persons or organisations holding personal information on computer files to register with the Data

Protection Registrar. Some countries have 'Freedom of Information Acts' which allow the individual to see any personal information stored in their own files, except where national security is thought to be threatened. It is generally accepted that the Data Protection Act falls far short of complete freedom of information.

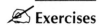 Exercises

1. Distinguish between *verification* and *validation*.
2. Using batch order processing as an example:
    (a) suggest four *data collection controls* to control the accuracy of data entering the system;
    (b) suggest three *validation checks* which could be applied to customer order details;
    (c) indicate any *file processing controls* which could be employed.
3. Draw a *system flowchart* to illustrate the batch processing of customer orders and the updating of stock, order and customer files.
4. With the use of an example, describe the *generation system* of security for tape files.
5. What is transaction logging?
6. With the aid of an example organisation, describe two methods to prevent *unauthorised access* to data.
7. What is data encryption and why is it important? Give and example to illustrate your answer.
8. (a) What is a computer virus?
    (b) Suggest two measures which an organisation can take to minimise the risk of damage from computer viruses.

Chapter 21

Health and safety

Although a computer is not inheriently dangerous, users should be aware of a number of potential risks to their safety and general health. Most employers have obligations (under Section 2 of the Health and Safety at Work Act, 1974) to protect the health, safety and welfare of their employees, by ensuring safe equipment, work systems and working environment. This legislative protection applies to work with a computer *workstation* (a visual display unit and its associated equipment and furniture), as it does to other work. In 1993, specific legislation was introduced to implement European Directive 90/270/EEC, "on the minimum safety and health requirements for work with display screen equipment". This section examines the potential hazards of using a computer workstation and the steps that can be taken to avoid them. The 1993 legislation recognises that good work organisation and job design, and the application of established *ergonomic* principles, can largely avoid the hazards to health and safety.

Ergonomics

Ergonomics is the "study of efficiency of workers and working arrangements" (Oxford English Dictionary). Although a separate science in its own right, certain aspects of ergonomics are being applied increasingly to the design of furniture associated with office computer systems, computer equipment for person/machine interfacing (e.g. screen displays and keyboards) and office and workstation layout.

It is generally recognised that, if workstation facilities and the working environment are inadequate, computer users will tend to be inefficient and may suffer from general fatigue and boredom. The increased emphasis on ergonomic design has come about because of the large increase in the number of computer users. The term *user* includes not only computer specialists, but also non-specialist users, such as data entry operators, clerks, accountants and managers.

Hazards to operator health and efficiency

In designing a suitable workstation, the designer needs to be aware of a number of potential hazards, which are described in the following paragraphs.

Visual fatigue

Various symptoms may indicate the onset of visual fatigue: sore eyes; hazy vision; difficulty in focusing when switching vision between near and distant objects; aching behind the eyes. Certain workstation features and user behaviour can contribute to visual fatigue. The screen display and the positioning of documents that are being transcribed, typically contribute to this fatigue. More specifically, the fatigue may be caused by one or more of the following.

- ❑ screen glare;
- ❑ poor character-definition on screen;
- ❑ excessive periods of screen viewing and consequent short distance focusing;
- ❑ screen flicker;
- ❑ screen reflection;

❑ insufficient or excessive ambient (surrounding) lighting;

❑ frequent, excessive eye movement when switching between screen and document.

Bodily fatigue

Tense and aching muscles or inflamed nerves, generally in the shoulders, neck, back, wrists or hands may result from:

❑ adopting a poor seating posture;

❑ bending frequently to reach various parts of the workstation;

❑ using a keyboard which is not at a comfortable height. *Repetitive strain injury* (RSI), or *carpal tunnel syndrome*, is now recognised as a disabling condition, which can result from intensive keyboard work. Products are available to support wrists and help users to avoid the injury. The nerves which lie down the edge of the hand can also become inflamed and painful, a condition known as *ulnar neuritis*.

❑ holding the head at an awkward angle to view the screen or a document.

Other hazards to health and safety

The proper design and positioning of a workstation can help prevent a number of potential hazards, generally relating to the use of equipment. The hazards may include:

❑ *electric shock*. A person may receive a live electric shock, from faulty equipment (such as incorrect earthing of the power supply), and from incorrect use of equipment (such as the removal of the machine's casing, without first isolating the machine from mains power). This form of electric shock will persist until the person breaks contact with the machine, or else the power is cut. Clearly, this hazard is life threatening, and although this is the primary concern, it will probably also cause damage to the machine.

❑ *static electric shock*. This is caused by the sudden discharge through any conducting material of static electricity, which may have built up in the body. The equipment earths the static electricity which the person has accumulated. A person may build up static electricity by walking on a nylon carpet. Sometimes, static electricity accumulates on the computer screen and a shock may be received when it is touched. If the screen is cleaned with special anti-static wipes, this problem should be avoided. Static electric shock is momentary and, whilst in exceptional circumstances it may injure someone, it is more likely to damage the equipment and, possibly, the stored data.

❑ *injury from impact*. For example, someone may bump against the sharp corner of a desk, be injured by dropping equipment when attempting to move it or be cut by sharp edges on equipment;

❑ *muscular or spinal strain*. Lifting heavy equipment may cause strained or torn muscles, or spinal injuries such as a 'slipped' disc;

❑ *burns, cuts or poisoning caused by equipment breakdown*. These injuries may result from fire or overheating of equipment.

Analysis of workstation requirements

No single standard exists for workstation design. The type of equipment and its layout will depend on, amongst other things, who is going to use it and how it is going to be used. So, before choosing an appropriate workstation design, information should be gathered on the following topics.

Users

The physical characteristics and abilities of potential users should, if possible, be identified. User features may include: gender; physical or mental handicap; age range; height; build. Obviously, it may not be possible to identify personally all members of a user group, in which case, information may be more generalised. Questions which could be asked include: Does the user group include males only, females only or both? What is the age range? Are there any handicapped users and if so, what are the handicaps? Are the physical characteristics of users similar or highly varied? In addition to identifying the features of current users, it is important to allow for possible changes. For example, there may be no wheelchair users at present, but business policy may result in their inclusion in the future.

Existing workstations

If there are workstations already in use within the organisation, then it is useful to determine if there are any good features to include, or bad features to avoid, in any new workstations. The general physical state of the old workstations should be determined. Questions to pose may include: "Have screen displays lost some clarity or steadiness?", "Is the seating still clean and serviceable?", "Are keyboards still fully operable?" The opinions of users should also yield useful information on the suitability of the existing workstations concerning, for example, seating comfort, positioning of equipment and reliability of hardware.

Workstation location and usage

The size of the room in which the workstation is to be located and the layout of existing furniture may place constraints on any design features. The various kinds of work to be carried out at a workstation may involve data entry involving transcription from source documents, use of large reference manuals, storage of file media, customer enquiries which involve customers viewing the screen display, side-by-side working with another member of staff, use of a mouse which requires a flat surface area for its movement, as well as activities which do not involve the use of a computer. There may be no other available work areas in the office, so sufficient space should be available at each workstation. It is also important to know how often particular activities are likely to be carried out and how long they will last.

Designing an appropriate workstation

Work surface

Height. A user should have thigh clearance amounting to at least 180mm, measured from the front surface of the seat, to the underside of the work surface. Obviously, this measurement can be obtained if the chair is adjustable in height and the work surface height does not require seat adjustment below its minimum height. The minimum clearance may be insufficient for someone to sit cross-legged, a position which he or she may wish to adopt for short periods, so some extra thigh clearance may be desirable. Typical heights of manufactured workstations are either 710mm for fixed or between 520mm and 750mm when adjustable. The standard 710mm which manufacturers use for a fixed height desk is based on the ideal writing height for an average male and does not take account of keyboard thickness.

Area. The work surface area required obviously depends on the nature of the work being carried out at the workstation. If transcription work is to be carried out, a *document holder* can be attached to one corner of the mobile workstation. Where more space is available, users may prefer that the document holder is positioned between the keyboard and the screen to reduce the amount of eye movement when alternately viewing the screen and the document. As with all computer equipment, a *matt surface* is desirable to avoid screen reflection and eye strain.

Chair

Where a fixed height desk of, say, 710mm is bought, then it is important that the chair's height is *adjustable* and that a footrest is available for persons of small stature. This is necessary for a comfortable keying height. At the same time, support is provided for the feet (if they are not supported, blood circulation in the legs may be impaired as pressure is exerted by the edge of the seat on the back lower thighs). The footrest should allow the thighs to be slightly raised above the front edge of the chair, thus avoiding 'pins and needles' in the legs and feet. An adjustable chair should be variable in height from 340mm to 520mm. Invariably, manufacturers produce workstation chairs which are adjustable for height and back, particularly lower back, support.

Screen display

In workstation design, the screen display has to be judged for its *quality* and its *position* in relation to the operator. Screen quality is measured for the clarity and steadiness of the images it displays. A high *resolution* screen is generally desirable, even for word processing work, but is of paramount importance if it is used for detailed design work. Several precautions can be taken to minimise eye strain if a poorer quality display is being used:

- ☐ appropriate lighting; this is examined in the next subsection;

- ☐ comparisons can be made with other screen displays (the clarity may deteriorate with age) and any deterioration reported;

- ☐ the use of a higher resolution screen, appropriate to the application and particularly where graphical work is involved;

- ☐ the correct adjustment of contrast and brightness controls. Filters can cut glare and improve character definition by preventing screen reflection from inappropriate lighting. However, their quality is highly variable and a good quality screen should avoid the problem of glare.

There are two major concerns regarding the *positioning* of the screen. First, there is an optimum viewing range. Second, its location should be aimed at minimising excessive head and eye movement. The distance between the user's eyes and the screen should, ideally, fall somewhere between 450mm and 500mm and the design should try to achieve a viewing distance within this range. However, eye strain is more likely to result from repeated re-focusing for lengthy periods, whilst attention is switched from the screen to a document on the desk top. This can be avoided by attempting to position documents approximately the same distance away as the screen. A document holder can be useful in achieving this aim, even if it is positioned to one side and thus requires some head movement to view the document. Some head movement helps to keep the neck and shoulder muscle loosened and avoids stiffness and aching in those areas. A user should try to look away from the screen occasionally, perhaps to the other side of the office, to avoid eye strain which stems from constant focusing at one distance.

Lighting

Natural light falling through office windows may, at times, be adequate for healthy and efficient working but there will be many occasions when it is either too dark or too bright. It is generally necessary to supplement the natural light with artificial lighting and control the entry of bright sunshine with window blinds. The following points provide some basic guidelines as to the artificial lighting requirements for a workstation;

- ☐ attempt to avoid glare. This can result if there is insufficient lighting and the screen's brightness contrasts sharply with the ambient level of brightness;

- ☐ reflection on screen can make it difficult to see the displayed characters and cause eye strain. The use of window blinds and non-reflective work surfaces and equipment can help.

Cabling

Cabling is needed to power individual systems, connect the component parts of system unit, printer, keyboard and screen and for communications purposes when separate systems are networked. Loose cable trailing beneath desks or across the floor can result in injury to staff who trip over it. If, in the process, hardware is pulled from a desk onto the floor, it is likely to be damaged and may result in loss of data and temporary loss of system use. Cabling should be channelled through conduit or specially designed channels in the workstation. Cable 'bridge' conduit is specially designed to channel cable safely across floor areas.

Office layout

If the designer has the luxury of starting from 'scratch', then the simplest approach to designing the layout is to make a scale drawing of the office on which the location of equipment and furniture can then be marked. Designated work positions should also be indicated. Numerous drawing and computer aided design packages make experimentation easy. Libraries of standard symbols (representing office equipment and furniture) are available, which the designer can select and locate on screen. The designer has to take into account a number of constraints which will dictate the location of some furniture and equipment. Fixed items should be placed on the drawing first so that those with fewer constraints can be tried in different locations until an optimum layout is achieved. Ideally, the designer should present two or three alternatives for consideration by management and office staff, whose opinions ought to be paramount. A number of factors should be taken into account when choosing the location of workstations:

❑ staff should not be obliged to work in areas which are subject to extremes of temperature, for example, next to radiators or near a frequently used door which creates a draught each time it is opened;

❑ computer equipment should not be placed next to a radiator as overheating may cause the system to malfunction;

❑ computer screens should be protected from direct sun-light which causes screen reflection and glare;

❑ there should be sufficient space for staff to move around the office without moving equipment or furniture;

❑ workstations should have sufficient space to allow routine maintenance and cleaning to be carried out;

❑ there should always be easy access to fire fighting equipment and fire exits should be kept clear.

✍ Exercises

1. What is meant by the term *ergonomics* and why is it important for the computing industry?
2. Identify two items of equipment which can be used to reduce the health risks for data entry operators and others who use computer systems intensively.
3. Draw a scale plan for a room layout which needs to accommodate 4 computer workstations and their users. Assume that the room is 7 × 5 metres, has a ceiling height of 3 metres, one exit door and that one of 7 metre walls has continuous window along its length. 2 × 2 metre radiators are fitted to the same wall.

Chapter 22

Privacy, fraud and copyright

Confidentiality is important for the protection of personal privacy and in the case of organisations, commercial advantage. For example, informing a competitor organisation about your employer's product development plans may be seriously damaging. Even if you have not signed a confidentiality agreement, you could be disciplined or dismissed from your job. Breaking confidence for monetary gain would be a prosecutable offence. The following paragraphs detail the legislation which exists to deter computer crime and protect personal privacy.

Computer Misuse Act (1990)

The Act identifies three categories of offence: (i) unauthorised access to computer material; (ii) unauthorised access with intent to commit or facilitate commission of further offences; (iii) unauthorised modification of computer material.

The Act deals with the general crime of 'hacking'. The first category of offence deals with unauthorised access to a computer system, its programs and data. An offence is committed if a person performs any computer function with the <u>intent</u> of securing unauthorised access to any program or data held in any computer. The second category covers the offence of persistent hacking. The third category covers the alteration of data to which a hacker has gained access. These crimes are punishable by prison sentences.

Computer fraud and protection measures

Computer fraud is invariably committed for financial gain, but unlike some forms of fraud, the perpetrator(s) will make considerable efforts to prevent discovery of any loss by the victim. The rewards for such efforts may be complete freedom from prosecution, or at least a delay in discovery of the fraud and a consequent chance of escape. Unless proper controls and checks are implemented, computer systems are particularly vulnerable to fraudulent activity, because much of the time processing and its results are hidden. The following section examines some methods for committing fraud and the measures which can be taken to foil them. To extract money from a financial accounting system requires its diversion into fictitious, but accessible accounts. To avoid detection, appropriate adjustments must be made to ensure that the accounts still balance. Sometimes, fraudulent activity may involve the misappropriation of goods rather than cash. Frequently, the collusion of several people is necessary to effect a fraud, because responsibility for different stages of the processing cycle is likely to be shared. Some common methods of fraud are given below.

Bogus data entry. This may involve entering additional, unauthorised data, modifying valid data or preventing its entry altogether. Such activity may take place during the data preparation or data entry stages.

Bogus output. Output may be destroyed or altered to prevent discovery of fraudulent data entry or processing.

Alteration of files. For example, an employee may alter his salary grading in the payroll file or adjust the amount owing in a colluding customers account.

Program patching. This method requires access to program coding and a detailed knowledge of the functioning of the program in question, as well as the necessary programming skill. By introducing additional code, in the form of a conditional subroutine, certain circumstances determined by the perpetrator can trigger entry to the subroutine, which may, for example, channel funds to a fictitious account.

Suspense accounts. Rejected and unreconciled transactions tend to be allocated to suspense accounts until they can be dealt with; fraud may be effected by directing such transactions to the account of someone colluding in the crime. Transactions can be tampered with at the input stage to ensure their rejection and allocation to the suspense/personal account.

An organisation can minimise the risk of computer fraud by:

Controlling access to computer hardware; in centralised systems with a limited number of specialist staff access can be readily controlled. On the other hand, if power is concentrated in the hands of few staff, then the opportunities for undetected fraud are increased. Distributed systems or centralised systems with remote access, for example through the Internet, may increase the number of locations where fraud can be perpetrated.

Auditing of data and procedures; until hard copy is produced the contents of files remain invisible and a number of auditing techniques can be used to detect fraudulent entries or changes.

Monitoring of the programming function; program patching can be controlled by division of the programming task, so that an individual programmer does not have complete responsibility for one application program. Unauthorised alterations to existing software can be detected by auditing utilities which compare the object code of an operational program with an original and authorised copy.

Data Protection Acts (1984 and 1998)

The Data Protection Act of 1984 states that a business or other organisation which holds personal information on their computer system must register with the Data Protection Registrar, the body that administers the act. The registration process requires identification of the classes of data held and the purposes for which they are to be used. For example, a business may hold personal data which includes information on lifestyle and income which it uses to target its marketing campaigns. A new UK Data Protection Act, passed in 1998 and which came into force on 1 March 2000, specifically concerns the processing of personal data on the Internet. The main provisions of each Act are given in the following sections.

Data Protection Act (1984)

Since the 1960s, there has been growing public concern about the threat that computers pose to personal privacy. Most countries, including the UK, have introduced legislation to safeguard the privacy of the individual. The Younger Report of 1972 identified ten principles which were intended as guidelines to computer users in the private sector. A Government White Paper was published in 1975 in response to the Younger Report, but no legislation followed. The Lindop Report of 1978 was followed by a White Paper in 1982 and this resulted in the 1984 Data Protection Act. Apart from public pressure concerning the protection of personal privacy, a major incentive for the Government to introduce the Act stemmed from the need to ratify the Council of Europe Data Protection Convention. In the absence of this ratification, firms within the UK could have been considerably disadvantaged in trading terms through the Conventions provision to allow participating countries to refuse the transfer of personal information to non-participating countries. The principles detailed in the Younger Report formed the foundation for future reports and the Data Protection Act. They are listed below.

❑ Information should be regarded as being held for a specific purpose and should not be used, without appropriate authorisation, for other purposes.

- Access to information should be confined to those authorised to have it for the purpose for which it was supplied.

- The amount of information collected and held should be the minimum necessary for the achievement of a specified purpose.

- In computerised systems which handle information for statistical purposes, adequate provision should be made in their design for separating identities from the rest of the data.

- There should be arrangements whereby a subject could be told about the information held concerning him or her.

- The level of security to be achieved by a system should be specified in advance by the user and should include precautions against the deliberate abuse or misuse of information.

- A monitoring system should be provided to detect violation of the security system.

- In the design of information systems, periods should be specified beyond which information should not be retained.

- Data held should be accurate. There should be machinery for the correction of inaccuracy and updating of information.

- Care should be taken in coding value judgements.

The White Paper which followed the Younger Report identified certain features of computerised information systems which could be a threat to personal privacy:

- The facility for storing vast quantities of data.

- The speed and power of computers make it possible for data to be retrieved quickly and easily from many access points;

- Data can be rapidly transferred between interconnected systems.

- Computers allow data to be combined in ways which might otherwise be impracticable.

- Data is often transferred in a form not directly intelligible.

The 1984 Data Protection Act sets boundaries for the gathering and use of personal data. It requires all holders of computerised personal files to register with a Registrar appointed by the Home Secretary. The holder of personal data is required to keep to both the general terms of the Act, and to the specific purposes declared in the application for registration.

Terminology

The Act uses a number of terms which require some explanation:

- Data. Information held in a form which can be processed automatically. By this definition, manual information systems are not covered by the Act.

- Personal data. That which relates to a living individual who is identifiable from the information, including any which is based on fact or opinion.

- Data subject. The living individual who is the subject of the data.

- Data user. A person who processes or intends to process the data concerning a data subject.

Implications

The requirements of the Act may result in an organisation having to pay more attention to the question of security against unauthorised access than would otherwise be the case; appropriate education and training of employees are also needed to ensure that they are aware of their responsibilities and are fully conversant with their roles in the security systems. The Act also provides the right of a data subject (with some exceptions) to obtain access to information concerning him or her. Normally, a data user must provide such information free of charge or for a nominal charge of around £10. From the individuals point of view, the Act can be said to have a number of weaknesses:

- ❏ Penalties for infringement of the rules are thought to be weak and ineffective.

- ❏ There are a number of exemptions from the Act. Some holders do not need to register and there are exceptions to the right of access to one's own file. There are also limits to confidentiality.

The Registrar is appointed by the Home Secretary and cannot therefore, be wholly independent.

Data Protection Act (1998)

"An Act to make new provision for the regulation of the processing of information relating to individuals, including the obtaining, holding, use or disclosure of such information." [16th July 1998 Data Protection Act]. The Act defines 'data' as information which is automatically processed, or is gathered with that intention, or is held in a structured filing system which is not automatically controlled. In other words, the Act covers manual filing systems which were not covered in the 1984 Act. The Act also refers to:

- ❏ the "data controller" as the person or persons who determine the purposes to which the personal data is put and the manner in which it is processed;

- ❏ the "data processor", meaning any person (other than an employee of the data controller) who processes the personal data;

The terms "data subject" and "personal data" retain the same meanings as stated in the 1984 Act. The 1998 Act additionally refers to "sensitive personal data", meaning personal information relating to racial or ethnic origin, political opinions, religious or similar beliefs, trade union membership, physical and mental health, sexual life, offences or alleged offences and court proceedings for such offences. There are a number of exemptions to registration, for example, when the data is held for national security, crime prevention or detection and certain tax purposes.

Copyright, Designs and Patents Act 1988

A computer program can now obtain the status of literary work and as such, retains protection for 50 years from the first publishing date. Computer software is now covered by the Copyright Designs and Patents Act 1988 and infringements include:

- ❏ the pirating of copyright protected software;

- ❏ the running of pirated software, in that a copy is created in memory;

- ❏ transmitting software over telecommunications links, thereby producing a copy.

The major software producers have funded an organisation called FAST (Federation Against Software Theft) which successfully lobbied for the inclusion of computer software into the above-mentioned Act. The law also covers material published on the World Wide Web, including images and materials used as part of a Web site's design. For example, you would be committing an offence if you copied images of products from a manufacturer's on-line brochure. Technically, an offence is also committed if you place a link in your own Web site to another site which contains copyright material, without the copyright holder's permission.

It is wise to assume that material is copyright protected unless there is a statement to the contrary. In the UK, copyright is created by the mere act of publication, although it is usual to include a notice of copyright ownership. You should make it standard practice to acknowledge the sources of information you include in your assignments, even though they are not to be made available to the public. If you produce material for publication, even through a web site, you must obtain permission from copyright holders for any material you include, such as published directories, extracts from reports or pictures taken, for example, from another web site or scanned from a manufacturer's catalogue.

✍ Exercises

1. A DIY retailer is launching a new e-commerce service to provide on-line shopping to its customers. The directors are concerned about the new service's vulnerability to crime.

    (a) Give two examples of crime which may damage the company.

    (b) Describe a legislative deterrent which may help to combat the threat.

    (c) Describe any measures the company can take to protect themselves from electronic crime.

    (d) The DIY company aims to gather marketing information from customers through the Web site. Identify the company's obligations under the Data Protection Acts (1984 and 1998).

    (e) Identify aspects of the DIY company's operations which will require careful attention to the Copyright, Designs and Patents Act (1988).

Unit 3 Assignments

3.1. Weaving a Web

Your County Council is developing a Web site to attract businesses to the area and also wishes to encourage people to move there. A number of Web pages will feature case studies of various organisations, designed to demonstrate the variety of employment opportunities and to attract employers to the County. You are part of a team gathering the data for these Web pages and your particular tasks are as follows.

1. Research organisations in your County (or elsewhere if necessary) and choose six, two for each of the following: *industrial*; *public service*; *commercial service*.

   One organisation in each pair should be significantly different in size from the other. For example, your two service organisations could be a bank and a firm of solicitors.

   (a) Create a table showing the six organisations classified as indicated.

   (b) Include a brief description of the main purposes of each organisation.

   (c) List the types of information each organisation uses as part of its primary purpose. Briefly explain how each type of information is used by the organisation and the forms in which it may be held (verbal, documentary or electronic).

   (d) Using the examples of the types of information you identified in (c), show how the size of an organisation can affect the types of information it holds.

2. Using the sample organisations chosen in 1. as illustrative examples:

   (a) Explain why organisations are necessary and the reasons for their formation.

   (b) Identify characteristics which are common to all organisations.

3. Select one of the organisations with which you are particularly familiar, or are able to research sufficiently to carry out the following tasks.

   (a) Draw and annotate an organisation chart, showing its functional and management structure.

   (b) Draw up a suitable table listing the main internal and external functions and the activities which are carried out within one of the internal functions.

   (c) Draw an information or data flow diagram, identifying the main internal and external functions and the primary information flows which take place between them.

   (d) Choose two directly related internal functions, and explain how the information flows between them are 'triggered' by particular events. Briefly describe the activities which are necessary to initiate, handle and receive each information flow between the two functions. Also identify any documents used as part of the process.

3.2. It isn't just about money

This assignment (which could usefully be undertaken as a team project) requires some research into the functional areas of a large clearing bank (or another type of large organisation with which you are familiar) to determine the data handling systems the bank is likely to use. For example, customer services comprise a number of different, but related systems:

> on-line telephone banking (touch tone or voice processing);
>
> account statement maintenance and production;
>
> charges calculation;
>
> personal insurance;
>
> mortgage services.

Some of these services can be provided by home visits from a personal account manager, who will make use of a notebook computer for the provision of information and completion of application forms.

1. Produce a table (using a word processor's table facility) of the systems you identify and for *each system*, indicate, with reasons, which processing method (*batch* or *transaction*) it would use. Use an example system to explain the batch and transaction processing methods and place the explanations beneath the table of systems already described.

2. Using several bank system examples, explain what is meant by a *single user* and a *multi-user* system.

3. Define the terms *centralised* and *distributed processing* and suggest reasons why modern banks favour a measure of distributed processing. Use the systems you have identified to support your suggestions.

4. Explain the function and general operation of the following types of data handling system and identify the applications of these systems in the clearing bank organisation: *bookings, payroll, ordering, invoicing, stock control, personal records*.

5. Using suitable examples from the bank's systems, explain the operation of the *system life cycle*.

Unit 4: Introduction to software development

Assessment Evidence Grid

Grade E	Grade C	Grade A
Write a brief report for a given specification stating the requirements and data needs based on what the system is to do.	Determine appropriate data types for a program and show how they are declared.	Evaluate and explain why procedural programs are developed and demonstrate an implementation of a procedural design.
Design a solution for a given set of requirements using appropriate text and graphical documentation tools.	Identify and use appropriate selection and iteration methods for programming problems.	Evaluate a program in terms of how well it relates to the original design.
Write simple linear programs that include suitable input/output statements, variable assignments and operators.	Produce technical documentation for a program.	Suggest ways in which a particular program could be improved.
Produce well designed programs that are clearly laid out and appropriately commented.	Use an appropriate tool to analyse a piece of code to ascertain its semantic correctness.	
Produce user documentation for a completed program including the user interface design.		
Produce suitable test data for a working program.		

Chapter 23
Program design

The single most important requirement of a computer program is that it runs without error at all times, since a program that either produces erroneous results or hangs up under certain circumstances is almost useless. Because of this stringent requirement, computer program design and production is a very skilled activity demanding meticulous attention to detail. It is not sufficient to address only the relatively easy problem of designing and implementing a program which produces the correct output when provided with ideal data. Rather, the program must be able to cope with non-ideal data such as that provided by a user who may be unfamiliar with its operation or data input requirements. Such a user might supply inappropriate input by, for example, entering alphabetic instead of numeric characters, and even experienced operators of the program might accidentally enter invalid data on occasions.

In fact there are many ways that a program could be presented with exceptional - that is, invalid or unreasonable - data and it is the responsibility of the program designer to allow for such. Consequently, the program design stage of program production, in which possible problems - and their solutions - are identified, is of vital importance. As a result, there are now a number of established program design methodologies to aid the program designer to produce well-crafted, error-free programs. The design method described here is a form of *structured programming* using *top-down, stepwise refinement*.

Two forms of notation that we will use to express solutions to design problems are *pseudocode* and *structure charts*; these are called *program design languages* (PDLs). Structure charts provide a graphical representation of a program, allowing its logical structure to be easily appreciated, whereas pseudocode, having a form similar to program instructions, aids program writing and testing.

Problem solving

Whether a problem is computer-related or otherwise, the strategy for solving it has essentially the same three main stages:(1) *understand the problem*, (2) *devise a solution*, and (3) *test the solution*. In addition, for program design tasks there is a further stage which is to (4) *document the solution*.

1. Understand the problem

This first stage requires a *thorough* understanding of the problem being addressed so that you can identify what assumptions can be made and what can't in order to test your solution in the correct context. Some problems are apparently straightforward but, when analysed with a view to producing a program design, become much more complex. As an example, consider the following outline program specification:

> Write a program to read in a date and convert it to the number of days from the start of the calendar year.

It sounds simple enough until you start to consider what the problem implies. For example, what format is to be used for the date? - 15th January, 1995 or 15 Jan 95, or 15/1/95, or 15-01-95 or 150195, or 950115, and so on. Is a particular format to be adopted and incorrectly formatted dates to be rejected, or is the program to attempt to interpret different formats? Are leap years to be considered when calculating the day number? Do you assume that the date is for the current year or can the date be for a different year? You may be able to think of more problems that could arise.

2. Design a solution

The method adopted here to design the solution involves tackling the problem in a number of steps. An outline program is designed first, showing the main modules of the program, and the order in which they are to be executed. Each main module is then reduced to a number of smaller, simpler, and more manageable components, and this process of refinement continues until the program designer judges that there is sufficient detail in the design for a programmer to be able to convert the design directly into a programming language. The process of reducing components into sequences of smaller components in stages is often termed *stepwise refinement*. Top-down, stepwise refinement encourages program design to be tackled methodically in a number of stages of increasing detail. Although structure charts and pseudocode are both suitable program design languages, we recommend that you adopt our approach of first using structure charts to produce your program designs in outline form and then translating them into detailed pseudocode prior to testing and subsequent conversion to program code.

An example of a simple structure chart and the equivalent pseudocode for the addition of two real numbers are shown in Figure 23.1. (Note that a *real* number is a number with a fractional part such as 23·456, whereas an *integer* is a whole number such as 32). Answer, a and b are called variables which serve a similar function to the symbols used in algebra - they are general, symbolic

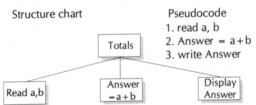

Figure 23.1. *Simple program design for addition of two real numbers*

representations of data that is to be processed. Thus, the pseudocode statement 1 in Figure 23.1 means 'read two values from the input device (such as a keyboard) and call them a and b respectively'. Statement 2 adds the two values and calls the result Answer. Statement 3 displays Answer on the output device (such as a display screen). By using variables rather than actual numbers, this sequence of statements defines how a computer is to deal with the addition of *any* two numbers. In addition to the problem solution itself, another part of the design is a *data table* which defines the purpose and type of the variables used in the solution. The data table (Table 23.1) would identify whether these variables were integers or real numbers and their purpose.

name	description	type
Answer	Holds the sum of the two numbers	real variable
a	First number entered	real variable
b	Second number entered	real variable

Table 23.1

3. Test the solution

This involves using test data to manually step through the solution statements so that the computed output can be compared with the expected output. For instance, the date example mentioned earlier should give an answer of 70 for 10th March 2000, assuming that the days are calculated from 1st January, 2000. This value would be compared with that provided by the design - if the answer was different then the apparent design fault would need to be investigated and corrected before continuing with further testing. The design of test data is considered in Chapter 24.

4. Document the solution

The documentation contains the following: (i) the problem statement; (ii) the top-level program design; (iii) the final detailed program design; (iv) the data table. These are produced during the course of the first three stages of program design. The examples in later sections show the form of this documentation.

Structured programming

Most current program design methodologies are based on *structured programming* concepts. Structured programming is generally associated with certain basic principles:

1. **Restricted use of control structures.** These are limited to three types: *sequence* consisting of instructions which are performed one after the other in the order that they appear in the program; *selection* of one set of instructions from several possible sets of instructions so that the program is able to deal with a number of different circumstances; *repetition*, or *iteration,* of a set of instructions using some kind of program loop. Restricting design to using only these three constructs does not necessarily produce error-free code, but it does help to produce a program which is clear and relatively easy to test.

2. **Modularity.** This is the subdivision of a program into easily identifiable and manageable segments, or *modules*. Each module should require no more than about one page of code. A module may be realised in the final program as one or more small subprograms. Using modules helps to clarify the logical structure of a program for human readers and, by incorporating subprograms, aids its construction.

3. **Top-down, stepwise refinement.** This program design method was described in the earlier section *Problem Solving.*

4. **Clear program format.** This is concerned with the layout of the program instructions. Each page of coding should contain clearly identifiable control structures and blocks of code. One main method of achieving this clarity of structure is by the consistent use of indentation showing the limits of loops, selections and blocks of instructions. Formatting standards apply both to pseudocode and actual program code.

5. **Comments.** The thorough use of comments within the pseudocode design and the actual program in order to explain the purpose of each variable and each few lines of logically related code.

6. **Simplicity.** Where there is a choice between a simple solution to a problem and a slightly more efficient solution which perhaps uses less code, then the simple solution is to be preferred. Straightforward, simple code is easier to test, modify and understand than obscure, 'clever' code.

Basic control structures

As explained earlier, structured programs are constructed using the three control structures sequence, selection and iteration. In order to illustrate how each of these is expressed and used in program design, consider the following programming problem:

Read a set of ten positive and negative numbers entered from a keyboard and find the separate totals of the positive numbers and the negative numbers. Print the two totals.

It is assumed that only valid real numbers such as $1 \cdot 2, -7 \cdot 3, 25, -6$ will be entered. The program can be considered to be a *sequence* of three simple modules:

1. **Initialise variables.** Two variables will be required: one for the total of the positive numbers and the other for the total of the negative numbers.

2. **Process the numbers**. This involves a loop to read numbers typed in from the keyboard until ten values have been entered. A count will be incremented every time a number is read in.

3. **Display the results**. This will involve writing out the two totals.

This top-level design is illustrated by the structure chart shown in Figure 23.2. The equivalent pseudo-code for the top-level design is in Listing 23.1.

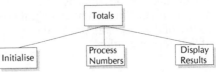

Figure 23.2 *Top level design as sequence of three modules*

Listing 23.1.

```
{Totals}
1    Initialise
2    Process numbers
3    Display results
```

The first refinement of the design results in the structure chart shown in Figure 23.3.

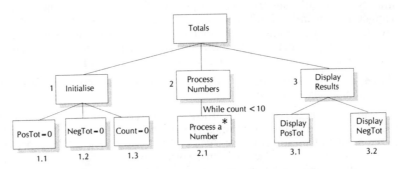

Figure 23.3. *First refinement showing an iteration*

The loop that reads the ten numbers, in other words the *iteration*, is indicated in the structure chart by an asterisk in the top right-hand corner of the component that is to be repeated. The condition governing the loop is written above this component; in this case the loop continues while the count variable has a value less than ten. The equivalent pseudocode is shown in Listing 23.2.

Listing 23.2.

```
{Totals}
1.1   PosTot=0
1.2   NegTot=0
1.3   Count=0
2     while Count < 10
2.1       Process Number
2     endwhile
3.1   write PosTot
3.2   write NegTot
```

Each of the Listing 23.1 statements, numbered *1*, *2* and *3*, have all been refined in Listing 23.2; statement *1* (initialise) has been replaced by three detailed instruction, *1.1*, *1.2* and *1.3*.

Similarly, statements *2* and *3* in Listing 23.1 have also been refined in Listing 23.2. (These statement level numbers reflect the depth of the structure diagram; a single statement level such as *1* indicates a top-level module, a statement number such as *1.2* indicate the second step of a refinement of level *1*. Number *2.3.1* indicates the first step of a refinement of statement *2.3*, and so on. A refinement of a statement is denoted by adding another level to the statement number.) Notice that the end of the loop is indicated by endwhile and the instruction inside the loop, Process Number, is indented. A loop thus translates into three pseudocode statements: one statement for the type of loop and the condition that governs it, another for the item that is to be repeated, and the third for the end of the loop. The final refinement is to expand Process Number, since this is the only statement that has not yet been fully defined: we need to show *how* a number is to be processed. The structure chart for the full design is shown in Figure 23.4.

The structure chart shows that the repeated component Process Number involves three steps: increment the count, read a number, and test the number to determine its sign. Positive numbers are to be accumulated in Pos-Tot and negative numbers are to be accumulated in NegTot. The test involves a *selection*, each independent choice being indicated by a small circle in the top right-hand corner of the box. The condition governing each choice is written above the

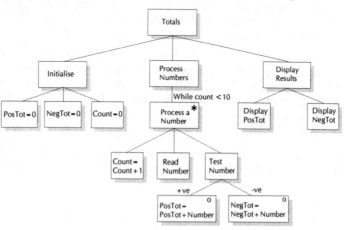

Figure 23.4. *Final refinement showing a selection*

appropriate box as shown. This version of the design needs no further refinement since it is now in a suitable form for conversion to pseudocode and subsequently to a programming language such as COBOL or C. The pseudocode in Listing 23.3 uses a select statement for the selection. If the condition following the first select is true, the statement or statements following are obeyed, otherwise the next select is considered. The endselect statement must be used to terminate the select statement. Note that the number of alternative sets of statements is not limited to two - as many as necessary can be chained together in this way. If some action is necessary when none of the select statements is true then the select when otherwise statement can be included before endselect.

Listing 23.3.   Totalling positive and negative numbers

```
{Totals}
1.1        PosTot = 0
1.2        NegTot = 0
1.3        Count = 0
2          while Count < 10
2.1          Count = Count + 1
2.2          Read Number
2.3          select
2.3.1a         when Number > 0
2.3.1b             PosTot = PosTot + Number
2.3.2a         when Number < 0
```

```
2.3.2b              NegTot = NegTot + Number
2.3          endselect
2            endwhile
3.1          write PosTot
3.2          write NegTot
```

The numbering follows the refinement levels of the structure charts. Thus if the first module is refined as a sequence of two statements, these statements are labelled *1.1* and *1.2*. In the case of an iteration, the start and end statements are given the same number. Thus in Listing 23.3, the `while` and `endwhile` both are labelled *2* showing that the iteration is the second top-level module in the program. The start and end statements of a selection are similarly labelled, but each option, which might involve a number of steps, has a small letter added to indicate that it is a step within the option. (For example, *2.3.1a* and *2.3.1b*).

In addition, in the examples that follow, where a structure chart step has been expanded in the pseudocode, each part of the expansion is also designated with a lower case letter. This frequently occurs when the structure chart shows that a value is to be entered by a user through a keyboard; the pseudocode might be expanded thus: *5.1* `read Number` becomes

```
5.1a  write 'Enter a number'
5.1b  read Number
```

This helps to prevent the structure chart from becoming too detailed and thus unclear. To complete the design, the three variables must be defined in a data table (see Table 23.2).

name	description	type
Count	Counts how many numbers have been entered	integer variable
PosTot	The sum of the positive value numbers	real variable
NegTot	The sum of the negative value numbers	real variable

Table. 23.2. *Definition of variables*

Summary

Figure 23.5 summarises the structure chart and pseudocode notation used for the three basic control structures, sequence, selection and iteration.

Iteration is shown in a commonly used alternative form in which the condition is expressed as `repeat..until <condition>`. In this form the condition is tested at the end of the loop rather than at the beginning; this means that the statements within the loop will be repeated at least once.

The `repeat..until` loop is illustrated in the worked examples.

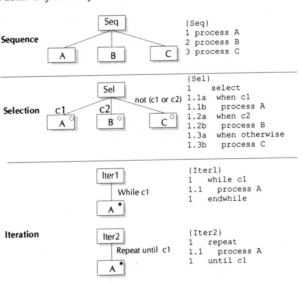

Figure 23.5. *The three basic control structures used in structured programming*

Worked examples

The worked examples presented in the next sections use a combination of structure charts and pseudocode to arrive at the final program design. Structure charts are used for the design refinements in order to express the overall logic in a clear, easily understandable form. The design is then presented in pseudocode, a form more suitable for testing and subsequent conversion to a programming language. At this stage some fine detail may also be added to the design. The program design technique presented here, rather than being targeted at a particular programming language such as COBOL, is in a form suitable for conversion to any one of a number of quite different high-level languages. Each of the following worked examples is in the format:

(i)   the problem statement;

(ii) any assumptions that have been made;

(iii) structure charts showing the top-level design and any further refinement stages;

(iv) pseudocode for the final design;

(v)   the data table for the complete design;

(vi) comments.

Reading and displaying information

Problem statement

Design a program which will accept from the keyboard a value representing a number of inches and display the equivalent number of centimetres.

Assumptions

1. The input is a valid real number.   2. There is no preferred format for the output.

Top-level design

The top-level design, shown on the right, now requires only minor refinements concerned with the precise form that the output is to take. This can be accomplished conveniently in pseudocode without the need to draw another structure chart.

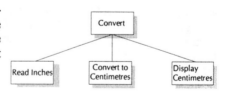

Pseudocode

```
{Convert inches to centimetres}
1a   write 'Enter the length in inches: ', <newline>
1b   read Inches
2    Centimetres = Inches*2.54
3a   write <newline>
3b   write 'A length of ', Inches, ' inches is equivalent to ',
                      centimetres, ' centimetres', <newline>
```

Data table

name	description	type
Inches	Value entered at the keyboard and converted to centimetres	real variable
Centimetres	The value to be output	real variable

Comments

`<newline>` indicates that the cursor is to move to the beginning of the next line.

Loops - Running totals

One very frequent programming task is to keep a running total when a number of values are read within an iteration (that is, *loop*). This next example illustrates the technique usually adopted to accumulate a total in a variable.

Problem statement

Design a program to read ten numbers from a keyboard and display their sum.

Assumptions

1. Exactly ten valid real numbers will be entered using a keyboard.

2. The sum of the numbers is to be accumulated as the numbers are entered, and thus there is no requirement to store them.

Top-level design

The top-level design is a simple sequence of three modules. The second module, `Process Numbers`, involves a loop which is to repeat a known number of times (namely 10). It can therefore be implemented using a count variable as shown in refinement #1.

Refinement #1

The variable `Total` is to be used to accumulate the sum of the ten numbers and therefore must start with an initial value of zero. `Count` is to start at 1 because it must be increased by one each time a new number is read. Each time through the loop a new number is read into the variable `Number` and then added to `Total` which accumulates the numbers. When `Count` reaches 10, the loop terminates.

Refinement #2

The statements required for processing a number and incrementing the loop control variable have been added; this represents the final structure chart form of the design.

Pseudocode

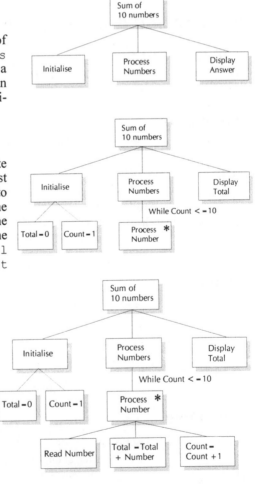

```
{Sum of 10 numbers}
1.1    Total = 0
1.2    Count = 1
2      while Count <= 10
2.1a     write <newline>, 'Enter
         number #', Count
```

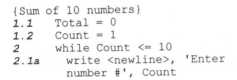

```
2.1b      read Number
2.2         Total = Total + Number
2.3         Count = Count + 1
2         endwhile
3         write <newline> , 'The sum of the 10 numbers is: ', Total
```

This pseudocode form of the final refinement is to make the program a little more user friendly by adding some text to prompt the user to enter a number - this is much better than presenting the user with a blank screen and expecting him/her to know exactly what to do. The final instruction adds some text to announce the answer.

Data table

name	description	type
Total	Accumulates the ten numbers	real variable
Number	Stores the latest number input	real variable
Count	The control variable for the loop	integer variable

Comments

1. Variables that are used as running totals and counts must always be initialised before a loop commences.

2. Control variables for loops are always of type `integer`.

3. A count variable is used to control the duration of a loop when the number of repetitions is known before the loop commences.

Loops - Rogue values

There are many occasions when the exact number of repetitions of a loop is not known in advance. Frequently loops are terminated when a special value is entered by the user. Such special values are often called 'rogue values'.

Problem statement

Design a program to read a set of numbers representing the cost of some purchased items. The end of the list is to be indicated by entering 0 for the cost. Display how many items were purchased and the total cost of the items.

Assumptions

1. The values entered will be valid real numbers   2. No negative numbers will be entered

Top-level design

The strategy used in this instance is to read a value before the loop represented by the module, `Process Items`, is started. The condition governing the continuation of the loop will be

While Amount > 0 and this means that Amount must have been assigned a value before the loop starts.

Refinement #1

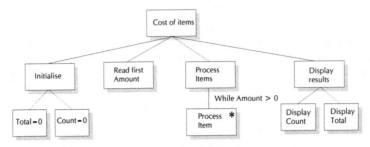

This refinement now shows that if the user initially enters zero for the amount, the loop is not executed at all because the condition, Amount > 0, is false. This is a very important characteristic of the while loop and a reason for not using the repeat..until loop construct in this instance.

Refinement #2

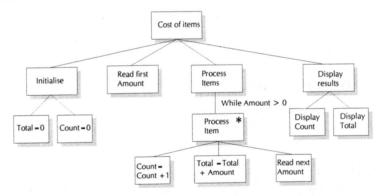

Processing an item requires a sequence comprising incrementing a count for the number of items, adding the current item's cost to the running total and finally obtaining another item cost. Again, if this latter amount is zero, the condition for continuing the loop becomes false and the loop is terminated. The results are then displayed.

Notice that the last statement executed in the loop is a read statement which obtains the data to be processed next. Since no further detail is required for the structure chart, this is the final refinement before writing the pseudocode.

Pseudocode

```
{Enter and total costs}
1.1    Total = 0
1.2    Count = 0
2.1a   write 'Enter the cost of the first item, or 0 to end'
2.1b   read Amount
3      while Amount > 0
3.1      Count = Count + 1
```

```
3.2      Total = Total + Amount
3.3a     write <newline>, 'Enter cost of next item, or zero to end'
3.3b     read Amount
3        endwhile
4.1a     write  <newline>,
4.1b     write  <newline>, Count, 'items were purchased'
4.2a     write <newline>
4.2b     write 'The total cost was: £', Total
```

The detail added to the pseudocode is again to improve communication with the user by displaying prompts such as that in statement *2.1a* and by using blank lines (that is, write <newline>) to improve the clarity of the output.

Data table

name	description	type
Total	Accumulates the cost of the items	real variable
Amount	Stores the current item's cost	real variable
Count	Counts the number of items	integer variable

Comments

Try to avoid using a while condition such as Amount <> 0 (not equal to zero) instead of Amount > 0 because real numbers may not be represented exactly within a computer; the representation of zero might not be **exactly** zero and the condition Amount <> 0 may still be true even when zero is entered for Amount.

Making decisions - the select statement

This example introduces the idea of taking one of several courses of action depending on the value of a variable read in from the keyboard. A loop is again terminated by testing for a rogue value, this time a negative value.

Problem statement

Design a program to accept a number of values representing student examination marks. Each mark is to be displayed as a grade as shown alongside. A negative value is to be used to indicate the end of the set of marks.

Mark	Grade
80 or over	Distinction
60 or over	Merit
40 or over	Pass
less than 40	Fail

Assumptions

The marks are entered as valid integers.

Top-level design

The third module in this sequence is an iteration which repeatedly reads and grades a mark until a negative mark is entered.

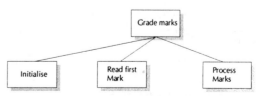

Refinement #1

The threshold values for the grades are assigned to integer constants. Any negative value entered will be regarded as the signal to terminate the program.

Refinement #2

The four actions comprising the selection statement, Grade, which determine the message to be displayed should not be considered as a sequence of tests; the selection notation simply shows which action is to be taken depending on the one condition which is true, and as such the four actions could have been drawn in any order.

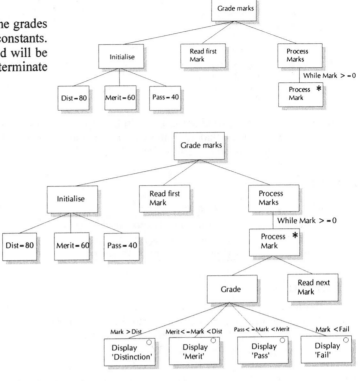

Pseudocode

```
{Grade marks}
1.1        Dist = 80
1.2        Merit = 60
1.3        Pass = 40
2.1a       write 'Enter the first mark(-1 to end):'
2.1b       read Mark
3          while Mark >= 0
3.1          select
3.1.1a         when Mark >= Dist
3.1.1b            write 'Distinction', <newline>
3.1.2a         when Mark >= Merit and Mark < Dist
3.1.2b            write 'Merit', <newline>
3.1.3a         when Mark >= Pass and Mark < Merit
3.1.3b            write 'Pass', <newline>
3.1.4a         when Mark < Pass
3.1.4b            write 'Fail', <newline>
3.1          endselect
3.2a         write 'Enter the next mark(-1 to end):'
3.2b         read Mark
3          endwhile
```

The three thresholds for the grades are stored in the integer constants Dist, Merit and Pass. The advantage of doing this rather than using the actual values 80, 60 and 40 respectively is that if any of these values need to be modified, they need only be changed in the initialisation module and nowhere else.

Data table

name	description	type
Dist	The distinction mark	integer constant = 80
Merit	The merit mark	integer constant = 60
Pass	The pass mark	integer constant = 40
Mark	The student's exam mark	integer variable

Comments

The precise form of a selection statement in a programming language can vary considerably; it is the responsibility of the programmer to choose the most appropriate form available in the target language that exactly represents the required logic.

Decisions - A menu program

Where a program offers a user a number of different options, a menu-based program structure is often employed. The options are displayed and the user is invited to choose one of them by, for example entering its first letter. The program then performs the requested operation and re-displays the menu after it is completed. One of the options always allows the user to exit the program. This example illustrates the structure of a program which presents the user with four options concerned with currency conversion.

Problem statement

Design a menu-based program to allow a user to choose between converting pounds sterling to German marks, American dollars or French francs. The program will ask the user to enter the number of pounds and it will display the equivalent amount in the chosen currency before returning to the menu. The menu is to appear at the top of a blank screen and appear as follows:

```
Currency conversion program

(M)arks
(D)ollars
(F)rancs
e(X)it

Which currency do you want to convert to Pounds?
```

Assumptions

1. Invalid choices (that is entering a letter other than M, D, F or X) will produce an error message and an invitation to try again.

2. Upper and lower case letters will be allowed.

3. The amount in pounds entered by the user will be a valid real number.

4. A single statement, ClearScreen, is available to blank the display screen.

Top-level design

The top-level design in this instance is very simple: the initialisation module sets the values for the three currency conversion factors and the remaining module, Main, repeatedly displays the user options and executes the one chosen.

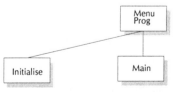

Refinement #1

Three constants used for the currency conversion calculations are defined at this point (don't rely on these figures for holiday plans!).

Further, the iteration is defined as a `repeat..until` loop with condition `c1`. Logical conditions governing loops and selections can be coded in this way so that defining their precise form can be deferred until the design has been completed. We will see later in refinement #3 that `c1` is the condition that indicates the user has chosen the exit option.

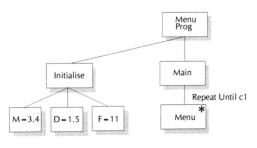

Remember that the `repeat` loop causes the statements within the loop to be repeated at least once, and that the test for continuing to repeat the statements is made at the end of the loop.

Refinement #2

This refinement now shows that the loop controls a sequence of two modules. The first, `Display menu`, repeatedly clears the display screen, shows the menu of options and then reads the user's choice. The second module is a selection statement which processes the option chosen. The final refinement defines the operation of each of the options and under what circumstances each is chosen.

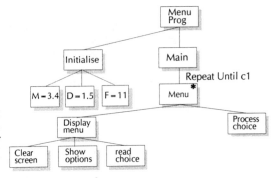

Refinement #3

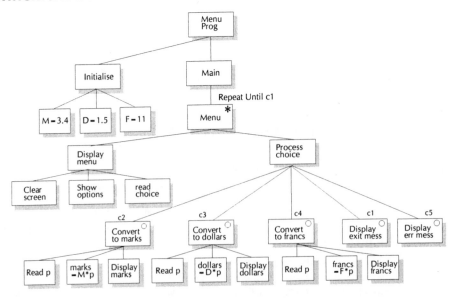

The first three options are concerned with the actual currency conversions. The fourth option displays a message to confirm that the user has chosen to exit the program. The final `select`

statement is only invoked if the user has entered an invalid choice, that is, the letter entered is not 'M', 'D', 'F' or 'X'. The condition codes $c1-c5$ are defined in the next table.

```
c1    choice = ('X' or 'x')
c2    choice = ('M' or 'm')
c3    choice = ('D' or 'd')
c4    choice = ('F' or 'f')
c5    choice <>  ('X' or 'x')or
                 ('M' or 'm')or
                 ('D' or 'd')or
                 ('F' or 'f')
```

Pseudocode

```
{Menu currency conversion}
1.1      M = 3.4
1.2      D = 1.5
1.3      F = 11
2        repeat
2.1.1      ClearScreen
2.1.2a     write 'Currency conversion program', <newline>
2.1.2b     write <newline>
2.1.2c     write '(M)arks'
2.1.2d     write '(D)ollars'
2.1.2e     write '(F)rancs'
2.1.2f     write <newline>
2.1.2g     write 'Which currency do you want to convert to pounds?'
2.1.3      read Choice
2.2        select
2.2.1a       when Choice = ('M' or 'm')
2.2.1b           write <newline>, 'Enter amount'
2.2.1c           read p
2.2.1d           Currency = M*p
2.2.1e           write ' = ', Currency, ' Marks'
2.2.1f           write <newline> 'Press <Enter> to return to menu'
2.2.1g           read key
2.2.2a       when Choice = ('D' or 'd')
2.2.2b           write <newline>, 'Enter amount'
2.2.2c           read p
2.2.2d           Currency = D*p
2.2.2e           write ' = ', Currency, ' Dollars'
2.2.2f           write <newline> 'Press <Enter> to return to menu'
2.2.2g           read key
2.2.2a       when Choice = ('F' or 'f')
2.2.3b           write <newline>, 'Enter amount'
2.2.3c           read p
2.2.3d           Currency = F*p
2.2.3e           write ' = ', Currency, ' Francs'
2.2.3f           write <newline> 'Press <Enter> to return to menu'
2.2.3g           read key
2.2.4a       when Choice = ('X' or 'x')
2.2.4b           write 'Exiting program..'
2.2.5a       when otherwise
2.2.5b           write 'Invalid option. Please try again'
2.2.5c           write <newline> 'Press <Enter> to return to menu'
2.2.5d           read key
2.2        endselect
2.3      until Choice = ('X' or 'x')
```

Data table

name	description	type
M	Conversion factor for pounds to marks	real constant = 3.4
D	Conversion factor for pounds to dollars	real constant = 1.5
F	Conversion factor for pounds to francs	real constant = 11
p	The number of pounds to convert	real variable
Choice	The user's menu choice	character variable
Currency	The equivalent value in the currency chosen	real variable
key	Dummy variable to accept the <Return> key	character variable

Comments

1. This is a good model for constructing menu-driven programs.

2. The manner of implementing the `select` statement can vary considerably with the target programming language. Pascal provides `if` and `case` statements which each have their particular advantages and disadvantages. The programmer is responsible for choosing the most appropriate selection construct from those available.

Chapter 24

Program testing, debugging and documenting

Once a program has been written, it must go through two stages in order to remove errors which almost inevitably will be present. No matter how much care has been taken in the design and coding of a program, it is still very likely to contain *syntax* errors, that is incorrectly formed statements, and probably errors in *logic* as well. *Debugging* is the term given to the process of detecting and correcting these errors or *bugs*.

The first stage in the removal of errors is the correction of syntax errors. Fortunately for the programmer, modern interpreters and compilers will provide a large amount of assistance in the detection of syntax errors in the source code. Badly formed statements will be reported by a compiler after it has attempted to compile the source code; an interpreter will report illegal statements as it attempts to execute them.

Logic errors, however, are largely undetectable by the translating program. These are errors which cause the program to behave in a manner contrary to expectations. The individual statements in the program are correctly formed, but when executed it does not operate correctly; it may give incorrect answers, or terminate prematurely, or not terminate at all. Hopefully, even the most puzzling logic errors, having been detected, eventually can be removed. But how can the programmer be confident that the program will continue to behave properly when it is in use? The answer is that the programmer never can be absolutely certain that the program will not fail. However, by the careful choice of test data in the second stage of the debugging process, the programmer can test the program under the conditions that are most likely to occur in practice.

Test data is designed to determine the robustness of the program: how well it can cope with unexpected or spurious inputs, as well as those for which it has been designed specifically to process. The purpose of *documentation* is to provide the user with all the information necessary to fully understand the purpose of the program and how that purpose has been achieved. The precise form that the documentation takes will be determined by a number of factors:

❑ The type of program.

❑ Who is likely to use the program.

❑ Whether it will be necessary to modify the program coding after it has been finally tested and accepted.

General guidelines for the contents of program documentation are at the end of this chapter.

Detecting logic errors

If after examining program code for a reasonable amount of time the cause of an error remains a mystery, there are a number of courses of action which probably will be much more productive than continuing to pore over the listing:

1. Ask a fellow programmer to listen while you explain the operation of the program and

the way it is behaving. Quite often you will see the cause of the error as you are making the explanation. Alternatively, your helper might recognise the type of error and its probable cause from his/her own experience, or might ask a question which makes you reconsider some aspect of the program which you have assumed to be correct or had no direct bearing on the problem. It is surprising how often this simple approach works.

2. Examine the values of key variables while the program is running by inserting temporary lines of code throughout the program to display the values of key variables. Comparison of the values actually displayed with expected values will normally identify the likely source of the error.

3. Use debugging utilities provided in the language itself or separately in the system software. Most high-level language development systems provide debugging aids. These allow the programmer to do such things as step through the program line by line and display the value of variables, or to insert break-points to interrupt the execution of the program so that the state of variables can be examined. It is the responsibility of the programmer to investigate the debugging aids available and make good use of them.

Test data

When the programmer feels that the more obvious program errors have been detected and removed, the next stage is to test the program using carefully selected data. The nature of the test data should be such that:

❏ every statement in the program is executed at least once;

❏ the effectiveness of every section of coding devoted to detecting invalid input is verified;

❏ every route through the program is tried at least once;

❏ the accuracy of the processing is verified;

❏ the program operates according to its original design specification.

In order to achieve these aims, the programmer must be inventive in the design of the test data. Each test case must check something not tested by previous runs; there is no point in proving that a program which can add successfully a certain set of numbers can also add another similar set of numbers. The goal is to strain the program to its limit, and this is particularly important when the program is to be used frequently by a number of different people. There are three general categories of test data:

1. *Normal data.* This is the general data which the program was designed to handle.

2. *Extreme values.* These test the behaviour of the program when valid data at the upper and lower limits of acceptability are used. The process of using extreme values is called 'boundary testing' and is often a fruitful place to look for errors. For numeric data this could be the use of very large or very small values. Text could be the shortest or longest sequence of characters permitted. A program for file processing could be tested with a file containing no records, or just a single record. The cases where zero or null values are used are very important test cases, frequently highlighting programming oversights.

3. *Exceptional data.* Programs are usually designed to accept a certain range or class of inputs. If invalid data is used, that is data which the program is not designed to handle, the program should be capable of rejecting it rather than attempting to process it. This is particularly important when the program is to be used by people other than the programmer, since they may be unaware of what constitutes invalid data. A programmer should from the outset assume that incorrect data will be used with the program; this may save a great deal of time looking for program errors which may actually be data errors.

Test logs

Once test cases have been devised, the program must be executed using the test data. The effect of using the test data is recorded in a *test log*. Since the point of program testing is to find errors, the log will indicate a <u>successful</u> test <u>if an error is found</u>, and an unsuccessful test otherwise.

The test log will form part of the documentation of the program so that if the program is subsequently modified, the same test data can be re-applied to ensure that no program errors have been accidentally introduced by the modifications. For each set of test data, the expected output must be determined before running the program so that it can be compared with the actual output produced by the program. The test log could be set out in tabular form as follows.

TEST LOG   **Date:**

Program name: **Version:**

Author: **Tested by:**

Test case	Expected output	Observed output	Result	Comments
1				
2				
3				
4				
etc				

Validation

At some point the programmer must decide that the program has had sufficient testing. He or she will be confident that the program will operate according to specification and without 'crashing' or 'hanging up' under extreme or unexpected circumstances; the reputation of a professional programmer relies on this. Prior to release, the final testing is then performed by the user for whom the program was developed. The programmer may have overlooked areas of difficulty because it is often hard to consider a problem objectively or entirely from the viewpoint of the user. If this is the case, that the operation of the program is not entirely satisfactory, the program will be modified and re-tested until all user requirements are met.

Program documentation requirements

The documentation produced for a program will depend on a number of factors. For instance, a program which validates a temporary file prior to creating it permanently will probably require a minimum of user interaction and only a small number of user instructions. However, at some later date, it might be necessary for the author of the program, or a different programmer, to modify it. This possibility means that the structure of the program will have to be explained in great detail, and test procedures to ensure its correct operation will need to be provided.

A general purpose program such as a spreadsheet, designed for people who just want to use the computer as a tool, will require extremely detailed instructions regarding its function and use. Such programs are generally accompanied by detailed user manuals and tutorials. On the other hand, users would not be expected (and definitely not encouraged) to modify the program coding; thus no details would be provided regarding the way the program has been written. This latter type of documentation would only be required for the people responsible for producing the program. In addition to the documentation requirements of users and programmers, there is a third category of person to be considered. These are people such as managers who are neither likely to use programs extensively nor want to attempt to modify them. They merely need to have an overview of the program - its function, capabilities, hardware requirements etc. Thus there are many factors governing the coverage of documentation, and for this reason in the next section it is only possible to provide a checklist of items which might reasonably be included.

Documentation checklist

The documentation for a simple program generally falls into four sections:

❑ Identification.   ❑ General specification.

❑ User information.   ❑ Program specification.

Most users will need access to the first three sections; in general the fourth section will only be needed if the program is to be modified. The amount of detail in each section will depend entirely on the particular application and, to some extent, the implementation language. COBOL, for example, is largely self-documenting: it contains an Identification Division containing all the information listed in the first section below; the Data Division of a COBOL program contains precise details regarding all of the files used by the program and which devices are required; the Procedure Division is written in 'English-like' sentences which are generally easy to understand, even by a non-programmer. Consequently, a program written in COBOL will generally require less documentation than one written in Pascal or C, languages which are not self-documenting. The following checklist is a guide to what might reasonably be included in the documentation for a program.

1. Identification.

❑ Title of program and short statement of its function.

❑ Author.

❑ Date written.

❑ Language used and version if relevant.

❑ Hardware requirements.

2. General specification.

❑ Description of the main action(s) of the program under normal circumstances.

❑ File specifications.

❑ Restrictions and/or limitations of the program.

❑ Equations used or references to texts explaining any complex procedures /techniques involved.

3. Program specification.

❑ Structure charts/flowcharts/decision tables.

❑ Annotated listing.

❑ Testing procedure including test classes and data with expected output and a test log.

4. User Guide.

❑ Installation instructions.

❑ Detailed explanation of the operation of the program.

❑ Tutorial.

❑ Screen shots.

❑ Troubleshooting guide.

Chapter 25
Pascal programming

This chapter addresses the task of developing a piece of software using the programming language Pascal. Here we look at Pascal in enough depth for you to be able to develop your own simple programs, provided of course that you have access to a Pascal compiler. The programs presented in this unit were written and tested using Borland's Turbo Pascal. However, apart from a small number of possible exceptions, the programs should work with any standard version of Pascal. Any special features of Turbo Pascal used in example programs are noted and explained; if you are not using Turbo Pascal, your version will most likely have very similar features that you can substitute, but you will need to refer to the appropriate language reference manual for the precise instruction format required. Turbo Pascal was chosen because it provides an ideal, easy to use environment for developing programs since it combines in one package all the tools required for the task. For example, it has: (i) an *editor* for creating and editing source programs; (ii) a *compiler* to check the syntax of a program, to report and identify errors and to produce object code; (iii) a *linker* to produce executable code; (iv) a *debugger* to help with locating runtime errors; (v) a *file manager* to allow you to quickly save, retrieve and print source programs.

The structure of a Pascal program

A Pascal program consists of four main parts: (i) the *name* of the program; (ii) a *declarations* section in which the programmer defines global *identifiers*. These are the variables and constants used in the program; (iii) *function* and *procedure definitions*; (iv) The main *procedural* part of the program which defines the sequence of instructions to be performed by the program. This section uses the identifiers, functions and procedures defined in the previous two sections of the program. It starts with the word begin and ends with end. Listing 25.1. shows the general structure of a Pascal program.

Listing 25.1.   General structure of a Pascal program

```
program Name(input, output);

   {Declarations of global variables and  and constants}

   {Procedures and functions definitions}

begin
   {The main body of the program containing a sequence of
   instructions to be performed}
end.
```

As a simple example to illustrate these ideas, Listing 25.2 shows a program which calculates the total cost of a purchased item by calculating VAT and adding it to the price of the item. The algorithm on which the program is based is as follows:

1.   *Ask the user to enter the price of the item*

2.   *Store the price*

3.   *Calculate the VAT at 17.5% (i.e. multiply the price by 0.175)*

4.   *Calculate the total price by adding the VAT to the price*

5.   *Display the total cost on the screen.*

Note that the line numbers preceding each line in the program are included in the example programs presented in this chapter simply for ease of reference to specific lines when describing them. *Line numbers are not part of the Pascal language and should not be included if you intend to compile and run the example programs.*

The operation of program `Example1`

Line *1* declares that this program is called `Example1` and `(input, output)` indicates that the program uses the keyboard for the input of data and the screen for the display of data.

Lines *2* **and** *3* declare that VAT is a *constant* value.

Listing 25.2.   A simple program to calculate the total cost of a purchase

```
 1     program Example1(input, output);
 2     const
 3       VAT = 0.175;
 4     var
 5       Price :real;
 6      .Tax :real;
 7       TotalCost :real;
 8     begin
 9       write('Enter price of the item');
10       readln(Price);
11       Tax:= Price*VAT;
12       TotalCost:= Price + Tax;
13       writeln('The total cost is:' , TotalCost:8:2);
14       end.
```

Lines *4 - 7* declare three *variables* `Price`, `Tax` and `TotalCost` (hence the word `var` on line *4*) each as being of type `real`. Variables are used to store data, which in this case are in the form of real numbers, that is, numbers which are not whole numbers. Every variable used in a Pascal program must be declared in this way.

Up to this point the programmer has defined a number of *identifiers* that will be used in the procedural part of the program which follows.

Line *8* indicates the beginning of the procedural part of the program, that is, the section of the program which states what operations are to be performed. This is the part of the program in which the tasks identified by the algorithm are coded.

Line *9* causes the message Enter price of the item to be displayed on the screen.

Line *10* causes the computer to pause and accept numeric data typed in to be stored in the variable `Price` before continuing.

Line *11* stores the result of `Price` multiplied by VAT in the variable `Tax`.

Line *12* stores the result of adding `Price` and `Tax` in `TotalCost`.

Line *13* then displays the text, 'The total cost is: ' followed by the value stored in `TotalCost`. The total cost is shown in a field of eight characters with two figures after the decimal point.

Finally in **Line** *14*, the word end followed by a full stop indicates the end of the program.

Some general remarks

Before going on to explore Pascal in more depth, it is worth mentioning a few general points at this stage:

1. Pascal does not distinguish between the use of capitals and lower-case letters. Thus it regards BEGIN, begin and Begin as being exactly the same.

2. Pascal uses the semicolon to indicate the end of an instruction, which is why you will see a semicolon at the end of most of the lines in a program. (You will quickly learn where a semicolon is not necessary). If you forget to terminate a complete instruction with a semicolon, the compiler will 'think' that the instruction is continued on the next line and, more often than not, it will say that there is an error in the next line.

3. It is a good idea to include comment lines (that is, text enclosed between '{' and '}') to describe the purpose of lines or sections of your program. Particularly for large, complex programs, this is very helpful if it is necessary to change the program at some later date.

4. Using spaces, blank lines and indentation can greatly improve the appearance and the clarity of a program, thus making the program easier to read and understand if it has to be modified later for any reason.

5. Programming involves meticulous attention to detail; omitting punctuation marks, including them in the wrong place or making spelling mistakes will usually lead to the compiler reporting syntax errors, but sometimes such slips might cause serious errors which are more difficult to detect, so be very careful to form instructions precisely.

Identifiers and data types

The term *identifier* is a general term used for *variables*, *constants* and other programmer-defined names such as *procedures* and *functions*. Variables and constants are always associated with a data *type*. Pascal requires that variables are given a type such as integer or real so that the necessary amount of memory can be reserved for their use.

Variables

A variable, which represents an item of data such as a single number, has a name and a current value. Variables are given names such as Amount, Total or Numb3 and are assigned values by program instructions. These values are stored in the memory of the computer and they are accessed whenever a variable is referenced in a program instruction. So, for example, in the instruction

```
Total := Price + Tax;
```

the value associated with the variable Price is added to the value of the variable Tax and the sum is then assigned to the variable Total. If in a previous instruction total had already been assigned a value, that value would be replaced by the new one.

Constants

Constants too are assigned values but only once after the word const preceding the main program. The constant VAT in Listing 25.2 is an example. Constants retain their values throughout the execution of a program; Pascal does not allow you to use a constant in an instruction which tries to change the value of the constant. Thus, if in Listing 25.2, you included an instruction such as

```
VAT := 0.2;
```

in the main program, the Pascal compiler would report an error. Notice that a constant is assigned a value using only the '=' sign without the ':'.

Special identifiers and reserved words

Certain words in Pascal are classed as *special*, or *standard, identifiers* because they perform the same function as programmer-defined identifiers but they are recognised by the compiler as being pre-defined and they are therefore to be used only in a certain context. Examples of special identifiers are the words write, writeln, read, readln, input and output. If you use any of these words for identifiers, for example by declaring

```
var
    Read :integer;
```

then Pascal will not necessarily regard this as a mistake, but you will have overridden the standard definition of read as an input instruction, and you will have to use it as an integer variable; you will not be able then to use read as an input instruction since, in effect, you will have redefined its function. The moral is to avoid using these special identifier names for your own, programmer-defined identifiers. Reserved words such as begin, end, real and program are words which are actually part of the Pascal language and are unavailable for use as identifiers. Pascal's reserved words and special identifiers are shown below.

Reserved words

and	array	begin	case	const
div	do	downto	else	end
file	for	function	goto	if
in	label	mod	nil	not
of	or	packed	procedure	program
record	repeat	set	then	to
type	until	var	while	with

Special identifiers

abs	arctan	boolean	char	chr
cos	dispose	eof	eoln	exp
false	get	input	integer	ln
maxint	new	odd	ord	output
pack	page	pred	put	read
readln	real	reset	rewrite	round
sin	sqr	sqrt	succ	text
true	trunc	unpack	write	writeln

Rules for naming identifiers

Pascal imposes a number of restrictions concerning the formation of names for identifiers:

1. The name must consist only of alphabetic and numeric characters.

2. The name must start with an alphabetic character.

3. The name must not be a special identifier or a reserved word.

Examples of valid identifiers

```
firstNum        NUMBER1         abc31            Counter     x
```

Examples of invalid identifiers

`12abc`	(starts with a numeric character)
`first-number`	(contains a non-alphabetic/numeric character)
`var 1`	(contains a space)
`End`	(a reserved word)
`READ`	(a special identifier)

Data types

As well as having names and values, variables are also given a *type*. Three commonly used types are `integer`, `real` and `char` (character). Data types are declared before the main program. For variables, the type must be shown after the name of the variable, as illustrated on lines 5-7 of Listing 25.2. More examples of type declarations are shown below.

```
var
    Amount          :real;
    CodeLetter      :char;
    NumberOfItems   :integer;
```

The type `real` means that these variables can be used for numbers such as 123.456, 0.22 or –9.93, that is, *signed* numbers that are not whole numbers. The computer holds `real` numbers in floating-point form so that very large, and very small numbers can be stored.

Signed whole numbers, that is, `integer` values are stored as two's complement binary values in the computer. Some examples of integers are 23, 0, –1, 32767 and –559.

Type `char` means that the named variable (`CodeLetter` in the example above) stores a single character such as 'a', 'D', '6' or '?'.

Turbo Pascal provides a further data type to handle *strings*. A string is simply a number of characters which are collected together and used as a unit. For example, a person's name is a string of alphabetic characters, and a stock number such as 100-234/ABC in a mail order catalogue is a string containing a mixture of alphabetic, numeric and special characters. String variable declarations are illustrated in the examples below.

```
    Surname         :string[20];
    StockNumber     :string[12];
    Address1        :string[30];
```

The number inside the brackets specifies the maximum number of single characters to be handled by the named variable.

A further standard data type is the type `boolean`. This type of variable has only one of two possible values, namely `true` or `false`. A boolean variable declaration is made as follows:

```
    Morevalues      :boolean;
```

Pascal provides the two reserved words `true` and `false` which can be used to assign a value to a boolean variable, as in:

```
    Morevalues:= true;
```

The use of boolean variables will be explored in a later section.

Performing calculations

Probably every program that you will ever write will contain at least one calculation, and this is true of the majority of programs. It is not surprising therefore that Pascal and other high-level languages make calculations easy to perform. Arithmetic instructions simply involve defining what arithmetic operations are to be performed on numeric identifiers and constants. The four common arithmetic operations: add; subtract; multiply; divide, use the symbols $+$, $-$, $*$ and $/$, respectively. The examples of arithmetic operations provided in Table 25.1 assume that the following data declarations have been made.

```
const
  PI      =3.14;
var
  Length, Width, Perimeter              :integer;
  Area, Radius, Gallons, Miles, Mpg     :real;
  a, b, c, x, y                         :real;
```

Expression	Pascal statement
$Area = length \times width$	`Area:= Length*Width;`
$Area = \pi r^2$	`Area:= PI*Radius*Radius;`
$Perimeter = 2 \times (length + width)$	`Perimeter:= 2*(Length + Width);`
$Mpg = gallons \div miles$	`Mpg:= Gallons/Miles;`
$x = 0$	`x:= 0;`

Table 25.1. Examples of arithmetic operations with real variables

All of the statements in Table 25.1 involve calculating a value using `real` or `integer` variables or a combination of `reals` and `integers`. Pascals rules concerning how such calculations may be expressed are called *assignment compatibility* rules. They state that a calculation which involves: (i) a mixture of integers and reals must be assigned to a real variable; (ii) only integers may be assigned to either an integer variable or a real variable. Another point to note is that Pascal provides two divide operators. The '/' divide operator may be used with any values, `real` or `integer`, but if both values are `integers`, the result is a `real` value and must be assigned to a `real` variable. The second divide operator, `div`, is only allowed to be used with integers. If the result of a division does not produce a whole number, the fractional part is ignored. In other words, the result is rounded down to the nearest integer. The remainder when one integer is divided by another is produced by the `mod` operator. Some examples should help to clarify these points and these are shown in Table 25.2.

Operands	Example	Answer	Answer type
`real/real`	`7.3/0.2`	`36.5`	`real`
	`0.5/0.25`	`2.0`	`real`
`real/integer`	`13.9/5`	`2.78`	`real`
`integer/real`	`1116/7.2`	`155.0`	`real`
`integer/integer`	`33/11`	`3.0`	`real`
	`33/10`	`3.3`	`real`
	`3/5`	`0.6`	`real`
`integer div integer`	`33 div 11`	`3`	`integer`
	`33 div 10`	`3`	`integer`
	`3 div 5`	`0`	`integer`

integer div real	Not allowed		
real div integer	Not allowed		
real div real	Not allowed		
integer mod integer	33 mod 10	3	integer
	10 mod 33	10	
integer mod real	Not allowed		
real mod integer	Not allowed		
real mod real	Not allowed		

Table 25.2. *Examples of divide operations*

Listing 25.3 is an example of the use of integer division. The program converts a number of seconds into hours, minutes and seconds.

Listing 25.3. The `div` and `mod` integer division operators

```
1    program ModAndDiv(input, output);
2      {Program to convert a time given in seconds
3       to hours, minutes and seconds}
4
5    const
6      SECONDSPERMINUTE    =60;
7      MINUTESPERHOUR      =60;
8
9    var
10     Hours          :integer;
11     Minutes        :integer;
12     Seconds        :integer;
13     Duration       :integer;
14     Temp           :integer;
15
16   begin
17     writeln;
18     write('Enter the time in seconds: ');
19     readln(Duration);
20     Seconds := Duration mod SECONDSPERMINUTE;
21     Temp := Duration div SECONDSPERMINUTE;
22     Minutes := Temp mod MINUTESPERHOUR;
23     Hours := Temp div MINUTESPERHOUR;
24
25     writeln;
26     writeln(Duration, ' seconds is: ');
27
28
29     write(Hours, ' hours ');
30     write(Minutes, ' minutes ');
31     writeln(Seconds, ' seconds.');
32   end.
```

On line *19* the user is requested to enter the time to be converted from seconds to hours, minutes and seconds. The number of seconds is stored in the variable `Duration`. The first stage in the calculation is to calculate the remainder when `Duration` is divided by the number of seconds per minute stored in the constant SECONDSPERMINUTE which has the value 60. Suppose, for example, the user entered the number 6573 when asked for the time in seconds. Line *20* would produce the value 6573 mod 60, that is, 33. This is assigned to the variable, Seconds. Next, the temporary variable Temp is given the value 6573 div 60, that is, 109. The remainder when this last number is divided by the number of minutes per hour, that is 60, gives the value for Minutes: 109 mod 60 = 49. The number of hours is calculated using 109 div 60 = 1. Thus, when the program is run, it produces the following output:

```
Enter the time in seconds: 6573 ⏎

6573 seconds is: 1 hours 49 minutes 33 seconds.
```

Operator precedence

The term *operator precedence* applies to the order in which the operators in an arithmetic expression are used. For example, to evaluate the expression

$$x = y + 3z$$

z is multiplied by 3 before the result is added to *y*; the multiply operator thus has precedence over the addition operator. If *y* had a value of 2 and *z* had a value of 4, *x* would be calculated as

$$x = 2 + 3 \times 4 = 2 + 12 = 14$$

The higher the precedence of an operator, the sooner it is used in the evaluation of an expression. The use of parentheses within an expression can alter the way a calculation is performed. So, in the above expression, to force the addition to be performed before the multiplication, we would write x = (y + 3) × z. This would result in y being added to 3 before multiplying by z. Thus,

$$x = (2 + 3) \times 4 = 5 \times 4 = 20$$

In Pascal, the operators * and / have equal precedence; this means that in an expression involving two or more of them, they are simply used in the order that they appear in the expression. These two operators have higher precedence than + and −. Again, + and − have the same precedence. As a further example, consider the program in Listing 25.4.

Listing 25.4.	Illustration of operator precedence

```
 1    program Example2(input, output);
 2    var
 3      x1 :real;
 4      y1 :real;
 5      n :integer;
 6    begin
 7      n:= 11;
 8      y1:= 5;
 9      x1:= 1.0/2.0*(y1 + n div y1);
10      writeln(x1:8:2);
11    end.
```

The order of evaluation of line *9* is as follows:

1.	1.0/2.0	i.e.	0.5
2.	n div y1	i.e.	11 div 5 = 2
3.	y1 + n div y1	i.e.	5 + 2 = 7
4.	1.0/2.0*(y1 + n div y1)	i.e.	0.5*7 = 3.5

Reading and displaying information

Practically every program requires that data are provided by some input device such as a keyboard and that results are produced on an output device such as a monitor. Pascal provides a number of instructions to simplify these operations. The example program in Listing 25.4 used three input-output instructions, namely `readln`, `writeln` and `write`. In this section we examine these instructions in a little more detail.

The `readln` instruction uses data provided by a standard input device such as a keyboard to assign values to variables . The word `input` inside the brackets after the program name at the beginning of a Turbo Pascal program tells the Pascal compiler that a keyboard is to be used to enter character-based data (see Listing 25.4 for an example). You use the readln instruction to read real numbers, integers, single characters or strings into appropriately declared variables. For example, the statement

```
readln(Price);
```

would cause the program to wait for the user to enter a number to be stored in the real variable price. The user presses the ENTER key (⏎) to signify the end of data entry. It is good practice to include a write instruction to precede readln to inform the user what information is required. So, for example, the statements

```
write('Please enter the price of the item: ');
readln(Price);
```

would cause the computer to display

```
Please enter the price of the item:
```

on the display screen and then, with the text cursor remaining on the same line, wait for the user to type in a value and press the ⏎ key. The `writeln` instruction is almost identical to `write`, except that the text cursor is automatically moved to the beginning of the line immediately following the line on which the message is displayed. Which one of the instructions `write` and `writeln` you use depends on how you want your output to appear. Listing 25.5 illustrates the use of `write`, `writeln` and `readln`.

Listing 25.5.   Using `write`, `writeln` and `readln` instructions

```
1     program convert1(input, output);
2       {Program to convert inches to centimetres }
3     const
4       CENTIMETRESPERINCH =2.54;
5     var
6       Centimetres  :real;
7       Inches       :real;
8     begin
9       write('Enter the length in inches: ');
10      readln(Inches);
11      Centimetres := Inches*CENTIMETRESPERINCH;
12      writeln;
13      write('A length of ', Inches:5:2,' inches');
14      write(' is equivalent to ');
15       writeln(Centimetres:5:2, ' centimetres');
16    end.
```

The program would produce the following output when run:

Enter the length in inches: *12* ⏎

A length of 12.00 inches is equivalent to 30.48 centimetres

Notice the different form of the `writeln` instruction on line *12*: it simply produces a single blank line when the round brackets are not used. This is useful for making your output clear and easy to read. The output shows that the user entered the number *12* followed by ⏎ when prompted to type in the length in inches.

In line *13*, `write('A length of ', Inches:5:2,' inches');`, the purpose of the numbers after the variable `Inches` is to control the number of characters printed, that is, the *field width* and the number of decimal places of the displayed variable. In this instance the field width, including the decimal point, is to be restricted to five, with two figures after the decimal point. When the variable is of type `integer`, only one figure representing the total number of digits to be displayed is provided. If the field width is larger than the item to be displayed, the output is padded with blanks. Using a field width of zero, as in `Inches:0`, or less than the number of digits in the number, causes the minimum number of digits to be displayed. Table 25.3 contains a number of examples using various output formats.

value	type	format	output	remarks
15.234	real	:10:1	`******15.2`	Six leading spaces are added
6.6666	real	:10:1	`*******6.7`	The figure after the decimal point is rounded up
6.6666	real	:0:2	`6.67`	The minimum number of digits is displayed
−8.3124	real	:0:3	`-8.312`	As above
234.56	real	:1	`2.3E+02`	Number is displayed in floating-point form
234.56	real	none	`2.3456000000E+02`	The maximum number of decimal places is displayed
123	integer	:5	`**123`	Two leading spaces included in the field
123	integer	:2	`123`	Minimum number of figures displayed and no leading spaces
'hello'	string	:10	`*****hello`	Strings are treated like integers
'hello'	string	:0	`hello`	As above

Table 25.3. *Examples of various output formats and their effects*

Note that the instructions that we have covered in this section, namely `readln`, `write` and `writeln`, are actually implemented as *standard procedures* which are explored later.

Loops

A very frequent programming requirement is to perform a set of instructions several times. Rather than writing the set of instructions several times (which is impractical for all but a small number of repetitions), they are controlled by a special instruction which causes them to be repeated as many times as desired. Such program constructs are called *loops*, and each repetition of a set of statements is often called an *iteration*. For example, suppose a program is required to read 10 numbers, add each one to a running total and then display the final total. The program in Listing 25.6 accomplishes this task using a loop.

Listing 25.6.	Using a loop to add numbers

```
1       program RunningTotal2(input, output);
2        {Program to add ten numbers }
3       var
4         Number        :real;
5         Total         :real;
6         Count         :integer;
7       begin
8         Total:= 0;
9         writeln('Enter ten numbers: ');
10        for Count:= 1 to 10 do
11        begin
12           readln(Number);
13           Total:= Total + Number;
14        end;
15        writeln('The total is: ', Total:10:2);
16      end.
```

Listing 25.6 uses a for loop to repeat the two instructions which repeatedly read a number and add it to a running total. The for loop requires that a control variable, called Count in this example, is defined as type integer. The control variable is automatically given the first value specified (1 in this example) and, each time the statements within the loop are repeated, it is increased by 1 until it finally reaches the second value specified (10 in this example). Thus the same program, but with the value 10 replaced by the required number, could be used to add any number of numbers. Statements to be repeated are enclosed between begin and end. Listing 25.7 is a further example of the use of the for loop.

Listing 25.7.	Using a for loop to display a conversion table

```
1       program ConvTab(input, output);
2        {Program to display a conversion table for inches to
3           centimetres using a for loop}
4       const
5         CONVERSIONFACTOR =2.54;
6         MAXINCHES =12;
7       var
8         Inches :integer;
9         Centimetres :real;
10
11      begin
12        writeln;
13        writeln('Inches':20, 'Centimetres':20);
14        writeln('——':20, '————':20);
15
16        for Inches:= 1 to MAXINCHES do
17           begin
18              Centimetres:= Inches*CONVERSIONFACTOR;
19              writeln(Inches:17, Centimetres:20:2);
20           end;
21      end.
```

The output produced looks like this:

```
    Inches      Centimetres
    ------      -----------
      1            2.54
      2            5.08
     etc           etc
     12           30.48
```

Notice that the end value in the `for` statement on line *16* is a `constant` called `MAXINCHES`; this could also have been defined as a variable used in a `readln` instruction.

A slight variation in the format of a `for` statement allows the count variable to go down from a high value to a low value. For example, you could write

```
    for i:= 12 downto 1 do ....
```

which would cause the variable `i` to start at 12 and go down to 1 in steps of 1.

The `for` statement is a very useful means of implementing a loop, but certain programming problems require a different approach to repeating a set of instructions. For example, consider the following outline program description:

Read a set of real numbers representing the cost of a number of items. Accumulate the total cost of the items until a value of zero is entered, then display the number of items purchased and their total cost.

Here it is not known how many times the loop is to be repeated: the user decides when to terminate the loop by entering a *rogue value,* (zero in this case). The rogue value is used in another type of loop instruction, the `while` instruction. Listing 25.8 shows how a `while` loop can be used in conjunction with a rogue value. The rogue value is defined as a constant on line *5*. Because the user may want to terminate the program immediately, without entering any values, the program asks for a purchase amount before entering the loop starting on line *18*. The `while` instruction requires that a true/false expression is included after the word 'while'. Thus the expression, `Amount > ROGUEVALUE`, will be true if `Amount` entered is greater than zero, and it will be false if `Amount` is not greater than zero, that is if it is equal to, or less than zero. When the expression is true, the statements between the immediately following `begin` and `end`, that is lines *20* to *23*, will be executed; as soon as the expression becomes false, the loop terminates and the program goes on to line *26*.

Notice that the last instruction in the lines to be repeated is the `readln` instruction to read another value: this means that because the next instruction to be executed is the `while` instruction, the value typed in by the user is immediately compared with the rogue value. This ensures that the rogue value is not processed as an actual data item.

Listing 25.8.   Using a `while` loop and a rogue value

```
1       program RogueVal(input, output);
2         {program to illustrate the use of a rogue value
3            to terminate a loop}
4       const
5         ROGUEVALUE =0;
6       var
7         Count :integer;
8         Amount :real;
9         Total :real;
10
11      begin
12        Total:= 0;
13        Count:= 0;
```

```
14
15        write('Enter the cost of the first item, or 0 to end :');
16        readln(Amount);
17
18        while Amount > ROGUEVALUE do
19           begin
20              Count:= Count + 1;
21              Total:= Total + Amount;
22              write('Enter the cost of the next item, or 0 to end :');
23              readln(Amount);
24           end;
25
26           writeln;
27           writeln(Count, ' items were purchased.');
28           writeln;
29           writeln('The total cost was: £', Total:0:2);
30      end.
```

Here is a typical output from the program:

```
Enter the cost of the first item, or 0 to end :23.45 ⏎
Enter the cost of the next item, or 0 to end :6.12 ⏎
Enter the cost of the next item, or 0 to end :5.99 ⏎
Enter the cost of the next item, or 0 to end :0 ⏎

3 items were purchased.
The total cost was: £35.56
```

Notice that the assignment instruction on line *20*, Count := Count + 1, is used as a means of counting the number of times the loop is executed. The instruction simply adds 1 to the variable, Count, each time the instructions within the loop are repeated. The true/false expression on line *18* in the while statement uses the *relational operator*, >, meaning 'greater than', to compare Amount with ROGUEVALUE. There are in fact six different relational operators that can be used in such logical expressions, and these are shown in Table 25.4.

relational operator	meaning
>	Greater than
>=	Greater than or equal to
<	Less than
<=	Less than or equal to
=	Equal to
<>	Not equal to

Table 25.4. *Relational operators used in logical expressions*

The operators in Table 25.4 are used according to the relationship to be established between two values. Whatever logical expression is used, the result of the comparison will either be true or false - if true, the while loop will repeat; if false the loop will terminate. More examples of the use of these operators are provided in the next section, which deals with the use of logical expressions in making program decisions.

Decisions

Suppose a program is required to display multiple-choice questions with one correct answer out of three possible choices. For example, one of the questions could be:

```
A BYTE is the name given to

    (a) Four bits
    (b) Eight bits
    (c) Sixteen bits

Your answer is:
```

The program is also required to display the message

```
Correct - well done!
```

if the answer is correct, and display a message such as

```
Sorry, the correct answer is (b)
```

if the answer provided is incorrect.

The program must therefore be able to take two alternative courses of action depending on the answer supplied. An if statement is one possible way of achieving this requirement. The appropriate form of the if statement is illustrated in Listing 25.9 which shows the Pascal code required to display the question above and provide the response appropriate to the letter 'a', 'b' or 'c', typed in.

Listing 25.9.   Using an if statement

```
 1     program Decisions1(input,output);
 2      {Program to illustrate the use of the if statement}
 3     var
 4      Answer       :char;
 5     begin
 6      writeln('Enter the letter corresponding to the ');
 7      writeln('correct answer for the following question:');
 8      writeln;
 9
10      writeln('A BYTE is the name given to');
11      writeln('(a) Four bits');
12      writeln('(b) Eight bits');
13      writeln('(c) Sixteen bits');
14      writeln;
15      write('Your answer is: ');
16      readln(Answer);
17
18      if Answer = 'b' then
19         writeln('Correct - well done!')
20      else
21         writeln('Sorry, the correct answer is (b)');
22     end.
```

The if statement extending over lines *18* to *21* shows how the program can take one of two possible courses of action depending on the value of a variable. We saw in the last section concerning the use of the while statement that logical expressions are either true or false. This is also the case with the logical expression Answer = 'b' in the if statement on line *18*. If the letter stored in the character variable Answer is the letter 'b', then the logical expression Answer = 'b' will be true, otherwise it will be false. If it is true, the statement following the word then is executed (that is, line *19*), otherwise the statement after else is executed (that is, line *21*). The general form of the if statement is

```
if {logical expression} then
    {statement 1}
else
    {statement 2}
```

Note that {statement 1} is the instruction that is performed if {logical expression} is true; {statement 2} is performed if {logical expression} is false. Note also that either {statement 1} or {statement 2}, or both of them, can be a block of instructions enclosed between begin and end as follows.

```
if Answer = 'b' then
  writeln('Correct - well done!')
else
  begin
    writeln('Sorry, the correct answer is (b)');
    writeln('There are eight bits in a byte');
  end;
```

Sometimes it is necessary to choose between more than just two courses of action in a program. For example, Listing 25.10 shows a program which converts a percentage mark to a pass, merit, distinction or fail grade. The program repeatedly accepts marks and converts them to grades until the mark entered is the rogue value –1 (or any negative integer value) signifying the end of the mark inputs. The rules that are used to determine the grade are as follows:

For a distinction the mark must be over 80.

For a merit the mark must be greater than or equal to 60 and less than 80.

For a pass the mark must be greater than or equal to 40 and less than 60.

Below 40 is a fail.

Listing 25.10. The if..else if construction

```
1      program Decision2(input, output);
2        const
3          DIST    =80;
4          MERIT   =60;
5          PASS    =40;
6
7        var
8          Mark    :integer;
9
10     begin
11       writeln;
12       write('Please enter the first mark(-1 to end): ');
13       readln(Mark);
14
15       while Mark >=0 do
16         begin
17           if Mark >= DIST then
18               writeln('Distinction')
19             else if (Mark >= MERIT) and (Mark < DIST) then
```

```
20                        writeln('Merit')
21              else if (Mark >= PASS) and (Mark < MERIT) then
22                        writeln('Pass')
23                        else writeln('Fail');
24        write('Please enter the next mark(-1 to end): ');
25        readln(Mark);
26     end;
27   end.
```

The if statement between lines *17* and *23* reflects this logic exactly. It is possible to chain if statements in this way to cope with quite complex lines of reasoning. Added flexibility is provided by the use of the logical and operator used for the the logical expressions on lines *19* and *21*. The and operator requires that both of the minor logical expressions it connects are true for the complete logical expression to be true. If either or both are false, then the whole expression is false. Logical operators are discussed in more detail in the next section. Here is a typical output from the program:

```
Please enter the first mark(-1 to end):46
Pass
Please enter the next mark(-1 to end):68
Merit
Please enter the next mark(-1 to end):32
Fail
Please enter the next mark(-1 to end):83
Distinction
Please enter the next mark(-1 to end):-1
```

Logical operators

Logical operators allow you to combine logical expressions. There are three logical operators in Pascal : and, or and not. An example of the use of the and operator was provided in Listing 25.10. The and and the or operators are always placed between two logical expressions, and they each combine these logical expressions to produce a value of true or false. Table 25.5 shows the rules that are applied by Pascal to determine whether a compound logical expression is true or false. This type of table is usually called a *truth table*.

(Expr 1)	(Expr 2)	(Expr 1) or (Expr 2)	(Expr 1) and (Expr 2)
true	true	true	true
true	false	true	false
false	true	true	false
false	false	false	false

Table 25. 5. *Truth table for the* **and** *and* **or** *logical operators*

Referring back to Listing 25.10 in the previous section, on line *19*, where the compound logical expression (Mark >= MERIT) and (Mark < DIST) is used to determine whether the mark is equivalent to a merit grade. In the expression, (Mark >= MERIT) is an example of (Expr 1) and (Mark < DIST) is an example of (Expr 2) shown in Table 25.5. The next table (Table 25.6) shows how the and operator combines these two logical expressions for a number of cases.

Mark	(Mark > = MERIT)	(Mark < DIST)	(Mark > = MERIT and (Mark < DIST)
45	false	true	false
86	true	false	false
67	true	true	true

Table 25. 6. *Truth table for the* **and** *logical operator.*

Thus, both logical expressions must be true for the complete expression to be true; with the or operator, however, only one of the expressions needs to be true for the complete expression to be true. For example, consider the program in Listing 25.11 which reads some text and counts how many vowels it contains. The program uses a for loop to test each letter in turn in the text against each possible vowel. If the current letter is a vowel, that is 'a', 'e', 'i', 'o' or 'u', a count is incremented.

Listing 25.11.   Illustrating the use of the or logical operator

```
1        program Vowels(input, output);
2        var
3           VowelCount        :integer;
4           Letters           :string[80];
5           LengthOfText      :integer;
6           c                 :integer;
7        begin
8           VowelCount:= 0;
9           writeln('Type text followed by ENTER: ');
10          readln(Letters);
11          LengthOfText:= length(Letters);
12
13          for c:= 1 to LengthOfText do
14             if (Letters[c] = 'a') or
15                 (Letters[c] = 'e') or
16                 (Letters[c] = 'i') or
17                 (Letters[c] = 'o') or
18                 (Letters[c] = 'u')
19             then
20                VowelCount:= VowelCount + 1;
21
22             writeln;
23             writeln('The text contained ', VowelCount, '
         vowels');
24          end.
```

The text is held in a string variable called Letters. Each letter in Letters is accessed by specifying its position within the text. For example, if the text entered was the string 'hello there', then Letters[1] is the letter 'h', Letters[2] is the letter 'e', Letters[3] is the letter 'l', and so on. The for loop control variable, c, starts at 1 and goes up in steps of 1 to the length of the string (11 for the string 'hello there'). The length of the string is determined by the pre-defined Pascal function length(), on line *11*, which requires a string as its single argument. (See the later section on Pascal functions for more detail about functions). Here is the output from the program when the string, 'the cat sat on the mat' is typed in:

```
Type text followed by ENTER: the cat sat on the mat ⏎
```

```
The text contained 6 vowels
```

Note that the program will only work with lower-case text. The reason is that lower-case letters 'a', 'b', 'c', etc are represented in a computer using a different set of codes from the equivalent upper-case letters 'A', 'B', 'C', etc.

The third logical operator is the not operator which simply reverses the logical value of a logical expression. Thus, the logical expression not (x > 3) is true only when x is less than or equal to 3. Similarly, the logical expression not (Balance <= 0) is true only when Balance has a value that is greater than zero. The truth table shown in Table 25.7 defines the operation of the not logical operator.

Expr	not Expr
true	false
false	true

Table 25.7. *Truth table for* **not** *logical operator*

More control statements

Listing 25.12 draws together two further Pascal control statements, namely the repeat..until and the case statements using a progam which allows you to convert Pounds Sterling into one of three foreign currencies: American Dollars, German Marks or French Francs. The repeat..until statement provides a third method of constructing a loop. It is similar to the while statement in that it uses a logical condition to determine when to exit the loop, but the difference is that the condition appears at the end rather than at the beginning of the loop. This means that the loop will be executed at least once, which is appropriate for this example in which the loop repeatedly executes instructions which display a menu and ask the user to choose one of the menu options. In this example, the repeat statement repeats the statements between lines *13* to *63* until the condition following the word until is true, that is, when the user enters the letter 'X' or 'x' to indicate the desire to exit the program.

Listing 25.12.   Using the case and repeat statements in a menu program.

```
1      program menu1(input, output);
2      uses CRT;
3      const
4        DOLLARS    =1.5;
5        MARKS      =3.4;
6        FRANCS     =11;
7      var
8        Choice     :char;
9        Currency   :real;
10       Pounds     :real;
11     begin
12       repeat
13         clrscr'
14          writeln('Currency conversion program');
15         writeln;
16         writeln('(M)arks');
17         writeln('(D)ollars');
18         writeln('(F)rancs');
19         writeln('e(X)it');
20         writeln;
21         write('Which currency do you want to convert to Pounds? ');
22         readln(Choice);
23         writeln;
24
25         case Choice of
26           'D', 'd':
27                 begin
```

```
28              writeln('Enter the amount to convert to Dollars');
29              readln (Pounds);
30              Currency:=Pounds*DOLLARS;
31              writeln('You would get ',Currency:0:0,
32                      ' Dollars for',Pounds:0:0, ' Pounds');
33              writeln('Press ENTER to return to the menu');
34              readln;
35            end;
36        'M', 'm':
37            begin
38              writeln('Enter the amount to convert to Marks');
39              readln(Pounds);
40              Currency:=Pounds*Marks;
41              writeln('You would get ',Currency:0:0,
42                      ' Marks for ',Pounds:0:0, ' Pounds');
43              writeln('Press ENTER to return to the menu');
44              readln;
45            end;
46        'F', 'f':
47            begin
48              writeln('Enter the amount to convert to Francs');
49              readln(Pounds);
50              Currency:= Pounds*FRANCS;
51              writeln('You would get ',Currency:0:0,
52                      ' Francs for ',Pounds:0:0, ' Pounds');
53              writeln('Press ENTER to return to the menu');
54              readln;
55            end;
56        'X', 'x':
57            writeln('Exiting program..');
58        else
59            begin
60              writeln('Invalid option. Please try again');
61              writeln('Press ENTER to return to the menu');
62              readln;
63            end;
64      end;
65    until (Choice = 'X') or (Choice = 'x');
66  end.
```

The `case` statement is an alternative method to the `if` statement for choosing between alternative courses of action wihin a program. It has the following general format:

```
case {variable name} of
    value list 1: statement 1;
    value list 2: statement 2;
    etc...
    ......
else statement N
end;
```

The `variable name` after the word `case` can be of type `integer`, `character` or `boolean`, but `string` and `real` variables *are not allowed*. Pascal matches the value of the variable against the values specified on the subsequent lines; when a match is found, the corresponding statement is executed after which the case statement is immediately exited without considering any remaining values. If there are no values that match the variable, the `case` statement does nothing unless the `else` option is used, in which circumstances, the supplied statement (shown as `statement N` above) is executed. Note that some versions of Pascal may not support the use of the `else` option: you may need to consult the language manual for your version of Pascal. In Listing 25.12, the `case` statement is used to select the block of statements corresponding to the menu option chosen by the user. The user can choose one of four options using the letters 'D', 'M', 'F' or 'X'; to allow for the possibility of either upper or lower case letters being entered, both are included in the `case` statement value lines. Here are some program fragments which should help to clarify the use of the `case` statement:

Example 1

```
var
  Month, Days    :integer;
.......
.......
case Month of
    1, 3, 5, 7, 8, 10, 12   :Days:= 31;
    4, 6, 9, 11             :Days:= 30;
    2                       :Days:= 28;
end;
```

`Month` contains a number corresponding to the month of the year, where January = 1, February = 2 ..... December = 12. The `case` statement is used to store, in the variable, `Days`, the number of days in the month whose number is stored in `Month`. Thus if `Month` contained the number 8 corresponding to August, `Days` would be assigned the value 31.

Example 2

```
var
  Smoker :boolean;
  ......
  ......
case Smoker of
  true :writeln('Smoking seriously damages your health!');
  false :writeln('Good for you!');
end;
```

If the boolean variable, `Smoker`, has been assigned a value of `true` prior to the `case` statement, the health warning will be displayed, otherwise the complimentary message 'Good for you!' will be displayed. This is equivalent to using the `if` statement

```
if Smoker then
  writeln('Smoking seriously damages your health!')
else
  writeln('Good for you!');
```

Note that it is because `Smoker` is a boolean variable having a value of `true` or `false`, that it can be used as a logical expression in an `if` statement as illustrated above.

Example 3

```
var
  Letter :char
  VowelCount :integer;
  ConsonantCount :integer;
  .....
  .....
case Letter of
  'a', 'e', 'i', 'o', 'u' : VowelCount:= VowelCount + 1;
```

```
    'A', 'E', 'I', 'O', 'U' : VowelCount:= VowelCount + 1;
    ',', '.', ';', ':', '(', ')', ' ':{No action required}
else ConsonantCount:= ConsonantCount + 1;
end;
```

Here the program adds one to a vowel count if `Letter` contains either an upper or lower case letter; otherwise it adds one to a consonant count. Punctuation marks, brackets and spaces are ignored. Note that using `if` statements to perform this task would be much more difficult.

Arrays

An *array* is a data structure which allows you to store a number of items of data without having to allocate separate variable names to them. Arrays, like all other identifiers, must be declared before they are used. For example, the following declaration is for an array of five integers:

```
var
    Array1    :array[1..5] of integer;
```

This single declaration is in effect defining five variables called `Array[1]`, `Array[2]`, `Array[3]`, `Array[4]` and `Array[5]`, each of which can store a single integer value. The integer value inside the square brackets is called the array's index, and it is allowed only to take the range of values specified in the declaration (1 to 5 inclusive in this example). Each of these identifiers can be used just like any ordinary integer variable. For instance, to set each of them to zero could be accomplished as follows:

```
Array[1]:= 0;
Array[2]:= 0;
Array[3]:= 0;
Array[4]:= 0;
Array[5]:= 0;
```

However, we could accomplish the same operation by using an integer variable as an *index* and by putting a single assignment statement in a `for` loop:

```
for i:= 1 to 5 do Array[i]:= 0;
```

Now the count variable `i` takes on the integer values 1 to 5 and again each element in the array is set to zero. The obvious advantage of using a variable for an index is that arrays can then be used very effectively within loops, and they allow the manipulation of as many or as few numbers as appropriate to the task in hand; notice that the same `for` loop could initialise 5000 array elements as easily as 5 elements:

```
for i:= 1 to 5000 do Array[i]:= 0;
```

This would be an exceedingly difficult task to accomplish without the use of an array. Listing 25.13 illustrates the use of an array of real numbers. The program reads five numbers into an array and then finds the position within the array of the smallest number. It then swaps this number with the first number in the list before displaying the re-ordered array.

Listing 25.13.   Using an array.

```
1    program TopList(input, output);
2    uses CRT;
3    const
4      MAXNUMS    =5;
5    var
6      Array1    :array[1..MAXNUMS] of real;
```

```
7     Temp           :real;
8     i              :integer;
9   begin
10    clrscr;
11    writeln('Enter ', MAXNUMS, ');
12    writeln;
13    for i:= 1 to MAXNUMS do
14      begin
15        write('Enter number ', i, ' and press ENTER :');
16        readln(Array1[i]);
17      end;
18    for i:= 2 to MAXNUMS do
19      if Array1[i] < Array1[1] then
20        begin
21            Temp:= Array1[1];
22            Array1[1]:= Array1[i];
23            Array1[i]:= Temp;
24        end;
25    writeln;
26    writeln('The new list is as follows:');
27    for i:= 1 to MAXNUMS do write(Array1[i]:10:2);
28  end.
```

Line *2* contains a non-standard statement which allows you to clear the screen by using the pre-defined *procedure* clrscr shown on line *10*. You may have to omit these two lines if you are not using Turbo Pascal. Note that *procedures* and the uses statement are discussed later.

The program first defines a constant MAXNUMS to be the maximum size of the real array, Array1. Lines *11* to *17* are to read in the ten numbers with appropriate user prompts. Thus the first number is read into Array1[1], the second into Array1[2], and so on up to the last number which is read into Array1[10]. The second for loop starting on line *18* compares each number in the array in turn with the first number; if one is found that is greater than the first, they are swapped over. By the time the last number in the array has been compared with the first one, the largest number is in the first position in the array.

A typical output from the program might be as follows:

```
Enter 5 numbers

Enter number 1 :5.7
Enter number 2 :3.9
Enter number 3 :9.1
Enter number 4 :1.7
Enter number 5 :98.4

The new list is as follows: 1.7   3.9   9.1   5.7   98.4
```

As a final example in this section on arrays, Listing 25.14 shows a program which uses a random number generator to select five lottery numbers in the range 1 to 49.

Listing 25.14.   Using random numbers and an array to generate lottery numbers

```
1     program Lottery(input, output);
2     uses CRT;
```

```
3
4    const
5      NUMOFNUMS       =5;
6      MAXNUM          =49;
7    var
8      LuckyNums       :array[1..MAXNUM] of integer;
9      Num             :integer;
10     i               :integer;
11     Count           :integer;
12
13   begin
14     clrscr;
15     writeln('Lottery random number generator');
16      writeln;
17
18     randomize;
19
20     for i:= 1 to MAXNUM do LuckyNums[i]:= 0;
21
22     for Count:= 1 to NUMOFNUMS do
23       begin
24         Num:= random(MAXNUM + 1);
25         while LuckyNums[Num] <>  0 do
26               Num := random(MAXNUM + 1);
27
28         LuckyNums[Num]:= Num;
29         write(Num:5);
30       end;
31
32     writeln;
33     writeln;
34     write('Press ENTER to exit program');
35     readln;
36   end.
```

The random numbers are generated using the pre-defined function `random(N)` which produces a random number in the range specified by its single integer argument, N, within the brackets. For example, `random(11)` would produce a random number between 1 and 10 inclusively. Thus the statement

```
    Num:= random(MAXNUM + 1);
```

assigns a random number between 1 and 49 to the variable Num. The `randomize` instruction on line *18* simply initialises the random number generator so that it does not produce the same sequence of random numbers every time the program is run. Line *20* initialises each element to zero in the array `LuckyNums[]` which is to be used to store the five random numbers. The reason for the `while` loop on lines *25* and *26* is to ensure that the same random number is not used more than once. The loop keeps generating random numbers until it finds one that has not been generated previously. For instance, if the first random number generated on line *24* was the number 36, then this would be stored in Num. The `while` loop will only generate another random number if `Luckynums[36]` contains zero, showing that 36 has not previously been generated. As soon as the `while` loop finds an empty slot, the number is stored in the array and immediately displayed on the screen. The process repeats until five different numbers have been generated.

Pre-defined procedures and functions

High-level languages almost invariably provide libraries of useful pre-written programs that are available to the programmer. These programs, which are often termed *pre-defined procedures* and *functions*, have previously been written, compiled and thoroughly tested so that they can be used by programmers with confidence that they are error-free.

In Turbo Pascal such libraries of programs are declared with the nonstandard instruction, uses, followed by the name the library file, or *unit*, as it is called. We have already used a unit called Crt containing the procedure clrscr which was used to clear the display screen Some library programs require you to provide information in the form of *parameters* at the time they are called. An example of such a program is the delay(T) procedure which requires you to supply a delay, T, in milliseconds inside the brackets. Functions always return an item of information when they are used. For example, in Listing 25.14 we saw that the function random(N) returned to the calling program a random number in the range 1 to N-1, where N is an integer value. Whatever the version, however, Pascal always provides a number of *standard procedures* and *functions* which are available without the need to declare them in programs. They comprise procedures and functions which are considered to be the most frequently used. It was noted earlier that readln, write and writeln are in fact such standard procedures, rather than instructions such as for and if which are integral parts of the Pascal language. Turbo Pascal keeps the standard procedures and functions, plus quite a few more, in a library unit called System which is automatically available when a program is compiled. Pascal's standard functions are described at the end of this chapter, and in addition we have provided further descriptions of a selection of procedures and functions that are available in some of Turbo Pascal's other units.

Simple user-defined procedures

Procedures are often called *subprograms* or *subroutines* because they form only part of a complete program. We saw in the previous section that Pascal provides a number of pre-written functions and procedures that you can use in your own programs, but it is also possible for you to write your own. These are called *user-defined* procedures and functions.

A Pascal procedure is very similar to a Pascal program, the main difference being that a procedure cannot stand by itself - it must form part of another program. Like identifiers such as constants and variables, procedures must also be declared at the beginning of the program before they are used. The structure of a program containing two procedures, called Procname1 and Procname2, would have the outline structure shown in Listing 25.15.

Listing 25.15.   The structure of a program containing two procedures.

```
1     program Progname(input, output);
2     const
3       {Progname constants are declared here}
4     var
5       {Progname variables are declared here}
6
7     procedure Procname1;
8     const
9       {Procname1 constants are declared here}
10    var
```

```
11      {Procname1 variables are declared here}
12      begin
13        {Procname1 code goes here}
14      end;
15
16      procedure Procname2;
17      const
18        {Procname2 constants are declared here}
19      var
20        {Procname2 variables are declared here}
21      begin
22        {Procname2 code goes here}
23      end;
24      begin
25        .......
26        .......
27        Procname1;
28        .......
29        .......
30        Procname2;
31        .......
32      end.
```

The two procedure definitions, shown in the shaded sections of the program, appear after the constants and variables declarations of the main program. The definitions of the procedures look exactly like a main program, each having their own constants and variables declarations (if required) and their own main code between begin and end.

The program in Listing 25.16 illustrates the use of simple procedures to cycle through three rudimentary pictures of faces in order to give the appearance of a face winking alternate eyes. The program uses three procedures, Face1, Face2 and Face3, each of which uses keyboard characters to display a face. The procedures are executed in the main program by simply naming them. Thus line *36* Face1 causes the instructions in procedure Face1 to be executed. The program then continues with line *37* delay(500), a pre-defined procedure which causes a delay of 500 milliseconds.

Listing 25.16.   Using procedures to make a face wink.

```
1       program Winker(input, output);
2       uses CRT;
3       var
4        i     :integer;
5
6       procedure Face1;
7       begin
8         clrscr;
9         writeln('   _ _   ');
10        writeln(' < 0 0 > ');
11        writeln('  | ^ |  ');
12        writeln('   \_/   ');
13      end;
```

```
14
15    procedure Face2;
16    begin
17     clrscr;
18     writeln('    _ _     ');
19     writeln(' < 0 o > ');
20     writeln('  | ^ |  ');
21     writeln('   \_/    ');
22    end;
23
24    procedure Face3;
25     begin
26     clrscr;
27     writeln('    _ _     ');
28     writeln(' < o 0 > ');
29     writeln('  | ^ |  ');
30     writeln('   \_/    ');
31     end;
32
33    begin
34    for i:= 1 to 10 do
35     begin
36        Face1;
37        delay(500);
38        Face2;
39        delay(500);
40        Face1;
41        delay(500);
42        Face3;
43        delay(500);
44     end;
45    end.
```

Each of the procedures uses the pre-defined `clrscr` procedure to clear the screen so that the face stays in the same place and appears to wink. Notice that the logic of the main program is easy to follow by the use of procedures - this is one of their major advantages. Another feature of this program is that although the procedure `Face1` is used twice, the code required for it appears only once in its definition. This economical use of program code is another major advantage of using procedures in programs.

Global vs local variables

Earlier we said that a procedure is allowed to have its own `var` declarations. When this is the case, the variables declared in the procedure are termed *local* variables. This means that these variables only have values while the procedure is being executed; once the procedure has been completed and control has returned to the main program, local variables cannot be accessed. On the other hand, *global* variables which are defined in the main program are always available, even to procedures, while the program is running. Note, however, that if a variable declared in a procedure has the same name as a variable declared in the main program, the local variable only, can be used in the procedure. These ideas are best illustrated with the aid of an example such as that shown in Listing 25.17.

Listing 25.17.   A program to illustrate the difference between global and local variables

```
1     program Scope(input, output);
2     uses CRT;
3     var
4        Greeting1      :string[20];
5
6     procedure Proc1;
7     var
8        Greeting1      :string[20];
9     begin
10      Greeting1:= 'How do';
11      writeln('Proc1':15, 'Greeting1':15, 'local ':15,
           Greeting1:15);
12    end;
13
14    procedure Proc2;
15    var
16      Greeting2      :string[20];
17        begin
18      Greeting2:= 'Hi ';
19      writeln('Proc2':15, 'Greeting2':15, 'local ':15,
           Greeting2:15);
20      writeln('Proc2':15, 'Greeting1':15, 'global':15,
           Greeting1:15);
21    end;
22
23    begin
24      clrscr;
25      writeln('Source':15, 'Variable':15, 'Scope':15, 'Value':15);
26       writeln;
27       Greeting1:= 'Hello ';
28      writeln('Main ':15, 'Greeting1':15, 'global':15,
           Greeting1:15);
29      Proc1;
30      Proc2;
31       end.
```

The program declares three string variables: Greeting1 which is a global variable defined on line *4*, Greeting1 a variable local to procedure Proc1 and declared on line *8*, and finally Greeting2, a local variable declared in Proc2 on line *16*. The main program assigns a value ('Hello') to Greeting1 on line *27* and displays it. Then, when Proc1 is executed, the local variable Greeting1 is assigned a different value ('How do') on line *10* and then displays that string. Finally, when Proc2 is executed, it displays the contents of the local variable Greeting2 followed by the global variable Greeting1. Note that an attempt to include a line such as

```
writeln(Greeting2);
```

after line *30* in the main program would result in an error since, once Proc2 has terminated, the local variable Greeting2 does not exist. Here is what the program produces as its output:

Source	Variable	Scope	Value
Main	Greeting1	global	Hello
Proc1	Greeting1	local	How do
Proc2	Greeting2	local	Hi
Proc2	Greeting1	global	Hello

Each line of the output indicates the source of the line, that is whether it is generated from the main program or from a procedure, the name of the variable whose value is being displayed, whether the variable is local or global, and the contents of the variable.

Using parameters in procedures

The 'wink' program shown in Listing 25.16 uses the simplest form of procedure which performs a task without any need to communicate with the main program. However, there will be many instances when you will want to use information available in the main program. As we saw in the previous section, global variables provide one means of accomplishing this, but for sound reasons current programming practice discourages the use of global variables for this purpose. Usually a much better method is to use procedures which have either *value parameters* or *variable parameters*.

Value parameters

Listing 25.18 is a modification of the program shown in Listing 25.16. Notice that another procedure, Wink(), has been included. This new procedure uses a *value parameter*, called Eye, which is defined within brackets after the procedure name on line *34*. A value parameter allows you to pass a value to a procedure from the main program or from another procedure. Thus, on line *47*, the value of the for loop variable k is passed to the procedure Wink. k takes the values 1, 2 and 3 which are used to decide which of the three procedures, Face1, Face2 or Face3 to execute. In effect, this causes each of the latter three procedures to be executed in turn. The outer for loop makes this cycle of three procedures repeat ten times. When one loop is controlled by an outer loop in this fashion, they are called *nested loops*.

Listing 25.18.   A program to illustrate the use of value parameters

---

```
1    program Winker2(input, output);
2    uses CRT;
3    var
4      i      :integer;
5      k      :integer;
6
7    procedure Face1;
8    begin
9      clrscr;
10     writeln('    _ _    ');
11     writeln(' < 0 0 > ');
12     writeln('  | ^ |   ');
13     writeln('    \_/    ');
14    end;
15
16   procedure Face2;
17   begin
18     clrscr;
```

```
19      writeln('    _ _    ');
20      writeln(' < 0 o > ');
21      writeln('  | ^ |  ');
22      writeln('   \_/   ');
23    end;
24
25    procedure Face3;
26      begin
27      clrscr;
28      writeln('    _ _    ');
29      writeln(' < o 0 > ');
30      writeln('  | ^ |  ');
31      writeln('   \_/   ');
32      end;
33
34    procedure Wink(Eye:integer);
35    begin
36      case Eye of
37         1 :Face1;
38         2 :Face2;
39         3 :Face3;
40      end;
41    end;
42
43    begin
44    for i:= 1 to 10 do
45      for k:= 1 to 3 do
46        begin
47           Wink(k);
48           delay(500);
49        end;
50    end.
```

The number of parameters that you can use in a procedure is not limited to one - you can use as many as you like as long as you declare them in the procedure definition and include them within the brackets when you call the procedure from the main program. For example, suppose that we wanted to include the pre-defined delay procedure on line *48* within the procedure Wink() as shown in the program fragment below.

```
procedure Wink(Eye:integer, Time:integer);
begin
  case Eye of
      begin
         1 :begin
              Face1;
              delay(Time);
            end;
         2 :begin
              Face2;
              delay(Time);
```

```
                        end;
                3 :begin
                        Face3;
                        delay(Time);
                    end;
        end;
```

Now Wink() has two value parameters and these would both be included in any call to the procedure, as shown in the example below.

```
        for i:= 1 to 10 do
            for k:= 1 to 3 do Wink(k, 500);
```

An important point about value parameters is that they provide a *one-way transfer of information* from the main program to a procedure. Variables used as value parameters when a procedure is called are unaffected by any processing that has occurred within the procedure; this is not the case, however, with *variable parameters*.

Variable parameters

Listing 25.19 is an example of a program which incorporates a procedure that uses a variable parameter.

Listing 25.19. A program to illustrate the use of variable parameters.

```
1      program VarParam(input, output);
2      var
3        Smaller      :real;
4        Larger       :real;
5
6      procedure Sort(var a, b:real);
7      var
8        Temp         :real;
9      begin
10       if a > b then
11          begin
12             Temp:= a;
13             a:= b;
14             b:= Temp;
15          end;
16       end;
17
18     begin
19        write('Enter two numbers: ');
20        readln(Smaller, Larger);
21        Sort(Smaller, Larger);
22        write('The sorted numbers are: ');
23        writeln(Smaller:10:2, Larger:10:2);
24     end.
```

The program simply sorts two numbers into ascending order of magnitude using a procedure. The procedure has two variable parameters, a and b, which it compares: if a is greater than b, the values in a and b are swapped over. The main program asks the user to enter two numbers, it calls the procedure using the two numbers stored in Smallest and Largest, and then displays them when the procedure has finished. Here is a typical run of the program:

```
Enter two numbers: 34.6 17.32 ⏎

The sorted numbers are: 17.32 34.6
```

Notice that the values contained in Smallest and Largest, which were exchanged in the procedure using the variables a and b, have been swapped over. Thus, *variable parameters allow a two-way exchange of data* between a program and a procedure.

User-defined functions

As well as being able to write your own procedures you can also devise your own functions. Functions also accept value or variable parameters, but in addition they require that you declare what type of value they return. So, for a function, you would need to write its first line using the following format:

```
function FunctionName(parameters):return type;
```

In addition, you must assign the return value to FunctionName somewhere within the function. For example, for a function called TriangleType which accepts three positive real numbers, in ascending order of magnitude, representing the three sides of a triangle and which returns an integer value of 0, 2 or 3 indicating how many of its sides are equal, the function definition in Listing 25.20 might be appropriate.

Listing 25.20.   A function to determine the type of triangle represented by three numbers

```
20    function TriangleType(a, b, c:real):integer;
21      var
22        Count      :integer;
23      begin
24        Count:= 0;
25        if a = b then Count:= Count + 1;
26         if b = c then Count:= Count + 1;
27         if c = a then Count:= Count + 1;
28        case Count of
29           0 :TriangleType:= 0;
30           1 :TriangleType:= 2;
31           2 :{not possible}
32           3 :TriangleType:= 3;
33         end;
34      end;
```

The three sides are passed as value parameters to the variables a, b and c. The if statements on lines *25* to *27* increment Count if any two sides are the same. The values that Count can assume are 0 for no sides equal, 1 if two sides are equal and 3 if all three sides are equal; a value of 2 is not possible when the three sides are arranged in ascending order of magnitude. The number of equal sides is stored in TriangleType by the case statement and it is this value which is returned by the function to the calling program. Note that because a function always returns a value it can be used like a variable in an arithmetic expression or in a logical expression or in a write statement. For example, it would be perfectly valid to write

```
if TriangleType(x, y, z) = 3 then writeln('Equilateral triangle');
```

Writing programs using procedures and functions

Listing 25.21 illustrates the use of user-defined procedures and functions in a program which allows two people to use the computer to play noughts and crosses. The program illustrates the use of procedures and functions appropriate to a variety of situations. The main program alternately gets X and O moves, checking each time for a winning or drawn position. The program terminates when someone has won or after nine moves have been made.

Listing 25.21. Noughts and crosses game

```
1    program Oxo(input, output);
2
3    {-----------------------------------------------------------------}
4    {A program which makes use of functions and procedures to allow }
5    {two players to play noughts and crosses. The computer checks    }
6    {for a win  or draw automatically, and ensures that illegal      }
7    {moves are not made. The board is a grid numbered 1 to 9. Each   }
8    {Player in turn selects a number and the grid is redrawn with    }
9    {the X or O in that position. X always starts first.             }
10   {-----------------------------------------------------------------}
11
12   uses CRT;{The screen handling unit to allow screen to be cleared}
13
14   var
15     Grid        :array[1..9] of char;
16     Move        :integer;
17     Count       :integer;
18     Winner      :boolean;
19     XMove       :boolean;
20
21   procedure InitGrid;
22   {-----------------------------------------------------------------}
23   {Sets up the board with the positions numbered from 1 to 9      }
24   {-----------------------------------------------------------------}
25
26   begin
27     Grid[1]:='1';
28     Grid[2]:='2';
29     Grid[3]:='3';
30     Grid[4]:='4';
31     Grid[5]:='5';
32     Grid[6]:='6';
33     Grid[7]:='7';
34     Grid[8]:='8';
35     Grid[9]:='9';
36   end;
37
38   procedure DrawGrid;
39   {-----------------------------------------------------------------}
40   {This draws the current board after every move                  }
41   {-----------------------------------------------------------------}
42
43   begin
44     clrscr;
45     writeln(' ',Grid[1], ' | ', Grid[2], ' | ', Grid[3]);
46     writeln('--|--|--');
47     writeln(' ',Grid[4], ' | ', Grid[5], ' | ', Grid[6]);
48     writeln('--|--|--');
49     writeln(' ',Grid[7], ' | ', Grid[8], ' | ', Grid[9]);
```

```
50    writeln;
51  end;
52
53  function CheckMove(Move:integer):boolean;
54  {-------------------------------------------------------------}
55  {This validates every move to make sure that a number         }
56  {from 1 to 9 is chosen and that the selected position is      }
57  {not already occupied by an X or O.                           }
58  {Parameters: Move - integer value parameter                   }
59  {Return value:boolean - true if valid, false if invalid move  }
60  {-------------------------------------------------------------}
61
62  begin
63    CheckMove:= true;
64    if (Move < 1) or (Move > 9) then
65      begin
66        writeln('Invalid position - number between 1 and 9');
67        CheckMove:= false;
68      end
69    else if (Grid[Move] = 'X') or (Grid[Move] = 'O') then
70      begin
71        writeln('This position has already been used');
72        CheckMove:= false;
73      end;
74  end;
75
76  function GetXmove:integer;
77  {-------------------------------------------------------------}
78  {Accepts the X move from the player. If the move is invalid, the}
79  {player is required to enter the move again.                  }
80  {Parameters: None                                            }
81  {Return value: Integer in the range 1 to 9                   }
82  {-------------------------------------------------------------}
83  var
84    Xpos            :integer;
85     ValidXMove      :boolean;
86  begin
87    repeat
88      writeln;
89      writeln('Enter position( 1 to 9 ) for X move');
90      readln(Xpos);
91      ValidXMove:= CheckMove(Xpos);
92    until ValidXMove;
93    GetXmove := Xpos;
94  end;
95
96  function GetOmove:integer;
97  {-------------------------------------------------------------}
98  {This accepts the O move from the player. If the move is      }
99  {invalid the player is required to enter the move again.      }
100 {Parameters: None                                            }
101 {Return value: Integer in the range 1 to 9                   }
102 {-------------------------------------------------------------}
103 var
104    Opos            :integer;
105    ValidOMove      :boolean;
106 begin
107    repeat
108      writeln;
109      writeln('Enter position( 1 to 9 ) for O move');
```

```
110        readln(Opos);
111         ValidOMove:= CheckMove(Opos);
112    until ValidOMove;
113    GetOmove:= Opos;
114 end;
115
116 function CheckForWinner :boolean;
117 {------------------------------------------------------------------}
118 {Checks for a line of Xs or Os in one of the 7 possible ways     }
119 {Determines whether row, column or diagonal contains the same    }
120 {character (ie an X or an O)                                     }
121 {Parameters: None                                                }
122 {Return value: Boolean - true if there is a winner, else false  }
123 {------------------------------------------------------------------}
124
125 begin
126    if   (Grid[1]=Grid[2])  and  (Grid[2]=Grid[3])  or
127         (Grid[4]=Grid[5])  and  (Grid[5]=Grid[6])  or
128         (Grid[7]=Grid[8])  and  (Grid[8]=Grid[9])  or
129         (Grid[1]=Grid[4])  and  (Grid[4]=Grid[7])  or
130         (Grid[2]=Grid[5])  and  (Grid[5]=Grid[8])  or
131         (Grid[3]=Grid[6])  and  (Grid[6]=Grid[9])  or
132         (Grid[1]=Grid[5])  and  (Grid[5]=Grid[9])  or
133         (Grid[3]=Grid[5])  and  (Grid[5]=Grid[7])
134    then         .
135         CheckForWinner:= true
136    else CheckForWinner:= false;
137 end;
138
139 begin   {Main program }
140    InitGrid;          {Call procedure to initialise the board }
141    Count:= 0;         {Counts the number of valid moves made  }
142    Winner:= false;    {Boolean variable which becomes true     }
143                       {when there is a winner                  }
144    XMove:= true;      {Keeps track of whose move it is:        }
145                                {true for X move                }
146                                {false for Y move               }
147    DrawGrid;          {Display the initial board position      }
148
149    {Loop to repeat the playing sequence                        }
150    while (Count < 9) and not Winner do
151      begin
152        case XMove of
153        true:               {Do this if it is X's move        }
154            begin
155              Move:= GetXmove;{Get the X move position          }
156              Grid[Move]:='X';{Store it in the data structure}
157              XMove:= false;  {Make it O's move next            }
158            end;
159        false:              {Do this if it is O's move        }
160            begin
161              Move:= GetOmove; {Get the O move position         }
162              Grid[Move]:= 'O';{Store it in the data structure}
163              XMove:= true;    {Make it X's move next           }
164            end;
165      end;
166
167    Count:= Count + 1;      {Increment count after every move}
168
169    DrawGrid;               {Show the current board position }
```

```
170
171     {Check to see if the game is a win or draw          }
172      Winner:= CheckForWinner;
173      if Winner
174        then writeln('End of Game:', Grid[Move], ' has won')
175      else if Count=9
176        then writeln('A draw');
177      end;
178
179      readln;
180 end.
```

The two procedures, InitGrid and DrawGrid, and the four functions, CheckMove, GetXMove, GetYMove and CheckForWinner, are described in the following sections.

InitGrid

This procedure initialises the character array, Grid[], which is a global array used throughout the program by every procedure and function. The procedure is used once only and does not require any parameters.

DrawGrid

This procedure draws the current board position. Initially the board is displayed like this:

```
1 | 2 | 3
--|---|--
4 | 5 | 6
--|---|--
7 | 8 | 9
```

The numbers are replaced by Xs and Os as the game progresses.

CheckMove

This function has a single integer value parameter called Move which represents the current player's choice of board position. The function first checks that the integer is in the range 1 to 9 before checking the contents of Grid[Move] to ensure that the position is not already occupied with an X or an O. If the move is valid, the function returns a boolean value of true, otherwise it returns false. CheckMove is used by the following two functions.

GetXMove

This function asks the X player to type in a number from 1 to 9 representing a board position. If the move is valid, the function terminates and the position entered by the player is returned as an integer value; if the move is invalid (see function CheckMove) the player is requested to try again.

GetOMove

This function asks the O player to type in a number from 1 to 9. Otherwise it is structurally identical to GetXMove.

CheckForWinner

This function checks individually the three rows, three columns and two diagonals, to see that they contain the same character. If one of these lines does contain the same character, then one of the players has won. For example, if the diagonal represented by Grid[1], Grid[5] and Grid[9] all contain an X, then the X player has won.

Advantages of using procedures and functions

All good programmers make full use of procedures and functions, and in fact their use is essential to the development of all but the most trivial programs. There are a number of good reasons for making this statement, including the following: (i) they allow a large, complex program to be built up from a number of smaller or more manageable units. This facilitates a team approach to program development by allowing each unit to be written and tested independently of the rest of the program; (ii) they can reduce the amount of code required for a program. Once a subprogram has been developed, it can be used as many times as required within a program using the same code; (iii) they can reduce the amount of time required to write a program if libraries of re-usable functions and procedures are available. This is much the same as building electronic circuits using standard electronic components.

Screen handling

Turbo Pascal's CRT unit contains a number of useful screen handling functions and procedures. We have already used two of the procedures in the unit: `clrscr` to clear the screen and `delay()` to make the computer pause while executing a program. More functions and procedures in the CRT unit are described below.

Window procedure

Defines a text window on the screen. The syntax of the procedure is

`Window(X1,Y1,X2,Y2)` where the four parameters are explained by the following diagram.

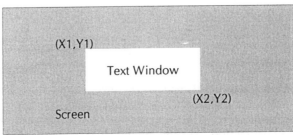

To set a text window containing ten lines at the top of the screen use

```
window(1,1,80,10)
```

To return the current window to the full screen size use

```
window(1,1,80,25)
```

ClrEol procedure

Clears all characters from the cursor position to the end of the line without moving the cursor. It uses the current text window.

DelLine procedure

Deletes the line containing the cursor in the current text window.

GotoXY procedure

Moves the cursor to X, Y, where X is the column and Y is the row relative to the top left corner of the current window which has the coordinates (1, 1). Thus to move the cursor to row 5, column 10, you would use `GotoXY(10,5)`.

InsLine procedure

Inserts a line in the current text window, above the line that the cursor is on.

TextColor procedure

This sets the colour for subsequently displayed text. There are sixteen colours and you can specify each one by name or by using the equivalent number as shown in the Table 25.8. Thus, to set the text colour to red, you could use either TextColor(Red) or TextColor(4).

By using the pre-defined constant, blink, you can make the text flash, for example, TextColor(Blue + Blink).

colour	value	colour	value	colour	value	colour	value
Black	0	Red	4	DarkGray	8	LightRed	12
Blue	1	Magenta	5	LightBlue	9	LightMagenta	13
Green	2	Brown	6	LightGreen	10	Yellow	14
Cyan	3	LightGray	7	LightCyan	11	White	15

Table 25.8.

TextBackGround procedure

This allows you to set one of sixteen different colours for the text background. The colours are shown in the table. Thus to set the background colour to light grey you could use either TextBackGround(LightGray) or TextBackGround(7). Note that if you clear the screen using clrscr after setting the background colour, the whole of the current text window will change to that colour.

Example program 1

The example shown in Listing 25.22 illustrates the use of text windows and text colours by drawing random windows of different colours.

Listing 25.22. Using text windows

```
1    program Screen1(input,output);
2
3    {-------------------------------------------------------------}
4    {Illustrates some screen handling facilities by              }
5    {drawing randomly sized and coloured windows                 }
6    {-------------------------------------------------------------}
7
8    uses CRT;
9    var
10     x       :integer;
11     y       :integer;
12     i       :integer;
13
14   begin
15     textbackground(Black);     {Clear screen}
16     clrscr;
17
18     for i:= 1 to 100 do
19        begin
```

```
20        {Draw random windows}
21          x := Random(60);     {Random x position}
22          y := Random(15);     {Random y position}
23          window(x, y, x + Random(10), y + Random(8));
24          textbackground( Random(16) + 1);
25          clrscr;      {Set window to random colour}
26                                {in the range 1 to 16}
27          delay(200); {Pause for 200 millisecs}
28        end;
29
30      end.
```

KeyPressed and Readkey

Two other useful functions to be found in Turbo Pascal's CRT unit are KeyPressed and ReadKey. KeyPressed returns a boolean value of true if there is a character in the keyboard buffer and false if the buffer is empty. The keyboard buffer is simply an area of memory which is used to store, temporarily, characters entered through the keyboard. KeyPressed can therefore be used to detect any use of the keyboard. A common application of KeyPressed is as a means of terminating a loop, as illustrated by the following program fragment.

```
repeat
     {instructions to be repeated}
until keypressed;
```

Each time through the repeat loop KeyPressed tests the keyboard buffer: if a key has been pressed, the keyboard buffer will have at least one entry, KeyPressed returns true and the loop terminates, otherwise KeyPressed returns false and the loop repeats once more.

Readkey allows you to capture a keystroke by reading the first character in the keyboard buffer. If the keyboard buffer is empty, it waits until a character is available and then returns its value. The advantage of using ReadKey rather than read or readln is that it is not necessary to press ⏎.

Example program 2

The program shown in Listing 25.23 echoes only numeric characters to the screen, ignoring characters that are not in the range 0 to 9. The repeat loop terminates as soon as the space bar is pressed.

Listing 25.23.   Using readkey.

```
1     program EchoNumbers(input,output);
2     {-----------------------------------------------------------}
3     {Program to display numeric digits entered at keyboard      }
4     {and to ignore any other characters typed. The program      }
5     {terminates when the space bar is pressed.                  }
6     {-----------------------------------------------------------}
7
8     uses CRT;
9
10    var
11      key     :char;
12
```

```
13    begin
14       repeat
15         key:= readkey;
16         if (key >= '0') and (key <='9') then write(key);
17       until key = ' ';
18      end.
```

Sound and NoSound

Finally, these two procedures allow you to use your computer's built-in speaker. Sound(Pitch) causes the speaker to emit a tone whose pitch is determined by the integer parameter, Pitch. Thus, Sound(500) produces a tone with pitch 500Hz. NoSound terminates the tone produced by Sound. Thus to produce a tone of 300Hz for half a second within a program you could use:

```
sound(300);
delay(500);
nosound;
```

Example program 3

As a final example Listing 25.24 uses all of the screen handling functions and procedures discussed in a program which measures how quickly you are able to press a key after being given a signal.

Listing 25.24.   Screen handling example.

```
1    program reflexes(input, output);
2
3    {-----------------------------------------------------------------}
4    {A program to illustrate some screen handling facilities.         }
5    {The user is invited to test his/her reflexes by pressing a key   }
6    {as quickly as possible. The average of three attempts is         }
7    {calculated and displayed in millisecond units.                   }
8    {-----------------------------------------------------------------}
9
10   uses crt;
11     const
12     ROW          =2; {The row base position for screen text         }
13     COLUMN       =5; {The column base position for screen text      }
14
15     var
16     i            :integer; {A for loop control variable             }
17     Total        :integer; {The total time for the three attempts   }
18   {.............................oOo..................................}
19
20     procedure FlushKeyboardBuffer;
21
22   {-----------------------------------------------------------------}
23   {This makes sure that there are no characters in the standard     }
24   {input buffer. The function readkey removes a single character    }
25   {from the keyboard buffer. Keypressed is true while there is at   }
26   {least one character in the buffer                                }
27   {-----------------------------------------------------------------}
28
29     var
30     key :char;
31
32     begin
```

```
33      while keypressed do
34        key:= readkey;
35    end;
36    {.........................oOo.............................}
37
38     procedure PressAnyKey;
39
40    {------------------------------------------------------------------}
41    {A procedure that waits until a key is pressed before        }
42    {continuing with the next instruction                        }
43    {------------------------------------------------------------------}
44
45     begin
46      FlushKeyboardBuffer;      {Ensure that the keyboard buffer is  }
47                                  {empty                             }
48        repeat until keypressed; {Do nothing until a key is pressed  }
49    end;
50    {.........................oOo.............................}
51
52    procedure instructions;
53
54    {------------------------------------------------------------------}
55    {Displays the instructions for using the program             }
56    {------------------------------------------------------------------}
57
58    begin
59      window(10,10,70,20);       {Define the text window            }
60      textcolor(yellow);         {Text colour set to yellow         }
61      textbackground(blue);      {Background text clour is blue     }
62      clrscr;
63      gotoxy(COLUMN, ROW);
64      writeln('Put your finger on any key and as soon as');
65      gotoxy(COLUMN, ROW+1);
66      writeln('this window changes colour, press it');
67      gotoxy(COLUMN, ROW+3);
68      writeln('You will get three tries and the program');
69      gotoxy(COLUMN, ROW+4);
70      writeln('will calculate your average response time');
71      gotoxy(COLUMN +5, ROW+6);
72      write('Press any key to begin');
73      PressAnyKey;
74    end;
75    {.........................oOo.............................}
76
77    function Time(attempt:integer):integer;
78
79    {------------------------------------------------------------------}
80    {Uses the delay() procedure to determine the response time in }
81    {milliseconds required for hitting the space bar.             }
82    {------------------------------------------------------------------}
83
84    var
85       Millisecs :integer;
86
87    begin
88      clrscr;
89      textcolor(yellow);
90      gotoxy(COLUMN, ROW);
91      case attempt of
92         1:write('First attempt starting..');
```

```
93         2:write('Second attempt starting..');
94         3:write('Third attempt starting..');
95     end;
96     randomize;              {Initialise the random number generator }
97
98     Millisecs:= 0;
99     delay(1000);            {Pause for one second before timing  }
100        textcolor(red + blink);
101        write(' NOW!');
102        delay(random(5000));  {Random delay of up to 5 seconds    }
103        FlushKeyboardBuffer;  {Make sure that there are no         }
104                             {characters in the keyboard buffer  }
105        textbackground(Red);
106        clrscr;             {The signal to press the space bar  }
107
108        repeat
109           delay(1);
110           Millisecs:= Millisecs + 1;{Count how many msecs expire }
111        until keypressed;             {Look for user hitting any key }
112        Time:= Millisecs;             {Return time taken to respond  }
113    end;
114 {..........................oOo...........................}
115
116 procedure Results(Average:real);
117
118 {————————————————————————————}
119 {Displays the average time taken over the three attempts    }
120 {————————————————————————————}
121
122 begin
123    textbackground(LightGray);
124    textcolor(Black);
125    clrscr;
126    gotoxy(COLUMN, ROW);
127    write('Your average response time was ', Average:5:0,
128             ' milliseconds');
129    gotoxy(COLUMN, ROW + 5);
130    write('Press any key to continue');
131    PressAnyKey;
132 end;
133
134 begin
135    Total:= 0; {Set the total time to 0 }
136    for i:= 1 to 3 do          {Repeat the trial three times        }
137    begin
138      Instructions; {Display the user instructions }
139      Total:= Total + Time(i);{Accumulate time for each trial     }
140    end;
141    Results(Total/3);          {Display result of the three trials}
142 end.
```

The main program starts on line *134*. The procedure Instructions explains that the user is to press a key as quickly as he/she can when a rectangular window changes colour. The function Time() times how long it took to do so in milliseconds. This time is added to a running total which accumulates the times for three attempts. Results() displays the average time the user took to respond. The program makes good use of user-defined functions and procedures, and the comments in the program Listing 25.24 explain their operation, but it is worth adding some further explanation regarding the procedure PressAnyKey and associated functions and procedures. As mentioned earlier, the buffer memory associated with the keyboard temporarily stores the values of key depressions made while the program is running, and these values can be accessed using the ReadKey function which extracts the first available character in the buffer. By repeatedly using this function to read single characters until there are no more left in the buffer, FlushKeyboardBuffer empties the buffer in preparation for using the KeyPressed function. This is to ensure that KeyPressed will detect only the next key depression and not any that have been made previously.

Reference section

This section describes a number of Pascal's standard functions and some of the additional functions provided by Turbo Pascal.

Standard Pascal functions

abs

Returns the absolute, that is unsigned, value of a real or integer value.

Examples

If x is a real variable then

1.   x:= abs (-3.7)   gives   x = 3.7

2.   x:= abs (24.3)   gives   x = 24.3

If i is an integer variable then

3.   i:= abs (-6)   gives   i = 6

4.   i:= abs (3.232)

is not allowed since the type of the returned value (real) is not the same as the type of the argument (integer).

exp

Returns the exponential of the argument, that is e^a, where a is the value of the parameter supplied in brackets and e is a mathemetical constant approximately equal to 2.72.

Example

If x is a real variable then

x:= exp (2)   gives   x = 7.39 (that is, $x=e^2$)

ln

Returns the natural logarithm of the argument, that is, the inverse of the exp function.

Example

If x is a real variable then

x:= ln (7.39)   gives   x = 2

sqr

Returns the square of the argument, that is x^2 , where x is the argument.

Examples

If x is a real variable then

1. `x:=sqr(-3.1)` gives x = 9.61
2. `x:=sqr(3.1)` gives x = 9.61

If i is an integer variable then

3. `i:=sqr(-6)` gives i = 36
4. `i:=sqr(3.232)`

    is not allowed since the type of the returned value (real) is not the same as the type of the argument (integer).

Sqrt

Returns the square root of the operand, that is $\sqrt{x}$, where x is a positive valued argument.

Examples

If x is a real variable then

1. `x:=sqrt(16.3)` gives x = 4.04
2. `x:=sqrt(-16.3)` is not allowed since x is negative

If i is an integer variable then

3. `i:=sqrt(16)` gives i = 4
4. `i:=sqrt(-16)` is not allowed since i is negative

sin

Returns the sine of the argument which must be in radians.

Example

Since 1 radian $= \dfrac{180}{\pi}$ degrees, to convert an angle from degrees to radians we must divide the angle by $\dfrac{180}{\pi}$ where $\pi \approx 3.1416$

Thus, if x is a real variable and we want the sine of 30^0, then

$\qquad$ `x:=sin(30/(180/3.1416))` gives x = sine(30^0) = 0.5

cos

Returns the cosine of the argument which must be in radians. See sin above for converting degrees to radians.

Example

If x is a real variable and we want the cosine of 30^0, then

$\qquad$ `x:=cos(30/(180/3.1416))` gives x = cosine(30^0) $\approx$ 0.87

Note that the sin and the cos functions can be used together for finding the tangent of an angle, since $\tan \theta = \sin \theta / \cos \theta$

arctan

Returns the arc tangent of the argument in radians. This is the inverse of finding the tangent of an angle.

Example

If x is a real variable and we want to find the arc tangent of 1 then

$$x := \texttt{arctan(1)} * (180/3.1416) \quad \text{gives} \quad x = \text{arctangent}(1) = 45^0$$

round

Returns the nearest integer type value to the real type value provided.

Examples

If i is an integer variable then

1. i := round (34.3)   gives   i = 34
2. i := round (34.8)   gives   i = 35

trunc

Converts a real type value to an integer type value by removing the fractional part of the real value.

Examples

If i is an integer variable then

1. i := trunc (34.3)   gives   i = 34
2. i := trunc (34.8)   gives   i = 34
3. i := trunc (.975)   gives   i = 0

ord

This gives the ASCII numeric value for characters.

Examples

If c is an integer variable then

1. c := ord ('a')   gives   c = 97
2. c := ord ('A')   gives   c = 65
3. c := ord ('?')   gives   c = 63

chr

Returns the character equivalent of a numeric code in the range 0 to 255

Examples

If c is an character variable then

1. c := chr (97)   gives   c = 'a'
2. c := chr (65)   gives   c = 'A'
3. c := chr (63)   gives   c = '?'

The following program prints the full character set:

```
program CharSet(input, output);
var
c :char;
i :integer;
begin
```

```
        for i:= 0 to 255 do
        writeln(i:10, chr(i):10);
    end.
```

odd

Returns TRUE if the argument is an odd number and FALSE if it is an even number. The argument must be an integer. The sign of the argument is ignored.

Examples

If t is a boolean variable then

1. t := odd(23)   gives   t = TRUE
2. t := odd(22)   gives   t = FALSE
3. t := odd(-23)   gives   t = TRUE
4. t := odd(0)   gives   t = FALSE
3. t := odd(7.5)   is not allowed since the argument must be an integer.

Some Turbo Pascal functions

These functions are always available in Turbo Pascal and do not require a unit declaration.

Length

Returns the length of a string.

Example

If s1 := '1234567' and len is an integer variable then

     len := length(s1)   gives   len = 7;

Concat

Joins together a number of strings. The strings are provided as arguments to the function.

Examples

If string variables s1, s2 and s3 have the values

```
s1= 'One, two, three o clock '
s2= 'four o clock '
s3= 'rock'
```

and s4 is another string variable then

     s4 := concat(s1, s2, s3) gives s4= 'One, two, three o clock four o clock rock'

Copy

This allows a set of characters, or a *substring*, to be copied from a string. It has the form:

     copy(Str, StartChar, NumOfChars)

where Str is the string from which the substring is to be copied,

StartChar is the position within Str from which to start copying and NumOfChars is how many characters are to be copied.

Examples

If s1 = 'Copy me please'

1. `s2:= copy(s1, 6, 2)`   gives   s2 = 'me'
2. `s3:= copy(s1, 1, length(s1))` gives   s3= 'Copy me please'

Pos

Returns the starting position of a substring within a string. Returns zero if the substring is not found.

Examples

1. `p:= pos('Koteikan, Windsor Tce', ',')` gives p=9
2. `p:= pos('abcde', 'z')`   gives p=0

Upcase

Converts a letter to capitals, that is, upper case. Non letters are not affected.

Examples

1. `Capital:= upcase('x');` gives   Capital='X'
2. `Capital:= upcase('X');` gives   Capital='X'
3. `Capital:= upcase('3');` gives   Capital='3'
4. `readln(Answer);`
5. `if upcase(Answer) = 'Y' then writeln('The Y key was pressed');`

(This is a good way to ensure that pressing both 'y' and 'Y' can be detected).

Random

Generates a random number in the range 0 to *n*-1 where *n* is the integer value supplied to the function.

Example

        `writeln(random(10) + 1)`

generates a random number between 1 and 10 inclusively.

Randomize

This is a procedure used in conjunction with random function described above. It initialises the random number generator using the system clock so that each time a program is run it does not generate exactly the same set of random numbers.

Programming Exercises

For each of the following problems, design, implement and thoroughly test the program.

Decisions

1. Read a number and display a message which states whether the number is positive, negative or zero.

2. Read a number and print it only if it is between 10 and 20.

3. Read a number followed by a single letter code. The number represents the price of an item and the code indicates whether tax is to be added to the price. If the code is "V" then the tax is 20% of the item's cost. If the code is "X" then the item is not taxed. Print out the total cost of the item.

4. Read three positive, non-zero integers which may represent the sides of a triangle. The numbers are in ascending order of size. Determine whether or not the numbers do represent the sides of a triangle.

5. Read in a single character and print a message indicating whether or not it is a vowel.

Loops

6. Write separate programs to produce conversion tables for:

    (i)   Inches to centimetres (1 to 20 inches, 1 inch = 2.54 centimetres);

    (ii) Pounds to kilograms (1 to 10 pounds, 2.2 pounds per kilogram);

    (iii) Square yards to square metres (10, 20 ,30,..., 100 sq yds 1yd = .91 m)

7. The cost and discount code of a number of items are to be entered by a user. The program must print out each item's cost, discount and cost less discount. The discount codes are as shown alongside. The program will terminate when the user enters 0 for the cost of the item. The program must then print the total cost of all the items entered.

Code	Discount
A	5%
B	10%

8. Write a program to repeatedly display a menu containing a number of options for converting between different units, plus one option to exit the program. The user must enter a number or letter corresponding to a menu item. Valid entries are to accept a numeric value from the user and apply and display the appropriate conversion, invalid entries are reported and the user is reminded about what choices are valid, and the exit option terminates the program. An example follows.

    > Menu

    1 Inches to centimetres

    2 Centimetres to inches

    3 Pounds to Kilograms

    etc

    4 Exit

    Please enter option number :

9. A program reads an integer representing the number of gas bills to be processed, followed by that number of customer details. Each set of customer details consists of a customer number, a single character code representing the type of customer and the number of units used. Customers are of type 'D' (domestic) or 'B' (business). Domestic customers are charged 8p per unit and business customers are charged 10p per unit. For each customer print the customer number, the number of units used and the cost of the gas used. Print the total number of units used for this batch of customers and the total amount charged.

10. Repeat the previous question assuming that all the domestic users are first and that separate totals are required for domestic and business users.

Strings

11. Read two strings and compare them. Print a message to indicate whether or not they are identical.

12. Repeat the previous problem but ignore case. For example, your program should regard the strings

    "Hello There", "HELLO THERE", and "hello there" as being identical.

13. Read a string representing a sentence and print the number of words in the sentence. Assume that words are separated by no more than one space and that there are no punctuation marks in the text.

14. Write separate programs to enter and store a string of up to 80 characters and then:

    (i)   Count the number of leading spaces;

    (ii) Count the number of trailing spaces;

    (iii) Count the number of embedded spaces;

    (iv) Count the number of leading, trailing and embedded spaces;

    (v)   Remove leading and trailing spaces from a string, and reduce multiple embedded spaces to single spaces.

15. Read a string containing a sentence and print the words in reverse order. For example, the sentence "the cat sat on the mat" would become, "mat the on sat cat the".

16. Read a string and determine whether it is purely alphabetic, purely numeric or a mixture of alphabetic and numeric characters.

Arrays

17. Read 15 values into a numeric array and then:

    (i)   print the contents the array;

    (ii) find the average of the numbers stored in the array;

    (iii) copy the array into a duplicate array, but in reverse order. Print the contents of both arrays.

18. Read a set of numbers and swap the first number with the largest in the set. Then, starting from the second value, find the largest number in the remaining list and swap it with the second value.

    Repeat this process until the list has been sorted into ascending order of magnitude.

Validation

19. Post codes have the following possible formats:

    (i)   aa99 9aa

    (ii) aa9 9aa

    (iii) a9a 9aa

    where *a* represents an alphabetic character and *9* represents a numeric character. Write a program to validate a post code, assuming that only uppercase letters are used and there is a single space separating the two parts of the post code.

20. As for the previous problem but allow upper and lower case letters, leading spaces, trailing spaces and more than one space between the two parts of the code.

Encoding

21. Many names that sound the same are often spelled differently and this can cause problems in information systems. For example, Waites, Waits and Whaites all sound the same though they are all spelled differently and contain different numbers of letters. A coding system called Soundex can be used to solve this problem by converting a name into a code based on the following algorithm.

   (i)   The first letter of the name is used as the first letter of the code.

   (ii) All subsequent vowels, and the letters H, W and Y are ignored.

   (iii) Double letters are replaced by single instances of the letter.

   (iv) Then this code, apart from the first character, is converted into a number by substituting the letters in the following table by numeric digits.

Letter	Substitute
BFPV	1
CGJKQSXZ	2
DT	3
MN	4
L	5
R	6

   (v)   The code is restricted to four characters including the leading letter.

   (vi) If the code is less than four characters it is padded with zeros.

22. Write a program to convert a name into its equivalent Soundex code. Some examples are given below.

   Morton becomes M635

   Morten becomes M635

   Waites becomes W320

   Whaites becomes W320

   Waits becomes W320

23. The table illustrates the Morse code.

A	. −	N	− .
B	− . . .	O	− −
C	− . − .	P	. − − .
D	− . .	Q	− − . −
E	.	R	. − .
F	. . − .	S	. . .
G	− .	T	−
H	. . . .	U	. . −
I	. .	V	. . . −
J	. − − −	W	. − −
K	− . −	X	− . . −
L	. − . .	Y	− . − −
M	− −	Z	− − . .

   (i)   Write a program to read in a word (or a sentence) and output it in Morse code.

   (ii) Add sound so that when a letter is pressed on the keyboard the appropriate Morse code is heard.

24. A form of encoding used on the Internet is called "rot13" encoding. It involves taking each letter of the alphabet and replacing it by the letter 13 positions further on in the alphabet as shown in the following table.

Letter	Replace with	Letter	Replace with	Letter	Replace with
A	N	J	W	S	F
B	O	K	X	T	G
C	P	L	Y	U	H
D	Q	M	Z	V	I
E	R	N	A	W	J
F	S	O	B	X	K
G	T	P	C	Y	L
H	U	Q	D	Z	M
I	V	R	E		

(i) Write a program to read a block of text and encode it using rot13. Spaces and punctuation marks do not need to be encoded.

(ii) Write a program to decode text which has been encoded using rot13.

(iii) Invent and implement your own encoding and decoding scheme using a different form of substitution.

An Introduction to Visual Basic

Overview

Even for experienced programmers, creating a program that runs under the latest Microsoft Windows *Operating System* can be a daunting task, particularly when using traditional programming languages such as Pascal, C or C++. Consequently, many program developers are using Visual Basic (VB) for application prototype development, or even for producing the final application program. The reason for the widespread adoption of VB is that it hides the complexities of Windows programming by the use of special graphical tools. These tools provide a convenient graphical user interface allowing complex windows components to be incorporated in a program with great ease.

Typically, a Visual Basic program is a collection of control objects that respond to user actions such as mouse operations and keyboard use. These actions generate events that are linked to program code. For example, a commonly used control is a *command button* that simulates a physical switch such as that used for door bells. 'Pushing' the button by clicking the mouse over it is a mouse-click event that can cause a specific section of code to be executed. Each type of control has one or more related events, each of which can be programmed. For this reason Visual Basic is classed as an *event-driven programming language*. The collection of control objects forms the user interface, the basis of most Visual Basic programs. Program design starts with creating the user interface which defines the functionality of the program. Then code is written to perform the required functions. Because control objects can be added to the user interface independently of other control objects, programs can be developed and tested in a modular fashion. A new control can be created, configured, modified, programmed and tested independently of existing controls. Moreover, the effects of any changes to the program can be examined immediately simply by clicking a button on the Visual Basic toolbar. This is one of the great strengths of Visual Basic, that programs can be created and modified very quickly and easily.

However, although VB can help novice programmers to produce professional-looking Windows programs relatively easily, it introduces a number of concepts additional to other more traditional languages. The VB programmer needs to know about objects, methods, properties and events in addition to such traditional programming concepts as variables, constants, control structures, files and subprograms. This brief introduction to programming in Visual Basic is in three parts:

1. **VB Programming Environment.** Later in this chapter we describe the VB environment and provide instructions for creating and running simple programs.

2. **Programming Basics.** Traditional programming concepts are examined using VB as the programming language. Once VB has been set up for the tutorial, the first example programs that illustrate programming concepts can be run without the complications of having to create procedures or screen objects.

3. **Introduction to Event-driven Programming.** A number of simple programs illustrate elementary event-driven programming principles. Objects such as Forms, Command buttons, List boxes and Text boxes are introduced.

Pre-requisites

To use this Visual Basic tutorial you need access to Microsoft Visual Basic version 4 or above running under Windows 95 or above, and you must be familiar with the Microsoft Windows 95/98/ME/2000 operating system. You should know how to run applications, maximise, minimise, resize and scroll windows, use a mouse to select and drag items and be able to save and load documents using standard File menu commands.

You also need to set up a simple project in Visual Basic, as explained after the next section, to be able to run the example programs in the next chapter, "Programming Basics".

The Visual Basic Programming Environment

The screenshot of the Visual Basic 6 programming environment shows the main features (described below) used in this introduction to VB. Note that in other versions of Visual Basic the toolbox, project window, properties window and form may initially appear in separate, movable windows.

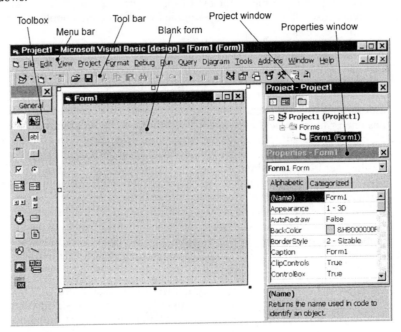

Menu and Toolbar

The Menu bar provides access to all of VB's utilities. We will mostly make use of the File, Edit, Debug and Run menus. The Toolbar provides quick access to some VB features. We will use some of these features in example programs.

Form

A Form is the container for user interface controls. These controls can be visually positioned and moved by using the mouse. Example programs that use forms are provided in *Event-driven Programming*.

Toolbox

The Toolbox allows you to select, position and configure various controls on a Form. It displays all the standard Visual Basic controls plus any custom controls and insertable objects you have added to your project with the Custom Controls dialog box. You can display ToolTips for the Toolbox buttons by selecting the Show ToolTips option in the Environment tab of the Options dialog box. To open the Toolbox, choose Toolbox from the View menu.

The tools used in this introduction to Visual Basic are briefly described below. You can learn about other tools from VB Help.

Pointer. This is the only item in the Toolbox that doesn't draw a control. Use it to resize or move a control after it has been drawn on a form.

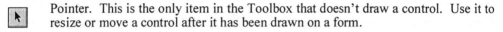 **PictureBox.** Use to display graphical images (either decorative or active), as a container that receives output from graphics methods, or as a container for other controls.

Label. Use for text that you don't want the user to change, such as a caption under a graphic.

TextBox. Use to hold text that the user can either enter or change.

Frame. Use to create a graphical or functional grouping for controls. To group controls, draw the Frame first, and then draw controls inside the frame.

CommandButton. Use to create a button the user can choose to carry out a command.

CheckBox. Use to create a box that the user can easily choose to indicate if something is true or false, or to display multiple choices when the user can choose more than one.

OptionButton. Use in a group of option buttons to display multiple choices from which the user can choose only one.

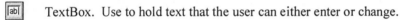 **ComboBox.** Use to draw a combination list box and text box. The user can either choose an item from the list or enter a value in the text box.

ListBox. Use to display a list of items from which the user can choose one. The list can be scrolled if it has more items than can be displayed at one time.

Timer. Use to generate timer events at set intervals. This control is invisible at run time.

DriveListBox. Use to display valid disk drives.

DirListBox (directory list box). Use to display directories and paths.

FileListBox. Use to display a list of files.

Shape. Use to draw a variety of shapes on your form at design time. You can choose a rectangle, rounded rectangle, square, rounded square, oval, or circle.

Line. Use to draw a variety of line styles on your form at design time.

Image. Use to display a graphical image from a bitmap, icon, or metafile on your form. Images displayed in an Image control can only be decorative and use fewer resources than a PictureBox.

OLE Container. Use to link and embed objects from other applications in your Visual Basic application.

CommonDialog. Use to create dialog boxes for operations such as opening, saving, and printing files, or selecting colours and fonts. CommonDialog is a custom control.

Project window

The Project window shows the project forms and modules and allows you to view code or forms.

To view the code associated with a form, click the code icon. To view the form itself, click the form icon.

Creating a project allows you to keep all of the files associated with the project together.

Properties window

Objects such as forms and controls used in a project have properties associated with them. For instance, the width, height and colour of a form are properties. The Properties window allows you to set and modify all of the properties associated with an object.

Setting up Visual Basic to run example programs in "Programming Basics"

You will need to create a simple project called "VBConcepts.vbp" to allow you to create and run the example programs given later in the chapter. To create the VBConcepts project, follow the instructions below:

First launch VB and start a new project.

1. Open the project window by pressing Ctrl+R.

2. If there is a Form in the project window delete it by clicking the mouse right-hand button and selecting "Remove".

3. Create a new Module (Menu: Insert|Module, VB4 or Menu: Project|Add Module, VB6). The code window for the module should appear.

4. Create a procedure called "Main" (Menu: Insert|Procedure.. VB4 or Tools|Add procedure.. VB6)

The code window should look much like this on the right.

5. Finally, open the Debug window by pressing Ctrl+G.

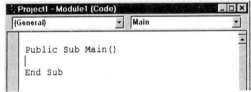

Now save the project as "VBConcepts".

Create and run example programs in "Programming Basics"

 In the next chapter, we will create example programs by first opening project *VBConcepts.vbp* and then entering code between the lines `Public Sub Main()` and `End Sub` in the code window. To run the program you click the ***Run*** button on the toolbar. Any output from the program will be shown in the Debug window. (**Note:** if the Debug window is not visible prior to running a program, press Ctrl+G).

Chapter 27

VB programming basics

This chapter introduces basic programming concepts common to languages such as Pascal and C/C++ as well as Visual Basic, the language used here. We cover the following subjects:

- Variables and Constants
- Performing calculations
- Arrays
- Data Types
- Loops
- Strings
- Simple input and output
- Decisions
- Visual Basic functions

A first VB program

As a simple example to illustrate creating and running a program, Listing 27.1 shows a program which calculates the total cost of a purchased item by calculating VAT and adding it to the price of the item.

The algorithm on which the program is based is as follows:

1. *Ask the user to enter the price of the item*

2. *Store the price*

3. *Calculate the VAT at 17.5% (i.e. multiply the price by 0.175)*

4. *Calculate the total price by adding the VAT to the price*

5. *Display the total cost on the screen.*

Listing 27.1.   A simple program to calculate the total cost of a purchase

---

```
Public Sub Main()
' ====== Program to calculate the total cost of an item ======
10 Const VAT = 0.175
20 Dim Price As Single
30 Dim Tax As Single
40 Dim TotalCost As Single
50 Price = InputBox("Enter price of the item")
60 Tax = Price * VAT
70 TotalCost = Price + Tax
80 Debug.Print "The total cost is: "; TotalCost
End Sub
```

Note: line numbers are optional in VB, and we have used them to allow us to describe the operation of the example programs in detail.

The operation of the program

The first two lines (without line numbers) identify the program. "Sub" stands for *Sub*program or *Sub*routine and "Main" is the name of the program (this will be the name of all our example programs in this tutorial). The single quotation mark identifies the rest of the line as a comment. Comments are ignored by VB and are used to annotate programs.

Lines *10* declares that VAT is a *constant* value.

Lines *20 - 40* declare three *variables* Price, Tax and TotalCost each as being of type single. (This means *single* precision real number - ie a number having figures after the decimal point). Variables are used to store data, which in this case are in the form of real numbers, that is, numbers which are not whole numbers. Every variable used in a VB program must be declared in this way.

Up to this point the programmer has defined a number of *identifiers* that will be used in the procedural part of the program which follows.

Line *50* causes the message 'Enter price of the item' to be displayed on the screen in an input box. That appears like this:

The user types in the value for the price of the item and then clicks OK or presses the Enter key on the keyboard. The value entered by the user is stored in the variable Price.

Line *60* stores the result of Price multiplied by VAT in the variable Tax.

Line *70* stores the result of adding Price and Tax in TotalCost.

Line *80* then displays the text, 'The total cost is: ' followed by the value stored in TotalCost in the Debug window. The Debug.Print statement indicates that the variables and/or text following is to be printed in the Debug window. As its name suggests, the Debug window is generally used for debugging , that is finding and correcting programs, but it is used in this context to simplify learning VB concepts. Print is known as a *Method* of the Debug window *Object*. We will be discussing *Objects* and *Methods* later in the tutorial.

Finally, End sub indicates the end of the program. When the program is run, if the user entered the value 20 in the input box, the output from the program would look like this:

Some general remarks

Before going on to explore VB in more depth, it is worth mentioning a few general points at this stage:

1. VB does not distinguish between the use of capitals and lower-case letters. Thus it regards Price, PRICE and price as being exactly the same.

2. It is a good idea to include comment lines - text beginning with a single quote (') - to describe the purpose of lines or sections of your program. Particularly for large, complex programs, this is very helpful if it is necessary to change the program at some later date.

3. Using spaces, blank lines and indentation can greatly improve the appearance and the clarity of a program, thus making the program easier to read and understand if it has to be modified later for any reason.

4. Programming involves meticulous attention to detail; omitting punctuation marks, including them in the wrong place or making spelling mistakes will usually cause VB to report a syntax error on a program line, but sometimes such slips might cause errors which are more difficult to detect, so be very careful to form instructions precisely.

5. Line numbers are used in VB as labels for the GOTO instruction. Our example programs contain line numbers only so that we can identify lines that we want to explain; you do not need to include these line numbers in your own programs.

6. The Debug window (also called the Immediate window) is mainly used as a debugging aid. In this tutorial we are using it to simplify showing the output from example programs. When VB programs are compiled into stand-alone applications, the debug window would not appear. Topics later in the tutorial will deal with more usual methods of displaying program output.

Identifiers and data types

The term *identifier* is a general term used for *variables*, *constants* and other programmer-defined names such as *procedures* and *functions*. Variables and constants are normally associated with a data *type*. *VB does not require that variables are given a type* such as `Integer` or `Single` but it is good practice do so by using `Dim` and `Const` declarations.

Variables

A variable, which represents an item of data such as a single number, has a name and a current value. Variables are given names such as `Amount`, `Total` or `Numb3` and are assigned values by program instructions. These values are stored in the memory of the computer and they are accessed whenever a variable is referenced in a program instruction. So, for example, in the instruction

```
Total = Price + Tax
```

the value associated with the variable `Price` is added to the value of the variable `Tax` and the sum is then assigned to the variable `Total`. If in a previous instruction `Total` had already been assigned a value, that value would be replaced by the new one.

Constants

Constants too are assigned values but only once after the word `Const`. The constant `VAT` in Listing 1 is an example. Constants retain their values throughout the execution of a program; VB does not allow you to use a constant in an instruction which tries to change the value of the constant. Thus, if in Listing 1, you included an instruction such as

```
VAT = 0.2;
```

in the main program, VB would report an error.

Reserved words

Words that form part of the VB language are not allowed to be used as identifier names. For instance, if you included in your program the line

```
Print = 3
```

VB would report an error because `Print` is a reserved word that is part of the VB language. VB also provides a large number of predefined constants that programmers can use but not change. Many, but not all, of these constants start with the letters vb, for example,

```
vbMultiSelectNone
```

Some of VB's reserved words are shown in the next table. You will soon learn to avoid using reserved words as identifiers by careful choice of identifier names, but be aware that illegal use of reserved words will cause an error.

Reserved words		
And	Wend	Not
Case	Next	Xor
End	Set	Until
Dim	To	Do
Or	Step	
If	Then	
For	Goto	
While	On	

VB imposes a number of restrictions concerning the formation of names for identifiers:

1. The name must consist only of alphabetic and numeric characters.

2. The name must start with an alphabetic character.

3. The name must not be a reserved word or predefined VB constant.

Examples of valid identifiers

```
firstNum     NUMBER1      abc31          Counter      x
```

Examples of invalid identifiers

```
12abc                (starts with a numeric character)
first-number         (contains a non-alphabetic/numeric character)
var 1                (contains a space)
End                  (a reserved word)
```

As well as having names and values, variables are also given a *type*. Three commonly used types are `Integer`, `Single` and `String`. Variable data types are declared before the variables are used in the program. For the purposes of this tutorial, we will use the `Dim` statement to declare variables, but note that this is not the only way it can be done.

The *type* must be shown after the name of the variable in the `Dim` statement. Some examples of type declarations are shown below.

```
Dim Amount As Single
Dim Address as String
Dim NumberOfItems As Integer, Count As Integer
```

The third example illustrates that more than one variable can be declared in a single `Dim` statement.

The type `single` means that these variables can be used for numbers such as $123 \cdot 456, 0 \cdot 22$ or $-9 \cdot 93$, that is, *signed* numbers that are not whole numbers. The computer holds `Single` numbers in 32-bit floating-point form so that very large, and very small numbers can be stored.

Signed whole numbers, that is, `Integer` values are stored as two's complement binary values in the computer. Some examples of integers are 23, 0, −1, 32767 and −559.

Type `String` means that the named variable (`Address` in the example above) can store a number of alphanumeric characters such as "24 Railway Terrace, Shilbottle, Countyshire".

A further standard data type is the type `Boolean`. This type of variable has only one of two possible values, namely `True` or `False`. A boolean variable declaration is made as follows:

```
Dim MoreValues As Boolean
```

VB provides the two reserved words `True` and `False` which can be used to assign a value to a boolean variable, as in:

```
Morevalues = True
```

The use of boolean variables will be explored in a later section. The following table shows all the data types supported by VB, including their storage sizes and ranges.

Data type	Storage size	Range
Byte	1 byte	0 to 255
Boolean	2 bytes	True or False.
Integer	2 bytes	−32,768 to 32,767
Long (long integer)	4 bytes	−2,147,483,648 to 2,147,483,647
Single (single-precision floating-point)	4 bytes	−3.402823E38 to -1.401298E−45 for negative values; 1.401298E-45 to 3.402823E38 for positive values
Double (double-precision floating-point)	8 bytes	−1.79769313486232E308 to −4.94065645841247E-324 for Negative values; 4.94065645841247E-324 to 1.79769313486232E308 for positive values.
Currency (scaled integer)		−922,337,203,685,477.5808 to 922,337,203,685,477.5807
Date	8 bytes	January 1, 100 to December 31, 9999
Object	4 bytes	Any Object reference
String (variable-length)	10 bytes + string length	0 to approximately 2 billion
String (fixed-length)	Length of string	1 to approximately 65,400
Variant (with numbers)	16 bytes	Any numeric value up to the range of a Double
Variant (with characters)	22 bytes + string length	Same range as for variable-length String
User-defined	Number required by elements	The range of each element is the same as the range of its data type

Performing calculations

Probably every program that you will ever write will contain at least one calculation, and this is true of the majority of programs. It is not surprising therefore that VB and other high-level languages make calculations easy to perform. Arithmetic instructions simply involve defining what arithmetic operations are to be performed on numeric identifiers and constants. The four common arithmetic operations: add; subtract; multiply; divide, use the symbols +, −, * and /, respectively.

The examples of arithmetic operations provided in Table 27.1 on the next page assume that the following data declarations have been made.

```
Const PI = 3.14
Dim Length As Integer, Width As Integer, Perimeter As Integer
Dim Area as Single, Radius as Single, Gallons as Single, Miles As
Single, Mpg As Single
Dim x As Single
```

Expression	VB statement
Area = length × width	`Area = Length*Width`
Area = $\pi \times$ radius^2	`Area = PI*Radius*Radius`
Perimeter = 2 × (length + width)	`Perimeter = 2*(Length + Width)`
Mpg = gallons ÷ miles	`Mpg = Gallons/Miles`
x = 0	`x = 0`

Table 27.1. *Examples of arithmetic operations with real variables*

Another point to note is that VB provides two divide operators. The '/' divide operator may be used with any values, real or integer, and it produces a real result, that is a non-integer value. The second divide operator, '\', produces an integer result. If the result of a division does not produce a whole number, the fractional part is ignored. In other words, the result is rounded down to the nearest integer. The remainder when one integer is divided by another is produced by the Mod operator. Some examples of different combinations of real and integer divisions are shown in Table 27.2. VB automatically rounds any non-integer values used with \ and Mod.

Operands	Example	Answer	Answer type
real / real	7.3 / 0.2	36.5	real
	0.5 / 0.25	2.0	real
real / integer	13.9 / 5	2.78	real
integer / real	1116 / 7.2	155.0	real
integer / integer	33 / 11	3.0	real
	33 / 10	3.0	real
	3 / 5	0.6	real
integer \ integer	33 \ 11	3	integer
	33 \ 10	3	integer
	3 \ 5	0	integer
integer \ real	33\3.3	11	integer
	33\3.8	8	integer
real \ integer	15.9\4	4	integer
real \ real	14.9/3.3	5	integer
integer mod integer	33 mod 10	3	integer
	10 mod 33	10	integer
integer mod real	10 mod 3.3	1	integer
real mod integer	14.4 mod 4	2	integer
real mod real	13.9 mod 3.3	4	integer

Table 27.2. *Examples of divide operations*

Listing 27.2 is an example of the use of integer division. The program converts a number of seconds into hours, minutes and seconds.

Listing 27.2. The \ and Mod integer division operators

```
Public Sub Main()
' ====== Program to illustrate integer division ======

' Declare identifiers
10 Const SECONDSPERMINUTE = 60
20 Const MINUTESPERHOUR = 60
30 Dim Hours As Integer
40 Dim Minutes  As Integer
50 Dim Seconds As Integer
60 Dim Duration As Integer
70 Dim Temp  As Integer

' Get the duration in seconds
80 Duration = InputBox("Enter the length of time in seconds")

'Calculate equivalent hours minutes and seconds
90 Seconds = Duration Mod SECONDSPERMINUTE
100 Temp = Duration \ SECONDSPERMINUTE
110 Minutes = Temp Mod MINUTESPERHOUR
120 Hours = Temp \ MINUTESPERHOUR

'Display the results
130 Debug.Print Duration; " seconds is: "
140 Debug.Print Hours; " hours "
150 Debug.Print Minutes; " minutes "
160 Debug.Print Seconds; " seconds."

End Sub
```

On line *80* the user is requested to enter the time to be converted from seconds to hours, minutes and seconds:

The number of seconds is stored in the variable Duration. The first stage in the calculation is to calculate the remainder when Duration is divided by the number of seconds per minute stored in the constant SECONDSPERMINUTE which has the value 60. Suppose, for example, the user entered the number 6573 when

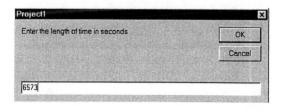

asked for the time in seconds. Line *90* would produce the value 6573 mod 60, that is, 33. This is assigned to the variable, Seconds. Next, the temporary variable Temp is given the value 6573 \ 60, that is, 109. The remainder when this last number is divided by the number of minutes per hour, that is 60, gives the value for

Minutes: 109 mod 60 = 49. The number of hours is calculated using 109 \ 60 = 1. Thus, when the program is run, it produces the following output:

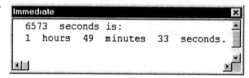

Operator precedence

The term *operator precedence* applies to the order in which the operators in an arithmetic expression are used. For example, to evaluate the expression

$$x = y + 3z$$

z is multiplied by 3 before the result is added to *y*; the multiply operator thus has precedence over the addition operator. If *y* had a value of 2 and *z* had a value of 4, *x* would be calculated as

$$x = 2 + 3 \times 4 = 2 + 12 = 14$$

The higher the precedence of an operator, the sooner it is used in the evaluation of an expression. The use of parentheses within an expression can alter the way a calculation is performed. So, in the above expression, to force the addition to be performed before the multiplication, we would write x = (y + 3) × z. This would result in y being added to 3 before multiplying by z. Thus,

$$x = (2 + 3) \times 4 = 5 \times 4 = 20$$

In VB, the operators *, /, div and mod have equal precedence; this means that in an expression involving two or more of them, they are simply used in the order that they appear in the expression. These four operators all have higher precedence than + and −. Again, + and − have the same precedence. As a further example, consider the program in Listing 27.3.

Listing 27.3.   Illustration of operator precedence

```
Public Sub Main()
' ====== Program to illustrate operator precedence ======

10 Dim x1 As Single
20 Dim y1 As Integer
30 Dim n As Integer

40 n = 11
50 y1 = 5
60 x1 = 1 / 2 * (y1 + n \ y1)

70 Debug.Print x1

End Sub
```

The order of evaluation of line *60* is as follows:

1.	½	i.e.	0.5
2.	n \ y1	i.e.	11 \ 5 = 2
3.	y1 + n \ y1	i.e.	5 + 2 = 7
4.	½* (y1 + n \ y1)	i.e.	0.5*7 = 3.5

The For..Next statement

A very frequent programming requirement is to perform a set of instructions several times. Rather than writing the set of instructions several times (which is impractical for all but a small number of repetitions), they are controlled by a special instruction which causes them to be repeated as many times as desired. Such program constructs are called *loops*, and each repetition of a set of statements is often called an *iteration*. For example, suppose a program is required to read 10 numbers, add each one to a running total and then display the final total. The program in

Listing 27.4 accomplishes this task using a loop.

Listing 27.4.   Using a loop to add numbers

```
Public Sub Main()
' ====== Program to add ten numbers    ======

' Declare variables
10 Dim Number  As Single
20 Dim Total As Single
30 Dim Count As Integer

' Initialise running total variable
40 Total = 0

' Get numbers and add to running total
50 For Count = 1 To 10
60   Number = InputBox("Please enter a number")
70    Total = Total + Number
80 Next Count

' Display final total
90 Debug.Print "The total is: "; Total

End Sub
```

Listing 27.4 uses a For loop to repeat the two instructions which repeatedly read a number and add it to a running total. The For loop requires that a control variable, called Count in this example, is defined as type integer. The control variable is automatically given the first value specified (1 in this example) and, each time the statements within the loop are repeated, it is increased by 1 until it finally reaches the second value specified (10 in this example). Thus the same program, but with the value 10 replaced by the required number, could be used to add any number of numbers. Statements to be repeated are enclosed between For and Next Count.

Listing 27.5 is a further example of the use of the For loop.

Listing 27.5.   Using a For loop to display a conversion table

```
Public Sub Main()
' ====== Program to display a conversion table for
'        inches to  centimetres using a For loop   ======

' Declare constants and variables
10 Const CONVERSIONFACTOR = 2.54, MAXINCHES = 12
20 Dim Inches As Integer
30 Dim Centimetres As Single


50 Debug.Print "Inches", "Centimetres"
60 Debug.Print "——", "———-"


70  For Inches = 1 To MAXINCHES
80    Centimetres = Inches * CONVERSIONFACTOR
90    Debug.Print Inches, Centimetres
100 Next Inches

End Sub
```

The output looks like this alongside. Notice that the end value in the `For` statement on line *100* is a constant called MAXINCHES; this could also have been defined as a variable, its value to be supplied by the user using an `InputBox` instruction.

Inches	Centimetres
1	2.54
2	5.08
3	7.62
4	10.16
5	12.7
6	15.24
7	17.78
8	20.32
9	22.86
10	25.4
11	27.94
12	30.48

A variation in the format of a `For` statement allows the count variable to go down from a high value to a low value. For example, you could write

```
For i= 12 To 1 Step -1
```

which would cause the variable `i` to start at 12 and go down to 1 in steps of 1.

The While..Wend statement

The `For` statement is a very useful means of implementing a loop, but certain programming problems require a different approach to repeating a set of instructions. For example, consider the following outline program description:

Read a set of real numbers representing the cost of a number of items. Accumulate the total cost of the items until a value of zero is entered, then display the number of items purchased and their total cost.

Here it is not known how many times the loop is to be repeated: the user decides when to terminate the loop by entering a *rogue value*, (zero in this case). The rogue value is used in another type of loop instruction, the `While` instruction.

Listing 27.6 shows how a `While` loop can be used in conjunction with a rogue value.

Listing 27.6.   Using a While loop and a rogue value

```
Public Sub Main()
' ====== Program to illustrate the use of a rogue value
'         to terminate a loop                              ======

' Declare constants and variables
10 Const ROGUEVALUE = 0
20 Dim Count As Integer
30 Dim Amount As Single
40 Dim Total As Single

' Initialise variables
50 Total = 0
60 Count = 0
' Get the cost of the first item
70 Amount = InputBox("Enter the cost of the first item, or 0 to end:")
' Loop to get the remaining items
80   While Amount > ROGUEVALUE
90     Count = Count + 1
100    Total = Total + Amount
110    Amount = InputBox("Enter the cost of the next item, or 0 to
end:")
120 Wend
' Display the restults
130 Debug.Print Count; "items were purchased"
140 Debug.Print "The total cost was: £"; Total
End Sub
```

The rogue value is defined as a constant on line *10*. Because the user may want to terminate the program immediately, without entering any values, the program asks for a purchase amount before entering the loop starting on line *80*. The While instruction requires that a true/false expression is included after the word 'while'. Thus the expression, Amount > ROGUEVALUE, will be true if Amount entered is greater than zero, and it will be false if Amount is not greater than zero, that is if it is equal to, or less than zero. When the expression is true, the statements between While and Wend, that is lines *90* to *110*, will be executed; as soon as the expression becomes false, the loop terminates and the program goes on to line *130*. Notice that the last instruction in the lines to be repeated is the instruction to read another value: this means that because the next instruction to be executed is the While instruction, the value typed in by the user is immediately compared with the rogue value. This ensures that the rogue value is not processed as an actual data item. Here is a typical run of the program:

```
Enter the cost of the first item, or 0 to end :23.45
Enter the cost of the next item, or 0 to end :6.12
Enter the cost of the next item, or 0 to end :5.99
Enter the cost of the next item, or 0 to end :0
```

Notice that the assignment instruction on line *90*, Count = Count + 1, is used as a means of counting the number of times the loop is executed. The instruction simply adds 1 to the variable, Count, each time the instructions within the loop are repeated. The true/false expression on line *80* in the While statement uses the *relational operator*, >, mean-

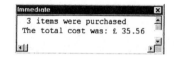

ing 'greater than', to compare Amount with ROGUEVALUE. There are six different relational operators that can be used in such logical expressions, and these are shown in Table 27.4.

relational operator	meaning
>	Greater than
>=	Greater than or equal to
<	Less than
<=	Less than or equal to
=	Equal to
<>	Not equal to

Table 27.4. *Relational operators used in logical expressions*

The operators in Table 27.4 are used according to the relationship to be established between two values. Whatever logical expression is used, the result of the comparison will either be true or false - if true, the While loop will repeat; if false the loop will terminate. More examples of the use of these operators are provided in the next part of this Topic, which deals with the use of logical expressions in making program decisions.

The If statement

Suppose a program is required to display multiple-choice questions with one correct answer out of three possible choices. For example, one of the questions could be:

```
A BYTE is the name given to

    (a) Four bits
    (b) Eight bits
    (c) Sixteen bits
```

```
Your answer is:
```

The program is also required to display the message

```
Correct - well done!
```

if the answer is correct, and display a message such as

```
Sorry, the correct answer is (b)
```

if the answer provided is incorrect. The program must therefore be able to take two alternative courses of action depending on the answer supplied. An If statement is one possible way of achieving this requirement. The appropriate form of the If statement is illustrated in Listing 27.7 which shows the VB code required to display the question above and provide the response appropriate to the letter 'a', 'b' or 'c', typed into the Input box that appears.

Listing 27.7.   Using an If statement

```
Public Sub Main()
' ====== Program to illustrate the use of the If statement =======


' Declare constants and variables
10 Dim Answer As String

' Ask the question
20 Debug.Print "Please enter a, b, c or d"
30 Debug.Print "in the Answer Box provided:"
40 Debug.Print
50 Debug.Print "A BYTE is the name given to"
60 Debug.Print "(a) Four bits"
70 Debug.Print "(b) Eight bits"
80 Debug.Print "(c) Sixteen bits"
90 Debug.Print

' Get the answer and display it
100 Answer = InputBox("Your answer is?", "Answer Box")
110 Debug.Print "You answered ("; Answer; ")"

' Check the answer and report
120 If Answer = "b" Then
130    Debug.Print "Correct - well done!"
140 Else
150    Debug.Print "Sorry, the correct answer is (b)"
160 End If

End Sub
```

The If statement extending over lines *120* to *160* shows how the program can take one of two possible courses of action depending on the value of a variable. We saw in the last Topic concerning the use of the While statement that logical expressions are either true or false. This is also the case with the logical expression Answer = "b" in the If statement on line *120*. If the letter stored in the character variable Answer is the letter 'b', then the logical expression Answer = "b" will be true, otherwise it will be false. If it is true, the statement following the word Then is executed (that is, line *130*), otherwise the statement after Else is executed (that is, line *150*). Notice the different form of the input box on line *100*:

```
100 Answer = InputBox("Your answer is?", "Answer Box")
```

The text after the prompt text ("Your answer is?") is the title of the input box shown alongside. The general form of the If statement is

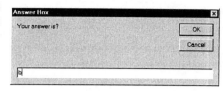

```
If {logical expression} Then
   {statement 1}
Else
   {statement 2}
End If
```

Note that {statement 1} is the instruction that is performed if {logical expression} is true; {statement 2} is performed if {logical expression} is false. Note also that either {statement 1} or {statement 2}, or both of them, can contain more than a single instruction, as illustrated below:

```
If Answer = "b" Then
   Debug.Print "Correct - well done!"
Else
   Debug.Print "Sorry, the correct answer is (b)"
   Debug.Print "There are eight bits in a byte"
End If
```

Sometimes it is necessary to choose between more than just two courses of action in a program. For example, Listing 27.8 shows a program which converts a percentage mark to a pass, merit, distinction or fail grade. The program repeatedly accepts marks and converts them to grades until the mark entered is the rogue value –1 (or any negative integer value) signifying the end of the mark inputs. The rules that are used to determine the grade are as follows:

For a distinction the mark must be equal to or over 80.

For a merit the mark must be greater than or equal to 60 and less than 80.

For a pass the mark must be greater than or equal to 40 and less than 60.

Below 40 is a fail.

Listing 27.8.   The If..Else If construction

```
Public Sub Main()
' ====== Program to illustrate the use of the If statement =======


' Declare constants and variables
10 Const DIST = 80, MERIT = 60, PASS = 40
20 Dim Mark As Integer, Grade As String

'Get the first mark
30 Mark = InputBox("Please enter the first mark(-1 to end): ",
"Marks")

' Check the grade
40 While Mark >= 0
50    If Mark >= DIST Then
60       Grade = "Distinction"
70    Else
80       If (Mark >= MERIT) And (Mark < DIST) Then
90        Grade = "Merit"
100       Else
```

```
110    If (Mark >= PASS) And (Mark < MERIT) Then
120       Grade = "Pass"
130     Else
140       Grade = "Fail"
150       End If
160   End If
170   End If

'Report mark and grade
180 Debug.Print "Mark: "; Mark, "Grade: "; Grade

' Get the next mark
190 Mark = InputBox("Please enter the next mark(-1 to end): ",
"Marks")
200 Wend

End Sub
```

The If statement between lines *50* and *170* reflects this logic exactly. It is possible to chain If statements in this way to cope with quite complex lines of reasoning. Added flexibility is provided by the use of the logical And operator used for the logical expressions on lines *80* and *110*. The And operator requires that both of the minor logical expressions it connects are true for the complete logical expression to be true. If either or both are false, then the whole expression is false. Logical operators are discussed in more detail in the next section. The output from the program for a set of four marks is shown on the right.

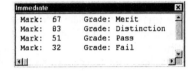

Logical operators

Logical operators allow you to combine logical expressions. There are three logical operators in VB: And, Or and Not. An example of the use of the And operator was provided in Listing 27.8. The And and the Or operators are always placed between two logical expressions, and they each combine these logical expressions to produce a value of true or false. Table 27.5 shows the rules that are applied by VB to determine whether a compound logical expression is true or false. This type of table is usually called a *truth table*.

(Expr 1)	(Expr 2)	(Expr 1) Or (Expr 2)	(Expr 1) And (Expr 2)
true	true	true	true
true	false	true	false
false	true	true	false
false	false	false	false

Table 27.5. *Truth table for the* **And** *and* **Or** *logical operators*

Look at Listing 27.8, on line *80*, where the compound logical expression (Mark >= MERIT) And (Mark < DIST) is used to determine whether the mark is equivalent to a merit grade. In the expression, (Mark >= MERIT) is an example of (Expr 1) and (Mark < DIST) is an example of (Expr 2) shown in Table 27.5.

The next table (Table 27.6) shows how the And operator combines these two logical expressions for a number of cases.

Mark	(Mark > = Merit)	(Mark < Dist)	(Mark > = Merit And (Mark < Dist)
45	false	true	false
86	true	false	false
67	true	true	true

Table 27.6. *Truth table for the* **And** *logical operator*

Thus, both logical expressions must be true for the complete expression to be true; with the Or operator, however, only one of the expressions needs to be true for the complete expression to be true. For example, consider the program in Listing 27.9 which reads some text and counts how many vowels it contains. The program uses a For loop to test each letter in turn in the text against each possible vowel. If the current letter is a vowel, that is 'a', 'e', 'i', 'o' or 'u', a count is incremented.

Listing 27.9.   Illustrating the use of the Or logical operator

---

```
Public Sub Main()
' ====== Program to illustrate the use of the Or operator =======

' Declare constants and variables
10 Dim VowelCount As Integer
20 Dim Letters As String
30 Dim LengthOfText As Integer
40 Dim c As Integer

' Initialise vowel count variable
50 VowelCount = 0

' Get the text to process
60 Letters = InputBox("Type text followed by ENTER: ", "Vowel count")
70 LengthOfText = Len(Letters)

' Count the number of vowels
80   For c = 1 To LengthOfText
90   If (Mid(Letters, c, 1) = "a") Or
         (Mid(Letters, c, 1) = "e") Or
         (Mid(Letters, c, 1) = "i") Or
         (Mid(Letters, c, 1) = "o") Or
         (Mid(Letters, c, 1) = "u") Then
100     VowelCount = VowelCount + 1
110   End If
120 Next c

'Display the results
130 Debug.Print "You entered "; Letters
140 Debug.Print "The text contains "; VowelCount; " vowels"
End Sub
```

The text is held in a string variable called Letters. Each letter in Letters is accessed by specifying its position within the text. For example, if the text entered was the string 'hello there', then Mid(Letters,1,1) is the letter 'h', Mid(Letters,2,1) is the letter 'e', Mid(Letters,3,1) is the letter 'l', and so on.

The function Mid allows us to access one or more characters from a string. The first item in the brackets is the string to search, the second is the position in the string to start, and the third is the number of characters to access. So Mid(Letters,5,2) would return two characters starting at position 5 and `Mid(Letters,c,1)` returns the single character at position c. The `For` loop control variable, c, starts at 1 and goes up in steps of 1 to the length of the string (11 for the string 'hello there'). The length of the string is determined by the VB function `len()`, on line *70*, which requires a string as its single argument. The output from the program when the string, 'the cat sat on the mat' is typed in, is shown on the right.

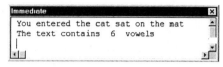

Note that the program will only work with lower-case text. The reason is that lower-case letters 'a', 'b', 'c', etc are represented in a computer using a different set of codes from the equivalent upper-case letters 'A', 'B', 'C', etc.

The third logical operator is the `Not` operator which simply reverses the logical value of a logical expression. Thus, the logical expression `Not (x >3)` is true only when x is less than or equal to 3. Similarly, the logical expression `Not (Balance <= 0)` is true only when `Balance` has a value that is greater than zero. The truth table shown in Table 27.7 defines the operation of the `Not` logical operator.

Expr	not Expr
true	false
false	true

Table 27.7. *Truth table for* `not` *logical operator*

The Select..Case statement

The `Select` statement is an alternative method to the `If` statement for choosing between alternative courses of action within a program. It has the following general format:

```
Select Case {expression}
Case value list 1
   statement 1
            Case value list 2
                statement 2
      etc...
      ......
Case Else
   statement N
Select End
```

The expression after `Select Case` can be a single variable or an expression involving several variables. VB matches the value of this single variable or expression against the values specified in the `Case` value lists; when a match is found, the corresponding statements are executed after which the `Select` statement is immediately exited without considering any remaining values. If there are no values that match the variable, the `Select` statement does nothing unless the `Else` option is used, in which circumstances the supplied statement or statements (shown as `statement N` above) are executed.

In Listing 27.10, the `Select` statement is used to find the number of days in a month given the month number (1 to 12):

Listing 27.10.   Illustrating the use of the Select statement

```
Public Sub Main()
' ====== Program to illustrate the use of the Or operator =======


' Declare constants and variables
10 Const Title = "Days in month"
20 Const Buttons = vbOKOnly
30 Dim Month As Integer
```

```
40 Dim Response As Integer

' Get month number
50 Month = InputBox("Enter a month number(1 to 12)", Title)

' Determine days in month
60   Select Case Month
     Case 1, 3, 5, 7, 8, 10, 12
70     Msg = "There are 31 days in month " & Month
     Case 4, 6, 9, 11
       Msg = "There are 30 days in month " & Month
     Case 2
       Msg = "There are 28 days in month " & Month
80   Case Else
90     Msg = "Invalid month number: " & Month
     End Select

' Report days in month using a message box
100 Response = MsgBox(Msg, Buttons, Title)
End Sub
```

`Month` contains a number corresponding to the month of the year, where January = 1, February = 2 ..... December = 12. The `Select..Case` statement is used to store, in the variable, `Days`, the number of days in the month whose number is stored in `Month`. Thus if `Month` contained the number 8 corresponding to August, `Days` would be assigned the value 31. The example uses a Message Box function on line *100* to display the number of days in the specified month. The message box displays a window with a title, a message and a single OK button as illustrated alongside.

A Message box can display a variety of different buttons that can be specified by using appropriate VB constants as shown below:

Constant	Value	Description
vbOKOnly	0	Display OK button only
vbOKCancel	1	Display OK and Cancel buttons
vbAbortRetryIgnore	2	Display Abort, Retry, and Ignore buttons
vbYesNoCancel	3	Display Yes, No, and Cancel buttons
vbYesNo	4	Display Yes and No buttons
vbRetryCancel	5	Display Retry and Cancel buttons

The function returns the value corresponding to the button that the user selects:

Constant	Value	Button chosen
vbOK	1	OK
vbCancel	2	Cancel
vbAbort	3	Abort
vbRetry	4	Retry
vbIgnore	5	Ignore
vbYes	6	Yes
vbNo	7	No

This allows us to take different forms of action depending on the button clicked. (See Listing 27.11). However, in our example this value is not used - we simply display a message and stop.

The message to display is stored in the variable Msg and is set according to the Case clause that corresponds to the Month entered by the user. Notice that to join together strings (*concatenate*) we use the & operator, as in line *70:*

```
70   Msg = "There are 31 days in month " & Month
```

In the next example we use another form of the Message box function in combination with the Select statement.

Listing 27.11.   Illustrating the use of the Select statement
---

```
Public Sub Main()
' ====== Program to illustrate the use of Select..Case =======

' Declare constants and variables
10 Const Title = "Smoking"
20 Const MsgYes = "Smoking is bad for you!"
30 Const MsgNo = "Good for you!!"
40 Dim Response As Integer

' Display message box
50 Response = MsgBox("Do you smoke?", vbYesNo, Title)

' Determine whether smoker or non-smoker and report
60   Select Case Response
     Case vbNo
70    Response = MsgBox(MsgNo, vbOKOnly, Title)
     Case vbYes
80    Response = MsgBox(MsgYes, vbOKOnly, Title)
     End Select

End Sub
```

If the user clicks the **Yes** button in the Message box that is displayed by line *70* variable, Response is assigned the value vbYes(6) ; if the user clicks the No button, Response is assigned the value vbNo (7). The Select statement then determines which button was clicked and displays the appropriate message.

Arrays

An *array* is a data structure which allows you to store a number of items of data without having to allocate separate variable names to them. Arrays must be declared before they are used. For example, the following declaration is for an array of five integers:

```
Dim Array(5) As Integer
```

This single declaration is in effect defining five variables called Array(1), Array(2), Array(3), Array(4) and Array(5), each of which can store a single integer value. The integer value inside the brackets is called the array's index, and it is allowed only to take the range of values specified in the declaration (1 to 5 inclusive in this example). Each of these identifiers can be used just like any ordinary integer variable. For instance, to set each of them to zero could be accomplished as follows:

```
Array(1) = 0
Array(2) = 0
```

```
Array(3) = 0
Array(4) = 0
Array(5) = 0
```

However, we could accomplish the same operation by using an integer variable as an *index* and by putting a single assignment statement in a For loop:

```
For i = 1 to 5
 Array(i)= 0
Next i
```

Now the count variable i takes on the integer values 1 to 5 and again each element in the array is set to zero. The obvious advantage of using a variable for an index is that arrays can then be used very effectively within loops, and they allow the manipulation of as many or as few numbers as appropriate to the task in hand; notice that the same For loop could initialise 5000 array elements as easily as 5 elements:

```
For i = 1 to 5000
 Array(i) = 0
Next i
```

This would be an exceedingly difficult task to accomplish without the use of an array.

Listing 27.12 illustrates the use of an array of real numbers. The program reads five numbers into an array and then finds the position within the array of the smallest number. It then swaps this number with the first number in the list before displaying the re-ordered array.

Listing 27.12.   Using an array

```
Public Sub Main()
' ====== Program to illustrate the use an array =======

' Declare constants and variables
10 Const MAXNUMS = 5
15 Dim Array1(MAXNUMS) As Integer
   Dim Temp As Integer
   Dim i As Integer

' Get the numbers
20 For i = 1 To MAXNUMS
30   Array1(i) = InputBox("Enter number " & i & " of " & MAXNUMS)
35 Next i

' Find the smallest and store in first array element
40 For i = 2 To MAXNUMS
50  If Array1(i) < Array1(1) Then
60    Temp = Array1(1)
70    Array1(1) = Array1(i)
80    Array1(i) = Temp
   End If
  Next i

' Print the new list
  Debug.Print "The new list is as follows: "
90 For i = 1 To MAXNUMS
   Debug.Print Array1(i);
  Next i
 End Sub
```

The program first defines a constant MAXNUMS to be the maximum size of the integer array, Array1. Lines *20* to *35* are to read in the five numbers with appropriate user prompts. Thus the first number is read into Array1(1), the second into Array1(2), and so on up to the last number which is read into Array1(5). The second For loop starting on line *40* compares each number in the array in turn with the first number; if one is found that is less than the first, they are swapped over. By the time the last number in the array has been compared with the first one, the smallest number is in the first position in the array. A typical run of the program might be:

```
Enter number 1 of 5 :5
Enter number 2 of 5 :3
Enter number 3 of 5 :9
Enter number 4 of 5 :1
Enter number 5 of 5 :8
```

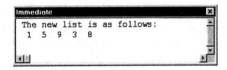

The output appears as shown alongside.

As a final example in this section on arrays, Listing 27.13 shows a program which uses a random number generator to select five lottery numbers in the range 1 to 49.

Listing 27.13.   Random numbers and array to generate lottery numbers

```
Public Sub Main()
' ====== Program to use random numbers
'        to generate 5 lottery numbers              ========

' Declare constants and variables
10   Const NUMOFNUMS = 5
20   Const MAXNUM = 49
30   Dim LuckyNums(MAXNUM) As Boolean
40   Dim Num As Integer
50   Dim i As Integer
60   Dim Count As Integer

'Display heading
     Debug.Print "Lottery random number generator"
     Debug.Print

' Initialise array
70   For i = 1 To MAXNUM
80      LuckyNums(i) = False
90   Next i

' Initialise count for numbers generated
100 Count = 0

' Initialise random number generator
110 Randomize

' Generate the lottery numbers
120 While Count < NUMOFNUMS
130   Num = Int(MAXNUM * Rnd()) + 1
140    If LuckyNums(Num) = False Then
150      Debug.Print Num;
160      LuckyNums(Num) = True
170      Count = Count + 1
180    End If
```

```
190   Wend

200   End Sub
```

The random numbers are generated using the function Rnd() which produces a random number less than 1 but greater than or equal to 0. To produce a random number in the range 0 to MAXNUM, we use the statement

```
130   Num = Int(MAXNUM * Rnd()) + 1
```

This instruction multiplies the random number by MAXNUM (i.e. 49) to produce a number in the range 0 to less than 49. The Int function then rounds this number down to the nearest integer, thus giving a number in the range 0 to 48. Then 1 is added to produce a number in the range 1 to 49. The randomize instruction on line *110* simply initialises the random number generator so that it does not produce the same sequence of random numbers every time the program is run. Lines *70-90* initialises each element to False in the array LuckyNums() which is to be used to record the five numbers that are generated.

The reason for the If statement on lines *140* to *180* is to ensure that the same random number is not used more than once. When a number is generated, the appropriate element in the LuckyNums array is checked to see if it has a value of False which indicates that the number has not been generated before. Then, to record that the number has been generated, that element is set to True in the LuckyNums array. For example, if the first random number generated on line *130* was the number 36, then this would be stored in Num. The If statement checks that 36 has not been used already by checking if LuckyNums(36) still has its initial value of False. If this is the case, 36 is displayed (line *150*), LuckyNums(36) is set to True and Count is increased by 1. Thus if 36 is generated again, the If statement will prevent it from being used. The While loop repeats until five different numbers have been generated. Here is an example from the output of Example 13:

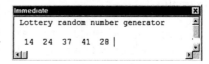

Strings

A string is a set of characters such as "24, Railway Terrace, Willington" or "Hello" or "123abc". Strings can be stored by string variables and they can be manipulated in various ways using special Visual Basic functions. In this section we will briefly review a number of common functions used for handling strings and then apply them in an example program.

Declaring strings and assigning strings to variables

Use the Dim statement to declare a variable as a string variable. For example, to declare the variable "Myname" as a string use the statement

```
Dim Myname As String
```

Declare Myname before it is used in the program.

There is no practical limit on the size of a string (up to about 2 billion characters).

To store characters in a string you simply use an assignment statement such as

```
Myname = "Ivar Peregrine Trews"
```

The right-hand side of this statement, that is the text in quotation marks, is called a string *literal*.

To clear a string variable, store the empty string, "" (double quotes with nothing between), in it:

```
Myname = ""
```

To join strings together (concatenate) use the & operator. The following example illustrates how to concatenate strings:

```
Dim Firstname As String,  Surname As String, Fullname As String
Firstname = "John"
Surname = "Smith"
Fullname = Surname &  ", " & Firstname
```

The variable `Fullname` would then contain the string "Smith, John"

String length - Len()

This function returns the length of a string, that is, the number of characters in the string.

Example

```
Mystring = "Hello there"
L = Len(Mystring)
```

(`L` would be assigned the value 11)

Substrings - Left(), Right() and Mid()

These three functions are used to extract parts of strings (*substrings*) from strings.

`Left(string,length)` returns a specified number of characters (`length`) from the left side of a string (`string`).

Examples

```
MyString = "Hello There"      ' Define string.
Str1 = Left(MyString, 1)      ' Returns "H".
Str2 = Left(MyString, 7)      ' Returns "Hello T".
Str3 = Left(MyString, 20)     ' Returns "Hello There".
```

`Right(string,length)` returns a specified number of characters (`length`) from the right side of a string (`string`).

Examples

```
MyString = "Hello There"      ' Define string.
Str1 = Right(MyString, 1)     ' Returns "e".
Str2 = Right(MyString, 5)     ' Returns "There".
Str3 = Right(MyString, 20)    ' Returns "Hello There".
```

`Mid(string, start, [length])` returns a specified number of characters (`length`) starting from position start in a string (`string`). `length` is optional and if omitted all characters from start to the end of the string are returned.

Examples

```
MyString = "Hello There"      ' Create text string.
Str1 = Mid(MyString, 1, 3)    ' Returns "Hel".
Str2 = Mid(MyString, 7, 5)    ' Returns "There".
Str3 = Mid(MyString, 7)       ' Returns "There".
Str4 = Mid(MyString, 5, 1)    ' Returns "o".
```

Searching strings - Instr()

InStr([start,]string1, string2[, compare]) returns the position of the first occurrence of string2 within string1 starting from position start in string1. The optional
parameter compare can be used to specify whether the search is to be case sensitive (compare
= 0) or not (compare = 1). If compare is omitted the comparison is case sensitive (binary
comparison). The start value is also optional - if omitted the search starts from the first character in string1. If the search string, string2, is not found in string1, the function returns
a value of 0, otherwise it returns the position of the first character of string2 within
string1.

Examples

```
MyString = "Information and Communications Technology"
Pos1 = Instr( MyString, "c", 0)      ' Returns 24 - case sensitive
Pos2 = Instr( MyString, "com", 1)    ' Returns 17 - case insensitive

Pos3 = Instr( MyString, "com")       ' Returns 0 - case sensitive
Pos4 = Instr( 25, MyString, "c")     ' Returns 34 - start position 25
```

Example program to illustrate string handling

This example program splits a sentence into separate words by looking for a space at the end of
a word. It is assumed that there are no extra spaces between words or any spaces at the beginning or end of the sentence, and that the sentence contains no punctuation marks.

Listing 27.14.   String handling

```
Public Sub Main()
' ====== Program to use illustrate the use of some string
'         handling functions                           =======
' Declare constants and variables
 Dim Sentence As String, Word As String
 Dim CurPos As Integer, SpacePos As Integer, L As Integer

' Get the sentence
10 Sentence = InputBox("Please type in a sentence")

' Add space at end to simplify coding
20 Sentence = Sentence & " "

' Set the starting point for searching sentence  ·
30 CurPos = 1

' Get the length of the sentence
40 L = Len(Sentence)

' Look for spaces and extract words
50   While CurPos < L
60     SpacePos = InStr(CurPos, Sentence, " ")
70     Word = Mid(Sentence, CurPos, SpacePos - CurPos)
80     Debug.Print Word
90     CurPos = SpacePos + 1  ' update search start position
100 Wend
End Sub
```

The user is requested to type in the sentence on line *10*. Line *20* adds a single space to the end of the sentence to simplify the programming required to extract single words. (this allows us to assume that all words in the sentence are followed by a space).

The starting position for the search is set at the beginning of the sentence on line *30*. CurPos will store the start position of each new word located.

On line *40* the length of the sentence is stored in the variable L.

The main part of the program is the While loop from lines *50* to *100*. The position of the next space in the sentence is located using the Instr() function. It is not necessary to use the compare option because a space does not have upper and lower case.

Line *70* extracts a word using the Mid() function. SpacePos contains the position of the space at the end of the word and CurPos is the position of the first letter in the word; thus the length of the word is given by SpacePos - CurPos.

Finally, the extracted word is printed, CurPos is set to the beginning of the next word and the loop repeats.

The loop ends when CurPos exceeds L, the length of the sentence.

Some Visual Basic Functions

We have already used a few functions in the example programs. The previous lottery number program used rnd() to generate random numbers and int() to convert a real number to an integer. We have also used the MsgBox() function to display a window and return a value to indicate which button the user clicked. Functions are pre-written subprograms that perform frequently required tasks. There are a great number of Visual Basic functions available to the programmer, and you can use the VB Help facility to research them and to see examples of how they can be used. Here we list and briefly describe a selection of them.

Function	Purpose
Abs	Returns the absolute value of a number
Asc	Returns the character code corresponding to the first letter in a string
Atn	Returns the arctangent of a number
Chr	Returns the character associated with the specified character code.
Cos	Returns the cosine of a number
CurDir	Returns the current path
Date	Returns the current system date.
Dir	Returns the name of a file or directory that matches a specified pattern or file attribute, or the volume label of a drive.
DoEvents	Yields execution so that the operating system can process other events
EOF	Returns a value that indicates whether the end of a file has been reached
Error	Returns the error message that corresponds to a given error number.

Exp	Returns e (the base of natural logarithms) raised to a power
Input	Returns characters from an open sequential or binary file
InStr	Returns the position of the first occurrence of one string within another
Int	Returns the integer portion of a number
IsNumeric	Returns a Boolean value indicating whether an expression can be evaluated as a number
Left	Returns a specified number of characters from the left side of a string
Len	Returns the number of characters in a string or the number of bytes required to store a variable
Log	Returns the natural logarithm of a number
Ltrim, Rtrim, Trim	Returns a copy of a string without leading spaces (LTrim), trailing spaces (RTrim), or both leading and trailing spaces (Trim)
Mid	Returns a specified number of characters from a string
MsgBox	Displays a message in a dialog box, waits for the user to choose a button, and returns a value indicating which button the user has chosen
Now	Returns the current date and time according to the setting of your computer's system date and time
Right	Returns a specified number of characters from the right side of a string
Rnd	Returns a random number
Sgn	Returns an integer indicating the sign of a number
Shell	Runs an executable program
Sin	Returns the sine of an angle
Space	Returns a string consisting of the specified number of spaces
Sqr	Returns the square root of a number
Str	Returns a string representation of a number
StrComp	Returns a value indicating the result of a string comparison
String	Returns a repeating character string of the length specified
Tan	Returns the tangent of an angle.
Timer	Returns the number of seconds elapsed since midnight.
Val	Returns the numbers contained in a string

Chapter 28

Introduction to event-driven programming

In this chapter we progress to using Visual Basic as a Windows Programming Application Generator rather than as a traditional programming language. To do this we need to begin to use *Forms* and *Controls*, and understand what is meant by *Event-driven* programming.

In Visual Basic, Forms and Controls are primary *Objects*. They are classed as Objects because they have characteristics that are typical of Object-Oriented Programming (OOP). In particular, Forms and Controls have *Properties*, *Methods* and *Events* associated with them. Properties define the appearance or behaviour of an object, Methods are procedures that perform actions associated with Forms and Controls, and Events are actions - such as user mouse clicks - that trigger the execution of program code.

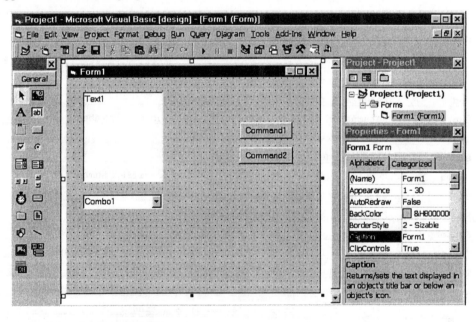

Forms and Controls

One of the great strengths of VB is the ease with which a complex graphical user interface can be constructed. The main component used for this is the Form on which Controls are placed. Controls are selected from the VB Toolbox and positioned on the form using the mouse. A Form and its Controls can be configured and modified using the Properties box. The screen shot above shows a Form (Form1) with the Toolbox on the left and the properties box on the right. There are four controls on the forms: two Command Buttons (Command1 and Command2), a Text Box (Text1) and a Combo box (Combo1).

Clicking on a control or a blank area of the form causes the properties box to display all of the properties for that object. These properties can be changed by clicking in the appropriate data cell to the right of the property name. For instance, the Form's Caption (the Caption is the text that appears in the title bar of the form) can be changed to, say, "MyForm" by editing "Form1".

To illustrate the creation of a simple Form and some associated Controls, we will design a program to perform a simple animation.

A Simple event-driven program - "Winking face"

When you launch VB and start a new project, you are automatically provided with a blank form called "Form1". Alternatively, if you wish you can add a Form to the current project by clicking the Add Form button on the toolbar. In this example we will start a new project and add three CommandButton controls to the blank Form. We will then use Click events to make the program respond to CommandButton Clicks. Our aim is to produce a Form as shown on the right.

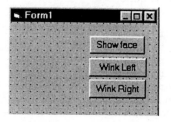

Creating the Form and Controls

To create the Form and Controls, follow the steps listed below:

1. Start a new project.
2. Click the CommandButton tool on the Toolbox.
3. Drag a rectangle in approximately the location shown. In the Properties window, change the Caption property to "Show face".
4. Repeat steps 2 and 3 for the two other buttons, changing their captions to those shown.
5. If necessary, resize the form by clicking a blank area on it and then dragging the bottom right-hand corner control node until the form is the required size.

Programming the CommandButtons

If you double click the "Show face" button, the code window will open:

The name of the button, "Command1", is displayed along with a blank procedure ("Command1_Click") for the Click event. The code that we will insert will be executed when Command1 (ie the "Show face" button) is clicked by the user when the program is running.

Add the following code to the Command1_Click event procedure:

```
Private Sub Command1_Click()
Form1.Cls
Form1.Print "    ---    "
Form1.Print " < 0 0 > "
Form1.Print "   | ^ |   "
Form1.Print "    \_/    "

End Sub
```

In this code we are calling two Form methods - `Cls` and `Print`.

`Form.Cls` clears Form1 of any text and graphics and `Form1.Print` prints the specified text.

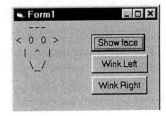

Now run the program. When you click the "Show face" button you should see a face that looks something like this (it may be a bit distorted but we will correct this later):

Next, add click event procedures for the other two Command buttons:

```
Private Sub Command2_Click()
Form1.Cls
Form1.Print "    ---    "
Form1.Print " < 0 o > "
Form1.Print "  |  ^  |   "
Form1.Print "    \_/    "
End Sub

Private Sub Command3_Click()
Form1.Cls
Form1.Print "    ---    "
Form1.Print " < o 0 > "
Form1.Print "  |  ^  |   "
Form1.Print "    \_/    "
End Sub
```

When you run the program again, all three buttons should now operate.

The face that appears will probably look different from those illustrated. The reason is that the default font for Form1 needs to be set to a font such as "Courier New". This property setting can be done manually using the Properties window for the form but, in order to illustrate the use of another event procedure, we will change the font with code.

To change the default font for Form1, do the following:

Double click on an empty area of Form1 to make the code window appear. The cursor will be in the blank `Form_Load` procedure. Add the line shown below:

```
Private Sub Form_Load()
   Form1.Font = "Courier New"
End Sub
```

Now, when you run the program, before Form1 appears, the `Form_Load` event procedure will be executed, thus setting the form font to Courier New. Then, when the Command buttons are clicked, the faces should appear undistorted.

ComboBox and TextBox Controls

The screenshot below shows a form containing two ComboBox controls and a TextBox control. A TextBox control, sometimes called an edit field or edit control, displays information entered by the user. In this example it allows a user to enter a currency amount to be converted to another currency. A ComboBox control allows users to enter information in the text box portion or select an item from the drop-down list portion of the control. The ComboBox controls in this example each provide the same drop-down list as shown next.

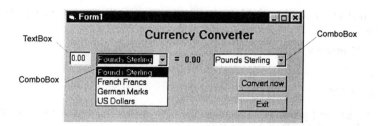

The form allows a user to enter in the TextBox control a number representing an amount of money in a currency specified by the first ComboBox. This amount is to be converted to the currency specified in the second ComboBox. When the "Convert now" command button is clicked, the equivalent amount of the target currency is calculated and displayed. For example, the next screenshot shows 230 Pounds Sterling converted to French Francs:

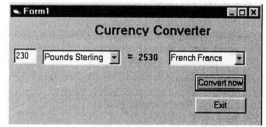

In this example we will:

- ❑ Create the form controls
- ❑ Configure the two ComboBox controls
- ❑ Create a global array to store exchange rates
- ❑ Initialise the program using the `Form_Load` event procedure
- ❑ Program the two Command buttons

Creating the Form and Controls

To create the Form and Controls, follow the steps listed below:

1. Start a new project.
2. Click the TextBox Control tool in the Toolbox
3. Drag a rectangle in approximately the location shown
4. In the Properties window, set the Text property to "0.00"
5. Click the ComboBox tool in the Toolbox
6. Drag a rectangle in the location shown for the leftmost ComboBox.
7. In the Properties window, set the Style property to "2 - Dropdown list"
8. In the Properties window, click in the List property box and Enter the following list of items: Pounds Sterling, French Francs, German Marks, US Dollars. You need to hold down the control key (Ctrl) while you press Enter after each item.
9. Repeat steps 5 - 8 for the second ComboBox
10. Click the Command Button tool in the Toolbox.
11. In the Properties window, change the Caption property to "Convert now"
12. Repeat steps 10 and 11 for the "Exit" button
13. There are three labels on the form: Label1, the Title ("Currency Converter"); Label2, the "=" sign; Label3, the converted amount immediately to the right of Label2. These

are created using the Label tool. Use the Caption property to change these labels as follows:

Label1: "Currency Converter"

Label2: "="

Label3: "0.00"

Also use the Font property to increase the size of the title and use the ForeColor property to change the colour of the title.

14. If necessary, resize the form by clicking a blank area on it and then dragging the bottom right-hand corner control node until the form is the required size.

Initialising the Form

When the program runs, the `Form_Load` event triggers. We will use this event to modify the two ComboBoxes so that they show the first item in the list of currencies, ie "Pounds Sterling".

We use the `ListIndex` property for the ComboBoxes to set the default item to the first one. Each item in a ComboBox has an index ranging from 0 to one less than the number of items in the list. In our case the items and indexes are shown in the first two columns of the table on the right.

Index	Item	ExchRate()
0	Pounds Sterling	1
1	French France	11
2	German Marks	4
3	US Dollars	1.5

The third column shows the appropriate exchange rates for the currencies stored in the array `ExchRate()`. This array is used in the currency conversion calculation explained later.

The code shown below sets the `ListIndex` values for both ComboBoxes to 0.

```
Private Sub Form_Load()

    Set each combo box to show the first item in the list
    Combo1.ListIndex = 0
    Combo2.ListIndex = 0

End Sub
```

Programming the Command Buttons

The code for the "Convert now" Command Button is shown below.

```
Private Sub Command1_Click()
' ===== Procedure to convert from one currency to another ======

' Declare variables used
10    Dim FromCurrency As Integer, ToCurrency As Integer
20    Dim AmountFrom As Single, AmountPS As Single, AmountTo As Single
      Dim ExchRate(4) As Single

' Set up exchange rates (these are not accurate figures!)
30    ExchRate(0) = 1      ' Pounds
40    ExchRate(1) = 11     ' Francs
50    ExchRate(2) = 4      ' Marks
60    ExchRate(3) = 1.5    ' Dollars
```

```
' Get the From and To currencies chosen
70    FromCurrency = Combo1.ListIndex
80    ToCurrency = Combo2.ListIndex

' Get the amount to convert from
90    AmountFrom = Val(Text1.Text)

' Convert to Pounds Sterling
100    AmountPS = AmountFrom / ExchRate(FromCurrency)

' Convert from Pounds to target currency
110    AmountTo = AmountPS * ExchRate(ToCurrency)

' Display equivalent amount by changing  Label3's caption
120    Label3.Caption = AmountTo

End Sub
```

The `Command1_Click` procedure contains the code required to convert from one currency to another. The method is to first convert the 'From' currency to Pounds Sterling by dividing by the exchange rate for that currency. Then this figure is converted to the 'To' currency by multiplying the number of Pounds Sterling by the exchange rate for the target currency. Lines *90* to *110* perform these calculations. The appropriate exchange rates are stored in the array `ExchRate()`, as shown in the earlier Table, so that the ListIndexes for the ComboBoxes matches the array indexes. For instance, if the user selects "German Marks" as the 'From' currency, this item's ListIndex is 2 and the exchange rate for Marks is stored in `ExchRate(2)`.

Line *70* determines the ListIndex for the 'From' Currency and line 80 determines the ListIndex for the 'To' currency.

Line *90* uses the Text property of the TextBox, `Text1`, to determine the amount of money to be used in the conversion. The `Val()` function converts a string to a numeric value that can be used in a calculation

Line *100* converts the 'From' currency to Pounds Sterling. Then on line *110*, this value is converted to the target currency.

Finally, the answer is displayed in `Label3` by using its Caption property.

Frames, OptionButtons and CheckBoxes

The next Form, shown on the next page, contains two Frames captioned "Select system required" and "Select options".

The first frame contains four OptionButtons that allow a user to select one computer system from the four choices available. When a user clicks one of a group of OptionButtons (sometimes called "radio buttons"), all of the other buttons are automatically deselected. In other words, a group of OptionButtons allow only one button in the group to selected at any one time. On the other hand, a user can select as many or as few CheckBoxes in a group as required.

The example Form shows the third OptionButton and two CheckBoxes selected. The Frame tool allows a number of OptionButtons or CheckBoxes to be collected together so that they operate as an independent group. Frames thus allow a single Form to contain several independent groups of these controls. The PC Configuration Calculator allows a user to select a PC system and a number of options. Whenever an OptionButton or a CheckBox is selected, the price of the system is immediately calculated and displayed. This facility allows a user to investigate the cost of different system configurations very quickly. The full listing of the program is shown on the next page.

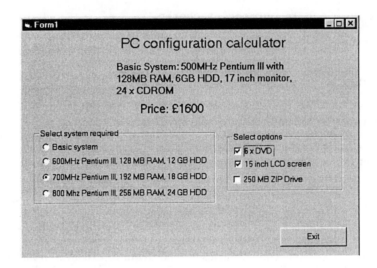

```
' ==== Global variables are defined here ====
10 Dim DVDOpt As Single
   Dim LCDOpt As Single
   Dim ZipOpt As Single
   Dim BasicCost As Single
   Dim SystemCost As Single
   Dim ExtraCost AS Single
```

```
Private Sub Command2_Click()
' Exit program
80 Unload Form1
End Sub
```

```
Private Sub Extras_Click(Index As Integer)
' CheckBox clicked
90 If Extras(0).Value = 1 Then
   DVDOpt = 100
   Else
   DVDOpt = 0
   End If

100 If Extras(1).Value = 1 Then
    LCDOpt = 500
    Else
    LCDOpt = 0
    End If

110 If Extras(2).Value = 1 Then
     ZipOpt = 150
    Else
    ZipOpt = 0
    End If

120 ExtraCost = DVDOpt + LCDOpt + ZipOpt

130 Call ShowCost
```

```
End Sub
```

```
Private Sub Form_Load()

' Initialise global variables when form loaded
140 DVDOpt = 0
    LCDOpt = 0
    ZipOpt = 0

' Initialise Cost variables
150 BasicCost = 600
    SystemCost = BasicCost

' Set first option (Basic system) as default
160 Option1.Value = True

' Display basic cost
    Label3.Caption = "Price: £ " & BasicCost

End Sub
```

```
Private Sub Option1_Click()
170 SystemCost = BasicCost
180 Call ShowCost
End Sub
```

```
Private Sub Option2_Click()
190 SystemCost = BasicCost + 200
200 Call ShowCost
End Sub
```

```
Private Sub Option3_Click()
210 SystemCost = BasicCost + 400
220 Call ShowCost
End Sub
```

```
Private Sub Option4_Click()
230 SystemCost = BasicCost + 600
240 Call ShowCost
End Sub
```

```
Public Sub ShowCost()
' Calculate system cost and display
250 Dim Price As Single
260 Price = SystemCost + ExtraCost
270 Label3.Caption = "Price: £" & Price
End Sub
```

Before looking at this program in more depth, we need to discuss *user-defined procedures* and *functions*, *parameters*, and the difference between *Global* and *Local* variables

User-defined Procedures

We have already used several Event Procedures in previous example programs. These are procedures that are linked to user interactions with a Form's controls. Visual Basic automatically provides empty procedures for all of a control's events. However, programmer-defined procedures can also be created. We can name and create code for our own procedures that are not directly linked to events. For example, in the program listing above, the procedure ShowCost has been created to calculate and display the cost of a computer system. It is invoked, or *called*, by a line such as

```
180 Call ShowCost
```

which causes VB to immediately execute the code in ShowCost before processing the next line. User-defined procedures allow us to split lengthy sections of code into manageable sizes, and also, most importantly, reduces the need to repeat code several times. Thus in the example program above for calculating the cost of a computer system, ShowCost is called from four other locations in addition to line *180*.

User-defined Functions

Functions, in addition to those that are provided by VB, can also be defined. Unlike Procedures, Functions can return a value calculated within the function's code. For example, look at the Function defined below:

```
Public Function Max(x, y)
If x > y Then
    Max = x
Else
    Max = y
End If
End Function
```

The Function Max() receives two numbers from code elsewhere in the program and determines the larger of the two. The value to be returned to the calling code must be assigned to the name of the Function, in this case, Max. To illustrate the use of this function, suppose that somewhere in a program is the line

```
Debug.Print "The larger of the two numbers, 3 and 5, is"; Max(3,5)
```

The value 5 would be displayed in the Immediate (Debug) window because the Function Max() returns the larger of the two numbers supplied to it. The two numbers supplied in brackets are called *Parameters* which are discussed next.

Parameters

A Parameter provides an important method of supplying data to a Procedure or Function. In the section on User-defined Procedures earlier we mentioned that one of their important uses was to avoid repeating code, and being able to use Parameters is essential to this. Passing data to a Procedure allows it to use different data each time it is used, thus greatly increasing its usefulness. For example, the Function Max() in the previous section allows any two numbers - not just 3 and 5 - to be compared. You will see several examples of using parameters in the next topic. (Visual Basic Case Study).

Global variables, Local variables and Scope

When we include a statement such as

```
Dim MyVar As Integer
```

in a procedure, it is classed as a *Local* variable. Local variables are available for use only within the procedure or function in which they are declared. In other words, the *Scope* of such a variable is limited to that procedure. For example, in the previous program listing, on line *250* the statement

```
250 Dim Price As Single
```

defines the Local variable `Price` which can be used only within the procedure `ShowCost`.

However, if a variable is defined in the *Declarations* section of a Form's program module (outside of any of the Form's procedure or functions), it can be used by any procedure or function in that module. For example, again referring to the previous program, the line

```
10 Dim DVDOpt As Single
```

occurs within the Declarations section of the Form and can therefore be used by any of the Form's procedures. Note that parameters used within functions and procedures are automatically local variables.

Creating the PC Configuration Calculator Form

Returning to the example program, we need to create two frames on the form and establish OptionButtons and CheckBoxes in them as shown in the screenshot below.

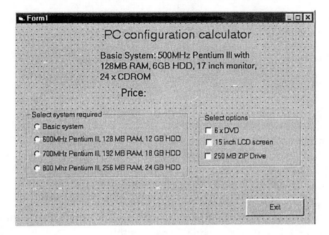

Proceed as follows:

1. Start a new project.

2. Double click the Frames tool to create a Frame on the form. This will be the "Select system required" Frame.

3. Position and size it to match the screenshot, and then set the caption property to "Select system required".

4. Now double click the OptionButton tool while the frame is selected. An OptionButton will appear in the frame. Set its Caption to "Basic system".

5. Create the three remaining OptionButtons in the same way, changing their Captions to those shown.

6. Next create the "Select options" Frame, and set its Caption.

7. Create the three CheckBoxes inside the frame. Set the name of each of the three checkboxes to "Extras" and set their captions to those required.

8. The title, basic system description and price are all labels (`Label1`, `Label2` and `Label3` respectively). Create these labels and change the text to that shown. Note that program code will be used to modify `Label3` to show the price of the system chosen by the user so allow space in the label for this.

9. Finally create a CommandButton and change its caption to "Exit".

The code for the PC Configuration Calculator

When the program starts, the Form_Load procedure is executed:

```
Private Sub Form_Load()

' Initialise Extras global variables
140 DVDOpt = 0
    LCDOpt = 0
    ZipOpt = 0

' Initialise Cost global variables
150 BasicCost = 600
    SystemCost = BasicCost

' Set first option (Basic system) as default
160 Option1.Value = True

' Display basic cost
    Label3.Caption = "Price: £ " & BasicCost

End Sub
```

This procedure initialises the global variables which will be used to calculate the cost of the system selected by the user. The cost of the basic system is set to £600 on line 150 and on line 160 the first OptionButton, Option1, is selected. Finally, the price of the basic system is displayed by setting the Caption for Label3 to the basic cost using the & operator to concatenate the literal "Price: £" and the value held in the variable BasicCost (i.e. 600).

When a user selects a PC system option from the "Select system required" frame, a click event associated with the relevant OptionButton is generated. Referring back to the program listing given earlier, you will see that the code is very simple. For example, when the second OptionButton is clicked, the following code executes:

```
Private Sub Option2_Click()
190 SystemCost = BasicCost + 200
200 Call ShowCost
End Sub
```

SystemCost and BasicCost are global variables defined in the Declarations section. The code simply adds 200 to BasicCost (which has been set to 600 in the Form_Load procedure) to give SystemCost. Similar code is used for the other three options. Then the user-defined procedure ShowCost is called. This procedure calculates the total system price, including extras, on line *260* and displays it in Label3:

```
Public Sub ShowCost()
' Calculate system cost and display
250 Dim Price As Single
260 Price = SystemCost + ExtraCost
270 Label3.Caption = "Price: £" & Price
End Sub
```

Every time an OptionButton or a CheckBox is clicked this procedure is called so that the new system price will be updated immediately.

The CheckBoxes procedure is handled using a different technique from that used for the OptionBoxes. Notice that we gave all of the CheckBoxes the same name, i.e. "Extras". This created a *Control Array* for the three CheckBoxes. A Control Array allows us to use a **single** event procedure no matter which control is clicked. The particular control within the Control Array that is clicked is identified by the `Index` parameter for the click event procedure, as shown below:

```
Private Sub Extras_Click(Index As Integer)
' CheckBox clicked
90 If Extras(0).Value = 1 Then
     DVDOpt = 100
   Else
     DVDOpt = 0
   End If

100 If Extras(1).Value = 1 Then
      LCDOpt = 500
    Else
      LCDOpt = 0
    End If

110 If Extras(2).Value = 1 Then
       ZipOpt = 150
    Else
       ZipOpt = 0
    End If

120 ExtraCost = DVDOpt + LCDOpt + ZipOpt

130 Call ShowCost
End Sub
```

This parameter is set to the appropriate control's index value by VB automatically when the control is clicked.

Each of the controls in a Control Array is assigned an integer value for its Index property during the design phase. You can manually set these values but VB automatically assigns values 0, 1, 2 etc for you. In this example we do not need to use the `Index` value since we need to find out whether each one of the CheckBoxes has been checked or unchecked. For instance, the `If` statement staring on line *90* determines whether the first CheckBox, `Extras(0)`, is checked - `Extras(0).Value = 1` - or unchecked. If it is checked, the user wants this extra included and the appropriate cost is recorded - `DVDOpt = 100`. If the CheckBox is unchecked, `DVDOpt` is set to zero. The same logic is applied to the other two CheckBoxes.

On line *120* the total cost of all extras is calculated and then the `ShowCost` procedure is used to display the new system cost.

Drag and Drop Events

The final example program in this topic illustrates the use of Drag and Drop events using the noughts and crosses game. The terms Drag and Drop refer to using the mouse to move a control from its current position and placing it somewhere else. A control is dragged by moving the mouse pointer over it, pressing and holding the mouse button and then moving the control with the mouse; the control is dropped in its destination position by releasing the mouse button.

In drag and drop operations there are two objects involved: the source object (a control) that is being dragged and the destination object (a form or control) that receives the dragged control when it is dropped. In our example, described below, the source objects and the destination objects are all CommandButtons. The code that controls drag and drop operations is placed in two different locations:

❑ the source object contains the code to start, stop and cancel dragging

❑ the destination object contains the code for the drop event.

For our implementation of the game of noughts and crosses we use the computer to display the game's grid and allow two players to position their O and X symbols. The program allows each player in turn to *drag* their symbol to a position on the grid and *drop* it there and then indicates whose turn is next. If the position has already been used, the move is rejected and the user is "beeped". The program also detects a winner or whether it is a drawn game after 9 moves. A screenshot of the game's Form is shown on the right.

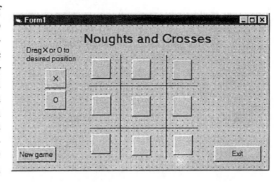

The first player drags the X button and drops it to a position on the grid. X appears in the required position. The X button becomes disabled and the O button becomes enabled allowing the second player to make a move. The next screenshot shows the position after the first player's third move:

If a player has three symbols in a horizontal, vertical or diagonal line, a congratulatory message appears. A message also appears if the game is drawn. The board is cleared for a new game by pressing the "New game" button.

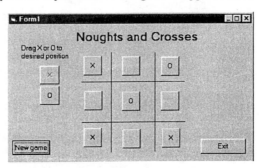

Creating the Noughts and Crosses Form

1. Start a new project and use the line tool to draw the grid lines.

2. Now create a CommandButton, size it and place it in the top left-hand corner of the grid. Clear its caption and name it OxoPos.

3. Now copy OxoPos to the clipboard (Ctrl C) and paste a copy of it to the Form (Ctrl V). You will be asked if you wish to create a Control Array. Answer "Yes" and position the new button to the right of the first one.

4. Paste the remaining 7 buttons (with Ctrl V again) and position them going from left to right. The Index value for the final button in the bottom right-hand corner should be 8.

5. Next, create the players' X and O CommandButtons. Name them OxoX and OxoO and change their captions to "X" and "O" respectively.

6. Create the "Exit" button.

7. Create the title label and use the ForeColor and Font properties to change the colour of the text and the size of the font.

8. Create the user instruction label that appears above the X and O CommandButtons.

9. Create new game button.

Coding the Noughts and Crosses Form

To simplify checking for a winning line of Os or Xs we will use an array called Grid() to record moves. Grid() is an array of nine integer values representing the nine positions on the grid as illustrated below:

Grid(0)	Grid(1)	Grid(2)
Grid(3)	Grid(4)	Grid(5)
Grid(6)	Grid(7)	Grid(8)

X moves will be stored as a value of 1 and O moves as −1; unused positions will contain zero. The next diagram shows a board position with the equivalent Grid() values:

Board position

X		O
	O	
X		X

Grid() values

1	0	−1
0	−1	0
1	0	1

We will test for a winner by finding the row, column and diagonal sums. A sum of 3 means that X has won and −3 means that O has won. Ignoring the sign of the sum, a value of 3 means that either X or O has won, i.e. there is a winner.

We will start by creating the code to initiate a drag operation when the mouse button is clicked over the X CommandButton. The X CommandButton is called OxoX and when it is clicked, the OxoX_MouseDown event procedure is executed. The code for this procedure is shown below:

```
Private Sub OxoX_MouseDown(Button As Integer, Shift As Integer, X As
Single, Y As Single)
' Initiate drag operation for X
  OxoX.Drag 1
End Sub
```

The parameters supplied by VB provide information regarding the button pressed, whether the Shift key was held down at the time, and the X and Y coordinates of the mouse pointer position when the button was clicked. In this example, we are only interested in the fact that OxoX was clicked. The code simply initiates a drag operation. This causes an outline of the button clicked to follow the movement of the mouse pointer while the mouse button is being held down.

The same coding principle applies to the O button:

```
Private Sub OxoO_MouseDown(Button As Integer, Shift As Integer, X As
Single, Y As Single)
' Initiate drag operation for O
  OxoO.Drag 1
End Sub
```

When the mouse button is released over one of the blank command buttons forming the game's grid, the `OxoPos_DragDrop` event procedure is triggered. This is the most complex part of the program, so we will discuss it in some detail.

```
Private Sub OxoPos_DragDrop(Index As Integer, Source As Control, X As
Single, Y As Single)
10   If OxoPos(Index).Caption = "" Then
20     OxoPos(Index).Caption = Source.Caption
30     Select Case Source.Name
40       Case "OxoO"
50         OxoO.Enabled = False
60         OxoX.Enabled = True
70         Grid(Index) = -1
80         Turns = Turns + 1
90       Case "OxoX"
100        OxoX.Enabled = False
110        OxoO.Enabled = True
120        Grid(Index) = 1
130        Turns = Turns + 1
140      End Select

150    Select Case Result()
160      Case "win"
170        MsgBox ("Well done, " & Source.Caption & ", you won!!")
180        OxoO.Enabled = False
190        OxoX.Enabled = False

200      Case "draw"
210        MsgBox ("Well played both of you - a draw")
220        OxoO.Enabled = False
230        OxoX.Enabled = False

240      Case ""
250    End Select

260 Else
270      Beep
280 End If
End Sub
```

Remember that because `OxoPos` is a Control Array when the `OxoPos_DragDrop` procedure is called VB provides the Index value of the control within the array that is the destination object of the Drop event. This will allow us to determine the position on the grid chosen by the user. In addition, the `OxoPos_DragDrop` procedure provides the Source control that has been dropped - either the X CommandButton or the O CommandButton - and the current mouse. We use the first two parameters in this procedure.

Line *10* determines whether the destination object has a blank caption. If this is the case, it means that that position in the grid has not yet been used and we can then set the caption of this control to X or O, depending on the Source object. However, if the caption is not blank, it means that it is either X or O and that grid position is not available. If this is the case, the else statement on line *270* emits a beep to indicate a problem and the procedure exits.

If the user's move is valid, the caption of the Destination control is changed to the caption of the Source control. Thus, if the user drags the X CommandButton over the middle position of the grid, `OxoPos(4)`'s caption will be changed to "X".

The Select statement starting on line *30* uses the Name property of the Source control to determine whether OxoX or OxoO was dragged and dropped. If it was an X move, Grid(Index) is set to 1, the X CommandButton is disabled, the O CommandButton is enabled and the variable Turns is incremented. Turns is used later to determine whether the game is a draw. If it was a O move, Grid(Index) is set to −1, the O CommandButton is disabled, the X CommandButton is enabled and the variable Turns is again incremented.

The next Select statement starting on line *150* uses the function Result() to determine whether the game has ended with a winner, whether it is a draw or whether the game has still not reached a conclusion. Result() - discussed below - returns one of three values:

1. "win" indicating that there is a winner - a congratulatory message for the winner is displayed and both X and O Command buttons are disabled to halt the game.

2. "draw" indicating that the game is drawn - a general congratulatory message is displayed and again both X and O Command buttons are disabled

3. "" (empty string) indicating that the game has not reached a conclusion - no action is taken.

The function Result() is shown next:

```
Public Function Result()

If Abs(Grid(0) + Grid(1) + Grid(2)) = 3 Or _
   Abs(Grid(3) + Grid(4) + Grid(5)) = 3 Or _
   Abs(Grid(6) + Grid(7) + Grid(8)) = 3 Or _
   Abs(Grid(0) + Grid(4) + Grid(8)) = 3 Or _
   Abs(Grid(2) + Grid(4) + Grid(6)) = 3 Or _
   Abs(Grid(0) + Grid(3) + Grid(6)) = 3 Or _
   Abs(Grid(1) + Grid(4) + Grid(7)) = 3 Or _
   Abs(Grid(2) + Grid(5) + Grid(8)) = 3 Then
   Result = "win"
Else
   If Turns = 9 Then
     Result = "draw"
   Else: Result = ""
   End If
End If

End Function
```

If there is a row, column or diagonal of Xs, the sum of the equivalent elements of the array Grid will add up to 3. For O's, the sum will be −3. The magnitude of the sum, ie the absolute value, in both cases will be 3. The expression Abs(Grid(0) + Grid(1) + Grid(2) finds the absolute value of the sum of the first row of Grid. The other similar expressions in the If statement find the absolute sums of the other 7 possible lines. Each of these expressions is compared with the value 3, and if any one of them has a value of 3, the If statement is true and Result returns "win". Note that the underscore character (_) is recognised as a continuation character to allow a long statement to be spread over more than one line.

If there is not a winning line, the variable Turns is checked. If it is equal to 9, this means that all of the grid positions are filled and, because there is no winner, the game must be a draw.

The "New game" Command button uses a loop to restore the grid to its initial state and to indicate that X is to start by Enabling X and Disabling O:

```
Private Sub NewGame_Click()
Dim i As Integer
For i = 0 To 8
 OxoPos(i).Caption = ""
 Grid(i) = 0
Next i
OxoX.Enabled = True
OxoO.Enabled = False
Turns = 0
End Sub
```

The "Exit" CommandButton simply closes the form:

```
Private Sub Exit_Click()
Unload Me
End Sub
```

Note that Me is a special VB word that represents the current object, that is, the Form in this instance. Finally, to establish `Grid` as a Global array so that it can be accessed by all of the Form's procedures and to do the same for `Turns`, the following two lines are included in the Declarations section:

```
Dim Grid(9) As Integer
Dim Turns As Integer
```

Programming Exercises

1. Create a Form similar to the "Winking face" program described earlier in this topic. Design your own shape to animate.

2. Repeat the previous exercise but use simple geometrical shapes to animate instead of text. You will need to use CommandButton clicks to change the properties of the shapes to be animated. You can use the Line tool to draw lines and use the X1, Y1, X2 and Y2 properties to change the position of the lines in code, and you can use the Shape tool to create and modify circles and squares.

3. Use the "Currency converter" program as a guide to producing a program that will convert between different units of measurement. For instance, you could convert between pounds, ounces, grams and kilograms, or between inches, feet, yards, metres and centimetres.

4. Extend the" PC Configuration Calculator" program to allow a user to select from a number of separate option categories such as faster processors, amount of additional RAM and larger Hard drives.

5. Write a program that uses a range of VB functions to simulate a scientific calculator. You could also provide the calculator with memory store and recall functions.

6. Write a simple vector drawing program that allows a user to drag and drop predefined shapes (eg squares and circles of different sizes) onto a drawing area on a form and then move them around.

7. Modify the "Noughts and Crosses" program so that a user can play the computer. To keep the coding as simple as possible, the computer's move can be chosen randomly from the available positions. You could later add some defensive tactics, such as blocking possible winning moves by detecting two of the same user's symbol in a vertical, horizontal or diagonal line and placing the computer's at the end of the line.

Unit 4 Assignment

4.1.

A program is required to read in three numeric values representing the three sides of a triangle. The numbers are to be entered from a keyboard one after the other, separated by one or more spaces and followed by pressing the Enter key. The program outputs a number of messages regarding the type of triangle that the three numbers represent:

- ☐ Invalid data: these values cannot be used to form a triangle;
- ☐ Invalid data: non-numeric input;
- ☐ Scalene;
- ☐ Isosceles;
- ☐ Equilateral;
- ☐ Obtuse;
- ☐ Right-angled.

The program may print out more than one message. For instance, if the three values were 3, 3, 5, the program should say that the triangle is 'Obtuse' and 'Isosceles'.

Task 1

Using a standard design methodology design the program. Your design should adhere to top-down, structured design principles and should include a data dictionary specifying the name, type, size and use of all identifiers used in the design.

Task 2

1. Use appropriate testing methods to devise test cases which would test the program thoroughly.
2. For each test case specify the expected output from the program.
3. You should assume that the program has code to validate the input so that it can detect invalid inputs. Your test data should cover every possible output from the program for invalid and valid data.

Task 3

Write the program using the design in Task 1.

After identifying and removing syntax and runtime errors, test the program using the test cases devised in Task 2. Keep a log of test results and of how errors were corrected and the program re-tested.

You will need to research the characteristics of each type of triangle in order to devise test data that represents each possible type of triangle.

Unit 5: Communications technology

Assessment Evidence Grid

Grade E	Grade C	Grade A
Distinguish between analogue and digital signalling and describe the role of a modem in computer communications.	Understand basic signal theory and how it affects the choice of transmission methods and media.	Evaluate current transmission methods and media and assess suitability of each for a particular communications channel.
Describe the main functions of a communications protocol.	Understand the differences between the various communication channels available.	Set up a PC to communicate via the Internet using appropriate hardware and software to enable Web-browsing and file transfers (FTP).
Identify the alternative forms of communication media and provide examples of their use in different forms of network.	Understand the selection criteria for LAN interconnection devices.	Explain the OSI seven layer model in relation to interconnection devices.
Describe and illustrated the role of the various components which make up a LAN.		Explain the functioning of the main LAN access control methods.
Draw the main LAN topologies and explain the difference between them in the ways that data flows around a network.		Identify and describe the functions of the main hardware and software elements which make up the Internet and World Wide Web.
Identify and describe the basic roles of a range of interconnection devices.		
Distinguish between the Internet and the World Wide Web and describe a range of services they provide.		

Chapter 29

Data communications

Telecommunications and data communications

The word *telecommunications* can be applied to any system capable of transmitting text, sounds, graphical images or indeed, data of any kind, in electronic form. The signals may travel along wires or they may be radio signals, which require no wires, but can travel through the atmosphere and space. The combination of computer and telecommunications technologies has profoundly affected the way computer systems and other communication devices are used.

To a computer, text, sounds and graphical images all constitute data, which it represents digitally, using the *binary* coding system. Although not all transmissions of digital data involve general-purpose computers, they are usually generated and controlled by digital computer technology. Data generated by a computer is already in digital form, but other data (the term is used in its broadest sense), such as sounds of human speech, or a photograph, need to be digitally encoded before transmission over a digital network. The term *data communications* can be applied to systems that combine the use of telecommunications and computer technologies.

Digital networks and user devices

Figure 29.1 illustrates the relationship between users and the various digital networks for computer, telephone, cellular mobile phone, radio and television transmissions.

The white circular band contains examples of the devices we use to switch information between the analogue forms we require into the digital forms needed by the networks. The analogue forms include, for example, pictures on television screens, text on a printout, pressure readings on a gauge, words spoken into a microphone, movement of a joystick, pictures received by a television camera, numbers displayed in a spreadsheet, spoken directions from a car's global positioning system (GPS) and temperature readings taken by a sensor. Some user devices, such as televisions, radios and cameras are still manufactured for use in analogue com-

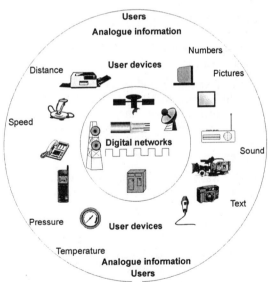

Figure 29.1. *Digital networks and user devices*

munications, but to use digital networks devices must use digital technology. It is anticipated that within the next few years any remaining analogue networks in the UK, notably for televison and radio, will become wholly digital.

Signalling

In this section we examine the principles of signalling between network devices. To transmit data electronically between two devices requires the use of a signalling method which is 'understood' by both the transmitter and receiver and is supported by the communication link (the *medium*) which connects them. There are two types of signal which can be transmitted along a medium, analogue and digital. Computer data is represented in *digital* form, so where the telecommunications systems support it, data is moved between remote computer systems as digitised signals. Although digital communications are now the norm, there are still some parts of our communications networks which are designed for analogue communication. The Public Switched Telephone Network (PSTN) is now primarily digital, but connections to it from most homes and small business premises are still analogue. For this reason, and because the principles of digital signalling are better understood with a foundation knowledge of analogue signalling, we briefly explain its principles here.

Analogue signals

Analogue comes from the word analogous, meaning similar. Thus, an analogue signal varies continuously in the same way as the information it represents. An analogue signal can vary in its amplitude and/or frequency.

Before we consider the transmission of computer data, it is helpful to look at the analogue representation of sound, which the telephone network was initially designed to carry. Figure 29.2 represents a simple sound sequence and shows a *sine* wave form with two characteristics, *amplitude* and *frequency*.

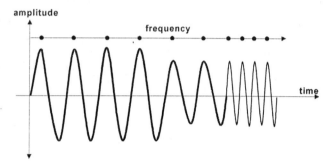

Figure 29.2. *Amplitude and frequency*

Amplitude determines loudness, or volume and frequency determines pitch. *Pitch* is commonly referred to in terms of high and low notes. Increasing frequency raises the pitch of a sound, whereas reducing it lowers the pitch. In the Figure, the amplitude and thereby the volume, begins at one level and is then reduced. Towards the end, the frequency and thereby the pitch, is increased. Frequency is measured according to the number of times a wave form is repeated per second, expressed as Herz (Hz) or cycles per second.

The PSTN was originally designed for voice transmission, using analogue electrical signals to represent what is spoken and heard at each end of a link. A telephone mouthpiece contains a diaphragm, which vibrates when struck by sound waves. These vibrations are converted into electrical signals which have a direct relationship to what is said. When the signals arrive at the earpiece on the receiving telephone, its diaphragm converts the impulses back into sound.

Electrical analogue signalling is subject to distortion from magnetic fields emanating from, for example, nearby electricity cabling. Unless the distortion is severe, the parties will still be able to communicate satisfactorily. Many radio stations still transmit using analogue signalling (because few of us have digital radios) and we are all familiar with the crackles and whistles which come from signal distortion.

Modems and analogue circuits

Signal distortion caused by line noise (interference) is one reason why computer data cannot be carried over analogue telephone circuits in the same way as the human voice. Distortion could easily prevent communicating computers from reliably distinguishing between 1's and 0's, the patterns of which are crucial to accurate transmission of data. It is the job of a device called a *modem* to convert the computer's 1's and 0's to an analogue form resembling that of speech signals.

Amplitude modulation

A binary sequence could be represented by *modulating* the amplitude of the wave, as shown in Figure 29.3.

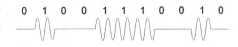

Figure 29.3. *Amplitude modulation*

Amplitude modulation (AM) signals can easily be corrupted by interference on the line and is not generally used for the transmission of computer data.

Frequency modulation

Frequency modulation uses one frequency for binary 1 and another frequency for binary 0, as shown in Figure 29.4.

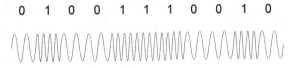

Figure 29.4. *Frequency modulation*

Frequency modulation is also known as *frequency-shift keying* (FSK). Modem transmission rates are measured in bits per second (bps) and FSK is still used for low speed transmissions up to 300 bps. Another modulation technique, TCM (Trellis Coded Modulation), which is mathematically complex and beyond the scope of this text, is used for today's high speed modems. TCM is a CCITT (see later) standard for modem communications. Other more complex methods include PSK (Phase Shift Keying) and QAM (Quadrature Amplitude Modulation).

Frequency bandwidth

The analogue sections of the telephone network are designed to carry voice signals ranging in frequency from 300 to 3000 Hz. This is known as the bandwidth. Referring back to Figure 29.2 of the sound wave, this means any sounds which are pitched outside of this range are lost. This is not a problem because, although the loss of some frequencies will alter the normal sound of a person's voice it is still perfectly intelligible to the listener. There is a problem in respect of digital signals, for which the analogue telephone network was not designed. For reasons which we do not need to explore here, digital signals generate frequencies outside of this range, including a frequency of 0Hz. If a digital signal is applied directly to an analogue line, the sine waves which represent the binary digits will be severely *attenuated* (weakened) and be so distorted as to be unrecognisable by the receiving device.

To overcome this problem, a *modem* (modulator-demodulator) is used to modulate the digital signal into an analogue form which will survive intact from transmitter to receiver. A modem acts as the interface between a computer and the analogue telephone connection to which it is attached. The modem for the transmitter device modulates the digital signal into the corresponding analogue form for transmission along the telephone line and the modem at the receiver device carries out the reverse operation. As Figure 29.5 shows, modems are capable of both functions, so that two way communications are supported.

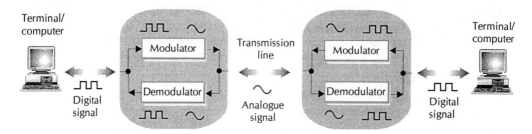

Figure 29.5. *Modems in a data communications link*

Digital communications

Where the network and user devices are wholly digital, analogue wave forms are not used. Instead, the communications medium carries two discrete (separate, distinct from one another) signals which correspond to the binary values of 1 and 0. For example, voltages of +12 volts and −12 volts may represent logical 0 and logical 1, respectively. Figure 29.6 illustrates the 'square wave' of a digital signal.

Figure 29.6. *Discrete signals for representing binary data*

Optical fibre, which is now widely used for digital communications, uses pulses of light rather than electricity to represent binary data. The information given in the next section applies to data communications generally, regardless of whether the transmission medium is analogue or digital.

Data communication modes

Direction of transmission

Communications media can be classified according to direction of transmission:

1.   *Simplex* mode allows communication in one direction only (Figure 29.7).

     This mode would appear to be suitable where no interactivity is required, for example, information displayed on an electronic motorway sign or an airport's flight arrivals and departures display. In

Figure 29.7. *Simplex transmission*

     practice, a *reverse channel* is always necessary to allow the receiving device to request the re-transmission of lost data (see Error Detection).

2.   *Half-duplex* (Figure 29.8) supports communications in both directions, but not at the same time; in other words there is only a single channel and the direction is switched after completion of transmission in the other direction. The mode is only suited to low volume data transmis-

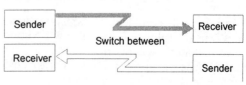

Figure 29.8. *Half-duplex transmission*

     sions where an immediate response is not required. For example, a shop may upload its daily order requirements to a central warehouse at the end of the day and receive confirmation of deliveries during the night. As with simplex, a reverse channel is needed to allow error control messages to be transmitted from receiver to transmitter during data transmission. A reverse channel is used purely for data transmission control and does not provide simultaneous two-way communication (see duplex).

3. *Duplex* (Figure 29.9) mode allows communication in both directions at the same time, as there are two channels permanently available. In interactive systems, where two way communication is continuously required, such as for telephone conversations, on-line enquiries and Internet shopping transactions, duplex is the only suitable mode.

Figure 29.9. *Duplex transmission*

Devices differ in the ways they communicate or talk with each other. The next section examines the principles of *serial* communications, which for practical and economic reasons are used in all remote communication systems. *Parallel* transmission, briefly described first, is only feasible for short distances such as for the connection between a computer and a locally attached printer.

Parallel transmission

Figure 29.10 illustrates the principle of *parallel transmission* with the data bits being transmitted in groups.

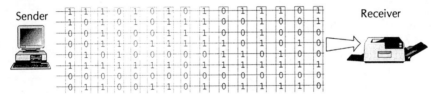

Figure 29.10. *Parallel transmission*

This is obviously quicker than sending the bits one after another (serially), but it is only practicable over short distances. Communication between a computer and its nearby peripherals can be carried out using parallel transmission, which is particularly important where high-speed devices, such as disk or tape units, are concerned. Microcomputer systems often use parallel transmission to communicate with a nearby printer.

Serial transmission

As Figure 29.11 shows, serial transmission sends the binary signals one after another in a serial fashion and is the only practicable method for communication over long distances. The principle problems with serial transmission concern the identification of the individual bits which make up a data stream and the division of bit groupings into words. A *word* is a given number of bits used as a standard unit. For example, a character within a data stream may comprise, say 7 or 8 bits, depending on the coding system in use. A commonly used coding system is ASCII, which uses 7 bits per character, plus a *parity* bit for error checking (see later). There are two techniques for achieving this separation of bits and words:

❏ asynchronous transmission;

❏ synchronous transmission.

Figure 29.11. *Serial transmission*

Asynchronous serial transmission

When a sending device transmits characters at irregular intervals, as does for example, a keyboard device, it is said to be transmitting *asynchronously*.

Although the characters are not sent at regular intervals, the bits within each character must be sent at regularly timed intervals. An example of asynchronous character format is shown in Figure 29.12. It can be seen that the line has two electrical states, representing 1 and 0.

To allow the receiver to identify individual characters, the transmitter signals the beginning of a character with a *start* bit and the end with a *stop* bit. In the Figure, the character comprises 7 data bits.

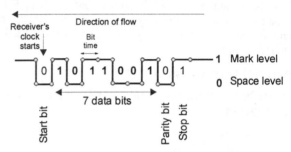

Figure 29.12. *Asynchronous character format*

The Figure also shows the use of a parity bit which was a simple but primitive method of detecting errors caused by noise on the transmission line. To provide an introduction to the topic of transmission error control, single bit parity checking is described in the next section. However, it should be noted that the sophisticated error detection and correction controls provided by high speed modems make the use of the single parity bit unnecessary. Figure 29.13 shows the current format of an asynchronous character.

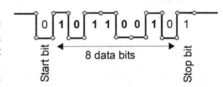

Figure 29.13. *Asynchronous character format without parity bit*

When no data is being transmitted the line is in its *idle* state, a condition maintained by a logical 1 output from the transmitter. This is known as the *mark* level.

When it is ready to send a character, the transmitter outputs a logical 0 signal, which drops the signal to *space*. Sensing this state, the receiver starts its clock after one *bit time* (for example, on a line operating at 9600 bits per second, one bit time is $1/9600^{ths}$ of a second) and counts off and samples the regularly timed bits that form a character. Even if the receiver's clock is not exactly in time with that of the transmitter, the bit-time is sufficient to allow each bit to be sampled and identified. If the receiver is out of synchronisation by no more than 5% then the system should still operate effectively.

When a stop bit is reached and the line returns to the mark level, the receiver switches back to its listening state. Although the transmission of individual bits requires fairly closely matched time control by transmitter and receiver, the presence of start and stop bits for each character permits the time interval between characters to be irregular, or asynchronous.

Modem frequency spectrum

A modem which uses frequency modulation (see Frequency Shift Keying or FSK earlier) will use different frequencies for logical 0 (space) and logical 1 (mark). For example, an early modem standard, CCITT (see Standards Authorities later) V21, used the following frequencies to provide full duplex, asynchronous transmission at 300 bps.

Modem operation		Space (logical 0)	Mark (logical 1)
Originate transmission	Transmit frequency	1180 Hz	980 Hz
Originate transmission	Receive frequency	1850 Hz	1650 Hz
Answer	Transmit frequency	1850 Hz	1650 Hz
Answer	Receive frequency	1180 Hz	980 Hz

Parity bit

The ASCII code (Chapter) is a useful 7-bit code for plain text transmission, but its error control facilities are primitive. An additional bit, known as the *parity bit* (in the left-most or most significant bit position), is attached to each character and can be used to detect *single bit* errors which may occur during data transfer.

There are two types of parity, odd and even, though it is of little significance which is used. If odd parity is used, the parity bit is set to binary 1 or 0, such that there is an odd number of binary 1s in the group. Conversely, even parity requires that there is an even number of binary 1s in the group. Examples of these two forms of parity are provided in Table 29.1.

7-bit characters	using odd parity	using even parity
1 0 0 1 0 1 0	**0** 1 0 0 1 0 1 0	**1** 1 0 0 1 0 1 0
0 1 0 1 1 0 1	**1** 0 1 0 1 1 0 1	**0** 0 1 0 1 1 0 1

Table 29.1. *Odd and even parity checking*

The parity bit is shown in bold. If even parity is being used and the receiving device identifies the grouping 10010100 then the presence of an odd number of binary 1s indicates an error in transmission. Provided that the number of bits corrupted is odd, all transmission errors will be detected. However, an even number of bits in error will not affect the parity condition and thus will not be revealed.

Asynchronous modem settings

Figure 29.14 shows the Connection tab for modem settings in Windows, with each character comprising 8 data bits and one stop bit. Because the modem uses its own error controls, a parity bit is not required.

Baud rate, bandwidth and data compression

The term *baud rate* refers to the line speed operating between two modems. For example, a 28,800 baud connection can transfer 28,800 bits per second (bps). The term *bandwidth* was used earlier in relation to the signal frequency range supported by an analogue circuit, but the term is also used in respect of digital communications, measured in bps. For example,

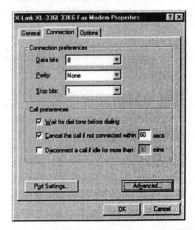

Figure 29.14. *Asynchronous modem settings*

a modem operating at 56 Kbits has twice the bandwidth of one operating at 28 Kbits. Bandwidth is important for modern communications because of the increased use of networks for the transmission of multimedia images. By using data compression, a modem can transfer a given amount of data with fewer bits, thus improving the rate of data throughput. Typically, a modem can receive data through the COM port (a PC's RS232 modem interface) at around four times the rate of the actual line. So, for example, using a connect speed of 28,800 baud, a modem could accept data from the COM port at 115,200 bps (4 × 28,800). Figure 29.15 shows the COM port set at this speed.

Figure 29.16 illustrates this relationship between line and modem speeds. The fastest modems will operate at 56 K (56 × 1024) bits per second and with data compression can achieve much higher effective data transfer rates (throughput). However, to achieve this maximum speed, the receiving modem must be able to operate at the same speed and use the same compression *protocols* (rules) to uncompress the data.

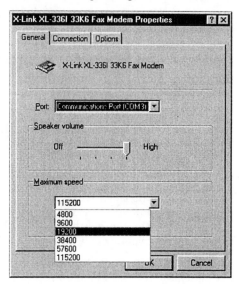

Figure 29.15. *Serial port settings*

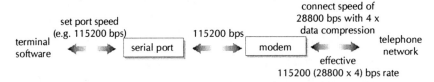

Figure 29.16. *Data compression allowing modem to handle more data through serial port*

As part of the data compression process, a modem will also strip out the start and stop bits which are still attached to each character for transmission through the COM port to the modem. This massively reduces the wasted transmission time which would otherwise be taken up by start and stop bits for each character. In earlier systems, these transmission overheads significantly reduced data throughput. For example, an early 2400 baud modem could transfer only 240 characters per second (cps), because each character required a minimum of 10 bits (1 start bit, 1 stop bit and 8 data bits). Without the start and stop bits, the rate would be 300 cps.

Although the technological advances in modems have permitted a radical increase in asynchronous data transmission performance, the sending PC is still having to attach start and stop bits to each character and there are circumstances when *synchronous* transmission provides a more efficient alternative.

V.90 Modem standard

Figure 29.17 illustrates a V.90 modem to Internet Service Provider (ISP) connection.

This most recent standard for analogue modems enables connection to the Internet at speeds of up to 56 Kbps (V.90 modems are labelled as such, but the theoretical maximum speed is 54 Kbps, because of technical restrictions). Previous modem standards were developed on the assumption that analogue modems would be used at each end of a link, and that the analogue/digital conversion processes at either end would limit the connect speed to 33.6 Kbps.

In fact, most computers are communicating via the Internet, using Internet Service Providers (ISP) who have wholly digital connections to the PSTN. Thus, analogue/digital conversions are only being carried out at one end of the link, for the analogue connection between the Internet user's computer and the local digital exchange on the PSTN.

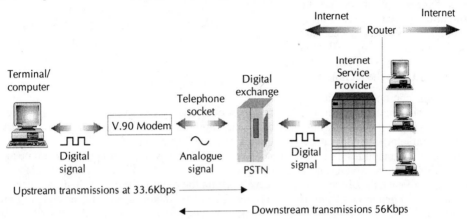

Figure 29.17. *Internet connection using a V.90 modem*

When a V.90 modem user accesses information on the Internet, the ISP's computer (provided it handles the V.90 standard) encodes it digitally for transmission to the users' PC, rather than using the modulation signalling techniques of analogue modems. This enables downstream transmission (from ISP to user's PC) at 56 Kbps. The higher speed allows the retrieval of complex Web pages incorporating images, sound and video sequences without excessive delays. Upstream (modem to ISP) transmissions are limited to 33.6Kbps, which for keystroke and mouse commands entered by the user, is perfectly adequate. The technical reason for the lower speed is that the V.90 modem uses the conventional V.34 modulation techniques for upstream transmission.

Pulse Code Modulation (PCM)

PCM has long been used for the digitisation of audio signals in particular (music CD recording) and samples an analogue wave form 8000 times per second. Figure 29.18 illustrates this process with each vertical line representing a sampling point.

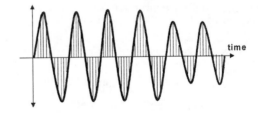

Figure 29.18. *PCM signal sampling*

Each sample point is encoded as a separate signal. For the journey from ISP to the user's local PSTN exchange, the data travels at 64 Kbps, but is then slowed to 54 Kbps when it is converted to the analogue waveform needed for the local connection to the user's PC. The user's V.90 modem can accept the PCM signals and convert them to the digital form required by the computer.

All connections via analogue modems are subject to variations in line conditions and the connect speed will frequently be below the modem's maximum speed. ISDN connections provide a quicker and more reliable service and are described later.

Synchronous serial transmission

The start and stop bits used in asynchronous transmission are wasteful, as they do not contain information. With higher speed devices or *buffered* (memory for the accumulation of data before it is transmitted) low-speed devices, data can be transmitted in more efficient, timed, or *synchronous* blocks. Figure 29.19 illustrates the technique.

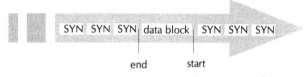

Figure 29.19. *Synchronous character format*

Most modems can operate synchronously or asynchronously, as required. In synchronous transmission, a data stream may be very long, so it is vital that the bit timing between transmitter and receiver is synchronised and that individual characters are separated. This can be achieved by using an additional transmission path to copy the transmitter's timings to the receiver. Alternatively, timing signals can be embedded within the data stream. These timing signals, referred to as SYN characters are placed at the beginning of each data block and at intervals within the block. If timing is lost, the receiver can re-time its bit groupings from the last received SYN character. Like the start and stop bits used in asynchronous transmission, SYN characters constitute an overhead and have to be stripped out by the receiver. Some computer terminals are designed for high speed data transmission and use synchronous transmission, but many others use asynchronous transmission. The data in a stream may consist of discrete text characters, coded in a character code such as ASCII, or it may be pure binary. Examples of pure binary data are found in graphic images, executable machine-code programs and numbers in floating point (Chapter 8) form. For character data streams, the allocation of a particular bit pattern to act, for example as a SYN character is not difficult. Obviously, for pure binary data, the binary patterns within the data block are not predictable and cannot, therefore, include embedded and unique SYN characters. HDLC (High-Level Data Link Control) is an example of a transmission protocol which is designed to overcome this problem.

HDLC frame structure

Each data block occupies a *frame* or *packet* which may vary in size, typically up to 4 Kb. An important standard for synchronous communications uses the HDLC frame structure, illustrated in Figure 29.19.

Figure 29.19. *HDLC frame structure*

The frame components are explained below.

❑ The *flag* fields mark the limits of the frame with the binary sequence 01111110. To ensure that this sequence always appears at the start of each frame and nowhere else, the transmitter inserts additional zeros if the reserved flag sequence happens to occur within the data area. This is know as *bit stuffing* or *zero insertion*. The receiver strips out (*unstuffs*) these extra zeros as part of the frame unpacking process. If a communication protocol uses a fixed frame size, bit stuffing may be used to extend frames which are shorter than the required length. A detailed description of bit stuffing is beyond the scope of this text.

❑ The *address* field occupies one or more bytes (1 byte = 8 bits) and contains the address of the destination device, or sometimes of the sending device. For example, when a central server wishes to communicate with an attached workstation, it will add the workstation's address to the frame. If the workstations only communicate with the central server and never directly with one another, then a transmitting workstation need only add its own address to the frame.

❑ The *control* field also occupies one or more bytes and identifies the type of frame. Apart from containing user data, some special frames may have a Supervisory control function, perhaps to control the flow of data across the network. The field also contains a sequence number to ensure that frames are not lost in transmission.

❑ The *data* field has no particular format and is simply the collection of bits which form the particular user data.

❑ The CRC (Cyclic Redundancy Check - see Error Controls) fields contain the result of an arithmetic calculation carried out on all the bits enclosed within the flag fields. The receiver carries out the same calculation and if it obtains the same result, it is almost certain that the contents of the frame have not been corrupted. If a CRC error is found, the frame is discarded and the transmitter has to send it again.

Short distance serial communications

A number of standards and products exist to allow serial communications between computers and between computers and input/output devices.

USB and Firewire

USB (Universal Serial Bus) is a massive improvement on the standard serial ports to which modems and other relatively slow devices are connected. USB transmits at up to 12 Mbps. Any common input/output devices, such as a scanner, printer or camera can be connected to one of the USB ports which are now standard in PC construction. USB allows 'plug and play' installation of devices and also supports 'hot plugging', which means that a device can be connected or disconnected without switching off the machine first. No device expansion card needs to be fitted.

Firewire is the main competitor to USB and also provides 'plug and play' device installation and 'hot plugging'. Its transfer rate of 400 Mbps compared with the 12 Mbps of a USB 1.0 connection, made it highly suitable for real-time video recording and playing, for which it was primarily designed. USB 2.0 offers transfer rates between 300 and 400 Mbps and enables it to compete with Firewire in the area of real-time video.

Bluetooth and IrDA

Bluetooth is a short range radio technology which is designed to allow wireless, voice and data communication between digital devices which are currently connected by cable. Thus, the technology can be used for connecting mobile phones, hand-held computers, as well as desktop PCs to WANs and LANs. Its low power requirements are ideal for battery-powered devices, such as mobile phones and communicating devices do not require a clear line-of-sight. Current infrared standards include IrDA for wireless, point-to-point, communication between stationary computer devices, but clear line-of-sight is necessary for it to work.

Communication standards

Standards authorities

The data communications industry has always had to deal with problems of *incompatible* standards. Standards have to do with all aspects of a communications system, including, for example, *hardware devices*, *encoding* of data and forms of *signals*. At first, the only computer systems available for use in data communications were mainframes and later, minicomputers. These computer systems were produced by a small number of very large manufacturers, the most important being IBM; they also produced communications devices that worked with their computers. In competition with one another, each manufacturer set the standards for use with its equipment. These *closed* systems prevented a customer from using equipment, produced by different manufacturers, in the same data communications system.

The huge expansion in the uses of data communications, both nationally and internationally has been made possible through the adoption of some common standards. Common standards lead to *open* systems, which allow users to use components from more than one manufacturer.

A number of bodies are concerned with the establishment of international standards and these are listed below. Frequently, a standard arises initially from the work of a particular manufacturer, and then, often because of the importance of the manufacturer, it is included in the recommendations of the standards authorities.

- ☐ CCITT. This is an acronym for Comité Consultatif Internationale de Télégraphie et Téléphonie an organisation that has its headquarters in Geneva, Switzerland. It is part of the United Nations International Telecommunications Union (ITU). The CCITT makes recommendations on most aspects of data communications, for example, modems (see earlier), networks and facsimile transmission or FAX and publishes them every four years. These recommendations usually obtain world-wide acceptance. CCITT's 'V' series of standards cover equipment used on telephone lines and its X series relate to digital packet transmission standards. Some examples of these standards are mentioned later in this chapter.

- ☐ ANSI is the acronym for American National Standards Institute. ANSI has long maintained a strong influence on standards in the computer and data communications industries. It is formed from industrial and business groups and is a member of the International Standards Organisation (ISO). Examples of its influence can be found in the fields of computer hardware and programming languages. For example, by conforming to ANSI standards, the FORTRAN, COBOL and C languages enable the production of computer software, which is largely *portable*. In other words, because each language is more or less universal, a program written in, for example, COBOL can be readily translated for use on any make of computer. In the area of microcomputer hardware, the ANSI standards define the SCSI (an acronym for Small Computer System Interface) parallel interface, for the connection of peripherals, such as disk drives and printers. The institute is also responsible for the ANSI.SYS *device driver*, a program that provides facilities for greater control of a computer console (screen and keyboard), than is possible with the MS-DOS operating system.

- ☐ IEEE is the acronym for the Institute of Electrical and Electronic Engineers. The organisation has set numerous standards for various aspects of telecommunications and computing. Notably, the IEEE has defined standards for local area network (LAN) protocols.

- ☐ The ISO (International Standards Organisation), has its headquarters in Geneva, Switzerland and is responsible for the definition of the Open Systems Interconnection (OSI) model. This model aims to ensure that any computer terminal is able to connect to any network and communicate with any other terminal, whether it is connected to the same or any other linked network. The OSI model is examined in greater detail in the section on Communications Protocols.

Communication protocols

We begin by looking at the protocols which are used for modem communications, typically between a home or small business user and an Internet Service Provider's server. Sending and receiving computers must use the same modem protocols and settings if they are to communicate reliably. Protocols are, essentially, sets of rules about how the two devices are to communicate. So, for example, if a modem is set to use 8 data bits, no parity bit and 1 stop bit (see earlier), the other modem will not be able to interpret the data unless it uses the same settings. Also, both modems must operate at the same speed. This is why, for example, when connecting to the Internet, the connect speed may vary, up to the maximum of the user's modem. The connect speed depends on the modem speed at the Internet Service Provider's site, when the dial-up connection is made. For communication between two devices, the protocol must establish as a minimum:

❑ the data transmission rate (measured in bits per second). If the devices have different maximum transmission rates, the rate is dictated by the slower of the two.

❑ whether both devices may transmit to each other simultaneously (in *full-duplex* mode) or one direction at a time (in *half-duplex* mode). In the latter case, the protocol must also allow determination of which device currently has *control of the communications link*.

❑ whether *synchronous* (data is sent in a stream with sender and receiver synchronised to identify when one character ends and another starts) or *asynchronous* (characters are sent at irregularly timed intervals, with start and stop bits to separate characters) transmission is to be used.

A protocol may also specify the form of *handshaking*, the method of data *flow control* and mechanisms for *error control* and *data compression*.

Handshaking, flow control

Handshaking means that communicating devices must have a common method of determining their presence and readiness to communicate. Although the details vary, a handshake can be illustrated simply by the following example. Suppose that device A wishes to communicate with device B. Device A signals "Hello Device B, are you there?", to which device B replies, "Yes, I am here A.". Finally, device A responds "I see that you are there B." The handshake should also define when each device has finished sending or receiving a message.

A flow control mechanism is needed to ensure that data transmission flows smoothly, that the communications channel is not overloaded and that the transmitting device does not send data more quickly than the receiver can handle.

All modern modems include hardware to do this, but if both modems do not support hardware flow control, then software (XON/OFF) must be used. When the receiving device's buffer is full, it sends an XOFF signal to the sending device, which then pauses transmission. Once the receiving device has cleared space in its buffer and is ready to receive again, it sends an XON signal to the sending device.

Error control and data compression

Although digital signals are infinitely more stable than their analogue equivalent, errors will occur and the communicating devices must have a means of detecting and re-transmitting them correctly. For transmission over analogue links (which are the norm for local connections to the public telephone network) error detection and correction is even more important and all modem error protocols are built in to the hardware. Data compression (see earlier) reduces the volume of data, allowing its speedier transmission.

Protocols can be implemented by software or hardware. Typically, dedicated network devices such as modems use hardware implementation, but general-purpose computers which have not been designed for connection to a particular network may have to set up transmission protocols through the communications software. Figure 29.14, earlier in this chapter, shows the protocol settings in Windows 98 for a dial-up connection to the Internet. The settings for eight data bits, no parity bit and 1 stop bit are standard for PC to modem communication. Other options, such as the use of 1.5 or 2 stop bits and varying numbers of data bits relate to largely obsolete terminal devices.

Example protocols

TCP/IP

TCP/IP (Transmission Control Protocol/Internet Protocol) is the standard for communication between Internet host computers and is probably the most well known. It is actually a suite of several protocols. The importance of the Internet for network communications means that all modern operating systems provide support for TCP/IP, including those PC and Macintosh computer systems and network operating systems such as Novell Netware. Unix, as the standard operating system for most Internet host computers, has the TCP/IP protocol built in.

SMTP

SMTP stands for Simple Mail Transfer Protocol and is the standard for e-mail transmissions between servers and between clients (user e-mail software) and servers on the Internet.

UDP

UDP or User Datagram Protocol is used for the broadcast of data over IP (Internet Protocol) networks but unlike TCP, does not require that a connection is first established between sender and receiver (point to point). In other words, the data is transmitted without any guarantee that it will reach its destination. For this reason, UDP is referred to as a *connectionless* protocol; TCP is a *connection-orientated* protocol, which means that the link between devices must be established before communication can begin. Ethernet local area networks also operate on a connectionless, broadcast principle.

X.25

This is a CCITT protocol for packet switching networks. X.25 Packet Switched networks allow remote devices to communicate with each other across high speed digital links without the expense of individual leased lines. Packet Switching is a technique whereby the network routes individual packets of data between different destinations based on addressing within each packet.

FTP

File Transfer Protocol (FTP) allows large amounts of information to be transferred between two computers very conveniently. FTP originated with the UNIX operating system and was used to transfer files of all types between remote computer systems. A popular application of FTP is for the uploading and downloading of Web site pages.

ASCII

This is only appropriate for *text* files, which contain no control characters. Thus it cannot be used to transfer files produced with a word processor, spreadsheet or graphics package. Neither can it transfer command (COM) or executable (EXE) files, or files in compressed (ZIP, for example) form. Apart from this, the protocol is not good at controlling errors.

Xmodem

This is a file-transfer protocol used for asynchronous communications. It is commonly used in communications packages. Its ability to find and correct errors makes it suitable for the transfer of files which must retain their integrity, such as program files.

Zmodem

This is one of the most advanced protocols, being much faster than Xmodem. Its error correction controls are absolutely reliable.

CCITT V42bis

This protocol includes a *data compression* (through encoding, data is reduced in volume) technique and error detection and correction. Both the sending and receiving modem must possess the error correction facility.

Error detection

Block check characters (BCC)

The idea of even and odd parity bits for each character is introduced earlier in this chapter 7 and is shown to be inadequate for the detection of even numbers of bit errors. Block check characters (BCCs) aim to conquer this problem by checking the parity of blocks of characters within a data transmission stream. BCCs may carry out *longitudinal* or *cyclic* redundancy checks.

Longitudinal redundancy checking (LRC)

By reference to Table 29.2, the principles of LRC can be explained as follows. Each BCC consists of a group of parity bits which carry out LRC. However, each LRC bit is a parity check on the corresponding bits in all the characters in a block. Thus, the first parity bit in the BCC relates to the bits which occupy the first position in each character in the block, the second parity bit in the BCC relates to the second position bits in each character in the block and so on. LRC ensures that multiple errors, whether even or odd, are likely to be discovered, so at the receiver end of the transmission, the parity of individual characters and blocks of characters is checked.

	7	6	5	4	3	2	1	0
	0	1	0	0	1	0	1	1
	0	1	0	0	1	1	1	0
	1	1	0	0	1	1	1	1
	1	1	0	1	0	1	0	0
	1	1	0	1	0	1	0	0
VRC (bit-7) on	1	1	0	1	0	1	1	1
each character	0	1	0	0	0	0	0	1
	1	1	0	0	1	0	0	1
	1	1	0	1	0	1	0	0
	1	1	0	0	0	1	0	1
	0	1	0	1	0	0	1	1
	1	1	0	1	0	1	1	1
	BCC to check LRC parity (per block)							

Table 29.2. *Vertical (VRC) and longitudinal redundancy checks (LRC)*

Cyclic redundancy checking (CRC)

The BCCs described previously treat a data block as a set of characters, whereas cyclic redundancy checking (CRC) uses a BCC which views each data block as a continuous *stream* of bits.

Firstly, the data block is regarded as one large binary number. That number is divided by another agreed binary number, the quotient is discarded and the remainder (sometimes referred to as a *checksum*) is attached to the data block as a BCC. Upon receipt of the data block, the receiver repeats the calculation used to generate the BCC and compares the result with the BCC attached by the transmitter; any difference between them indicates some corruption of the block. CRC is easy to implement in hardware and detects a very large proportion of all potential errors. CRC is also used by a number of file transfer protocols, including Zmodem (see earlier).

Hamming code, which is beyond the scope of this text, is capable of detecting and correcting transmission errors. Codes which allow the receiver to both detect and correct errors are known as *forward error-correcting codes* (FECs). The majority of data transmission systems do not use FECs and favour the use of powerful CRC techniques to detect errors, even though the receiver then has to request re-transmission of the incorrect data. The alternatives for requesting re-transmission are described in the next section.

Error correction

Echoplex (echo checking)

Echoplex was used in asynchronous communications, for low speed, *dumb* (no processing power of its own) terminals connected to a remote host computer. When a character is transmitted (in other words, when a key is pressed) the host device immediately sends it back to be displayed on the dumb terminal's screen. If the displayed character does not match the character selected from the keyboard, the operator should detect this; the host device can be advised, by the terminal operator, to ignore the incorrect character, by the sending of an agreed *control* character. Clearly, the method is slow and crude. A character could have been received correctly by the host device and an error could corrupt it on its way back. The operator has no way of knowing how and at what point an error occurred. Another disadvantage is that error correction is manual; in an interactive system, the user needs to rely on automatic error control and correction.

Automatic repeat request (ARQ)

When a receiver detects an error it must tell the sending device to re-transmit the erroneous data; this is known as *automatic repeat request* (ARQ). The technique is most appropriate to the handling of data streams, that is, synchronous communications, in conjunction with cyclic redundancy checking (CRC - see earlier). ARQ can take one of three forms:

Stop and wait ARQ or *ACK and NAK*. With this form the receiver acknowledges every block of data, with ACK if it detects no error and NAK if an error is detected. The sending device cannot send the next block until an acknowledgement is received. Any NAK block is re-transmitted repeatedly, if necessary, until an ACK is received.

Go-back N ARQ. With this form, a block is only acknowledged if an error is detected. The sending device can continue transmitting without waiting for an acknowledgement. When a NAK is received, the block in which the error occurred is identified and that block, plus any transmitted since (N blocks), must be re-transmitted.

Selective-repeat ARQ. This is the most sophisticated form of ARQ, in that blocks transmitted since the erroneous block (correct ones are not acknowledged), do not have to be sent again. Thus the sender only re-transmits the identified block and then continues from where it left off, when the NAK was received.

Transmission media

Cables of various types, radio and light waves can be used to carry the data between communicating devices. Each such medium has particular qualities which make it suitable for a particular task. For example, the mobile phone network, by definition, cannot rely entirely on physical cabling and uses radio communications for transmissions to and from mobile phones. The following sections describe the major transmission media.

Physical cabling

Unshielded twisted-pair (UTP) cable

UTP cable is formed from strands of wire twisted in pairs. It predates any other method and is still extensively used for standard telephone or telex terminals. Each twisted pair can carry a single telephone call between two people or two machines. Although twisted-pair cable is generally used for analogue signal transmission, it can be used successfully for digital transmission. Variation in the lengths of wire within pairs can result in signals being received out of phase (mis-timed), but this can be overcome by the frequent use of *repeaters*. The repeaters refresh the signal as it passes to maintain its consistency. Although transmission rates permitted by such cable are lower than for some other media, including co-axial and optical fibre, they are acceptable for many computer applications. Its low cost and ease of installation make it a popular choice for local area networks and for the analogue connections to the PSTN.

Coaxial cable

Coaxial cable is resistant to the transmission interference which can corrupt data transmitted via twisted-pairs cable. It thus provides a fast, relatively interference-free transmission medium. Its construction consists of a central conductor core which is surrounded by a layer of insulating material. The insulating layer is covered by a conducting shield, which is itself protected by another insulating layer. During network installation, the cable can be cut and connections made, without affecting its transmission quality. The quality of cable can vary and some low quality cable is unsuitable for data transmission over long distances. On the other hand, high quality cable can be quite rigid and difficult to install in local networks, where space is limited. Despite this difficulty, it is an extremely popular choice for LANs.

Optical fibre cable

Optical fibre cable consists of thousands of clear glass fibre strands which transmit light or infra-red rays instead of electrical signals. The data is transmitted by a light-emitting diode (two-state signals) or injection-laser diode. Bandwidth is measured in gigabits per second and repeaters are only required after around 60 miles (copper cable requires repeaters every 3 or 4 miles). The other end of the cable has a detector which converts the light pulses into electrical pulses suitable for the attached device. Optical fibre cable is slightly more expensive than electrical cable, is used widely in WANs, but is also finding increasing use in LANs, particular for network backbones.

Public switched telephone network (pstn)

The *pstn* is the main telecommunications network for the United Kingdom. It was originally designed for voice transmission, using analogue electrical signals; these electrical signals represent what is spoken and heard at each end of a link. A telephone mouthpiece contains a diaphragm, which vibrates when struck by sound waves. The vibrations are converted into electrical impulses and are sent over the network to the earpiece on the receiving telephone; a diaphragm in the earpiece converts the impulses back into sound.

Much of the pstn is now digital, in particular the national trunk network and call switching exchanges; the analogue connections are mainly confined to the pstn's local links to homes and businesses. Digital voice transmission uses coded patterns of digital impulses, which are similar to those used to represent computer data. To transmit computer data over analogue sections of the pstn, requires use of a *modem* (see earlier).

Types of telecommunications lines

Dedicated lines

These can be leased from British Telecom and provide a permanent connection for devices in a network. They provide high transmission rates and are relatively error-free. They are only cost-effective for high volume data transmission, or when a permanent link is vital to the users. Charging is by a flat rate rather than when calls are made.

Dial-up or switched lines

These are cheaper, but support lower transmission rates than leased lines. They are more cost effective than leased lines for low-volume work and allow the operator to choose the destination of transmissions.

Switched digital network systems

Public switched data network (psdn)

The psdn, owned by British Telecom (BT) is a *packet switching* (see later) service. Modems are not required and transmission performance is better than that achievable over the partially ana- logue pstn. The service conforms to the CCITT (see Standards Authorities) standard known as the X.25 protocol and for this reason is often referred to as the X.25 network. A major benefit of using this CCITT standard is that the network can be used for international communications. The protocol is steadily being replaced by ATM (see later).

Circuit switching

In any network, setting up a connection between two devices may involve circuit switching. For example, if a network is busy a connection may be established through a series of switches, from one circuit to another, over an alternative route. Thus the actual distance the signals travel may be greatly in excess of the geographical distance between the two points. Charges, whether the connection is for voice or data, will be made according to the geographical distance be- tween the devices (local, medium, long distance), rather than the distance the signals actually have to travel through the various switches.

Packet switching

The main components of a packet switching network are: high speed data lines; packet switch- ing exchanges (PSEs); packet assembler/disassembler (PAD); packet terminal. With the use of a specialised computer, called a *packet terminal*, a customer can create the packets and connect directly to the network through a dedicated dataline.

If the customer is not using a packet terminal, a dial-up connection is used and the data has to go through a *packet assembler /disassembler* (PAD). This device converts data to and from the networks protocol as it enters and leaves the network. Figure 29.20 illustrates these features.

The principles of packet switching are as follow. Messages are divided into data packets, which are then directed through the network to their destination under computer control. Besides a *message* portion, each packet contains data concerning:

- ❑ the destination address;
- ❑ the source identification;
- ❑ the sequence of the packet in the complete message;
- ❑ the detection and control of transmission errors.

The progress of a packet is monitored and controlled by *packet switching exchanges* (PSE) located at each *node* in the network. A node is a junction of network lines, which could be a computer or a computer terminal or other device.

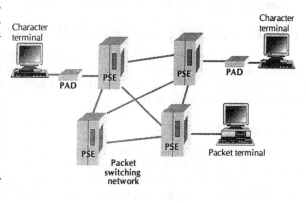

As a packet arrives at a node, the exchange checks the addressing instructions and unless it corresponds to its present location, forwards it on the most appropriate route. Each node has an *input queue*, into which all arriving packets are entered (even those which are addressed to the node itself) and a number of *output queues* (to allow for the possibility of network congestion).

The route may be determined by one of a number of *routing strategies*:

Figure 29.20. *Packet switching network*

❑ *hot potato*. The packet is sent as quickly as possible to the shortest output queue; such packets are not unduly delayed, although they may not be transmitted on the most direct route;

❑ *pre-determined routing*. With this method, the routing details are included in the packet itself, each switching exchange forwarding the packet according to the embedded instructions;

❑ *directory routing*. Each switching exchange has a copy of a routing table to which it refers before forwarding each packet. The appropriate output queue is determined from the table and the packet destination.

Network traffic information is continually transmitted between the various nodes, so that each switching computer has information to allow, for example, the avoidance of congested routes. Figure 29.21 illustrates how a network structure provides alternative routes by which a packet may reach its destination.

If a network is structured as shown in Figure 29.21, a packet sent from terminal T(2) to terminal T(6), would go into the input queue of packet switching exchange PSE (a). Depending on the routing strategy and network traffic conditions, the packet could be directed to an output queue leading to any of the other PSEs. If PSE (e) was inoperative, the alternative routes would be cut drastically; in fact the packet would either have to go through PSEs (b), (c) and (d), in that sequence, or direct from PSE (a) to PSE (d).

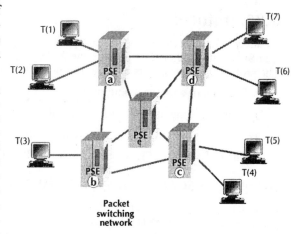

Figure 29.21. *Routing in a packet switching network*

Packet switching allows packets relating to a single message, to be transmitted on different routes. This may be necessary, either because of the breakdown of some routes, or because of variations in traffic conditions over different routes.

Packet switching versus circuit switching

Packet switching networks maximise use of network connections and provide a cheaper, more reliable and efficient, though slightly slower, alternative. Circuit switched connections are ideal for the transmission of data in real-time, when the delays inherent in a packet switching network would not be acceptable.

Message switching

As the name suggests, this type of network deals with identifiable and complete messages, in contrast to a packet switched system where the destination user nodes are responsible for re-assembling their packets into complete messages upon receipt. A number of points can be made when comparing and contrasting packet switching and message switching networks:

- both use a store and forward principle; each node in the network has storage facilities for the accumulation of data prior to its onward transmission and the intelligence to examine the destination data before forwarding it;

- packet switching networks treat data transparently. Individual packets generally do not contain complete messages and the network does not recognise connections between packets, except from identification of their destination. The destination user nodes are left with the responsibility of re-assembling individual packets into complete messages;

- the store and forward facilities in message switching networks need to be much larger than those for packet switching systems, because complete messages must be accumulated at each point of transfer in the network;

- message switching requires increased processing time at intervening nodes while messages are accumulated before onward transmission;

- message switching provides users with greater confidence that messages will be transmitted and received in complete form.

X.25 protocol

As already mentioned, the psdn uses a packet switching protocol, known as X.25. The CCITT (see Standards Authorities) provide the X.25 protocol for interfacing terminals with a psdn. The protocol provides users with the following facilities.

- Division of a message into packets.

- Error checking and re-transmission of any packet affected by an error.

- An addressing format that allows international transmission.

- The PSEs control the transmission of packets through the network.

Integrated services digital network (ISDN)

Many forms of data, including text, voice and video images, can be digitised and an Integrated Services Digital Network (ISDN) is designed to allow the *integrated* transmission of these various data forms over the same network. An Integrated Services Digital Network exists in various forms in different countries, although the ultimate aim is to achieve an international system. It is defined as a wholly *digital* system, with end-to-end digital connections and digital exchanges throughout. ISDN has become achievable because the telephone network has become largely digital. The public telephone network is, by far, the largest communications network, so once it is fully digitised, every business and home user will have access to ISDN services. British Telecom's ISDN began with a pilot scheme in 1985, which was extended in 1986 and has continued to develop since. The network provides three types of access:

❑ *single-line* IDA (integrated digital access). The user gains access with *Network Terminating Equipment* (NTE);

❑ *line adapter module* (LAMs). A LAM allows two terminals to simultaneously share the same, two-wire, connection; this could provide a cheap method of communicating with a remote computer system;

❑ *multi-line* IDA, which provides 30 independent channels, each being capable of transmitting voice or data.

ADSL (Asynchronous Digital Subscriber Line)

ADSL is a relatively new service, similar to ISDN, which operates over standard telephone lines and provides Internet access at around 10 times the speed of a conventional modem. As with ISDN, simultaneous voice communication is also provided. Transmissions are separated at the telephone exchange to channel the voice calls through the standard public switched telephone network and the computer transmissions through fibre optic connection to the user's Internet Service Provider.

Multiplexed network services

Kilostream

An alternative to packet switching is to use *multiplexing*. The Kilostream service uses this technique for data transmission. The service provides a high speed direct link between two points. Data can pass in both directions at the same time; this is known as *full duplex* mode. The main link can transmit data at a rate of 2048 megabits per second (Mbits/s); this allows a number of low speed terminals to be connected to the high speed link through separate low speed links, each transmitting at either 128 kilobits per second (Kb/s) or 64 Kb/s. The signals from each terminal can then be merged for transmission along the high speed link, using a technique known as *time division multiplexing* (TDM).

The process of multiplexing is carried out by a *terminal multiplexer*. At the receiving end of the link, the signals are separated out for transmission along low speed lines connected to their respective terminals. The terminal multiplexer at each end of the link can carry out the functions of multiplexing (combining signals) and demultiplexing (separating the signals). This is obviously necessary for full duplex operation.

Multiplexers fall into two broad categories according to the methods used to combine signals and separate them:

❑ *Time Division Multiplexing (TDM)*, as the term suggests, provides a *time slice* on the higher-speed line for each terminal. The multiplexer has a number of registers, one per low-speed channel. Each register can store one character. The multiplexer scans each register in sequence, emptying the contents into a continuous stream of data to be transmitted. A multiplexer will send a null character whenever it finds an empty slot. TDM is used for digital networks. Figure 29.22 illustrates the time division multiplexing of signals from three terminals to a remote mainframe computer.

❑ *Frequency Division Multiplexing (FDM)* differentiates between the data signals sent from different devices by using a different *frequency range* for each. This can be likened to tuning a radio or television to receive particular programmes. So that any given radio programme does not interfere with the transmissions of another (although, they sometimes do), it is assigned a frequency that is not too close to the other assigned frequencies. In the same way, when a data transmission channel is multiplexed to accommodate signals from separate devices, some space must be left between the frequency ranges to avoid confusion of signals. Spaces between the different frequency ranges are know as *guard bands*. FDM relates to analogue signalling.

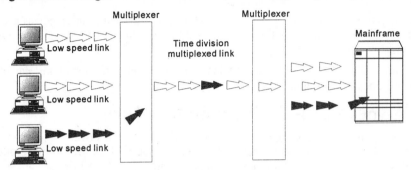

Figure 29.22. *Multiplexed link*

Megastream

This service is similar to Kilostream, except that no terminal multiplexing equipment is provided. Data can be transmitted at 2.048, 8, 34 or 140 Mbits/s. A user can choose to use the high speed circuit directly or multiplex the circuit, such that a number of low speed channels are made available across the link. Each separate lower speed channel can then be used to carry data or some may be left for the transmission of digitised speech.

Satstream

This digital data service provides customers with a small dish aerial to allow radio transmission of data, through a communications satellite. Customers are thus able to connect with networks in Western Europe.

ATM (Asynchronous Transfer Mode) and virtual networking

ATM evolved partially from the X.25 protocol and offers high bandwidth, packet switching and multiplexing support. ATM's bandwidth can handle data, video and voice transmissions through a single communication link. Its support for TCP/IP and other protocols allows ATM to handle a variety of traffic and services across network backbones, WANs (including the Internet), LANS and desktop computer connections. ATM makes maximum use of the available bandwidth by using virtual networking. This means that different logical networks can be created over the same physical network. For example, if the departments of an organisation are located in different parts of the country and are not connected to the same network segment, they can still be given access to the same set of network resources through a virtual network. Virtual network management software is needed to allow the administrator to view the physical network topology and create the logical views required by the organisation. Graphical user interface (GUI) software allows the administrator to use drag and drop functions to move network nodes and create the desired logical structure.

Optical communications and WDM

The high bandwidth of optical fibre (see earlier) makes it suitable for multiplexing. WDM (Wavelength Division Multiplexing) modulates signals to create several channels within the light spectrum and is the digital equivalent of FDM (frequency division multiplexing) used with analogue transmissions on coaxial cable. Even greater bandwidth can be obtained with D(Dense)WDM. It is protocol independent and can carry, for example, IP (Internet Protocol), ATM (Asynchronous Transfer Mode) and Ethernet traffic at rates between 100 megabits/sec and 2.5 gigabits/sec.

Connecting to a remote mainframe

In organisations with mainframe computers, it is often desirable for staff with microcomputers on their desks to be able to communicate with the mainframe via those systems. With non-IBM systems, where the host computer uses asynchronous transmission, the connection can be made via the RS232C (this refers to a standard used in most serial communications) serial transmission port, located at the back of the microcomputers system casing. However, the most common mainframe systems, IBM and ICL in particular, use synchronous communications, so special terminal emulation cards are required.

Thus, microcomputer workstations can be converted to mainframe terminals using a technique called emulation. A terminal emulation card is fitted into one of the expansion slots in the microcomputers system casing. If there are a number of terminals to be connected, the microcomputer is then connected, via a coaxial cable, to a terminal cluster controller. The controller is linked to a front-end processor (usually a minicomputer, dedicated to handling incoming and outgoing communications for the mainframe), which is itself connected to the mainframe computer. In this way, a microcomputer can, for example, be converted into an emulation of an IBM 3270 terminal.

The advantage of using a microcomputer as a mainframe terminal is that it can also be used on a stand-alone basis for local processing tasks, such as word processing or spreadsheet work. The terminal emulation package ensures that the mainframe responds in the same way as it would to a dedicated terminal. Security mechanisms, such as passwords, prevent users of emulated terminals from carrying out processes which are forbidden to users of dedicated terminals. However, the microcomputer's facility for local storage and processing can present serious security problems for the mainframes data and various mechanisms have to be included to prevent unauthorised updates. Where emulated terminals are to be linked to a mainframe via a wide area network, adapter cards are available which combine the terminal emulation with the gateway software, to access the intervening network.

Wireless networks

Television and radio broadcasting

When a television studio broadcasts a programme, the signals are carried to television receivers through a network of transmitters; radio programmes are broadcast from a studio in a similar fashion. An out-of-date term for a radio is a wireless; thus the transmissions in these broadcast networks are all carried out without the use of wires, that is, as *radio waves*. Radio waves vary in *frequency* and different frequency bands are used for different kinds of broadcasting. It is beyond the scope of this text to go into detail concerning these frequency bands, but the abbreviations VHF (very high frequency) and UHF (ultra-high frequency) should be familiar. The term *broadcast* is used because the radio wave signals can be received by any number of receivers within the broadcast area. The geographical area which can be reached by a broadcasting station depends on which method is used, namely:

❑ *cable* connections; this is an exception here as it clearly involves the use of wire or cable;

❑ *terrestrial* transmitters;

❑ *communications satellites*.

A broadcasting company may use a combination of cable, terrestrial and satellite transmitters to distribute its programmes. For example, the American company WTBS, in Atlanta, Georgia uses satellite to transmit low-cost sports and entertainment programmes to cable systems across the USA. Cable broadcasting, as the term indicates, uses physical cabling and is only economic over a limited area, such as a large city. However, in combination with satellite broadcasting, cable television plays an important role. Although terrestrial transmitters allow a much larger broadcast area than cable, satellites are essential to modern television broadcasting. Within the UK, pictures and monophonic sound are transmitted as analogue signals. The BBC has developed and transmits, NICAM stereo sound and digital aerial services, using digital encoding techniques.

Television broadcasting allows the transmission of *moving pictures*, *sound* and *data* to television receivers within the area served by a broadcasting station. Database services provided by television are *one-way* only, to television receivers and are collectively known as *Teletext* (see Network services). The BBC teletext service is known as Ceefax. To access these services a television receiver must have a Teletext *decoder*.

Microwave transmissions and communications satellites

Microwaves are super-high frequency (SHF) radio waves and can be used where transmitter and receiver are not in sight of one another. The communication path must be relatively obstruction-free. Microwaves can also be transmitted, through earth transmitters, to communications satellites; microwaves can penetrate cloud. Earth stations must be no more than 25-30 miles apart, because humidity in the atmosphere interferes with microwave signals. Each station in a communication path acts as a *repeater* station. Obviously, it is impractical to build sufficient repeater stations to deal with all transmissions, so communications satellites are essential. Once a satellite has received a signal, it amplifies it and sends it back to earth. Satellite communications are now fairly common and provide a cheaper and better trans-ocean transmission medium than undersea cable. Apart from television broadcasting, satellites form an essential part of the international telephone network. Voice and data messages are digitally transmitted as packets (see Packet Switching). There are three basic types of satellite:

❑ GEO (geosynchronous earth orbit). A GEO satellite remains fixed above a given point on the earth's surface. This means that a terrestrial station, once set to point at the satellite, does not require further adjustment. It is the most expensive to build and launch, but its powerful transmitters mean that few are needed to maintain global coverage. It also has an orbital life in excess of 12 years. A weakness of GEO satellite communication is *latency*, or propagation delay. A transmission passed via a GEO satellite from one terrestrial station to another takes more than two tenths of a second, which may make it unsuitable for use in high speed networks, but suitable for television broadcasting, mobile communications and global positioning services (GPS).

❑ MEO (medium earth orbit). A MEO satellite moves relative to a point on the earth's surface. This means that ground-based stations must have tracking equipment to maintain contact with a MEO. Global coverage requires the use of more MEOs than is the case for GEOs, but they are cheaper to build and launch and the transmission delay is insignificant. Its orbital life is between 6 and 12 years.

❑ LEO (low earth orbit). A LEO satellite moves quickly relative to a point on the earth's surface and many are needed to provide global coverage. LEOs are the cheapest to build and launch, provide the greatest bandwidth and suffer from virtually no transmission delay. However, a LEO satellite may have a lifespan of only 5 years.

Applications of satellite communication

Undersea cabling used to be the only way of connecting telephone networks on different continents but satellite communication provides a much cheaper alternative. Satellites also make it feasible and cost effective to extend networks to geographically remote and poorer countries which do not have established telecommunications systems. Satellite communications have been used in television broadcasting for over thirty years by traditional aerial delivery networks and cable networks. The bandwidth available through satellite communications allows the transmission of hundreds of television channels. Today, Direct Broadcast Satellite (DBS) allows television networks to transmit direct to individual users. A DBS satellite is geosynchronous and can transmit up to 150 channels, using digital signals to provide high quality reception to consumers.

Satellite communications allow ship to shore communications, linking a ship to a land-based receiver/transmitter anywhere in the world; aircraft use a similar service. A satellite phone can be used, even in the most remote parts of the world for voice and data communications; Inmarsat, for example, provides for ISDN communication. Global positioning services (GPS) can be used by ships, aircraft and land vehicles to determine their precise geographical position. Multiple geosynchronous satellites triangulate their signals to produce geographical coordinates.

Weather forecasting involves reporting, predicting, and studying the weather, including temperature, moisture, barometric pressure, and wind speed and direction. Satellites are vital for the rapid collection and transmission of meteorological data from the many terrestrial and atmospheric sources which contribute to more accurate weather forecasting.

Cellular telephone networks

These networks use *cellular radio* communications, which operate in the UHF (ultra-high frequency) band. Local *base stations* allow cellphone (hand-held or vehicle-based) users to access the pstn. Each base station covers a *cell site*, an area within which it can pick up cellphone signals. Within the UHF band, signals can penetrate buildings and other barriers, but a user must be within a few miles of a transmitter, particularly in urban areas, where the largest numbers of users tend to be found. Thus, a base station in a rural area, serving fewer users, can cover a larger cell site than is possible in an urban area. Computers are used to allow links to be maintained even while the caller is moving from one transmission area to another. Thus, when a base station receives a signal from a cellphone, it monitors the strength of the signal continuously to determine if it is still the most suitable base station to handle the transmission. Obviously, if the user is driving while making a call, a different base station may be handling the call at different points on the journey. The only effect of these changes is a brief (about one-fifth of a second) interruption to the call as the switch is made to a different base station. Major cellular radio operators in the UK are Orange, Cellnet and Vodaphone.

New generation mobile phones

Apart from voice transmission, mobile phones can be used to transmit text messages and those that support Internet Protocol (IP) or the newer WAP (Wireless Application Protocol - see later) can be used to access Internet services, albeit very slowly. The delivery of Internet services through mobile networks is hampered by the mobile phone itself, with its slow processor, poor battery life, mono display and awkward keypad, as well as by limited bandwidth.

The development of broadband mobile networks and more sophisticated phones is vital if the full potential of the Internet's multimedia content is to be made as accessible through a mobile phone as it is through a PC. In the meantime, services are largely text-based and perfectly adequate for the viewing of such information as travel, weather, sport results, share prices and the delivery of bank, ticket and message services.

New generation mobile phones are making use of larger flip-up screens with touch-sensitive input and handwriting recognition as additions to the usual keypad.

WAP and WML (Wireless Markup Language)

Although mobile phones have been able to access Web pages coded in HTML for some time, a WAP-enabled mobile can use its WAP browser to access pages coded in WML, a language specially designed to take account of the limitations of mobile networks and phones. Access to the Internet must be provided through a *gateway* which supports the WAP protocol. All the major cellular networks provide WAP gateways to allow their users to access Internet data services and as the market expands it is likely that conventional Internet Service Providers (ISPs) will provide a similar service. Once cellular networks are able to provide the bandwidth (see UMTS later) presently available to PC users, full Java-enabled HTML content will be easily accessible to mobile phone users and the need for WAP and WML is likely to be reduced.

Use of satellites in cellular networks

In common with other communication networks, digital signalling has largely replaced analogue signalling. Each cell in a network provides a number of communication channels. In the case of analogue signalling each channel occupies a separate frequency band (frequency division multiplexing or FDM). Digital networks divide the cells into channels by time slot (time division multiplexing). When a network is busy, all the channels in a particular cell may be occupied, preventing other callers from using that cell. Satellites which are operating within a different bandwidth to the cell are able, when they have free bandwidth, to provide extra channel space for overloaded terrestrial cells. Digital cellular networks provide better performance (analogue networks can be subject to cross call interference) and more channels.

GSM and UMTS

GSM (Global System for Mobile communications) is the European standard for digital mobile communications and is the most widely used digital standard in the world today. Mobile phones which use the GSM standard are equipped with a SIM (Subscriber Information Card) which is a *smart* card for storing the phone number, personal security key and other information necessary for handset operation. The SIM provides levels of security which were not possible with first generation, analogue handsets, as well as the facility to make calls from any country which supports the GSM standard. The SIM can also be used to store personal phone numbers, signal missed calls, notify receipt of voice mail, text messages and so on. GSM also allows notebook and palmtop computers to be communicate with GSM handsets.

Users of analogue phones are vulnerable to eavesdropping, but GSM networks use encryption algorithms to scramble the digitised voice signals before transmission between the handset and the GSM transmitter site. The information stored in the SIM card enables the voice signals to be decrypted so that the user hears what the connected caller actually says.

Like the ISDN (see earlier) standard, GSM allows information to be transmitted in different forms through a single network. Thus, GSM provides integrated voice, data, fax and text message services, as well as services such as call forwarding, speed dialling (popular numbers can each be assigned to a single key press) and the selected blocking or receipt of calls, for example, based on location or time. GSM is regarded as second generation wireless technology.

UMTS (Universal Mobile Telecommunications System) is the planned third generation standard for mobile communications, with increased bandwidth (up to 2 Mbps). As a *broadband* network, UMTS is designed to carry multimedia (voice, data, pictures and video) information, a facility which is not feasible with the bandwidth of current GSM standards. Although a WAP phone can be used to access the Internet for e-mail, only WAP sites can be visited and these are largely text-based.

UMTS will be supported by all fixed, wireless and satellite networks, making it possible for the mobile phone to be used as the primary user device for communicating with computer-based systems of all kinds. A competing standard being developed in the USA and with similar aims, is called 'BlueTooth'.

Inter-networking components

The term inter-networking is used to describe the formation of integrated systems, through the connection of separate networks, locally and remotely. This enables organisations to construct organisation-wide information and communications systems, even if sections of it are a few or thousands of miles apart. This section looks at the devices used to make connections between local area networks (LANs) and between LANs and wide area networks. In general, these devices deal with the:

- ❏ connection of networks operating on different protocols;

- ❏ connection of LANs to LANs;

- ❏ connection of LANs to WANs;

- ❏ connection of networks of different architecture, cabling and protocol;

- ❏ routing of packets (see packet switching earlier) along the most efficient path;

- ❏ conversion between different packet formats, protocols and transmission speeds.

Computer networking is a relatively new industry and terminology is not entirely standardised. For this reason, definitions of terms, such as bridge, router and gateway can vary from one manufacturer's specification to another. Some devices, for example, combine the features of bridges and routers and are referred to as bridge/routers. Bearing this in mind, the following definitions are generally accepted.

Repeaters

Repeaters allow the effective length of a LAN cable to be increased. For example, the maximum length of an Ethernet segment is restricted because of signal loss and distortion which occurs as a data packet travels along the cable.

A repeater re-strengthens, that is, *re-amplifies* the signal and resets its timing, so that the effective length of the segment can be increased (see Figure 29.23).

It is also used to enable a signal to travel to another segment of a network. A repeater can normally connect any kind of cable medium:

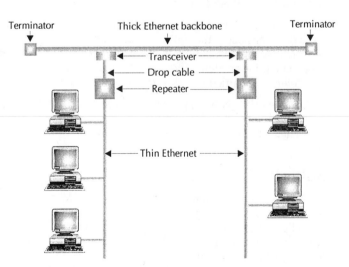

Figure 29.23. *Repeaters connecting segments*

thick or thin Ethernet, twisted pair or optical fibre. In relation to the Open Systems Inter-connection (OSI) model, referred to at the end of this chapter, a repeater works at the Physical level and only needs to know how to interact with the physical transmission medium.

Bridge

A bridge is used to connect two LANs of the same type, that is, two IBM token ring or two Ethernet LANs. This is known as *local inter-networking*. Packets crossing such a link are *forwarded* by the bridge device. Some bridges are *protocol transparent* and the otherwise similar networks can be using different protocols, for example, IPX (Novell) or IP (Internet Protocol). They can also be used to divide large networks into smaller segments. Segmenting large networks can improve administrative control and the performance of the separate segments. In the latter case, the bridge can be configured such that only data which needs to cross the bridge actually does. For example, if there are two segments, one for the Sales department and the other for Accounts, the data traffic for each function will be isolated within the respective segments, except when data needs to travel between the two. This improves the performance of each segment and thus the effectiveness of the whole network. A bridge operates at the Data Link Layer in the OSI model.

Hubs and switches

A hub has multiple ports to allow devices (or other network segments) to share a common connection point to the LAN cable. Some hubs are passive and simply pass packets between the devices and the network cable, but others provide device status information which allows, for example, a technician to identify a faulty device and disconnect it without affecting the operation of the remainder of the network. A hub contains devices called *switches* which forward packets from one segment to another.

Gateway or router

A gateway, or router, is used to connect two LANs of different (they do not have to be) type ; thus, for example, an Ethernet LAN can be connected to a Token Ring LAN, or the connection may be Ethernet to Ethernet. The LANs may be remotely connected through, for example, a packet switching WAN, with a gateway at each LAN's entry point to the WAN.

The term *router* is used to signify that the device is more intelligent than a bridge, in that it makes decisions about the route a data packet (by reference to its destination address) should follow to reach its destination; in this way, packets can be made to take the most efficient path. It may determine an alternative route for a packet, in the event of, for example, congestion or breakdown on a particular link. Networks may have different architectures and protocols.

A LAN using IPX (Novell) protocol can use a gateway to allow users access to, for example, a remote IBM network, which uses SNA protocol, through the Kilostream packet (X.25 protocol) switching network. In the OSI model (see later), a router operates at the Network Layer level.

Multiplexer

A multiplexer allows a number of low-speed devices to share a high-speed line, as illustrated in Figure 29.24. The messages from several low-speed lines are combined into one high-speed channel and then separated out at the other end by a demultiplexer. In two-way transmissions, both these functions are carried out in one unit at each end of the higher speed channel. Multiplexers send data from multiple sources along a single, high speed, communications link by dividing it into different channels, allocated as time slots. A brief time slot it given to each of a succession of terminals in which to send a block of data. The transmission rate of each terminal is relatively slow and limited by the speed of its human operator, so the high speed link can easily accommodate the transmissions of many terminals. The multiplexed link's capacity is known as its *bandwidth* (the rate at which data can be sent, measured in bits per second). The process of dividing this bandwidth into many channels is known as *time division multiplexing* (TDM - see earlier).

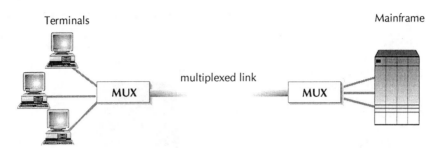

Figure 29.24. *Multiplexers to allow several terminals to use a single link*

Concentrator

A concentrator is a type of multiplexer which greatly increases data throughput by increasing the number of low-speed channels and instead of transmitting a null character, empties the contents of the next full register. The data from each low-speed device is identified by extra identification bits and this constitutes an overhead.

Front-end-processors (FEP)

A front-end-processor is the most sophisticated type of device for communications control and is usually a minicomputer held at the site of a mainframe host computer. Its main task is to handle all the communications traffic, leaving the mainframe free to concentrate on other processing tasks. Its main tasks include:

❑ parity checking;

❑ stripping of overhead characters (e.g. start and stop bits) from serial transmission;

❑ conversion from serial to parallel transmission and vice versa;

❑ network control;

❑ network accounting;

❑ character conversion.

Communications software

Various programs are available to provide users with different ways of communicating with remote computer systems. The following examples are used to illustrate typical communication services on the Internet:

❑ Internet Explorer, a Web browser;

❑ Hyperterminal, for logging in to Telnet BBS (Bulletin Board Services);

❑ Cute FTP (File Transfer Protocol) for transferring files to or from an FTP server;

❑ Microsoft Outlook for e-mail and newsgroups.

Hyperterminal

This Windows program allows connection to any remote computer, to which the user has authorised access. The program includes a dialler so connection can be made directly to another computer, but more usually the connection is indirect via an Internet Service Provider (ISP). Hyperterminal can be used as a Telnet client and thereby access Telnet BBS (Bulletin Board Services). A BBS site may offer a variety of services, including for example, various files for downloading, e-mail facilities, a discussion forum, or simply an information service. *Telnet* is designed to allow remote terminals to operate in the same way as those which are locally attached and has been in use since before the introduction of the World Wide Web. One such Telnet site is illustrated in Figure 29.25.

Notice that the status bar at the bottom of the screen identifies the terminal type as VT100, which provides basic text facilities.

The Hyperterminal package terminal settings were set to AutoDetect before the connection was made and the Telnet site changed that setting to VT100. Other terminal types are shown in the Settings tab in Figure 29.26. Some operating systems, including VAX and Unix, provide a built-in Telnet *client* and do not require the use of an additional package.

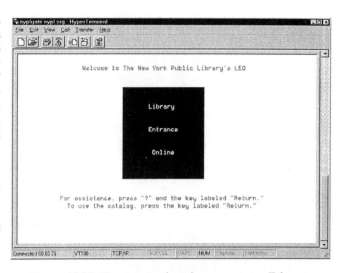

Figure 29.25. *Hyperterminal used to connect to a Telnet site*

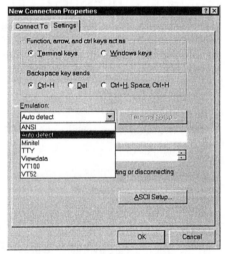

Figure 29.26. *Terminal types available with Hyperterminal*

Many users access Telnet services via a Web browser which automatically *calls* the Telnet client into action, as illustrated in Figure 29.27. The New York Library web site in the Figure has a hyperlink "Leo via Telnet" which launches the Telnet client as shown. Many Telnet sites allow visitors to sign in as "guest".

Hyperterminal can also be used for sending or receiving text and binary files. Apart from plain text files without any formatting all other file types must be

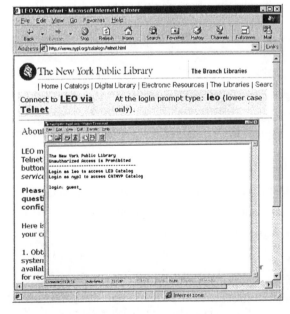

Figure 29.27. *Telnet session from a Web site link*

transferred in binary format, using one of the protocols available in Hyperterminal. Figure 29.28 shows the drop-down list of protocols for sending binary files.

Normally, the communications software on the receiving computer needs to be set to receive the file using an agreed protocol.

With the facility to transfer almost any type of file as an e-mail attachment, the use of Hyperterminal for these purposes is extremely limited. In addition, a much more widely used protocol, File Transfer Protocol or FTP is the standard for most remote file transfers.

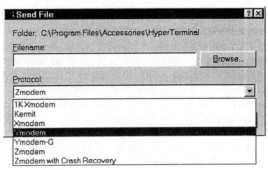

Figure 29.28. *Protocols for sending binary files*

All Internet ISPs support the protocol and for Web site maintenance, an FTP package is an essential piece of software. To make a Web site available to the world, its pages must be uploaded to an Internet server and for maintenance pages will need to be downloaded, modified and uploaded again. An FTP package such as CuteFTP is designed to communicate with the FTP server which hosts Web sites. Figure 29.29 shows an FTP package being used to upload pages to a Web site. The left panel shows the directory structure of the local machine and the right panel shows the relevant part of the directory structure on the Web server. The bottom panel shows the pages queued for uploading.

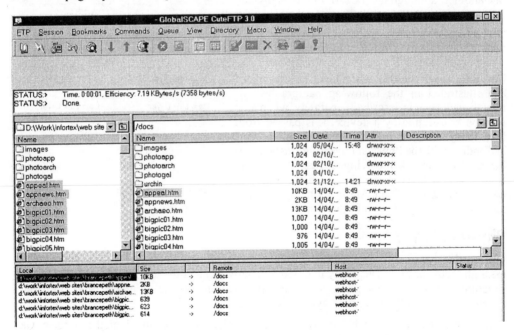

Figure 29.29. *FTP software uploading Web pages tp the Web server*

The OSI (open systems interconnection) model

Many computer devices are now designed for use in networked systems. Manufacturers are now tending to conform to standard protocols that make their equipment compatible with a variety of user networks. *Closed* networks, that are restricted to one manufacturer's equipment and standards, are not attractive to the user, because it restricts the choice of equipment which can be used. The aim of standardisation is to achieve more open systems which allow users to select from a wider range of manufacturers' products. A Reference Model for Open Systems Interconnection (OSI) has been under development by the International Standards Organisation (ISO) since 1977. Other standards, including SNA (IBM's System Network Architecture) and Ethernet, are largely incompatible with one another. Certain standards in the OSI model have been set by manufacturers as their commercial products have gained in popularity. The TCP/IP model, which is the dominant one for Internet communications and precedes the OSI model are largely compatible with one another, although the TCP/IP model is divided into fewer layers. Figure 29.30 shows the hierarchy of layers which make up the OSI model and the equivalent layers which make up the important TCP/IP model used in TCP/IP Networks.

The functions of the OSI model layers are described and illustrated in the following paragraphs. Although each layer is described separately, when data is to be transmitted by a device, it is passed from layer to layer, beginning with the Application Layer and ending with the Physical Layer, within the sending device itself. A receiving device passes data from layer to layer, beginning with the Physical Layer and ending with the Application Layer. These sequences are illustrated in Figure 29.31.

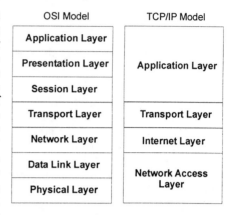

Figure 29.30. *OSI and TCP/IP models*

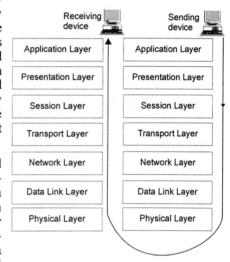

Figure 29.31. *Data passes through protocol layers*

Physical Layer

The Physical Layer encompasses the hardware used to connect a network device to the network medium (cable or radio frequency in a wireless network) and the transmission of the raw, unstructured binary signals through the communication channel. Figure 29.32 illustrates components within the Physical Layer which, in summary, relates to:

❏ The unstructured, raw bit stream passing through the network medium, that is, the cable (or radio frequency in a wireless network) and the signalling methods (voltage levels etc.) used to transmit it.

❏ The transmission medium itself (the cable or radio frequency).

❏ Non-intelligent devices, such as repeaters or passive hubs, used to connect separate segments of network cable.

☐ Communication mode on the line, whether half duplex or duplex.

☐ The function and position of pins within connectors which attach a network device to the network medium. Network interface cards (NIC) standards are set within the Physical Layer.

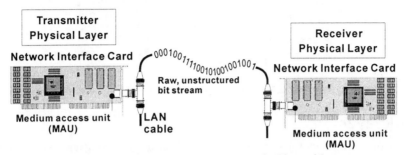

Figure 29.32. *Hardware components at the Physical Layer*

The Ethernet cabling standard, IEEE 802.3 Type 10Base5 (transmission rate of 10 Mbps) falls within the Physical Layer.

Data Link Layer

The Data Link Layer accepts the unstructured bit stream from the Physical layer and packages it into *frames*. Figure 29.33 illustrates the structure of an Ethernet IEEE 802.3 frame.

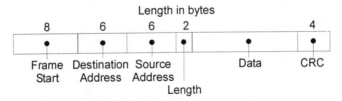

Figure 29.33. *Structure of an Ethernet frame*

This layer is responsible for ensuring that frames are error free when they pass between devices on the network. After sending a frame, the Data Link Layer of the transmitting device waits for an acknowledgement from the Data Link Layer in the destination device. The CRC (Cyclic Redundancy Check) field holds a value calculated by the sending device and errors can be detected by the receiving device using the same calculation. If the CRC values don't match, the frame is retransmitted. The techniques used for the receipt and acknowledgement of data by a receiver device, are determined by the Data Link Layer.

In Ethernet networks, the Destination Address is also known as the MAC (Media Access Control) Address and is unique to a particular network device. For example, to be used as a network device, a PC must have an installed Network Interface Card (NIC) or network adapter which has a unique MAC address. If written down, a 64 bit MAC address is written as 6 hexadecimal numbers, separated by colons, for example, 12:9B:02:C4:89:13. Where multiple networks are connected to a single host computer, it is identified by the same MAC address for all. The processes within the Data Link Layer are illustrated in Figure 29.34. A bridge is an example of a Data Link Layer device, used to handle traffic between two similar or dissimilar LANs.

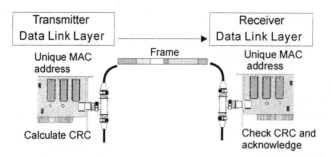

Figure 29.34. *Processes handled at Data Link Layer*

Network layer

The function of the Network Layer is to perform the logical addressing and routing of information to destination devices around the network and also from one network to another.

Physical addresses are used in LANs to transmit data to intended destination devices, but this requires that each device on the network 'listens' to all messages passing through the network. Clearly, this is not possible for devices attached to the Internet and other wide area networks, so a system of logical addressing (IP addressing) is used instead. Thus, the physical address of a device on the Internet needs to be converted to a logical IP address which may include three levels: network ID; subnet ID; and host ID; the host ID is the part assigned to the individual computer attached to the network..

Figure 29.35 illustrates some of the processes which fall within the Network Layer. Concerning the IP protocol, it should be mentioned that, as part of the TCP/IP protocol *stack*, it falls within the Internet Layer of the TCP/IP model, which is equivalent to the Network Layer in the OSI model. Apart from the IP protocol, examples of other Network Layer protocols include IPX (Novell networks), NetBEUI (extended NetBIOS protocol) and ICMP (Internet Control Message Protocol).

Devices operating at the Network Layer include routers, brouters (bridge/routers) and switches. Examples of protocols concerned with routing include RIP (Routing Internet Protocol) and IGMP (Internet Group Management Protocol).

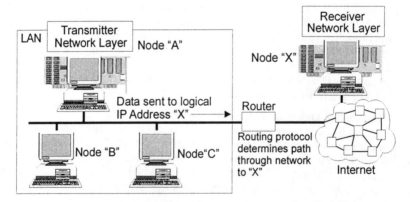

Figure 29.35. *Processes within the Network Layer*

Transport Layer

When necessary, the Transport Layer divides longer messages into smaller packets before transmission, reassembles them at the receiving end into complete messages and ensures that packets are received in sequence and free of errors. Also, the Transport Layer at the destination device sends acknowledgement of message receipt. Figure 29.36 illustrates the main operations carried out within the Transport Layer.

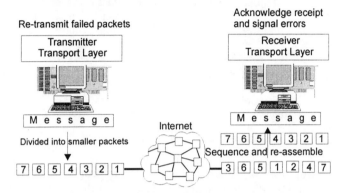

Figure 29.36. *Packet division and re-assembly*

The Transport Layer is relevant to the inter-network, or wide area network which separates communicating devices. The protocols at this level are either *connection-orientated*, that is, they ensure delivery and acknowledgement of all transmissions, or *connectionless*. Figure 29.37 illustrates the principles behind connection-orientated protocols.

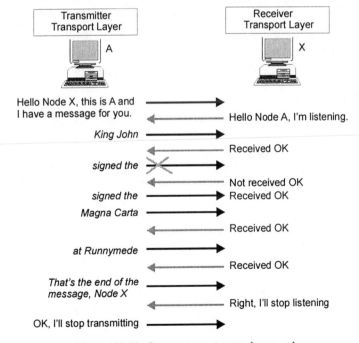

Figure 29.37. *Connection-orientated protocol*

Note that as the packets are routed through the intervening network, they may not arrive in the exact sequence as shown in the figure. Figure 29.38 shows the operation of connectionless protocols, the significant feature being the reduced certainty that the message will be received intact. To counter this weakness, connectionless protocols rely on the application to control transmission errors.

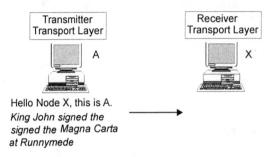

Figure 29.38. *Connectionless protocol*

TCP (Transport Control Protocol) is part of the TCP/IP protocol stack used for Internet communications and is therefore the most important example of the connection-orientated type. UDP (User Datagram Protocol) is an example of a connectionless protocol, which is faster than TCP but not as reliable.

Session Layer

Allows two applications to establish, use and disconnect a connection between them called a *session*. The Session Layer also provides:

- [ ] name recognition to ensure that only the designated parties can take part in the session;
- [ ] checkpoints in the data stream to cater for breakdown in the link and re-transmission since the last checkpoint.

Examples of sessions are file transfer and interactive login to a remote host.

Presentation layer

This layer covers standards on how data is presented to the end-user devices. The aim is to ensure that different devices, which may be using data in different formats, can communicate with one another. In other words, data is translated into a *platform independent* format. The Presentation Layer can, for example, handle conversions between ASCII and EBCDIC character codes. It may also carry out encryption to ensure data security during transmission over vulnerable telecommunication links and data compression to improve the efficiency use of bandwidth.

The presentation layer also attempts to deal with conversions between terminals which use different line and screen lengths and different character sets.

Application layer

This is the highest layer in that it is closest to the user. It supports the transfer of information between end-users, applications programs and devices. Several types of protocol exist in this layer, including those for specific applications, such as e-mail and those for more generalised applications, such as accounting, directory services, network management, entry control and user identification. The applications layer hides the physical network from the user, presenting a user-orientated view instead. For example, the user need not know that several physical computers are involved when accessing a database. Example protocols within the Application Layer include MIME (Multi-purpose Internet Mail Extensions), SMTP (Simple Message Transfer Protocol), FTP (File Transfer Protocol) and DNS (Domain Name Service). Figure 29.39 illustrates the use of e-mail protocols within the Application Layer.

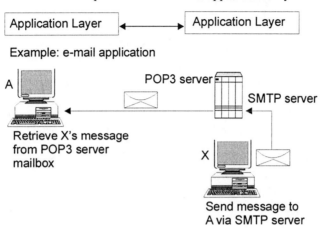

Figure 29.39. *Use of e-mail protocols within Application Layer*

The purpose of layering

Layering allows the separation of system components into the physical and a range of logical levels and makes them independent of one another. This separation facilitates the development and production of platform (different hardware and operating systems) components which can communicate with one another. For example, by using a common language to write network card drivers, the same network card can then handle different network protocols, say IPX (Novell) and TCP/IP (Internet Protocol).

✍ Exercises

1. Give two examples of information which are commonly transmitted in digital form, but are presented to users in analogue form.
2. (a) Distinguish between the amplitude and frequency of a sine wave signal and sketch a diagram showing how each could be used to represent binary data.
   (b) Briefly explain the concept of frequency bandwidth and the role of the modem in the transmission of computer data over analogue sections of the PSTN.
3. Why is a duplex connection the favoured option for most data communications applications?
4. Suggest organisations and applications which would be likely to use:
   (i) leased lines
   (ii) dial-up connections.
   to access external networks. Justify your choice in each case, indicating how the link would be used.
5. Distinguish between asynchronous and synchronous serial transmission and suggest circumstances when each may be appropriate.
6. Why does data compression require a distinction to be made between baud rate and the rate of data throughput?

7. What main characteristic distinguishes the V.90 modem standard from its predecessors?

8. With the use of a simple sketch, illustrate the technique of pulse code modulation (PCM).

9. Briefly explain the concepts of *handshaking* and *flow control* and state why they are a necessary part of data communications.

10. Identify two methods of error checking.

11. Identify three types of cabling used in data communications.

12. Briefly explain the principles of packet switching.

13. Distinguish between packet and message switching.

14. What is meant by time division multiplexing (TDM)?

15. What major advantage will the new UMTS standard for mobile communications provide over the existing GSM standard?

16. Briefly identify the role of the following internetworking components: *repeater, bridge, router, hub, front-end processor.*

17. State the primary purpose of each of the following communications software products: *HyperTerminal; Cute FTP; Microsoft Outlook.*

18. (a)   What is the main pupose of the OSI model?

    (b)   List the 7 layers it contains.

Chapter 30

Computer networks

Networking computer systems has the effect of decentralising computer processing and improving communications within and between organisations and between organisations and individuals. Some computer networks use dedicated intelligent terminals or microcomputer systems to permit some independent processing power at sites remote from the *host* computer, to which they are connected. Other networks distribute even more processing power by linking microcomputer, minicomputer, mainframe and supercomputer systems. They are sometimes referred to as *distributed processing* systems. Networks can be configured to suit almost any application, from the provision of a world-wide airline reservation system to home banking. *Nodes* (connection points in the network) may only be a few feet apart and limited to a single building, or they may be several thousand miles apart.

Local and wide area networks

Computer networks can be classified according to their geographical spread. A network confined to, say, one building, with microcomputer workstations distributed in different rooms, is known as a *local area network* (LAN). One particular type, known as a ring network can extend over a diameter of around five miles. A computer network distributed nationally or even internationally makes use of telephone and sometimes, satellite links, and is referred to as a *wide area network* (WAN). In large organisations with several branches, it is common practice to maintain a LAN at each branch for local processing requirements and to link each LAN into a WAN covering the whole organisation. In this way, branches of an organisation can have control over their own processing and yet have access to the organisation's main database at headquarters. In addition, inter-branch communication is possible.

Network architecture

The architecture of any network includes definition of: its *components*, both hardware and software, identified by *name* and *function*; the ways the components are connected and communicate with one another. The architecture of wide area networks (WANs) is described in Chapter 29 and the following primarily relates to local area networks (LANs). However, the section on Network Topologies does relate, in part, to WANs.

LAN architecture

It is important that the components are combined in such a way that the LAN can be: *extended*. The LAN must be capable of providing for new users and new equipment, as the need arises; *upgraded* to take advantage of new technologies which can improve network performance; *connected* to other LANs, both local and remote and Wide Area Networks.

LAN architecture comprises hardware and software, both for the control of the LAN communications and as an interface between the LAN and its users. In order that all components are compatible and operate as a coherent system, it is important that they conform to agreed standards (Chapter 29). This means that LAN producers have to take account of generally agreed standards for equipment linking and data communications, so that as new products come onto the market, the user is not left with a system which cannot take advantage of them.

Unfortunately, a number of different standards exist and this means that the decision on which type of LAN to purchase is not always straightforward.

Hardware components

Figure 30.1 shows a simple *client-server* LAN and identifies the main hardware components: *workstation*; *file server*; *printer server*; network *cabling*. The way in which they are connected defines its general *topology* or physical shape.

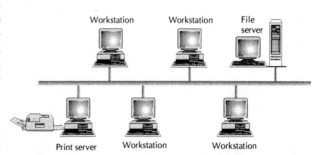

LAN Workstation

A *workstation* gives a user access to a LAN and its facilities. A workstation comprises a *microcomputer* with a *network card*, which fits into an *expansion slot* inside its system

Figure 30.1. *Main components of a local area network*

casing. The network card enables workstations to communicate across the network, and with the *file server* (see later). The card converts computer-generated data into a form suitable for transmission over the LAN and as such is an *interface*. The card is operated with a network card *driver*.

Servers

The general function of servers is to allocate shared resources to other nodes on the network. There are a number of different types of server, classed according to the resources they control.

File server

The file server is usually a specially configured microcomputer, with a network card, more memory and disk storage, as well as a more powerful processor than is needed for a workstation. It has to control access to shared storage, directories and files. In addition, it controls the exchange of files between network users. Most network software provides *multiple device* support. This means that file servers can support several disks, allowing file storage capacity on the LAN to be increased beyond that of the file server's integral hard disk. Except for the smallest of networks LANs are typically supported by multiple servers.

Print server

A print server (there may be several) accepts and queues jobs from workstations; the user may be informed when printing is complete. The print server may also provide certain print management functions, for example, to attach priorities to different print jobs so that certain jobs are printed before others, no matter what their positions in the queue. A print server will be configured to:

- ❑ support the use of particular printers;
- ❑ service particular printer *queues*; users with the right to use a particular print queue can then place their jobs in that queue.

Communications server

If a LAN is to have access to external networks or databases, a communications server is required. Generally, the communications server can establish a temporary link with remote computers or users on other networks (see Remote Inter-networking).

Network topologies

Computer networks can be categorised according to their physical shape or topology. Each terminal in a network is known as a *node*. If a central computer controls the network it is known as the *host* computer. The topology of a network is the *arrangement* of the nodes and the ways they are interconnected. The communication system within a network is known as the *subnet*. Data can be transmitted around the subnet either on a *point-to-point* basis or through a *broadcast* channel. If point-to-point transmission is used, the data passes through each device in the network. Thus, if two devices wish to communicate, they must do it indirectly, via any intervening devices. Each device must have the facility to store the entire message and forward it when the output channel is free. If a broadcast channel is used, a common communication channel is shared by all devices in the network. This means that any message sent by a device is received by all devices. The message contains the address of the device intended to receive it, so that the other devices can ignore it. There are a number of recognised network topologies and some of the most common are described below.

Star network

A star topology means that each node is connected, by separate connections to a computer at the centre, known as the *hub*. Figure 30.2 shows a LAN in a star topology. It is also a popular topology for a WAN. In this structure, all messages pass through the host (probably a mainframe or minicomputer) computer, which interconnects the different devices on the network. So, in this topology the host computer at the hub has a *message switching* function. Messages are transmitted point-to-point. The topology is particularly useful for intercommunications between pairs of users on the network (via the host). The network may consist of numerous computer systems (the nodes), connected to a larger host computer which switches data and programs between them.

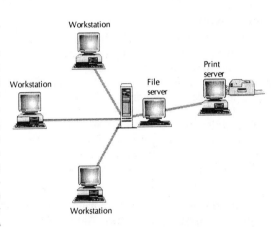

Figure 30.2. *Star topology*

The star computer network is by far the most popular for WANs, because most large organisations start with a central computer at the head office, from which branch computer facilities are provided through the telephone network. The main aim is to provide computer communication between the branches and head office. Most other network topologies aim to provide communication between all devices on a network. The star topology can also be used for a LAN.

The *advantages* of a star network topology are as follow:

☐ It is suitable for WANs where organisations rely on a central computer for the bulk of processing tasks, perhaps limiting the nodes to their local processing needs and the validation of data, prior to transmission to the central computer;

☐ Centralised control of message switching allows a high degree of security control;

☐ Each spoke in the star is independent of the rest and a fault in a link or device in one spoke, can be identified by the computer at the hub;

☐ The data transmission speeds used can vary from one *spoke* (a link from the hub to a node) to another. This is important if some spokes transmit using high speed devices, such as disk, whilst others transmit from low speed keyboard devices. The method of transmission may also vary. For example, one node may only require access to the network at the end of each day, in which case a *dial-up* connection may be sufficient. A dial-up connection uses the public telephone network and the user only pays for the time taken for transmission. Alternatively, other nodes may require the link for most of the working day, in which case a permanent *leased line* is appropriate. Leased lines provide a more reliable transmission medium and also allow higher speeds of data transmission.

The main *disadvantages* inherent in star networks are as follow:

❏ The network is vulnerable to hub failures which affect all users. As a distributed processing system, some processing is still possible at the nodes but inter-node communication is lost when the host computer fails;

❏ For a WAN, the control of communications in the network requires expensive technology at the hub, probably a mini or mainframe computer. Complex operating and communications software is needed to control the network.

Ring network

The ring topology is specifically designed for use with a LAN and is not suitable for a WAN. A ring network connects all the nodes in a ring, as illustrated in Figure 30.3. The *Cambridge Ring*, developed at Cambridge University, has no host computer and none of the nodes need have overall control of access to the network. In practice, a monitoring station is used for the control of data transmission in the network. Messages in a ring network flow in one direction, from node to node.

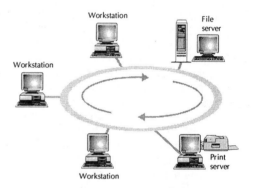

Figure 30.3. *Ring topology*

The ring consists of a series of repeaters, which are joined by the physical transmission medium (twisted pair, co-axial, or fibre-optic cable). The choice of medium depends on the distances to be covered and the desired transmission rates. Fibre-optic cable allows the greatest distances to be covered and the highest transmission rates. Repeaters are used to regenerate messages as they pass around the network. The use of repeaters allows a ring network to cover larger distances than is possible for other topologies. In fact, recent developments using fibre optic cable allow a ring with a range of about 100 kilometres, which makes it a *metropolitan area network* (MAN). The user devices are connected to the repeaters. A message from one node, addressed to another, is passed continually around the ring until the receiving node flags that it is ready to accept it. Acceptance of a message is determined by its *destination address*, which is examined by each node it passes. If the destination address matches the node's own address, the node takes the message; otherwise, the node repeater regenerates the signal to be passed to the next node in the ring. Data is transmitted in mini-packets of about 40 bits and contains the address of the sending node, the address of the destination node and some control bits. A variation on the Cambridge ring is the IBM ring, which uses a different protocol to allow better control of message flow on the network; the two protocols, *empty slot* and *token passing* are described in Network Access Protocols. The ring network presents advantages:

❏ There is no dependence on a central host computer as data transmission around the network is supported by all the devices in the ring. Each node device has sufficient intelligence to control the transmission of data from and to its own node;

❑ Very high transmission rates are possible; 10 megabits/sec is typical;

❑ Routing between devices is relatively simple because messages normally travel in one direction only around the ring;

❑ The transmission facility is shared equally amongst the users.

The main disadvantages are as follow:

❑ The system depends on the reliability of the whole ring and the repeaters, although it can be designed to bypass any failed node;

❑ It may be difficult to extend the length of the ring because the physical installation of any new cable must ensure that the ring topology is preserved.

Star/ring network - IBM token ring

The *IBM Token Ring* Network is a star-based topology, with a hub or *multiple access unit* (MAU) to which all the workstations are connected. The movement of data is, however in a *logical ring*. All signals between workstations are through the MAU. The star/ring structure has a major advantage over the basic ring. If one workstation breaks down, or the connection with the MAU is broken, other workstations are not affected (except that they cannot communicate with the damaged workstation). Failure of the MAU will prevent operation of the network. The Cambridge ring structure, described earlier, is prone to complete failure if one workstation fails (the continuous ring is broken).

Bus network

The bus network topology is illustrated in the Figure 30.4. With a bus topology, the workstations are connected to a main cable (known as the *bus* or trunk), along which data travels. The ends of a bus are not connected, so that data has to travel in both directions to reach the various nodes on the network. The bus topology makes the addition of new devices straightforward, either by attachment to the existing cable or to cable which can be added at either end.

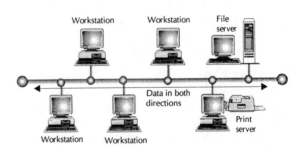

Figure 30.4. *Bus topology*

The main bus standard is known as *Ethernet*. The term *station* tends to be used rather than node for this type of network. The communications subnet uses a *broadcast* channel, so all attached stations can hear every transmission. As is the case in the ring network, there is no host computer and all stations have equal priority in using the network to transmit. The maximum length of a single bus *segment* is 500 metres and 100 stations can be attached to it. Segments can be specially linked to form larger configurations, up to a maximum of about 12 kilometres. Transmission speeds of 10 megabits/second are obtainable. The bus network provides certain benefits:

❑ If a node malfunctions, it simply stops communicating; it doesn't prevent the rest of the network from working;

❑ The attachment of devices is straightforward and the cable can be extended, if necessary; additional *segments* can be linked to extend the network.

The main drawback is that if a part of the Ethernet cabling develops a fault, the whole network (assuming it consists of a single segment) fails.

Bus-star network

This is a mixed topology designed to provide a high speed bus backbone via which multiple, slower, star networks can communicate with one another.

Mesh network

The nodes of a mesh network are fully interconnected. The mesh topology is not found in LANs, but is typical of the public switched telephone network (pstn) and WANs. Its complexity requires the use of switching techniques to route data through the network.

Network cabling - the transmission medium

In order to share resources on a network, servers, workstations and other devices must be connected; although wireless radio media are possible, most LANs use physical cabling, which acts as the *transmission medium*. The physical layout of the cabling should conform to one of the basic *topologies*: star, ring or bus. The type of cable used depends on the chosen topology and the rules governing the transmission of data through the cable (the *protocol*). The cabling standards of Ethernet and Token Ring, described below, are also LAN protocols.

Ethernet cabling

Ethernet is one the two most widely accepted standards (the other is Token Ring) for specifying how data is placed on and retrieved from a LAN. An Ethernet-equivalent standard is IEEE 802.3, which also uses Ethernet cable, but packets data slightly differently for transmission through the cable.

Ethernet cable falls into the following main categories:

❑ Fast (100Base-TX) Ethernet supports a bandwidth of 100 megabits per second (Mbps) and uses Unshielded Twisted Pair (UTP) or Shielded Twisted Pair (STP) cable. The maximum length which can be used in a single network segment is 100 metres.

❑ 100Base-FX uses optical fibre cable, operates at 100 Mbps, with a maximum segment length of 1000 metres.

❑ Gigabit Ethernet supports 1000 Mbps. The 1000BaseT standard is intended for use with UTP cabling and a maximum segment length of 100 metres, whilst the 1000Base-CX standard requires the use of copper core coaxial cable for distances up to 25 metres. Gigabit Ethernet can also be used with optical fibre cable to support greater distances and operate as network *backbones*.

❑ Thick Ethernet coaxial cable, with a diameter of 10mm has a solid copper core conductor. A single network segment can be 500 metres and supports the attachment of 100 devices. The cabling conforms to the IEEE 802.3 Type 10Base5 standard. The transmission rate is 10 megabits (10,000,000 bits) per second (Mbps).

❑ 10BaseT Standard Ethernet. The T stands for *twisted pair*. The Unshielded Twisted Pair (UTP) cabling used is much cheaper than the thick, coaxial Ethernet cabling, but provides the same transmission rate of 10 Mb/s and being the same as most telephone cabling, it is easier to install.

Token ring cabling

Used in *IBM token ring* networks use twisted pair cabling, either two pairs or four, depending on data transmission requirements. A single IBM Token Ring network will support up to 260 network devices at rates of 4, 16 and 100 Mbps over shielded twisted pair (STP), unshielded twisted pair (UTP and fibre-optic cable. Up to eight rings can be connected using *bridges*.

Fibre-optic cabling and FDDI

Cable of this type is available for use with any of the network types, but provides greater *bandwidth* and permits transmission over greater distances, without the use of *repeaters*. Fibre Distributed Data Interface (FDDI) is a fibre optic standard with bandwidth of over a Gigabit (1024^3) per second. FDDI is also a token ring standard, but operates with two counter rotating rings and workstations may be attached to one or both rings. FDDI is used widely for network backbones. A *backbone* is the part of a network which carries the main traffic and connects, for example, the LANs in different departments of an organisation.

Cable bandwidth

Digital bandwidth is measured in bits per second and indicates the volume of data which can be transmitted over a communications link in a fixed time. Bandwidth is important because is determines the practicability of using remote communications for modern user applications. High bandwidth is not a crucial consideration for users who wish to exchange the occasional text email, but it is fundamental to the success of businesses with more complex and high volume communication needs.

For example, a multi-sited organisation may need use its communications links to the Internet for the transmission of complex documents containing high quality images, voice communications and video conferencing. To meet these requirements the organisation would need dedicated, high speed links from each site to a 'backbone' (a major communications link) in the Internet In summary, bandwidth can be:

- ☐ Baseband. In a baseband network, a transmitting device uses the whole bandwidth (frequency range), so only one signal can be carried at any one time. This means that, for a brief moment, a transmitting device has exclusive use of the transmission medium. In general, broadband networks are suitable for networks which only transmit data signals.

- ☐ Broadband. Broadband networks provide a number of frequency bands or channels within the total bandwidth (*frequency division multiplexing*) and thus allow simultaneous use by different devices on the network. Generally, one channel is dedicated to the user workstations, leaving others free for transmitting video pictures for the security system, voice communication, television pictures and so on.

Cable-device connection

A number of different devices are used to make the connection between network devices, such as workstations and servers, and the transmission medium. The particular components used will depend on the type of network (for example, Ethernet or Token Ring); even for the same type of network, there are a range of connection alternatives. This paragraph only details the main categories of connection component, which are:

- ☐ *network card* (adapter), which is the *interface* for linking a network device to all other resources on the network; this is fitted into an expansion slot inside each workstation and other network devices. A device attaching to a Token ring network needs a different type of network card, from one attaching to an Ethernet network. A notebook or portable computer can be connected using its PCMCIA (Personal Computer Memory Card International Association) slot and a special network adapter;

- ☐ *Ethernet transceiver*; this device implements the CSMA/CD access protocol (see Access protocols). It is external from the network device and is connected to the network card and the Ethernet network cable. Although most network cards already contain a transceiver chip, *thick* Ethernet connections need an external transceiver. Thin Ethernet connections simply use the transceiver chip on the network card;

❏ *BNC connector*. Figure 30.5 illustrates its appearance; this is one of several types of connector used for *thin* Ethernet cable. There are BNC male and female connectors for linking sections of cable and T connectors for attaching devices to the cable. *Thick* Ethernet cabling uses a stronger screw coupling for cable connections (N-series connectors);

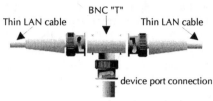

BNC "T"
Thin LAN cable   Thin LAN cable
device port connection

❏ *Terminator*; this is an electrical resistor which must be attached to each end of an Ethernet network segment (see Bus Topology);

Figure 30.5. *BNC "T" connector*

❏ *Multiple Access Unit* (MAU). This is the central component of a star/ring topology and is used in the IBM Token Ring network (see Star/Ring Network).

Connecting and extending LANs

Although there are limitations to the range of a LAN and the number of devices which can be attached, imposed by the performance ability of the network transmission medium, networks can be connected to one another and extended. LANs set up separately can be connected permanently, or data transmission between them can be restricted, for special user or system requirements. The devices used in this area of LAN architecture are described in Chapter 29.

Software components

Apart from physical components identified in the previous section, various types of software are also needed and these are described in the following sections.

Network operating system

A network operating system typically includes functional components to set-up, monitor and administer:

❏ The *directory* and *file* system on the server; directories are used to organise the storage of programs and data held on the file server's hard drive(s). Some directories are for the storage of the network operating system; others contain application programs and some directory space is allocated for the storage of user's data.

❏ *User login* and activity. A user must be identified by the network operating system before being given access to the network. The supervisor *creates* users and assigns a user-id to each. A user may also be assigned to a *user-group*, for example, Sales or Marketing. To access a network, a user must login at a workstation, which will require the entry of a *user-id* and possibly, a *password*. The precise conditions can be set by the network supervisor; certain time periods can be set when users are not allowed to log into the network; the time restrictions can be applied to all users, specific groups or individuals. The resources available to any given user can also be controlled through the login procedure.

❏ *User access* to applications and data files. Typically, users are assigned *rights*, sometimes as individuals, but more usually as members of a group. These rights relate to directories and files; in other words, the rights determine whether, for example, a user is allowed to delete or copy files in a particular directory. Access rights to *network executables*, that is application programs, only allow the programs to be run.

❑ *Network printing*; users can be given access to a shared printer, through a print *queue*; each queue is controlled by a printer server, which directs the jobs to a network printer under its control.

❑ *Electronic messaging*; this is a LAN version of electronic mail and provides a mailbox facility for inter-user communication.

❑ *Network backup*. This task, although important to users, because it may prevent the loss of important work, or network facilities, is a task carried out on a regular basis by the network supervisor.

All these tasks are the responsibility of the *network supervisor* or *administrator* who has special rights of access, not available to others. Usually, these tasks are carried out through a system console; any computer on the network can be used for this purpose, but, usually it will be secure in a separate location. Although printing, electronic messaging, applications and limited file management are available to users, their rights should not extend to the amendment of these facilities.

Workstation operating system

Each workstation has its own local operating system, such as MS-DOS or Windows95 to control processing; once an application is retrieved from the file server, the workstation must be able to run it.

Network connection software

The network connection software must be loaded into the workstation RAM (usually from the its integral hard drive, during start-up), before the workstation can be logged onto the network. This software remains in the workstation RAM as long as it is logged onto the network. A program which remains resident like this is referred to as a TSR (terminate and stay resident) program. There are usually several components to the connection software, each having a separate function. Two major functional components are the:

❑ *Communication protocol*. This is the set of rules for transmitting data through the network; it ensures that devices can successfully communicate with one another by using the same language. Example protocols are: IPX (Novell Netware); TCP/IP (Internet); SNA (IBM).

❑ *LAN driver*, which controls the network card fixed inside the workstation. LAN drivers which conform to the ODI (Open Data-link Interface) standard can accept data from the network in any of the standard communication protocols, listed in the previous paragraph. This means that workstations of different operating system types (MS-DOS, Macintosh, UNIX etc.) can be attached to the same LAN and share its resources.

Network access protocols

Empty slot technique

This system is appropriate for networks in the shape of rings or loops, where messages are passed point-to-point in one direction. One or more empty *slots* or *packets* circulate continuously around the ring. When a device has information to transmit, it loads it into the slot, which carries it to its destination. At the time of loading, the destination address is placed in the slot and a full-empty flag is set to full. As the slot is passed from one repeater to another, no attempt will be made to load the slot as long as the flag is set to full. When the slot reaches the destination device, the devices repeater reads the information without clearing the slot. Before passing it on, the repeater sets a received message flag in the slot. When the slot again reaches the sending device, the flag is set to empty. The destination device can check that the message was received by checking the received flag. If the message was not successfully received, perhaps because the destination device was not listening, the sender device can check the acknowledgement flag and re-transmit in the next slot.

Token passing technique

This technique is also used for ring networks. An imaginary *token* is passed continuously around the ring. The token is recognised as such by the devices, as a unique character sequence. If a device is waiting to transmit, it catches the token and with it, the authority to send data. As long as one device has the token, no other device can send data. A receiving device acknowledges the receipt of a message by inverting a 1-bit field. Token Ring employs this method.

Carrier sense multiple access (CSMA)

CSMA is used on broadcast systems such as the bus network. Each device is theoretically free to transmit data to any other device at any time. Before attempting to transmit, a device's network card polls the network path to ensure that the destination device is free to receive data and that the communications channel is free. A device wishing to transmit must wait until both conditions exist. Generally such delay will be no more than a few millionths of a second.

- ❑ CSMA *Collision Detection* (CSMA-CD). Because of the possibility of collision through simultaneous transmission, a collision detection mechanism is used. When collision does occur, the devices involved cease transmission and try again some time later. In order to avoid the same collision, each device involved is made to wait a different time. If a number of retries prove unsuccessful, an error will be reported to the user. Ethernet (IEEE 802.3 Standard) networks (see Network Cabling) use a form of CSMA/CD.

- ❑ CSMA *Collision Avoidance* (CSMA-CA). This strategy attempts to improve on that of CSMA-CD, which allows a device to place a packet onto the network path as soon as its network card detects it as being free. In the time between the test (measured in fractions of a microsecond) and the placing of the packet onto the path, another device's network card may have detected the path as free and be about to place another packet onto it. CSMA-CA seeks to remedy this problem by requiring a device's network card to test the path *twice*, once to see if the path is free and a second time, after alerting the device that it may use the network, but before the packet is placed onto the path.

Aloha

This protocol is used in satellite and terrestrial radio communications and in its primitive form is prone to collisions, because user devices can transmit at any time. A time slot version helps to reduce collisions by requiring that a user device can only transmit at the start of a time slot. Aloha was the basis for the Ethernet network protocols.

Benefits of computer networks

The general benefits are:

- ❑ sharing of appropriate *software*, *hardware resources* and common *data*;

- ❑ sharing of *processing* activity;

- ❑ *connectivity*; this is a very broad term used to categorise facilities and devices which support connection and communication between otherwise incompatible systems or devices. For example, a *terminal emulation* card, which enables a microcomputer to communicate with a remote IBM host computer, falls into this category;

- ❑ accessible services for *security*, *user support* and *system maintenance*.

Sharing hardware and software

In a LAN, particularly, there are opportunities to share hardware and software. This is because resources tend to be distributed over a small area; it is reasonable to ask users to share a printing resource if the printers serving them are within the same room, or perhaps in an adjacent room. It could be argued that the rapid fall in hardware costs has, to a certain extent, reduced the need for sharing peripherals, such as hard disk drives and printers. Although the prices of hard drives have fallen, the heavy demands of modern software and the increasing number of applications, ensures matching increases in demand for on-line storage. It is now common for microcomputer systems, even at the cheaper end of the market, to have their own hard disk storage with capacities measured in gigabytes (1024^3 bytes).

Although printers are becoming much cheaper, increasing numbers of users are demanding the high quality output (and sometimes colour) provided by top quality printers; printers at the top of the quality range are still relatively expensive. In summary, a number of factors concerning computer usage, storage and printing confirm that resource sharing remains a major purpose of a LAN.

❑ Applications. The range of computer applications and the number of users is continually increasing.

❑ Software packages. The increasing sophistication of software means that large amounts of disk space are needed for each package. Network versions of a package are cheaper (per user) than those for stand-alone systems.

❑ Storage technologies. Optical storage and high performance hard drives are capable of storing thousands of megabytes (gigabytes or gb) and are still relatively expensive. Individual users, each with their own hard disk-based microcomputer, are unlikely to make use of the several hundred megabytes available on each machine. A shared, large volume, hard or optical drive can satisfy the storage needs of all users.

❑ Printers. Most users require only occasional use of a printer, so there is little point in providing one for each. This is particularly the case for colour printers. A laser printer can produce the high quality output demanded by many applications and it operates at speeds which allow sharing to take place, without unreasonable delay for users.

❑ Other devices, such as scanners and plotters are relatively expensive and are likely to be used only occasionally.

Sharing data

A major benefit of all types of network concerns the sharing of data, frequently from centralised databases. This purpose is made particularly clear by the expansion of *Internet*, the world-wide network described in Chapter 31. Data can also be regarded as a resource, so sharing it can bring similar benefits to those available from sharing hardware. For example, a common data store supports the use of a *database* system, which itself reduces the need for data duplication.

Traditional computer processing methods require that each application has its own files and this results in the duplication of many data items and the updating process. For example, in a retail business both the stock control and purchasing departments make use of commodity details such as Stock Codes, Descriptions and Prices; if separate files are maintained by each department, a change in, for example, the Price of a commodity requires more than one input.

Limiting access to shared storage

The sharing of data files presents some problems which need to be tackled. Firstly, access to some data may have to be restricted to particular users. Although the aim of networks is to provide computer access to as many users as possible, procedural and software controls can be built in to limit entry to the system, or to particular files or processes. Network software allows the network administrator to vary the rights of users, according to the kinds of access they require to particular applications or files.

Another problem with sharing files is that several users may attempt to update the same data at the same time. This can lead to corruption of data. To combat this problem, network software usually provides a facility for locking individual records while they are being updated. Thus, if a particular record is being altered, it is locked and made inaccessible by any other user until the updating process is complete.

Sharing processing activity

Host computer with intelligent terminals

A host computer with intelligent terminals allows processing to be carried out at remote sites; as such it comes under the heading of WAN. The distribution of processing work may be very limited, such that the majority is processed by a central computer. For example, terminals connected to a remote host computer often have their own processing power, file storage and printing facilities. Usually, before being transmitted to the host computer for the updating of files, *transaction* data will require some *validation* and other accuracy checks and this can be done at the terminal. Microcomputers equipped with suitable software are often used to *emulate* mainframe intelligent terminals, with the added advantage of being useable as stand-alone systems, when not communicating with the mainframe. Alternatively, the work may be equally shared amongst a number of powerful computer systems, which then merge the results of their separate efforts.

Client-server network

A *client-server* LAN aims to exploit the full processing power of each computer in the network, including the *file server* and the user workstations or *clients*. This is effected by dividing the processing tasks between a client and a server. The client, a microcomputer in its own right (as opposed to the *dumb* terminal found in older mainframe systems) provides the user with a completely separate facility for running applications. The file server which could be a microcomputer, minicomputer, or mainframe, enhances the client component by providing additional services.

These services are traditionally offered by minicomputer and mainframe systems operating a *time-sharing* operating system; they include shared file management, data sharing between users, network administration and security. The major benefit of a client-server network is that the power of the client and server machines is used jointly to carry out the processing of an application. Interactive activities, for example, construction of a spreadsheet or the word processing of a report, are carried out by the client machine; having logged onto the network, the user can load the required applications software from the file server. Backup and file sharing security, relating to the application, can be handled by the server. Printing tasks can also be queued and handled as a shared printer becomes available. This task is handled by one or more *print servers*, which can be dedicated devices, or microcomputers assigned to the task. Except for small LANs, most operate on the client-server principle.

Peer-to-peer network

With a peer-to-peer configuration, it is not necessary to have a file server; instead all the workstations on the network contribute to the control of the network. Thus, any workstation can supply or use resources of others, as required. Unfortunately, this has the effect of slowing performance; in addition it means that files are not held centrally and this complicates file management.

Operating systems, such as Windows 2000 Professional allow networks to be set up as peer-to-peer or as client-server, although there are specific products, such as Windows 2000 Server which are aimes specifically at a client-server setup.

Network development

Developing a network involves similar stages to those used in information system development, including initial investigation of the problem, feasibility, analysis, design and implementation. The design process should identify requirements for equipment, such as file servers, network cards and cabling, a suitable topology or mix of topologies and appropriate network and communications software. The objective is to satisfy the requirements of the client business and produce a sustainable and reliable network which also meets necessary performance criteria, such as minimum downtime, data transfer rates, etc.

Design criteria

The main design criteria are as follows.

- ❑ Traffic. Rather like a roads sytem, a computer network's design should be specified in terms of the volume of transmissions it is required to support. This may be determined by the number of simultaneous user connections that need to be supported and the likely mix of user applications (e-mail, word processing, graphics, imaging etc). Clearly, a network which has to support occasional email communications, but is primarily providing a facility to share applications software stored on a server, will not require the bandwidth (data transfer rate) of a network which is used for the exchange of numerous, large document, image or sound files.

- ❑ Speed. This is determine by traffic levels and bandwidth. Transmission of large files, such as video, requires the use of broadband communication, that is a bandwidth which will allow the transfer of such files in an acceptable time.

- ❑ Cost. A business will require a return on its investment within a reasonable time. This means the the money spent on developing and maintaining a network must result in additional profit, or at least allow the business to break even on its investment. Typically this may be achieved by, for example, lower overheads, increased productivity or improved customer service.

- ❑ Reliability. This is fundamental to the success of a network. Clearly, a network which fails frequently and perhaps for extended periods will not result in improved productivity or reduced costs. If the network is crucial to the provision of customer services, then its failure will probably result in loss of business.

- ❑ Security. The importance of security cannot be over-emphasised, particularly if there are access points outside of the business premises, for example, through the Internet. Security failures can result in loss or corruption of data, fraud, sabotage or in the case of personal data, prosecution under the Data Protection Act.

Assessing user requirements

The design criteria outlined above must be measured against the *functionality* the network is to provide. The term functionality refers to all the tasks the network is to perform, including for example, business applications, such as word processing, accounts and stock control, e-mail, Internet access, Web site hosting and e-commerce. A business can benefit from networking even if its requirements are very simple, such as being able to share documents without the chore of copying files to floppy disk or some other backup medium.

Network design should also cater for growth in usage, if such growth is envisaged. For example, a network may begin with the connection of three PCs via a hub, the cost of which is fairly small. The business may decide that there is a likelihood that further PCs may be connected and buy an 8-port hub in preference to a 4-port hub.

To achieve acceptable network performance, an assessment needs to be made of the load that the applications and other functions will put on the network. Clearly, a network which supports the exchange of a few small document files each day will not require the investment needed to support complex database applications or, for example, the hosting and management of a busy e-commerce site.

Network size and complexity

The size of the network should be determined by the number of users and the level of use. In measuring the number of users, you would need to allow for the possibility that some access points may be shared because their level of use is low enough to allow it. If business efficiency is like to be compromised because some staff are having to queue to use the network then an increase in the number of access point need to be considered. Equally, if the range of user applications is wide, delays may be caused at a shared access point as each user may need to load a different application when their turn arrives.

To allow the network to grow or be connected with other networks, components should be compatible with the widest possible range of products.

The term *connectivity* refers to a network's ability to communicate with other networks and typically this is via an Internet connection. The type of connection needs to take into account bandwidth requirements and the type of external network. In the case of a small business, a dial-up connection to an Internet Service Provider (ISP) may be adequate, but a larger business may need a permanent, leased line and investment in additional hardware such as *bridges* and *routers*, to connect to both private and public networks.

Small networks can be built without sophisticated technical support and with relatively small capital investment, but large networks with external connections may require considerable investment and technical expertise.

Network type and components

As detailed earlier in this chapter, commonly available network types are Ethernet, Token Ring and ATM, although most small networks are based on Ethernet, for which there are a number of bandwidth and cabling variations, including for example, 100 Base-TX, Gigabit Ethernet and 10/100 Base-T. If applications include use of multimedia applications, such as video and image processing and the consequent transfer of large files, a higher bandwidth solution is likely to be needed.

Choice of network type and bandwidth option may have an effect on which cable type is needed, but consideration may also need to be given to ease of installation. For example, co-axial cable is more inflexible and difficult to install in restricted spaces than twisted pair cable. Other hardware components include, network server, client workstations, hubs, bridges, routers, network cards and other basic elements of a network.

Software decisions relate to choice of network operating system, Microsoft Windows and Novell Netware products being currently the most important, network compatible client applications (most applications are available as network or stand-alone versions) and network management and backup software.

✍ Exercises

1. Identify the main *components* of a LAN and briefly explain the function of each.
2. Identify one advantage and one disadvantage of each of the following network topologies: *star; ring; bus.*
3. How does the *Token Ring* network overcome a weakness of the basic ring topology?
4. Name the main *Ethernet cable standards*, and the performance specification of each.
5. (i) Differentiate between *baseband* and *broadband* networks.
   (ii) Suggest, by reference to applications, why broadband networks will become increasingly important.
6. Identify four functions of a *network operating system.*
7. What is meant by a workstation's *local operating system*?
8. In the context of network connection software, briefly describe the functions of the:
   (i) *communication protocol;*
   (ii) *LAN driver.*
9. Outline the operation of the following network access protocols:
   (i) *empty slot;*
   (ii) *token passing;*
   (iii) *CSMA/CA.*
10. A major benefit of a network is its facilities for *resource sharing.* Identify the particular resources which can be shared and the benefits such sharing brings for an organisation and its users.
11. Distinguish between a *client-server* and *peer-to-peer* network operating system.

Chapter 31

The Internet

The Internet is a world-wide network composed of thousands of smaller regional networks scattered throughout the globe. A common set of communication protocols enables every computer connected to the Internet to interchange information with every other computer so connected. On any given day it connects tens of millions of users in over 65 countries. Over the last 25 years, the Internet has grown to include government and educational institutions, and, more recently, commercial organisations.

Though there are companies which help manage different parts of the networks which tie everything together, there is no single governing body which controls what happens on the Internet. The networks within different countries are funded and managed locally according to local policies.

The Internet began in early 1969 under the experimental project ARPAnet. ARPA (Advanced Research Projects Agency, later known as the Defence Advanced Research Projects Agency) wanted to demonstrate the feasibility of building computer networks over a wide area such that the loss of a number of hosts on that network did not disrupt it. So ARPA initially interconnected four computers and linked them with Internet Protocol (IP), and the Internet grew from there. In the 70's and 80's U.S. universities began to link with DARPAnet so that it could be used for academic research and in 1991 the U.S. government lifted its ban on commercial use of the Internet. The considerable business opportunities provided by the Internet ensure that it will continue to grow.

Today the Internet is a huge collection of different, intercommunicating networks funded by commercial, government and educational organisations. It has developed to handle larger volumes of data, software has become more powerful and user-friendly, and the types of services available have grown.

All types of computers make up the hardware connected on the Internet. They vary from PCs, Macintoshes and UNIX workstations to minicomputers, mainframes and supercomputers. Anyone who wants to have access to the enormous amount of information available regionally or around the world can use the Internet. They can access electronic libraries, receive periodicals, exchange ideas, read the news, post questions with newsgroups, examine the weather (from reports or satellite photos), obtain the latest stock market prices and currency exchange rates, and access public government information on trade, laws, research and other subjects. It is likely that in the very near future, every school will be connected to the Internet, an Internet connection in your house will be no more unusual than a telephone line and, if you run a business, the Internet will be a vital tool (see E-commerce).

Uses of the Internet

The Internet is essentially a tool for transferring information between computers. This can be achieved in numerous ways and for various purposes. For example, *E-mail* is a convenient, quick and cheap alternative to the postal system for business and personal correspondence; *File Transfer Protocol (FTP)* allows large amounts of information to be transferred between two computers very conveniently; *Usenet,* the world-wide collection of interest groups, or *Newsgroups*, allows groups of people with similar interests to exchange views and information.

Another important use of the Internet is the remote control of computer systems via *Telnet*.

The *World-Wide Web* provides a uniform means of accessing and transferring information in the form of hypermedia documents. Accessing these documents does not require any particular machine or operating system. These and other Internet services are discussed in the following sections. A rapidly expanding application of the Internet is e-commerce, or on-line trading, between businesses and between businesses and consumers; this topic is examined at the end of this chapter. Note that programs used on the Internet can be classified as being either *server* or *client*. Server programs operate at Internet sites where the particular Internet service being used is provided; the program which is used to access a site, on a home PC for example, is the client program. For instance, a Web server at a Web site processes requests made by client programs called Web *browsers*.

The World-Wide Web

Abbreviated to the Web and WWW, this is the fastest growing Internet service. Though the World-Wide Web is mostly used on the Internet, the two terms do not mean the same thing. The Web refers to a world-wide collection of knowledge, while the Internet refers to the physical side of the global network, an enormous collection of cables and computers.

The World-Wide Web uses the Internet for the transmission of hypermedia documents between computer users connected to the Internet. As with the Internet, nobody actually owns the World-Wide Web. People are responsible for the documents they author and make available publicly on the Web. Via the Internet, hundreds of thousands of people around the world are making information available from their homes, schools, colleges and workplaces. The aim of WWW is to make all on-line knowledge part of one interconnected web of documents and services.

The World-Wide Web began in March 1989, when Tim Berners-Lee of the European Particle Physics Laboratory (known as CERN, a collective of European high-energy physics researchers) proposed the project as a means of distributing research results and ideas effectively throughout the organisation. The initial project proposal outlined a simple system of using networked hypertext to transmit to members of the high-energy physics community. By the end of 1990, the first piece of Web software had been introduced on a NeXT machine. It had the capability to view and transmit hypertext documents to other people on the Internet, and came with the capability to edit hypertext documents on the screen. Since then many people throughout the world have contributed their time writing Web software and documents, or telling others about the Web.

The World-Wide Web is officially described as a wide-area hypermedia information retrieval initiative aiming to give universal access to a large universe of documents. What the World-Wide Web (WWW, W3) project has done is provide users on computer networks with a consistent means to access a variety of media in a simplified fashion. With the aid of a popular software interface to the Web, called a *browser* (described later), the WWW has changed the way people view and create information. The first true global hypermedia network, it is revolutionising many elements of society, including commerce, politics, and literature.

Hypertext and hypermedia

The operation of the Web relies mainly on *hypertext* as its means of interacting with users. Hypertext is basically the same as ordinary text - it can be stored, read, searched, or edited -with an important exception: hypertext contains links to other places within the same document or to other documents. A Web browser indicates text links by the use of colour or by underlining. For example, Figure 31.1 shows part of a Web site home page which contains underlying links to other documents. Each link takes the user to a different document, although the second hypertext link simply directs attention to a point further down the same page.

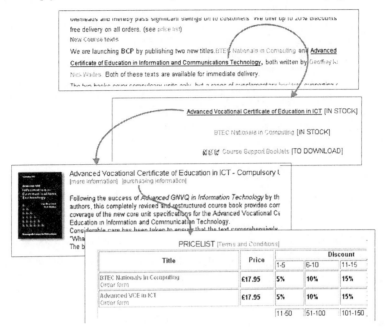

Figure 31.1. *Three linked hypermedia documents*

The first document would be retrieved from the WWW using a browser and the user, by pointing and clicking with a mouse on a link, will cause the browser to retrieve the appropriate document automatically, no matter where it is located.

Figure 31.2 shows a browser displaying a *hypermedia* document with three buttons which, when clicked with a mouse, would demonstrate sound, graphics and video files.

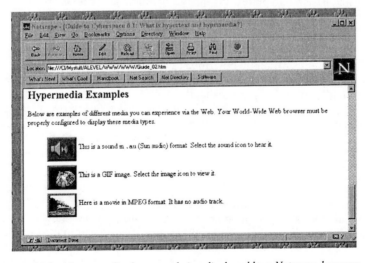

Figure 31.2. *A hypermedia document being displayed by a Netscape browser*

Hypermedia is hypertext with a difference - hypermedia documents contain links not only to other pieces of text, but also to other forms of media, namely sounds, images, and movies. Images themselves can be selected to link to sounds or documents. Hypermedia simply combines hypertext and multimedia.

The appearance of a hypermedia document when it is displayed by a browser is determined partly by the browser which provides a certain amount of control over such things as text fonts and colours, but mainly by the language used to encode the document. This language is *Hyper-Text Mark-up Language* (HTML).

Web browsers

These are graphical interface client programs to help users to navigate through the Web, to transmit and to receive information from other users or information providers. By using a browser, the user does not have to know the format and location of the information: he or she simply jumps from site to site by clicking on hypertext links. Examples of commercially available browsers are Netscape's *Navigator* and Microsoft's *Internet Explorer.*

Although there are many different ways to represent a document on the screen, it is often called a *page*. Usually, those responsible for creating a given collection of interrelated documents also create a special document which is intended to be viewed first - one that contains introductory information and/or a master menu of documents within that collection. This type of document is called a *home page* and is generally associated with a particular site, person, or named collection. The example document has underlined hypertext phrases. These phrases are hyperlinks (or links) - typically, clicking on one of them with a mouse will cause another document to appear on the screen, which may hold more images and hyperlinks to other places. There is no single way to represent text which is linked to other things - some browsers underline, others use special colours, and many give the user a variety of options. Images which are part of the document and are displayed within the page are called *inline images*.

There is usually a toolbar at the top or bottom of the screen. This contains buttons which perform frequently used operations. For example, a set of navigation buttons is provided because a user might go to many different pages by selecting links in hypertext and there needs to be some method of retracing one's steps and reviewing the documents that have been explored.

How the Web works

Web software is designed around a distributed client-server architecture. A Web client (called a Web browser if it is intended for interactive use) is a program which can send requests for documents to any Web server. A Web server is a program which, upon receipt of a request, sends the document requested (or an error message if appropriate) back to the requesting client.

Using a distributed architecture means that a client program may be running on a completely separate machine from that of the server, possibly in another room or even in another country. Because the task of document storage is left to the server and the task of document presentation is left to the client, each program can concentrate on those duties and progress independently of each other. Since servers usually operate only when documents are requested, they put a minimal amount of workload on the computers on which they run. Here is an example of how the process works:

1. Running a Web client program, such as a browser, the user selects a hyperlink in a piece of hypertext connecting to another document - Java Programming for example.

2. The Web client uses the address associated with that hyperlink to connect to the Web server at a specified network address and asks for the document associated with Java Programming.

3. The server responds by sending the text and any other media within that text (pictures, sounds, or video clips) to the client, which the client then renders for presentation on the user's screen.

The World-Wide Web is composed of thousands of these virtual transactions taking place per hour throughout the world, creating a web of information flow. Web servers are now beginning to include encryption and client authentication abilities, allowing them to send and receive secure data and be more selective as to which clients receive information. This allows freer communications among Web users and ensures that sensitive data is kept private. In the near future, it will be harder to compromise the security of commercial servers and educational servers which want to keep information local.

The language which Web clients and servers use to communicate with each other is called the *HyperText Transfer Protocol* (HTTP). All Web clients and servers must be able to 'speak' HTTP in order to send and receive hypermedia documents. For this reason, Web servers are often called HTTP servers.

The standard language the Web uses for creating and recognising hypermedia documents is the Hypertext Mark-up Language (HTML). One of the major attractions of using HTML is that every WWW browser can 'understand' it, no matter what machine the browser is being run on. This means that Web page developers do not need to worry about producing different versions for different computer platforms.

Uniform Resource Locators

The World-Wide Web uses what are called Uniform Resource Locators (URLs) to represent hypermedia links and links to network services within HTML documents. It is possible to represent nearly any file or service on the Internet with a URL. The first part of the URL (before the two slashes) specifies the method of access. The second is typically the address of the computer which the data or service is located on. Further parts may specify the names of files, the port to connect to, or the text to search for in a database. A URL is always a single unbroken line with no spaces.

Sites which run World-Wide Web servers are typically named with a "www" at the beginning of the network address.

Here are some examples of URLs:

```
http://www.nc.edu/nw/book.html
```

Connects to an HTTP server and retrieves an HTML document called 'book.html' in a directory called 'nw'

```
file://www.nc.edu/sound.au
```

Retrieves a sound file called 'sound.au' and plays it.

```
file://www.abc.com/picture.gif
```

Retrieves a picture and displays it, either in a separate program or within a hypermedia document.

```
file://www.bcd.org/dd/
```

Displays the contents of directory 'dd'.

```
ftp://www.wer.uk.co/pub/file.txt
```

Opens an FTP connection to www.uk.co and retrieves a text file.

```
gopher://www.hcc.hawaii.edu
```

Connects to the Gopher at www.hcc.hawaii.edu.

```
telnet://www.nc.edu:1234
```

Telnets to www.nc.edu at port 1234.

```
news:alt.hypertext
```

Reads the latest Usenet news by connecting to a news host and returns the articles in the "alt.hypertext" newsgroup in hypermedia format.

Most Web browsers allow the user to specify a URL and connect to that document or service. When selecting hypertext in an HTML document, the user is actually sending a request to open a URL. In this way, hyperlinks can be made not only to other texts and media, but also to other network services. Web browsers are not simply Web clients, but are also full-featured FTP, Gopher, and telnet clients (see later for a discussion of these Internet services).

WWW search engines

The WWW is a vast, distributed repository of information, and more is being added to the Web each day. However, the only consistent characteristics of the information available are the manner in which it is coded, that is, in HTML, and the way in which it can be located, that is, by using URLs.

To access this huge bank of information, dispersed over the entire world, and locate specific information on a certain subject, there are numerous information retrieval utilities which provide access to databases of Web page details. These *search engines* allow Web users to enter search criteria in the form of keywords or phrases and they retrieve summaries of all database entries satisfying the search criteria. Of the many information retrieval services available, some of the most well known include *Excite*, *Lycos* and *Yahoo*.

Figure 31.3 shows the Yahoo search engine being used to find information on shiatsu. The search produced short summaries of numerous Web pages containing the keyword shiatsu, the first few of which are shown in Figure 31.4. Clicking on any of the links shown as underlined headings would cause the browser to retrieve the appropriate page which might also have links to further pages containing related information.

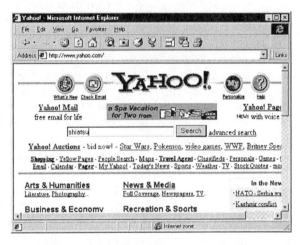

Figure 31.3. *A keyword entered in the Yahoo search engine*

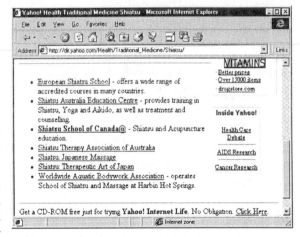

Figure 31.4. *A partial list of the result of searching for the keyword 'shiatsu'*

E-mail

The most used application of the Internet is electronic mail, or *e-mail* as it is widely known. E-mail is primarily used to send and receive text-based messages such as personal or business letters, orders, reports and statements.

To use Internet e-mail, access to a computer which is connected to the Internet and has e-mail software is required. Most commercial Internet service providers include e-mail facilities in their subscriber services. Subscribers are given an identifying code called an e-mail *address*. The service provider collects and forwards mail sent from that address and holds mail to be received by that address until able to deliver it. The service provider thus acts like a post office, and in fact there is a close analogy between the way which e-mail is implemented and the traditional manual postal system (which is disparagingly termed 'snail mail' by e-mail devotees). The same principles apply to e-mail users who do not rely on commercial service providers - messages are automatically forwarded from users to their destinations and incoming mail is stored on their service provider's computer until the user is able to accept it. The process of composing and sending an e-mail message is as follows:

1. The message to be sent is composed (usually off-line) using some form of text editor.

2. A *mailer* program is used to connect to the Internet and transmit the message to its destination computer. The mailer examines the code containing the address to which the message is to be sent and makes a decision regarding how the message should be routed to the destination before sending it on its way.

3. The message is automatically passed from computer to computer until it arrives at the recipient's *mailbox* which is generally a special directory used for storing messages which are waiting to be read.

4. The recipient accesses his/her mailbox and removes any messages which have arrived.

Because e-mail is delivered by electronic means, it is much faster than the manual system, taking minutes or seconds rather than days to arrive at practically any destination in the world. Though the technology which makes e-mail possible is complex, from a user's viewpoint e-mail is simple to use and extremely useful. See the chapter on Software Tools for more information on email and email software.

FTP

File Transfer Protocol (FTP) provides the facility to transfer files between two computers on the Internet. There are thousands of FTP sites all over the Internet with data files, software, and information for almost any interest. See the chapter on Software Tools for more information on FTP and FTP software.

Closely associated with FTP, *Archie* is a program which periodically searches all FTP sites on its master list, and stores the filenames it finds in a central database. This information is then made available to users to retrieve via FTP. This, in common with other types of search engines found on the Internet, provides a convenient method of locating items of information which could be in an FTP site anywhere in the world.

Telnet

Telnet allows you to use a remote computer system from your local system. For example, an employee of an organisation which is on the Internet and supports Telnet working, could use the firm's computer system from home. The employee would simply Telnet the employer's computer system using his/her home PC and, once connected, could run programs available on the remote system. The Telnet software provides an interface window through which commands can be issued and results displayed.

This *virtual terminal* allows the remote computer to be controlled as if it were the local computer. Any task which can be performed on a workstation connected directly to the remote computer can also be done using a Telnet connection.

Usenet

Usenet is a large collection of newsgroups, of which there are many thousands. Newsgroups allow people with common interests to exchange views, ask questions and provide information using the Internet. Almost anything you care to find can be found as a newsgroup, which acts like a community bulletin board spread across millions of computer systems world wide. Anyone can participate in these groups, and moderation ranges from strict to none. Everything imaginable is discussed, from selling and trading goods and services, to discussing the latest episode of a popular TV show. Subscribers can read news articles, and reply to them - either by posting their own news articles, or by sending E-mail to the authors. Since Usenet news is not limited to any political or geographic boundaries, it provides the possibility of being able to interact with an enormous number of individuals. See the chapter on Software Tools for more information on newsgroups and *newsreader* software.

IRC

IRC, or *Internet Relay Chat*, is a multi-user talk program. IRC allows several people to simultaneously participate in a discussion over a particular channel, or even multiple channels. There is no restriction to the number of people who can participate in a given discussion, or the number of channels which can be formed over IRC. All conversations take place in real time and IRC has been used extensively for live coverage of such things as world events, news and sports commentary. It is also an extremely inexpensive substitute for long distance calling.

Intranets and Extranets

An intranet is a private Internet which uses Internet software and the TCP/IP protocols. Its appearance is that of the Web and the familiar browser is its user interface. 'Out of the box' Web servers provide a convenient and relatively cheap method of developing internal network requirements and many organisations have built intranets as part of their overall Internet strategy. Employees are usually familiar with the Web and require little training to access the resources they need on the company intranet. Web tools, such as HTML editors, are relatively cheap and application development only becomes expensive when large and complex databases are needed, as in the case of an on-line store's product database.

An intranet may be developed on private corporate LANs or WANs but organisations frequently wish to provide appropriate and limited access to clients and suppliers and develop an outward facing extension for those purposes. As an intra/Extranet, outside access only requires entry of the appropriate user-id and password.

E-commerce

Many businesses including, for example, supermarkets, travel agents, wine merchants, booksellers and car sales companies now sell their products through e-commerce web sites. With a computer, Internet connection and Web browser, consumers can visit these virtual stores and view, select and pay for goods which can often be delivered within 24 to 48 hours. Until the 1960s it was common practice for shops to make home deliveries or orders taken over the telephone and Internet shopping has the potential to reduce the volume of traffic visiting, for example, out of town shopping centres. It is extremely unlikely that demand for conventional 'bricks and mortar' will disappear because Internet shopping provides no social interaction and many consumers will wish to view and handle many types of goods before buying.

More formally, e-commerce can be defined as "conducting business transactions over electronic networks". E-commerce is fundamentally changing the way business operates. Because of e-commerce, businesses of all sizes are changing their internal operations and their relationships with suppliers and customers. When properly implemented, e-commerce can improve the efficiency of all stages of the business process, from design and manufacture to retailing and distribution.

E-commerce is playing a major role in the establishment of a global economy. The major catalyst for the expansion of international electronic retailing is the Internet. Its users, the number of which is rapidly increasing, can communicate with the Web sites of countless organisations all over the world, and it is through these *World Wide Web* sites that companies can provide 'on-line stores'. The Web-based on-line stores are accessible by Web browsers, such as Microsoft Explorer and Netscape Communicator. An Internet store provides all the facilities that the customer needs, including a product catalogue, a 'virtual shopping basket' and a secure credit card payment system.

The importance of e-commerce

E-commerce makes the location and size of a business less important - even irrelevant - to its market. The global market is accessible to small and large businesses alike. E-commerce can remove the need for traditional retail outlets by bringing a business into direct contact with its customers.

In an increasingly competitive and global economy, business success depends on knowing what customers will buy and how to satisfy their needs better than the competition. Success is most likely if there is close cooperation between the business, its suppliers and its customers. E-commerce, made possible by the Internet and other emerging communication technologies, is crucial to the achievement of this closer cooperation.

To obtain a competitive edge, the best businesses are using new technology to clarify customer demand, more precisely target marketing efforts, tighten business processes and investigate new methods of distribution. Large businesses are making similar demands of their suppliers and expect them to be fully integrated into their information networks. Similar demands are even being made of customers, in that some companies are limiting some goods and services to those with Internet access.

The Parliamentary Under Secretary of State for Small Firms, Trade and Industry recently declared that, "In markets where the traditional model can be turned on its head overnight, where a business can move from start-up player to global player in a matter of months, it is vital that all companies, whatever their sector of business, whether large or small, understand how electronic commerce can bring them competitive advantage – and use that knowledge."

Business benefits

Businesses can benefit tremendously from e-commerce in many important ways:

- ❑ Expensive printed catalogues and service guides can be replaced by a single, up-to-date electronic product database that is accessible at all times.

- ❑ Many businesses use mail shots to inform customers of new products or special offers. However, mail shots are time consuming and expensive. But when the latest information is always available on a web site, existing customers can obtain up-to-date information on new products or services at any time. This can result in significant savings.

❑ Through search tools and customer profiles, information can be tailored to customer requirements on demand.

❑ The supply chain is shortened so delivery times and costs are reduced.

❑ Staffing costs can be a fraction of those for conventional sales outlets. For example, Web site software can handle routine sales transactions automatically, leaving sales staff to deal with more complex orders.

❑ E-commerce also provides opportunities for entirely new products and services. These include network supply and support services, web site design and hosting, and various types of on-line information services.

❑ A business can maintain closer contact with its customers and suppliers, and direct communication allows improved pre- and post-sales support.

E-commerce should not be seen simply as an add-on. The greatest benefits are obtained by businesses that change their organisation and processes to take full advantage of the opportunities provided by e-commerce.

Customer benefits

Customers can gain considerable benefits from electronic commerce:

❑ The range of products that can be bought on-line is continually being extended. There are virtual stores all over the Internet offering a wide range of goods, including books, wine, newspapers, cakes, computer hardware, software and even cars. Similarly, numerous services are available on-line. These include education, entertainment and information services.

❑ The customer has the convenience of 24-hour home shopping and access to a wider range of goods and services than is conventionally available within their locality.

❑ A conventional shopping chain rarely offers its full product range at every shop, whereas a virtual shop can make its full product range available globally.

❑ The customer is given global choice. If a product or service is available from a number of suppliers, the customer can choose without regard to geographical location.

❑ The customer benefits from lower prices. Electronic commerce drastically reduces transaction costs. A transaction involving human interaction may be measured in £s, but the same transaction carried out electronically can cost a few pence.

❑ The customer enjoys rapid response to orders. Direct supply from manufacturer to customer can also be effected with mail order or telephone order catalogues, but the human and paper-based transactions are more costly and involve longer delays than is possible with e-commerce.

❑ For products that can be delivered electronically, such as software, video and newspapers, the time delay between order and delivery can be reduced to an absolute minimum, and intermediaries in the traditional supply chain are entirely redundant.

By bringing products and services to the home, electronic commerce also has the potential to benefit the disabled, the elderly and those living in remote areas.

Internet Service Providers

Types of ISPs

An Internet Service Provider (ISP) is a business which acts as the interface between the Internet and Internet users. Although some larger organisations will find it worthwhile to invest in all the necessary hardware and software and technical support required for direct connection, this is not a practical option for individual users and many smaller organisations. Some ISPs do not provide their services publicly and not for commercial gain. For example, larger academic institutions such as colleges and universities will usually have their own Internet servers and the necessary communications routing equipment to act as an ISP solely for their own staff and students.

Commercial ISPs can be categorised according to the connection services they provide and the charges they make. Although many ISPs will fall into more than one category, the following broad divisions can be identified:

1. **Free access.** Such ISPs (TescoNET is an example) do not charge for providing the Internet connection but usually require a registration process which allows them to gather a certain amount of marketing information. Their revenue may come from a percentage of the call charges when their Help lines are called (often these are at a premium rate, rather than a standard local rate). Many users of such ISPs are ICT novices and frequently need to call for assistance. Revenue may also come from advertising; the registration and setup process will normally make the ISP's home page the default page in the browser and on the assumption that many users will not know how, or even want, to change this setting, they will be viewing the home page every time they connect to the Internet. The ISP can monitor their home page visitor statistics and use its popularity to persuade advertisers to pay for space. To retain loyalty to their home page, the ISP will include popular services, such as channel guides to the Web for shopping, leisure, entertainment, chat rooms, newsgroups and so on. The ISP connection is normally via a local rate telephone number (08457 numbers are charged at local rate even if a caller is far distant from the ISP). Although the ISP is not making a charge for Internet access, users are still paying local telephone call charges for any connection time to the Internet.

2. **Unmetered.** Some ISPs, AOL and BT Internet for example, provide free access and for a flat, monthly rate, users can be connected to the Internet for as long as they like without additional telephone charges. The monthly rate varies depending on whether the unmetered access is restricted, commonly to evenings and weekends, or unrestricted. This is an alternative to the 'pay as you go' system which applies to 'free access' connection and is worthwhile provided that Internet usage would have used up at least the monthly subscription in telephone call charges.

3. **Subscription.** The services provided by free access and unmetered ISPs may be too limited or slow for some business users and a subscription ISP may be more suitable. For an ISP to charge a subscription for access to the Internet it should be able to demonstrate a quality and reliability of service which is superior to non-subscription ISPs. More is said about services and reliability later.

Services provided

Some services are standard to all types of ISP and as indicated above, subscription ISPs must provide additional services to justify their charges.

ISPs offering 'free' and unmetered access may also provide a number of additional services, typically including:

1. Free e-mail address(es). Often, the registration process includes allocation of an e-mail address. For example, a "Alan Dunn", registering with BT Internet, may be offered Alan.Dunn@btinternet.com or A.Dunn@btinternet.com. E-mail services may be provided as *hotmail* or *pop3*.

    Hotmail means that the user can pick up messages from any computer with an Internet connection and browser, although there may be no facility for off-line preparation of messages before transmission and downloading to a local PC before they are opened. If the user's mailbox is stored on a POP3 server (POP stands for Post Office Protocol), then e-mail software such as Microsoft Outlook Express (see Chapter on Software Tools) can be used to set up an Account for the downloading of messages, off-line reading and message preparation. BTInternet, for example, provides both hotmail (which it refers to as Web Mail) and POP3 mail for use with e-mail software.

2. Free server space for storing Web pages. To be viewed by users of the World Wide Web, a Web site (comprising Web pages with navigation facilities to connect them) must be located on an Internet server. The uploading of Web pages from their creator's PC is accomplished with FTP (File Transfer Protocol) software (see Chapter on Software Tools). To be viewable by a browser, the pages must be coded in HTML, although additional features to control their operation may be programmed using, for example, Java Script or Java.

3. Access to 'chat' or discussion rooms . These are stored on the Internet server and record messages from users as contributions to a discussion. Once logged into a chat room, users can simultaneously view contributions from other users and add their own comments accordingly. Most chat rooms require use of the Internet Relay Chat (IRC) protocol, although sites do provide alternatives, based on subsets of the IRC protocol.

4. Access to newsgroups. These are hosted on news servers and use a bulletin board approach to allow users to view contributions and post up their own. The chapters on the Internet and Software Tools provide more information on newsgroups and newsgroup software.

5. Technical support. As explained earlier, free access or unmetered ISPs also provide free technical support except that calls to the telephone Help line are often charged at a premium rate, a percentage of which contributes to the ISP's revenue. In that the users of such ISPs are often novices, technical support can prove expensive. On the other hand, email technical support is normally free. ISPs may also provide on-line technical support, making use of FAQs (Frequently Asked Questions) to explain the solutions to commonly experienced problems. Generally, to take advantage of on-line support requires a level of user confidence and expertise which may be beyond many first-time buyers of purchase. Subscription ISPs can be expected to provide free technical support by phone, without use of a premium rate number, or on-line.

Quality and reliability of service

For most private users, the quality of service can be measured according to the level of first-time connections (when the number is not engaged), the speed with which server-side login procedures are completed and the typical connection speed. To make the latter measurement fair, a user's modem must support the fastest connection speeds offered by the ISP. The fastest modems presently available are 56Kbits/sec V90 modems and most ISPs support the V90 standard (see Chapter 29).

An ISP's performance will tend to vary over time as the number of its users expands or contracts, or investment is made in new network and communications equipment and maintenance staff. For example, a new ISP is likely to have surplus capacity and at first users may well experience 100% first-time connection and a consistently high connect speed. The good performance may well increase the number of users at a rate which does not allow the ISP to expand its facilities to meet demand, so leading to a drop in the level of first-time connections and poorer connect speeds.

The Internet side of the ISP's connection will also affect the experience of its users. Some ISPs will be connected to faster Internet *backbones* (these are the primary communications links for the Internet) than others and the quality and performance of the servers and communications equipment they use will also vary.

Users of ISDN connections can rely on a consistent connect speed of 64 Kbits/sec. BT's Highway connection box provides two channels for Internet connection and by using both channels (at the double the call cost) subscribers can connect to the Internet at 128 Kbits/sec.

A reliable ISP service will ensure that connection services are always available. Loss of service may result from failure of the ISP's server, although to qualify as an ISP requires the ownership of two servers which are permanently connected to the Internet. Of course, loss of service may result from factors which are outside of the ISP's control, for example, the breakdown of a section of the telephone network.

Reliability may also be measured in respect of email and web hosting services. For example, mailbox settings may be corrupted or lost, resulting in missed messages and failure of a Web server will prevent access to the Web sites and pages it hosts. Web servers need to 'locked' at various times to allow for maintenance or upgrade work and the frequency with which this happens will be a measure of reliability. Clearly, for an e-commerce business, frequent lockouts may result in loss of business, both temporarily and permanently.

Subscription ISPs should be able to guarantee levels of service which are better than those of the free or unmetered ISPs, but for most private users and many small business users the payment of a subscription is probably not justified.

Subscription ISPs usually provide a wider range of services and facilities, including for example, unlimited Web server space, dedicated (to one subscriber) Web servers, unlimited mailboxes, email forwarding and leased line connections.

Connecting to the Internet

Connecting to the Internet is very easy now. Most new PCs come with the required hardware and software already installed. It is only necessary to plug in a telephone line, install a browser program and run the installation program supplied on CD ROM by an Internet Service Provider (ISP). Probably the browser will also be available on the CD ROM since the two major browsers, Microsoft's *Internet Explorer* and Netscape's *Navigator*, are free. However, for people who have a PC that is not Internet ready, this chapter explains basic hardware and software requirements and possible alternatives.

Using an Internet Service Provider (ISP)

Figure 31.5 shows a PC connected to the Internet via a remote service provider which is itself a LAN (Local Area Network). The PC connects to the service provider using a modem and the telephone system. The service provider is directly connected to the Internet by means of a *router,* a computer which provides the link to special data transmission lines required to access the Internet. A large organisation might have its own direct link to the Internet, but many private users rely on commercial service providers for the connection, for which they must pay a subscription. Some service providers do not charge a subscription but generate revenue from advertising and a percentage of telephone call charges received from subscribers who take advantage of the telephone help lines they run for their clients.

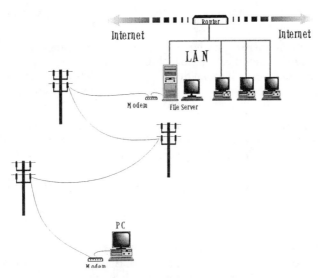

Figure 31.5. *PC connected to a server for access to the Internet*

Modem, ISDN or ADSL?

A PC connects to a service provider using a modem, ISDN adapter or some other interface device, and the telephone system. The Internet Service Provider (ISP) is directly connected to the Internet by means of a *router*, a computer which provides the link to special data transmission lines required to access the Internet. A large organisation might have its own direct link to the Internet, but many private and small business users rely on commercial service providers for the connection, for which they may have to pay a subscription.

Many service providers do not charge a subscription but generate revenue from advertising and a percentage of telephone call charges received from subscribers who take advantage of the telephone help lines they run for their clients. The most recent modem standard, V.90 and the ISDN and ADSL services are described in Chapter 29.

Hardware costs

Modems are relatively cheap and still provide the most cost-effective method of Internet connection for private and small business users. For BT's Highway service there is a relatively small installation charge, the cost of the ISDN card and an increased rental for the multiple lines the come with the service. The availability of ADSL connections is still very limited and costs will initially be high, but as with all technologies, wider availability and usage should bring costs down.

Software requirements

Modern operating systems include utility programs for some types of WAN communications. The Windows operating system includes Hyperterminal, a program which allows connection to any remote computer to which the user has authorised access and the sending or receiving of files. Before sending or receiving a file, the user must specify whether the file is text or binary (such as an image or program file) and if the latter, the communications protocol to be used; this must be one that is recognised by the remote computer.

A Dialup Networking 'wizard' guides the user through the process of setting up a connection to a WAN such as the Internet. The settings needed to establish a connection with a Service Provider's Internet server include: telephone number, communication device (modem or ISDN adapter), the type of server (e.g. Internet, Windows 2000 etc or Unix), Internet server address and the communication protocol (TCP/IP).

Apart from built-in utilities, there exist a number of application packages that provide more sophisticated communications facilities. These include Web browsers, graphical interface client programs to help users to navigate through the World Wide Web, to transmit and to receive information from other users or information providers. Examples of commercially available browsers are Netscape's *Communicator*, Microsoft's *Explorer.*

There are also communication packages specially designed for communication with FTP (File Transfer Protocol) sites. Internet Service Providers (ISPs) use these sites to allow the remote management of client web sites hosted by them. The site owner uses the FTP package (see chapter on Software Tools) to connect to the ISP's FTP server and is then able to download web pages, modify them and then upload the amendments. The changes to the web site are immediate.

The importance of bandwidth

Digital bandwidth is measured in bits per second and indicates the volume of data which can be transmitted over a communications link in a fixed time. Bandwidth is important because is determines the practicability of using remote communications for modern user applications. High bandwidth is not a crucial consideration for users who wish to exchange the occasional text email, but it is fundamental to the success of businesses with more complex and high volume communication needs. For example, a multi-sited organisation may use its communications links to the Internet for the transmission of complex documents containing high quality images, voice communications and video conferencing. To meet these requirements the organisation would need dedicated, high speed links from each site to a 'backbone' (a major communications link) in the Internet.

Internet Services

Information

It is generally accepted that we live in an "information age", one in which individuals and organisations have increased ease of access to information on a myriad of subjects from all parts of the world. Strictly, to be defined as such, information should be useful to the recipient and it is clear that much is not useful and arrives unsolicited as junk mail and email. The Internet undoubtedly gives access to the largest information source (the World Wide Web or WWW) but it requires considerable skill and patience to filter out the useless from the useful. The WWW uses the Internet for the transmission of hypermedia documents between computer users connected to the Internet. As with the Internet, nobody actually owns the World-Wide Web. People are responsible for the documents they author and make available publicly on the Web. Via the Internet, hundreds of thousands of people around the world are making information available from their homes, schools, colleges and workplaces. The aim of WWW is to make all on-line knowledge part of one interconnected web of documents and services.

Many Web sites contain information which is so specialised as to be only relevant to a small number of users and exist more for the gratification of their creators than anyone else. Fortunately, there are also numerous Web sites dedicated to the provision of high quality information and facilities to make its retrieval more efficient. Clearly, it is not feasible to produce a full classification here but we list below a few important examples.

❑ Government. www.open.gov.uk not only provides documents on government policies, legislation, the work or government departments etc., but also provides access to other public sector organisations, both nationally and at local level. In the Organisation

Index, for example, you will find links to information on or the Web sites of Aberdeen City Council, Air Accidents Investigation Branch, Animal Procedures Committee, Arts Council of England and the United Kingdom Atomic Energy Authority, amongst the thousands of entries. Most Western democratic governments now have Web sites for the provision of public information.

❑ Transport and travel. www.baa.co.uk, which is the Web site of the British Airports Authority provides comprehensive information on British airports and their services, including, for example, complete schedules for flights to or from British airports. www.thetrainline.com provides journey planning facilities, seat reservations and on-line payment.

❑ News. www.bbc.co.uk, the official Web site of BBC is one of the most popular home pages in the UK and provides information on all aspects of its programming, including news, weather, entertainment, sport, games and education.

❑ Academic. As centres of research, universities commonly use their Web sites to publish academic reports and research documents as well as teaching notes, study and support material for their students. www.cam.ac.uk, the Cambridge University Web site provides its own information resources, plus links to others in the UK and around the world (see Figure 31.6).

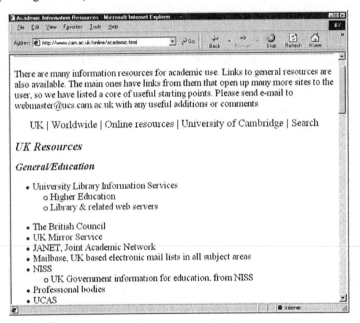

Figure 31.6. *The Cambridge University site with academic links*

❑ Professional bodies. Although the Web sites of many professional bodies are of particular interest to their members, there are some which are also useful to the general public. For example, the British Acupuncture Council and the Society of Homeopaths both provide extremely useful background information for those considering alternative health therapy. The Law Society (www.lawsociety.org.uk) provides information for its members but also gives guidance on choosing a solicitor and Rules of Conduct which govern solicitors.

Education

Computer-based education has been developing over many years and there is a wealth of exciting and useful interactive products, particularly in the area of primary education. The main barrier to placing such materials on the Internet is the limited bandwidth available to most schools and colleges and the development of an Information Super Highway is fundamental to the growth of Internet-based education.

One area in which the Internet is already playing an important role is in the provision of distance learning and the sharing of resources between different learning centres. For example, with video conferencing it is possible for students in a remote area to receive specialist language teaching from a teacher in a major city school or college or for students in separate schools to collaborate on a project. Newgroups and discussion forums also provide a medium for such collaboration.

The BBC and Open University have been at the forefront of distance learning collaboration for many years and continue to develop new an exciting materials for delivery electronically, including over the Internet.

Newsgroups and email

These have been dealt with at the beginning of the chapter.

Banking

Internet banking services are now provided by all the major banks and the facility to manage accounts remotely is one which is appealing to many businesses and individuals. Typically, an on-line banking service allows, for example:

- ❑ on-line application to use the service;
- ❑ open new accounts, including those exclusive to the Internet service;
- ❑ application for loans;
- ❑ share dealing;
- ❑ inter-account transfers;
- ❑ payments to third-party accounts;
- ❑ viewing of balances and statements;
- ❑ ordering of stationery.

If account charges are incurred, these are often less than those for a conventionally operating account. Naturally, the security controls are stringent and, for example, an account transfer or payment must be authorised by entry of the user's password, even though a User-ID and password will already have been entered when first accessing the service. From login to exit all communications between the user's computer and the Bank are carried out via a secure server (see the Chapter on Internet Security).

Buying and selling Goods

Portals

A portal is a web page, normally provided by a free Internet Service Provider, which has become hugely popular as a browser home page. Its popularity stems from its provision of information and resources demanded by the users, such as shopping, travel, news, education and games channels. If an e-business provides products or services which the portal site owners consider will help to make their site 'sticky', that is encourage users to return, then they may include a link to it. The marketing exposure which an e-business receives via a portal is in proportion to the portal site's popularity.

Portal sites are the Web equivalent of shopping complexes or American shopping malls, but with wider ranges of products, information sources etc. Often the home page lists major categories of products and services, such as Autos, Computers, Education, Finance and so on. Many search engines have converted themselves into portals.

For an e-business, the benefits of being found within a portal site are the number of visitors who arrive at the portal and the location of the e-business within a clearly defined category of product or service.

Obtaining a presence in a portal depends on whether a business's particular product or service is adding value to the portal. Some portals will include a business if it allows them to host their Web site. Others will charge by taking a percentage of the income that the business takes in through the site.

Although search engines are important, portals can be an important way for a business to become known, simply because the portals are regularly visited.

Portals with an industry focus

Portals can specialise in one area called an "affinity site". www.propertymall.com is a good example, claiming 15,000 visitors a month. A property firm is more likely to be found by those visitors if located within the portal. Property Mall charges according to the number of visitors the business receives - less than 200 a month and the business pays nothing. The portal will include the company's profile and a link to its Web site. It also offers other services, such as a Jobs, News and Property Finance to attract visitors. Portals become popular by giving added value.

Other affinity sites: www.timberweb.co.uk www.teacouncil.co.uk www.breworld.com

Portals with a geographical focus

www.fish4.co.uk is a good example, but it will not promote any particular sites, simply including a link each one.

✍ Exercises

1. Distinguish between the *Internet* and the *World Wide Web*.
2. (i) What is the purpose of a *browser*?
   (ii) Give two examples of the use of *hyperlinks*.
   (iii) Distinguish between *hypertext* and *hypermedia*.
   (iv) What does *HTML* stand for and what is its purpose?
3. Give a well-known example of a *URL* (Uniform Resource Locator).
4. What is the purpose of a *search engine*? Name three.
5. Define the terms *Intranet* and *Extranet* and suggest applications of each for an organisation.

Unit 5 Assignments

5.1. Data communications

This assignment requires reference to the Pilcon Polymer Case Study, given below.

Pilcon Polymers

Pilcon Polymers is a manufacturer of plastic containers of all kinds. Its Head Office, factory and main warehouse are in Peterlee, County Durham, but it also has distribution warehouses in Leeds, Birmingham, Milan and Cologne. The company also has regional office and wholesale outlet facilities in Glasgow, Leeds, Belfast, Swansea and Birmingham. Across the whole organisation, Pilcon employ 450 people, of whom 350 are in administrative, marketing, sales or clerical roles. The manufacturing processes are highly automated, so the factory only employs 50 people, whose main tasks relate to machine minding and maintenance. 25 staff are employed in warehouse operations and the remaining 25 research, design and develop new products. The UK centres each have a regional manager, who is responsible for the marketing, wholesale and distribution operations in his or her region. The Milan and Cologne centres have a warehouse and distribution manager who responds to instructions from Head Office in Peterlee. Physical stock control operations need to be carried out in the Milan and Cologne warehouses, but the records of stocks held of the continental warehouse stocks issues and receipts are all held by Head Office. Marketing and sales operations are all carried out from the UK, so the Milan and Cologne centres do not employ staff in these roles. Payroll and personnel management are functions handled by the Peterlee Head Office. The main functions carried out in Peterlee are:

research and development (R&D); *product design and manufacture*; *product testing* and *quality control*; *sales* and *marketing*; *personnel*; *payroll*; *financial accounting* (sales, purchasing and so on); *stock control*; *sales order processing*.

The UK centres also take regional responsibility for these functions, except for R&D, product design and manufacture, product testing and quality control. Management information produced by these regional functions is regularly transmitted to Head Office, to allow assessment of regional efficiency and profitability, as well as a corporate view of performance to be obtained. Each month, the warehouses in Milan and Cologne need to transmit their orders to replenish stocks; these orders may involve several hundred different stock items. Goods are transported by rail and road. There may also be a need for an emergency order to be transmitted (the goods can then be flown out). Peterlee also wish to send information to Milan and Cologne, but the communications do not need be interactive (both ways at the same time). Local area networks are installed in all the United Kingdom offices and are linked across communications networks.

The following Tasks concern the investigation of various aspects of data communications and networks, in the context of the case study. Present the information you gather, in the process of the following activities, in a word processed report.

Tasks

1. Use a suitable package to draw a block diagram showing the various data communications and network links between the regional and continental centres of the business. Include the title 'Pilcon Polymers – Communications' and a company logo of your own design.

2. Describe *simplex*, *half duplex* and *duplex* modes of communication and explain which modes are appropriate for the circumstances outlined in the case study.

3. State, with reasons, whether serial or parallel communications would be employed between the offices and warehouses of Pilcon Polymers.

4. Synchronous and asynchronous communications are also used in data communications systems. Explain the difference between these two forms and, by reference to the various needs of Pilcon Polymers, argue when each might be most appropriate.

5. Annotate the diagram prepared in Task 1, to illustrate your explanation of these technical terms. You should use vector drawing tools. Embed the image as an object within the report document.

6. The criteria of transmission speed and data integrity (uncorrupted - without error) are vital to the usefulness of data communications. With reference to Pilcon and using example circumstances, explain why this is so. Also explain the role of modems and protocol parameters (flow control, stop bits, parity and other error checking techniques) in achieving speed and integrity.

7. Apart from data transfer, Pilcon want to make use of various network services. These include: electronic mail; video and teleconferencing; file transfer; bulletin board services (BBSs); databases, electronic data interchange (EDI); integrated services digital network (ISDN). Briefly explain the function of each of these services. Identify those services, which you judge could be of use to Pilcon Polymers, and develop your explanations with example applications.

5.2. Networks and applications

Tasks

1. Use *vector* graphics drawing tools and bit map *clip art*, to produce a simple guide to network topologies. The guide should include text to annotate the graphics. The final product should fold into a multi-page, A5, booklet (short edge across the top) and include a title page.

2. This Task requires a team approach to research and report on computer networks. It also requires the *merging* of separate document files of a consistent format and the use of *presentational graphics* software to summarise main points in your investigation. A team could have four members, one being the team leader responsible for the co-ordination and integration of the work of individual team members. The terms of reference for the investigation are:

    types of networks, with examples. Also describe the features of each and organisational types for which they are appropriate;

    network *components* and *topologies*, together with examples of network products, their topologies and the *protocols* they support; network and PC magazines are a good source;

    benefits of the various types of network and the applications each has for particular organisations.

    The team could focus on a particular organisational type, such as an airline, a bank, DIY store, or college and highlight the important role of the Internet and the services which provide such benefit for many organisations.

    The assignment should provide opportunities for practising a variety of research methods and sources, team discussions and the development of team building qualities.

Unit 6: Systems analysis and design

Assessment Evidence Grid

Grade E	Grade C	Grade A
Summarise the stages of the systems life cycle and identify some of the methods used for systems analysis.	Show a detailed knowledge of the stages of the system life cycle and of the methods used to undertake a systems investigation.	Evaluate your systems investigation, describing what went well and what went less well, and suggesting how you investigative methods could have been improved.
Write an outline problem definition for a specified problem.	Record in detail the information gathered from the systems investigation using appropriate documents and techniques. Include a detailed problem definition.	Give details of alternate solutions to the problem and justify your selection of a solution including analysis of its organisational impact.
Undertake the systems analysis of a specified problem using an appropriate technique (such as interview, observation or questionnaire).	Provide full and detailed documentation in support of your proposed solution to the specified problem, including a cost benefit analysis.	Use appropriate technical language clearly and correctly as part of coherent narratives. Include suitable graphical images to enhance your written work.
Record the findings of the analysis in a logical way.	Produce a full and detailed test plan for testing the designed system. The test plan will contain predicted and actual results, and will cover all pathways and normal and extreme data.	Produce a design which is based on a formal structured methodology but also makes effective use of less formal illustrations to ensure that design features are communicated unambiguously and clearly to users.
Design an outline solution to a specified problem.		
Produce a test plan for the inputs to completed system design.		

Chapter 32

Systems development: basic concepts

Information systems

To properly understand the processes involved in the development of an information system, it is important to be clear about what is meant by the term 'system' and then more specifically, 'information system'. A system can be defined as "an organised body of interrelated parts" and we can see examples of systems all around us. In the natural world, there are galaxies, solar systems, plants, animals and of course, the human body. The word 'organised' in the definition is important in that it emphasises the need for all the parts to work effectively together. Man-made systems include, for example, forms of government, social systems, such as family, clubs and societies, manufacturing systems for clothing and car production, and information systems to handle payroll, stock control or order processing. In this Unit, we are concerned with the development of information systems which are essential to the functioning of business organisations. In the case of computerised information systems, the "interrelated parts" which make up an information system include:

1. people. Above all, information systems are about people, the users and the specialists, such as systems analysts and designers and programmers who are concerned with creating and maintaining systems. Users include corporate managers and staff at all levels of the organisation, although individual involvement may be direct or indirect and vary in degree. For example, a warehouse manager uses information from the stock control system, but it is operational staff who enter data and produce summary stock reports. Sometimes, 'users' include customers and suppliers, or other external agencies.

2. technology - hardware and software needed for the automated aspects of the system.

3. clerical and administrative procedures. Although a computerised system automates many processes, users need to be trained to use it properly and to follow procedures which optimise its effectiveness. Typically, there are procedures for:

    (i) data entry, perhaps involving the completion of data input forms, or the initial entry of transactions onto magnetic disk;

    (ii) dealing with system messages or error reports. Users must be able to respond correctly if errors or delays in processing are to be avoided.

    (iii) preventing data loss or disclosure of confidential information. For example, if user passwords are not properly protected and changed regularly, unauthorised access may allow accidental or malicious damage to the system. Similarly, failure to adopt the set backup procedures may result in significant loss of data and in some circumstances, failure of the business.

    (iv) dealing with system outputs. Report summaries and other outputs need to be distributed promptly (much business information becomes worthless if it is out-of-date). Similarly, for example, a system which produces a summary of overdue invoices will not be effective if no one uses it to chase customers for payment.

Systems analysis and design

As is explained later, although the term "systems analysis and design" is commonly used to refer to the whole development process, it really identifies just two stages within the process.

In business, systems analysis and design is the process of investigating an information system, existing or new, with a view to determining how best to manage the various procedures and information processing tasks that it involves. Though it frequently means considering the use of a computer system to replace some manual operations, this need not always be the case. The *systems analyst*, whose job it is to perform the investigation, might recommend the use of a computer to improve the efficiency of the information system under consideration, but he/she might equally well decide that a manual system is adequate, or even preferable. Thus, the intention in systems analysis is to determine how well a business copes with its current information processing needs, and whether it is possible to improve the procedures involved in order to make it more efficient, or more profitable, or both. Systems design involves planning the structure of the information system to be implemented. In summary,

❑ analysis determines what the system should do and

❑ design determines how it should be done.

System life cycle

This Unit is concerned with the development, testing and maintenance of business information systems, such as those described in Unit 3. The entire process, from the birth of the idea for a new or modified system to its installation, use and continued maintenance, is referred to as the *system life cycle*, one version of which is illustrated in Figure 32.1.

It is the stages shown in this version which we will follow in this Unit. If you research several books on the subject, you will find different versions which broadly cover the same stages but include more or less detail. Figure 32.2 shows an alternative and less detailed version of the traditional system development life cycle.

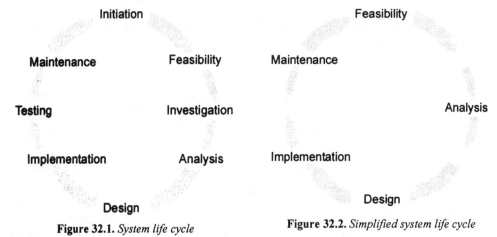

Figure 32.1. *System life cycle*

Figure 32.2. *Simplified system life cycle*

Structured systems analysis

Information systems have developed in ways which make their modification, as user requirements change, as straightforward as possible. Structured systems analysis methods became popular in the late 1970s as a response to difficulties with information systems which proved to be inflexible and very difficult to modify. Structured methods focus on data rather than processes because although the processing requirements of users change frequently, the underlying data structures tend to change little. This can be best illustrated by two examples.

1. A sales system reads the customer file, which has this structure, to address invoices.

Name	Address	Credit limit

The business extends its range of products and wishes to target its advertising mailshots more effectively using demographic data (social/income groups). This requires use of the post code and separate lines of the address which at present are combined in a single field. A structured approach would have focused on the data and identified the separate elements of the address, instead of the requirements of a single application for invoice addressing.

2. A business keeps records of external training courses which may be helpful to staff, who can attend them on a voluntary basis. Following a review of staff development policy, the business decides to link salaries and promotion to which staff are formally trained and educated. This requires a link, which does not exist at present, between the personnel system and the records of training courses.

A structured approach would have identified a potential relationship between Courses and Staff Training records and allowed for a link between the two systems. In a relational database, this link would be achieved by a common field or fields in each of the Course and Staff Training tables. This is illustrated in Figure 32.3. The process of identifying relationships between data is known as *entity-relationship modelling* (see Chapter 36).

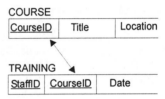

Figure 32.3. *Establishing a relationship*

Systems development methodologies

Systems development involves the use of various specialists, most importantly, systems analysts and systems designers (the roles are sometimes combined). In more recent years these specialists have usually undergone formal training in the use of one or more *methodologies* which are designed to improve the efficiency of the system development process and the quality of information systems. (The quality of an information system can be measured in a variety of ways, for example, it may reduce staffing costs, or it may improve the quality of its service, or it may simply be more pleasant for people to use.)

Most methodologies provide for a *structured* approach and the name of one methodology reflects this - SSADM (Structured Systems Analysis and Design Method). In this book, the examples used to illustrate various stages of system development are based on SSADM tools and techniques. SSADM covers all stages of the system life cycle shown in Figure 32.2, apart from Implementation.

✍ Exercises

See end of Chapter 34.

Chapter 33

The Feasibility Study

Although it is not always essential to carry out a feasibility study, if it is not absolutely clear that the proposed system is going to be worthwhile and cost-effective, then it is extremely desirable. A feasibility study involves many aspects of systems analysis, but on a smaller scale. Before embarking on a development project, a business should be clear as to how it will contribute to business objectives (increased profitability, improved efficiency, better customer service etc) and if several system developments are proposed, their order of priority. The feasibility study should attempt to provide answers to the following questions.

1. How much will the new system cost?
2. What are its objectives? (see below)
3. When would it be completed?
4. How will it be developed? (Staffing implications, methodology, etc).

The structured analysis techniques used in the full analysis and design stages can also be used during the feasibility study. On completion of a feasibility study, the client (which may be the employer if development is 'in-house') should be presented with a Feasibility Report (see later in this chapter).

Meeting business objectives

It is important for a business to be clear about its overall objectives and how the proposed system(s) will contribute to their achievement. For example, two major business objectives may be to improve the delivery of customers' orders and to minimise the stock levels which tie up valuable cash resources. The achievement of these objectives may involve contributions from several different information systems and the list may include the following.

- ❑ Stock Control - records stock movements and controls stock levels.
- ❑ Purchasing - responsible for the ordering of new supplies from suppliers.
- ❑ Sales Order Processing - receives customers' orders and initiates the process of order fulfilment.
- ❑ Purchase Ledger - the accounting record of amounts owed and paid to suppliers of stock.
- ❑ Invoicing - the production of invoices requesting payment from customers for goods supplied.
- ❑ Sales Ledger - the accounting record of amounts owing by and received from customers for goods supplied.

Development priorities

It is not generally advisable or even practicable to attempt the development of more than one or two applications at the same time, even if they are closely linked. In any case, it is likely that some applications make a greater contribution to the achievement of the required business objectives than do others. Thus, the applications which are going to bring greatest benefit to the business should be developed first.

Individual system objectives

Before any single application can be computerised, it is necessary to establish its objectives clearly because users may have become so used to its procedures that they no longer question their purpose. It is self-evident that before any informed judgements can be made on the design of a computerised system, the objectives of the relevant application must first be clearly understood. The following list for stock control serves to illustrate the definition of such objectives.

☐ To maintain levels of stock which will be sufficient to meet customer orders promptly.

☐ To provide a mechanism which removes the need for excessive safety margins of stock to cover customer orders. This is usually effected by setting minimum stock levels which the computer can use to report variations below these levels.

☐ To provide automatic re-ordering of stock items which fall below minimum levels.

☐ To provide management with up-to-date information on stock levels and values of stocks held.

The Feasibility Report

The feasibility report should include the following sections.

Terms of reference

These are statements of the purpose of the proposed system, as agreed by management and detail the business objectives to be achieved, for example:

☐ the improvement of customer service, such that orders are delivered within 24 hours of order receipt;

☐ the provision of more up-to-date management information on current stock levels and projected customer demand;

☐ a tighter control of the business's cash resources, primarily through better stock management.

Applications considered for computerisation

The applications which may assist the achievement of the business objectives set out in the Terms of Reference are listed, for example: stock control; purchasing; sales order processing; invoicing; accounts. The scope of the system should be clearly stated so that the boundaries of the investigation are clearly marked.

System investigations

For each application under consideration there should be:

☐ a description of the existing system;

☐ an assessment of its good and bad points. For example, the sales order processing system may be slow to process customer orders and this results in poor delivery times, which in turn causes customers to take away their business;

☐ an estimate of the costs of the existing system. For example, apart from the cost of staffing, an estimate has to be made of the cost of lost business, which could be avoided with an improved system.

Statement of user requirements

This section should detail, in general terms, those aspects of each application which need to be improved and a broad outline of how each system may operate following development. Of course, it is still possible that not all applications will benefit from computerisation but can be improved by other methods.

Costs of development and implementation

These will include both capital costs and revenue or running costs. Capital costs are likely to be incurred for the following:

- ❑ computer hardware;
- ❑ systems software and software packages (either 'off-the-shelf' or 'tailor-made');
- ❑ installation charges for hardware and software;
- ❑ staff training.

Revenue costs include those for the maintenance and insurance of the system. In addition, unless there are existing computer specialists in the organisation, additional suitable staff may need to be recruited.

Timescale for implementation

This will depend on the scale of the operation, the type of application and whether or not packaged software is to be used.

Expected benefits

These are more difficult to quantify than the costs but may include, for example:

- ❑ estimated savings in capital expenditure on photocopiers or office space.
- ❑ more efficient stock management allows customer service to be maintained whilst keeping stock levels lower. This releases valuable cash resources and reduces possible interest charges on borrowed capital;
- ❑ expansion in business turnover, without the need for extra staff and reduced overtime requirements.

Other considerations

The staff have to support any development for it to be properly successful and this usually means consultation at an early stage in the feasibility study and the provision of a proper staff training programme. Customers must also be considered. For example, when a customer receives a computer-produced invoice it should be at least as easy to understand as the type it replaced. Assuming that the feasibility study concludes that the proposed computerisation is worthwhile, according to the criteria set out in the report, then more detailed investigation and design can follow.

 Exercises

See end of Chapter 34.

System life cycle: an overview

In this chapter, we provide an overview of the stages within the system life cycle introduced in Chapter 32. Though the steps in the system life cycle may appear separate and in strict order, in practice they may be performed in a different order, or even be difficult to distinguish one from another; sometimes one part of the system will be in the process of being implemented while another is still being analysed.

The system development stages illustrated in the diagram may be repeated a number of times during the life of a system. Each time a significant change or improvement is required, the cycle is repeated.

Initiating a development project

The initiation of a project to introduce a new information system, or modifying an existing one, can be part of a:

❑ *planned strategy* towards the improvement of a business's performance, competitiveness, profitability and so on. (Business strategy is part of corporate management's role, although ideas for change may also come from lower down the decision-making pyramid. With a planning strategy, the business will continually review its information systems and attempt to seek improvement. This does not mean that every change can be immediately undertaken; there may be many reasons for delaying or shelving a project, for example, excessive cost, consequent disruption to normal business or shortage of the necessary staff skills to make best use of the system. In the latter case, for example, a graphic design company may wish to take advantage of the sophisticated features provided by new design software, but the design staff may require extensive and costly training to make use of it.

❑ an *unplanned approach*. Although a planned, strategical approach is desirable, developments are sometimes initiated on a piecemeal basis, perhaps in response to extreme overload on existing procedures. For example, a business may key in customer orders and unless more staff are employed, customers will have to wait longer before receiving their goods. An improved system may well avoid this and the need for extra staff, but making changes under pressure will make success less likely than would be the case with a planned strategy.

Here are some examples of business pressures which may initiate new system development:

(i) A business is expanding and to cope with the increased workload it appears that the only the alternative to computerisation is increased staffing.

(ii) A business is growing at such a rate that more information is needed to manage it properly. To obtain the information manually is too time-consuming and by the time it has been gathered is probably out-of-date.

(iii) Staff are being asked to work regular and increasing amounts of overtime and back-logs of work are building up.

(iv) Customers are complaining about the speed and quality of the service provided.

(v)   Where stock is involved, it is difficult to keep track of stock levels and while some customer orders cannot be filled because of stock shortages, other stock is 'gathering dust' on the shelves.

(vi)   A great deal of advertising literature is constantly reminding business management that they are out-of-date and at a disadvantage with their competitors.

(vii)   Other businesses which provide a similar service use an improved system.

Examples (i), (ii) and (iii) suggest that the business is operating successfully and needs to take on extra staff or streamline its systems. Examples (iv) and (v) may be symptomatic of generally poor business management and in such cases, system changes alone may not solve the problems. Examples (vi) and (vii) may tempt the management to computerise simply 'to keep up with the Jones's'. Although a system development programme which results directly from one or more such pressures may be completely successful and worthwhile, the pressure itself should not be the reason for change. Instead, management should establish the organisational objectives they wish to achieve through the envisaged system development.

Feasibility study

Before an organisation embarks on a costly project involving the development of a new information system, it is necessary to determine whether the system is possible to achieve and, if so, whether there will be sufficient benefits in doing so. The main part of this investigation is called a *feasibility study*. However, even before the feasibility study commences, it will be necessary to fully clarify what is being proposed. The systems analyst dealing with the proposal will talk with the people who have initiated the project in order to determine exactly what they have in mind and their reasons.

Once the proposal has been fully clarified, the feasibility study can be undertaken. The feasibility study is usually carried out by a team of people with experience in information systems techniques, with a knowledge of the type of system being proposed and who are skilled in systems analysis and design. The team will be responsible for determining whether the potential benefits of the proposed system can justify the costs involved in developing it. It may be that the consequences of not adopting the new system make the change essential. For example, if a company is unable, through volume of work, to deal with customers effectively, the latter may take their business to more efficient competitors. It then becomes essential to the company's survival to improve its information system.

The feasibility study must also establish whether the new system can operate with available technology, software and personnel. In most instances, for example where a currently manual system is to be replaced or improved by using a computer system, the existing technology will most probably exist, but a new, innovative idea might require hardware or software that don't exist. If this is the case, the feasibility study team will attempt to determine whether the new items can be developed within a reasonable time.

The feasibility study should, as a minimum, be able to answer the following questions:

(i)   How much is the new system likely to cost?

(ii)   What is the new system expected to achieve?

(iii)   How will the new system be produced? (In terms, for example, of staff and equipment resources and the processes to achieve its completion.)

(iv)   How long will the project take?

The study should also consider how well the system will be received by the people who will have to use it. This must have been a prime concern, for instance, of the first analysts who considered the use of cash points such as those now commonly provided by banks and building societies: would customers trust them and would they be sufficiently easy to use?

The feasibility study should be documented in a Feasibility Report, which is examined in more detail in Chapter 33.

Investigation and analysis

If the feasibility study produces a favourable report, the next stage, that of making a detailed analysis of the current system (if it exists), will commence. The systems analyst will investigate, collect and document information on all aspects of the current system:

- ❏ what services are being offered;
- ❏ what tasks are being performed;
- ❏ how they are being performed;
- ❏ how frequently they are done;
- ❏ how well they are done;
- ❏ what staff are involved and the nature of their involvement
- ❏ what is lacking in the system;
- ❏ any faults with the system;
- ❏ how the system can be improved.

Every requirement for the new system and every pitfall to be avoided or shortcoming remedied needs to be documented.

Finding the answers to these questions requires the analyst to talk to all the people involved in operating the current system, from ordinary employees to managers and directors. This will frequently involve the use of questionnaires as well as personal interviews with employees, the study of manuals and reports, the observation of current working practices, and the collection and study of forms and other documents currently used. As this process is going on, the analyst will be starting to form views on how the new system should work in order to overcome the problems with the current system. In SSADM terminology, the analysis is referred to as Requirements Analysis

Requirements specification

On completion of the analysis stage, the gathered information can be used to draw up a proposal which clearly presents what the new or modified system is meant to do and achieve. In SSADM terminology, this proposal document is known as a Requirements Specification.

Detailed design considerations should be left until the Design stage but some design aspects, such as the need for bar code scanning for an EPOS (electronic point of sale) system, may be obvious and can be taken for granted. Some parts of the design may be constrained by the need for compatibility with existing hardware and software. Otherwise, creating a precise design at this stage is unwise because as the development proceeds new design possibilities or unforeseen 'glitches' are almost certain to arise.

Although the systems analyst is responsible for drawing up the Requirements Specification, he or she needs to ensure that users are closely involved in its development. The systems analyst should listen carefully to users and ensure that their comments and suggestions have been properly interpreted before incorporating the information into the specification.

Design

This stage produces the details of how the system will meet the requirements identified in the previous analysis stage. A major part of this stage involves identifying the inputs to the system (what they are and how they are to be captured), and the outputs from the system, such as reports, invoices, bills and statements. The designers will also specify in detail what files will be needed, their structures and what devices and media will be used to store them. All this information will be written down in the form of reports, tables and diagrams. Such diagrams as system flow charts and data flow diagrams will be used to show how the overall system is integrated. The system designers will also provide detailed specifications on what the software is required to do so that programmers in the next stage will have a clear idea of what they are expected to produce.

Implementation

In this stage the system designers will actually install the new system, putting new equipment into operation, installing and setting up software, creating data files and training people to use the system. A common practice is to run the new system in parallel with the old one to ensure that if anything does go wrong, the business will not come to a grinding halt.

Maintenance

When a system has become fully operational, there will still be the possibility of unforeseen events causing problems. Feedback from users on general usability, shortcomings and error conditions, the latter being recorded in a fault log detailing date, time and nature of error. The system developers will therefore need to be available to deal with any problems that do arise, as well as making modifications as circumstances change. If an outside firm has developed the system, this *system maintenance,* normally will be subject to a separate financial arrangement such as an annual charge.

During maintenance some parts of the system may be temporarily unavailable and the organisation must have contingency plans if it is to continue to function effectively. For hardware maintenance the organisation should either maintain a backup system or if this is too costly have leasing arrangements for temporary hardware replacement. With the latter option, the hardware will have to be configured and software installed before maintenance on the main system begins. Software maintenance should be carried out on a duplicate system to prevent interference with the live applications. If possible, installation of the newly modified software should take place outside of working hours, and if changes are significant, a suitable change-over method needs to be adopted. A period of diagnostic testing and monitoring can then follow to ensure that the maintenance changes are working properly.

✍ Exercises

These questions also relate to Chapters 32 and 33.

Using suitable examples, explain the importance of the main parts which form an information system.

2. With the use of a suitable example, briefly explain what is meant by *structured systems analysis*.

3. What does SSADM stand for?

4. Briefly describe each of the following stages in the System Life Cycle:
   ☐ Project initiation
   ☐ Feasibility study
   ☐ Investigation and analysis
   ☐ Requirements specification
   ☐ System design
   ☐ Implementation
   ☐ Maintenance

5. Suggest four possible reasons for a company undertaking computerisation of one or more of its systems.

6. Using stock control as an example, list possible objectives for computerisation.

7. List the main sections that might be included in a feasibility report.

Chapter 35

Fact-finding methods

Although information is being gathered throughout the life of a development project, even through to the maintenance stage, when users are asked for feedback on system performance, most fact-finding takes place during the analysis stage. Clearly, unless full information on system requirements is gathered during analysis, then there is little prospect of designing a system which properly meets users' needs. There are several methods which can be used to gather facts about a system: (i) interviewing; (ii) questionnaires; (iii) examination of records and procedure manuals; (iv) examination of documents; (v) observation.

Each method has its own particular advantages and disadvantages and the method or methods chosen will depend on the specific circumstances surrounding the investigation, for example, the size of the business, the number of staff employed and their location and distribution.

Interviewing

This method has much to recommend it, in that the facts can be gathered directly from the person or persons who have experience of the system under investigation. On the other hand, a business with a number of geographically distributed branches makes the process of extensive interviewing expensive and time-consuming. Further, interviewing skills need to be acquired if the process is to be effective. The interviewer needs to know how to gain the confidence of the interviewee and ensure that the information which is given will be of value in the design of the new system. Questions need to be phrased unambiguously in order that the interviewee supplies the information actually required and a checklist of points will help to ensure that all relevant questions are asked. Of course, the interview may need to stray from the points in the checklist, if it becomes apparent that the interviewee is able to provide relevant information not previously considered. For example, clerical procedures may be designed quite satisfactorily but may be made less effective because of personality conflicts between staff. Such tensions may only be revealed through personal interview. The interviewer also needs to detect any unsatisfactory responses to questions and possibly use alternative methods to glean the required information. Unsatisfactory responses include:

❑ Refusal to answer. Such refusal may indicate, for example, that set procedures are not being followed and that the member of staff does not wish to be 'incriminated'.

❑ Answer with irrelevant information. It may be that the question is ambiguous and has to be re-phrased in order to elicit the required information.

❑ Answer with insufficient information. If a system is to be designed which covers all foreseeable user requirements and operational circumstances, it is important that the analyst has all relevant information.

❑ Inaccurate answer. The interviewer may or may not be aware that an inaccurate answer has been given but it is important that other sources of information are used to cross-check answers.

A formal record of each interview should be kept, detailing time, location, those in attendance and their roles in the business. Specific details of procedures, for example, on the handling of order forms by a sales clerk need to be recorded. It may also be helpful to relate the role of each interviewee to an organisation chart, which you may need to amend in the light of responses to your questions.

Questionnaires

Questionnaires are useful when only a small amount of information is required from a large number of people, but to provide accurate responses, questions need to be unambiguous and precise. The questionnaire has a number of advantages over the interview:

- ❑ each respondent is asked exactly the same questions, so responses can be analysed according to the pre-defined categories of information;

- ❑ the lack of personal contact allows the respondent to feel completely at ease when providing information, particularly if responses are to be anonymous;

- ❑ questionnaires are particularly suited to the gathering of factual information. for example, the number of customer orders received in one week;

- ❑ it is cheap, particularly if users are scattered over a wide geographical area.

A number of disadvantages attach to the use of questionnaires:

- ❑ questions have to be simple and their meaning completely unambiguous to the respondents;

- ❑ if the responses indicate that the wrong questions were asked, or that they were phrased badly, it may be difficult to clarify the information, particularly if the respondents were anonymous;

- ❑ without direct observation it is difficult to obtain a realistic view of a system's operation. The questionnaire often provides only statistical information on, for example, volumes of sales transactions or customer enquiries.

More detail on the design of questionnaires is provided in Unit 1.

Examination of records and procedure manuals

If existing procedures are already well documented, then the procedure manuals can provide a ready-made source of information on the way procedures should be carried out. It is less likely, however, that procedures will be documented in the smaller organisation. In any event, it is important to realise that procedures detailed in manuals may not accord entirely with what actually happens. The examination of current records and the tracing of particular transactions can be a useful method of discovering what procedures are carried out.

Special purpose records which may involve, for example, the ticking of a box when an activity has been completed, can be used to analyse procedures which are causing delays or are not functioning efficiently. The use of special purpose records imposes extra burdens on staff who have to record procedures as they happen and the technique should only be used when strictly necessary.

Examination of documents

It is important that the analyst examines all documents used in a system, to ensure that each:

- ❑ fulfils some purpose, that is, it records or transmits information which is actually used at some stage. Systems are subject to some inertia, for example, there may have been a 'one-off' requirement to record and analyse the geographical distribution of customers over a single month and yet the summary document is still completed because no-one told the staff it was no longer necessary;

❏ is clear and satisfies its purpose, for example, a form may not indicate clearly the type of data to be entered under each heading. In any case, it may well require re-designing for any new system which is introduced.

The documents, which should include, for example, source documents, report summaries, customer invoices and delivery notes, help to build a picture of the information flows which take place from input to output.

Document analysis form

This form is used to record information about the various documents, such as order forms, summary reports and invoices, which have been examined during systems analysis. Document analysis, in combination with other information gathering techniques, is an important way of discovering how an existing system operates.

The NCC (National Computing Centre) has produced a standard form for document analysis, called the Clerical Document Specification, although you can design your own to suit the particular system under investigation. A slightly modified version of the NCC document analysis form is shown in Figure 35.1. The bold headings are part of the blank standard recording form and the italicised text identifies the completed entries. The entries of such forms are likely to be handwritten unless the forms are stored as templates on computer.

The example in Figure 35.1 shows recorded details for an invoice which is clearly used in an existing computerised system. Most of the entries are self explanatory, although the Value Range column may require some clarification. The Picture definition, using 9 to represent a digit and A to represent an alphabetic character comes from the COBOL programming language which uses Picture to define field types. If the value range is mixed (alphanumeric characters), then X is used, for example X(25) represents a field with a maximum of 25 alphanumeric characters. This format is not used in the example, blank entries making it implicit that it is a mixed character field.

Observation

It is most important to observe a procedure in action, so that irregularities and exceptional procedures are noticed. Observation should always be carried out with tact and staff under observation should be made fully aware of its purpose, to avoid suspicions of 'snooping'.

The following checklist identifies some of the features of office procedures and conditions which may usefully be observed during an investigation:

❏ office layout - this may determine whether the positioning of desks, filing cabinets and other office equipment is convenient for staff and conducive to efficient working;

❏ work load - this should indicate whether the volume of documents awaiting processing is fairly constant or if there are peak periods of activity;

❏ delays - these could show that there are some procedures which are constantly behind schedule;

❏ methods of working - a trained observer can, through experience, recognize a slow, reasonable or quick pace of working and decide whether or not the method of working is efficient. It is important that such observations should be followed up by an interview to obtain the co-operation of the person under observation;

❏ office conditions - these should be examined, as poor ventilation, inadequate or excessive temperatures, or poor lighting can adversely affect staff efficiency.

Often the observation will be carried out in an informal way but it may be useful on occasion to, for example, work at a user's desk, so as to observe directly the way that customer orders are dealt with. It is important to realise that a user may 'put on a performance' whilst under observation and that this reduces the value of the information gathered.

Document description		System	Name	Sheet
Invoice		Sales	INV	1
Stationery ref:	**Size**	**Number of copies**		**Method of preparation**
bcp04	A4	2		Computer printed
Filing seq	**Medium**	**Prepared / maintained by**		
Order Ref	Ring binder	Head Office		
Frequency of preparation		**Retention period**		**Location**
As orders occur		6 years		Accounts manager
Volume(s)	**Minimum**	**Maximum**	**Av/Abs**	**Growth rate/fluctuations**
(weekly)	15	80	35	10% growth per annum
Users/ recipients	**Purpose**			**Frequency of use**
Customers Accounts manager	To record debt of customer (1 copy) To request payment (1 copy)			Daily
Ref	**Item**	**Picture**	**Value range**	**Source of data**
1	Customer name	X(25)		Customer file
2	Invoice address	X(75)		Customer file
3	Order Ref	9(5)	00001 to 99999	Automatic counter
4	Cust Order No	X(12)		Customer order
5	Order received	99/99/99	Date rec'd	Accounts clerk
6	Order despatched	99/99/99	Date despatched	Accounts clerk
7	Item Code	A999	(A, B or C) 001 to 005	Product file
8	Description	X(20)		Product file
9	Quantity	999	1 to 999	Customer order
10	Unit Price	£99.99	£10 to £80	Product file
11	Order value	£9(6).99		Computer calculated
12	VAT	£9(5).99		Computer calculated
13	Total inc VAT	£9(7).99		Computer calculated
Author	**Notes**			
PRS **Date** 13/02/02	2 copies of the invoice are generated immediately following entry of a customer order, together with a Delivery Note (Stationery ref:bcp02). The Order Ref is generated by a counter field, which is also the primary key field for the Order table.			

Figure 35.1. *Example of a completed document analysis form*

Chapter 36

Recording analysis information

Systems analysts can make use of a number of techniques to record and illustrate the way systems operate, generally in a logical rather than physical way. This chapter introduces diagramming techniques for recording data flows, entity-relationship modelling and the use of data dictionaries and CASE tools in the analysis process.

Diagrams and illustrations produced at the analysis stage will form part of the Requirements Specification, a proposal document which sets out what a new system should do and achieve. At the design stage, the systems designers will usually adapt those diagrams and produce new ones to create the detailed design of the new system. You will be shown examples of the use of these tools and techniques in the Design Tutorial in Chapter 38.

Document flow diagram

Document flow diagrams may be used in the early stages of analysis before the more detailed work required for data flow diagrams is started. Document flow diagrams illustrate the movement of documents connected with the system under analysis.

To help you understand the diagrams which appear in the following sections, 'rich picture' representation of the operations in a typical trading business is provided in Figure 36.1, on the next page.

Before drawing such a diagram, or a formal document flow diagram, it is useful preparation to create a table which details all data movements, the sender and recipient of each and the document used.

Table 36.1 lists the document flows associated with stock purchases and customer sales, illustrated in Figures 36.1 and 36.2.

Source	Document	Recipient
Customer	Order form	Sales clerk
Sales clerk	Delivery note	Goods despatch supervisor
Goods despatch supervisor	Delivery note (+ goods)	Customer
Goods despatch supervisor	Stock issued note	Stock clerk
Sales clerk	Copy customer order	Accounts receivable clerk
Accounts receivable clerk	Sales invoice	Customer
Goods requisition clerk	Requisition	Purchase order clerk
Purchase order clerk	Purchase order	Supplier
Supplier	Delivery note (+ goods)	Goods in clerk
Purchase order clerk	Copy purchase order	Accounts payable clerk
Supplier	Invoice	Accounts payable clerk

Table 36.1. *Document flows for stock, sales and purchasing*

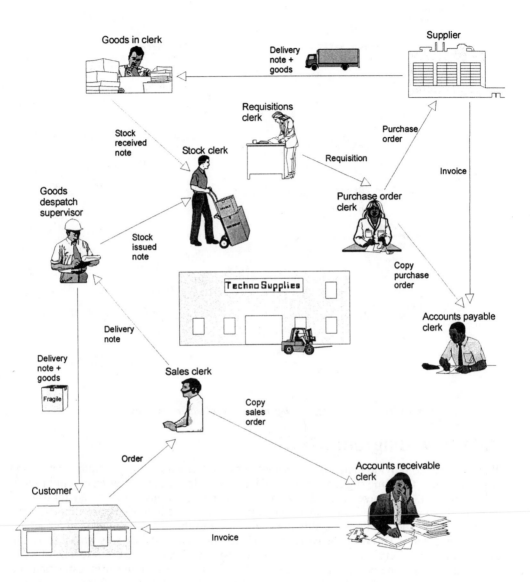

Figure 36.1. *'Rich picture' representation of operations in a typical trading business*

Figure 36.2 shows the document flow diagram. In contrast to the data flow diagrams described later, the only symbols used in document flow diagrams are the ellipse and the data flow arrow. The processes detailed in data flow diagrams are not included.

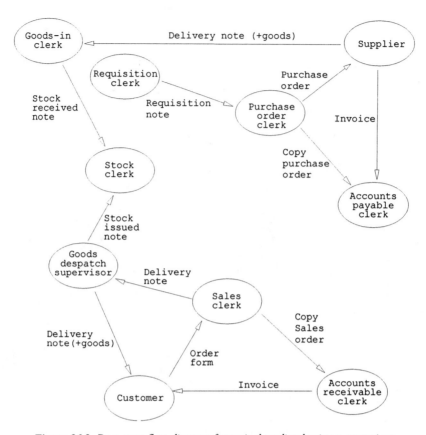

Figure 36.2. *Document flow diagram for typical trading business operations*

Data flow diagram (DFD)

DFDs are used to provide pictorial representations of information systems, both existing and proposed, and as the name suggests show the data flows within an organisation or within a limited section of it. They have the advantage over written descriptions of being easy for users to understand and provide analysts with a generally recognised method of documenting systems. However, written descriptions are still an essential part of the analysis and design processes. The level of detail in DFDs can be varied to produce a *hierarchy* of diagrams which, at the top level, give a broad overview, perhaps of the whole business. One or more lower level DFDs can then be used to provide progressively greater detail about the system under investigation and development, such as Sales Order Processing or Personnel. As will be seen from the examples in the Design Tutorial in Chapter 38, DFDs can be used to represent both 'physical' and 'logical' views of systems.

DFDs can be used at various stages in the analysis and design process. In the early stages, they will be at a high level and may, for example, show little detail except for a department's general function, such as sales accounting or stock control; later, DFDs may be drawn at a lower, more detailed level, to show for example, the checking of a customer's account before sending an invoice reminder or statement of account. Standard symbols (from SSADM) for the drawing of data flow diagrams are illustrated and explained in the following paragraphs.

External entities

Figure 36.3 shows an External Entity symbol with example entries. External entities can be people, organisations or other information systems which receive data from or send data to the system under examination. Examples include suppliers, customers and agencies such as banks and Customs and Excise. As the Figure shows, the external entity symbol is an ellipse and contains two types of entry, a name (e.g. customer, supplier) and a unique identifier (a single letter). It is important to remember that the Name of the external entity refers to a type and not an occurrence of the type. So, for example, if a business has several suppliers, the entity 'Supplier' refers to any of them.

Figure 36.3. *External entity*

Processes

Figure 36.4 shows a Process symbol with example entries. Choice of 'Process name' is important in that it will be used to label a precise stage in a system's operation. For example, within a Sales system, a number of processes can be identified, such as 'Enter order', 'Print delivery note', 'Check invoice', 'Mark invoice as paid'. Some processes will be manual and others will be computerised. Process names should be meaningful above all, but should be kept as brief as possible. As the symbol means 'process' it is not helpful to use names like 'Process order' - this may mean, for example 'Check order', 'Stamp order' or 'Key in order'. The Location box is only used for physical modelling, that is, when the business function which is to carry out the process is known. A logical model would not show location.

Figure 36.4. *Process*

A process indicates that data has been changed in some way. It can be helpful to view processes as business activities triggered by *events*. For example, the arrival of a customer order into a business will trigger a number of activities or processes, such as 'Check order', 'Check customer credit status', 'Stamp date received', 'Check stock availability' and so on.

Data stores

Figure 36.5 shows a Data Store symbol with example entries. The 'name' given to a data store should clearly identify the contents not the physical store itself. In the Figure, the name is 'Sales', but other possible examples include, 'Orders', 'Purchases' and 'Customers'. It is not appropriate or useful to use names such as 'Disk', 'Folder' or 'Filing cabinet', as they don't tell us anything about the data itself.

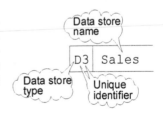

Figure 36.5. *Data store*

The data store type is identified as follows:

- ❏ D stands for Digitised data store, or computerised store (magnetic disk, CDROM, etc).

- ❏ M stands for Manual data store, such as a ring binder or filing cabinet.

- ❏ T(M) represents Transient (Manual) data store. An example of temporary data storage area is a filing tray which is used for newly received order forms, before they are passed to the Order Processing section.

- ❏ T stands for Transient (Computerised) data store such as is used in batch processing systems. For example, cheque payments received from customers may be entered onto a temporary file and then used to update the customer records, in a single operation, on the day the money is to be banked.

As Figure 36.5 shows, the data store type letter is combined with a digit to give it a unique identifier (in the Figure, D3).

Data flows

Figure 36.6 shows a Data Flow arrow with an example description. Data flows can be used to represent the movement of data between objects within the system and with external entities. Data can only flow between certain pairs of objects. Figure 36.7 shows the objects which can be connected by a data flow arrow.

Figure 36.6. *Data flow*

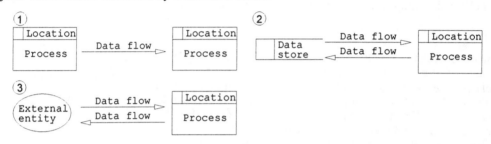

Figure 36.7. *Permitted data flows*

Notice that there is a Process in every pair. This is because data must undergo some process to move through the system. For example, the data for a customer order could not move independently from the T(M) data store of the plastic in-tray to the D data store of the computerised order file, but may undergo several processes, such as stamping, checking and keying in. Even in a completely manual system, a process is involved in every data flow. To illustrate the use of these symbols, we provide two example data flow diagrams illustrating the trading operations of a typical business organisation. The first is a Level 1 DFD and the second, at Level 2, provides more detail on the operation of Sales. Sometimes, these levels may be preceded by a Level 0 DFD, otherwise known as a *context diagram*.

Context diagram

A context diagram shows no details of processes and the system is regarded as a 'black box' with data flows to and from external entities. Context diagrams are useful as a means of defining the boundaries of the project before more detailed work begins. An example is shown in Figure 36.8 for a trading (buying and selling) system

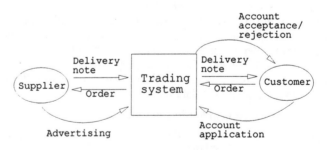

Figure 36.8. *Context diagram (Level 0 DFD)*

Example Level 1 DFD

Figure 36.9 is an example of a Level 1 DFD for showing the main trading operations of a typical business. It is an example of a physical model and a location is identified in every process box. If you find it difficult to relate the diagrams which follow to real procedures in a business, then look again at the simplified pictorial representation in Figure 36.1.

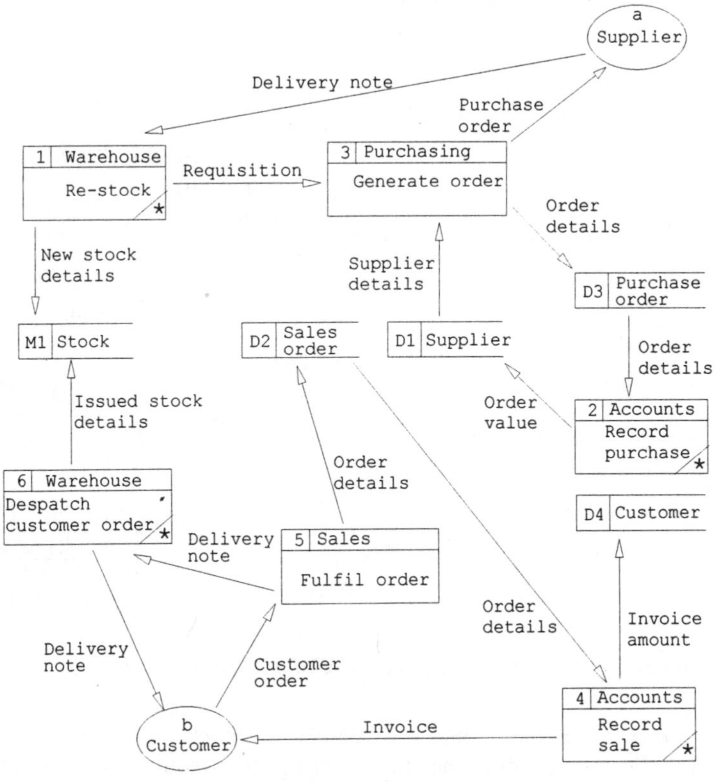

Figure 36.9. *Level 1 data flow diagram*

Study Figure 36.9 carefully and note the following important points:

❑ The unique identifier in a process box does not indicate sequence of processes, but simply a precise way of identifying each process. For example, in Figure 36.9 processes 2 and 4 both occur in the location Accounts and have names that may be confused - 'Record sale' and 'Record invoice'.

❑ Not all the activities related to trading operations are shown. For example, there is no reference to payment of invoices, either to suppliers or from customers. This detail could be added, but for the purposes of the system which is to undergo more detailed examination, such additional detail may not be considered relevant by the analyst/designer. The diagram could have been drawn in a variety of different ways, and only detailed knowledge of the way a particular business works will allow for an accurate representation.

❑ Notice that some of the process boxes have an asterisk and diagonal line in the corner; this is to indicate an *elementary item*, one for which no further detail needs to be added. The decision as to whether an item is elementary depends on practical, thorough knowledge of how the business and its systems operate. For example, a process named 'Check order' may simply mean "Read it to check that it has all the necessary details". However, if it also means "Check customer account and credit limit" and "Check stock availability" then it is not an elementary item and further detail needs to be added, preferably in a lower level DFD

We now explain some of the detail in the previous data flow diagram. Figure 36.10 shows part of the Level 1 DFD associated with stock purchasing.

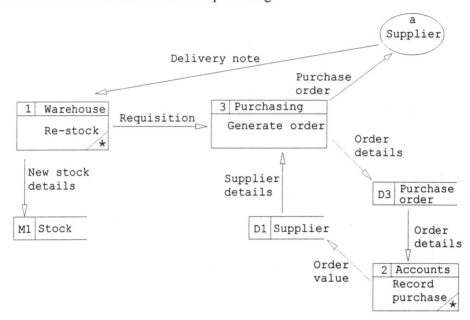

Figure 36.10. *Part of Level 1 DFD dealing with stock and purchasing activities*

1. Process 1 `Restock` assumes that the Warehouse stock control system has already highlighted that certain products need re-ordering, so a requisition is produced and the data flow `Requisition` passes it to Process 3 `Generate order` in the Purchasing office.

2. Process 3 `Generate order` requires a data flow from data store D1 `Supplier` (D indicates computerised storage) for details of suppliers. This will allow selection of a supplier and retrieval of name and address and other details needed to generate the order.

   There is clearly insufficient detail for a proper understanding of the process 3 `Generate order`, so a Level 2 DFD would be needed to analyse it further. Possible details include, for example, 'Check current supplier prices' (to obtain the most competitive price), 'Check delivery times' (to ensure quickest delivery) and 'Check credit' (to determine that amounts already owing to the chosen supplier do not exceed the credit limit).

3. Process 3 `Generate order` shows that the order details are recorded and a data flow `Order details` passes them to data storage D3 `Purchase order`.

4. The data flow `Purchase order` passes the data to the external entity a `Supplier` (remember, the a acts as a unique identifier). An external entity represents a type, Supplier in this case, not an occurrence of a type (not a particular supplier).

5. Process 2 `Record purchase` requires a data flow `Order details` from the data store D3 `Purchase order` so that they can be recorded in the appropriate supplier account (as a debt or amount owing by the business). Thus, the data flow `Order value` passes from process 2 `Record purchase` to data store D1 `Supplier`.

6. The data flow `Delivery note` passes from the external entity a `Supplier` to the process 1 `Restock` at the Warehouse. Obviously, the goods would accompany the

delivery, but as they don't constitute data no reference is made to them.

7. The data flow `New stock details` shows that when the delivery note (and goods) are received, the data store `M1 Stock` is updated.

The data store `M1 Stock` is a manual filing system and when the order is received the relevant item quantities will need to be adjusted. A manual stock system often uses documents called Bin cards located at the storage point for each product category in the warehouse. When stock of a particular product is received or issued, an entry is made on the bin card and the running total is adjusted accordingly.

Using Figure 36.11, we now look at that part of Figure 36.9 which deals with sales and stock.

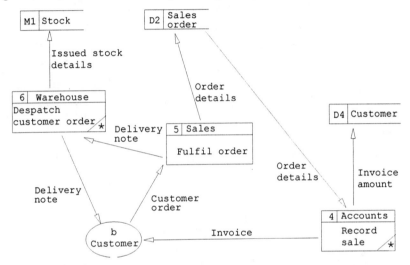

Figure 36.11. *Part of Level 1 DFD dealing with customer sales and stock issues*

The diagram can be explained as follows.

1. External entity `b Customer` connects to process `5 Fulfil order` with the data flow `Customer order`.

2. The data flow `Order details` passes the data from process `5 Fulfil order` to data store `D2 Sales order`, which is used to record customer orders.

3. The process `6 Despatch customer order` needs the data flow `Delivery note` from process `5 Fulfil order`. A delivery note details the delivery name and address as well as a list of what is to be sent to the customer.

4. Process `6 Despatch customer order` connects to the external entity `b Customer` with the data flow `Delivery note` (in practical terms the delivery note accompanies the goods).

5. Data flow `Order details` ensures that the data store `D2 Sales order` is updated by the process `5 Fulfil order`.

6. Process `4 Record sale` uses the data flow `Order details` to access the data store `D2 Sales order`. These details enable the production of an invoice.

7. Data flow `Invoice amount` allows the process `4 Record sale` to update the data store `D4 Customer`, which contains details of customers and the amounts they owe to the business.

8. Data flow `Invoice` connects process 4 `Record sale` to external entity b `Customer`. This informs the customer of the amount owing for the order.

Example Level 2 DFD

Figure 36.12 focuses on the process 5 `Fulfil order`. Notice that the process symbol itself is shown enlarged to enclose all the details not shown in the Level 1 DFD. Some details have been added which were not shown in the Level 1 DFD.

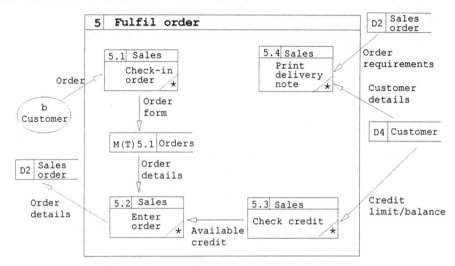

Figure 36.12. *Level 2 data flow diagram for process* 5 `Fulfil order`

The diagram can be further explained as follows.

1. Process 5.1 `Check-in order` receives the data flow `Order` from the external entity b `Customer`. In this case, the process happens to involve the stamping (received date) and cursory check for validity (properly completed with customer details, delivery address, products and quantities etc) of incoming orders before they are placed in an in-tray (a manual data store). This is represented by the data flow `Order form` which connects process 5.1 `Check-in order` to the temporary data store `M(T)5.1 Orders`.

2. Process 5.2 `Enter order` receives the data flow `Order details` from the data store `M(T)5.1 Orders`. This can be assumed to be a keying operation as the data flow `Order details` connects the process 5.2 `Enter order` to the computerised data store `D2 Sales order`.

3. Process 5.2 `Enter order` receives the data flow `Available credit` from process 5.3 `Check credit`, which itself receives the necessary data flow `Credit limit/balance` from data store `D4 Customer`. This means that the order entry process uses a further process checking a customer's available credit before the order is accepted.

4. Process 5.4 `Print delivery note` receives two data flows, `Customer details` from data store `D4 Customer` and `Order requirements` from data store `D2 Sales order`.

Note that only objects directly associated with the process under examination are shown and that any processes with the asterisk in the bottom right corner do not require further analysis.

In summary, the following guidelines for drawing DFDs should be helpful.

❑ Drawing DFDs is an *iterative* process, in that it will take several attempts, redraws and refinements to reach a satisfactory outcome. When you are drawing a DFD, it will help if you attempt to explain its logic to someone else, thereby clarifying your own thoughts and most probably, highlighting errors in the process.

❑ A Level 1 DFD does not have to cover all aspects of a business and if it did, would probably be less detailed than this example. Too much detail makes a diagram difficult to follow and it is normally necessary to have at least one and possibly more lower level DFDs. Nevertheless, sufficient detail must be shown to give an accurate picture of the way the various systems interact.

❑ Try not to have too many crossing data flow lines as this makes the diagram confusing. You will probably have to move objects around several times before your reach a satisfactory result. It is a good idea to locate data stores in the centre and external entities around the edge.

❑ Although further, lower level DFDs may be needed for proper analysis of system operations, you should find that the systems you study can be properly analysed with only Level 1 and Level 2. Generally, you will only require one Level 1 DFD, but several Level 2 DFDs may be needed to properly analyse all the processes identified at Level 1.

Entity-relationship models

An entity-relationship diagram is the product of entity-relationship modelling (ERM), which is itself a valuable aid to database design. In SSADM, the term Logical Data Model (LDM) is used, but uses the same components.

Using the data store symbol, the physical DFDs described in the previous section identify the methods (manual, temporary or computerised) used to store the various files in a system. They also show the processes on data as it moves through the various business functions or departments. However, they do not show the underlying structure of the data which is processed. Without further analysis, the direct implementation of a data flow diagram may result in duplication of data, as well as inconsistencies between similar records held in various parts of the business. Suppose, for example, that the Sales and Stock Control department hold separate records on the products in which the business trades. If a manufacturer changes the specification of a product, this may be communicated to the Stock Control department, which updates its records, leaving the Sales staff with the wrong information. A major aim of structured analysis and in particular, logical data modelling, is to focus on the structure of data, rather than on the processes it is to undergo. An entity-relationship model focuses on the data stores identified in data flow diagrams and shows relationships between them.

To use the modelling technique effectively, the following definitions need to be understood.

❑ *Entity.* The term equates with an object, or 'class of things' which is of interest or relevance to the organisation, for example, Supplier, Customer, Stock. An entity will normally equate with a file, or in the case of a relational database, a table. An entity *occurrence* is normally synonymous with a *record* in a file or database table.

❑ *Relationship.* Entities are connected by relationships. For example, an Employee works for a particular Department, although each Department may have many Employees. A model will also show the *degree* of the relationship between pairs of entities. As is explained later, this may be one-to-one, one-to-many (or the reverse, many-to-one), or many-to-many. It is apparent that the Employee / Department example given above has a many-to-one relationship. In the physical implementation of a model, relationships are established between tables in a database or traditional files with the use of common fields to link them. For example, to link an Employee table with a Department table, the

Employee table definition would include the primary key (say, DeptID) for the Department table.

☐ *Attribute.* An entity has properties, or attributes, which are identified as being of interest to users. In the physical implementation of an entity-relationship model, attributes become fields in records.

We now examine the components of entity and relationship in more detail.

Entity

An entity is any subject about which an organisation needs to hold information. Figure 36.13 shows two examples of related entities and occurrences of each. As explained previously, an entity equates with a file or database table and an occurrence of the type equates with a record.

Entity type: SUPPLIER					
ID	**Name**	**Address**	**Town**	**County**	**Postcode**
3766	Organic Foods	4 Main Street	Hexham	Northumberland	NE22 3LD
3767	Mary's Cookies	3 End Road	Corbridge	Northumberland	NE24 2DS
Entity type: PURCHASE ORDER					
ID	**Date sent**	**Supplier ID**	**Value**		
0065	13/4/2002	3766	£2544.88		
0066	14/4/2002	3766	£120.44		

Figure 36.13. *Example related entity types and occurrences of each*

As the examples show, each entity has a number of associated *attributes*, but each occurrence of a particular entity has the same attributes. In other words, every record in a particular file or database table contains the same fields.

Figure 36.14 shows an entity symbol for Supplier and PurchaseOrder. (The symbol shape is from the SSADM methodology, but you may find it simpler just to use rectangles without the rounded corners.) The label inside the symbol must be unique within the particular model.

In SSADM, attributes are not shown within the entity symbol, but are dealt with in an accompanying textual description. Otherwise it is perfectly acceptable to show the attributes if the analysis has progressed to a point where such detail has been established. Figure 36.15 shows Purchase Order with its attributes.

Supplier   Purchase Order

Figure 36.14. *Entities*

PURCHASE ORDER

ID	Name	Address	Town	County	Postcode

Figure 36.15. *Entity with attribute details included*

Relationship

Figure 36.16 shows how the relationship which exists between the Supplier and Purchase Order entities is represented.

Figure 36.16. *Many to one relationship*

The 'crow's foot' symbol indicates a *degree* of relationship, in particular the 'many' side of a relationship. More is said about degree of relationship later. A *name* is used to indicate the nature of the relationship. In the Figure, this is used to say that "many different orders may be placed with a single supplier". In reverse, it means that "each purchase order must only be placed with one supplier". It is not always possible to find a relationship name which makes sense in both directions, which is why textual description is also important.

The importance of entity relationships

The pictorial representation of common business operations, shown in Figure 36.1, demonstrates clearly that functions within a business interact with one another, creating a network of relationships. These relationships exist because of common data requirements, such as the need for customer information in Sales, Marketing, Customer Services and so on, or the need for product information in Sales, Stock Control and Purchasing.

The task of entity modelling is to identify and illustrate all relationships that exist between the entities in a business and with external entities, such as suppliers and customers. If relationships are not identified there is the risk that data will be duplicated, for example, with Sales and Marketing holding separate copies of customer records. This would not only be wasteful of storage, but could lead to inconsistencies in data values if information updates happen to go to only one function. This may cause inefficiencies, such as sending flyers to the wrong address, or damaging mistakes, such as sending advertising to recipients who have repeatedly requested to be removed from the mailing list.

Degree of relationship

Degree of relationship may be one-to-one, one-to-many, many-to-one or many-to-many.

One-to-one relationship

A one-to-one relationship between entities is relatively uncommon, but here are a few examples:

☐ Employee and National Insurance record. Every person aged 16 or over who is working or has been registered for work has a unique National Insurance Number.

☐ Husband and wife.

☐ Patient and medical history. Each hospital patient develops a unique medical history and each medical history can only relate to one hospital patient.

☐ Autobiography and author. An autobiography is a written account of the author's own life.

Figure 36.17 shows the last example as an entity-relationship diagram.

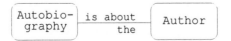

Figure 36.17. *One-to-one relationship*

One-to-many or many-to-one relationship

Many can mean one or more. One-to-many or many-to-one relationships (simply switch the entities around) are the most common. Here are a few examples.

❑ Doctor and patient. Each patient can only registered with one doctor at any one time, but a doctor has many patients.

❑ Customer and order. Each customer can place many orders, but each order relates to only one customer.

❑ Bookshop customer and book. A customer may buy many books, but each copy of a book can only be bought by one person.

❑ Ward and patient. Each ward can contain many patients, but each patient can only be in one ward.

❑ Order and order line. Each order may have many order lines (several products may be listed on a single order) but each order line (for example, 6 boxes of Stabilo, red, HB, pencils) must relate to a particular order (it is not relevant that another customer order includes the same item and quantity).

Figure 36.18 illustrates the last example. Note the 'crow's foot' to indicate the *many* side.

Figure 36.18. *One-to-many relationship*

Many-to-many relationship

Many-to-many relationships cannot be implemented in a relational database which only supports a two-dimensional, 'flat file' structure. Once identified, many-to-many relationships must be converted to one-to-many and how this is achieved is explained later in this section. Here are some examples pairs of entities with a many-to-many relationship.

❑ Author and book. A publisher may publish many books by the same author and each book may have one or more authors.

❑ Staff member and in-house training course. Each staff member may attend many in-house training courses and each course may be attended by many staff members.

❑ Student and course. A student may be enrolled on more than one course and each course may have many students.

This last example is symbolised in Figure 36.19.

Notice that the relationship name only makes sense in one direction and that if the entities are reversed then the name "enrols" would be more appropriate. The order in which you place the entities is not important and the choice depends on which seems to make most sense for the particular application under analysis.

Figure 36.19. *Many-to-many relationship*

Establishing the degree of a relationship is not always straightforward and you need to take into account the specific business and application being analysed. For example, the relationship between Student and Course could be many-to-one if a student can only enrol on one course. Otherwise, a many-to-many relationship exists.

Resolving many-to-many relationships

The Student and Course entity relationship model is used here to illustrate the method used to resolve a many-to-many relationship. As stated earlier, many-to-many relationships cannot be used directly in a relational database or other 'flat file' (2-dimensional) structures, except in a very limited and inefficient way, as illustrated by Figure 36.20.

Impracticality of using repeated fields

The necessary relationship to allow production of student lists could be established by including, say, 3 Course Code fields in each Student record, as illustrated in Figure 36.20.

STUDENT						
Student ID	Surname	......	Sex	Crse Code 1	Crse Code 2	Crse Code 3
01311	Carter	......	M	PTAS01	PTAS02	PTAS07
01312	McDonald	......	M	PTGC04	PTGC06	
etc	etc	etc	etc			

Figure 36.20. *Problems of using repeated Course Code fields*

To produce a student list for a particular course, the Student table can be scanned for records which contain the relevant Course Code. Although this model could be implemented, for example, in a relational database, there are potential difficulties with the approach: What if a student enrolled on 4 or even more courses? Clearly, the difficulty would be even greater if, instead of repeating Course Code in the Student table, the Student ID field were repeated in the Course table.

Although the above solution is possible, it is not a good solution and breaks the first rule of *data normalisation* (see next section), that there should be no repeating groups. Normalisation is a process designed to make the storage and use of a database more efficient and generally involves 3 stages, although only the first stage (First Normal Form) needs to be covered here.

Normalisation - a practical solution

To explain how to resolve the difficulty, we use continue with the example of the Student and Course entity relationship model. The entities, together with sample occurrences are shown in Figure 36.21.

COURSE				
Course Code	Title	Level	Duration	Course Leader
PTAS01	French	AS	1 year	G. Depardieu
PTAS02	Italian	AS	1 year	M. Pollini
etc	etc	etc	etc	etc

STUDENT				
Student ID	Surname	Forename	Date of Birth	Sex
01311	Carter	James	18/06/81	M
01312	McDonald	Myrtle	23/03/82	M
etc	etc	etc	etc	etc

Figure 36.21. *Course and Student entities with sample occurrences*

To produce student lists for a particular course, for example, it must be possible to connect a particular Course record (entity occurrence) to all the Student records registered for that course. To remove the need for any repeated fields, a new entity must be created to act as a link between the existing entities.

This new entity will have a many-to-one relationship with each of the other entities and the model can now be drawn as in Figure 36.22.

Figure 36.22. *Using a new entity to transform a many-to-many relationship*

The new entity should be given a name which indicates its intermediary role. In the case of the Student and Course entities, the new entity can be called Enrolment (or Registration, for example), because this is the event which connects a student with a course.

The relationships can now be expressed as:

1.   A student may be named in one or more enrolments

2.   A course has one or more enrolments.

3.   An enrolment refers to only one student on a single course.

Figure 36.23 which follows shows how the entities could be structured in a relational database.

COURSE

Course Code	Title	Level	Duration	Course Leader
PTAS01	French	AS	1 year	G. Depardieu

STUDENT

Student ID	Surname	Forename	Date of Birth	Sex
01311	Carter	James	18/06/81	M

ENROLMENT

Student ID	Course Code	Date
01311	PTAS01	09/09/2002

Figure 36.23. *Relational database structure using a link table*

Each entity must have one attribute which will contain a unique value in every entity occurrence. More familiarly, each table must contain a field (or fields) which can act as the primary key to uniquely identify each record. Thus, in Figure 36.23, the Course table uses Course Code (underscored), Student uses Student ID and Enrolment uses both. This *composite* key acts as primary key in the Enrolment table and provides the necessary links with the Course and Student tables. An alternative would be to use another field, say Enrolment Number, as the primary key but the Student ID and Course Code fields would still need to be present to provide the links with the other tables.

First Normal Form (1NF)

The process of transforming many-to-many relationships and the consequent removal of repeating fields or groups of fields is the first stage of data *normalisation*. Thus, the tables in

Figure 36.23 are said to be in First Normal Form. Two further stages are normally followed, but they are beyond the scope of this Unit.

Example entity model

Figure 36.24 shows a model which could be used as the basis for an Academic database.

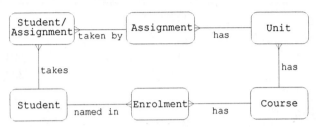

Figure 36.24. *Entity model for an Academic database*

The relationships between Student, Enrolment and Course were dealt with in the previous section, so the rest of the model is explained below.

1. Course and Unit. Each Course has many Units, but each Unit relates to only one Course.

2. Assignment and Unit. Each Unit has a number of Assignments, but each Assignment relates to only one Unit.

3. Student, Assignment and Student/Assignment. The latter entity is acting as the link between Assignment and Student, which would otherwise have a many-to-many relationship (each Student takes many Assignments and each Assignment is taken by many Students). This is an other example of the first stage of normalisation to First Normal Form (no repeating groups of fields). The Student/Assignment entity could be viewed more practically as the Grade entity, in that the link is needed to record student assignment grades. The entity data could be structured as shown in Figure 36.25 for use in a relational database.

STUDENT/ASSIGNMENT			
Student ID	Assignment No	Unit No	Grade
01311	4	6	B

Figure 36.25. *Link table for recording student assignment grades*

Data dictionary

This is also known in SSADM as the *data catalogue*. A data dictionary system is an ICT department's own information system, with the database administrator, systems analysts and programmers as the main users. An essential part of the system design process is to maintain a data dictionary. Its main function is to store details of all the data items which are to be included in the information system. Such details can be wide ranging, but should include, as a minimum:

(i) field names and the table(s) in which they occur;

(ii) field definitions, including field types and lengths;

(iii) additional properties, concerning, for example, data formats and validation controls;

(iv) synonyms. Sometimes, the same field occurs in more than one table, but using different names. Generally it is better not to use synonyms.

The dictionary's main role is to ensure consistent data usage; if synonyms are used (different data names may be used by different functional areas of an organisation to refer to the same field), the dictionary must record their use accordingly to prevent duplication. A typical example dictionary for the Course and Student entities, taken from the Academic database shown in Figure 36.24, is shown in Figures 36.26, 36.27.

COURSE				
Field name	CourseCode	Title	Level	CourseLeader
Data type	text	text	text	text
Field size	3	25	1	30
Validation rule	>=100 and <=200			
Validation text	Range 100 to 200		Range 1 to 4	
Required	Yes	No	No	No
Indexed	Yes (no duplicates)	No	No	No

Figure 36.26. *COURSE data dictionary definition*

STUDENT					
Field name	StudentID	Sname	Fname	DOB	Sex
Data type	text	text	text	date	text
Field size	4	25	15		1
Validation rule	>=1000 and <=9999			<=now()-15	M or F
Validation text				invalid date	invalid
Required	Yes	No	No	No	No
Indexed	Yes (no duplicates)	No	No	No	No

Figure 36.27. *STUDENT data dictionary definition*

Process models

Although data flow diagrams identify processes, they do not show how they will be carried out. Process models allow the detail of processes to be analysed and illustrated.

Process models describe tasks that can be broken down into logical sequences of activities. Such models can be used to describe computer processing tasks that require computer programs, purely manual systems or combinations of both. There are many forms of process models; here we describe four of them: structured English; structure charts; flowcharts; decision tables.

Structured English

Structured English, and a similar form of notation (not discussed here) called pseudo-code, uses a technique called top-down, stepwise refinement to analyse and describe processes. Structured English involves first describing a task in terms of a sequence of simpler tasks each of which, in turn, is further broken down into simpler tasks. This process of successive refinement of tasks continues until there is sufficient detail for the resulting description to be of practical use. In the case of describing a solution method for a computer programming task, that is defining an *algorithm*, the task refinement process halts when there is sufficient detail to allow the algorithm to be easily converted into a computer program; this is usually when a task is one simple action that cannot easily be refined further. Keywords such as if, while and do, are used to specify standard programming constructs. Line indentation and delimiters such as endif and endwhile are used to designate the extent of blocks of instructions governed by keywords..

To illustrate the syntax of Structured English and its use in defining a computer programming problem, we will analyse the following example:

The sales details for a number of company sales representatives are held as a set of records in a computer file. Each record in the file contains the following data:

- ❑   name (of rep)
- ❑   item-code (a six-digit numeric code)
- ❑   units-sold (number of units of this item sold)
- ❑   value (value of this sale)

There may be several such records in the file for each sales representative. The records in the file are ordered according to sales representative, ie all the records for a particular salesperson are grouped together, and they are in alphabetical order of sales representative name. Sales representatives receive commission on their total sales value. This commission depends on the code of the item sold. For codes of 100000 - 199999 commission is calculated at 10%, for codes of 200000 - 299999 the commission is 15% and for codes of 300000 - 399999 the commission is 20%.

A report is to be produced giving the total sales value and commission due to each salesperson, and the grand totals of sales values and commissions for all the salespersons. The report is to have the following structure:

ACME COMPUTER SERVICES
SALES REPORT March 2000

Salesperson	Total sales value	Commission
Moray, R	1334.90	133.49
Scott, P Y	2452.76	245.28
Smith, J	1213.55	121.36
Williams, I	1668.22	166.82
Winns, J R	1167.23	116.72
Tyson, M	932.34	93.23
GRAND TOTALS	8769.00	876.90

The file to be processed has the form illustrated below:

Name	Item	Sold	Value
Moray, R	100232	5	725.00
Moray, R	301567	3	609.90
Scott, P Y	200234	2	1204.40
Scott, P Y	223045	1	605.00
Scott, P Y	301067	4	652.20
Smith, J	122077	5	1213.55
Winns, J R	356099	8	400.00

Winns, J R	367234	4	334.00
Winns, J R	100034	2	433.23
Tyson, M	301023	8	932.34

Adopting a top-down approach, that is first identifying the main processes involved in producing the report, the report program can be described as a sequence of three tasks:

```
report program
        1. print headings
        2. process report body
        3. print grand totals
END report program
```

Each of these three steps needs to be further refined, particularly the second step which involves processing a file of records.

```
report program
1. print headings
        1.1. print page headings
        1.2. print column headings
2. process report-body
    while more sales reps to process do
        2.1. process salesrep records
        2.2. print detail line
        2.3. Accumulate sales value and commission grand totals
    endwhile
3. print grand totals
        3.1. print sales value
        3.2. print commission
end report program
```

This second level of refinement introduces a processing loop which is defined by while..endwhile. Because there are a number of sales reps, step 2 involves repeatedly processing the records for each rep and printing the details for that rep. All of the steps between while and endwhile are repeated until there are no more reps to process..

After this second level of refinement, the first and the third tasks are sufficiently detailed. However, the second step still requires more detail. Firstly, we need to define step 2.1., how to process a sales rep's records.

```
2.1 process salesrep records
    while more sales records do
        2.1.1. read sale value
        2.1.2. add sale value to sales total
        2.1.3. calculate commission
        2.1.4. add commission to commission total
    endwhile
```

This step involves another loop in which each record in turn for the current rep being is read. The record is processed by accumulating the rep's sales value for the item just read and calculating and accumulating the commission due for that sale. This process repeats until there are no more records for that rep. Steps 2.2.and 2.3, shown below, are then completed.

```
2.2. print detail line
        2.2.1. print sales rep name
        2.2.2. print total sales value
        2.2.3. print total commission
2.3. Accumulate sales value and commission grand totals
```

```
      2.3.1. add total sales value to sales value grand total
      2.3.2. add total commission to commission grand total
```

The final level of refinement is to specify precisely how commission is calculated. We refine step `2.1.3 calculate commission` as follows:

```
2.1.3 calculate commission
        2.1.3.1 case item-code
                100000 to 199999: calculate commission @ 10%
                200000 to 299999: calculate commission @ 15%
                300000 to 399999: calculate commission @ 20%
        endcase
```

The value of item-code determines which one of the three possibilities is selected so that the appropriate commission will be calculated.

We are now in a position to define the complete algorithm for the report program:

```
report program
1. print headings
      1.1. print page headings
      1.2. print column headings
2. process report-body
    while more salesreps to process do
        2.1. process salesrep records
        while more sales records to process do
            2.1.1. read sale value
            2.1.2. add sale value to sales total
            2.1.3. calculate commission
                2.1.3.1 case item-code of
                  100000 to 199999: calculate commission @ 10%
                  200000 to 299999: calculate commission @ 15%
                  300000 to 399999: calculate commission @ 20%
                endcase
            2.1.4. add commission to commission total
        endwhile
        2.2. print detail line
            2.2.1. print sales rep name
            2.2.2. print total sales value
            2.2.3. print total commission
        2.3. accumulate sales value and commission grand totals
            2.3.1. add total sales value to sales value grand total
            2.3.2 add total commission to commission grand total
    endwhile
3. print grand totals
    3.1. print sales value
    3.2. print commission
end report program
```

Note that the only actions that are performed are those that are not further refined. For instance, in step 3 above, 3.1 and 3.2 define precisely how to `print grand totals`, and step 3 itself is simply a description of the two refined steps, not an action to be performed.

Structured English constructs

Our example illustrates the three Structured English constructs of:

❑ Sequence - a set of instructions performed in order of appearance

❑ Selection - the `case` statement used for calculating commission

❑ Iteration - the `while` statements that defined instructions to be repeated

In the following amplifications of these three terms, the word *statement* refers to a single instruction which can either be a single action, a selection or an iteration. As you will see, this means that any one of the above three constructs can contain, nested within the block of instructions that it governs, any of the other constructs. Thus these three simple constructs are capable of being used to define algorithms of almost any degree of complexity.

Sequence

This is simply one or more actions performed in the order in which they appear. For instance, the following four actions constitute a sequence:

```
2.1.1. read sale value
2.1.2. add sale value to sales total
2.1.3. calculate commission
2.1.4. add commission to commission total
```

Selection

This involves selecting one course of action from two or more when a decision needs to be made. In our example, the commission rate for a sales item was determined by the item's code number. The `case` statement used specified that the commission was to be selected from three alternatives which depended on the value of `item-code`:

```
2.1.3 calculate commission
    2.1.3.1 case item-code of
        100000 to 199999: calculate commission @ 10%
        200000 to 299999: calculate commission @ 15%
        300000 to 399999: calculate commission @ 20%
    endcase
```

Each case in a `case` statement can comprise a number of statements, not just one.

An alternative form of selection statement is the `if` statement which is more convenient when there are only one or two possible courses of action. The `if` statement has the form:

```
if <conditional expression> then
    <statements>
else
    <alternative statements>
endif
```

If the `<conditional expression>` is true, then the first statement or block of statements is performed, otherwise the alternative statement or statements are performed. For example, we could write

```
if tax-code = 4 then
      VAT=17.5%
else
      VAT=0%
endif
```

Iteration

This is another name for performing a loop in which a block of statements are repeated until a specified condition is true. In our example, this took the form of a `while` statement that defined a loop for processing each sales rep in turn. The condition that specified when to exit the loop and continue with the next statement following `endwhile` was

(**while**) more sales reps to process *(do)*

Another example of a `while` loop is shown below.

```
set count = 0
while count is less than 10 do
    .........
    add 1 to count
endwhile
```

This is a loop which repeats exactly ten times before exiting. The count is called a *variable* whose value can be modified within the algorithm. In this case, `count` is incremented every time the loop instructions are repeated and it is used within the `while` condition to determine when the loop is to be exited.

Note that if the `while` condition is already true before the `while` statement is encountered, the loop exits without obeying any of the instructions within the loop.

Alternative forms of loops, such as `repeat..until` and `for..next` are sometimes used as alternatives to the `while` loop; however, they are really just variations of `while` that are useful when the target computer language contains similar constructs.

Structure charts

A Structure Chart is a diagrammatic form of a Structured English algorithm. Rectangles organised into a tree structure are used to represent the problem solution. Again, sequence, selection and iteration constructs are nested within one another to enable complex problem solutions to be illustrated. Figure 36.28 shows the sales rep problem that was discussed in the previous section as a Structure chart.

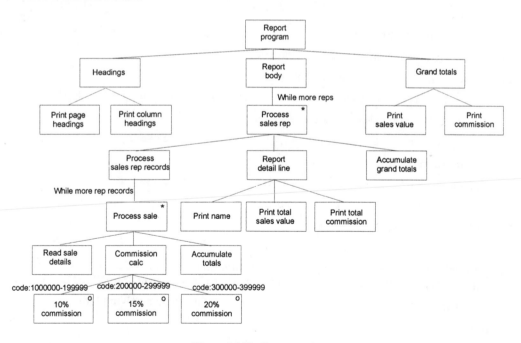

Figure 36.28. *Structure chart*

Note the symbols '*' and 'o' placed in top right-hand corners of some of the rectangles to indicate iterations and selections respectively. In the case of a selection, only one of the circle boxes is chosen, depending on the condition indicated above the boxes. The asterisk indicates that all boxes connected to it are to be repeated while the specified condition is true. Structure charts are also developed using top-down, stepwise refinement as discussed earlier. Their use is illustrated in more detail in Unit 4, Introduction to Software Development.

The structure chart is read from top to bottom and left to right, the rectangles that are not further refined being actions to perform.

Thus the order of execution of the actions shown in the chart is:

```
1. Print page headings

2. Print column headings

3. Read sale details 1 for sales rep 1

4. Calculate 10% or 15% or 20% commission depending on item code 1

5. Accumulate value and commission totals

6. Read sale details 2 for sales rep 1

7. Calculate 10% or 15% or 20% commission depending on item code 2

8. Accumulate value and commission totals

        (repeat steps 3-8 for rest of records for sales rep 1)

9. Print summary line for sales rep 1

10. Accumulate grand totals for sales value and commission

11. Read sale details 1 for sales rep 2

12. Calculate 10% or 15% or 20% commission depending on item code 1

13 Accumulate value and commission totals

14. Read sale details 2 for sales rep 2

15. Calculate 10% or 15% or 20% commission depending on item code 2

16. Accumulate value and commission totals

        repeat steps 11-16 for rest of records for sales rep 2

17. Print summary line for sales rep2

18. Accumulate grand totals for sales value and commission

        repeat for rest of sales reps

19. Print sales value grand total

20. Print commission grand total
```

Being a graphical interpretation of a problem, Structure Charts can provide a more convenient and easily understood interpretation of a problem than that obtained using Structured English.

The Flowchart, discussed in the next section, is also a visual problem solving tool.

Flowcharts

A flowchart can be used to represent any well-defined sequence of activities. In the context of computer programming, a flowchart is used to convey in diagrammatic form, the logic, processing operations and flow of control required of a computer program.

Flowcharts are used by programmers in two main ways:

   ❏ to plan the structure of a program before it is written;

❑ to describe the structure of a program after it has been written.

The first use is primarily for the benefit of the programmer to aid program design; the second use is to document program structure in a form that anyone with an understanding of the symbols used will be able to understand.

However, a flowchart can be used to convey a sequence of events unconnected to computer programming. The next example illustrates such a use. Though rather frivolous, Figure 36.29 illustrates how a flowchart can show the logical order in which the actions involved in "Questioning a Suspicious Person" are to be performed by a police constable.

To read the flowchart you follow the direction indicated by the arrows. A diamond shaped box indicates a point where a decision, leading to one of two different routes, has to made. The question to be asked at a decision point is written inside the box, and the only possible answers are indicated on the two lines leading from the decision symbol. The question inside the box needs to be phrased in such a way that there can be only two possible answers such as Yes (Y) and No (N) or Male (M) and Female (F), as illustrated in the figure.

Loops, that is, repeated sections of the flowchart, are indicated by lines leading back to a previously encountered section. For example, the policemen is required to say "Hello" three

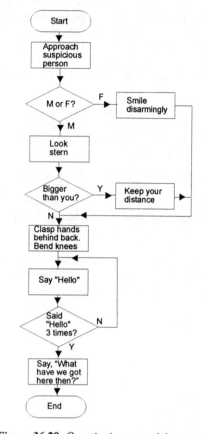

Figure 36.29. *Questioning a suspicious person*

times, so this is shown by a loop in which the question, "Said Hello 3 times?" is asked inside a decision box. After going around the loop three times, the answer to the question is "Yes" and you can continue to the next box. If a flowchart is too big to be shown as a single diagram, it can be split into a number of sections using connectors shown by circles containing numbers (Figure 36.30) or letters. When you come to a connector you simply continue at the next section starting with the same number or letter.

When a flowchart is being used to represent the operation of a computer program, it is usual to use one further symbol for input or output operations, that is, where information has to be read in to the computer or is to be produced by the computer so that it can be read by us.

The minimum set of symbols used in flowcharts is shown in Figure 36.30.

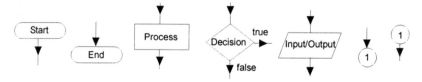

Figure 36.30. *Basic flowcharting symbols*

The oval symbols are used to indicate the start or end of a process. The rectangle represents a calculation or other processing operation, the nature of which is written inside the box. The diamond shape shows that a decision is to be made between two alternatives, and the criteria for making the decision is shown inside the symbol. Any input or output operations are shown by the parallelogram. Finally, a small circle containing a number or letter is used to split a large flowchart into smaller parts.

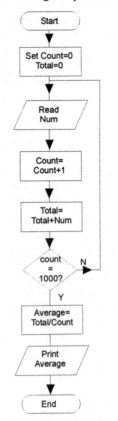

Now suppose that the requirement is to write a computer program to read and calculate the average of one thousand numbers. Figure 36.31 illustrates how a flowchart can summarise a lengthy process by using a loop.

Notice that the arrows on the lines joining the symbols show the direction to follow when reading the flowchart, and that the decision box provides the means by which a loop can be introduced. This example introduces the idea of using a variable, namely Count, as a counter which starts at a value of zero and increases by one every time a number (Num) is read. The expression, Count = Count + 1, is a   form that is used very frequently in computer programming, and it simply means that the value of Count is to be replaced by its current value plus one. That is, Count is to be incremented by 1. A third variable, Total, also initially set to zero, accumulates the numbers as they are read in: Total = Total + Num simply means "replace the value of Total by its current value plus Num."

When 1000 numbers have been read, Count will be equal to 1000 and Total will be the sum of all the numbers. The average value is found by dividing the sum of the numbers by the number of numbers, that is, Total ÷ Count.

For example, if the first five numbers to be read in were 3,2,4,6 and 9, then the table on the right shows the how the values change for the three variables Count, Num and Total

Figure 36.31. *Flowchart to find average of 1000*

When 1000 numbers have been read, Count will be equal to 1000 and Total will be the sum of all the numbers. The average value is found by dividing the sum of the numbers by the number of numbers, that is, Total ÷ Count.

Decision boxes can also show how to cope with different situations that might occur during some processing activity. For instance, suppose that a program is required to calculate the selling price for some item which may or may not be VAT rated. The flowchart fragment in Figure 36.32 shows how this situation could be represented.

Count	Num	Total
0		0
0 + 1 = 1	3	0 + 3 = 3
1 + 1 = 2	2	3 + 2 = 5
2 + 1 = 3	4	5 + 4 = 9
3 + 1 = 4	6	9 + 6 = 15
4 + 1 = 5	9	15 + 9 = 24

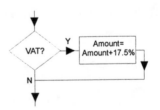

Figure 36.32. *Using a decision box*

Decision tables

As an alternative, or even supplement, to a flowchart, a program designer might use a decision table to define the logical requirements of a program. A decision table identifies possible combinations of conditions that might arise, and defines what action must be taken in each case.

Suppose that a bank uses the following procedure for determining charges on transactions for its deposit account customers:

There is a charge of 50p for each cash withdrawal unless the account is in credit by at least £100, in which case there is no charge. If the customer would become overdrawn as a result of the cash withdrawal, the transaction is not allowed and no charge is made. The maximum cash withdrawal allowed at any one time is £50. If the transaction is a deposit, no charge is made. A decision table for the logic might look like this:

Cash withdrawal?	y	y	y	y	y	y	y	y	n	n	n	n	n	n	n	n
Withdrawal>£50?	y	y	y	y	n	n	n	n	y	y	y	y	n	n	n	n
Balance<£100?	y	y	n	n	y	y	n	n	y	y	n	n	y	y	n	n
Withdrawal>Balance?	y	n	y	n	y	n	y	n	y	n	y	n	y	n	y	n
Charge 50p						x										
No Charges							x	x	x	x	x	x	x	x	x	x
Refuse withdrawal	x	x	x	x	x											

Conditions are phrased as questions and appear in the top left-hand quarter of the table. All possible combinations of the answers (Yes or No) are listed in the top right-hand quarter. All possible actions are listed in the bottom left-hand quarter. An x in the bottom right quarter indicates under what combinations of conditions the action is to be performed.

Taking, for example, the sixth column of y/n combinations, it shows that

> IF   it is a cash withdrawal
>
> AND   the withdrawal is not greater than £50
>
> AND   the balance is less than £100
>
> AND   the amount of the withdrawal is not greater than the current balance
>
> THEN   make a charge of 50p

Notice that some combinations of conditions are not relevant. For example, if a cash withdrawal is greater than £50, then the final two conditions are irrelevant. Irrelevant conditions are indicated by dashes:

Cash withdrawal?	y	y	y	y	y	y	y	y	n	n	n	n	n	n	n	n
Withdrawal>£50?	y	y	y	y	n	n	n	n	-	-	-	-	-	-	-	-
Balance<£100?	-	-	-	-	y	y	n	n	-	-	-	-	-	-	-	-
Withdrawal>Balance?	-	-	-	-	y	n	-	-	-	-	-	-	-	-	-	-
Charge 50p						x										
No Charges							x	x	x	x	x	x	x	x	x	x
Refuse withdrawal	x	x	x	x	x											

Notice also that several combinations are now repeated so that the table could be summarised as follows:

Cash withdrawal?	y	y	y	y	n
Withdrawal>£50?	y	n	n	n	-
Balance<£100?	-	y	y	n	-
Withdrawal>Balance?	-	y	n	-	-
Charge 50p			x		
No Charges				x	x
Refuse withdrawal	x	x			

When drawing decision tables it is important to ensure that all combinations of conditions have been included. The maximum number of combinations is calculated as follows:

Number of conditions	Combinations
2	2x2=4
3	2x2x2=8
4	2x2x2x2=16
5	2x2x2x2x2=32
etc	

There is also a certain way of writing these combinations so that all of them are covered:

1. Determine the maximum number of combinations;

2. Halve this number;

3. Along the first condition line write this number of y's followed by the same number of n's until the line is complete;

4. Halve this number;

5. Repeat steps (3) and (4) until the final condition line consisting of alternate y's and n's has been completed.

For example, suppose there are 3 conditions, then the number of combinations is 2x2x2 = 8. Half of this is 4. Therefore the first line is

>   y y y y n n n n

The second line will consist of two y's followed by two n's alternating to the end of the line:

>   y y n n y y n n

The last line has one y and one y alternating:

>   y n y n y n y n

Thus the decision table will have the form

Condition 1	y	y	y	y	n	n	n	n
Condition 2	y	y	n	n	y	y	n	n
Condition 3	y	n	y	n	y	n	y	n
Actions								

CASE (computer-aided software engineering) tools

Software engineering is a concept which recognises the fact that the principles of engineering normally applied to other disciplines, can be highly relevant to the 'engineering' of information systems; the parameters for the effectiveness and quality of an information system have to be set at the design stage, if users' needs are to be properly met. A CASE tool can loosely refer to any software tool used in the development of information systems, for example:

- ❑ language processors (compilers and interpreters);
- ❑ fourth generation languages (4GLs);
- ❑ graphics programs to allow analysts to draw DFDs or ERMs.

A more precise definition of the term requires reference to the typical features of CASE proprietary software; complete CASE packages or toolkits are commercially available to aid the systems analyst and/or programmer in system development.

A CASE toolkit would normally contain components for:

- ❑ diagram construction;
- ❑ data dictionary development and control;
- ❑ interface and source code generation;
- ❑ project management.

Diagram construction

This tool is essential for the support of a structured systems methodology. The graphical facilities allow the drawing, storage and modification of diagrams and charts, such as data flow diagrams (DFDs), entity-relationship models (ERMs) and structure diagrams (for program development).

Data dictionary

Being particularly important in the development of database systems for the control and consistency of data, the function of data dictionaries is described and illustrated earlier.

Interface generation

Interface generators support the preparation of prototypes of user interfaces, such as screen dialogues, menus and reports.

Source code generation

These tools allow the automated preparation of computer software, in other words, the conversion of a system specification into the source code of a chosen programming language, which can then be compiled into executable object or machine code. CASE tools for code generation are general purpose and are, as a consequence less efficient in the production of source code than specialised applications generators; most code generators will only produce, say, 75% of the code automatically, leaving the rest to be hand-coded by a programmer.

Project management

Such tools support the scheduling of analysis and design activities and the allocation of resources to the various project activities.

Integrated CASE tools

CASE tools can be used as separate, discrete elements or as a complete system. The integrated use of CASE tools can best be managed through windowing software, which allows, for example, the simultaneous viewing of data flow diagrams and data dictionary entries on screen. Integration also has the benefit of allowing data from one component of the toolkit to be transferred to another, for example, data dictionary entries to entity-relationship diagrams.

✍ Exercises

1. List and briefly describe five fact-finding methods (see Chapter 35).
2. Obtain a sample input or output document for an information system, analyse its contents and record you analysis on a Document Analysis Form, similar to that shown at the end of Chapter 35.
3. By reference to Table 36.1, draw a document flow diagram to trace the use of one business document.
4. With the use of examples, define the terms: *external entity*, *process*, *data store* and *data flow*, in the context of data flow diagrams.
5. Which data flow diagram symbol (apart from the flow arrow) must be present in every data flow?
6. In the context of data flow diagrams, what is an *elementary item*?
7. Distinguish between a Level 1 DFD and a Level 2 (or lower) DFD.
8. What is the general purpose of an entity-relationship model?
9. With the use of an illustrative example, define the terms *entity*, *relationship* and *attribute*.
10.
    (i)   What is meant by the term *degree of relationship*?
    (ii) Why is one type of relationship problematic for relational database implementation of a model and how can the problem be resolved? Illustrate your answer with an example.
11. What is the purpose of a *data dictionary*?
12. In top-down design, what is the name given to the process of replacing the program components by sequences of smaller components?
13. Name and briefly describe four different forms of process model.
14. What are the three control structures used in structured English?
15. Try drawing a flowchart for a common task, such as making a cup of tea or cooking a soft-boiled egg.
16. Produce a flowchart and decision table for the following problem:
    A company bills its customers on the last day of each month. If the bill is paid before the start of the second week of the next month, the customer is given a discount of 5%. If the account is settled after the second week but before the last week, the customer is charged the amount of the bill. Payment after the beginning of the last week of the month results in an interest charge of 5%.
17. Give three examples of CASE tools.

Chapter 37

Requirements specification

At the end of the analysis stage, the systems analyst should have a thoroughly documented record of what the users want from the proposed system. The documentation will be a mixture of narrative description and diagrams of various types, including those already described in Chapter 36.

Specification features

To communicate the findings to users a Requirements Specification should be prepared. It should be:

1. readily understood by users and as free of ambiguity as possible. Before design begins, it is crucial that the users are quite clear about the analyst's conclusions. This is a simple rule which applies to all transactions between a provider and a consumer. If you ask someone to clean your windows, it is fairly straightforward to agree whether this includes the upstairs windows, or just the ground floor, but it is more difficult to come to an unambiguous understanding of the design for a house, simply because the problem is more complex and as a non-specialist you may not properly understand architectural drawings. Of course, the architect can help by producing artistic impressions or a computerised, 3D 'walk through'.

   To determine whether the user has properly interpreted a specification, it is a good idea to ask him or her to talk you through the Requirements Specification and clarify any point where you think they have misunderstood. For example, suppose that you have recorded that "At the end of the Company's financial year, the Sales system will produce a report of the sales for the year, with monthly totals and a grand total." You may have meant that the report would only contain summary totals when in fact the user thought you meant that the report would also include all the sales transaction within each month. Of course, the confusion in this example could be avoided by producing a sample of the report in the Specification.

2. achievable, affordable and practical. Although the systems analyst should be focusing on the business objectives which the system is meant to achieve, the Requirements Specification should not suggest a solution which the business cannot afford, or is impractical because of, for example, the physical constraints of the office premises or the limited skills of staff.

Presenting alternative solutions

There is always a number of possible solutions to a given problem and it is important to present users with alternatives. This is because there is usually a trade-off between the degree of functionality provided by a system (what it will do) and its cost. For example, option A may meet every business objective required by management, but option B costs half as much and can be implemented in half the time with the sacrifice of one aspect of a business objective. Put simply, a system which automates additional tasks, for example in order processing, and saves the business an average of 5 minutes each day may not be worth the additional cost. The decision on which solution is chosen may be influenced by:

❑ how much the business can afford to invest;

❑ how quickly the system will repay that investment. This is not always easy to measure, but an attempt should be made. Suppose, for example, that a business has to spend £20,000 on a system which takes 6 months to develop and implement and then another 3 years for increased productivity to bring the required return. The business must make sure that it will not run short of cash for the day-to-day running of the business during that period.

❑ the technical competence of the staff who are to use the system. For example, a small architectural firm may decide to do all its work using computer-aided design (CAD), but the staff may need an extensive training period to make effective use of the software. In the meantime, jobs have to be completed by traditional methods, until a sufficient level of skill has been reached to complete an entire job with the CAD system. An alternative could be to allocate CAD work to the most technically competent architect and to use it only for relatively small jobs.

It is important to keep an open mind about alternative solutions and not to present users with a single, "this is the only way" solution. Users should be encouraged to concentrate on what they want the system to do, to think creatively and should be discouraged from simply wanting a copy of the old system, but using the latest technology. In this way, new benefits may be obtained which were impractical or impossible with the old system. Context and high level data flow diagrams, or even less formal pictorial or 'rich picture' representations are extremely useful for communicating ideas to users.

Making the decision

It is not up to the systems analyst to make the decision on which option to choose. Apart from presenting the alternatives and pointing out the pros and cons of each, the decision should be left to the client. The 'client' will be the proprietor or partners in a business, or in the case of a limited company, the Board of Directors. The client should take careful account of the actual users, operational, supervisory and management but the final decision must be left to the person or persons who are paying for the development. Effectively, the analyst needs to be able to say, "I presented you with viable and effective alternatives, but you decide which one to implement". Apart from allocation of responsibility for the decision, users must not feel that they are using a system for which they have no responsibility. Their commitment to its success will be greater if they feel that they have been closely involved and have received sufficient information to make a considered decision.

Prototyping

Prototyping is a method providing users with a 'taster' of the appearance of a proposed system, without commitment to full development. A prototype is, in effect, a first try at manufacturing a newly designed product; it is not expected to be perfect, but will form a basis for future development and design improvements. Car manufacturers do this when trying to incorporate revolutionary features and technologies into a new car.

A prototype of an information system allows users to test it for achievement of their desired objectives. Prototyping can take place at various stages of the system development cycle, but its use must be planned and anticipated to ensure maximum feedback is obtained from users. In the early stages, a prototype may be developed to test the appropriateness of screen dialogues, without constructing the main files, whilst later it may include a section of database and some applications software. Prototyping is expensive, in terms of time and resources and is unlikely to be used where user requirements are well established or the system is fairly standard.

Development costs

Labour costs include the time of specialists such as analysts, designers and programmers, as well as users who have to spend time providing information to the developers or perhaps testing at various stages of design and before full implementation. The development time affects labour costs, but will also affect the general operation of a business and may bring other costs of, for example, slower response time to customer orders. The development time also has a significant effect on cashflow. During development, costs have to be met even though there will be no system benefits to provide return on the investment until after implementation.

Hardware costs may be significant or minimal, depending on whether the systems is able to make use of existing computer hardware. However, the speed with which technology continues to develop often means that every new system needs to take advantage of the most recent hardware. Other costs may result from:

- ❏ a requirement for software development or purchase
- ❏ need for user training;
- ❏ necessary alterations to office layout and new furniture;
- ❏ a need to recruit new staff with specialist knowledge and skills;
- ❏ liability to redundancy payments for staff whose work is to be done by the system;
- ❏ a need for parallel running or other methods of ensuring that the system operates effectively before full implementation.

Projected benefits

These are more difficult to quantify than the costs but may include, for example:

- ❏ increased productivity, thus reducing unit costs and increasing profitability;
- ❏ lower running costs, particularly if the older systems were subject to regular breakdown and required frequent repair and maintenance;
- ❏ expansion in business turnover, without the need for extra staff and reduced overtime requirements.

Contents of the requirements specification

The Requirements or Functional Specification is part of the contract between the client and the analyst/designer and should be signed by the client. Typically, the Specification may contain the following sections:

- ❏ Outputs from the system - content, format and layout of screen and printed outputs;
- ❏ Inputs to the system - sources of data, data types and formats, procedures (clerical and machine-assisted);
- ❏ System performance - response times, work throughput (e.g. number of transactions per hour), procedures for system recovery in the event of hardware or software failure (for example, use of backup files or systems);
- ❏ Operating procedures - for example, start-up and shutdown, backup, virus protection, access security.

Chapter 38

Systems design tutorial

This Tutorial guides you through the various stages of a design, using the example of Accounts Receivable (Sales Accounting) for Trade Cycles, a cycle wholesaler. The general business structure is similar to the typical trading business used in Chapter 36 to illustrate the systems analysis stage.

Before illustrating the various stages of design, we now describe the role and operation of an Accounts Receivable section within the Accounts Department of a business, in this case, a cycle wholesaler.

The system: Accounts Receivable

The role of Accounts Receivable system is to record amounts owing by customers who buy goods on credit, which is usual with trade customers, and to handle the processes of issuing invoices and receiving payment. These records are held in the Sales Ledger or, as it may also be referred to, the Customer Accounts file.

We now illustrate the procedures and processes involved in Sales Order Processing, using the example of a cycle shop and a cycle wholesaler. Suppose that the Rough Rider cycle shop wishes to buy stock from a particular wholesale supplier, Trade Cycles, for the first time.

The procedures and the particular role of the Accounts Receivable section may involve the steps illustrated in Figure 38.1 (not every detail is shown) and described below. Although we are using the example of one particular customer, the procedures would apply to all such customer transactions with Trade Cycles

Such a "rich picture" illustration is extremely useful for communicating with users in the initial stages of design, although it does not comply with any particular methodology. For your own understanding of the formal design stages which follow in this Tutorial, you should make sure that you thoroughly understand the application being designed and the illustration should be of help.

1. The proprietor of Rough Rider wants to apply for an account and trade credit terms and a form is faxed or e-mailed from Trade Cycles.

2. Rough Rider completes and returns the application, which may require, for example, bank account details, date company established, trade references and other information to establish the reliability and credit worthiness of the business.

3. Trade Cycles sends for trade references provided by Rough Rider.

4. Trade reference replies are received by Trade Cycles. (It is assumed here that the replies are satisfactory, but a procedure would be needed to deal with credit account refusal. We will not include that complication here.)

5. Accounts Receivable sets up a customer account for Rough Rider. Trade terms are agreed which, for example, require orders to be paid for within 30 days of the invoice date. A credit limit, sufficient to cover the value of orders that the customer will place within one month, will also be agreed.

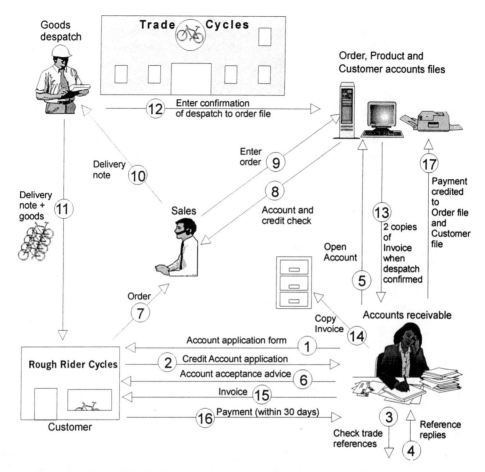

Figure 38.1. *Rich picture illustrating order processing and invoicing*

6. Trade Cycles advises Rough Rider that an account has been opened.

7. Rough Rider sends an order on its own headed stationery to Trade Cycles.

8. Sales accesses the customer account to check available credit.

9. Sales enters the order details to the Order file and Rough Rider's Account is debited with the order value.

10. Sales section generates a delivery note and passes it to Despatch.

11 The required stock is allocated and then despatched to Rough Rider.

12. Despatch updates the Order file to confirm that goods have been despatched.

13. Accounts Receivable checks the order file daily and for those with confirmed despatch, 2 copies of each invoice are printed, including that for Rough Rider.

14. A copy of the invoice is filed under "Unpaid Invoices". (Such manual records are normally needed when the business accounts are prepared and audited at the end of the financial year)

15. The other copy of the invoice is sent to Rough Rider.

16. Within 30 days of the invoice date, Rough Rider should send a payment in settlement of the debt to Accounts Receivable. It is essential that the invoice number is quoted so that the payment can be applied to the correct invoice, in case other orders have been placed during the month by Rough Rider.

17. Upon receipt of the payment, Accounts Receivable inputs the amount to the appropriate order in the Sales Order file; this amount is then automatically credited to the account of Rough Rider in the Customer Accounts file (this update is not included within the design which follows). When payment is received and the customer's account updated, the relevant hard copy invoice can be stamped "PAID" and re-filed under "Paid Invoices" (such manual procedures must be designed but are not included in this tutorial).

Stages of design

In the following sections you will be guided through the following steps in the design of the Accounts Receivable system for Trade Cycles:

- ❏ establishing the system boundary;
- ❏ output and input design;
- ❏ logical data design (entity modelling);
- ❏ database table design;
- ❏ process design.

System boundary - accounts receivable

The *system boundary* should have been identified during the analysis stage, but it is vital that the limits of the development are clearly defined before design work starts.

Identifying inputs and outputs

The data flow diagram in Figure 38.2 shows the boundary between the Accounts Receivable and its related functions in the sales order processing and invoicing system. The boundary allows easy identification of inputs and outputs for the target system. Arrows which flow towards Accounts Receivable are inputs to the system, whilst outputs are indicated by outward flow arrows.

Figure 38.2 is focused on the Accounts Receivable application as this allows us to illustrate the design stages more clearly than would be possible with a more extensive system boundary. In reality, it is likely that the design would have a wider focus because, as Figure 38.1 shows, the other aspects of sales order processing and invoicing are closely linked with Accounts Receivable. Figure 38.1 shows the complete process from the initial request for a credit account, through the placing of an order, invoicing of the customer and final settlement of the account. If we were designing the complete system, those processes would be included within the system boundary and also show inputs and outputs with Sales and Despatch.

Output design - Accounts Receivable

Figure 38.2 identifies three outputs which are explained below.

1. Order details. This is screen output and allows the Accounts Receivable clerk to identify which orders have been despatched but for which customers have not yet been invoiced. Identification of such orders requires a search of the order file. As each order is displayed, the clerk can choose an option to print two copies of an invoice, one of which is sent to the customer, the other being retained in a manual file (such clerical,

non-computerised procedures will be part of the completed design specification, but are not included here). Order records are updated when the invoices are printed to ensure that they are not included in later invoice print runs.

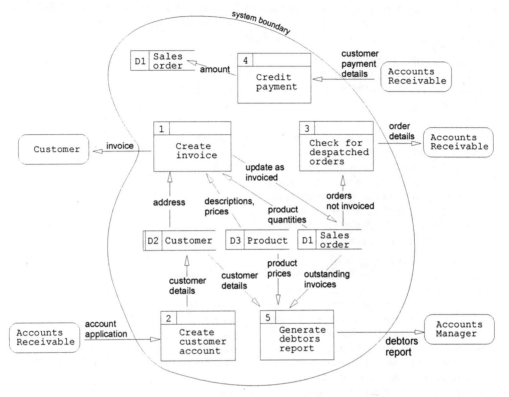

Figure 38.2. *System boundary identifying inputs to and outputs from Accounts Receivable*

2. Sales invoice. An invoice is printed and sent to the customer after the despatch of an order has been confirmed. In the case of Rough Rider, this will have to be settled within 30 days of the invoice date. The process requires access to three files:

    (i)   Customer file for address details

    (ii)   Order file for details of products and quantities ordered.

    (iii) Product file for product prices.

    These elements will be examined in more detail later in process and file/database design.

3. Debtors report. This is a report listing of all unpaid and overdue invoices as at a specified date. The Accounts Manager uses the information to monitor customer debts, allow chasing of overdue accounts and to provide early warning of debts which may become 'bad'.

Each of the above outputs needs to be analysed in terms of the:

❑ data items required as output;

❑ form of the output, for example, whether or not printed copy is required;

☐ volume of data with each output and the frequency of the output. This information assists decisions on the type and number of output devices required.

The data items then form part of the output design with the addition of, for example, labels and headings on a printed report. We now look at the data requirement, forms of output and the designs for each of the outputs identified from Figure 38.2.

1. **Order details**. The output should contain the following data items, which should be recorded in the data dictionary as shown in Table 38.1 (9 indicates a digit).

   The output is only used to alert the Accounts Receivable clerk of orders for which invoices have not yet been produced and not all the above information is essential to that task. Customer Name and Order Value, for example, would allow the clerk to check that these details agree with the invoice once it is printed.

Data item	Type	Length
Order number	9999	
Customer account code	9999	
Customer name	text	30
Order value	9999.99	
Date despatched	date	8
Date invoiced	date	4

Table 38.1.

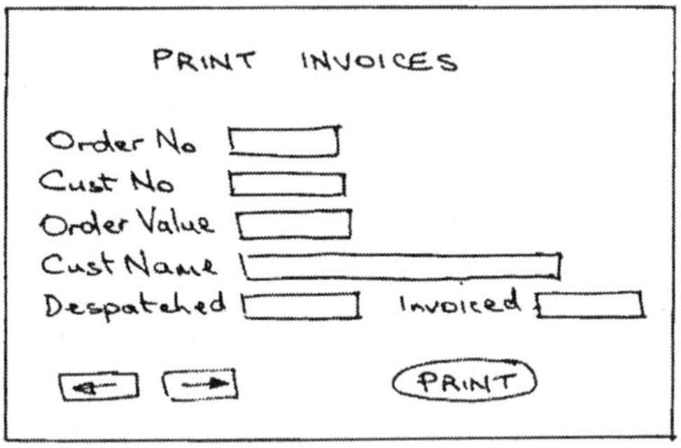

The form of the output is on screen and there is no requirement for the details to be printed. Concerning the volume of output for this example, we assume that it can be managed by a single operator and that the task is undertaken towards the end of each day, so that invoices can be sent with the afternoon post. The screen design can be produced by hand or with word processing or CASE (Computer Aided Software Engineering) software. A hand-prepared example layout is shown in Figure 38.3.

Figure 38.3. *Screen layout for display of orders for which invoices are to be printed*

2. **Sales invoice**. The output should contain the following data items, which should be recorded in the data dictionary as shown in Table 38.2 (the number in brackets indicates the number of digits, for example, 9(3) means 999).

Data item	Type	Length
Order number	9999	
Customer order number	text	15
Order received	date	8
Order despatched	date	8
Customer name	text	25
Invoice address	text	50
Invoice post code	text	9
Item code	text	5
Item description	text	30
Quantity	999	
Unit price	999.99	

Line value	9(6).99	
Order value	9(7).99	
VAT	9(6).99	
Total inc VAT	9(7).99	
Payment terms	text	20

Table 38.2.

The form of the output is printed, although a screen preview could also be provided to allow visual checking before printing.

As mentioned earlier and illustrated in Figure 38.2, the invoice draws data from three different data stores, namely the Order file, Customer file and Product file. As will be detailed in process design, some items, for example, Order value and VAT, will be calculated from other stored values. The shaded rows identify repeated data items (a customer may order several different products items on one order) an issue which is dealt with later in entity modelling.

The invoice will also include static data which is embedded into the template, such as the company details for Trade Cycles, column headings and other labelling. A word processed design for the invoice, with example data, is shown in Figure 38.4.

Trade Cycles Limited

Unit 4, Thames Ind Estate
Henley, Oxon, OX4 3NG
Telephone: 01465 326140
Fax: 01465 326102
Email: sales:tradecycles.co.uk
www.tradecycles.co.uk

Rough Rider Cycle Shop
23 Hartsfell Road
Cartmel
Cumbria
CU2 3LS

Order No:	1299
Customer Order No:	PO1893811
Order received:	13/12/01
Order despatched:	18/12/01

Item Code	Description	Quantity	Price	Value
cc311	Amazon RB	15	323.00	4845.00
cc522	Krakatoa MB	3	220.00	660.00

Order value	5505.00
VAT	963.38
Total inc. VAT	6468.38

Trade Cycles Limited
Registered in England: 4136472
VAT Reg. No: 746 316724

Figure 38.4. *Word processed invoice design*

3. **Debtors report.** The output should contain the following data items, which should be recorded in the data dictionary as shown in Table 38.3.

Data item	Type	Length
Customer account number	9999	
Customer name	text	25
Order number	9999	
Order value	9(7).99	
Due	date	8

Table 38.3

The form of the output is printed, although screen output could be provided for quick reference without printing hard copy.

Figure 38.5 shows a design for the report. The date of the report would be provided by the computer system (system date), the amount due would be calculated as for the invoice and the 'late' * marker would be inserted on each line where the Due date is earlier than the report date. These aspects will be dealt with later in the process design section.

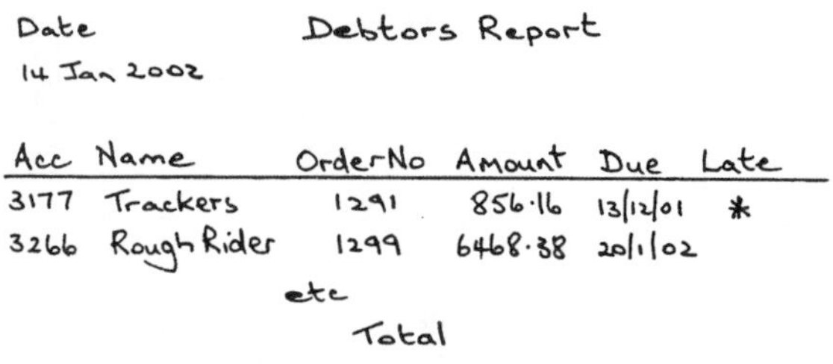

Figure 38.5. *Hand-prepared design for Debtors Report*

Input design - general guidelines

Before we deal with the specific design requirements for the Accounts Receivable system, there are a number of general design requirements with which you need to be familiar. Input design requires attention to the following:

- source(s) of data. It may, for example, originate from a customer, a supplier, or another department in the business;

- contents. For example, the individual items of data that appear on a supplier's invoice;

- forms of data. The data may arrive, for example, by telephone, letter, or a standard form such as an order form or supplier's invoice;

- volume and frequency of inputs. For example, the number of orders received daily or weekly.

- user interface design (Chapter 39).

The design of appropriate input methods also has to take account of various tasks associated with the collection and entry of data to a system:

- recording. For example, the completion of a customer order form following receipt of a customer order by telephone;

- transmission or communication. For example, the order details may need to be transferred to another department or branch of the business for encoding and computer processing or they may be keyed in directly at the point of collection;

- visual checking. It may be, for example, that a customer order has no quantities entered;

- encoding. Verification procedures need to be designed to prevent transcription errors when data is encoded onto a computer storage medium for processing. In high volume, batch entry systems, verification is computer-assisted and involves a double keying operation.

- validation. Data is checked by a data vet program against set limits of validity, for example, account numbers may have to fall between a particular range of values.

Thus, design decisions need to be made concerning: (i) data collection procedures; (ii) methods for the transmission of data to the place of processing; (iii) data entry, data verification and data validation procedures.

Data collection

The designer needs to be aware of the available input technologies. These can be divided into two categories, keyboard entry and data capture technologies such as bar code reading, optical character reading (OCR) and optical mark reading (OMR), which allow direct input to the computer from specially designed input forms.

Keyboard entry is the most common method of input and requires the transcription of data from source documents. These can be designed to minimise the possibility of transcription errors at the data collection stage.

Direct input uses methods such as bar code and optical mark reading.

Bar codes are pre-encoded and are thus immune from errors of transcription (assuming that the bar code is correct in the first place). Optical mark reading requires that pencil marks are used to indicate particular values from a limited set on a pre-designed form. Although no keyboard entry is required, mistakes may be made by the originator of the document and good design is therefore important.

Data transmission

It may be that no data transmission is necessary because the data is processed at the point of collection. For example, customer orders may be recorded on order forms at the sales desk and then taken into the next room for keying into the computer. Alternatively, the data may have to be transmitted some distance, perhaps to another floor of the building or to another building some miles away. A fundamental decision has to be made, whether to localise processing at the points of collection, or to use a central facility with data communications links from each location.

Data entry

The data entry method chosen will depend on the data collection methods used and may involve keyboard transcription from source documents or data may be captured directly from bar codes, OCR (optical character recognition) or OMR (optical mark recognition) type documents. Where keyboard transcription is used, verification and validation procedures are likely to be interactive, in that the data entry operator has to respond to prompts on screen and make corrections as and when the system indicates. Most small business computer systems will be used for on-line processing, where transactions are processed immediately with master files at the data entry stage. Consequently, validation and verification have to be carried out immediately prior to the processing of each transaction.

On-screen verification and validation

At the end of each transaction entry, the operator is given the opportunity to scan the data on the screen and to re-enter any incorrect entries detected. This usually takes the form of a message at the bottom of the screen which is phrased in a way such as Verify (yes or no).

Character, data item and record checks, such as range and mode checks, can be made each time the RETURN key is pressed during data entry. For example, the screen may prompt for the entry of an account number, which must be 6 digits long and be within the range 000001 to 500000. Any entry which does not conform with these parameters is erased and the prompt re-displayed for another attempt. Appropriate screen dialogue to allow the data entry operator to enter into a 'conversation' with the computer is a crucial part of the input design process and is dealt with as a separate topic in Chapter 39.

Batch data entry

The type of keyboard transcription used will be affected by the type of input data. Where, for example, files only need to be updated weekly, transaction data may be batched and entered onto magnetic disk for processing at a later stage in one update program run.

Input design - Accounts Receivable

Figure 38.2 identifies three inputs which are explained below.

1. New customer account. A standard form is completed by each new customer and the details are then input to the Customer file to create a new account. Two designs are needed, one for the account application form and the other for the screen input of new account details.

2. Customer payment. When payment is received in settlement of a sales invoice, the amount is entered to the Customer file to reduce the amount owing.

Each of the above inputs needs to be analysed in terms of the:

☐ data items required as input.

☐ form of the data, for example, whether a standard input form is used or, in the case of call centre, for example, the inputs follow from a telephone dialogue;

☐ volume of data with each input and the frequency of the input. This information assists decisions on the type and number of input devices required.

The data items then form part of the input design with the addition of, for example, the labels and headings which form part of a screen dialogue.

1. **New customer account.** The input should contain the following data items, which should be recorded in the data dictionary as shown in Table 38.4.

Data item	Type	Length
Customer account number	9999	
Name	text	25
Address	text	50
Post code	text	10
Telephone	text	15
Contact name	text	25
Credit term	99	
Credit limit	999999	
Balance	99999.99	

Table 38.4

Input is taken from data on the completed account application form, although not all the data from the form is entered. For example, the details of trade references are used to check on the customer's credit worthiness but are not stored on computer. The credit term (30 days, for example) and the credit limit are entered after agreement between the customer and the Accounts Manager, taking into account the customer's order requirements. The balance (amount owing) will be entered at £0.00 when the account is first opened. Figure 38.6 shows a hand-prepared design for the customer account application form. The boxed entries will contain the values for input to the Customer file. Some are labelled "leave blank" and will be completed by Trade Cycles following receipt of the application.

A design for the screen input of new customer accounts is shown in Figure 38.7.

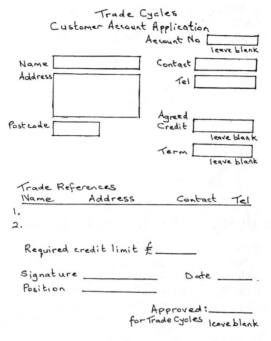

Figure 38.6. *Design for Customer Account Application*

Figure 38.7. *New customer account input screen*

2. **Customer payment.** Having received an invoice, the customer sends payment to reach Trade Cycles within the agreed credit term (say, 30 days), accompanied by a *payment advice* which identifies the payment with the relevant Trade Cycles Order number (this appears on the invoice - Figure 38.4).

The data items needed for payment input are shown in Table 38.5 and should be included in the data dictionary.

Data item	Type	Length
Order No	9999	
Payment amount	99999.99	
Payment type	text	8

Table 38.5

Although these are the only data items which have to be input, the dialogue may show details of customer name (accessed from the Customer file via the Order file) to allow a level of verification that the payment is being credited to the correct order and thereby to the correct customer. A design for the screen is shown in Figure 38.8.

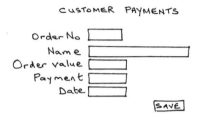

Figure 38.8. *Customer payment input screen*

Logical data design - Accounts Receivable

Reference is made to the various files from which outputs are drawn and to which inputs are applied, but no detail has been given so far on the ways that the data may be structured to allow these necessary connections between files. For example, the invoice in Figure 38.4 uses data from the Order, Product and Customer file and the next section shows how these necessary connections, or relationships, between files (or tables in the case of a relational database implementation) can be specified. The topic of Entity (relationship) Modelling is fully described in Chapter 36.

Entity model

We have already established that there are three main objects of interest, or entities, associated with the Accounts Receivable system: Order, Customer and Product. We have also referred to Order Line which, as illustrated below, is needed to resolve the many-to-many relationship which exists between Order and Product. The entity model with the three original entities is shown in Figure 38.9.

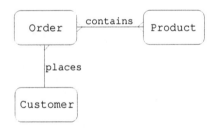

Figure 38.9. *Entity model including many-to-many relationship*

The many-to-many relationship between Order and Product can be expressed as follows. "Each order may contain many product items and each product item may appear in many orders." This relationship will not allow direct implementation in a flat file or relational database system and the first stage of normalisation (First Normal Form) must be applied to resolve the it. In First Normal Form the data must have no repeating groups.

The entity Order Line can be placed between the Order and Product entities to create many-to-one relationships with each, as shown in Figure 38.10.

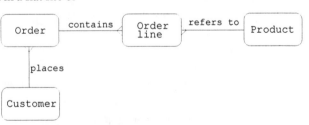

Figure 38.10. *Entity model in First Normal Form*

As the relationship between Customer and Order is already one-to-many ("each customer may place many orders, but each order only relates to one customer"), the entity model is in First Normal form and can be directly implemented with a relational database.

Each entity in the model equates with a relational database table and the relationships can be further illustrated by including the attributes (fields) for each entity in the model, as shown in Figure 38.11.

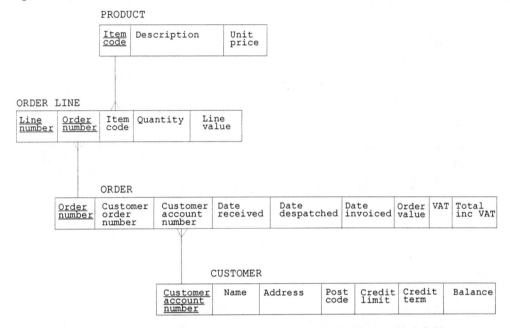

Figure 38.11. *Entity model showing attributes, unique identifiers and link fields*

The Figure shows how the Order Line entity is linked to the Product entity by the Item Code attribute and to the Order entity by the Order Number attribute.

Each entity must have one attribute which can be used to uniquely identify an entity occurrence (record). These unique identifiers are underscored in the Figure. Note that Order Line needs Line Number and Order Number as a composite identifier. This is always necessary for an entity which is created to resolve a many-to-many relationship. In database terminology, Order Number in the Order Line entity is known as a *foreign key*.

Data dictionary

The entries for the data dictionary have been illustrated at various stages of the design tutorial, but a complete definition of all data items should be included in the final system specification. Once implemented, the system will need to provide different data requirements as users' needs change and the data dictionary needs to reflect all such changes.

The data dictionary is vital for the maintenance of data consistency across a database and must be kept up-to-date. If, for example, a new application appears to require a new data item, the dictionary should be checked to ensure that it does not already exist. This can be necessary if different departments in an organisation use different names to refer to what is actually the same data item.

Process design - Accounts Receivable

Process design focuses on the process boxes which are found in data flow diagrams, where they appear simply as 'black boxes' with no explanation of how data is transformed at each stage. In process design, the designer/programmer can make use of a number of *process models*, already described earlier in this chapter. As illustrated by the examples in that section, a programmer would need to define all processes, including those, for example, to accept input, read sequentially through a series of records, sort or filter records according to some criterion, carry out calculations and print headings and summary totals. If implementation is planned with the use of a programming language, such as Pascal, COBOL or a database programming language, the process models would need to cover every stage from input to output.

When implemented in a relational database without programming, such detailed specification is unnecessary because the database management system (DBMS) can take care of the routine tasks of record handling. So, the models provided here are limited in scope, but sufficient for our purposes.

Rather than use structured English, we will give a narrative description of the process, followed by the appropriate SQL (Structured Query Language) statements. This has the benefit of providing a similar form of expression to structured English, with the added benefit that SQL statements can be interpreted directly by the database management system.

Process models are illustrated for following processes identified in Figure 38.2.

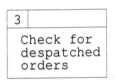

This process could be an option within a menu-based system. Running the option will scan the Order file and retrieving (SELECT) records where the Date Despatched field is not blank (Is Not Null) and the Date Invoiced is blank (Is Null).

For each retrieved record, the date can be entered and the Print Invoice option chosen (the day's data may be entered automatically as soon as the print option is chosen). The SQL statement could be of the following form.

```
SELECT Order.OrderNo, Order.CustOrdNo, Order.CustAccNo, Order.DateRec,
Order.DateDes, Order.DateInv, Order.PaymentAmt, Order.DatePaid
FROM [Order]
WHERE (((Order.DateDes) Is Not Null) AND ((Order.DateInv) Is Null));
```

The SELECT keyword is followed by the field names, each being prefixed by the table name in which they are located, in this case Order. This determines the contents of each displayed record. The FROM keyword states which table is used and WHERE is followed by the criteria for selection.

```
1
    Create
    invoice
```

Figure 38.2 shows that this process needs access to three files, Customer for the address details, Product for prices and Sales Order for order details. If we look at the entity model in Figure

38.11, it is apparent that a relational database would involve the use of a fourth file, or more properly, table (Order Line). The need for all these tables in actual implementation arises from the fact that the line and total order values are calculated 'on the fly' and are not held as permanent values in the Order file.

The previous process 'Check for despatched orders' is followed by this process which generates and prints the invoices. The SQL statement may be formed as follows.

```
SELECT Customer.Name, Customer.Address, Customer.Postcode,
Order.CustOrdNo, Order.DateRec, Order.DateDes, OrderLine.LineNo,
OrderLine.OrderNo, OrderLine.ItemCode, OrderLine.Quantity,
Product.ItemCode, Product.Description, Product.UnitPrice,
[UnitPrice]*[Quantity] AS [value]
FROM ((([Order] INNER JOIN OrderLine ON Order.OrderNo =
OrderLine.OrderNo) INNER JOIN Product ON OrderLine.ItemCode =
Product.ItemCode) INNER JOIN Customer ON Order.AccNo = Customer.AccNo;
```

INNER JOIN is a commonly used operation and merges information from tables where values in the link fields are common to both tables. The SQL word ON is followed by criteria. Thus, the selected fields from the Order table are combined with fields from the:

- ☐ OrderLine table when the OrderNo in the Order table matches with OrderNo in the Order Line table;

- ☐ Product table when ItemCode in the Order Line table matches with ItemCode in the Product table;

- ☐ Customer table when AccNo in Order table matches with AccNo in the Customer table.

Non-standard procedures

Most processes will follow standards suitable for their particular circumstances. For example, before an order is processed, stock items ordered are checked for availability. It is important, however, that the investigation identifies and notes any non-standard procedures. For example, what procedure is followed when there is an insufficient quantity of an ordered item to completely fulfil a customer order? It may be that some customers will take part-orders, whilst others require the full quantity of an item or none at all. If non-standard procedures are needed, it is important to know their complexity, how often they are used and what extra information is required. Ideally, a system should be designed to cope with all possible circumstances, but cost sometimes forces a compromise. If cost prohibits the inclusion of certain system features, for example, the ability to deal with part-orders, then it is important that the business is aware of such limitations so that it can modify its business objectives.

✍ Exercises

1. Define the term *system boundary*, explain its importance and how it can be used to identify system inputs and outputs.

2. Identify a range of input methods and provide an example of an application for which each is suitable.

3. With reference to a suitable example, identify the main aspects of input design.

4. With the use of an illustrative example, explain why data must be in First Normal Form before implementation of a design with a relational database.

Chapter 39
User interface design

The movement from centralised to distributed systems and the expansion in microcomputer usage has spawned the need for a variety of approaches to the design of *user interfaces* (UIs) which fulfil the requirements of an increasing population of computer users, the majority of whom are not computer specialists. When all computer processing was controlled by small numbers of experts, in centralised data processing departments, there was little pressure for UI design to be particularly 'friendly'. This is probably a major reason why many people used to regard computers with some suspicion and apprehension. UIs are also variously known as *human-computer* and *man-machine* interfaces. UI design is now recognised as being of critical importance and is usually the yardstick by which a system is judged; poor UI design can seriously affect a user's view of a system's functionality. Several design principles can be identified:

- ❏ it should be a product of collaboration between the designer and the users;
- ❏ user, not designer, convenience should be paramount;
- ❏ the interface should be of consistent design throughout the system;
- ❏ built-in help and advice should be accessible at different levels, depending on the degree of assistance required.

Interface metaphors
Through the use of metaphors, an interface can present a system's facilities in a form familiar to the user. A number of metaphors are commonly employed.

Desktop metaphor
As the term indicates, the UI relates everyday desktop or office facilities to routine computer tasks such as loading, saving or deleting files. The following representations are usual:

- ❏ filing cabinets for disc drives;
- ❏ documents for files;
- ❏ folders for directories;
- ❏ waste paper baskets or bins for the deletion of files from backing storage.

Control panel metaphor
A screen control panel may include a variety of elements, such as: *buttons* for initiating actions, for example, print; *switches* for setting options on and off, for example, a grid on a spreadsheet; *radio buttons* for choosing from ESGs (exclusive selection groups), for example, A5/A4/A3 documents sizes; *sub-panel menu* of buttons or switches to select, for example, system default settings; *lights* to indicate some active event, for example, printing; *signs* displaying, for example, which file is currently active; *sliders*, to vary for example, RGB (red green blue) colour mixes.

WIMP interfaces

An acronym for Windows, Icons, Menus, Pointing (alternatively, Windows, Icons, Mice and Pull-down menus), the WIMP concept stems from original work by Xerox PARC Laboratories in the mid-1970s and was first employed on Apple Lisa and Macintosh computer systems. Since then a number of WIMP orientated UIs have been developed, notably, GEM, MS-Windows, ARC and Sun. Such interfaces have a number of characteristics and features:

❑ the necessary skills are easy to grasp and the systems are easy to use;

❑ multiple windows for switching between tasks (multi-tasking);

❑ full-screen interaction allows quicker command execution than is usually possible through a *command line interpreter*;

❑ control panels (see previous section).

However, as a relatively new concept, there are no standards for the design of WIMP-based products. Certain difficulties in their design may be experienced:

❑ although multiple windows are useful for task switching, too many windows can be confusing;

❑ designing icons which unambiguously tell the user of specific functions can be difficult and some may need to be augmented with text support, perhaps in a help window.

The graphical user interface (GUI) used on modern operating systems uses the WIMP design principles.

Graphical user interface (GUI)

Figure 39.1 shows the graphical user interface for the Windows 2000 operating system.

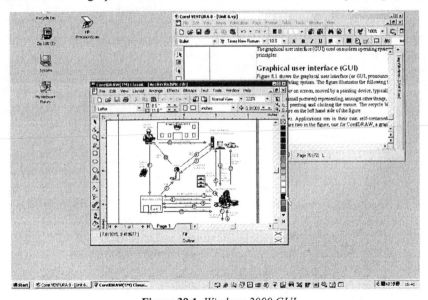

Figure 39.1. *Windows 2000 GUI*

The figure illustrates the following features of a GUI:

❑ a *pointer* on screen, moved by a pointing device, typically a *mouse*.

❏ *icons* (small pictures) representing, amongst other things, programs, which can be run by pointing and clicking the mouse. The recycle bin, browser and system icons are on the left hand side of the figure.

❏ *windows*. Applications run in their own self-contained areas called *windows*. There are two in the figure, one for CorelDRAW, a graphic design program and another for Corel Ventura, a desktop publishing package.

Most users are not really interested in the technical details of a computer's operation and simply want to use it. However, to do so effectively, a user must learn routine maintenance tasks, such as creating folders, copying files and formatting disks as well as the use of the particular applications they need. A GUI is designed to make these tasks easier as follows.

❏ Methods of doing things are more *intuitive*. This means that a user can often anticipate what certain actions with the mouse will do. For example, selecting a file with a mouse pointer and dragging it to an *icon* (small picture) of a dustbin has the effect of deleting the selected file.

❏ Applications running under a GUI have common features, so, for example, it is easier to transfer skills learned using a word processor to those needed for a spreadsheet.

The hardware needed to run GUI systems needs to be of higher specification, in terms of disk space, RAM capacity, processor speed and screen resolution, than is the case for text-orientated systems. Most modern applications software use a GUI, but there are still applications, such as for till checkouts and machine control displays which are text based and accordingly they require reduced hardware specifications.

Menu systems

A menu of options is displayed, from which a user can make a selection. Menus are only appropriate where a limited range of options is available at any one time, although the selection of an item may cause the display of a further sub-menu. Commonly, each option is identified by a single letter or number which has to be keyed to select the option. Some packages, typically those running under the MS-DOS operating system, use a menu system which allows selection of an option either by highlighting the option with the cursor and pressing the 'enter' key or simply by keying the first letter of the option (without the need for confirmation). The problem for all such systems is to design each menu such that the first letter of each option is unique in that menu. The use of main menus which give access to sub-menus, each of which in turn may provide access to further sub-menus, follows a hierarchical structure. A number of design principles may be employed:

❏ Provided a simple mechanism is available for the user to return to the main menu, then several levels of menu can be used without the user becoming 'lost'. Commonly, the Esc key allows the user to work backwards from lower level menus to the main menu. Alternatively, each sub-menu may include an option 'Return to Main Menu'.

❏ The designer of a menu structure should limit the number of options displayed in a menu to a maximum of about eight, at which point, a sub-menu should be considered for further options. An excessive number of options on screen at one time looks untidy and may be rather intimidating to the user.

Pull-down menus

This method generally displays the main menu along the top of the screen and is popularly associated with WIMP orientated systems. When an option is selected with the cursor or mouse pointer, the range of sub-options associated with it are 'pulled down' and displayed.

Menu systems provide a number of benefits:

- ❏ all possibilities are presented as a command list;
- ❏ minimal typing is required;
- ❏ error trapping is simple;
- ❏ inappropriate choices can be withheld from the user;
- ❏ context sensitive help can be provided.

The drawbacks are that:

- ❏ they can be tedious for experienced users;
- ❏ an extended hierarchy of menus can be difficult for the user to follow;
- ❏ a large number of choices may require the use of several screens, as is the case, for example, with viewdata systems.

Form-fill dialogue

This type of dialogue requires that the screen layout matches the associated input document as closely as possible. The operator is then able to make the entries in the same logical progression as the hand-filled form. A number of features are usually evident:

- ❏ boxed in areas indicate fields for data entry;
- ❏ form headings are protected and cannot be overwritten by the user;
- ❏ cursor movement is restricted to the variable data entry points adjacent to each heading.

A number of design features can be applied to the data entry process:

- ❏ with fixed length data items, for example, a 6-digit account number, the cursor skips automatically to the next field as soon as the last character is entered;
- ❏ with variable length data items, the TAB key is pressed by the user when an entry is complete. This causes the cursor to skip to the next field;
- ❏ when all entries have been made, the user scans the screen to ensure all entries appear correct and the confirms them by pressing 'return';
- ❏ if errors are discovered before the 'return' key is pressed, a mechanism is available to enable corrections to be made.

The form-fill method is inappropriate when system responses are displayed which may obscure the screen headings or entries. Thus, if an invalid entry is made, the system should 'bleep' to indicate that a correction is required, without displaying an error message or display the message in a status line at the bottom of the screen; users should be well trained and aware of the valid data formats, so the need for help messages should be minimal.

Natural language dialogue

This type of dialogue is frequently used in database systems to allow users to specify their requirements in a 'natural' language style. The construction of the language is a complex process and many systems only allow the use of strictly limited syntax and sentence construction. Thus although the language can be described as 'natural', there is limited flexibility to allow different users to form requests in a way which is natural to each. As a result, the casual user may become frustrated by having to rephrase requests in attempts to resolve ambiguities. Queries tend to be verbose and speech recognition may provide useful support in the future.

Mnemonic driven dialogue

This design is suitable for highly trained users carrying out specialised tasks. Virtually no explanatory prompts are provided. A typical example can be found in airline reservation systems. The operator can carry out a variety of tasks relating to seat reservations using only brief mnemonic (memory aid) representations for the input. For example, in response to a customer enquiry, the operator requests a list of flights which may satisfy the customer's requirements. These may be:

```
Departure Date: 23rd June
Departure Time: 2.30pm
Departure From: London
Destination City: New York, USA
```

The operator's screen entry may appear as follows:

```
? A23JUNLHRNYCJFK1430
```

The string of characters is in strict sequence according to function. Thus: A = Available; 23JUN = 23rd June; LHR = London, Heathrow Airport; NYCJFK = New York City, John F. Kennedy Airport; 1430 = 2.30pm or up to one hour earlier or later. The system then displays any flights which satisfy these criteria, together with details of seats available, arrival times, type of aircraft etc. The operator can, if requested, immediately make a reservation for the customer with a similar mnemonic command.

Communication of errors

Where data validation is to be performed at the time of data entry, it is important that the interface facilitates error detection and correction. Before designing error dialogues, the following points should be noted.

❑ A screen which leaves error messages on screen and re-displays the prompt beneath is untidy and confusing to the user.

❑ Repeated rejection of data without any explanation can be extremely frustrating. Such systems are only suitable for properly trained users who know the forms of input expected.

❑ Validation alone cannot ensure accuracy. Proper input document design, staff training and clerical checking are also vital. Users should be made aware of what validation is and its limitations, otherwise they may come to think of the system as infallible.

❑ It can save considerable frustration if the system is 'transparent' in terms of upper and lower case characters. In other words, entries are not made invalid simply because they are upper or lower case. Even if characters are to be output in only one case, the conversion can be carried out by the software.

❑ Where inexperienced users are involved, it may be useful if the system produces appropriate help messages from a file on disk. This facility is provided with many general-purpose packages.

❑ Error messages should be concise but detailed enough to allow the user to correct the error.

❑ Whilst using an application program, the user should not be presented with an error message directly from the operating system; as far as possible, all errors should be capable of being handled by the application and communicated via it to the user.

Other design considerations

It is important that the interface presents screen prompts and responses in a way which aids interpretation and to this end:

❏ any dialogue should follow a logical progression appropriate to the user, the activity and in the case of data entry, to the input document;

❏ spacing is important. Full use should be made of the screen space available;

❏ the interface should, as far as possible, be consistent across all applications in a given user area. This is particularly desirable when several packages are being used in a general application area such as accounts. The dialogue for sales ledger, purchase ledger, stock control and so on, should follow a similar structure. Many integrated packages allow the user to learn basic dialogue structure which allows rapid transfer of skills from one part of the package to another;

❏ techniques of highlighting such as brightness variation, blinking and colour coding should be used sparingly. Brightness variation should be limited to two levels, bold and normal as other variations will be difficult to detect. The blinking of a field on screen to attract the user's attention can be useful provided it does not continue once appropriate action has been taken.

 Exercises

1. Study the graphical user interfaces (GUIs) of various software packages and identify examples of *control panel* metaphor elements, such as switches, buttons, lights and radio buttons.

2. With reference to a particular GUI, identify tasks which appear to use intuitive methods.

3. (i) Examine a range of GUI packages and note those task features, such as opening files which are common to all.

   (ii) What benefits does this use of common features have for users?

4. (i) Describe two important principles for the design of menu systems.

   (ii) Examine two versions of the same package and identify changes the manufacturer has made to the menu structure. New features will have been added and resulted in some menu changes, but others may have been made to improve usability of the package. Study the changes and judge whether they have made the package easier or more difficult to use.

5. Describe a suitable application for *form-fill* dialogue.

6. Describe an application which may benefit from the use of *natural language* and suggest major difficulties which inhibit the use of truly 'natural language'.

7. Why is it beneficial to use simple text displays for supermarket checkouts?

8. Input errors have to be communicated to the user in a way which is appropriate to the application and the experience of the user. Suggest the kind of on-line support which is appropriate for communicating input errors to the following users:

   (i) Supermarket checkout operator using a simple text display.

   (ii) System administrator communicating with the operating system through a command line interpreter.

   (iii) Airline booking clerk using an in-house booking system.

   (iv) Graphic designer using a general-purpose graphics package.

   (v) Accounts clerk using an off-the-shelf accounts package with a GUI.

Chapter 40

System specification - Accounts Receivable

This chapter provides a completed specification for the Accounts Receivable system used in the Systems Design Tutorial in Chapter 38. The precise headings used in a specification may vary with the system and its complexity, but the headings used here are typical.

System description

The Account Receivable system is responsible for:

1. Opening new customer acccounts.

2. Producing and sending out invoices following the despatch of ordered goods to customers.

3. Applying payments received from customers to the Order file and thereby to the Customer accounts file.

4. Generating a variety of management reports, for example, debtor and overdue invoice lists.

System objectives

The system should:

1. Ensure that new customer credit accounts are only opened after completion of a standard application form, the checking of trade references and authorisation by the Accounts Manager.

2. Provide verification procedures and validation controls to ensure the integrity and accuracy of all input data.

3. Allow the Order file to be checked for the despatch of orders, so that invoices can be generated after despatch, rather than when an order is placed.

4. Integrate with a computerised Sales system to allow automatic generation of invoices and management information reports which draw on shared data sources.

5. Allow payments received from customers to be input to the Order file and that the payment is then automatically applied to the Customer file to reduce the amount owing.

Data flows

At this point we could include a 'rich picture' specification, a context (Level 0 DFD) diagram and lower level DFDs. A Level 1 DFD with system boundary is illustrated in Chapter 38.

User procedures

1. New customers requiring a credit account should be sent the New Account Application Form.

2. The Accounts Receivable clerk should check the trade references provided by the new account applicant. Replies should be referred to the Accounts Manager who will agree or modify the credit limit requested by the customer.

3. The Accounts Receivable clerk should enter the customer details using the New Customer Account application and advise the customer that an account has been opened and that an order may be placed.

4. The Accounts Receivable clerk should use the Create Invoice application to produce invoices to send to customers (2 copies are printed and one should be filed manually in Order number sequence) and the Credit Payment application to input payments received in settlement of invoices.

5. Weekly, or upon request, the Accounts Receivable clerk should run the application to generate a Debtors Report and pass it to the Accounts Manager.

Output specification

The system outputs are:

- ❑ despatch order details (screen);
- ❑ sales invoice (printed);
- ❑ debtors report (printed).

(The designs are provided in Chapter 38.)

Input specification

The system inputs are:

- ❑ new customer account;
- ❑ customer payments received.

(The designs are provided in Chapter 38.)

Data model

The entity model is illustrated in Chapter 38 and identifies 4 entities which are to be implemented as relational database tables: Order, OrderLine, Product and Customer.

Data dictionary

The entries for the four tables identified in the entity model are included. For details of key and relationship fields, refer to the entity model which includes attribute names in Chapter 38. As the design is to be implemented as a relational database, such as Microsoft Access, the field definitions for each table are provided in a form required by that package. The validation rules are also included as a basis for the Test Plan.

ORDER	OrderNo	CustOrderNo	CustAccNo
Data type	Autonumber		Number
Field size	Long integer	15	Long integer
Format			
Input mask			
Validation rule			
Validation text			
Required	Yes	No	Yes
Indexed	Yes (no duplicates)	No	No

	DateRec	DateDes	DateInv
Data type	Date	Date	
Field size			
Format	Medium date	Medium date	Medium date
Input mask			
Validation rule		>=DateRec	
Validation text		Invalid date	
Required	No	No	No
Indexed	No	No	No

ORDERLINE	LineNo	OrderNo	ItemCode	Quantity
Data type	Autonumber	Number	Text	Number
Field size		Long integer	5	Long integer
Format				
Input mask			LL000	
Validation rule				>0
Validation text				Invalid
Required		No	No	No
Indexed	Yes (no dup)	No	No	No

CUSTOMER	AccNo	Name	Address
Data type	Autonumber	Text	Memo
Field size	Long integer	30	
Format			
Input mask			
Validation rule			
Validation text			
Required	Yes	No	No
Indexed	Yes (no duplicates)	No	No

	PostCode	CreditLimit	CreditTerm
Data type	Text	Currency	Number
Field size	10	Zero decimal places	Integer
Format			
Input mask			00
Validation rule		>=200 and <=30000	30 Or 60 Or 90
Validation text			Invalid term
Required	No	No	No
Indexed	No	No	No

PRODUCT	ItemCode	Description	Price
Data type	Text	Text	Currency
Field size	5	30	2 decimal places
Format			
Input mask	LL000		
Validation rule			
Validation text			
Required	Yes	No	No
Indexed	Yes (no duplicates)	No	No

Process specification

Process models, for example, structured English would be included here.

There are 5 processes: 1 Create Invoice, 2 Create Customer Acount, 3 Check Despatched Orders, 4 Credit Payment, 5 Generate Debtors Report. Two of the processes are expressed in SQL in Chapter 38.

System flowchart

The way in which the system will use hardware can be illustrated with the use of system flowcharts. We would include one for each of the processes identified in the previous paragraph. A flowchart for the Create Invoice process is provided alongside.

Standard symbols are used to represent a keyboard, monitor, storage and documents.

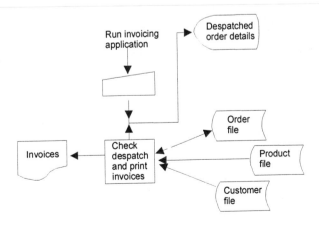

Implementation plan

This section would detail the sequence and time of the stages leading to implementation. These stages, with target dates, could include the following although the precise list would depend on the complexity of the problem, the degree of consultation required and business targets which will need to take account of, for example, cash flow requirements and possible new staff requirements.

- ❑ approval of detailed design specification;
- ❑ software development and hardware purchase;
- ❑ associated clerical and procedural documentation;
- ❑ staff training;
- ❑ system testing;
- ❑ going 'live'.

Equipment

This section will detail the computer hardware, furnishing, cabling installation and layout alterations which may be needed for the new system

Test plan

Guidance on testing is provided in the Introduction to Software Development Unit. You will need to refer to the data types and validation parameters detailed in the data dictionary to design suitable test data. Apart from testing the input validation controls, you need to ensure that outputs bring the expected results. For example, the Create Invoice process needs to be tested to ensure that order line values are correct given test unit prices and quantities.

Chapter 41

System implementation, maintenance and review

There are several clearly identifiable areas which require attention in the implementation of a new system, including: file conversion; system testing; staff training; changeover plan - going live.

File conversion

All records to which the computer requires access must be transferred to the appropriate backing storage medium. Records may include those concerning, for example, customer accounting and stock control. The encoding of large files is a time-consuming process and because live transaction data will be continually changing the values in the master files, they may need to be phased into the computer system in stages. In a stock control system, for example, records for certain categories of stock item may be encoded and computer processed, leaving the remainder to be processed by existing methods and encoded at a later stage. If a business has inadequate staffing to cope with the encoding exercise, a computer bureau may be used. Where possible, the bureau's staff should carry out the work on site because the records will be needed for the continued operation of the business. In favourable circumstances, a large scale encoding exercise may be undertaken to initially create the file and then, through an application program, transactions which have occurred since the encoding began can be used to update the file to reflect the correct values. Users will have to be made aware of which records have already been encoded into the system, so that they can properly update them as transactions occur. An additional problem is that records in their existing state may not conform with the file layouts designed for the new system and the data may have to be copied onto special-purpose input forms to assist with accurate encoding.

System testing

Before a system is made fully operational it should be thoroughly tested, generally in stages. If reputable and popular packaged software is being used, then provided it is being used with a wholly compatible hardware configuration, its reliability can probably be assumed. It is essential, however, that the user tests the system with real data from the business. With tailor-made systems, the testing needs to be more complex and lengthy. Once the reliability of the system has been tested, the user should run it with historical data, for which the results of processing are already known. The computerised results can then be checked for accuracy and consistency against the known manual results.

Staff training

The education and training of the users of a system is vital if it is to be operated correctly and the full benefits are to be obtained.

Generally, although managerial staff will not carry out routine data entry, except in the event of staff sickness, they should possess skills in the operation of a terminal, desk-top or notebook microcomputer, to allow them, for example, to make database enquiries. The supplier should provide training for everyone connected with the computer system, so that they are aware of its functions and are confident in its use. In the main, this will consist of computer operating skills for data entry staff, but those receiving computer output need to know what to expect and to be able to interpret it readily. Deciding when to carry out the training can be difficult. If too early, some staff will have forgotten what they have been taught by the time the system is introduced. If too late, staff may feel panicked because they have not been properly prepared.

System changeover

Switching from the old to the new system can be carried out in stages or all at once. There are three generally recognised approaches to going live: parallel running; pilot running; direct changeover.

Parallel running

With this approach, the old and new systems are run concurrently and the results of each are compared with the other for accuracy and consistency. The old system is not abandoned until the user has complete confidence in the reliability and accuracy of the new one. Obviously, parallel running places a great administrative strain on the business, in that staff are effectively doing many of the jobs twice. Any inconsistencies in results have to be cross-checked and the source of errors located (they may result from the old or the new system). The major advantage of parallel running is that the old system can be used whenever the computer system crashes or fails to function as it should. However, the two systems cannot operate together indefinitely and "Murphy's Law" will probably ensure that some errors only become apparent after the old system has been abandoned. In conclusion, it can be said that parallel running provides a safe, but expensive and time consuming, method of switching systems. It is unlikely that many businesses will use it for any extended period, except where system failure would be completely catastrophic.

Pilot running

This strategy requires that only a portion of live transactions go through the new computerised system, the rest being processed by the old method. Thus, for example, the transactions for one section of the business, or a sample of transactions from the whole business, could be used to test the system. This is a reasonably safe strategy but again, the transactions which cause errors may be amongst those which do not pass through the computer system.

Direct changeover

This is the riskiest option in that the new system completely replaces the old, without any interim parallel or pilot running. Its major benefit is the lack of administrative costs experienced with the other two methods. The potential costs can be severe, in that system failure could mean complete loss of data access and business failure. To minimise these risks, changeover should be preceded by careful system testing and thorough staff training. It is also helpful if the changeover is carried out during a slack period so that staff are not under pressure. The considerable cost of parallel and pilot running mean that this, the riskiest strategy, is often used in small businesses.

System maintenance

Following its initial introduction, a system will not remain static and dealing with the necessary changes is termed *system maintenance*. Problems will probably become apparent as the system is operated but even if they do not, the information needs of the business will probably change after a time. Some changes will come from within the business, as staff and management identify new possibilities for the system, whilst others may be forced upon the organisation because of changes in the strategies of competitors or government legislation. The most important catalyst for change is probably the desire for better and more timely information by management, to assist their decision-making and planning. Maintenance may concern updating of hardware or amendment of software. The hardware purchased should be expansible and the software should, ideally, be flexible enough to allow amendments to be made. Often, where packaged software is used the manufacturer provides, either free or more usually for an additional payment, upgraded versions of the software with extra features (this can be a supplier-led method of system maintenance).

System review

The final phase of the system development process is the assessment of the completed system. In this *review*, or *evaluation*, a number of factors are examined, including:

- How well the system is performing with reference to the needs that were initially identified.
- The final cost of the system compared to its original budget.
- The time taken to complete the work.

Even after the system is fully operational its performance is continually *monitored* throughout its life. At some stage, monitoring will identify needs that are no longer satisfied by the current system, and the system development process will begin once more with a preliminary study.

Unit 6 Assignments

6.1 Systems analysis

This assignment is based on the Barford Properties case study given below. You may wish to carry out further research into the operation of a local estate agency.

Case study

Barford Properties is a small firm of estate agents, with three partners, each one specialising in a particular aspect of the business. The specialisms are:

- ❏ property valuation;
- ❏ mortgage, insurance and conveyancing;
- ❏ marketing.

There are five sales negotiators and a potential buyer or vendor is assigned to one sales negotiator. The partner responsible for marketing has an assistant. These staff are directly responsible to the partners. An office manager is responsible for two accounts staff and one administrative clerk. Two secretaries are also employed, with a range of duties including general correspondence, and the production of property descriptions (including photographs).The agency operates a number of functions, as follows:

- ❏ Property valuations. When a client first approaches the agency with a request to handle the sale of their property, the responsible partner visits the property to assess its market value. The establishment of a selling price is usually a matter for negotiation. The client has a minimum figure in mind, which may coincide with the valuation assessment by the agency. If the valuation is less than the minimum figure put forward by the client, they are advised to lower the asking price accordingly. However, the final decision is made by the client. The asking price may be reviewed, depending on the response or otherwise of potential buyers. In making the assessment, the agency draws on its local experience, but also on data concerning regional and national trends in the housing market.

- ❏ Property sales. Once an asking price is agreed, fees are settled. Charges vary according to the value of the property, as the agency takes a percentage of the ultimate selling price, plus costs of advertising. Other charges for conveyancing work are also made. The sales negotiator assigned to a vendor handles their routine enquiries and correspondence to keep them informed of progress. If a client is not satisfied with progress and wants a different asking price, for example, he or she is referred to one of the partners.

- ❏ Marketing. This section deals with the placing of advertisements in local and national newspapers and property journals. It also organises the window displays and property details leaflets which are given out to interested buyers.

- ❏ Mortgage, conveyancing and insurance services (the agency acts as a broker). Buyers of properties handled by the agency are offered these services, and many clients make use of them, particularly if they are first-time buyers. The agency does not have Independent Financial Adviser status and mortgages are arranged with the Barford and Bamford Building Society. Property, mortgage protection and endowment insurances are obtained from the Buzzard Life Insurance Company.

- ❏ Financial accounting. This section handles all the customer accounts and deals with receipts and payments flowing between the agency, building societies, solicitors and insurance companies.

A brief outline of the procedures involved in a property sale is given below.

1. The initial request from a client wishing to sell a property is dealt with by the responsible partner, who makes an appointment to visit the property. Details of location, type, agreed asking price, number of rooms and so on are recorded. Photographs are also taken.

2. The property details are transcribed onto one of two standard forms, depending on whether the property is residential or business. This process is carried out in the Property Sales section.

3. The staff categorise the property according to basic criteria, including property location, type, size, quality, number of rooms and price range. These basic details are transcribed onto record cards, which are the initial point of reference when a potential buyer makes an enquiry.

4. To match prospective buyers with properties for sale, a Buyer Clients file is maintained. Details of suitable properties are sent (using a mailing list) to potential buyers.

5. When a buyer expresses an interest in a property, a viewing appointment is arranged between the buyer and the vendor (if the property is empty, one of the partners will accompany the buyer).

6. If a buyer expresses interest, they are asked to make an offer, which is then put to the vendor for consideration. Apart from the offer price, other factors are considered; for example, whether, the buyer has a property to sell.

7. Once a sale is agreed, solicitors take over the process of carrying out the various conveyancing operations and agreeing a completion date, when payment is made and the property ownership changes hands. When this is completed, the agency requests payment of the fees by the vendor. Buyers are not charged by the agency, although they do incur conveyancing costs.

Task 1

Produce a plan of the *systems life cycle stages*, which you will need to follow. Explain the purpose of each stage and the general activities it involves.

Task 2

Identify the user categories who would be expected to have access to the records and analyse their requirements.

Task 3

Undertake a *feasibility study* of the proposal. Define the *purpose* of the Property Sales System and establish its *objectives*. Other systems within the estate agency, which may interact with it, also need to be identified. Produce a word processed *feasibility report*.

Task 4

Briefly describe the standard techniques for gathering users' system requirements, select the technique(s) you consider most appropriate for the estate agency proposal and explain your choice. Design and use appropriate software to produce, a *questionnaire* for gathering information from buyers. It should identify Barford Properties and establish a corporate style. The aim of the questionnaire is to establish which types of information on houses they most need in the initial stage of an enquiry and the form(s) in which they would like the information to be presented to them. You also want to know which types of house and price ranges are most in demand and the number of houses each respondent has bought. Most people have bought at least one house, so you should obtain around 20 *responses*. You should make use of any software you consider appropriate to produce the questionnaire.

Task 5

Use a *spreadsheet* to analyse your findings and produce useful statistics. Produce two types of *chart* from these statistics, using *spreadsheet graphics* facilities.

Task 6

Use a suitable *graphics package*, to draw an *organisation chart* to represent the divisions of responsibility in the agency; it is likely to be a fairly 'flat' structure.

Task 7

Draw an *information flow* diagram (using vector drawing tools), showing the *functional* areas of the agency and the information flows between them. These should cover all information systems in the agency, including property for sale records, viewing appointments, accounts, buyer and vendor records, and connections with outside bodies, such as solicitors, banks and building societies and the Land Registry.

Task 8

Analyse the Property Sales system, and word process a requirements specificat.ion. It must include appropriate digrammatic representations (such as document flow diagrams, document analysis forms, rich picture illustrations and data flow diagrams). Your analysis should detail the current: *data collection methods* and *inputs*; *documents used*; *operations* and *decisions*; *storage*; system *outputs*. Also, include in your report, *recommendations* for a computerised system. These should:

- [ ] **describe** the different types of system (for example, batch processing, transaction processing, information storage and retrieval) and make an argued recommendation for a particular type;

- [ ] **detail** *input* (including form, source and collection method), *processing* (form of processing activity), *storage* and *reporting* requirements of the system; you should also detail expected *volumes* of data and *frequency* of input and outputs;

- [ ] **identify** *expectations* of the system.

- [ ] **costs** and **savings** of a new system, identifying resources needed and any constraints on its development or use.

Task 9

Obtain user comments on your analysis and **make modifications**, as necessary.

6.2 System design

These activities are based on the Barford Properties Case Study at the end of this Developmental Exercise section and builds on the feasibility report and requirements specification produced in 6.1. These tasks lead to the production of a system design for the Property Sales system. To begin with you are required you to demonstrate your knowledge of the terminology associated with this subject.

Task 1

Word process (using table facilities) a *glossary*, listing and briefly describing the following elements of a system specification: *input specification; output specification; process specificat'on; resources; constraints; first normal form (1NF) data model.*

Task 2

Produce a system specification in the following stages. At each stage, include an explanation of its purpose and the specification element(s) it comprises.

a. **Refine** and **re-draw** thevarious data flow and other diagrams produced in 6.1 and identify the *entities* which form the Property Sales system. Draw the entity model. **Produce** *data definitions* for each entity, and if necessary *normalise* to first normal for (1NF). **Establish** a *data dictionary* and **record** the details.

b. **Produce** an *input specification*, detailing data source(s), capture methods; screen layouts, verification, validation parameters.

c. **Produce** an *output specification*, with designs for screen and printed reports.

d. **Produce** a *process specification* (if appropriate, use decision tables to refine the efficiency of processes). Use at least one of the following methods to define the process(es): *structured English; structure diagram, flow chart.*

e. **Identify** and **describe** resource implications of the specification, including hardware, software, people, time scale for implementation and costs.

Task 3

Describe the *alternative information technology methods*, which may be used to implement the specification and **suggest** for *which aspect of development* each may be appropriate (with reasons; otherwise indicate as inappropriate).

Task 4

Evaluate the design and outline alternative solutions. Justify your choice of design.

Task 5

Produce a full and detailed test plan, based on the data definitions and input screens which formed part of your design solution.

6.3 Process models

For each of the following problems, produce a flowchart, structure chart, structured English or a decision table, as indicated in brackets.

Decisions

1. Read a number and display a message which states whether the number is positive, negative or zero. (Flowchart)

2. Read a number and print it only if it is between 10 and 20. (Flowchart)

3. Read a number followed by a single letter code. The number represents the price of an item and the code indicates whether tax is to be added to the price. If the code is 'V' then the tax is 20% of the item's cost. If the code is 'X' then the item is not taxed. Print out the total cost of the item. (Structured English)

4. Read three positive, non-zero integers which may represent the sides of a triangle. The numbers are in ascending order of size. Determine whether or not the numbers do represent the sides of a triangle. (Decision table)

5. Extend the previous question to determine the type of triangle if one is possible with the values provided. Assume that the only types of triangles to consider are: *scalene* - no equal sides; *isosceles* - two equal sides; *equilateral* - three equal sides. (Decision table)

6. Read in a single character and print a message indicating whether or not it is a vowel. (Structure chart)

Loops

7. To produce conversion tables for:
    (i)   Inches to centimetres (1 to 20 inches, 1 inch = 2·54 centimetres);
    (ii) Pounds to kilograms (1 to 10 pounds, 2.2 pounds per kilogram);

    (iii) Square yards to square metres: 10, 20 , 30,..., 100 sq yds (1yd = ·91 m)
        (Structured English)

10. A program reads an integer representing the number of gas bills to be processed, followed by that number of customer details. Each set of customer details consists of a customer number, a single character code representing the type of customer and the number of units used. Customers are of type 'D' (domestic) or 'B' (business). Domestic customers are charged 8p per unit and business customers are charged 10p per unit. For each customer print the customer number, the number of units used and the cost of the gas used. Print the total number of units used for this batch of customers and the total amount charged.

    (Structured English)

11. Repeat the previous question assuming that all the domestic users are first and that separate totals are required for domestic and business users. (Structure chart)

Index

E

Echoplex, 368
E-commerce, 205,414
   benefits for consumers, 206
   benefits of business, 205
   social and employment costs, 206
EDI, 182
EDO DRAM, 92
EDO RAM, 95
EFT, 183,220
EFTPOS, 183
EISA, 98
Electronic data interchange (EDI), 182
E-mail, 17 - 18,181,406,412
   benefits of, 182
   encryption, 18
   etiquette, 17
   smiley, 18
Encoding of data, 187
Encryption, 18,183,219
Entity, 452
   external, 445
   model, 484
   model example, 457
   occurrence, 456
   relationship
      diagram, 451
      modelling, 429,451,453,455,457
Ergonomics, 222
Error
   punctuation, 20
   spacing, 20
   typographical, 20
Error communication, 492
Errors
   absolute, 251
   logic, 251
Ethernet, 379 - 380,395 - 396
Event-driven programming language, 305
Excess codes, 87
Expansion board
   installation, 129
   slots, 124
Expansion card, 94 - 95
Exponent, 79,81
External code, 70
Extranet, 183,413

F

Fact-finding methods, 438 - 440
FAX, 184
Feasibility
   report, 431 - 432

   study, 430,432,434
Feasibility study, 434
Fetch-execute cycle, 133
Fibre Distributed Data Interface (FDDI), 397
Fibre optic cable, 369
Field
   definition, 457
   name, 457
File, 187 - 188,224
   controls, 215
   conversion, 499
   master, 216
   processing controls, 211
   protection ring, 217
   server, 392
   transaction, 216
   Transfer Protocol (FTP), 366,406,412
Financial
   accounting, 170
Financial accounting, 191,193,195
Findings, 17
Firewall, 183
First Normal Form (1NF), 456,484
Fixed point numbers, 78 - 80,84
   number range and precision, 79
Fixed terminal identifier, 219
Flash memory, 94
Flat structure, 169
Flip chart, 24
Flip-flop, 63 - 64,66,68
Floating point
   addition, 82 - 83
   arithmetic, 72,82 - 83,85,87
   arithmetic precision, 84
   conversion to denary, 81
   multiplication and division, 86 - 87
   number representation, 79 - 81
   storage, 81
   subtraction, 83 - 84
Floppy disk, 113
   connector, 126
   drive installation, 129
Flow control, 365
Flowcharts, 464
Font
   sans-serif, 4
   serif, 4
Foreign key, 485
Format, 189
Form-fill dialogue, 491
Forms layout, 226
Forward referencing, 136
FPM RAM, 93
FPM SIMM, 125